Economic Growth with Income and Wealth Distribution

Other books by the author:
SYNERGETIC ECONOMICS

CAPITAL AND KNOWLEDGE: DYNAMICS OF ECONOMIC STRUCTURES WITH NON-CONSTANT RETURNS

DIFFERENTIAL EQUATIONS, BIFURCATIONS, AND CHAOS IN ECONOMICS

ECONOMIC GROWTH THEORY

DISCRETE DYNAMICAL SYSTEMS, BIFURCATIONS AND CHAOS IN ECONOMICS

Economic Growth with Income and Wealth Distribution

Wei-Bin Zhang

© Wei-Bin Zhang 2006

All rights reserved. No reproduction, copy or transmission of this publication may be made without written permission.

No paragraph of this publication may be reproduced, copied or transmitted save with written permission or in accordance with the provisions of the Copyright, Designs and Patents Act 1988, or under the terms of any licence permitting limited copying issued by the Copyright Licensing Agency, 90 Tottenham Court Road, London W1T 4LP.

Any person who does any unauthorized act in relation to this publication may be liable to criminal prosecution and civil claims for damages.

The author has asserted his right to be identified as the author of this work in accordance with the Copyright, Designs and Patents Act 1988.

First published 2006 by
PALGRAVE MACMILLAN
Houndmills, Basingstoke, Hampshire RG21 6XS and
175 Fifth Avenue, New York, N. Y. 10010
Companies and representatives throughout the world

PALGRAVE MACMILLAN is the global academic imprint of the Palgrave Macmillan division of St. Martin's Press, LLC and of Palgrave Macmillan Ltd. Macmillan® is a registered trademark in the United States, United Kingdom and other countries. Palgrave is a registered trademark in the European Union and other countries.

ISBN-13: 978–0–230–00478–8 hardback
ISBN-10: 0–230–00478–4   hardback

This book is printed on paper suitable for recycling and made from fully managed and sustained forest sources.

A catalogue record for this book is available from the British Library.

Library of Congress Cataloging-in-Publication Data

Zhang, Wei-Bin, 1961–
  Economic growth with income and wealth distribution / Wei-Bin Zhang.
    p. cm.
  Includes bibliographical references and index.
  Contents: Contents: Growth and distribution – One-sector growth (OSG) economies with capital accumulation – Growth with human capital and knowledge – Growth with heterogeneous households – Multi-sector growth economies – Multiple sectors and heterogeneous households – Multi-region growth economies – Multi-country growth economies.
    ISBN 0–230–00478–4 (cloth)
  1. Economic development. 2. Income distribution. I. Title.

HD75.Z457 2006
338.9–dc22   2005056518

10 9 8 7 6 5 4 3 2 1
15 14 13 12 11 10 09 08 07 06

Printed and bound in Great Britain by
Antony Rowe Ltd, Chippenham and Eastbourne

Contents

List of Tables and Figures ix

Preface xii

1 Growth and Distribution 1
1.1 The Walrasian economic system 3
1.2 The Solow growth model 8
1.3 The Ramsey growth model 14
1.4 A post-Keynesian model of growth and distribution 21
1.5 A representative consumer approach in the Ramsey theory 23
1.6 The overlapping-generations (OLG) model 27
1.7 Timescales, changeable speeds, and economic theory 30
1.8 The structure of the book 33

2 One-Sector Growth (OSG) Economies with Capital Accumulation 37
2.1 The one-sector growth model 38
2.2 The OSG model with the Cobb-Douglas functions 47
2.3 The OSG model in discrete time 53
2.4 Growth with endogenous leisure 58
2.5 Public goods and returns to scale 66
2.6 Home production in the OSG model 71
2.7 Environment and growth 74
2.8 The OSG model with population 79
2.9 Money and economic growth 82
2.10 A small open economy with capital accumulation 89
    2.10.1 The model with general production and utility functions 89
    2.10.2 The dynamics with the Cobb-Douglas functions 93
    2.10.3 Autarky interest rates and the trade pattern 96
2.11 Theoretical foundations of the utility function 99
2.12 Relations with traditional approaches to consumer behavior 102
    2.12.1 The Keynesian consumption function 102
    2.12.2 The life cycle hypothesis 105
    2.12.3 The permanent income hypothesis 106

v

	2.12.4 The Solow model	108
	2.12.5 The Ramsey growth model	111
Appendix		112
	A.2.1 Economic dynamics with fertility and old age support	112

3 Growth with Human Capital and Knowledge 119

- 3.1 The AK-OSG model with learning by doing 121
- 3.2 Growth with capital accumulation and education 124
  - 3.2.1 The OSG model with endogenous human capital 125
  - 3.2.2 The dynamics and multiple equilibrium points 128
  - 3.2.3 The path-dependent motion of the system by simulation 132
  - 3.2.4 The impact of educational policy 134
  - 3.2.5 The impact of the propensity to save 138
- 3.3 Growth with learning by doing and research 140
- 3.4 Development with monopolistic competition 150
- 3.5 Product variety and growth 159
- 3.6 Variety of consumer goods and growth 165
- 3.7 From Malthusian stagnation to demographic trends of advanced economies 169
- Appendix 172
  - A.3.1: Proving Proposition 3.2.1 172

4 Growth with Heterogeneous Households 174

- 4.1 The OSG model of two-type households 177
  - 4.1.1 The OSG model of two-type households 177
  - 4.1.2 Equilibrium and stability 180
  - 4.1.3 Different levels of human capital 184
  - 4.1.4 Preference differences 185
- 4.2 The OSG model with heterogeneous groups 186
- 4.3 Growth with knowledge and multiple groups 191
- 4.4 Persistence of inequality with poverty traps 195
- 4.5 A growth model with human capital and income distribution 199
- 4.6 On modeling group differences 204
- Appendix 206
  - A.4.1 Proving Proposition 4.1.1 206

5 Multi-Sector Growth Economies 209

- 5.1 The Uzawa two-sector model 210

5.2	A two-sector growth model with endogenous saving	214
	5.2.1 The model	214
	5.2.2 The motion of the economic system	217
	5.2.3 The dynamics with the Cobb-Douglas production functions	219
	5.2.4 Simulate the model	222
	5.2.5 Comparative dynamic analysis by simulation	224
5.3	A two-sector growth model with labor supply and consumer durables	226
	5.3.1 The model with endogenous leisure and consumer durables	227
	5.3.2 The dynamics with the Cobb-Douglas production functions	229
	5.3.3 Simulate the model	233
5.4	Knowledge accumulation and economic structure	239
5.5	Conclusions	243
	Appendix	243
	A.5.1 The dynamics with general production functions	243

6 Multiple Sectors and Heterogeneous Households 248

6.1	The two-sector two-group model	249
6.2	Dynamics with the Cobb-Douglas production functions	252
6.3	Simulating the model	257
6.4	Further discussions	269
	Appendix	271
	A.6.1 The two-sector multi-group model with general production functions	271

7 Multi-Region Growth Economies 275

7.1	Leisure, amenity, and capital accumulation	278
	7.1.1 The model with time, amenity, and capital accumulation	279
	7.1.2 Simulate the three-region economy	286
	7.1.3 Parameter changes and regional economic structures	292
7.2	Regional economic structure with endogenous knowledge	299
	7.2.1 The regional model with economic structure	302
	7.2.2 The equilibrium structure and stability	305
	7.2.3 The creativity and the regional economic structure	309
7.3	On regional dynamics with capital and knowledge	313
	Appendices	314
	A.7.1 Proving Lemma 7.1.1	314
	A.7.2 Proving Proposition 7.2.1	318
	A.7.3 Proving Proposition 7.2.2	321

8 Multi-Country Growth Economies — 323
- 8.1 The Ricardian trade theory — 324
- 8.2 The neoclassical theory and the Heckscher-Ohlin theory — 327
- 8.3 A two-country trade model with capital accumulation — 332
  - 8.3.1 The trade model — 335
  - 8.3.2 Behavior of the dynamic system — 337
  - 8.3.3 Some special cases — 340
- 8.4 A multi-country trade model with heterogeneous households — 343
  - 8.4.1 The trade model with heterogeneous households — 344
  - 8.4.2 The world economic dynamics — 347
  - 8.4.3 The three-country two-group economy — 350
  - 8.4.4 Comparative dynamic analysis — 354
- 8.5 International trade with capital and technology — 363
  - 8.5.1 The trade model with capital and knowledge accumulation — 366
  - 8.5.2 The dynamics of the trade system — 368
  - 8.5.3 The global economy in the autarky system — 372
  - 8.5.4 Comparing the autarky and trade systems — 373
- 8.6 On trade and income and wealth distribution — 376
- Appendix — 380
  - A.8.1 Equilibrium and stability conditions in the two-country economy — 380

9 Endless Complexity — 383

Notes — 389

Bibliography — 403

Index — 429

List of Tables and Figures

Tables

1.7.1	Change speeds of economic variables	32
2.12.1	Historical gross saving rates as a percentage of the GNP	109

Figures

1.2.1	Intensive form of the aggregate production function	11
1.2.2	Evolution of capital–labor ratio in the Solow model	13
1.3.1	The dynamics of the Ramsey model	17
2.2.1	Indifference curves and the propensity to hold wealth	48
2.2.2	Optimal choice	49
2.2.3	Optimal saving with different propensities to own wealth	49
2.2.4	The impact of changes in the interest rate	50
2.2.5	Evolution of capital–labor ratio in the OSG model	52
2.2.6	Dynamics of growth rate in the OSG model	53
2.3.1	The dynamics in the OSG model	57
2.4.1	Behavior of the model over time	66
2.4.2.	The propensity to use leisure, σ, increases from 0.25 to 0.30	67
2.5.1	Stable and unstable steady states	70
2.6.1	Evolution of capital stocks in the home production model	74
2.8.1	The interaction between wealth and the population	81
2.9.1	The Tobin effect	88
2.10.1	Convergence toward the equilibrium point	94
2.10.2	The impact of the international interest rate, $0 < r^* < 0.15$	95
2.10.3	The impact of the propensity to save, $0.1 < \lambda < 0.9$	96
2.10.4	The differences in the two economies as r^* changes, $0 < r^* < 0.15$	99
2.10.5	The differences in the two economies as λ changes, $0 < \lambda < 0.9$	100
A.2.1.1	The unique fixed point for $\rho > 0$	116

A.2.1.2　Fixed points for $\rho < 0$ 118

3.0.1　Indexes of business productivity (1977=100, 1960–94) 119
3.0.2　Disposable personal income (DPI) per capita, 1960–94 120
3.1.1　Sustained growth in the AK-OSG model 123
3.2.1　The two sectors exhibit different returns to scale effects 131
3.2.2　Path-dependent economic evolution 133
3.2.3　Path-dependent development as education is discouraged ... 137
3.2.4　An increase in the propensity to save 139
3.3.1　$\xi_j^{\xi_j} \lambda_j^{\lambda_j}$ as a function of λ_j with $\xi_j + \lambda_j = 1$ 145
3.5.1　The dynamics with product variety 164

4.0.1　Enlarged wage differences in the US, 1979–96 176
4.2.1　The time-dependent paths of the key variables 190
4.2.2　The poorest group improves human capital and increases the propensity to save 192
4.4.1　Multiple steady states and persistent income inequality 198
4.5.1　Three possible equilibrium points and their stability 203

5.2.1　Simulating the two-sector model 223
5.2.2　λ rises from 0.65 (solid lines) to 0.70 (dashed lines) 225
5.2.3　A_i rises from 1.1 (solid lines) to 1.4 (dashed lines) 226
5.3.1　The existence of a unique equilibrium point 234
5.3.2　The motion of the variables over 50 years 235
5.3.3　λ rises from 0.82 (solid lines) to 0.84 (dashed lines) 237
5.3.4　As A_i rises from 1.3 (solid lines) to 1.5 (dashed lines) 238

6.3.1　The motion of the system 259
6.3.2　As A_i rises from 0.7 (solid lines) to 0.82 (dashed lines) 261
6.3.3　As h_1 rises from 9 (solid lines) to 10 (dashed lines) 262
6.3.4　As h_2 rises from 2 (solid lines) to 3.5 (dashed lines) 264
6.3.5　As N_1 rises from 1 (solid lines) to 1.5 (dashed lines) 265
6.3.6　As N_2 rises from 5 (solid lines) to 6 (dashed lines) 266
6.3.7　As λ_1 rises from 0.87 (solid lines) to 0.89 (dashed lines) 267
6.3.8　As λ_2 rises from 0.75 (solid lines) to 0.79 (dashed lines) 268

7.1.1	The existence of positive solutions of $\Omega(k_1) = 0$	291
8.4.1	The existence of positive solutions of $\Omega(k_1) = 0$	352
8.4.2	The motion of the global economy	355
8.4.3	Group $(1, 1)$ improves its human capital ($h_{11}: 12 \Rightarrow 13$)	357
8.4.4	The other groups are affected differently ($h_{11}: 12 \Rightarrow 13$)	358
8.4.5	Group $(3, 2)$ improves its human capital ($h_{32}: 1 \Rightarrow 2$)	359
8.4.6	The other groups are affected differently ($h_{32}: 1 \Rightarrow 2$)	359
8.4.7	Group $(1, 1)$ increases its propensity to save ($\lambda_{11}: 0.87 \Rightarrow 0.88$)	361
8.4.8	Group $(3, 2)$ increases its propensity to save ($\lambda_{32}: 0.65 \Rightarrow 0.7$)	362
8.4.9	Group $(1, 1)$'s population is increased ($N_{11}: 2 \Rightarrow 2.2$)	364
8.4.10	Group $(3, 2)$'s population is increased ($N_{11}: 20 \Rightarrow 22$)	365

Preface

With regard to the lack of a satisfactory theory of personal income distribution, Irving Fisher (1912) observes:

> No other problem has so great a human interest as this, and yet scarcely any other problem has received so little scientific study.

The situation remained little improved over the years. In 1975, Atkinson (1975: 258) summarized the survey of the study about growth and income distribution as follows:

> ... far too little is known about this central subject. This is an indictment of economics, but it is also a challenge.

As observed by Atkinson and Bourguignon (2000), there is no unified theory of income distribution, not to mention both income and wealth distribution within a single analytical framework. This situation is mainly due to the fact that economics does not have a proper dynamic economic theory, which explains interactions of various economic forces within a consistent framework. This book attempts to propose an economic growth theory with income and wealth distribution, based on the analytical framework recently proposed by Zhang.[1] The reader may wonder why important problems related to growth with income and wealth distribution have remained very little examined. Theoretically, the issues related to growth and income and wealth distribution are difficult because they are genuinely multidimensional and dynamic and have to be examined within an analytical framework in which the economy is treated as a whole (rather than a collection of unconnected parts as typically reflected in many economic textbooks or books of collected papers on the topic). I explain the current situation of the economic theory as follows:

> Various fields in economics live in isolation from each other. Students trained in one sub-field often do not have a shared understanding of the fundamentals of the others. When economists from each sub-field are busy with pursuit of learning, they do not converge upon a common framework but find themselves in divergent directions.[2]

The unconnected but harmonious coexistence of the theories for the same economic system in the same research and education institutions over such a long period of time contains the necessity and certainty for producing a higher theory, which unifies these traditional theories within a compact framework.

This book attempts to make some progress by propounding a dynamic general equilibrium model which explains the determinants of income and wealth distribution over time. I will endeavor to overcome some of the difficulties in modeling growth with income and wealth with an alternative approach to the consumer. Although my main purpose is to create a growth theory with income and wealth distribution based on my analytical framework, the book also introduces some other models on the subject of growth and distribution.

This book provides a powerful – but easy to operate – engine of analysis that sheds light not only on economic growth and distribution per se, but on many other dimensions that interact with growth and distribution, including education, research policy, and knowledge creation and utilization. Building and analyzing various tractable and flexible models within a compact whole, the book helps the reader to visualize economic life as an endless succession of physical capital accumulation, human capital accumulation, innovation wrought by competition, and government intervention. The book starts with a growth theory in which capital accumulation is the key element for economic growth. I differ from the traditional growth theories in that I introduce a novel economic mechanism to determine consumers' decisions on consumption and saving. The novel utility maximization solves the problem that there is no profound rational decision mechanism for consumers in the Solow model and avoids the complication that the Ramsey growth theory brings about. Through numerous examples, I demonstrate that the novel utility functions help us to analytically handle many economic problems in a consistent manner. I also simulate some of models. The recent surge of simulations in growth theory has been impelled by current developments in computer processing, algorithm design, software, and data storage. Since growth models are described by nonlinear differential equations, simulation by computer provides an effective way to describe time-dependent paths of these systems.

I would like to thank Editors Katie Button and Philip Tye at Palgrave Macmillan for effective co-operation. I completed this book at the Ritsumeikan Asia Pacific University, Japan. I am grateful for the university's free academic environment. I take great pleasure in expressing my gratitude to my wife, Gao Xiao, who also helped me to draw some of the figures in the book.

Wei-Bin Zhang
Beppu-Shi, Spring 2006

1
Growth and Distribution

Living conditions, income and wealth vary among people, cities, regions, and countries. It is important to study how persistent disparities in aggregate growth rates across nations, regions, or groups of people have led to differences in welfare and happiness. Does more equal distribution of income and wealth encourage national economic growth? What role does the public education or other public expenditures play in the relationship between inequality and growth? Does a higher personal saving rate of one type of household benefit or harm economically other households in the economy? Will income/wealth inequality among the individuals or regions be reduced as an economy expands? Does everyone benefit from economic globalization? Is globalization sustainable? Will globalization and technological progress enlarge or reduce inequalities among nations, regions, or individuals? One may ask many similar questions related to growth and income and wealth distribution.

Income and wealth distribution affects allocation of scarce resources and economic growth, and economic growth leads to changes in the distribution. The issues related to economic growth and distribution are the main concerns of classical economists such as Ricardo and Marx. But there are only a few growth models with income and wealth distribution. The situation is described by Atkinson and Bourguignon (2000: 5) as follows:

No unified theory of income distribution actually exists. Even though several titles of books and articles announce quite ambitiously the state of such a "theory of income distribution", they typically refer to only one part of what actually be covered by such a theory: the determination of wages in the labor market, factor shares, the accumulation of wealth, etc. Rather than a unified theory, the literature thus offers a series of building blocks with which distribution issues are to be studied. Because of the natural complexity of the subject, however, no serious attempt at integrating them has really been made.

Economic theory is supposed to explain mechanisms and to provide intellectual insights into important issues such as relations between growth and distribution. The development of growth theory has created a wide array of different theories, concepts, and results. Nevertheless, the growth theory has been split between partial and conflicting representations of economic growth. Diverse growth models have co-existed but not in a structured relationship with each other. Economic students are trained to understand economic phenomena by several incompatible theories one after another in the same course. In order to overcome incoherence, we need a general theoretical framework which enables us to account for the phenomena explained by the current theories in a unified manner in order to draw together all the disparate branches of growth theory with income and wealth distribution into a single organized system of knowledge. This book is to undertake a theoretical integration of well-established growth theories with income and wealth distribution. Our integration is based on conceptual integration. We analyze growth phenomena in different subfields with a few basic concepts and assumptions.

The theory proposed in this study is influenced by traditional economics. The three following modeling frameworks in theoretical (mathematical) economics are important in order to appreciate our approach to economic growth with structure and distribution. The first approach is the Arrow-Debreu equilibrium theory which mainly deals with the equilibrium of demand and supply in a perfectly competitive environment (Arrow and Hahn, 1971; Debreu, 1959). In this approach, monetary variables such as prices and wages are determined by the interdependence between demand and supply. The second theory is the neoclassical growth theory.[1] This approach emphasizes long-run aspects of economic dynamics. How capital is accumulated over time and what kinds of effects capital stocks may have on the economic structure are two of its main concerns. Monetary variables are treated as fast variables in comparison to real variables in the dynamic system. At each point in time, the monetary variables are determined at their marginal values and real variables evolve over time. In modern nonlinear dynamic terms, the monetary variables are "enslaved" by dynamics of the real variables such as population and capital dynamics. The third approach deals with the distribution of income and wealth between workers and capitalists, explaining Marx's economic system.[2] In this approach, the behavior of individuals is conditioned by their class. It is the relationship between long-run growth, profit and the saving propensities of the social classes that this approach is mainly concerned with. Our classification of the population into groups is strongly influenced by this school. We agree that the existence of differences among the population is an important force for economic development; but we do not see that groups are always in conflict. In general, there are either conflicts or mutual benefits among groups, depending on institutional structures and economic conditions in the system. This chapter introduces the Walrasian system, the Solow model, the Ramsey model, the post-Keynesian growth model, and a growth model in discrete time.

1.1 The Walrasian economic system

The standard static Walrasian model describes competitive equilibrium by taking as given the distribution of all productive factors in the economy. This is a key model for us to see how prices and exchanges are determined in free markets. As the Walrasian system is discussed in textbooks in microeconomics, I only briefly describe some main features of the theory. The Walrasian system is important for judging the validity of dynamic economic theory in the sense that a dynamic economic theory will contain the Walrasian theory as a special case.

We now formalize the competitive structure of the economy by supposing that consumers act to maximize utility subject to their budget constraints and that firms seek to maximize profit. Both consumers and firms are price takers.[3] We assume that there is a fixed and finite number n of commodities (and services) in the economy.

Producers

Consider that there is a fixed number J of firms. We index them by the set $\Gamma = \{1, \cdots, J\}$. Let $y^j \in R^n$, $j \in \Gamma$. If commodity k is an input used by firm j, we have $y_k^j < 0$; if commodity k is an output produced by firm j, we have $y_k^j > 0$. To describe the technological possibilities in production, we make the following assumptions on production possibility sets.

Assumption 1.1.1
Suppose each firm possesses a production possibility set, Y^j, $j \in \Gamma$. We assume

1. $0 \in Y^j \subseteq R^n$.
2. $Y^j \cap R_+^n = \{0\}$.
3. Y^j is closed and bounded.
4. Y^j is strongly convex.[4]

The first of these conditions guarantees that firm profits are bounded below by zero; the second that production of output always requires some inputs. The closed part of the third condition imposes continuity, meaning that the limits of possible production plans are themselves possible production plans. The bounded part of the third condition is made mainly for convenience of analysis. The strong convexity is strict but it rules out constant and increasing returns to scale in production and ensures that a maximum of firm profits exists and is achieved from a unique production plan.

Each firm faces fixed commodity prices $p \geq 0$ and chooses a production plan to maximize profit. Thus, each firm solves the problem

$$\max_{y^j \in Y^j} p \cdot y^j. \tag{1.1.1}$$

As the objective function is continuous and the constraint set is closed and bounded, a maximum of firm profit will exist. So for all $p \geq 0$ let

$$\Pi_j(p) \equiv \max_{y^j \in Y^j} p \cdot y^j \tag{1.1.2}$$

denote firm j's profit function. It is known that $\Pi_j(p)$ is continuous on R_+^n. The strong convexity ensures that the profit-maximizing production plan, $y^j(p)$, is continuous.

Theorem 1.1.1
If each Y^j satisfies Assumption 1.1.1, then for every price $p \gg 0$, the solution to the firm's problem (1.1.1) is unique and denoted by $y^j(p)$. Moreover, $y^j(p)$ is continuous on R_{++}^n. Moreover, $\Pi_j(p)$ is well-defined and continuous on R_+^n.

It can be shown that the maximum firm profits are homogeneous of degree one in the vector of commodity prices. Each output supply and input demand function is homogeneous of degree zero in prices. We neglect any possible externality in production between firms. We define the aggregate production possibilities set

$$Y \equiv \left\{ y \mid y = \sum_{j \in I} y^j, \ y^j \in Y^j \right\}.$$

If each Y^j satisfies Assumption 1.1.1, then the aggregate production possibility set, Y, also satisfies Assumption 1.1.1.

Consumers
Let there be I consumers, indexed by i. Let $I \equiv \{1, \cdots, I\}$ index the set of consumers and let u^i denote i's utility function over the consumption set R_+^n.

Assumption 1.1.2
Utility u^i is continuous, strongly increasing, and strictly quasi-concave on R_+^n.

In a private ownership economy, consumers own shares in firms and firm profits are distributed to shareholders. Consumer i's shares in firm j entitle her to some proportion $0 \leq \theta^{ij} \leq 1$ of the profits of firm j. We should have

$$\sum_{i \in I} \theta^{ij} = 1, \ \forall j \in \Gamma.$$

In this exchange economy, a consumer's income can arise from two sources – from selling an endowment of commodities already owned and from shares in the profit of any number of firms. If $p \geq 0$ is the vector of market prices, the consumer's budget constraint becomes

$$p \cdot x^i \leq p \cdot e^i + \sum_{j \in I'} \theta^{ij} \Pi^j(p).$$

Introduce

$$m^i(p) \equiv p \cdot e^i + \sum_{j \in I'} \theta^{ij} \Pi^j(p).$$

The consumer's problem is

$$\max_{x^i \in R_+^n} u^i(x^i) \quad \text{s.t.} \quad p \cdot x^i \leq m^i(p). \tag{1.1.3}$$

Theorem 1.1.2
If each Y^j satisfies Assumption 1.1.1 and if u^i satisfies Assumption 1.1.2, then a solution to the consumer's problem (1.1.3) exists and is unique for all prices $p \gg 0$. Denoting it by $x^i(p, m^i(p))$, we have furthermore that $x^i(p, m^i(p))$ is continuous in p on R_{++}^n.

Equilibrium
We examined the behavior of consumers and producers with prices fixed. We now examine the existence of equilibrium. We introduce excess demand for commodity k as

$$z_k(p) \equiv \sum_{i \in I} x_k^i(p, m^i(p)) - \sum_{j \in \Gamma} y_k^j(p) - \sum_{i \in I} e_k^i.$$

The excess demand vector is

$$z(p) \equiv (z_1(p), \cdots, z_n(p)).$$

A vector $p^* \in R_{++}^n$ is called a Walrasian equilibrium if $z(p^*) = 0$.

Theorem 1.1.3[5]

Consider the economy $(u^i, e^i, \theta^{ij}, Y^j)_{i \in I, j \in \Gamma}$. If each u^i satisfies Assumption 1.1.2 and each Y^j satisfies Assumption 1.1.1, and $y + \sum_{i \in I} e^i \gg 0$ for some aggregate production vector $y \in \sum_{j \in \Gamma} Y^j$, then there exists at least one price vector $p^* \in R_{++}^n$ such that $z(p^*) = 0$.

We may also discuss the dynamics of the system through the construction of Walrasian tâtonnement, which is important for understanding the dynamics and stability of competitive economies in the short term.[6]

The Walrasian system is the most elegant and useful economic theory as far as short-run economic mechanisms of perfectly competitive economies are concerned. In this sense, a dynamic theory of perfect competitive economy should include the Walrasian economic system as a special case so that when the whole system achieves or remains at its stationary state, it should be identical to the Walrasian economic system.

Except issues related to monetary variables (such as supply and demand of money and price dynamics), information, and international and interregional trade, the Walrasian system assumes many factors to be fixed. For instance, the number of commodities and services is changeable, rather than fixed as in the theory. The number of firms is not fixed. Population is changeable. People will die and babies will be born. Distribution is not fixed. The assumption of perfect competition may be invalid. Monopoly or monopolistic competition is a main feature of modern industries. Environment brings about externalities. Infrastructures may be associated with increasing returns to scale in economic dynamics. Human capital accumulation, technological change, and knowledge creation all have close interdependent relationships with economic systems.

As the Walrasian system is useful/insightful and theoretically beautiful for short-run competitive economies, we might argue that a theory of perfectly competitive economies should include the Walrasian system as a special case. When talking about developing a new theory, I am aware of the following criteria of a theory proposed by Kuhn (1977):

A theory should be: (1) accurate within domain; (2) consistent internally and with other currently accepted theories; (3) a broad scope allowing its consequences to extend beyond the particular observations, laws or subtheories it was initially designed to explain; (4) simple but able to bring order to the phenomena that in its absence would be individually isolated and, as a set, confused; and (5) fruitful to disclose new phenomena or previously unnoted relationships among those already known.[7]

These five characteristics – accuracy, consistency, scope, simplicity and fruitfulness – for evaluating the adequacy of economic theory are important as they make us aware of the limitations of different economic theories.

We may consider that various schools of economic theory are to introduce some other factors or forces to the Walrasian system.[8] We mention a few factors which are fixed in the Walrasian system and have been chosen as endogenous variables in some economic theories:

Capital – the neoclassical growth theory is to consider capital stocks as endogenous variables; nevertheless, the neoclassical growth theory fails to develop tractable analytical frameworks for analyzing economies with heterogeneous households and multiple production sectors.

Population – the dynamics of the population at micro as well as macro levels are the main concerns of population economics;

Knowledge-related variables — technology, knowledge, education level, skill, human capital are now the main concerns of economic theory;

Environment, energy, and resources — these variables are also treated as endogenous variables in some economic models;

Preferences – rapid changes of fashions and tastes are a main character of modern society;

Values, customs, and institutions — these variables are the key variables of the so-called institutional economics.

In the remainder of this chapter, we review a few dynamic economic theories in which some of the exogenous variables in the Walrasian theory are endogenous variables. The theory in this book will treat not only the Walrasian theory, but also those theories as special cases.

1.2 The Solow growth model

In his Nobel Lecture in 1987, Solow (2000: x) stated what he felt about traditional growth theory:

> Growth theory, like much else in macroeconomics, was a product of the depression of the 1930s and of the war that finally ended it. So was I. Nevertheless, it seemed to me that the story told by these models felt wrong. An expedition from Mars arriving on Earth having read this literature would have expected to find only the wreckage of a capitalism that had shaken itself to pieces long ago. Economic history was indeed a record of fluctuations as well as of growth, but most business cycles seemed to be self-limiting. Sustained, though disturbed, growth was not a rarity.

Most neoclassical models are extensions and generalizations of the pioneering works of Solow (1956) and Swan (1956).[9]

First, we describe the behavior of the production sector.[10] Time is represented continuously by a numerical variable which takes on all values from zero onwards ($t \geq 0$). Let $K(t)$ denote the capital existing at each time t and $N(t)$ the flow of labor services used at time t for production. Capital is malleable in the sense that one need distinguish neither its previous use nor the factor productions of its previous use. Malleable capital can be transferred quickly from a production process appropriate at one level of factor intensity to a different process appropriate to a different capital intensity. We use the conventional production function to describe a relationship between inputs and output. The function, $F(t)$, defines the flow of production at time t. The production process is described by some sufficiently smooth function

$$F(t) = F(K(t), N(t)).$$

We assume that $F(K(t), N(t))$ is neoclassical. We note that time does not enter the production function directly, but only through $K(t)$ and $N(t)$. In the rest of this book, we omit time subscripts and in the subsequent analysis whenever no ambiguity results. A production function $F(K, N)$ is called neoclassical if it satisfies the following conditions:

(1) $F(K, N)$ is nonnegative if K and N are nonnegative;
(2) $F(0,0) = 0$;
(3) marginal products, F_K and F_N are nonnegative;

(4) there exist second partial derivatives of F with respect to K and N;
(5) the function is homogeneous of degree one

$$F(\lambda K, \lambda N) = \lambda F(K,N),$$

for all nonnegative λ;
(6) the function is strictly quasi-concave.

Here, we say that the function $F(x)$ with $x = (K,N)$ is strictly quasi-concave if for any $x_1 \geq 0$ and $x_2 \geq 0$, $0 < \lambda < 1$, and for any c, if $F(x_1) \geq c$ and $F(x_2) \geq c$, then

$$F[\lambda x_1 + (1-\lambda)x_2] \geq c,$$

with equality iff $x_1 = x_2$. A concave function appears like a hill. Consider, for example, setting an eggshell on end and cutting it in half. The top half would constitute a concave function.

For the production function $F(K,N)$ we define the homogeneity of degree n for capital and labor inputs as follows:

$$F(\lambda K, \lambda N) = \lambda^n F(K,N)$$

where λ is an arbitrary nonnegative number. When $n = 1$, we say that the production function has constant returns to scale. It is linearly homogeneous or homogeneous of degree one. It simply means that if all inputs are changed in a given proportion, then output also changes in the same proportion. The same definition applies to any number of inputs. When we assume output to be related to infrastructures, knowledge, and land, in addition to labor and capital, we have the same concept of homogeneity. When $n > (<) 1$, we say that the production function displays increasing (decreasing) returns to scale. It should be noted that increasing and decreasing returns to scale are not confined to a homogeneous function.

We assume that the production function exhibits constant returns to scale, meaning that if all inputs rise in some proportion, output will increase in the same proportion. A doubling of the amount of both capital and labor used in production doubles the amount of output produced. We can check directly that a linear homogeneous production function $F(K,N)$ has the following properties:

10   Economic Growth with Income and Wealth Distribution

(i) The production function can be written in terms of per capita output as a function of per capita capital

$$\frac{F}{N} = F(k,1) \equiv f(k), \quad k \equiv \frac{K}{N}. \tag{1.2.1}$$

Output per worker depends only on the amount of capital employed by one worker. Equation (1.2.1) is called the intensive form of the aggregate production function. It is also referred to as the perworker production function.

(ii) The slope of $f(k)$ represents the marginal product of capital, i.e.

$$F_K = \frac{\partial F}{\partial K} = \frac{\partial(F/N)}{\partial(K/N)} = f'(k) > 0.$$

(iii) The marginal product of labor can be obtained by $f(k)$ as follows:

$$F_N = \frac{\partial F}{\partial N} = \frac{\partial(NF/NK)}{\partial(N/K)} = \frac{\partial(f(k)/k)}{\partial(1/k)} = f(k) - kf'(k) > 0.$$

(iv) The Euler Theorem holds:

$$KF_K + NF_N = F.$$

We depict intensive form $f(k)$ of the aggregate production function in Figure 1.2.1. As we move out to the right along the production function, the output per worker increases as the capital/labor ratio, $k(t)$, rises. The shape of $f(k)$ in the figure reflects the assumption that there are diminishing returns to increases in $k(t)$. The increment to output per worker declines as capital per worker rises. The slope of the production function becomes flatter from left to right. This means that although more capital always leads to more output, it does so at a decreasing rate.

We assume (identically numerous) one production sector. Its goal of economic production is to maximize its current profit

$$\pi(t) = p(t)F(t) - r(t)K(t) - w(t)N(t),$$

where $p(t)$ is the price of product, $r(t)$ is the rate of interest, and $w(t)$ is the wage rate.

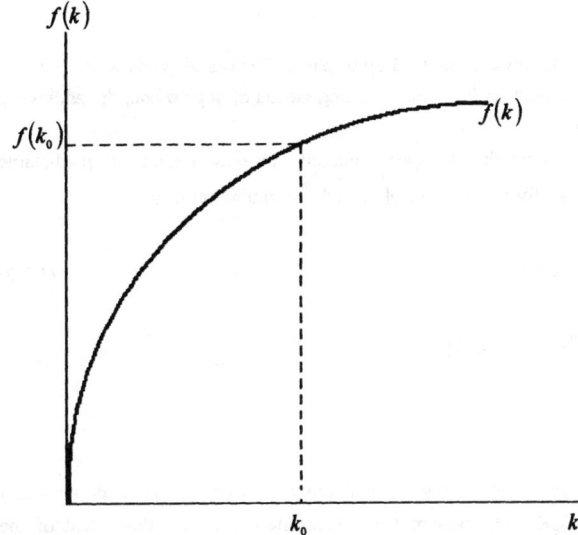

Figure 1.2.1 Intensive form of the aggregate production function

We assume that the output good serves as a medium of exchange and is taken as the numeraire. We thus set $p(t) = 1$ and measure both wages and rental flows in units of the output good. The rate of interest and the wage rate are determined by the markets. Hence, for any individual firm r and w are given at each point in time. The production sector chooses the two variables, K and N, to maximize its profit. Maximizing π with regards to K and N as decision variables yields

$$r = F_K = f'(k), \quad w = F_N = f(k) - kf'(k).$$

We assume that factor markets work quickly enough so that our system always displays competitive equilibrium in factor markets. Thus we always have

$$w(t) = F_N, \quad r(t) = F_K.$$

These equations show that the production factors are paid according to their marginal product. Since we assumed that the production function is homogenous of degree one, we have $KF_K + NF_N = F$, or

$rK + wN = F$.

This means that the total revenue is used up to pay all factors of production. We thus conclude that if the production function is homogeneous of degree one, the adding-up requirement is satisfied.

The Solow model assumes that the agents regularly set aside some fairly predictable portion of its output, $\hat{s}$, for the purpose of capital accumulation; hence

$$\dot{K}(t) = \hat{s}F(t) - \delta_k K(t). \tag{1.2.2}$$

The consumption, $C(t)$, is given by

$$C(t) = (1 - \hat{s})F(t).$$

It is worthwhile introducing Solow's recent comments on the linear depreciation function of capital, $\delta_k K$. This assumption makes depreciation independent of the details of the history of technological change and past gross investment, even though this is known to be empirically inaccurate. Solow (1999) introduces a way to relax this assumption. Define a nonincreasing survivorship function, $\phi(a)$, with $\phi(0) = 1$ and $\phi(+\infty) = 0$. Here, $\phi(a)$ stands for the fraction of any investment that survives to age a. Then if $I(t)$ (which is assumed to equal $\hat{s}F(t)$) is gross investment

$$K(t) = \int_0^\infty \hat{s}F(t-a)\phi(a)\,da.$$

Now differentiation with respect to time and one integration by parts with respect to a leads to

$$\dot{K}(t) = \hat{s}F(t) - \hat{s}\int_0^\infty F(t-a)d(a)\,da,$$

where

$$d(a) \equiv -\frac{d\phi(a)}{da}$$

is the rate of depreciation at age a. The net investment at time t depends on the whole stream of gross investments. If we specify $\phi(a) = \exp(-d_k a)$, then

$$\dot{K}(t) = \hat{s}F(t) - d_k K(t).$$

This is reduced to the Solow capital accumulation equation.

As the production function is neoclassical, one can reduce equation (1.2.2) to the following single differential equation:

$$\dot{k}(t) = \hat{s}f(k(t)) - (n + \delta_k)k(t).$$

We illustrate the dynamics of the capital–labor ratio in Figure 1.2.2. It can be seen that the dynamic system has a unique stable equilibrium.[11]

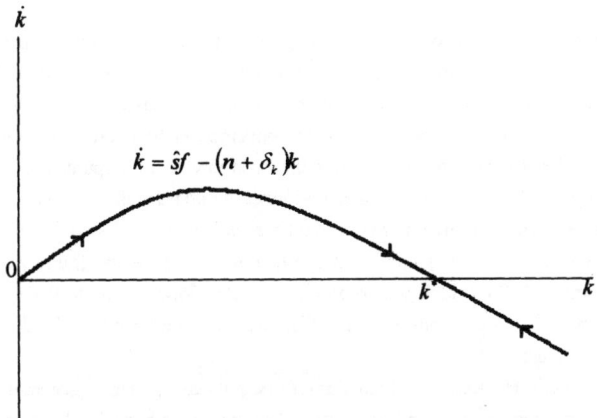

Figure 1.2.2 Evolution of capital–labor ratio in the Solow model

Although the Solow model is an important analytical framework for analyzing economic growth, the main problem for the model is that it lacks a rational mechanism for explaining household behavior. When faced with the choice of multiple goods (like leisure and services), the Solow model does not provide a mechanism for households to make a decision. Any realistic macroeconomic model should be ready for extensions to cases of multiple goods and capital. Many extensions of the Solow

14   *Economic Growth with Income and Wealth Distribution*

model in the 1960s and 1970s have limited implications because of the lack of a rational mechanism for household behavior. Because of this character, the Solow model is not a generalization of the Walrasian system. Nevertheless, it explains the capital accumulation which the Walrasian system cannot explain. There is a need for a theory which deals with the problems which both the Walrasian theory and the Solow growth theory explain.

1.3 The Ramsey growth model

There are two main modeling frameworks in the neoclassical growth theory, the Solow model and the Ramsey growth model, with capital accumulation. The main difference between the two approaches is related to consumers' behavior. Solow (2000: x) explained:

> I know that even as a student I was drawn to the theory of production rather than to the formally almost identical theory of consumer choice. It seemed more down to earth.

The Solow model initiated a new course of development of economic growth theory by using the neoclassical production function and neoclassical production theory, still maintaining the traditional way of dealing with consumer behavior in dynamic analysis. The Solow model introduces a plausible consumption function with some empirical support. The Ramsey model assumes the economy to be populated by a single immortal representative household that optimizes its consumption plans over infinite time in the sort of institutional environment that will translate its wishes into actual resources allocation at any point in time. We now introduce the framework initiated by Ramsey in 1928, which was proposed and developed as a story about centralized economic planning (Ramsey, 1928). The Ramsey model was refined by Cass (1965) and Koopmans (1965).

We assume a one-sector economy in which 1 unit of output can be used to generate 1 unit of household consumption, or 1 unit of additional capital. Each household consists of one or more adults who are employed in the competitive labor market and receive wages for providing labor services. A household is imagined as an immortal extended family. The households receive interest income on assets, purchase goods for consumption and save by accumulating additional assets. Each household maximizes utility and incorporates a budget constraint over an infinite horizon. Denote by $C(t)$ the total consumption at time t and $c(t) \equiv C(t)/N(t)$ is consumption per worker. It is assumed that the labor market clears at any point in time and each adult supplies 1 unit of labor services per unit of time. Households take the net rate of return $r(t)$ on assets and the wage rate $w(t)$ paid per unit of labor services as given in the competitive markets.

Most aspects of the Ramsey model are similar to the Solow model. The variables, $Y(t)$, $K(t)$, $N(t)$, $k(t)$, $w(t)$, $r(t)$, in the Ramsey model have the same meanings as in the Solow model. The production process, marginal conditions, and population growth are the same as in the Solow model. Different from the Solow model which assumes that the agents regularly set aside some fairly predictable portion of its output for the purpose of capital accumulation, the Ramsey model endogenously determines saving and consumption. The firms maximize the present value of profits. Since firms rent capital and labor services and have no adjustment costs, there are no intertemporal elements in the firm's optimal behavior. Maximizing the profit with K and N as variables yields the same conditions as in equation (1.2.1).

We now describe households' behavior. In the Ramsey approach, households' decisions on saving are represented by assuming that consumers maximize the discounted value of their flow of utility, using a constant rate of impatience. The extended family is assumed to grow at an exogenously given rate n. Let the number of adults at time 0 be unity, the family size at time t is

$$N(t) = e^{nt}.$$

Each member supplies one unit of labor per unit time, without disutility. The household's preference is expressed by an instantaneous utility function, $u(c(t))$, where $c(t)$ is the flow of consumption per person. Let the discount rate for utility be denoted by ρ. For simplicity, specify $u(c)$ as

$$u(c) = \frac{c(t)^{1-\theta} - 1}{1 - \theta}, \quad \theta > 0, \tag{1.3.1}$$

where θ is a parameter, $u' > 0$, $u'' < 0$, and u satisfies the Inada conditions: $u' \to \infty$ as $c \to 0$ and $u' \to 0$ as $c \to \infty$.

Assume that each household maximizes utility U as given by

$$U = \int_0^\infty u(c(t)) e^{nt} e^{-\rho t} dt, \quad c(t) \geq 0, \quad t \geq 0.$$

16 Economic Growth with Income and Wealth Distribution

The household makes the decision subject to a lifetime budget constraint. We denote the net assets per household by $k(t)$, which is measured in units of consumables. The total income at each point in time is equal to $w + rk$. The flow budget constraint for the household is

$$\dot{k}(t) = w(t) + r(t)k(t) - c(t) - nk(t) = f(t) - c(t) - nk(t). \tag{1.3.2}$$

The equation means that the change rate of assets per person is equal to per capita income minus per capita consumption and the term, nk. It is assumed that the credit market imposes a constraint of borrowing, the present value of assets must be asymptotically nonnegative, that is

$$\lim_{t \to \infty} \left[k(t) \exp\left\{ -\int_0^t (\rho - n) \, dv \right\} \right] \geq 0.$$

The present-value Hamiltonian is given by

$$J = u(c)e^{-(\rho-n)t} + \overline{\lambda}(w + rk - c - nk),$$

where $\overline{\lambda}$ is the present-value shadow price of income. The first-order conditions are

$$\frac{\partial J}{\partial c} = 0 \implies \overline{\lambda} = u' e^{-(\rho - n)t},$$

$$\frac{d\overline{\lambda}}{dt} = -\frac{\partial J}{\partial k} \implies \frac{d\overline{\lambda}}{dt} = -(\rho - n)\overline{\lambda}. \tag{1.3.3}$$

The transversality condition is given by

$$\lim_{t \to \infty} [\overline{\lambda}(t) k(t)] = 0.$$

By equation (1.3.3), we can derive

$$r = \rho - \frac{u''c}{u'} \left(\frac{1}{c} \frac{dc}{dt} \right). \tag{1.3.4}$$

This equation says that households choose consumption so as to equate the rate of return r to the rate of time preference ρ plus the rate of decrease of the marginal utility of consumption, u', due to growing per capita consumption, c. Inserting equation (1.3.1) into equation (1.3.4) yields

$$\dot{c}(t) = \frac{r(t) - \rho}{\theta} c(t) = \frac{f'(k) - \rho}{\theta} c(t). \tag{1.3.5}$$

The trajectory of the economy is determined by equations (1.3.2) and (1.3.5). The phase diagram in $c(t)$ and $k(t)$ is shown by Figure 1.3.1. Along the vertical line defined by $f'(k^*) = \rho$, the change rate of consumption per capita is equal to zero, that is, $\dot{c}(t) = 0$. The consumption per capita increases to the left of the curve and falls to the right. Along the locus defined by $c(t) = f(t) - nk(t)$, the change rate of the capital–labor ratio equals zero. The capital–labor ratio falls above the curve and increases below it. With the requirement $\rho > n$ (without which the utility becomes unbounded along feasible paths), the intersection of the two curves determines a unique steady state, (k^*, c^*).

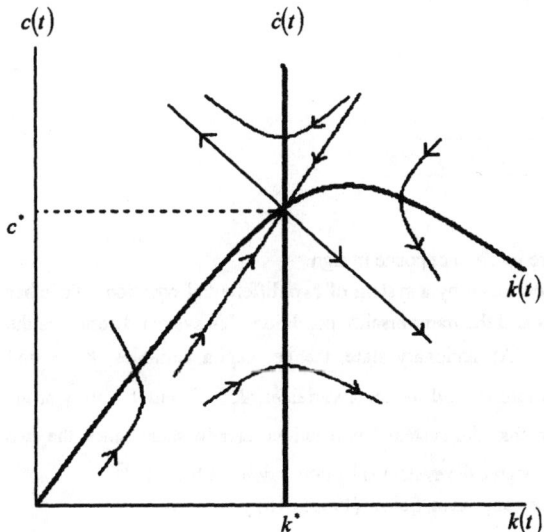

Figure 1.3.1 The dynamics of the Ramsey model

18 Economic Growth with Income and Wealth Distribution

The local stability of the $c-k$ system is determined by the characteristic roots of the following matrix of the coefficients of $k(t)$ and $c(t)$ equations linearized around the equilibrium point

$$J \equiv \begin{bmatrix} \dfrac{\partial \dot{k}}{\partial k} & \dfrac{\partial \dot{k}}{\partial c} \\ \dfrac{\partial \dot{c}}{\partial k} & \dfrac{\partial \dot{c}}{\partial c} \end{bmatrix} = \begin{bmatrix} f' - n & -1 \\ \dfrac{f''c}{\theta} & 0 \end{bmatrix}.$$

We have

$$\operatorname{tr}(J) = f' - n = \rho - n > 0, \quad |J| = \frac{f''c}{\theta} < 0. \tag{1.3.6}$$

The characteristic equation is

$$\phi^2 - \operatorname{tr}(J)\phi + |J| = 0.$$

Inserting equation (1.3.6) into the above equation yields

$$\phi^2 - (\rho - n)\phi + \frac{f''c}{\theta} = 0.$$

We solve

$$\phi_{1,2} = \frac{(\rho - n) \pm \sqrt{(\rho - n)^2 - 4f''c/\theta}}{2}.$$

The characteristic roots are real and opposite in sign.

The Ramsey model is controlled by a system of two differential equations. Together with the initial conditions and the transversality condition, this system determines the path of the two variables. At stationary state, the per capita variables, k, c and $y\,(\equiv Y/N)$, grow at the rate 0, and the level variables, K, C and Y, grow at the rate, n. It can be shown that the system has a unique steady state. Since the two eigenvalues have opposite signs, the system is locally saddle-path stable.[12]

With regard to the Ramsey approach, Solow (1999: 646) points out:

These formulations all allocate current output between consumption and investment according to a more or less mechanical rule. The rule usually has an economic interpretation, and possibly some robust empirical validity, but it lacks "microfoundations". The current fashion is to derive the consumption-investment decision from the decentralized behavior of intertemporal-utility-maximizing households and perfectly competitive profit maximizing firms. This is not without cost. The economy has to be populated by a fixed number of identical immortal households, each endowed with perfect foresight over the infinite future. No market imperfections can be allowed on the side of firms.

The Ramsey modeling framework is analytically more complicated than the Solow model – it is perhaps due to the analytical intractability associated with the approach that many important dynamic economic issues have not been studied with an integrated approach. Any concrete problem results in a complicated analytical problem incapable of being thoroughly analyzed. For instance, the Solow model is one-dimensional, while the Ramsey model is two-dimensional. The equilibrium of the Ramsey is a saddle point for the two-dimensional differential equations. If the initial values of the two variables are located anywhere but on the saddle path, the resulting trajectory is nonoptimal for the household (or else ultimately infeasible). The appropriate path for this economy is along the saddle path, which leads asymptotically to the equilibrium. If we are only interested in steady states and neglected issues about stability and dynamic paths, the Solow model is similar to the Ramsey model; but the former is usually simpler.

The form of utility formulation in the Ramsey optimal growth theory is given by

$$\int_0^\infty U[C(t)]e^{-\rho t}\, dt.$$

The specified form means that the household's utility at time 0 is a weighted sum of all future flows of utility. The parameter, ρ (≥ 0), is defined as the rate of time preference. A positive value of ρ means that utilities are valued less the later they are received. There are two assumptions involved in the Ramsey model. The first is that utility is additional over time. Although we may add capital over time, it is unrealistic to add utility over infinite time. Intuitively it is not reasonable to add happiness over time. It is well known in utility theory that when we use the utility function to describe consumer behavior an arbitrary increasing transformation of the function would result in identical maximization of the consumer at each point in time. Obviously, the above formulation will not result in an identical behavior if U is subjected to arbitrarily different increasing transformations at different times. The second implication of the above formation is that the parameter, ρ, is meaningless if utility is not additional over time.

It should be noted that Ramsey interpreted the agent as a social planner, rather than a household. The planner chose consumption and saving for current and future generations. Ramsey assumed $\rho = 0$ and considered $\rho > 0$ "ethically indefensible". If $\rho = 0$, by equation (1.3.5) consumption per capita always grows if the interest rate is positive irrespective of whether wealth grows or falls. A fundamental difference between the Solow model and Ramsey model is that the Solow model has a stable equilibrium point, while the standard Ramsey model has a saddle equilibrium point. This implies that for the Ramsey theory, a simple economy (without changes in knowledge, population, preference, or any other changeable returns to scale effect) is always unstable. This dynamic character is due to the fact that a household takes account of welfare in an infinite time horizon in making any decision, while a firm calculates the profit quite differently.

The Solow model determines consumption as follows:

$$c(t) = (1 - \hat{s}) f(k(t)).$$

Taking the derivatives of this relation with respect to t yields

$$\dot{c}(t) = (1 - \hat{s}) f'(k) \dot{k}(t).$$

The change in consumption is related to the rate of interest; but the direction is not affected by the rate of interest. The rational household has increasing, stationary, or decreasing consumption according to whether the wealth rises, is stationary, or falls. The consumer adapts consumption level not according to the difference between the interest rate and discount rate for utility as the Ramsey model predicts. According to the Solow model theory, a Japanese consumer would consume more, irrespective of low interest, if his wealth increases; he would consume less, irrespective of a high interest rate, when his wealth falls. On the other hand, the Ramsey model predicts

$$\dot{c}(t) = \frac{f'(k) - \rho}{\theta} c(t).$$

This implies that the difference between r and ρ determines whether households choose a pattern of per capita consumption that rises, stays constant, or falls over time. That is, the optimizing household has increasing, stationary, or decreasing consumption according to whether the current real interest rate exceeds, equals, or falls short of the utility discount rate. According to this result, consumption always falls if the interest rate is low and the utility discount rate is high. As observed by Maital and Maital (1994):

> There is, however, strong empirical evidence that for most of us, the marginal rate of time preference exceeds the rate of interest, often by a large margin... Kurz found empirically measured subjective interest rates as high as 60%.

Since the value of ρ cannot be empirically identified, it is difficult to judge the merit of the Ramsey model.[13] Many studies are conducted to determine the value of the discounting rate, ρ. The Ramsey model has played an important role mainly in the development of economic theory.

In 1937 Paul Samuelson published an article on discounted utility. Since then, discounted utility was rapidly adopted as the framework of choice for intertemporal decisions. It is worth citing from Samuelson's following caution against applying utility to the study of welfare (Samuelson, 1937: 161):

> Any connection between utility as discussed here and any welfare concept is disavowed.

It is nowadays common to use utility in modeling and comparing welfare. Samuleson (1937: 159) elucidates:

> It is completely arbitrary to assume that the individual behaves so as to maximize an integral of the form envisaged in [the discounted utility model].

This reservation does not affect the dominant role of the discounted utility.

This book will use an alternative utility function not only because the validity of the discounted utility concept has been questioned from philosophical, psychological or/and empirical aspects,[14] but also because many obviously significant issues, such as growth with heterogeneous households and growth with interregional dynamics, can hardly be properly discussed with the concept as having become evident in the history of theoretical economics in the last 40 years.

1.4 A post-Keynesian model of growth and distribution

The previous two sections introduced the two key models in growth theory. Nevertheless, the models do not take account of differences among households. This section introduces a principal modeling approach to issues related to growth and distribution. Kaldor (1955) first formulated this theory in his seminal article in

1955. In 1962, Pasinetti reformulated the Kaldor model and introduced explicitly the assumption of steady growth. He also suggested a change in the saving function of workers and set the interest rate equal to the profit rate. After the publication of these seminal works, many articles about the issue were published.[15] The key feature of this theory is that it puts the population into different groups, whose consumption and saving behavior are homogeneous within each group and are different among groups.[16]

The model represented here was developed by Sato.[17] The population is classified into workers and capitalists. It is assumed that the capitalists' propensity to save is equal to unity, and the workers' propensity to save is equal to the relative profit share. The wage rate, $w(t)$, and the profit rate, $r(t)$, are given by

$$r = f'(k), \quad w = f(k) - kf'(k),$$

where $f(k)$ is the per capita output level and $k(t)$ is the per capita capital. The output is distributed between wages and profits

$$Y = rK + wN.$$

The relative share of capital is given by $h \equiv rK/Y$. Denote by K_c and K_w the equities held by capitalists and workers, respectively. We have

$$K = K_c + K_w = zK + (1-z)K,$$

where z is the capitalists' share of wealth, $z \equiv K_c/K$. The workers' total income is given by $wN + rK_w$ and the capitalists' total income by rK_c. Assume that the capitalists' saving rate is s_c and the workers' saving rate is s_w, where we require

$$0 \leq s_w < s_c \leq 1.$$

As

$$\dot{K}_c = s_c rK_c, \quad \dot{K}_w = s_w(wN + rK_w),$$

we have

$$\frac{\dot{k}}{k} = (s_c - s_w)zf' + \frac{s_w f}{k} - n, \qquad (1.4.1)$$

where n is the fixed population growth rate. Differentiating $z \equiv K_c/K$ with respect to time results in

$$\frac{\dot{z}}{z} = (s_c - s_w)(1-z)f' - s_w\left(\frac{f}{k} - f'\right). \qquad (1.4.2)$$

The dynamics consist of equations (1.4.1) and (1.4.2). An equilibrium point is determined by

$$(s_c - s_w)zf' + \frac{s_w f}{k} - n = 0,$$

$$(s_c - s_w)(1-z)f' - s_w\left(\frac{f}{k} - f'\right) = 0.$$

We thus have $f' = n/s_c$, which is independent of the workers' propensity to save in balanced growth. It is straightforward to carry out traditional comparative statics analysis with regard to parameter changes. Here, we omit further analysis. As in the Solow model, this approach does not have a suitable behavioral mechanism for consumers. Nevertheless, this is one of the analytical frameworks, which explicitly introduced heterogeneous households into formal economic growth theory.

1.5 A representative consumer approach in the Ramsey theory

As the Ramsey model provides a rational mechanism of household behavior, it is reasonable to expect that the one-sector Ramsey model has been extended to economies with multiple sectors and/or heterogeneous households over the years.

The Ramsey growth model with heterogeneous households tends to result in dynamically intractable problems. A typical model of the Ramsey approach is reflected in Becker's model of heterogeneous households (Becker, 1980). The model forges a link between income distribution, wealth distribution, and economic growth. Becker verifies a conjecture of Ramsey (1928). The model demonstrates that if an agent's lifetime utility function over an infinite horizon is represented by a stationary, additive, discounted function with a constant pure rate of time preference, then the income distribution is shown in the long-run steady state to be determined by the lowest discount rate. The household (for instance, a single household) with the lowest rate of discount owns all the capital and earns a wage income; all other households (for instance, two million households) receive a wage income. Indeed, there are variants of the Ramsey model in which the long-run distribution of wealth can be nondegenerate. For example, progressive taxation or monopolistic power of the dominant household can be factors for the existence of equilibrium points with a nongenerate wealth distribution.[18]

Caselli and Ventura propose a representative consumer (RC) model of distribution with heterogeneous households.[19] Assuming that heterogeneous households have an identical discounting rate of utility in the Ramsey utility function, they show how to introduce various sources of consumer heterogeneity in one-sector representative consumer growth models.[20] We now introduce the model by Caselli and Ventura.

The economy has many infinitely lived consumers, indexed by $j = 1, \cdots, J$. The number J is so large that any concrete individual is small in the sense his choices have negligible effects on aggregate quantities and prices.[21] Let $c_j(t) \in R^+$ denote the after-tax private consumption of agent j at date t and let

$$c(t) \equiv (c_1(t), \cdots, c_J(t)),$$

be the vector of consumptions. For simplicity, we omit the time indexes when this is not confusing. The average consumption is

$$\bar{c} = \frac{1}{J}\sum_{j=1}^{J} c_j.$$

The utility of consumer j is given by

$$U_j = \int_0^\infty \frac{(c_j + \beta_j g)^{1-\theta} - 1}{1-\theta} e^{-\rho t}\, dt,\ \theta, \rho > 0, \tag{1.5.1}$$

where $\beta_j \in R^+$ and $g(t) \in R^+$.[22] The term, $\beta_j g$, is interpreted as the value of the publicly provided goods that the consumer receives in terms of the private consumption good. Introduce

$$\beta \equiv (\beta_1, \cdots, \beta_J)$$

and normalize

$$\frac{1}{J}\sum_{j=1}^{J}\beta_j = 1.$$

We refer to g as the average consumption of publicly provided goods. We define x as the growth rate of g. Let $a_j(t) \in R^+$ denote the stock of financial assets of consumer j at date t and let

$$a(t) \equiv (a_1(t), \cdots, a_J(t)).$$

We denote by $\pi_j \in R^+$ the skill level of agent j and let

$$\pi \equiv (\pi_1, \cdots, \pi_J)$$

and

$$\frac{1}{J}\sum_{j=1}^{J}\pi_j = 1.$$

Let $r(t) \in R^+$ and $w(t) \in R^+$ denote the after-tax rate of return on assets and the average after-tax wage rate. Also, let $p \in (0,1]$ be equal to one minus the proportional consumption tax. We define ϕ as the growth rate of p. We can now write consumer j's flow budget constraint

$$\dot{a}_j = ra_j + w\pi_j - \frac{c_j}{p}. \tag{1.5.2}$$

Maximizing U_j subject to constraint (1.5.2) implies the following Euler equation

$$\dot{c}_j = \frac{r - \rho + \phi}{\theta}(c_j + \beta_j g) - \beta_j \dot{g}. \tag{1.5.3}$$

Integrate the above equation

$$c_j + \beta_j g = \mu \left[a_j + \int_t^\infty \left(\pi_j w + \frac{\beta_j g}{p} \right) \exp\left(-\int_t^\tau r\, dv \right) d\tau \right], \quad (1.5.4)$$

where

$$\mu = \int_t^\infty \frac{1}{p} \exp\left\{ \int_t^\tau \frac{1}{\theta} [r(1-\theta-\rho+\phi)] dv \right\} d\tau.$$

Equation (1.5.4) states that the total consumption is a fraction of the total wealth. It can be seen that the variable μ is independent of the characteristics of the consumers.

We now show that the sum of all consumers behaves exactly as if the economy contained a single consumer with average asset holdings, skills, and taste parameters. The average equations of equations (1.5.2) and (1.5.4) are given by

$$\dot{a} = ra + w\pi - \frac{c}{p}, \quad (1.5.5)$$

$$c + \beta g = \mu \left[a + \int_t^\infty \left(w + \frac{g}{p} \right) \exp\left(-\int_t^\tau r\, dv \right) d\tau \right]. \quad (1.5.6)$$

As shown by Caselli and Ventura, one may determine distribution of income and wealth with the above two equations and some additional conditions for determining g, w, p and r. As our purpose is to illustrate the way in which the RC theory solves distributive issues, we refer further analysis of the model to Caselli and Ventura. It can be seen that this modeling framework is not effective when we take account of variations in households' preferences. As empirical studies have shown the existence of great differences in impatience among households and the Ramsey approach proves futile for dealing with the issues, it is necessary to look for alternative ways to explain the reality. In fact, as shown in a recent survey on studies of estimating individuals' discount rates by Frederick et al. (2002), rates differ dramatically across studies, and within studies across individuals. There is no convergence toward an agreed-on rate of impatience. It is estimated, for instance, by Warner and Pleeter (2001) that individual discount rates vary between 0 and 70 percent per year.[23]

1.6 The overlapping-generations (OLG) model

The overlapping-generations model is another key modeling framework in economic dynamics. This approach is basically the discrete version of the Ramsey model. Since the approach allows people to live in two periods and people behave differently in each period,[24] economic growth problems related to physical capital accumulation and/or human capital can be constructed in such a way that models are analytically tractable. This tractability is perhaps the main reason for the popularity of the analytical framework.

This section introduces the model of finite-horizon households.[25] It is common to assume, in the OLG analytical framework, that each person lives for only two periods.[26] People work in the first period and retire in the second. If one thinks of reality, one period perhaps lasts over 30 years. As we neglect any possibility of transfers from government or from members of other generations, people consume in both periods; they pay for consumption in the second period by saving in the first period. The cohort that is born at time t is referred to as generation t. Members of this generation are young in period t and old in period $t+1$. At each point in time, members of only two generations are alive. Each person maximizes lifetime utility, which depends on consumption in the two periods of life. It is assumed that people are born with no assets and do not care about events after their death; they are not altruistic toward their children, and therefore, do not provide bequests or other transfers to members of the next generation. Their lifetime utility is specified as

$$U(t) = \frac{c_1^{1-\theta}(t) - 1}{1 - \theta} + \left(\frac{1}{1+\rho}\right)\frac{c_2^{1-\theta}(t+1) - 1}{1 - \theta}, \qquad (1.6.1)$$

where $\theta > 0$, $\rho > 0$, $c_i(t)$ is consumption of generation i, $i = 1, 2$. Each individual supplies one unit of labor inelastically while young and receives the wage income $w(t)$; he does not work when old. Let s_t stand for the amount saved in period t. The budget constraint for period t

$$c_1(t) + s(t) = w(t). \qquad (1.6.2)$$

Let $r(t+1)$ denote the interest rate on one-period loans between periods t and $t+1$. In period $t+1$, the individuals consume the savings plus the accrued interest:

$$c_2(t+1) = (1 + r(t+1))s(t). \qquad (1.6.3)$$

For each individual, $w(t)$ and $r(t+1)$ are exogenous; he chooses $c_1(t)$ and $s(t)$ (and, hence c_2,) subject to equations (1.6.2) and (1.6.3). Substitute equations (1.6.2) and (1.6.3) into the utility function to delete $c_1(t)$ and $c_2(t+1)$:

$$U(t) = \frac{(w(t)-s(t))^{1-\theta}-1}{1-\theta} + \left(\frac{1}{1+\rho}\right)\frac{(1+r(t+1))^{1-\theta}s^{1-\theta}(t)-1}{1-\theta}.$$

The first-order condition with respect to $s(t)$ is

$$s^{-\theta}(t)(1+r(t+1))^{1-\theta} = (1+\rho)(w(t)-s(t))^{-\theta}, \qquad (1.6.4)$$

which also implies, under equations (1.6.2) and (1.6.3)

$$\frac{c_2(t+1)}{c_1(t)} = \left(\frac{1+r(t+1)}{1+\rho}\right)^{1/\theta} \qquad (1.6.5)$$

Solve equations (1.6.4)

$$s(t) = \frac{w(t)}{\varphi(t+1)}, \qquad (1.6.6)$$

where

$$\varphi(t+1) \equiv 1 + \frac{(1+\rho)^{1/\theta}}{(1+r(t+1))^{(1-\theta)/\theta}} > 1.$$

We obtain

$$s_r \equiv \frac{\partial s(t)}{\partial r(t+1)} = \left(\frac{1-\theta}{\theta}\right)\left(\frac{1+\rho}{1+r(t+1)}\right)\frac{s(t)}{\varphi(t+1)},$$

$$s_w \equiv \frac{\partial s(t)}{\partial w(t)} = \frac{1}{\varphi(t+1)}, \quad 0 < s_w < 1. \qquad (1.6.7)$$

We see

$$s_r \begin{cases} > 0 & \text{if } \theta < 1, \\ = 0 & \text{if } \theta = 1, \\ < 0 & \text{if } \theta > 1. \end{cases}$$

Firms' behavior is the same as in the Solow model. They have the neoclassical production function, $y(t) = f(k(t))$, where

$$y(t) \equiv \frac{Y(t)}{N(t)}, \quad k(t) \equiv \frac{K(t)}{N(t)},$$

where $N(t)$ is the number of young people, $Y(t)$ is the total output, and $K(t)$ is the total capital. The marginal conditions are

$$r(t) = f'(k(t)) - \delta_k, \quad w(t) = f(k(t)) - k(t)f'(k(t)), \tag{1.6.8}$$

where δ_k is the depreciation rate of capital.

In the closed economy, households' assets equal the capital stock. Aggregate net investment equals total income minus total consumption:

$$K(t+1) - K(t) = w(t)N(t) + r(t)K(t) - c_1(t)N(t) - c_2(t)N(t-1). \tag{1.6.9}$$

Substituting equations (1.6.8) into equation (1.6.9), we get

$$K(t+1) - K(t) = F(K(t), N(t)) - C(t), \tag{1.6.10}$$

where

$$C(t) = c_1(t)N(t) + c_2(t)N(t-1).$$

From equations (1.6.9), (1.6.2), and (1.6.3), we obtain

$$K(t+1) = s(t)N(t) + (1 + r(t))(K(t) - s_{t-1}(t)N_{t-1}(t)).$$

Assume that the economy starts with the condition

$$c_2(1)N(0) = (1 + r(1))K(1),$$

which is equivalent to $K(2) = s(1)N(1)$ with equations (1.6.9) and (1.6.2). Hence, the above equation becomes

$$K(t+1) = s(t)N(t),$$

which means that the savings of the young equal the next period's capital stock. We can write this equation in per capita terms:

$$k(t+1) = \frac{s(t)}{1+n}.$$

Substituting $s(t)$ in equation (1.6.6) into the above equation yields

$$k(t+1)\left[1 + \frac{(1+\rho)^{1/\theta}}{(1+r(t+1))^{(1-\theta)/\theta}}\right] = \frac{w(t)}{(1+n)}, \qquad (1.6.11)$$

in which we use the definition of $\varphi(t+1)$. In the case that utility is logarithmic ($\theta = 1$), it can be shown that equation (1.6.11) becomes

$$k(t+1) = \frac{1}{(1+n)(2+\rho)}[f(k(t)) - k(t)f'(k(t))]. \qquad (1.6.12)$$

The system has a unique equilibrium and it is stable.

1.7 Timescales, changeable speeds, and economic theory[27]

Economics consists of many schools, even though the economic world is one. The parallel existence of multiple schools implies the existence of a higher theory which treats all meaningful schools as special cases and perhaps provides some new insights. My book, *Synergetic Economics*, published in 1991 as a part of Professor Hermann Haken's Synergetics book series, shows that the time is mature for constructing a more general economic theory because of the recent rapid developments of nonlinear theory and computers. Synergetic economics emphasizes timescales and changeable speeds of various economic variables in economic evolution. We now briefly describe relations between timescales and speeds in economic analysis.

As time passes, economic issues with which economists are concerned have shifted. Even since the time of Adam Smith, the economic variables that economists have dealt with appear to have been invariant. But the ways in which these variables are combined and the speeds at which they change have constantly varied and the dominant economic doctrines have shifted over time and space. The complexity of economic reality is constantly increasing in modern times. This is partially because of the expanded capital and knowledge stocks of mankind. Knowledge, in the fields of philosophy, arts, literature, music, technology and sciences, expands man's imagination and extends the possibilities of human action, not to mention that the knowledge reservoir can directly satisfy the desires of an unlimited number of people at the same time. Knowledge is not only power and sources of wealth, but also the most durable capital good for the human mind. Increases in machines, housing and infrastructures have enriched the human environment, increased accessibility to various locations, and enlarged the variety of human behavior. The explosion of knowledge and capital has resulted in complicated fields of human interactions.

Time is at the center of the chief difficulty of almost every economic problem. The role of time in decision-making and action is becoming increasingly complicated as the variety of action and social networks is expanding. It is a difficult issue to decide the length of time which affects a particular decision making since each kind of human decision is made with different timescales and two people may have different timescales with regard to the same kind of decision making. Because of the high variety of human behavior and timescales, in order to analyze a single person's economic behavior as a whole we have to conduct the analysis within a framework with varied timescales. Human behavior is connected in direct or indirect ways in fields of human action; but we may miss the interdependence between some elements if we do not properly recognize the role of time.

If we examine the complexity of economic evolution from a historical perspective, we may argue that mankind has experienced three economic structural transformations – from a hunting society to an agricultural one, an agricultural society to an industrial one, and an industrial society to an information/knowledge-based one. These transformations are still occurring in different nations in different forms at different speeds. Each of these economic systems has certain corresponding dominant ideologies such as religions, socialism, and capitalism. At each turning point there tend to be great conflicts among different social classes, though forms of conflict are affected by geographical conditions, cultural traditions, the international environment, and other factors. As an illustration of applying the concept of speed of change in analyzing economic structural changes, we may select three basic variables, the population, capital, and knowledge. As shown in Table 1.7.1, these three variables may be roughly considered to be changeable at different speeds in different societies.

Table 1.7.1 Change speeds of economic variables

Society Variables	Agricultural	Industrial	Knowledge
Population	fast	fast/slow	slow
Capital	slow	slow/fast	fast
Knowledge	slow	slow/fast	fast

It may be argued that if we are interested in examining agricultural economies, we may concentrate on studying population (and power struggle) dynamics. But the analytical conclusions about agricultural economies cannot be applied to explain the economic dynamics of industrialized economies, as capital is the dominant variable of industrial economies. Similarly the analytical conclusions about capital-based societies cannot be applied to explain economic phenomena of knowledge-based societies. In fact, from studies of the history of economic analysis,[28] it is clear that many economic ideas were created at a time when societies were faced with new economic problems (such as structural transformation) and thus required new ideas to solve those problems. We may thus expect a certain correspondence between the creation of economists' ideas and historical conditions.

Another dimension in analysis is space. Man, action, capital, knowledge, and time can become culturally and socially meaningful only if we locate them over space. Each human being is born into a unique existence and each piece of land has its unique attributes in affecting human action. Space means individual characteristics and accordingly requires refined classification. This is particularly important in analyzing modern economies. Fast technological changes, richness of material living conditions, complicated international interactions, and many other modern phenomena have increased the complexity of spatial economies. Subsystems such as ecological, economical and social subsystems, which could once be decomposable as separate elements in analyzing the social system at least in the short term over a homogeneous space, have to be treated as a part of the whole system. Economic relations cannot be recognized if we do not explicitly introduce spatial and temporal dimensions. Without a spatial dimension, we can hardly analyze actual processes of, for instance, how the Japanese economy may actually affect the world economy. In fact, the choice of spatiotemporal scale is a delicate and obligatory process and must be made before actual study of any special economic problem. The explicit awareness of this necessity is important for understanding both economic reality and the structure of economics. For instance, for human life what is good to one's taste (assessment on a short timescale) may be harmful to one's health (assessment on a longer timescale). One can hardly explain differences between Keynes and Schumpeter's economic visions without differentiating their temporal scales. Temporal scales in the economist's vision have complicated interdependent relationships with actual analyses and abstraction of reality.

1.8 The structure of the book

Contemporary economic theory includes a number of separated subtheories. It is more desirable to have one compact theoretical framework than multiple separate theories to explain various aspects of reality. I have made efforts to examine various aspects of national economies with a few concepts within a consistent framework.[29] This book explores complex interdependence between economic growth and income and wealth distribution. The book is organized as follows.

Chapter 2 first proposes the one-sector growth (OSG) model with capital accumulation which plays the key role in making some progress in economic theory along the lines of the neoclassical growth theory. Section 2.1 studies the OSG model. Section 2.2 further explains the OSG model with the Cobb-Douglas utility and production functions. Section 2.3 examines the OSG model in discrete version. In Section 2.4, we introduce time distribution between leisure and labor into the OSG model. Section 2.5 introduces public goods into the OSG model and shows possible increasing returns to scale in the dynamic system. Section 2.6 examines the one-sector economic system in which capital stocks are employed both for economic and home production. Section 2.7 introduces environment into the OSG model. Section 2.8 studies interactions between economic development and population growth. Section 2.9 introduces money into the OSG model and examines issues related to money neutrality. Section 2.10 studies the dynamics of a small open economy. Section 2.11 discusses the theoretical foundations of the utility function proposed in this study. Section 2.12 examines relations of our approach to consumers and traditional theories about behavior of households. The traditional theories reviewed here include the Keynesian consumption function, the life cycle hypothesis, the permanent income hypothesis, the consumption function in the Solow model, and the utility maximization approach by Ramsey. In Appendix A.2.1, we present a growth model with endogenous fertility and age support.

Chapter 3 introduces endogenous human capital and knowledge into growth theory. We emphasize the interdependence between economic growth and knowledge creation and utilization. Section 3.1 combines the traditional AK growth model with technological change and the OSG approach to consumer behavior. The simple modeling framework generates possible infinite economic growth. Section 3.2 examines the interdependence between education and economic growth. The human capital growth may come from two sources – Arrow's learning by producing and Uzawa's learning through education. We show how path-dependent economic phenomena can be created when three learning sources exhibit different returns to scales. Section 3.3 introduces knowledge utilization and creation into the OSG model. Sections 3.4–3.7 study some models with knowledge utilization and creation under imperfect competition. Section 3.4 studies Romer's growth model with endogenous knowledge under monopolistic competition. Section 3.5 studies endogenous growth based on intentional industrial innovation. The model is proposed by Grossman and Helpman. In this approach, research is treated as an ordinary economic activity that requires the input of resources and responds to profit opportunities. Returns to R&D are possible because of the monopoly rents from imperfectly competitive products markets. Section 3.6 introduces a growth model with a variety of consumer products. The idea is to introduce a variety of consumer goods into the utility function that parallels the treatment of a variety of intermediate products in the production function as in the previous section. Section 3.7 examines a growth model, proposed by Galor and Weil, that captures the historical evolution of population, technology, and output. The economy evolves three regimes that have characterized economic development: from a Malthusian regime (where technological progress is slow and population growth prevents any sustained rise in income per capita) into a post-Malthusian regime (where technological progress rises and population growth absorbs only part of output growth) to a modern growth regime (where population growth is reduced and income growth is sustained).

Chapter 4 introduces heterogeneous households into one-sector growth economies. We emphasize the interdependence of growth and income and wealth distribution among various households. The chapter is organized as follows. Section 4.1 examines a dynamic interdependence of two groups with different productivities and preferences within the OSG framework. Section 4.2 studies the OSG model with any number of types of households. Section 4.3 introduces knowledge creation and utilization to the two-group model. Section 4.4 illustrates a widely used approach to issues related to growth with inequality. The sample model is proposed by Moav. The model demonstrates persistence of inequality. In this model, the evolution of income within each dynasty in society is governed by a dynamical system that generates a poverty trap equilibrium point along with a high-income equilibrium point. Section 4.5 is concerned with interactions between human capital accumulation, economic growth, and inequality. In Section 4.6, we discuss issues related to how to aggregate labor input of heterogeneous labors.

Chapter 5 deals with multi-sector growth economies with a homogeneous population. Section 5.1 introduces the Uzawa two-sector growth model. Section 5.2 reexamines the economic issues in the Uzawa model with the utility function proposed in this study. Different from the Uzawa model in which consumer behavior is treated in the

Growth and Distribution 35

same way as in the Solow model, our model determines the consumer's decision on saving and consumption with the assumption of utility maximization. Section 5.3 examines the interdependence between economic growth and economic structure with labor supply and consumer durables. Section 5.4 introduces endogenous knowledge into the growth model with economic structure. We identify conditions for existence of multiple equilibrium points and examine stability conditions of different equilibrium points.

Chapter 6 studies one-sector group models of heterogeneous groups. Chapter 5 examined multi-sector growth models with homogeneous population. It is a natural step to combine the main ideas of the previous two chapters to examine economic dynamics with multiple sectors and heterogeneous households. Section 6.1 defines the two-sector two-group model. Section 6.2 analyzes the behavior of the model when the production functions take on the Cobb-Douglas form. Section 6.3 simulates the model analyzed in Section 6.2. Section 6.4 concludes the chapter. The appendix analyzes the dynamics of the model with general production functions.

It may be said that traditional growth theories have failed to provide proper analytical frameworks for analyzing regional issues. As regional economic dynamics are characterized by relatively free movement of people, goods, and production factors, it tends to be more difficult to analyze regional issues than interregional ones. Chapter 7 develops a few interregional models which explicitly include three spatial factors: land, amenities, and services. Section 7.1 develops a multi-region model with leisure, amenity, and capital accumulation as endogenous variables. As it is difficult to explicitly analyze the behavior of the model, we simulate the motion of the system. Section 7.2 introduces a two-region model and each region has two production sectors. Both capital and knowledge are endogenous variables in the model. We demonstrate possible path-dependent regional economic evolution and carry out comparative statics analyses with regard to some parameters. Section 7.3 discusses some issues about regional economic development with capital and knowledge.

Chapter 8 is concerned with economic development with economic interactions among multiple countries. Section 8.1 introduces Ricardian trade theory. In Section 8.2, we review the Heckscher-Ohlin theory. Section 8.3 develops a two-country growth model with capital accumulation within the OSG framework. Section 8.4 extends the model of the previous section to the case that the world consists of multiple countries and each country has any number of types of households. Section 8.5 examines interactions of capital and knowledge within a two-country modeling framework. Section 8.6 discusses trade and income and wealth distribution.

Chapter 9 concludes the study by pointing out important issues for future research within the framework proposed in this study. These issues are related to, for instance, democracy and distributional justice, scale effects of endogenous population, networks and infrastructures, knowledge and human capital, variety of capital, people, and natural resources, preference structures, government policy, unemployed production factors, conditions of capital mobility and people migration, and dynamics of monetary variables.

2
One-Sector Growth (OSG) Economies with Capital Accumulation

The previous chapter introduced some key models in economic growth theory. As mentioned before, this book will make a contribution to the study of growth with income and wealth distribution by proposing an alternative approach to consumers. This chapter introduces the basic model in our alternative approach to economic growth and development with income and wealth distribution. The main deviation from traditional approaches is the introduction of an alternative approach to modeling consumer behavior. As observed by Frederick et al. (2002: 383–84)

> The [discounted utility] model, which continues to be widely used by economists, has little empirical support. Even its developers – Samuelson, who originally proposed the model, and Koopmans, who provided the first axiomatic derivation – had concerns about its descriptive realism, and it was never empirically validated as the appropriate model for intertemporal choice.
> ... [D]eveloping descriptively adequate models of intertemporal choice will not be easy.

Although the validity of the Ramsey approach has been questioned over the years, it is quite another matter to create a more effective alternative, even though researchers in various fields have attempted to introduce more realistic models over the years.[1]

We start investigating economic growth with an economy of one production sector and one type of household. We introduce a number of ideas basic to the later discussion. In the rest of this book, we use the OSG framework to stand for the one-sector growth model developed in this chapter and its variation extensions. With regard to production, almost all the aspects of the OSG model are similar to the Solow or Ramsey one-sector growth model. It is assumed that there is only one (durable) good in the economy under consideration. Households own assets of the economy and distribute their incomes to consume and to save. Production sectors or firms use inputs such as labor with varied levels of human capital, different kinds of capital, knowledge, and natural resources to produce material goods or services. Exchanges take place in perfectly competitive markets. Production sectors sell their product to households or to other sectors and households sell their labor and assets to production sectors. Factor markets work well; factors are inelastically supplied and the available factors are fully utilized at every moment. This means that the qualities of factor services do not vary with changes in factor prices. At any point in time all existing land, labor, and capital are offered for use regardless of what rent, wage, or rate of interest prevail. Saving is undertaken only by households, which implies that all earnings of firms are distributed in the form of payments to factors of production, labor, managerial skill and capital ownership. We omit the possibility of hoarding of output in the form of nonproductive inventories held by households. All savings volunteered by households are absorbed by firms for the accumulation of capital. We require savings and investment to be equal at any point in time.

This chapter is organized as follows.[2] First, the one-sector growth (OSG) model with capital accumulation is proposed. Section 2.2 studies the OSG model with the Cobb-Douglas utility and production functions. Section 2.3 examines the OSG model in discrete version. In Section 2.4, we introduce time distribution between leisure and labor into the OSG model. Section 2.5 introduces public goods into the OSG model and shows possible increasing returns to scale in the dynamic system. Section 2.6 examines the one-sector economic system in which capital stocks are employed both for economic and home production. Section 2.7 introduces environment into the OSG model. Section 2.8 studies interactions between economic development and population growth. Section 2.9 introduces money into the OSG model and examines issues related to money neutrality. Section 2.10 studies the dynamics of a small open economy. Section 2.11 discusses the theoretical foundations of the utility function proposed in this study. Section 2.12 examines relations of our approach to consumers and some traditional theories about the behavior of households. The traditional theories reviewed here include the Keynesian consumption function, the life cycle hypothesis, the permanent income hypothesis, the consumption function in the Solow model, and the utility maximization approach by Ramsey. In Appendix A.2.1, we present a growth model with endogenous fertility and age support.

2.1 The one-sector growth model

The production sector is identical to that in the Solow model defined in Section 1.3. Let $K(t)$ denote the capital existing at each time t and $N(t)$ the flow of labor services used at time t for production. The production function, $F(t)$, defines the flow of production at time t. In this chapter, the production process is described by some sufficiently smooth function

$$F(t) = F(K(t), N(t)).$$

We assume that $F(K(t), N(t))$ is neoclassical.

We assume (identically numerous) one production sector. Its goal of economic production is to maximize its current profit

$$\pi(t) = p(t)F(t) - (r(t) + \delta_k)K(t) - w(t)N(t),$$

where $p(t)$ is the price of product, $r(t)$ is the rate of interest, $w(t)$ is the wage rate, and δ_k is the fixed depreciation rate of capital. We assume that the output good serves as a medium of exchange and is taken as the numeraire. We thus set $p(t) = 1$ and measure both wages and rental flows in units of the output good. The rate of interest and wage rate are determined by the markets. Hence, for any individual firm r and w are given at each point in time. The production sector chooses the two variables K and N to maximize its profit. Maximizing π with regards to K and N as decision variables yields

$$r + \delta_k = F_K = f'(k), \quad w = F_N = f(k) - kf'(k), \tag{2.1.1}$$

in which $k(t) \equiv K(t)/N(t)$. We assume that factor markets work quickly enough so that our system always displays competitive equilibrium in factor markets. Thus we always have

$$w = F_N, \quad r + \delta_k = F_K.$$

Since we assumed that the production function is homogeneous of degree one, we have

$$KF_K + NF_N + \delta_k K = F,$$

or

$$rK + wN + \delta_k K = F. \tag{2.1.2}$$

This result means that the total revenue is used up to pay all factors of the production.

We now describe the behavior of consumers. Consumers make decisions on choice of consumption levels of services and commodities as well as on how much to save (in terms of wealth and education). There is no single purpose for people in saving. Wealth may be accumulated for different reasons such as the capitalist spirit, old age consumption, providing education for children, power and social status. In order to provide a proper description of endogenous savings, we should know how individuals perceive the future. Different from the optimal growth theory in which utility defined over future consumption streams is used, we do not explicitly specify how consumers depreciate future utility resulting from consuming goods and services. In our approach, preferences for future consumption are reflected in the consumer's current preference structure over current consumption and saving.

Consumers obtain income

$$Y = rK + wN, \qquad (2.1.3)$$

from the interest payment rK and the wage payment wN. We call Y the current income in the sense that it comes from consumers' daily toils (payment for human capital) and consumers' current earnings from ownership of wealth. The current income is equal to the total output as we neglect any taxes at this initial stage. The sum of income that consumers are using for consuming, saving, or transferring is not necessarily equal to the temporary income because consumers can sell wealth to pay, for instance, for current consumption if the temporary income is not sufficient for buying food and touring the country. Retired people may live not only on the interest payment but also have to spend some of their wealth. The total value of wealth that consumers can sell to purchase goods and to save is equal to $p(t)K(t)$, where $p(t) = 1$. Here, we assume that selling and buying wealth can be conducted instantaneously without any transaction cost. The disposable income is equal to

$$\hat{Y}(t) = Y(t) + K(t). \qquad (2.1.4)$$

It should be noted that in equation (2.1.4), like $Y(t)$, the value of wealth, $K(t)$, is a flow variable. The disposable income is used for saving and consumption.

At each point in time, consumers would distribute the disposable income between saving, $S(t)$, and consumption of goods, $C(t)$. The budget constraint is given by

$$C(t) + S(t) = \hat{Y}(t). \qquad (2.1.5)$$

In our model, at each point in time, consumers have two variables to decide upon. A consumer decides how much to consume and to save. Equation (2.1.5) means that consumption and savings exhaust the consumers' disposable income. The slope of the budget line is equal to -1, i.e. $dS/dC = -1$.

We assume that the utility level, $U(t)$, that the consumers obtain is dependent on the consumption level of commodity, $C(t)$, and the saving, $S(t)$:

$$U(t) = U(C(t), S(t)). \tag{2.1.6}$$

A typical consumer is to choose his most preferred bundle $(c(t), s(t))$ of consumption and saving under his budget constraint. Here, $c \equiv C/N$ and $s \equiv S/N$. The utility-maximizing problem at any time is defined by

$$\underset{c,s \geq 0}{\text{Max}} \; U(c(t), s(t))$$

$$\text{s.t.} \; c(t) + s(t) = \hat{y}(t), \tag{2.1.7}$$

in which $\hat{y}(t) \equiv Y(t)/N(t) + k(t)$. The following proposition holds.

Proposition 2.1.1
Let $U(c,s): R_+^2 \to R^1$ be a C^1 function that satisfies the monotonicity assumption, which says that $\partial U/\partial c > 0$ and $\partial U/\partial s > 0$ for each (c, s) satisfying the constraint set in problem (2.1.7). Suppose that (c^*, s^*) maximizes U on the constraint set. Then, there is a scalar $\overline{\lambda}^* > 0$ such that

$$\frac{\partial U}{\partial c}(c^*, s^*) \leq \overline{\lambda}^*, \; \frac{\partial U}{\partial s}(c^*, s^*) \leq \overline{\lambda}^*.$$

We have $\partial U/\partial c = \overline{\lambda}^*$ if $c^* \neq 0$ and $\partial U/\partial s = \overline{\lambda}^*$ if $s^* \neq 0$. If both $c^* > 0$ and $s^* > 0$, then

$$\frac{\partial U}{\partial c}(c^*, s^*) = \overline{\lambda}^*, \; \frac{\partial U}{\partial s}(c^*, s^*) = \overline{\lambda}^*.$$

Conversely, suppose that U is a C^1 function, which satisfies the monotonicity assumption and that $(c^*, s^*) > 0$ and the first-order conditions. If U is C^2 and if

$$|\overline{H}| = \begin{vmatrix} 0 & 1 & 1 \\ 1 & U_{cc} & U_{cs} \\ 1 & U_{sc} & U_{ss} \end{vmatrix} = 2U_{cs} - U_{cc} - U_{ss} > 0,$$

then (c^*, s^*) is a strict local solution to the utility maximization problem. If U is quasi-concave and $\nabla U(c, s)$ for all $(c, s) \neq (c^*, s^*)$, then (c^*, s^*) is a global solution to the problem.

The proof of this proposition and other general properties of the problem can be found in standard textbooks of microeconomics or mathematical economics.[3]

We now specify some properties of U. We require that U is a C^2 function, and satisfies $U_c > 0, U_s > 0$ for any $(c, s) > 0$. Construct the Lagrangian

$$L(c, s, \overline{\lambda}) = U(c, s) + \overline{\lambda}(\hat{y} - c - s).$$

The first-order condition for maximization is

$$U_c = U_s = \overline{\lambda}, \quad \hat{y} - c - s = 0. \tag{2.1.8}$$

The bordered Hessian for the problem is

$$|\overline{H}| = \begin{vmatrix} 0 & 1 & 1 \\ 1 & U_{cc} & U_{cs} \\ 1 & U_{sc} & U_{ss} \end{vmatrix} = 2U_{cs} - U_{cc} - U_{ss}.$$

The second-order condition states that given a stationary value of the first-order condition, a positive $|\overline{H}|$, is sufficient to establish it as a relative maximum of U. It is known that the bordered Hessian is identical with the endogenous-variable Jacobian. Hence, if $|\overline{H}|$ is not equal to zero, we can directly apply the implicit function theorem to the problem. That is, the first-order condition has a solution as C^1 functions of the disposable income, $\hat{y}$. Take the derivatives of equations (2.1.8) with respect to $\hat{y}$:

$$U_{cc} \frac{dc}{d\hat{y}} + U_{cs} \frac{ds}{d\hat{y}} = U_{sc} \frac{dc}{d\hat{y}} + U_{ss} \frac{ds}{d\hat{y}},$$

One-Sector Growth (OSG) Economies with Capital Accumulation

$$1 = \frac{dc}{d\hat{y}} + \frac{ds}{d\hat{y}}.$$

We solve these functions

$$\frac{ds}{d\hat{y}} = \frac{U_{sc} - U_{cc}}{2U_{cs} - U_{ss} - U_{cc}},$$

$$\frac{dc}{d\hat{y}} = \frac{U_{sc} - U_{ss}}{2U_{cs} - U_{ss} - U_{cc}}.$$

We see that $0 < ds/d\hat{y} < 1$ and $0 < dc/d\hat{y} < 1$ in the case of $U_{sc} \geq 0$ under the second-order condition of maximization. We denote an optimal solution as a function of the disposable income

$$(c(t), s(t)) = (c(\hat{y}(t)), s(\hat{y}(t))).$$

The vector $(c(\hat{y}(t)), s(\hat{y}(t)))$ is known as the Walrasian (or ordinary or market) demand function, when it is single-valued for all positive disposable income.

It appears reasonable to consider population as independent of economic conditions, as a first approximation. We assume that the population dynamics is exogenously determined in the following way:

$$\dot{N}(t) = nN(t) \Rightarrow g_N = n, \tag{2.1.9}$$

where n is a constant and g_x ($\equiv \dot{x}/x$) is the growth rate of variable x. We use the symbol g_x to stand for the growth rate in the rest of the book if without special explanation. Here, we neglect variations in labor productive potential due to, for instance, technical progress, education, learning through working, and learning through leisure. The assumption of a constant population growth rate has been widely used in the literature of economic growth. This rules out economic factors that may affect birth and death rates.

The change in households' wealth is equal to the net savings minus the wealth sold at time t, i.e.

$$\dot{K}(t) = s(\hat{y}(t))N(t) - K(t). \tag{2.1.10}$$

Inserting

$$\dot{k}(t) = \frac{\dot{K}(t)}{N(t)} - nk(t),$$

into equation (2.1.10) yields

$$\dot{k}(t) = s(\hat{y}(k)) - (1+n)k(t) \qquad (2.1.11)$$

where

$$\hat{y}(k(t)) = \frac{\hat{Y}(t)}{N(t)} = f(k(t)) + k(t).$$

In a stationary state, we have: $s(\hat{y}(k)) = (1+n)k$.
We now show that this equation has a unique solution. Define

$$\Phi(k) \equiv \frac{s(\hat{y})}{(1+n)k} - 1, \quad k \geq 0. \qquad (2.1.12)$$

When k is approaching zero, $\hat{y}\,(=f(k)+k)$ is approaching zero and hence $s(\hat{y})$ is coming near zero. As $0 < s'(\hat{y}) < 1$ and $f'(k) \to \infty$ as $k \to 0$, we have

$$\lim_{k \to 0} \frac{s(\hat{y})}{(1+n)k} = \frac{s'(0)(f'(0)+\delta)}{(1+n)} > 1. \qquad (2.1.13)$$

When k is approaching positive infinity, $\hat{y}$ is coming to positive infinity. As $0 < s'(\hat{y}) < 1$ and $f'(k) \to 0$ as $k \to +\infty$, we have

$$\lim_{k \to +\infty} \frac{s(\hat{y})}{(1+n)k} = \frac{s'(+\infty)(f'(+\infty)+\delta)}{(1+n)} < 1.$$

Taking derivatives of equation (2.1.12) with respect to k yields

$$\frac{d\Phi}{dk} = \left[\frac{s'(\hat{y})k(f'(k)+1)}{s(\hat{y})} - 1 \right] \frac{s(\hat{y})}{(1+n)k^2}.$$

We now show that $d\Phi/dk < 0$ for $k > 0$. To prove this, we use $ds/d\hat{y} < 1$ and the inequality $f'(k) < f(k)/k$ (which also guarantees $w > 0$). By $s(\hat{y}(k)) = (1+n)k$ and the definition of $\hat{y}$, we have

$$\frac{s'(\hat{y})k(f'(k)+1)}{(1+n)s(\hat{y})} < \frac{s'(\hat{y})(f(k)+k)}{(1+n)s(\hat{y})} = \frac{s'(\hat{y})\hat{y}}{(1+n)s(\hat{y})} < 1, \qquad (2.1.14)$$

where we use $s'(\hat{y}) < 1$ and $\hat{y}/s(\hat{y}) \leq 1$ to guarantee the right inequality. We thus conclude that $d\Phi/dk < 0$ for $k > 0$. The equation, $\Phi(k) = 0$, has a unique solution for $k > 0$ because of equations (2.1.13), (2.1.14), and $d\Phi/dk < 0$. We now demonstrate that the unique stationary state is stable.

For the steady state to be stable, the following conditions must prevail:

$$\left.\frac{d[s(\hat{y}(k)) - (1+n)k]}{dk}\right|_{k=k^*} = s'(\hat{y})(f'(k)+1) - (1+n) < 0. \qquad (2.1.15)$$

From the equilibrium condition and inequalities (2.1.14), we have

$$\frac{s'(\hat{y})(f'(k)+1)}{1+n} = \frac{s'(\hat{y})k(f'(k)+1)}{s'(\hat{y})} < 1. \qquad (2.1.16)$$

Accordingly, inequality (2.1.15) is satisfied. Summarizing the above discussions, we obtain the following theorem.

Theorem 2.1.1
Given a neoclassical production function and a utility function that is a C^2 function, and satisfies $U_c > 0, U_s > 0$ for any $(c(t), s(t)) > 0$. Let the bordered Hessian be positive for any nonnegative $(c(t), s(t))$. Then the capital-labor ratio converges monotonically to a unique positive steady state. The unique stationary state is stable.

The stability guaranteed above is local. We now show that if $s(\hat{y})$ is concave in $\hat{y}$, then the system is globally stable. Because of $d^2c/dy^2 = -d^2s/dy^2$ by the equation $1 = dc/d\hat{y} + ds/d\hat{y}$, concavity of s implies convexity of c. From the first-order conditions, it is straightforward to give those conditions under which s is concave; we omit the expression because we lack a clear economic interpretation.

Asymptotic stability can be proved by applying Lyapunov's theorem.[4] Define the Lyapunov function

$$V(x(t)) \equiv x(t)^2,$$

where

$$x(t) \equiv k(t) - k^*$$

and k^* is the equilibrium value. We have $V(x) \geq 0$ and $V(x) = 0$ iff $x = 0$. Differentiation of $V(x(t))$ with respect to t gives

$$\dot{V} = 2x\dot{k} = 2x\{s(\hat{y}(k)) - (1+n)k\} = 2x\{s(\hat{y}(k^* + x)) - (1+n)(k^* + x)\},$$

where we use equation (2.1.11). By concavity of $f(x + k^*)$

$$f(k^* + x) \leq f(k^*) + xf'(k^*).$$

According to its definition, $\hat{y}(k)$ is also concave in k. Hence,

$$\hat{y}(k^* + x) \leq \hat{y}(k^*) + x\hat{y}'(k^*).$$

Since $ds/d\hat{y} > 0$, we have

$$\dot{V} \leq 2x\{s(\hat{y}(k^*) + x\hat{y}'(k^*)) - (1+n)(k^* + x)\}.$$

Concavity of $s(\hat{y})$ estimates

$$\dot{V} \leq 2x\{s(\hat{y}) + x\hat{y}'(k^*)s'(\hat{y}) - (1+n)(k^* + x)\}.$$

By $s(\hat{y}(k)) = (1+n)k$ at equilibrium, we rewrite the above inequality:

$$\dot{V} \leq 2x^2(1+n)\left\{\frac{s'(\hat{y})(f'(k^*) + \delta)}{(1+n)} - 1\right\}.$$

By inequality (2.1.16), we conclude that $dV/dt < 0$ if $x \neq 0$ and $dV/dt = 0$ at $x = 0$. Hence, the equilibrium point, $k = k^*$, is asymptotically stable. To interpret the analytical results, we will specify the functions in the next section.

2.2 The OSG model with the Cobb-Douglas functions[5]

This section solves the OSG model when the production and utility functions are taken on the Cobb-Douglas functions

$$F(t) = AK^{\alpha}(t)N^{\beta}(t), \ \alpha, \beta > 0, \ \alpha + \beta = 1,$$
$$U(t) = C^{\xi}(t)S^{\lambda}(t), \ \xi + \lambda = 1, \ \xi, \lambda > 0, \quad (2.2.1)$$

where A is a number measuring overall productivity, and α, β, ξ, and λ are parameters. The marginal conditions for the production sector are

$$r = \alpha A k^{-\beta} - \delta_k, \ w = \beta A k^{\alpha}, \ f = Ak^{\alpha}. \quad (2.2.2)$$

As our approach to consumer behavior is new, we explain some properties of the utility function. It is convenient to describe preferences graphically by using a construction of indifferent curves. The indifference curve through a bundle $(C(t), S(t))$ consists of all bundles of the variables that leave the consumer indifferent to the given bundle. The marginal rate of substitution (MRS) measures the slope of the indifference curve at a given bundle of variables. It can be interpreted as the rate at which a consumer is just willing to substitute a small amount of saving for consumption goods. Taking the total differential of the utility function, keeping utility constant, yields

$$dU(C, S) = \frac{\partial U}{\partial C} dC + \frac{\partial U}{\partial S} dS = 0.$$

Accordingly, we have

$$\text{MRS} = \frac{dS}{dC} = -\frac{\partial U/\partial C}{\partial U/\partial S} = -\frac{\xi}{\lambda}\frac{S}{C}.$$

The algebraic sign of the MRS is negative: if you save more you have to consume less in order to keep the same level of utility.

The preference represented by $U = C^\xi S^\lambda$ is described in Figure 2.2.1. In Figure 2.2.1a, we illustrate the indifference curve for $\xi = 0.5$ and $\lambda = 0.5$. In Figure 2.2.1b, we illustrate the indifference curves for $\xi = 0.2$ and $\lambda = 0.8$. Different values of the parameters, ξ and λ, lead to different shapes of the indifference curves. The greater the propensity to own wealth, the more patient the consumer. The consumer behavior which is described in Figure 2.2.1a is less patient than that described in Figure 2.2.1b.

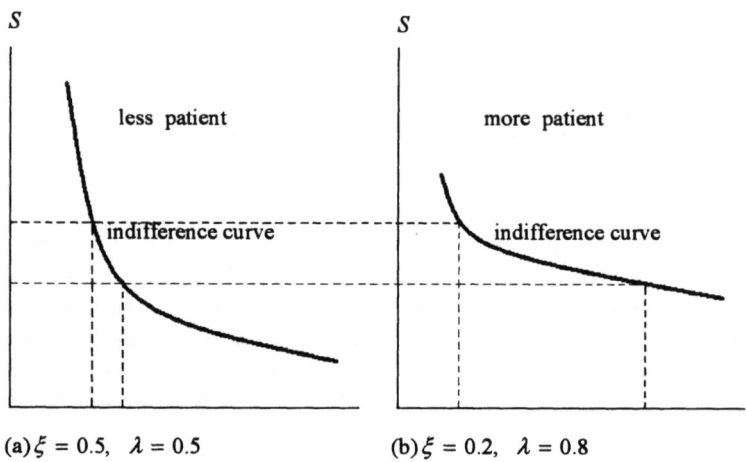

(a) $\xi = 0.5$, $\lambda = 0.5$ (b) $\xi = 0.2$, $\lambda = 0.8$

Figure 2.2.1 Indifference curves and the propensity to hold wealth

It is straightforward to solve the optimal choice of the consumers as

$$C^*(t) = \xi \hat{Y}(t), \quad S^*(t) = \lambda \hat{Y}(t). \tag{2.2.3}$$

The optimal choice is illustrated in Figure 2.2.2.

In Figure 2.2.1, we illustrate how values of the propensity to save λ determine the shapes of the indifference curve. Figure 2.2.3 illustrates how values of λ affect optimal solutions. As the consumer's propensity to save becomes higher, out of the same disposable income the consumer saves more.

One-Sector Growth (OSG) Economies with Capital Accumulation   49

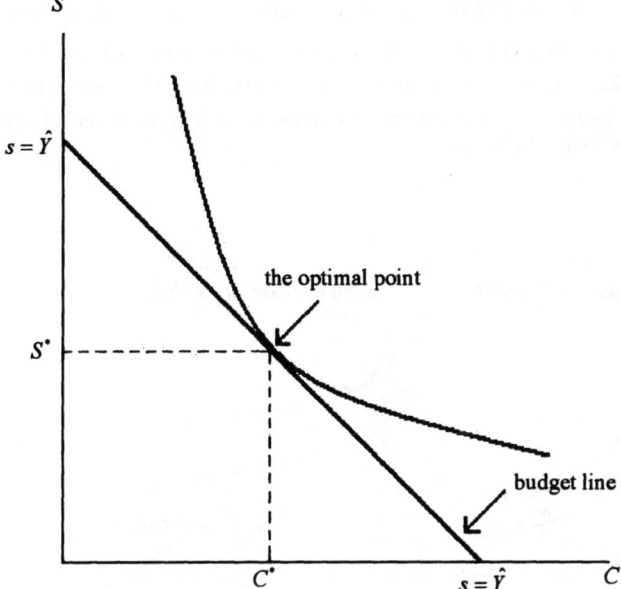

Figure 2.2.2 Optimal choice

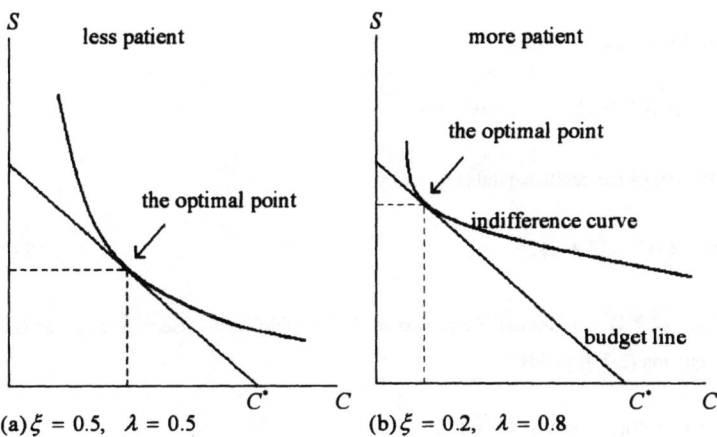

(a) $\xi = 0.5, \ \lambda = 0.5$ (b) $\xi = 0.2, \ \lambda = 0.8$

Figure 2.2.3 Optimal saving with different propensities to own wealth

50   Economic Growth with Income and Wealth Distribution

In Figure 2.2.4, we see that as $\hat{Y}(t)$ increases, both $C(t)$ and $S(t)$ are increased. An increase in $\hat{Y}(t)$ may be caused either by increases in the interest rate, or the wage rate, or the wealth. If $r(t)$, $w(t)$, or $K(t)$ is increased, both $C(t)$ and $S(t)$ are increased. For instance, as the interest rate increases, the budget line is shifted right-upwards parallel to the original line.

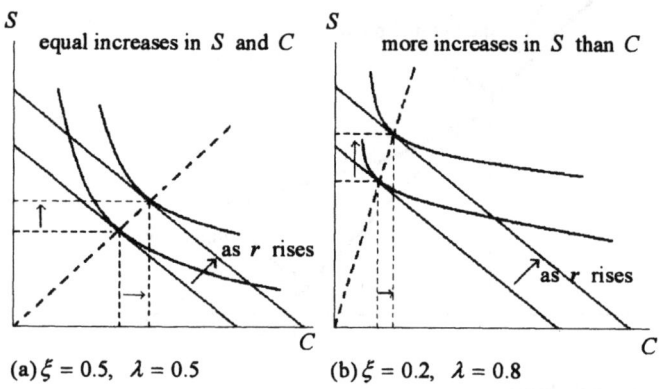

Figure 2.2.4 The impact of changes in the interest rate

By equations (2.2.3), we have

$$c = \xi(Ak^\alpha + k), \quad s = \lambda(Ak^\alpha + k).$$

The motion of per capita capital is given by

$$\dot{k} = \lambda A k^\alpha - (\xi + n)k. \qquad (2.2.4)$$

Equation (2.2.4) is a Bernoulli equation in the variable $k(t)$. Inserting $z(t) = k^\beta(t)$ into equation (2.2.4) yields

$$\dot{z} + (1-\alpha)(\xi + n)z = (1-\alpha)\lambda A,$$

which is a standard first-order linear differential equation. The solution is given by

$$z(t) = \left(z(0) - \frac{\lambda A}{\xi + n}\right) e^{-\beta(\xi + n)t} + \frac{\lambda A}{\xi + n}.$$

Substituting $z(t) = k^\beta(t)$ back to the solution, we obtain

$$k^\beta(t) = \left(k^\beta(0) - \frac{\lambda A}{\xi + n}\right) e^{-\beta(\xi + n)t} + \frac{\lambda A}{\xi + n},$$

where $k(0)$ is the initial value of the capital-labor ratio, $k(t)$. This solution is what determines the time path of $k(t)$. Once we know $k(t)$, all the other points are explicitly determined at any point in time.

As $t \to +\infty$, the exponential expression will approach zero. Consequently, letting $t \to +\infty$ yields the unique steady-state capital ratio

$$k^* = \left(\frac{\lambda A}{\xi + n}\right)^{1/\beta}. \tag{2.2.5}$$

The capital-labor ratio will approach a constant as its equilibrium value. This steady state varies directly with the propensity to save, λ, the technology, A, and inversely with the propensity to consume, ξ, and the population growth rate, n.

The dynamics is depicted in Figure 2.2.5. Since equation (2.2.4) contains two terms, $\lambda A k^\alpha$ and $(\xi + n)k$, we plot them as two separate curves. The $(\xi + n)k$ term, a linear function of $k(t)$, will show up in the figure as a straight line, with a zero vertical intercept and a slope equal to $(\xi + n)$. The term, $\lambda A k^\alpha$, plots as a curve that increases at a decreasing rate. Based upon these two curves, we can measure the value of the change rate $\dot{k}$ for each value of $k(t)$ by the vertical distance between the two curves. The two curves intersect when the capital-labor ratio arrives at the steady state. As shown by the figure, the capital-labor ratio will always reach a positive steady state. For instance, if $k(t)$ starts at some value less than k^*, $\lambda A k^\alpha$ is greater than $(\xi + n)k$. When this extra amount $\lambda A k^\alpha - (\xi + n)k$ is converted into capital, the capital-labor ratio will rise. As shown in Figure 2.2.5, $k(t)$ increases towards k^*. We can similarly explain the falling of the variable $k(t)$ when it starts at some value greater than k^*.

$\lambda A k^\alpha$, $(\xi + \lambda)Ak^\alpha$

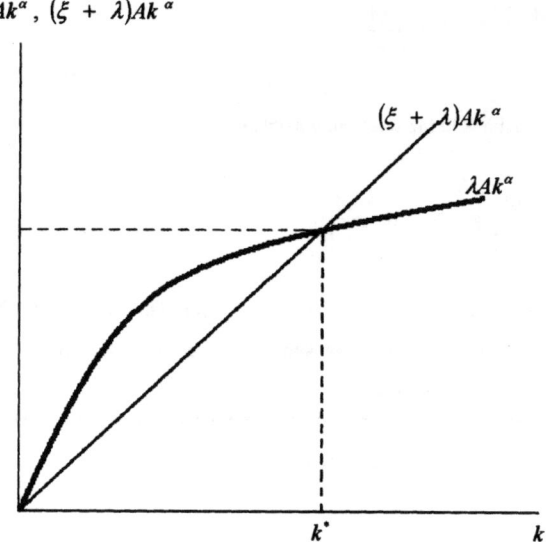

Figure 2.2.5 Evolution of capital-labor ratio in the OSG model

The right-hand side of equation (2.2.4) first increases and then decreases, and eventually becomes and remains negative. These imply that there exists a unique $k^* > 0$ such that $k'(t) > 0$ when $k'(t) < k^*$, $k'(t) = 0$ when $k'(t) = k^*$, and $k'(t) < 0$ when $k'(t) > k^*$. Thus k^* is a globally asymptotically stable equilibrium for $k(t)$.

To see motion of the growth rate, dividing equation (2.2.4) by $k(t)$ we obtain growth rate $g_k(t)$ of per capita capital as

$$g_k(t) \equiv \frac{\dot{k}(t)}{k(t)} = \lambda A k^{-\beta}(k) - (\xi + n).$$

Here, $g_k(t)$ stands for growth rate of per capita capital at time t. The above equation says that the growth rate of per capita capital equals the difference between two terms, $\lambda A k^{-\beta}$ and $\xi + n$, which we plot against k in Figure 2.2.6. The first curve is downward-sloping and the second term is a horizontal line. The vertical distance between the curve and the line equals the growth rate of per capita capital. As shown before, there is a unique equilibrium. The figure shows that to the left of the steady state, the curve lies above the line. Hence, the growth rate is positive and k increases over time. As k rises, the growth rate declines. Finally, k reaches k^* as the growth rate becomes zero. An analogous argument demonstrates that if the system starts from the right of the steady state, the growth rate is negative. As k declines, the growth rate rises and finally becomes zero.

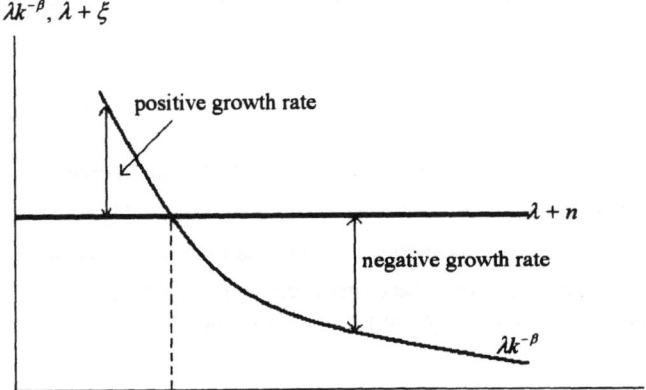

Figure 2.2.6 Dynamics of growth rate in the OSG model

When the economy has reached stationary capital intensity, capital per capita will remain the same as time passes, but the stock of capital, $K(t)$, continues to grow infinitely at the same predetermined rate as the labor force, n. The sustainable growth rate of the model is exogenously given by n. This can be confirmed by

$$K(t) = k^* N_0 e^{nt}, \quad F(t) = f(k^*) N_0 e^{nt}, \quad C(t) = c(k^*) N_0 e^{nt}.$$

2.3 The OSG model in discrete time[6]

The neoclassical growth theory is developed in both continuous and discrete versions. Similarly, our alternative approach is developed in both continuous and discrete versions. Because of the character of our alternative utility function, it is straightforward to change discrete models to continuous models, and vice versa.[7] The continuous version requires knowledge about differential equations, while the discrete version requires knowledge about difference equations.

We now represent the OSG model in discrete time. The economy has an infinite future. We represent the passage of time in a sequence of periods, numbered from zero and indexed by $t = 0, 1, 2, ...$ Time 0, referring to the beginning of period 0, represents the initial situation from which economy starts to grow. The end of period $t-1$ coincides with the beginning of period t; it can also be called time t. We assume that transactions are made in each period.

The model assumes that each individual lives forever. As before, the population grows at rate n; thus

$$N_t = (1+n)N_{t-1}.$$

Each individual supplies one unit of labor at each time t. Production in period t uses as inputs an amount of capital, K_t, and an amount of labor services, N_t. It supplies an amount of goods, Y_t. Here, production is assumed to be continuous during the period, but then uses the same capital that existed at the beginning of the period. The production function is $F_t = F(K_t, N_t)$. The marginal conditions are

$$r_t + \delta_k = f'(k_t), \quad w_t = f(k_t) - k_t f'(k_t), \tag{2.3.1}$$

where

$$k_t \equiv \frac{K_t}{N_t}, \quad f_t \equiv \frac{F_t}{N_t} = F(k_t, 1).$$

As in the OSG model in continuous time, the consumer is to choose his most preferred bundle of consumption and saving, (c_t, s_t), under his budget constraint. The utility maximizing problem at any time is defined by

$$\underset{c_t, s_t \geq 0}{\text{Max}} \ U(c_t, s_t)$$

$$\text{s.t. } c_t + s_t = \hat{y}_t \equiv f(k_t) + k_t.$$

The optimization problem is the same as the model in continuous time. Here, we will not repeat the proof. We denote an optimal solution as a function of the disposable income

$(c_t, s_t) = (c(\hat{y}_t), s(\hat{y}_t))$.

The wealth accumulation is given by

$$K_{t+1} - K_t = s(\hat{y}_t)N_t - K_t.$$

That is

$$K_{t+1} = s(\hat{y}_t)N_t.$$

Dividing the two sides of this equation by N_{t+1} yields

$$k_{t+1} = \frac{s(\hat{y}_t)}{1+n}.$$

This mapping controls the motion of the system with general production and utility functions. A stationary state for the growth progress is a capital-labor ratio, k^*, that satisfies

$$k = \frac{s(\hat{y})}{1+n}. \tag{2.3.2}$$

To solve the above equation, define

$$\Phi(k) \equiv \frac{s(\hat{y})}{(1+n)k} - 1, \quad k \geq 0. \tag{2.3.3}$$

When k is approaching zero, $\hat{y} \, (= f(k) + k)$ is also approaching zero, and hence $s(\hat{y})$ is coming near zero. As $0 < s'(\hat{y}) < 1$ and $f'(k) \to \infty$ as $k \to 0$

$$\lim_{k \to 0} \frac{s(\hat{y})}{(1+n)k} = \frac{s'(0)(f'(0)+1)}{(1+n)} > 1. \tag{2.3.4}$$

When k is approaching positive infinity, $\hat{y}$ is coming to positive infinity. As $0 < s'(\hat{y}) < 1$ and $f'(k) \to 0$ as $k \to +\infty$, we have

$$\lim_{k\to+\infty}\frac{s(\hat{y})}{(1+n)k}=\frac{s'(+\infty)(f'(+\infty)+1)}{(1+n)}<1. \qquad (2.3.5)$$

Taking derivatives of equation (2.3.3) with respect to k yields

$$\frac{d\Phi}{dk}=\left[\frac{s'(\hat{y})k(f'(k)+1)}{s(\hat{y})}-1\right]\frac{s(\hat{y})}{(1+n)k^2}.$$

We now show that $d\Phi/dk<0$ for $k>0$. To prove this, we use $ds/d\hat{y}<1$ and the inequality $f'(k)<f(k)/k$ (which also guarantees $w>0$). By equation (2.3.1) and the definition of $\hat{y}$, we have

$$\frac{s'(\hat{y})k(f'(k)+1)}{(1+n)s(\hat{y})}<\frac{s'(\hat{y})(f(k)+k)}{(1+n)s(\hat{y})}=\frac{s'(\hat{y})\hat{y}}{(1+n)s(\hat{y})}<1,$$

where we use $s'(\hat{y})<1$ and $\hat{y}/s(\hat{y})\leq 1$ to guarantee the right inequality. We thus conclude that $d\Phi/dk<0$ for $k>0$. The equation $\Phi(k)=0$ for $k>0$ has a unique solution because of equations (2.3.4), (2.3.5), and $d\Phi/dk<0$. We now demonstrate that the unique stationary state is stable.

For the steady state to be stable, it is sufficient to show

$$-1<\frac{s'(\hat{y}^*)(f'(k^*)+1)}{1+n}<1.$$

As the steady-state values, k^* and $\hat{y}^*$ are positive, $s'(\hat{y}^*)>0$ and $f'(k^*)$ are positive. The left inequality always holds. To prove the right inequality, we use $ds/d\hat{y}<1$ and the inequality $f'(k^*)<f(k^*)/k^*$ (which also guarantees $w_t>0$). By equation (2.3.1) and the definition of $\hat{y}$, we have

$$\frac{s'(\hat{y}^*)(f'(k^*)+1)}{1+n}<\frac{s'(\hat{y}^*)(f(k^*)/k^*+1)}{1+n}=\frac{s'(\hat{y}^*)\hat{y}^*/k^*}{1+n}=\frac{s'(\hat{y}^*)\hat{y}^*}{s(\hat{y}^*)}.$$

Since $s'(\hat{y})<1$ and $\hat{y}/s(\hat{y})\leq 1$, we see that the right inequality of inequalities (2.3.3) is satisfied.

Theorem 2.3.1

Given a production function that is neoclassical and a utility function that is a C^2 function, and satisfies $U_c > 0, U_s > 0$ for any $(c_t, s_t) > 0$. Let the bordered Hessian be positive for any nonnegative $(c_t, s_t) > 0$. Then the capital-labor ratio converges monotonically to a unique positive steady state. The unique stationary state is stable.

We conclude that the unique steady-state is stable. Figure 2.3.1 shows the relation between k_{t+1} and k_t, which we express by

$$k_{t+1} = \Psi(k_t).$$

The slope of $\Psi(k_t)$ is infinite at $k_t = 0$ and diminishes toward a constant. The function $\Psi(k_t)$ crosses the 45-degree line at the steady-state value, k^*. The capital stock monotonically approaches its unique steady-state value as time passes. The steady state is stable because the curve, $\Psi(k_t)$, is always upward sloping, and it crosses the 45-degree line from above.

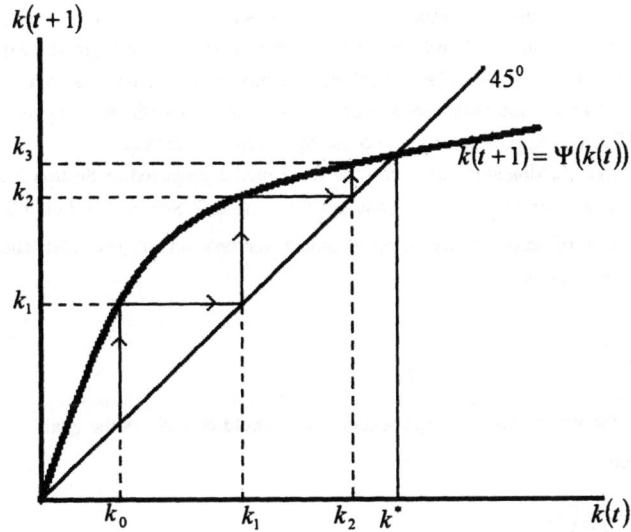

Figure 2.3.1 The dynamics in the OSG model

We introduced the OLG model in Section 1.5. It can be seen that our model is similar to the OLG model as far as stationary states are concerned. A careful reader might have already noticed that it is easy to relate the discrete OSG model and the OLG model. For instance, if we consider that people live only two periods in the OSG model as in the OLG model, then the saving $s(t)$ plus its interest is equal to the consumption level of the second period. Then, our OSG model with a certain form of the utility function generates the same dynamic behavior as the OLG model. Although the OSG model generates the same dynamic behavior as the OLG model, the OSG model does not employ the concept of discounted utility or discount preference rate.

From now on, we are mainly concerned with continuous models. We will show that the OSG model can generate the same dynamic behavior as the Ramsey model or Solow model by making the propensity to change related to income and wealth in certain ways.

2.4 Growth with endogenous leisure

Time distribution between leisure and work is constantly changing as living conditions and work environment are changed. The implications of economic rationality in the allocation of time have been made explicit in a formal and rigorous theory of the subject since Becker published his seminal work in 1965.[8] There have been studies on the interdependence between the productivity of a person's labor, his income, the price of leisure time, and time allocation. There is an immense body of empirical and theoretical literature on economic growth with time distribution between home and nonhome economic and leisure activities.[9] Nevertheless, it has become clear that economic growth models with labor supply in the traditional Ramsey approach tend to become analytically intractable.

We now introduce endogenous time into the OSG model proposed in Section 2.1. Almost all the aspects of the following model are the same as in Section 2.1. Let $N(t)$ stand for the flow of labor services used at time t for production. The total labor force, $N(t)$, is now given by

$$N(t) = T(t)N_0,$$

where $T(t)$ is the work time of a representative household and N_0 is the total labor force. Introduce

$$f(k(t)) \equiv F(k(t), 1),$$

where $k(t) \equiv K(t)/N(t)$. The production sector chooses the two variables $K(t)$ and $N(t)$ to maximize its profit. The marginal conditions are given by

$$r(t) + \delta_k = f'(k(t)), \quad w(t) = f(k(t)) - k(t)f'(k(t)). \tag{2.4.1}$$

Let $\bar{k}(t)(\equiv K(t)/N_0)$ stand for per capita wealth. According to the definition of $k(t)$ and $\bar{k}(t)$, we have

$$\bar{k}(t) = k(t)T(t).$$

Now the current income is given by

$$y(t) = r(t)\bar{k}(t) + w(t)T(t).$$

The per capita disposable income is given by

$$\hat{y}(t) = y(t) + \bar{k}(t).$$

The disposable income is used for saving and consumption. At each point in time, a consumer would distribute the total available budget among saving, $s(t)$, and consumption of goods, $c(t)$. The budget constraint is given by

$$c(t) + s(t) = \hat{y}(t) = r(t)\bar{k}(t) + w(t)T(t) + \bar{k}(t). \tag{2.4.2}$$

Denote by $T_h(t)$ the leisure time at time t and the (fixed) available time for work and leisure by T_0. The time constraint is expressed by

$$T(t) + T_h(t) = T_0.$$

Substituting this time constraint into the budget constraint yields

$$w(t)T_h(t) + c(t) + s(t) = \bar{y}(t) \equiv r(t)\bar{k}(t) + w(t)T_0 + \bar{k}(t). \tag{2.4.3}$$

Here, we may interpret the variable $\bar{y}(t)$ as the potential disposable income since it is equal to the disposable income $\hat{y}(t)$ when all the available time is spent on work (i.e. $T = T_0$). For a given level of $T_h(t)$ at t, as

$$\bar{y}(t) = \hat{y}(t) + w(t)T_h(t),$$

we see that the potential disposable income, $\bar{y}(t)$, is equal to the sum of the disposable income, $\hat{y}(t)$, and the leisure cost, $w(t)T_h(t)$.

In our model, at each point in time, consumers have three variables to decide upon. We assume that the utility level, $U(t)$, that the consumers obtain is dependent on the leisure time, T_h, the consumption level of commodity, $c(t)$, and the saving, $s(t)$, as follows:

$$U(t) = T_h^\sigma(t)c^\xi(t)s^\lambda(t), \quad \sigma, \xi, \lambda > 0, \quad \sigma + \xi + \lambda = 1, \tag{2.4.4}$$

where the parameters σ, ξ, and λ are elasticities of the utility with respect to the leisure time, consumption, and saving. For consumers, wage rate, $w(t)$, and rate of interest, $r(t)$, are given in markets and wealth, $k(t)$, is predetermined before the decision. Maximizing $U(t)$ in (2.4.4) subject to the budget constraint (2.4.3) yields

$$w(t)T_h(t) = \sigma\bar{y}(t), \quad c(t) = \xi\bar{y}(t), \quad s(t) = \lambda\bar{y}(t). \tag{2.4.5}$$

We call σ the propensity to use leisure time, ξ the propensity to consume, and λ the propensity to own wealth. We call them "propensities" as they are equal to the proportions of the "potential disposable income" that are spent on the corresponding variables.

We now find the dynamics of capital accumulation. According to the definition of $s(t)$, the change in the household's wealth is given by

$$\dot{\bar{k}}(t) = s(t) - \bar{k}(t) = \lambda\bar{y}(t) - \bar{k}(t). \tag{2.4.6}$$

We have constructed the model. To examine the dynamic properties of equation (2.4.6), from the definition of $\bar{y}(t)$ and equations (2.4.1) we obtain

$$\bar{y} = (f'(k) - \delta_k)\bar{k} + (f(k) - kf'(k))T_0 + \bar{k}. \tag{2.4.7}$$

Substituting equation (2.4.7) into $w(t)T_h(t) = \sigma \bar{y}(t)$ yields

$$(\xi + \lambda)(f(k) - kf'(k))T_0 = (f'(k) + \delta)\sigma \bar{k} + (f(k) - kf'(k))T,$$

where we use equation (2.4.1), $\sigma + \xi + \lambda = 1$, and

$$T(t) + T_h(t) = T_0,$$

and $\delta \equiv 1 - \delta_k$. Inserting $\bar{k}(t) = T(t)k(t)$ into the above equation, we solve

$$T(t) = \frac{(f(k) - kf'(k))(\xi + \lambda)T_0}{(f'(k) + \delta)\sigma k + (f(k) - kf'(k))}, \tag{2.4.8}$$

where $f - kf' > 0$ for any positive k. We see that for any positive k, $0 < T(t) < T_0$. This also guarantees

$$0 < T_h(t) \, (= T_0 - T(t)) < T_0.$$

We see that $T(t)$ is uniquely determined as a function of $k(t)$.
From equation (2.4.7), we have

$$\lambda \bar{y}(t) - \bar{k}(t) = (\lambda f'(k) + \delta \lambda - 1)\bar{k} + (f(k) - kf'(k))\lambda T_0.$$

Insert $\bar{k}(t) = T(t)k(t)$ and equation (2.4.8) into the above equation:

$$\lambda \bar{y}(t) - \bar{k}(t) = \left[\frac{k(\lambda f' + \lambda \delta - 1)(\xi + \lambda)}{(f' + \delta)\sigma k + (f - kf')} + \lambda\right]T_0(f - kf). \tag{2.4.9}$$

Take derivatives of $\bar{k}(t) = T(t)k(t)$ with respect to t:

$$\dot{\bar{k}}(t) = \dot{T}k + T\dot{k}. \tag{2.4.10}$$

62 *Economic Growth with Income and Wealth Distribution*

This equation expresses how the change in per capita wealth is related to the changes in the labor intensity and the labor time. From equation (2.4.8), we have

$$\dot{T}(t) = -\left[\frac{(f - kf')(f' + \delta) + (f + \delta k)kf''}{[(f' + \delta)\alpha k + (f - kf')](f - kf')}\right]\sigma T(t)\dot{k}(t).$$

Insert the above equation into equation (2.4.10):

$$\dot{\bar{k}}(t) = \left[\frac{(f - kf')^2 - (f + \delta k)\alpha k^2 f''}{((f' + \delta)\alpha k + (f - kf'))^2}\right](\xi + \lambda)T_0 \dot{k}, \qquad (2.4.11)$$

where we use equation (2.4.8). As $f - kf' > 0$ and $f'' \leq 0$ for any $k > 0$, we see that the sign of $\dot{\bar{k}}$ is the same as that of $\dot{k}$. Combining equations (2.4.6), (2.4.9), and (2.4.11), we get a nonlinear differential equation in k as follows:

$$\dot{k} = \frac{(\alpha k f^* + 1)^2}{1 - \alpha k^2 f'' f^{*2}/(f + \delta k)}\left[\frac{k(\lambda f' + \lambda \delta - 1)}{\alpha k f^* + 1} + \frac{\lambda(f - kf')}{(\xi + \lambda)}\right], \qquad (2.4.12)$$

where

$$f^*(k(t)) \equiv \frac{f'(k(t)) + \delta}{f(k(t)) - k(t)f'(k(t))} > 0, \quad \forall k(t) > 0.$$

The differential equation (2.4.12) contains a single variable, $k(t)$. The following lemma says that for any positive solution of equation (2.4.12), all the other variables in the dynamic system are uniquely determined.

Lemma 2.4.1

For any positive $k(t)$, all the other variables are uniquely determined at any point in time by the following procedure: $T(t)$ by equation (2.4.8) $\rightarrow T_h = T_0 - T \rightarrow \bar{k} = kT \rightarrow r$ and w by equations (2.4.1) $\rightarrow \hat{y}$ by equation (2.4.2) $\rightarrow \bar{y}$ by equation (2.4.3) $\rightarrow c$ and s by equations (2.4.5).

The lemma guarantees that the dynamics of the system are determined by the differential equation (2.4.12). We now show that this system has a unique positive

One-Sector Growth (OSG) Economies with Capital Accumulation 63

equilibrium point and the system is stable. An equilibrium point of the differential equation is determined by

$$\frac{k(\lambda f' + \lambda\delta - 1)}{\sigma k f^* + 1} + \frac{\lambda(f - kf')}{(\xi + \lambda)} = 0.$$

Insert $f^* = (f' + \delta)/(f - kf')$ into the above equation:

$$\frac{f}{k} = \frac{\xi}{\lambda} + \delta_k. \qquad (2.4.13)$$

As f is a neoclassical production function, the above equation has a unique positive solution, denoted by k^*. From the differential equation (2.4.12), we calculate

$$\dot{k}\Big|_{k=k^*} = \frac{\lambda}{(\xi + \lambda)}\left(-\frac{f - kf'}{\sigma k f^* + 1} + f_1 f''\right)\left[\frac{(\sigma k f^* + 1)^2}{1 - \sigma k^2 f'' f^{*2}/(f + \delta k)}\right], \qquad (2.4.14)$$

in which

$$f_1 \equiv \frac{\sigma k(1 + kf^*)}{\sigma k f^* + 1} - \frac{\lambda(f - kf')}{(\lambda f' + \lambda\delta - 1)} - k = \frac{-(\xi + \lambda)k}{\sigma k f^* + 1} - \frac{\lambda(f - kf')}{(\lambda f' + \lambda\delta - 1)}$$
$$= -\frac{[((\xi + \lambda)(\lambda\delta - 1) + \sigma\lambda\delta) + \lambda f/k]}{(\lambda f' + \lambda\delta - 1)}(f - kf').$$

As $f - kf' > 0$ and $f'' < 0$, we see that $\dot{k}\Big|_{k=k^*}$ is negative if $f_1 \geq 0$. Inserting (2.4.13) into the term

$$(\xi + \lambda)(\lambda\delta - 1) + \sigma\lambda\delta + \frac{\lambda f}{k}$$

in the definition of f_1 yields

$$(\xi + \lambda)(\lambda\delta - 1) + \sigma\lambda\delta + \lambda\frac{f}{k} = 0,$$

where we use $\sigma + \xi + \lambda = 1$ and $\delta = 1 - \delta_k$. Hence, $f_1 = 0$. We thus conclude that the dynamic system has a unique stable equilibrium.

Proposition 2.4.1
The dynamic system has a unique stable equilibrium.

We now examine impact of changes in some parameters.[10] First, we introduce technological change by specifying $f(k) = Ah(k)$, where A describes the level of technology. Taking derivatives of (2.4.13) with respect to A yields

$$\frac{dk}{dA} = \frac{kf}{(f - kf')A} > 0,$$

where $f/k - f' > 0$. As technology is improved, the capital intensity, k, is increased. From (2.4.8), we obtain

$$\frac{dT}{dA} = -\frac{((f - kf')f' + kff'')(f + \delta k)kT\sigma}{A(f - kf')^2[(f' + \delta)\sigma k + (f - kf')]}.$$

The sign of dT/dA is the same as that of $(f - kf')f' + kff''$. As $(f - kf')f' > 0$ and $kff'' < 0$, the impact is ambiguous. If f takes on the Cobb-Douglas form, i.e.

$$f = Ak^\alpha,$$

then $dT/dA = 0$. If we use the following constant elasticity of substitution (CES) production function

$$f = A(ak^\rho + 1)^{1/\rho},$$

where $\rho < 1$, a and A are positive, we calculate

$$(f - kf')f' + kff'' = a\rho A^2 k^{\rho-1}(ak^\rho + 1)^{2/\rho-2}.$$

We see that if $\rho > 0$, then $dT/dA > 0$; if $\rho = 0$, then $dT/dA = 0$; and if $\rho < 0$, then $dT/dA < 0$. By $\bar{k} = kT$, we have

$$\frac{d\bar{k}}{dA} = k\frac{dT}{dA} + T\frac{dk}{dA}.$$

If the improvement in technology increases work time, then per capita wealth definitely increases; otherwise the impact is ambiguous. From equations (2.4.1), we obtain

$$\frac{dr}{dA} = \frac{f'}{A} + f''\frac{dk}{dA}, \quad \frac{dw}{dA} = \frac{w}{A} - kf''\frac{dk}{dA} > 0.$$

The wage rate is increased due to technological improvement; but the impact on the rate of interest is ambiguous. The impact on the output level is given by

$$\frac{df}{dA} = \frac{f}{A} + f'\frac{dk}{dA} > 0.$$

We now simulate the model to illustrate different patterns of time value and distribution over time.

For simplicity, we specify the production function by $f = Ak^\alpha$. We specify the following parameters:

$$A = 0.7, \ N_0 = 1, \ T_0 = 24, \ \alpha = 0.35, \ \delta_k = 0.03, \ \lambda = 0.5, \ \sigma = 0.25. \quad (2.4.15)$$

With the initial condition of $k(0) = 1$, we simulate the motion of $T(t)$, $k(t)$, $\bar{k}(t)$, $f(t)$, $c(t)$, $T(t)f(t)$, $r(t)$ and $w(t)$ over a period of 10 years. Figure 2.4.1 depicts the motion of these variables during the given period. Figure 2.4.1a shows that work time declines as time passes. Figure 2.4.1b shows that the capital intensity and per capita wealth increase over time. As demonstrated in Figure 2.4.1c, as the capital intensity increases, the per capita consumption, the per capita output Tf, and the per capita output in per unit of time rise. Figure 2.4.1d predicts that the wage rate rises and the rate of interest declines.

We now examine impact of changes on dynamic processes of the system. First, we examine the case that all the parameters, except ρ, are the same as in (2.4.15). We increase the propensity to use leisure from 0.25 to 0.30. The simulation results are demonstrated in Figure 2.4.2. The solid lines in Figure 2.4.2 are the same as in Figure 2.4.1, representing the values of the corresponding variables when $\sigma = 0.25$; the dashed lines in Figure 2.4.2 represent the new values of the variables when $\sigma = 0.30$.

Figure 2.4.2a shows that as the propensity to enjoy leisure increases, the work time decreases. Figure 2.4.2b demonstrates that as the work time declines, the capital intensity and per capita wealth increase in the long term. As shown in Figure 2.4.2c, both the per capita consumption and the per capita output income fall. In Figure 4.3.2d, we see that the wage rate increases and the rate of interest falls.

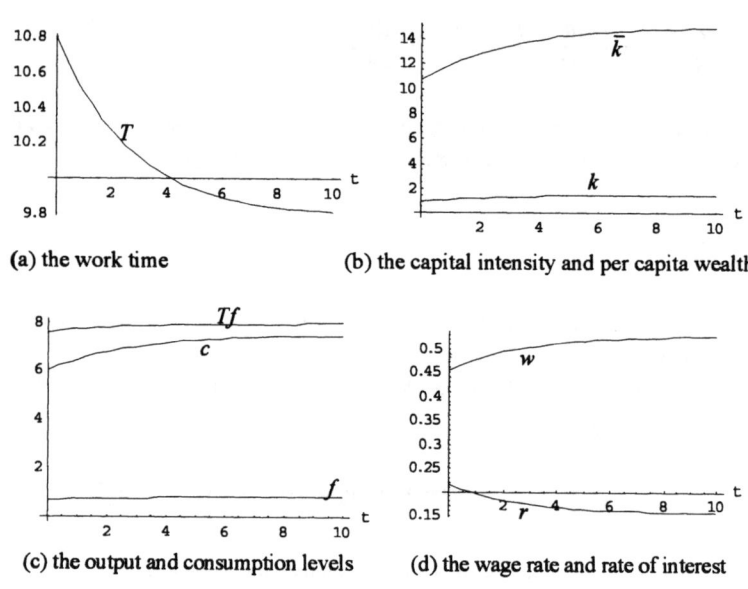

(a) the work time

(b) the capital intensity and per capita wealth

(c) the output and consumption levels

(d) the wage rate and rate of interest

Figure 2.4.1 Behavior of the model over time

2.5 Public goods and returns to scale

Infrastructure is public investment in roads, sewers, airports, and even includes education. Infrastructures provide widespread benefits to consumers and raise the return on private investment and productivity of production sectors. It is argued that recent inadequate public investment in infrastructure has been the major cause of the productivity slowdown in the United States. Barro (1991) finds a negative and significant effect of the level of public consumption as a percentage on economic growth rates of countries.[11] Although he asked for less government intervention, Adam Smith never said that government should not intervene in economic activity at all. The problem is not only how much the government intervenes but also how it spends its resources. Government can affect both physical capital formation and human capital accumulation. Government expenditures on health, nutrition, and education can be considered as an investment in the sense that they will lead to a more productive force in the future. The quantity and quality of public infrastructure – roads, airports, railways, ports, military defense systems, schools, public hospitals, and the like – are essential for the welfare of people and efficiency of production. It should be noted that for an economy as a whole, formation of government capital is not necessarily conducive to economic growth as it abstracts private use of capital. It is important for us to show under what conditions an increase in formation of public infrastructures would stimulate economic growth.

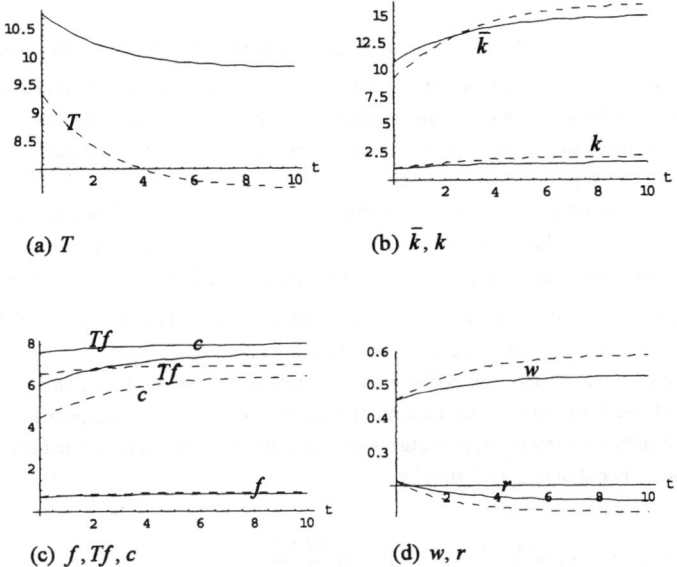

Figure 2.4.2 The propensity to use leisure, σ, increases from 0.25 to 0.30

This section will introduce (public) infrastructure into the OSG model.[12] The production function now includes, together with private inputs, those government inputs that will affect the level of output. For simplicity, we only consider a single type of public physical capital. The economy consists of industrial and public sectors. The industrial sector is the same as in the OSG model, except that infrastructures will affect productivity. The population is constant and homogeneous; each worker is employed in either of the two sectors. The production function is

$$F(t) = G^v(t)K_i^{\alpha_i}(t)N_i^{\beta_i}(t), \quad \alpha_i + \beta_i = 1, \quad \alpha_i, \beta_i > 0, \quad v \geq 0,$$

where α_i, β_i, and v are parameters, and

$F(t) =$ the output of the industrial sector at time t;
$K_i(t) =$ the capital stocks employed by the industrial sector;
$N_i(t) =$ the labor force employed by the industrial sector;
$G(t) =$ the (service) level of the public sector.

We interpret the variable, $G(t)$, as public goods such as physical and institutional infrastructures. The aggregate public goods are supplied by the government and are taken as given by the firms. Despite increasing social returns to scale, the function allows us to maintain the assumption of perfect competition in the goods market since the technology exhibits constant returns to scale for any given level of public goods, which firms cannot control. It is reasonable to assume that production efficiency will be improved as the service level of the public sector is improved; it seems that doubling the service level will not double the output with fixed $K_i(t)$ and $N_i(t)$. That is, the parameter v should be less than one. Because public service is freely available to firms, it is not a decision variable for the industrial sector.

The government finances the public sector by imposing taxes on, for instance, the outputs of the firms, the capital income, the labor income, and consumptions. We assume that the government imposes taxes only on the firms.[13] The after-tax returns of capital and labor at time t are given by

$$r(t) + \delta_k = (1-\tau)\frac{\alpha_i F(t)}{K_i(t)}, \quad w(t) = (1-\tau)\frac{\beta_i F(t)}{N_i(t)}, \qquad (2.5.1)$$

where $r(t)$ is the rate of interest, $w(t)$ is the wage rate, and τ $(1 > \tau \geq 0)$ is a fixed tax rate on the producers.

Introduce $\hat{Y}(t) = Y(t) + K(t)$ and specify the utility function as follows:

$$U(t) = G(t)^\vartheta C(t)^\xi S(t)^\lambda, \quad \vartheta, \xi, \lambda > 0.$$

One-Sector Growth (OSG) Economies with Capital Accumulation

The optimal solution is

$$C(t) = \xi \rho \hat{Y}(t), \quad S(t) = \lambda \rho \hat{Y}(t),$$

where $\rho \equiv 1/(\xi + \lambda)$. Substituting $S = \lambda \rho \hat{Y}$ into $\dot{K} = S - K$ yields

$$\dot{K}(t) = \lambda \rho Y(t) - \rho \xi K(t).$$

We now describe the public sector. In this model, we assume that the public sector is financially supported by the government's tax income. The capital stocks and workers employed by the public sector are paid at the same rates that the private sector pays the services of these factors. This is possible because factor markets are free and competitive. The government may have various objectives in providing public services. It is commonly assumed that the government will maximize the social welfare over a certain period of time in determining scales and scope of its intervention. The public sector has a fixed income, because the tax rate is fixed and the public sector has no income resource except the private sector. The public sector is assumed to behave effectively in the sense that it will use the income to maximize public services. We neglect possible inefficiency, such as official corruption, of the public sector. The production function of the public sector is given by

$$G(t) = K_p^{\alpha_p}(t) N_p^{\beta_p}(t), \quad \alpha_p + \beta_p = 1, \quad \alpha_p, \beta_p > 0,$$

where $K_p(t)$ is the capital and $N_p(t)$ is the labor force employed by the public sector.

For the given tax rate τ, the public sector is faced with the budget constraint

$$w(t)N_p(t) + r(t)K_p(t) = \tau F(t).$$

Maximizing the public services under the budget constraint yields

$$\frac{\alpha_p N_p(t)}{\beta_p K_p(t)} = \frac{r(t)}{w(t)}.$$

The factors are fully employed:

70   Economic Growth with Income and Wealth Distribution

$$N_i(t) + N_p(t) = N, \quad K_i(t) + K_p(t) = K(t).$$

We have thus built the model. We summarize the main analytical results by Zhang (2005a: 122) in the following theorem.

Theorem 2.5.1
The dynamics of the economic system are governed by the one-dimensional differential equation. The dynamic system has a unique equilibrium. Moreover, if $x < (>) 0$, where $x \equiv \alpha_i + \alpha_p v - 1$, the unique equilibrium is stable (unstable).

We illustrate the stability conditions in Figure 2.5.1.

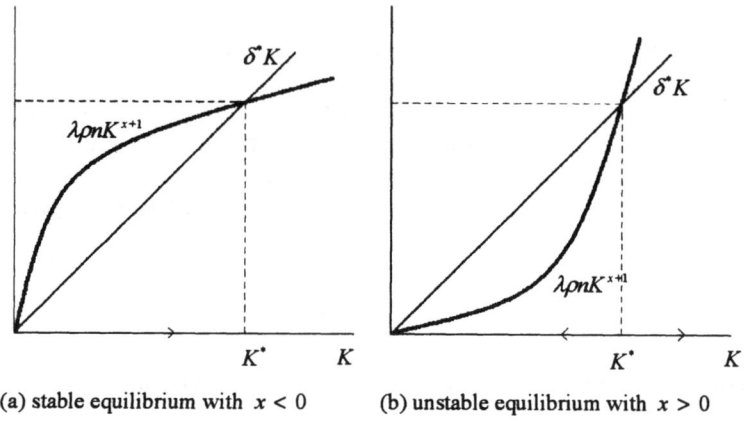

(a) stable equilibrium with $x < 0$ (b) unstable equilibrium with $x > 0$

Figure 2.5.1 Stable and unstable steady states

The parameter, x, determines stability of the system. From $x = \alpha_i + \alpha_p v - 1$, we see that this parameter measures net increasing returns to scale in capital accumulation. For instance, let us examine what happens to the capital accumulation equation when we double capital stocks. If we double the capital stocks, then capital inputs in the two sectors are exactly doubled because of the Cobb-Douglas technologies and perfectly competitive input factor markets. The level of public service is 2^{α_p} times as much as the old level of services because capital input is doubled. This means that productivity of the industrial sector is $2^{\alpha_p v}$ times as high as the old level. On the other hand, the output will increase 2^{α_i} times as much as the initial output because of the increase in capital stocks in the industrial sector. Consequently, as the total capital doubles, the total output will be $2^{\alpha_i + \alpha_p v}$ times as much as before. We see that if $\alpha_i + \alpha_p v < (>) 1$ (that is, $x < (>) 0$), the capital accumulation exhibits increasing (decreasing) returns to scale. If the capital accumulation exhibits decreasing returns to scale, the system becomes stable.

It can be shown that in the case of $x < 0$, the traditional view on savings is valid – an increase in the propensity to save, λ, tends to increase income; in the case of $x > 0$, the steady state is lowered. The following corollary summarizes the results.

Corollary 2.5.1
In the case of $x < (>) 0$, an increase in the propensity to hold wealth, λ, has the following impact on the equilibrium values of the variables: (1) K and Y rise (fall); C may be either increased or reduced; (2) N_i and N_p are not affected; (3) K_i and K_p rise (fall); (4) F and G increase (decline); and (5) r falls (rises); and w rises (falls).

2.6 Home production in the OSG model

Becker (1965) and Lancaster (1966, 1971) introduce the concept of the household production function. Instead of receiving utility directly from goods purchased in the market, they assumed that consumers derive utility from the attributes possessed by these goods, and then only after some transformation is performed on these market goods. A typical example is that the consumers purchase raw food in the market but they derive utility from the consumption of the completed meal, which has been produced by combining the raw food with labor and time in some environment. In *Treatise on the Family*, Becker (1981) emphasized the importance of division of labor and gains from specification. Becker applies the concept of household production functions to describe the possibility of producing household commodities with varied inputs. Household commodities include nonmarket goods including children, prestige, envy, health, and pleasures of the senses. These goods are produced with market goods and labor time of household members as inputs. Some goods, such as living space, household heating and lighting, and shared automobile trips are jointly consumed and can be considered as local public goods which enter simultaneously into the utility functions of all family members. It is argued that the because of benefits of shared public goods marriage yields a utility surplus over living separately. The well-being of children is treated as a household public good that enters the utility of both parents whether these parents are married or divorced.[14] Perceiving the household as a firm and applying microeconomic theories about firm behavior to the household, Becker examined specification within the household, comparative advantage, returns to scale, factor substitution, human capital, and assortative mating. Each member of the family can use time either for household labor or market labor and the family can purchase market goods either to consume or to use them as inputs in the household production function.

The OSG model in this section views the family as production units in economic analysis.[15] In addition to enjoyment, households also supply labor services, recreation, spiritual experiences, as well as conventional goods of the do-it-yourself variety. Household activities are conducted within houses as well as outside. These activities not only consume goods (like eating fruit and vegetables) but also utilize machines like videos, TVs, cookers, cars, and the like. This section extends the one-sector growth model proposed in Section 2.1 to endogenously determine capital distribution between industrial production and housing.

Except for home production, most aspects of this model are the same as the OSG model. The parameters, δ_k, N, and the variables, $K(t)$, $F(t)$, $w(t)$, $r(t)$, and $C(t)$ are defined as in the OSG model. Total capital, $K(t)$, is distributed between the industrial sector and home use. We denote by $K_i(t)$ and $K_h(t)$ respectively the capital stocks employed by the industrial sector and households. The production function is

$$F_i(t) = K_i^\alpha N^\beta$$

where α and β are parameters. The marginal conditions are

$$r(t) + \delta_k = \frac{\alpha F(t)}{K_i(t)}, \quad w(t) = \frac{\beta F(t)}{N(t)}. \qquad (2.6.1)$$

We assume that $U(t)$ is dependent on the consumption level, $C(t)$, the housing, $K_h(t)$, and the saving, $S(t)$, in the following way:[16]

$$U(t) = C(t)^\xi K_h(t)^\eta S(t)^\lambda, \quad \xi, \eta, \lambda > 0.$$

Similar to the budget constraint in the OSG model, the budget constraint is

$$C(t) + r(t)K_h(t) + S(t) = \hat{Y}(t) \, (= Y(t) + K(t)).$$

Maximizing $U(t)$ subject to the budget constraint yields

$$C(t) = \xi\rho\hat{Y}(t), \quad rK_h(t) = \eta\rho\hat{Y}(t), \quad S(t) = \lambda\rho\hat{Y}(t), \quad (2.6.2)$$

where $\rho \equiv 1/(\xi + \eta + \lambda)$.

The above equations mean that the housing consumption and consumption of the good are positively proportional to the net income and wealth, and the saving is positively proportional to the net income but negatively proportional to the wealth. Substituting $S(t)$ in equation (2.6.2) into $\dot{K}(t) = S(t) - K(t)$ yields

$$\dot{K}(t) = sY(t) - \delta K(t),$$

where $s \equiv \lambda\rho$ and $\delta \equiv (\xi + \lambda)\rho$. Capital is fully employed:

$$K_i(t) + K_h(t) = K(t).$$

We have thus built the one-sector growth model with home capital. It can be shown that the dynamics can be described by the motion of a single variable, $K(t)$, as follows:

$$\dot{K}(t) = s^*F(\Lambda(K)) - \delta^*K(t), \quad (2.6.3)$$

where $\Lambda(t)$ is a function of $K(t)$ and s^* and δ^* are parameters.

Proposition 2.6.1
For any given (positive) level $K(t)$ of the total capital stocks at any point in time, all the other variables in the system are uniquely determined as functions of $K(t)$. The dynamics of $K(t)$ are given by equation (2.6.3). The dynamic system has a unique stable equilibrium.

The system with home capital has similar dynamic properties to the OSG model, even though its internal structure is more complicated than that of the OSG model. This model provides detailed information about the dynamics of the components of the national product. The dynamics are illustrated in Figure 2.6.1.

74 *Economic Growth with Income and Wealth Distribution*

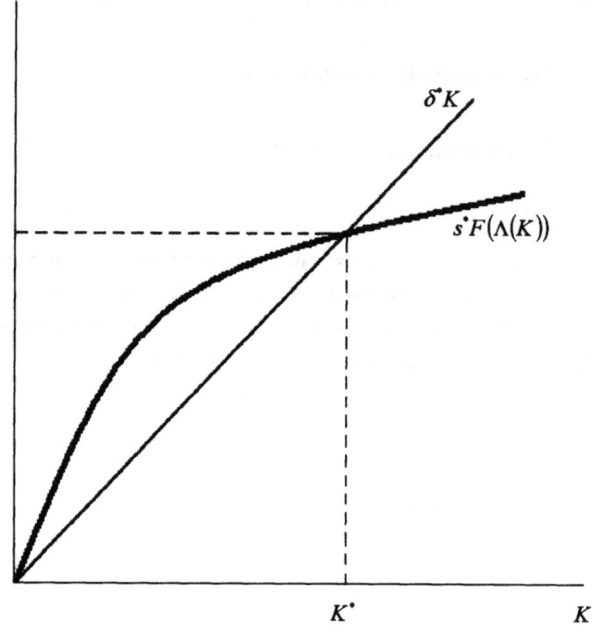

Figure 2.6.1 Evolution of capital stocks in the home production model

2.7 Environment and growth[17]

Energy, natural resources, and environmental pollution are necessary factors of production and consumption. Traditional growth theory neglected issues related to energy, natural resources, and environmental pollution. However, as economics was faced with the challenge of OPEC and the doomsday predictions of the Club of Rome in the 1970s, economists made efforts to introduce energy, natural resources, and environmental pollution into the neoclassical growth theory. Interdependence between capital accumulation and energy, natural resources, and environmental pollution was examined. In the 1990s, as the new growth theories were developed, economists have emphasized the various implications of knowledge creation and diffusion on the dynamics of energy, natural resources, and environmental pollution.

As dynamic interactions among these variables are too complicated, this section provides some insights into economic sustainability by examining the trade-offs between economic growth, consumption, and pollution. We neglect technological change in this initial stage.[18] Both production and consumption may pollute the environment. Economic growth often implies worsening environmental conditions. Growth also implies a higher material standard of living which will, through the demand for a better environment, induce changes in the structure of the economy to improve the environment. As a society accumulates more capital and makes progress in technology, more resources may be used to protect, if not improve, the environment. It is clearly observed that a country at the beginning of its economic development will be experiencing a worsening of the environment, while a country in which growth has taken place over a longer period of time will be adjusting its patterns of growth in such a way that the environment in fact improves. Trade-offs between consumption and pollution have been extensively analyzed since the publication of the seminal papers by Plourde (1972) and Forster (1973). Issues related to interdependence between economic growth and the environment have been examined from different perspectives.[19] This section introduces the dynamics of the environment and environment policy into the OSG model.

The economic system consists of production and environmental sectors. The production sector is similar to the OSG model. The environmental sector employs labor and capital to purify the environment. The government pays the environmental sector's costs of labor force and capital. The government's income comes from taxing the industrial sector. Factor markets are perfectly competitive and labor and capital are always fully employed. The population, N, is fixed. The variables, $K(t)$, $F(t)$, $N_i(t)$, $K_i(t)$, $C(t)$, $S(t)$, $r(t)$, and $w(t)$, are defined as in Section 2.1. We introduce

$N_e(t)$ and $K_e(t)$ = the labor force and capital stocks employed by the environmental sector;

$E(t)$ = the level of pollutant stocks; and

τ = the fixed tax rate, $0 < \tau < 1$.

There are two factor inputs, capital and labor, in economic production. We assume that environmental quality may affect the productivity of production units such as hotels, restaurants and hospitals and cause deterioration of machines. We specify the production function as follows:

$$F(t) = K_i(t)^\alpha N_i(t)^\beta \exp(-h_p E), \quad \alpha + \beta = 1, \quad \alpha, \beta > 0, \quad h_p \geq 0.$$

The term, $\exp(-h_p E)$, in $F(t)$ means that productivity is negatively related to the pollution level. The marginal conditions are given by

$$r(t) + \delta_k = \frac{(1-\tau)\alpha F(t)}{K_i(t)}, \quad w(t) = \frac{(1-\tau)\beta F(t)}{N_i(t)}. \tag{2.7.1}$$

We now describe the dynamics of the stock of pollutants, $E(t)$. We assume that pollutants are created through two sources, production and consumption. Pollutants may be reduced in two ways. Nature may "treat" certain pollutants in a similar way to that of waste treatment plants. Some of pollutants may naturally disappear without any human effort. Pollutants may be treated by using capital and labor. We specify the dynamics of the stock of pollutants as follows:

$$\dot{E}(t) = q_f F(t) + q_c C(t) - Q_e(t) - q_0 E(t),$$

in which q_f, q_c, and q_0 are positive parameters and

$$Q_e(t) = f(E) K_e^u N_e^v,$$

where u and v are positive parameters, and $f(E)$ (≥ 0) is a function of E. The term, $q_f F$, means that pollutants that are produced during production processes are linearly positively proportional to the output level.[20] The term, $q_c C$, means that in consuming one unit of the good the quantity, $q_c C$, is left as waste. The parameter, q_c, depends on the technology and environmental sense of consumers. The parameter, q_0, is called the rate of natural purification. The term, $q_0 E$, measures the rate that nature purifies the environment. The term $K_e^u N_e^v$ in Q_e means that the purification rate of the environment is positively related to knowledge utilization efficiency, capital and labor inputs. The function, $f(E)$, implies that the purification efficiency is dependent on the scale of pollutants at time t. It is not easy to generally specify how purification efficiency is related to the scale of pollutants. For simplicity, we specify f as follows: $f(E) = q_e E^v$, where $q_e > 0$ and $v > 0$ are parameters. The function has the following properties:

$$f(0) = 0, \quad \lim_{E \to \infty} f(E) = \infty, \quad \frac{df}{dE} > 0, \quad \frac{d^2 f}{d^2 E} < 0.$$

When E is large, the specified functional form is problematic. At this initial stage of the investigation, we accept the above specified form. In order to describe the behavior of households, we define a variable

$$E^* = E_0 - E,$$

where E_0 is called the threshold of pollution level. For instance, consumption of nuclear-generated electricity brings about the creation of radionuclides that cause death or severe mutation when threshold concentrations are exceeded. Electricity production using coal creates atmospheric CO_2 concentrations which, at sufficiently high levels, may cause dramatic changes. We assume that the critical level is known.[21]

We assume that the disutility that the society experiences from pollution is a continuous function of the environmental pollution stock. It is assumed that the utility level, $U(t)$, that a typical household obtains is dependent on the consumption level of commodities, $C(t)$, the environmental condition, $E^*(t)$, and the saving, $S(t)$. The utility function is specified as follows:

$$U(t) = E^*(t)^\varsigma C(t)^\xi S(t)^\lambda, \quad \varsigma, \xi, \lambda > 0,$$

in which ς, ξ, and λ are respectively the propensities to enjoy the environment, to consume goods, and to own wealth. As in the OSG model, the budget constraint is

$$C + S = \hat{Y}.$$

Maximizing $U(t)$ subject to $C(t) + S(t) = \hat{Y}(t)$ yields

$$C(t) = \xi \rho \hat{Y}(t), \quad S(t) = \lambda \rho \hat{Y}(t), \tag{2.7.2}$$

where $\rho \equiv 1/(\xi + \lambda)$. It is assumed that the saving is equal to investment. Substituting $S(t)$ in equation (2.7.2) into $\dot{K}(t) = S(t) - K(t)$ yields

$$\dot{K}(t) = \lambda \rho Y(t) - \xi \rho K(t). \tag{2.7.3}$$

We now determine how the government determines the number of the labor force and the level of capital employed for purifying pollution. The government budget is given by

$$r(t)K_e(t) + w(t)N_e(t) = \tau F(t).$$

We assume that the government will employ the labor force and capital stocks for purifying the environment in such a way that the purification rate achieves its maximum under the given budget constraint. The government's problem is given by

$$\text{Max} Q_e(t) = f(E)K_e^u N_e^v \quad \text{s.t.: } rK_e + wN_e = \tau F.$$

The optimal solution is given by

$$rK_e = \tau u v_0 F, \quad wN_e = \tau v v_0 F,$$

where

$$v_0 \equiv \frac{1}{u+v}.$$

We assume that labor and capital are fully employed:

$$K_i(t) + K_e(t) = K(t), \quad N_i(t) + N_e(t) = N.$$

We have thus defined the model. We can represent the dynamics of the economic system in terms of the two following differential equations:

$$\dot{K} = \alpha_0 \lambda \rho K^\alpha N^\beta \exp(-h_p E) - \xi \rho K,$$
$$\dot{E} = \lambda_i K^\alpha N^\beta \exp(-h_p E) + q_c \delta \xi \rho K - \lambda_e E^v K^u N^v - q_0 E,$$

where

$$\alpha_0 \equiv \alpha^\alpha \beta^\beta, \quad \lambda_i \equiv \alpha_0 (q_f + q_c \xi \rho), \quad \lambda_e \equiv q_e \alpha_e^u \beta_e^v.$$

Proposition 2.7.1
The dynamic system has a unique stable equilibrium point in the case of $h_p = 0$.

In the case of $h_p = 0$, it is straightforward to prove the proposition. In the case of $h_p > 0$, it is possible that the system has multiple equilibrium points.

2.8 The OSG model with population

We now suggest a possible dynamics for population growth.[22] Except for population dynamics, the model is the same as in the OSG model. We will not repeat the assumptions and definitions of the variables. In the Malthusian growth model the population grows at a constant rate times the current population, with no limitations on its resources. The following logistic growth model

$$\dot{N}(t) = nN(t)(m - qN(t))$$

takes account of the limiting effects of natural resources upon population growth. However, in a human society resources are endogenous variables. To analyze how production affects population growth, Haavelmo suggests the following model:[23]

$$\dot{N}(t) = nN(t)\left(1 - q\frac{N(t)}{Y(t)}\right),$$

where $Y(t)$ is the level of production of the society. Haavelmo further assumed that

$$Y(t) = N(t)^{\theta}, \quad 0 < \theta < 1.$$

This population model is valid for an agricultural economy where no capital accumulation is allowed. Zhang (1994) extended the Haavelmo population dynamics

$$\dot{N}(t) = nN(t)\left[C(t)^{b} - qN(t)\left\{\frac{N(t)}{Y(t)}\right\}^{\theta}\right], \qquad (2.8.1)$$

where n, q, b, and θ are nonnegative parameters. By equation (2.2.10), we have

$$C = \xi(Y + K).$$

When $b = 0$ and $q = 0$, the model is identical to the Malthusian population model. When $\theta = 0$, and $q > 0$ and $b = 0$, it is identical to the logistic model. When $b = 0$ and $q > 0$, the model is identical to the Haavelmo model. We now interpret our population dynamics. In equation (2.8.1), we interpret C^b as the capacity for supporting the population. This implies that the population which can suitably live (or survive) in a society is dependent upon the current level of consumption. This is similar to the effects of consumption upon the growth rate of the population. The term $qN(K/N)^\theta$ expresses how wealth makes a contribution as a checking force of the population growth. It means that the richer the society becomes, the more expensive it is for the society to support its people. This is observed in industrialized societies. If $0 < b < 1$, there are decreasing effects of consumption upon the population capacity. Doubling the current level of consumption will not double the capacity for supporting the people. This case seems acceptable for a developed economy. In a developed economy, each person will consume more because of increased needs for health caring, education, leisure, housing, privacy, and travel. If $b > 1$, there are increasing effects of consumption upon the population capacity. Doubling the current level of consumption will more than double the capacity for supporting the people. For instance, if people's material consumption consists only simple shelter and food, it is possible to have situations that double consumption would more than double the capacity. We will see that this parameter plays a key role in determining the stability of the dynamics.

The capital accumulation is the same as that in the OSG model. The capital accumulation is characterized by decreasing returns as the population is fixed and $\alpha < 1$. Although endogenous population is introduced, since $\alpha + \beta = 1$ (which does not generate a case of increasing return in the capital accumulation), the system will not exhibit instability if the population dynamics do not exhibit increasing returns. We now look at the population dynamics. Because $N(N/F)^\theta$ does not exhibit increasing returns in either K or/and N, this term will not create increasing returns in the system. Accordingly, there is only one possible term, C^b, for the system to exhibit increasing returns. This happens only when $b > 1$. We will prove this. If we consider that $b < 1$ fits for industrial economies and $b > 1$ may be suitable for poor countries, we may expect that the system will behave stably as in the OSG model in the case of $b < 1$; and the system will be unstable, like poverty traps observed in the extended Solow model, in the case of $b > 1$. From these discussions, we see that b should be considered as an endogenous variable in analysis of economic structural transformation.

It can be shown that the dynamics of $K(t)$ and $N(t)$ are given by the following two-dimensional differential equations:

$$\dot{K}(t) = \lambda A K(t)^\alpha N(t)^\beta - \xi K(t),$$

$$\dot{N}(t) = nN(t)\left[\xi^b\left(AK(t)^\alpha N(t)^\beta + \delta K(t)\right)^b - \frac{qN(t)}{A^\theta K(t)^{\alpha\theta}}^{1+\alpha\theta}\right]. \quad (2.8.2)$$

Proposition 2.8.1
The dynamic system has a unique equilibrium point. If $0 \leq b < 1$, then the unique equilibrium point is stable. If $b > 1$, then the equilibrium point is unstable.

Here, we specify the parameter values as follows:

$$\alpha = 0.3, \ \delta_k = 0.05, \ \lambda = 0.65, \ b = 0.3, \ q = 0.4, \ \theta = 0.4, \ A = 0.7, \ n = 1.5. \quad (2.8.3)$$

We simulate the motion of the system with the initial condition, $K(0) = 1.2$ and $N(0) = 0.8$, for 15 years. The simulation results are given in Figure 2.8.1. In the first few years, wealth tends to decline but the population grows. After the population reaches 1.45, the growth of the population slows down and wealth begins to increase.[24]

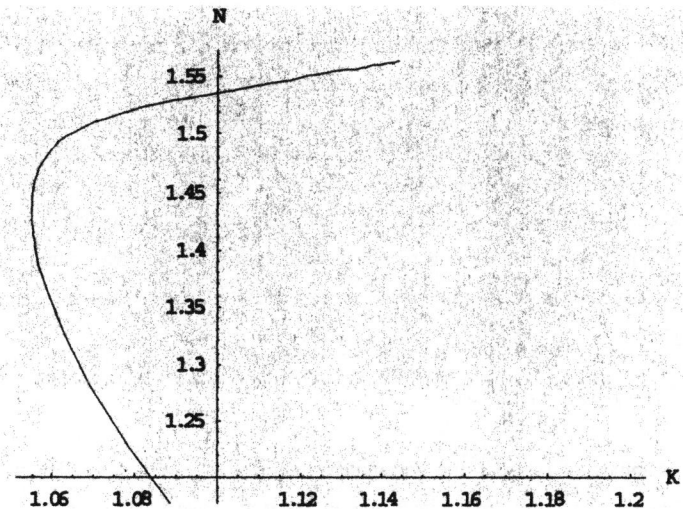

Figure 2.8.1 The interaction between wealth and the population

The model in this section derives the population dynamics, not based on the utility-maximization mechanism. A large part of the contemporary literature on growth and population dynamics is based on assumptions that households determine birth rates under utility-maximization assumptions. In Appendix 2.1 to this chapter, we provide an economic growth model with proposed endogenous population. This model also hints at possibilities of extending our model to build population dynamics upon utility-maximization principles.

2.9 Money and economic growth

Modern analysis of the long-term interaction of inflation and capital formation begins with Tobin's seminal contribution in 1965. Tobin deals with an isolated economy in which outside money competes with real capital in the portfolios of agents within the framework of the Solow model.[25] Since then, many growth models of monetary economies have been built within the OLG framework.[26] This section introduces money within the OSG framework. We present the model in discrete time, as in Section 2.3. The population, N, is constant. Production is achieved through a neoclassical constant return to scale technology. The real interest rate and the wage of labor are given as before by

$$r(t) + \delta_k = f'(k(t)), \quad w(t) = f(k(t)) - k(t)f'(k(t)). \tag{2.9.1}$$

For simplicity of expression, we normalize $N = 1$. There is some initial capital stock, k_0, that is owned equally by all individuals at the initial period.

We assume that agents have perfect foresight with respect to all future events and capital markets operate without friction. The government levies no taxes. Money is introduced by assuming that a central bank distributes at no cost to the population a per capita amount of fiat money $M(t) > 0$. The scheme according to which the money stock evolves over time is deterministic and known to all agents. With μ being the constant net growth rate of the money stock, $M(t)$ evolves over time according to

$$M(t) = (1 + \mu)M(t - 1), \quad \mu > 0.$$

At the beginning of period t the government brings $M(t) - M(t - 1)$ additional units of money per capita into circulation in order to finance all government expenditures via seigniorage. For the seigniorage mechanism to work, injections of the additional units of money take place before the other markets open. Let $m(t)$

stand for the real value of money per capita measured in units of the output good. Then, we may rewrite the above equation as

$$g(t) = \frac{M(t) - M(t-1)}{P(t)} = \frac{\mu}{1+\mu} m(t). \tag{2.9.2}$$

In this model, money acts as a pure store of value. The demand for money relies exclusively on the speculative conjecture that the future exchange value of money in terms of goods will be positive because people will express a positive demand for money in the future. In the absence of uncertainty and with money not being explicitly required for transaction purposes, this bubbly view implies that in a monetary equilibrium the return on money needs to be equal to the return on competing assets such as claims on productive investment projects. In period t, each consumer receiving the per capita nominal money stock, M, believes that money will be exchanged at the expected future price, $p^m(t+1) > 0$. The price of money $p^m(t)$ is in terms of goods or it expresses the amount of goods that can be purchased by one unity of money in each period t. According to the definitions, we have

$$P(t) = \frac{1}{p^m(t)}.$$

A necessary condition for a monetary economy to exist is that the price of money must be positive. If money has a positive value, people have an opportunity to save in money. According to the definition of the price of money, the deflation rate $P(t)/P(t+1)$ coincides with the real return on money. In a competitive economy the absence of arbitrage opportunities entails equality of return on assets

$$\frac{P(t)}{P(t+1)} = 1 + f'(k(t+1)) - \delta_k.$$

As

$$\frac{P(t)}{P(t+1)} = \frac{P(t)}{P(t+1)} \frac{M(t+1)}{(1+\mu)M(t)} = \frac{m(t+1)}{(1+\mu)m(t)},$$

the above balance condition becomes

$$1 + f'(k(t+1)) - \delta_k = \frac{m(t+1)}{(1+\mu)m(t)}. \tag{2.9.3}$$

The consumer obtains income in period t from the interest payment, $r(t)k(t)$, and the wage payment, $w(t)$,

$$y(t) = r(t)k(t) + w(t), \tag{2.9.4}$$

where $y(t)$ is called the current income. We define the disposable income as the sum of the wealth, $a(t)$, and the current income, i.e.

$$\hat{y}(t) \equiv y(t) + a(t), \tag{2.9.5}$$

where

$$a(t) = k(t) + m(t).$$

The budget constraint is given by

$$c(t) + s(t) = \hat{y}(t).$$

For simplicity, we take the Cobb-Douglas utility function to describe consumers' preferences:

$$U(t) = c^\xi(t)s^\lambda(t), \quad \xi + \lambda = 1, \quad \xi, \lambda > 0,$$

in which ξ and λ are respectively the propensities to consume goods and to own wealth. The households maximize the utility function subject to the budget constraint. We solve the optimal choice of the consumers as

$$c(t) = \xi \hat{y}(t), \quad s(t) = \lambda \hat{y}(t). \tag{2.9.6}$$

According to the definitions, the per capita wealth in period $t+1$, $a(t+1)$, is equal to the saving made in period t minus the wealth in period t, i.e.

$$a(t+1) = s(t) - a(t).$$

By the above equation and $a(t) = k(t) + m(t)$, we have

$$k(t+1) = s(t) - m(t+1). \qquad (2.9.7)$$

The economy starts to operate at $t = 0$. Each member in period 0 is endowed with $M(-1)$ units of money and owns k_0 ($= K(0)/N(0)$) units of physical capital. The labor force N is exogenously given. We will show that the above equations allow us to calculate recursively all the $k(t)$ and $m(t)$.

We now show that the motion of the system may be expressed in three-dimensional difference equations. Government spending is given by equation (2.9.2). From equations (2.9.5) and (2.9.6), we obtain

$$s(t) = \lambda(y(t) + k(t) + m(t)).$$

Substituting equations (2.9.1) and (2.9.4) into the above equation yields

$$s(t) = \lambda(f(k(t)) + \delta k(t) + m(t)), \qquad (2.9.8)$$

where $\delta \equiv 1 - \delta_k$. Substituting equation (2.9.8) into equation (2.9.7), we obtain

$$k(t+1) = \lambda(f(k(t)) + \delta k(t) + m(t)) - m(t+1). \qquad (2.9.9)$$

From equation (2.9.3), we obtain

$$m(t+1) = (1 + \mu)[\delta + f'(k(t+1))]m(t). \qquad (2.9.10)$$

Definition 2.9.1

Given the initial capital stock k_0 and the initial money stock $M(-1)$, a *competitive equilibrium* is given by a sequence of quantities $\{m(t), c(t), s(t), g(t), k(t+1)\}$ and a sequence of prices $\{r(t), w(t), P(t)\}$ such that for all periods $t = 0, 1, 2, \cdots$: (i) competition ensures that factors get paid their marginal products according to equations (2.9.1); (ii) given $M(t) = (1 + \mu)M(t-1)$, the budget constraint (2.9.2) of the government is satisfied; (iii) given the price consequence, agents solve optimally the decision problem (2.9.7) subject to equation (2.9.6); (iv) the evolution of money balances satisfies (2.9.10); (v) investments and savings are matched by equation (2.9.7); and (vi) all markets clear with the equilibrium conditions being as following:

86 Economic Growth with Income and Wealth Distribution

labor market: $w(t) = f(k(t)) - k(t)f'(k(t))$;
money market: $m(t) = M(t)/P(t)$;
goods market: $f(k(t)) + k(t) = g(t) + \delta_k k(t) + c(t) + k(t+1)$.

Equilibrium can be further classified as *inside* and *outside money equilibrium*: an inside money equilibrium is associated with a situation in which outside balances are zero; an outside money equilibrium is associated with positive outside money balances.

We now examine the dynamic properties of the difference equations, (2.9.9) and (2.9.10). At inside money equilibrium with $m(t) = 0$, we have

$$k(t+1) = \lambda(f(k(t)) + \delta k(t)).$$

Government spending is reduced to zero. As shown before, this system has a unique stable equilibrium given by

$$\frac{f(\bar{k})}{\bar{k}} = \frac{\xi + \delta_k \lambda}{\lambda}. \qquad (2.9.11)$$

We are mainly interested in the monetary economy which is characterized by the three difference equations (2.9.2), (2.9.9) and (2.9.10). As (2.9.9) and (2.9.10) do not contain $g(t)$, we treat $g(t)$ as an exogenous variable. In fact, once $m(t)$ is determined, we determine $g(t)$ by (2.9.2).[27] Dynamics of the monetary economy are described by (2.9.9) and (2.9.10). We may rewrite the system as follows:

$$k(t+1) = \lambda(f(k(t)) + \delta k(t) + m(t)) - m(t+1),$$
$$m(t+1) = (1+\mu)(\delta + f'(k(t+1)))m(t). \qquad (2.9.12)$$

A steady state of the monetary economy is given by

$$k = \lambda(f(k) + \delta k) - \xi m,$$
$$1 = (1+\mu)(\delta + f'(k)). \qquad (2.9.13)$$

From $1 = (1+\mu)(\delta + f'(k))$, we get

$$f'(k) = \delta_k - \frac{\mu}{1+\mu}. \qquad (2.9.14)$$

From the properties of f, we see that if $\delta_k > \mu/(1+\mu)$, equation (2.9.14) has a unique solution, denoted by k^*. From the first equation in (2.9.13), we solve

$$m^* = \left(\frac{f(k^*)}{k^*} - \frac{\xi}{\lambda} - \delta_k\right)\frac{\lambda k^*}{\xi}. \qquad (2.9.15)$$

For $m^* > 0$, we should require $f(k^*)/k^* > \xi/\lambda + \delta_k$. Comparing equations (2.9.11) and (2.9.15), we see that the monetary economy has a unique equilibrium if

$$\frac{f(k^*)}{k^*} > \frac{f(\bar{k})}{\bar{k}}. \qquad (2.9.16)$$

As $d(f/k)/dk = (f' - f/k)/k < 0$ because of strict concavity of f, f/k strictly decreases in k. Hence, (2.9.16) implies $\bar{k} > k^*$ if both $\bar{k}$ and k^* exist. As f' decreases in k, we see that if $f'(\bar{k}) < \delta_k - \mu/(1+\mu)$, then $\bar{k} > k^*$. In summary, we have the following proposition.

Proposition 2.9.1
Suppose that the inside competitive equilibrium has a unique nontrivial steady state $\bar{k} > 0$. Then, the monetary economy has a unique steady state k^* if the following inequality holds:

$$f'(\bar{k}) < \delta_k - \frac{\mu}{1+\mu}.$$

The steady state is a saddle point.[28]

From (2.9.14), we get

$$f''\frac{dk^*}{d\mu} = -\frac{1}{(1+\mu)^2} < 0.$$

If the rate of monetary expansion μ is permanently raised, then the per capita capital stock in the new monetary steady state is higher than before. That is, the Tobin effect prevails.[29] This is illustrated as in Figure 2.9.1. As μ is shifted, the accumulation equation

$$k = \lambda(f(k) + \delta k + m) - m$$

is not affected; the arbitrage relation

$$1 = (1 + \mu)(\delta + f'(k))$$

is shifted by lowering the return on real balances via increased inflation taxation. To rebalance the arbitrage relation, the composition of the portfolios of agents needs to be readjusted in favor of capital. In the new steady state, the capital stock will be higher than before.

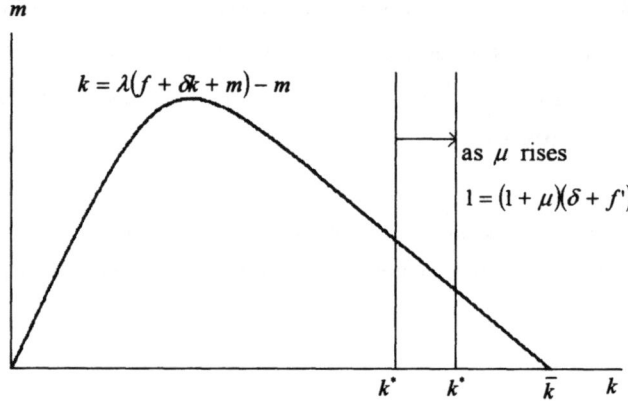

Figure 2.9.1 The Tobin effect

Although we will not be further concerned with demand and supply of money in our analysis of growth and income and wealth distribution, it is important to introduce money and inflation into models with distribution as various groups of people or nations may be affected differently by change in monetary policies or exchange rates. Our analytical framework allows further examination of these topics.

2.10 A small open economy with capital accumulation

This section describes the dynamics of a small country economy.[30] An open economy can import goods and services and borrow resources from the rest of the world or exports goods and services and lend resources abroad. For convenience of illustration, assume that there is a single good in the world economy and the price of the good is unity.

2.10.1 The model with general production and utility functions

The production sector is identical to that in the OSG model for the closed economy. Let $K(t)$ denote the capital stocks employed by the economy at time t and N ($=1$) the flow of labor services used at time t for production.[31] The production function $F(t)$ defines the flow of production at time t. We assume that $F(K(t),N)$ is neoclassical. Let $w(t)$ stand for the real wage rate and $r^*(t)$ the real interest rate for borrowing or lending in the world capital market at time t. For illustration, we fix the interest rate during the study period. The marginal conditions are

$$r^* + \delta_k = f'(k(t)), \quad w(t) = f(k(t)) - k(t)f'(t), \qquad (2.10.1)$$

in which $k(t) \equiv K(t)/N$. We assume that factor markets work quickly enough so that our system always displays competitive equilibrium in factor markets. As r^* is fixed, we see that both $k(t)$ and $w(t)$ are functions of r^* as

$$k = g(r^*), \quad w = h(r^*).$$

It is straightforward to show $dg/dr^* = 1/f'' < 0$ and $dh/dr^* = -g < 0$. That is, as the rate of interest rises, both the capital density and the wage rate fall.

We now describe the behavior of consumers. Denote by $\bar{k}(t)$ the wealth per capita at time t. A typical consumer obtains current income

$$y(t) = r^*\bar{k}(t) + w(t),$$

from the interest payment $r\bar{k}$ and the wage payment w. We call $Y(t)$ ($\equiv y(t)N$) the current income. Introduce $B(t)$ as the value of the economy's net foreign assets at t and define $b(t) \equiv B(t)/N$. According to the definitions, we have

$$\overline{K}(t) = K(t) + B(t).$$

That is

$$\overline{k}(t) = k(t) + b(t).$$

As

$$Y(t) = r^*\overline{K}(t) + wN = F(t) - \delta_k K(t) + E(t), \qquad (2.10.2)$$

where $\overline{K}(t) \equiv \overline{k}(t)N$, $E(t) \equiv r^*B(t)$ and we use

$$r^*K(t) + w(t)N = F(t) - \delta_k K(t).$$

The current income of the households is equal to the sum of the economy's net output, $F - \delta_k K$, and the country's interest earned on foreign assets, r^*B. The gross national product (GNP) is measured as the sum of the value of the net output produced within its borders and net international factor payments. The GNP is given by $F + E$. The output produced within the country's geographical borders is called the gross domestic product (GDP). The GDP is given by F. A country's current balance at time t is the change in the value of its net claims over the rest of the world – the change in its net foreign assets. If $\dot{B}(t) > 0$, the economy as a whole is lending (in this case we say that the current account balance is in surplus); if $\dot{B}(t) < 0$, the economy as a whole is borrowing (the current account balance is in deficit); and if $\dot{B}(t) = 0$, the economy as a whole is neither borrowing nor lending (the current account balance is in balance).

The disposable income is given by $\overline{Y}(t) = Y(t) + \overline{K}(t)$. From equation (2.10.2), we have

$$\overline{Y}(t) = (1 + r^*)\overline{K}(t) + wN = w_0 N + (1 + r^*)B(t), \qquad (2.10.3)$$

where

$$w_0 \equiv (1 + r^*)g + h.$$

Here, we require $\bar{Y}(t) > 0$, i.e.

$$\bar{K}(t) + F(t) > -r^* B(t) + \delta_k K(t).$$

The requirement means that the sum of the economy's total assets and output is more than the sum of the interest payment to the rest of world and the capital depreciation. Otherwise, the economy has nothing to consume after paying the two parts.

The disposable income is used for saving and consumption. At each point in time, consumers would distribute the disposable income between saving, $S(t)$, and consumption of goods, $C(t)$. The budget constraint is given by

$$C(t) + S(t) = \bar{Y}(t). \tag{2.10.4}$$

A typical consumer is to choose his most preferred bundle $(c(t), s(t))$ of consumption and saving under his budget constraint. Here, $c \equiv C/N$ and $s \equiv S/N$. The utility-maximizing problem at any time is defined by

$$\underset{c,s}{\text{Max}} \ U(c,s)$$
$$\text{s.t.} \ c(t) + s(t) = \bar{y}(t). \tag{2.10.5}$$

We denote an optimal solution as a function of the disposable income

$$(c(t), s(t)) = (c(\bar{y}(t)), s(\bar{y}(t))).$$

The change in the households' wealth is equal to the net savings minus the wealth sold at time t, i.e.

$$\dot{k}(t) = s(\bar{y}(k)) - \bar{k}(t). \tag{2.10.6}$$

From $\bar{y}(t) = w_0(r^*) + (1 + r^*)b(t)$ and $\bar{k}(t) = g(r^*) + b(t)$, for any fixed level of r^*, we see that the national economic dynamics are determined by the following motion of per capita foreign assets:

$$\dot{b}(t) = s(w_0(r^*) + (1 + r^*)b(t)) - g(r^*) - b(t). \tag{2.10.7}$$

In a stationary state

$$s(w_0(r^*) + (1 + r^*)b) = g(r^*) + b.$$

We now show that this equation has a unique solution. Define

$$\Phi(b) \equiv s(w_0(r^*) + (1 + r^*)b) - g(r^*) - b. \tag{2.10.8}$$

The condition $\bar{Y} \geq 0$ is guaranteed if

$$b \geq \tilde{b} \equiv -\frac{w_0(r^*)}{1 + r^*}.$$

We have $\Phi(\tilde{b}) = h/(1 + r^*) > 0$. As $0 < s'(\bar{y}) < 1$, for sufficiently large b, we may have $\Phi(b) < 0$. As $\Phi'(b) = (1 + r^*)s' - 1$, we have $\Phi'(b) < 0$ if r^* is small and s' is properly smaller than unity.[32] If $\Phi(b) < 0$ and $\Phi'(b) < 0$ for $b \geq \tilde{b}$, the dynamic system has a unique equilibrium point. Let b^* stand for an equilibrium point. As

$$\left.\frac{\partial \dot{b}}{\partial b}\right|_{b=b^*} = \Phi'(b^*) = (1 + r^*)s' - 1,$$

we see that if $\Phi'(b) < 0$, the dynamic system has a unique stable equilibrium point.

In the case of $\Phi'(b) < 0$ at the equilibrium point we can examine effects of change in the rate of interest. Take derivatives of $\Phi'(b) < 0$ with respect to r^*

$$\Phi' \frac{db}{dr^*} = -(w_0(r^*) + b)s' + \frac{dg}{dr^*} = \frac{1 - (1 + r^*)s'}{f''} - bs', \tag{2.10.9}$$

where we use

$$\frac{dw_0}{dr^*} = g + (1 + r^*)\frac{dg}{dr^*} + \frac{dh}{dr^*} = \frac{1 + r^*}{f''} < 0.$$

Using $\Phi' < 0$, $0 < s' \leq 0$, $f'' < 0$ and $1 > (1 + r^*)s'$, we have: $db/dr^* > 0$. As the rate of interest increases, the value of the country's net foreign assets rises. As

$$\frac{d\bar{y}}{dr^*} = \frac{1+r^*}{f''} + b + (1+r^*)\frac{db}{dr^*},$$

we see that the sign of $d\bar{y}/dr^*$ is ambiguous in general. As the impacts on c and s are in the same direction as on $\bar{y}$, we need additional conditions in order to explicitly judge the impacts on c and s.

2.10.2 The dynamics with the Cobb-Douglas functions

To illustrate the analytical results and to simulate the model, we now examine the model with the following utility and production functions:

$$F(t) = AK^\alpha(t)N^\beta, \ \alpha, \beta > 0, \ \alpha + \beta = 1,$$
$$U(t) = c^\xi(t)s^\lambda(t), \ \xi + \lambda = 1, \ \xi, \lambda > 0. \qquad (2.10.10)$$

From $f = Ak^\alpha$ and equations (2.10.1), we solve

$$k = r_0^{1/\beta}, \ w = \beta A r_0^{\alpha/\beta}, \qquad (2.10.11)$$

where

$$r_0 = \frac{\alpha A}{r^* + \delta_k}.$$

We have $\bar{y} = w_0 + (1+r^*)b$, where $w_0 = (1+r^*)k + w$. The optimal choice of households is given by

$$c = \xi \bar{y}, \ s = \lambda \bar{y}.$$

From equation (2.10.7), $s = \lambda \bar{y}$ and $\bar{y} = w_0 + (1+r^*)b$, we have

$$\dot{b} = \lambda w_0 - r_0^{1/\beta} - (\xi - \lambda r^*)b. \qquad (2.10.12)$$

94 Economic Growth with Income and Wealth Distribution

Assume $\xi - \lambda r^* > 0$. From the definitions of ξ and λ and the rate of interest should be small, it is reasonable to require $\xi > \lambda r^*$. The solution of the linear differential equation is given by

$$b(t) = (b(0) - b^*)e^{-(\xi - \lambda r^*)t} + b^*, \quad (2.10.13)$$

where

$$b^* \equiv \frac{\lambda w_0 - r_0^{1/\beta}}{\xi - \lambda r^*}.$$

As $\xi - \lambda r^* > 0$, we conclude that as $t \to +\infty$, $b(t) \to b^*$. In the long term, the system approaches its equilibrium position. Figure 2.10.1 depicts the foreign asset dynamics with different initial conditions. We see that if the initial foreign asset is above the equilibrium level, it decreases over time, and vice versa.

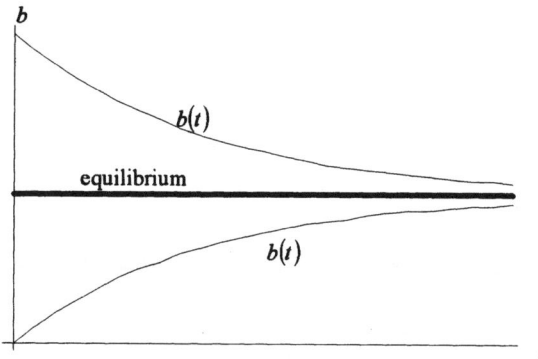

Figure 2.10.1 Convergence toward the equilibrium point

Lemma 2.10.1

Assume $\xi - \lambda r^* > 0$. The dynamic system has a unique stable equilibrium point.

As $\xi - \lambda r^* > 0$, the sign of b^* is the same as that of $\lambda w_0 - r_0^{1/\beta}$. From $w_0 = (1 + r^*)r_0^{1/\beta} + \beta A r_0^{\alpha/\beta}$, we see that the equilibrium value of b^* is positive if

$$r^* > \frac{\alpha \xi}{\lambda} - \beta \delta_k, \qquad (2.10.14)$$

where we also use $r_0 = \alpha A / (r^* + \delta_k)$. We conclude that if the propensity to save is high, it needs a higher level of the interest rate to keep the above inequality. Moreover, the above equation implies that in the long term, whether or not the economy owns wealth employed by other countries is independent of its productivity parameter, A.

We simulate the model to illustrate how the equilibrium values are affected by parameters. First, we examine the impact of r^* on the equilibrium values. We specify the other parameters as follows:

$$\alpha = 0.35, \ A = 1, \ \lambda = 0.7, \ \delta_k = 0.05. \qquad (2.10.15)$$

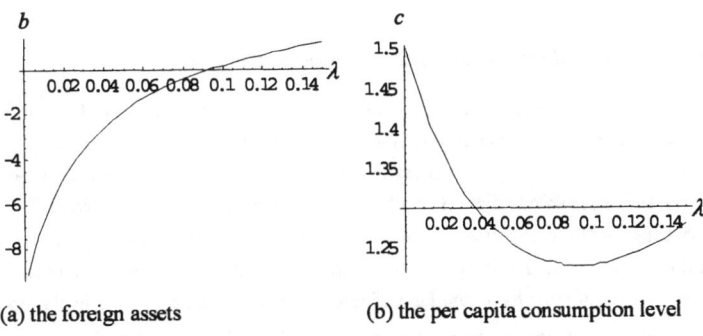

(a) the foreign assets   (b) the per capita consumption level

Figure 2.10.2 The impact of the international interest rate, $0 < r^* < 0.15$

The effects of changes in the rate of interest are shown in Figure 2.10.2. We now allow λ to vary, with $r^* = 0.03$ and the values of the other parameters specified as (2.10.15), we have the effects of change in the propensity to save as in Figure 2.10.3.

As the propensity to save rises, both the foreign assets and the consumption level increase. It should be noted that in an autarky economy, a rise in the propensity to save reduces per capita consumption level when the propensity to save is high. As the economy in trade is faced with a fixed rate of interest, accumulated wealth will not reduce the return rate from wealth as in the autarky case.[33]

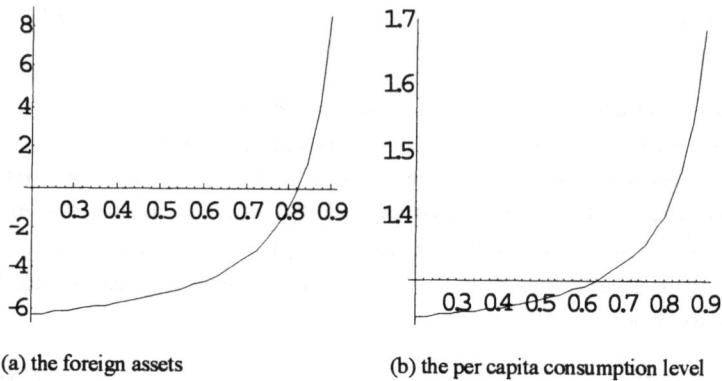

(a) the foreign assets (b) the per capita consumption level

Figure 2.10.3 The impact of the propensity to save, $0.1 < \lambda < 0.9$

2.10.3 Autarky interest rates and the trade pattern

We are concerned with an open economy where the rate of interest is fixed in an international market. In order to describe the impact of trade on national economic growth, it is proper to compare two extreme types of economies – a completely open economy and an isolated economy with the same preference and technology.[34] The key concept for the comparison is the autarky real interest rate, that is, the rate of interest that prevails in an economy barred from international borrowing and lending.

As the two economies have similar variables, if x is a variable value in the open economy, then $\hat{x}$ stands for the corresponding variable value in the autarky economy. We assume that the two economic systems have the same preference and technology, which are specified as in (2.10.10). From Section 2.10.3, we know that the dynamics of the open economy are described by

$$f(t) = Ak^\alpha(t), \quad k = r_0^{1/\beta}, \quad w = \beta A r_0^{\alpha/\beta}, \quad U(t) = c^\xi(t)s^\lambda(t),$$
$$\bar{y}(t) = w_0 + (1 + r^*)b(t), \quad c(t) = \xi \bar{y}(t), \quad s = \lambda \bar{y}(t), \quad \bar{k}(t) = k(t) + b(t),$$
$$b(t) = (b(0) - b^*)e^{-(\xi - \lambda r^*)t} + b^*, \qquad (2.10.16)$$

where

$$r_0 = \frac{\alpha A}{r^* + \delta_k}, \quad w_0 = (1 + r^*)r_0^{1/\beta} + \beta A r_0^{\alpha/\beta}.$$

From Section 2.10.2, we know that the dynamics of the autarky economy are described by

$$\hat{f}(t) = A\hat{k}^\alpha(t), \quad \hat{r}(t) = \alpha A \hat{k}^{-\beta}(t) - \delta_k, \quad \hat{w}(t) = \beta A \hat{k}^\alpha(t),$$
$$\hat{\bar{y}}(t) = A\hat{k}^\alpha(t) + \delta \hat{k}(t), \quad \hat{c}(t) = \xi \hat{\bar{y}}(t), \quad \hat{s}(t) = \lambda \hat{\bar{y}}(t),$$
$$\hat{k}(t) = \left[\left(\hat{k}^\beta(0) - \frac{\lambda A}{\xi_k}\right)e^{-\beta \xi_k t} + \frac{\lambda A}{\xi_k}\right]^{1/\beta}, \tag{2.10.17}$$

where $\xi_k \equiv 1 - \lambda \delta > 0$. The equilibrium value of $\hat{k}(t)$ is given by

$$\hat{k} = \left(\frac{\lambda A}{\xi_k}\right)^{1/\beta}$$

First, we are interested in comparing the equilibrium values of the two systems. From

$$\hat{r} = \frac{\alpha \xi_k}{\lambda} - \delta_k = \frac{\alpha \xi - \beta \lambda \delta_k}{\lambda},$$

we see that $\hat{r} - r^* > (<) 0$ if $\alpha \xi / \lambda > (<) r^* + \beta \delta_k$, that is

$$\frac{\alpha}{r^* + \alpha + \beta \delta_k} > (<) \lambda.$$

We conclude that for the autarky economy's equilibrium rate of interest to be greater than the internationally fixed interest rate (i.e. $\hat{r} > r^*$), we should require that the economy's propensity to save is properly small or the international interest rate is small. In the remainder of this section, our discussion is limited to the case of

$$\alpha > \lambda(r^* + \alpha + \beta \delta_k).$$

Under this condition, we have $\hat{r} > r^*$. Under $\alpha / (r^* + \alpha + \beta \delta_k) > \lambda$, we have

$$b^* = \frac{\lambda w_0 - r_0^{1/\beta}}{\xi - \lambda r^*} = \frac{((\alpha + r^* + \beta\delta_k)\lambda - \alpha)r_0^{1/\beta}}{\alpha(\xi - \lambda r^*)} < 0.$$

The equilibrium value of foreign assets is negative because of the low propensity to save. From $\hat{r} > r^*$, $r = \alpha A k^{-\beta} - \delta_k$ and $\hat{r} = \alpha A \hat{k}^{-\beta} - \delta_k$, we see that the capital intensity of the open economy is higher than the capital intensity of the autarky economy, i.e., $k > \hat{k}$. We have $f > \hat{f}$ and $w > \hat{w}$. From

$$\bar{y} = (1 + r^*)r_0^{1/\beta} + \beta A r_0^{\alpha/\beta} + (1 + r^*)\frac{((\alpha + r^* + \beta\delta_k)\lambda - \alpha)r_0^{1/\beta}}{\alpha(\xi - \lambda r^*)},$$

$$\hat{\bar{y}} = A\left(\frac{\lambda A}{\xi_k}\right)^{\alpha/\beta} + \delta\left(\frac{\lambda A}{\xi_k}\right)^{1/\beta},$$

we have

$$\frac{\bar{y} - \hat{\bar{y}}}{r_0^{1/\beta}} = (1 + r^*) + \frac{(r^* + \delta_k)\beta}{\alpha} + (1 + r^*)\frac{((\alpha + r^* + \beta\delta_k)\lambda - \alpha)}{\alpha(\xi - \lambda r^*)}$$
$$- \frac{\xi_k \tilde{r}}{\lambda} - \delta\tilde{r} = \frac{\beta(r^* + \delta_k)}{\alpha(\xi - \lambda r^*)} - \frac{\tilde{r}}{\lambda}, \qquad (2.10.18)$$

in which

$$\tilde{r} \equiv \left(\lambda\left(\frac{r^* + \delta_k}{\alpha\xi_k}\right)\right)^{1/\beta} < 1$$

(under $\alpha/(r^* + \alpha + \beta\delta_k) > \lambda$). In general, we cannot judge the sign of $\bar{y} - \hat{\bar{y}}$. As

$$\bar{c} - \hat{\bar{c}} = \xi(\bar{y} - \hat{\bar{y}}),$$

the impact of trade on the long-term consumption is ambiguous.

Lemma 2.10.2
If $\alpha/(r^* + \alpha + \beta\delta_k) > (<) \lambda$, then the autarky economy's equilibrium rate of interest is higher (lower) than the internationally fixed interest rate. The capital

intensity, per capita output, and wage rate in the trade economy are higher (lower) than the corresponding variables in the autarky economy.

We now simulate the model to illustrate the behavior of the economy. First, we examine the effects of the international interest rate. We specify the other parameters as in (2.10.15). As r^* rises, the difference between the international interest rate and the interest rate in the autarky system rises. When r^* reaches near 0.094, the difference changes its sign from negative to positive. From Figure 2.10.4, we see that free trade will always benefit the economy in terms of (long-term) per capita consumption.

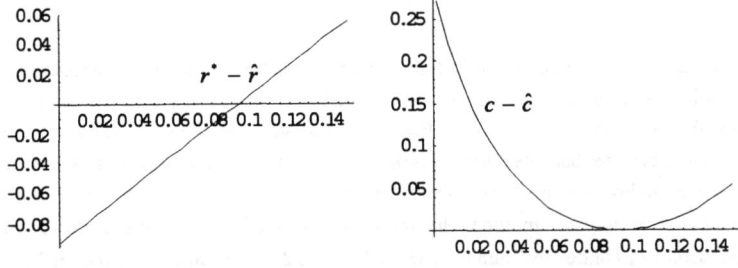

(a) the difference in the interest rates   (b) the difference in per capita consumption

Figure 2.10.4 The differences in the two economies as r^* changes, $0 < r^* < 0.15$

We now allow λ to vary, with $r^* = 0.05$ and the values of the other parameters specified as (2.10.15), we have the effects of change in the propensity to save as in Figure 2.10.5. As the propensity to save rises, the difference between the international interest rate and the interest rate in the autarky system rises. When r^* reaches near 0.76, the difference changes its sign from negative to positive. We see that free trade benefits the economy in terms of (long-term) per capita consumption.

2.11 Theoretical foundations of the utility function

We now provide some insights into utility functions accepted in the OSG model. We show that it is possible to specify manifested forms of consumers' preference structures by the utility function proposed by this study.[35]

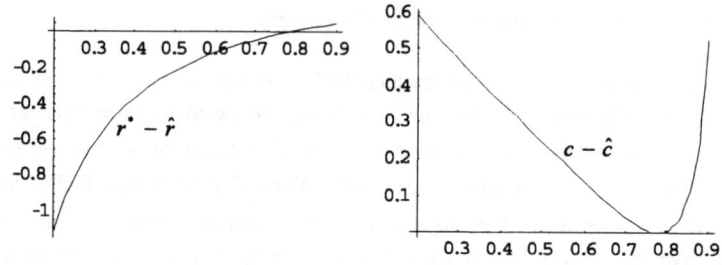

(a) the difference in the interest rates   (b) the difference in per-capita consumption

Figure 2.10.5 The differences in the two economies as λ changes, $0 < \lambda < 0.9$

We assume that at any point in time the consumer has preferences over alternative bundles of commodities, which can be divided into goods, services, and time distribution of the consumer. The behavioral rule consists of maximization of these preferences under budgets restrictions of finance, or time, or human capital, or energy.

A commodity is characterized by its location, date at which it is available and its price. At each point in time, the consumer is faced with a commodity bundle consisting of (finite) real numbers $\{x_j(t)\}$, $j = 1, 2, \cdots, m$, indicating the quality of each commodity. The commodity space consists of commodity bundles. Here, we omit issues related to spatial location. Let us denote the price of commodity j by $p_j(t)$. For simplicity, we omit the time index of x and p except in some circumstances. Both commodity vector, x, and price vector, p, can be represented by points in Euclidean space R^m, i.e. $x \in R^m$ and $p \in R^m$. The value of the commodity bundle at any point in time is given by

$$p(t)x(t) = \sum_j p_j(t)x_j(t).$$

Obviously, some bundles of the commodity space may be excluded as consumption possibilities. The consumption set, denoted by X, consists of all consumption bundles in which are possible. Let us assume that the value of his consumption should not exceed his income, $w(t)$, at each point in time. The budget set

$$\beta(p, x, t) \equiv \{x \in X \mid px \leq w\},$$

is the set of possible consumption bundles whose value does not exceed the income.

The consumer has tastes and desires. They are important in analyzing why the consumer chooses a bundle from the consumption set. Mathematically, we represent the preference structure by the consumer's preference relation, $\succeq_t$, at each point in time which is a binary relation on X. For any two bundles, $x(t)$ and $y(t)$, $x \in X$ and $y \in X$, $x \succeq y$ means that x is at least as good as y at time t. Before discussing the relation between the preference relation and utility functions, we introduce the following axioms.

Axiom 1 (Reflexibility)

For all $x \in X$, $x \succeq x$, i.e. any bundle is as good as itself.

Axiom 2 (Transitivity)

For any three bundles, x, y, z in X such that $x \succeq y$ and $y \succeq z$ it is true that $x \succeq z$.

Axiom 3 (Completeness)

For any two bundles x and y in X, $x \succeq y$ or $y \succeq z$.

Axiom 4 (Continuity)

For every $x \in X$ the upper contour set $\{y \in X | y \succeq x\}$ and the lower contour set $\{y \in X | x \succeq y\}$ are closed relative to X.

A preference relation $\succeq$ which satisfies the first three axioms is a complete preordering on X and is called a preference order. A bundle x is said to be strictly preferred to a bundle y, i.e. $x \succ y$ iff $x \succeq y$ and not $y \succeq x$. A bundle x is said to be indifferent to a bundle y, i.e. $x \sim y$ iff $x \succeq y$ and $y \succeq x$. The indifference relation defines an equivalent relation on X, i.e. $\sim$ is reflexible, symmetric, and transitive. We always assume that X includes at least two bundles x' and x'' such that $x' \succ y''$. In order to solve the problem of the representability of a preference relation by a numerical function, we introduce the concept of utility function.

Definition 2.12.1

Let X denote a set and $\succeq_t$ a binary relation on X at time t. Then a function u from X into real R is a representation of $\succeq$, i.e. a utility function for the preference relation $\succeq_t$, if, for any two points x and y, $u_t(x) \geq u_t(y)$ iff $x \succeq_t y$ at point in time t.

It seems that Pareto was the first to recognize that arbitrary increasing transformation of a given function would result in identical maximization of a consumer. From the above definition we see that for any utility function u_t and any increasing transformation $f: R \to R$ the function $v_t = f \circ u_t$ is also a utility function for the same preference relation $\succeq_t$. The following theorem is referred to in Debreu (1959) or Rader (1963).

Theorem 2.12.1
Let X denote a topological space with a countable base of open sets and $\succeq$ a continuous preference order defined on X, i.e., a preference relation that satisfies Axioms 1-4. Then there exists a continuous function u.

The above theorem shows that under certain conditions the concepts of utility and of the underlying preferences may be used interchangeably to determine demand at any point in time. The above theorem is referred to any point in time. It does not involve how to calculate the future. When applying to our cases, we assume that a consumer is to choose consumption, $C(t)$, and saving, $S(t)$, with the disposable personal income, $\hat{Y}(t)$, at each point in time t.

2.12 Relations with traditional approaches to consumer behavior

We now examine the relations of our alternative approach to consumer behavior with some traditional approaches in economic dynamic analysis.

2.12.1 The Keynesian consumption function

The OSG model with the Cobb-Douglas utility function determines the relationship between consumption and disposable personal income

$$C(t) = \xi \hat{Y}(t) = \xi Y(t) + \xi K(t).$$

We now discuss possible relations between our model and the Keynesian consumption function.

In the *General Theory*, Keynes postulated that current consumption expenditure has a stable relation to current income and that a greater proportion of income is saved as real income rises. Keynes (1936) argues

... men are disposed, as a rule and on the average, to increase their consumption as their income increases, but not by as much as the increase in their income.

This statement by Keynes stimulated many empirical works to derive the consumption function. Many attempts were made to correlate aggregate consumption expenditures over time with aggregate disposable income and other variables. The traditional Keynesian consumption function posits that consumption is determined by current disposable income, i.e.

$$C(t) = a + bY(t), \quad a > 0, \quad 0 < b < 1,$$

where a and b are constant, $C(t)$ is real consumption at time t, and $Y(t)$ is real disposable income (which is the same as the current income in our model), which equals GNP minus taxes. It can be seen that if we swap the real disposable income in the Keynesian model with the disposable personal income in our model, we see that the Keynesian consumption function with $a = 0$ is identical to the consumption derived from our rational choice assumption. Since Y in the Keynesian consumption function is the current consumption in our model, we cannot see further relations between the two approaches without further exposition.

The parameter, b, is the marginal propensity to consume, which measures the increase in consumption in association with per unit increase in disposable income. The intercept, a, measures consumption at a zero level of disposable income.

Because of the intercept, the Keynesian consumption is not a proportional relationship between consumption and income. The ratio of consumption to income is termed the average propensity to consume (APC), i.e.

$$\text{APC} = \frac{C}{Y} = b + \frac{a}{Y}.$$

The average propensity to consume declines as income increases. The average propensity to consume is greater than the marginal propensity to consume, by the amount of a/Y. The ratio of saving to income is termed the average propensity to save (APS), i.e.

$$\text{APS} \equiv \frac{Y-C}{Y} = 1 - b - \frac{a}{Y}.$$

We have

$$\text{APC} + \text{APS} = 1.$$

As Y increases, the average propensity to save rises.

The Keynesian consumption function is based on the assumption that consumption reacts only to actual levels of income. It is known that the permanent income hypothesis would relax the Keynesian assumption. We now show that the Keynesian assumption is related to, but different from, the implications of our rational choice theory with consumption and saving. One of the implications of the Keynesian assumption is that the intercept a is independent of any change in wealth and other factors. Consider two persons, A and B, who started to work 5 years ago with the same conditions and the same preference. Their preferences were invariant during the period. Person A has accumulated a large amount of wealth during this period; but person B accumulates little. At the end of the period, they both lose their jobs. If the interest rate is almost zero, both persons A and B have no income. According to the Keynesian consumption function, at this moment when they lose their jobs or are retired, persons A and B should enjoy the same level of consumption (which is given by the intercept a). Nevertheless, intuitively this is invalid as person A is richer than person B. It is reasonable to see that person A consumes more than person B. Our theory will solve this problem.

We connect the two theories by treating a in the Keynesian model as a wealth-related variable. If we assume that the intercept a is dependent on wealth and marginal propensity to consume, b, is related to the propensity to consume, ξ, in the following way:

$$a = \xi K(t), \quad b = \xi,$$

then the Keynesian consumption function is identical to the consumption function in the OSG model. We may call our consumption function a generalized Keynesian consumption function. We can define the APC and APS, denoted by $\bar{c}(t)$ and $\bar{s}(t)$, respectively, for the OSG model in the same way as in the Keynesian consumption function. In the OSG model

$$\bar{c}(t) = \text{APC} \equiv \frac{C}{Y} = \frac{\xi(Y+K)}{Y} = \xi + \xi\frac{K}{Y},$$

$$\bar{s}(t) = \text{APS} \equiv \frac{S-K}{Y} = \frac{\lambda Y - \delta K}{Y} = \lambda - \xi\frac{K}{Y},$$

where we use $\xi + \lambda = 1$. It should be noted that according to the definition of the APS

$$\bar{s}(t) = \text{APS} \equiv \frac{S(t) - K(t)}{Y(t)} = \frac{\dot{K}(t)}{Y(t)}.$$

The APC in the OSG model rises as wealth increases or as current income declines; the APS in the OSG model rises as wealth falls or as current income rises. It should be noted that APC + APS = 1. It is possible for the APS to be negative in the OSG model.

2.12.2 The life cycle hypothesis

The life cycle hypothesis is to explain the empirical work on consumption functions.[36] It has been observed that the relationship between consumption and current income would be nonproportional and the intercept of consumption function is not constant over time. As stated by Modigliani (1966)

> The point of departure of the life cycle model is the hypothesis that consumption and saving decisions of households at each point in time reflect a more or less conscious attempt at achieving the preferred distribution of consumption over the life cycle, subject to the constraint imposed by the resources accruing to the household over its lifetime.

Consumption depends not just on current income but also on the long-term expected earnings over their lifetime. The general form of the aggregate consumption function implied by the life cycle hypothesis is

$$C(t) = b_1 w(t) + b_2 \widetilde{Y}(t) + b_3 K(t), \tag{2.12.1}$$

where b_1, b_2, and b_3 are nonnegative parameters and

$C(t) =$ consumption at time t;

$w(t)$ = the individual's labor income at time t;

$\tilde{Y}(t)$ = the average labor income expected over the remaining years during which the individual plans to work;

$K(t)$ = the value of presently held assets.

To apply equation (2.12.1) to examine actual consumer behavior, it is necessary to make further assumptions about the way in which individuals form expectations concerning lifetime labor income. Ando and Modigliani assumed

$$\tilde{Y}(t) = \beta w(t), \quad \beta > 0. \tag{2.12.2}$$

Individuals expect their future income flows through deciding the value of parameter β, which measures the ratio between the average labor income in the future and the current income. Under equation (2.12.2), equation (2.12.1) becomes

$$C(t) = (b_1 + \beta b_2)w(t) + b_3 K(t). \tag{2.12.3}$$

In the OSG model, consumption (in terms of per capita) is given by the generalized Keynesian consumption function

$$C(t) = \xi \hat{Y}(t) = \xi w(t) + \xi(r(t) + \delta)K(t), \tag{2.12.4}$$

if we specify $N = 1$. We see that both equations (2.12.3) and (2.12.4) show that consumption is positively related to labor income and wealth. The OSG model does not require that each household have at all times a definite vision of the family's future size and composition, the life expectancy, the entire lifetime profile of the income from birth to death, and even the future emergencies, opportunities and the like. It can be seen that our approach does not impose such strict information about the future, even though it can take any important information into consideration by changing preference parameters, $\xi(t)$ and $\lambda(t)$.

2.12.3 The permanent income hypothesis

According to Friedman (1956, 1957), consumption is proportional to permanent income, $Y^p(t)$, as follows:

$$C(t) = \kappa Y^p(t),$$

where κ is the positive factor of proportionality. Permanent income is expected average long-term income from human and nonhuman wealth. To implement the permanent income hypothesis, it is necessary to make some assumptions about how individuals form long-term expectations about income. Friedman assumed that individuals revise their initial estimate of permanent income from period to period in the following manner:

$$Y^p(t) = Y^p(t-1) + j(Y(t) - Y^p(t-1)), \quad 0 < j < 1,$$

which states that in each period individuals adjust their estimate of permanent income by a fraction j of the discrepancy between actual income in the current period and the prior period's estimate of permanent income.

Following Romer (1996), we illustrate the essence of the permanent income hypothesis. Let us consider an individual who lives for T periods. The individual has initial wealth of Y_0 and labor incomes of $Y_1, Y_2, ..., Y_T$ in the T periods of lifetime. The individual takes these as given. Under the assumption that the individual's discount rate of utility is zero, lifetime utility is equal to the sum of the level of utility over each period. That is

$$U = \sum_{t=1}^{T} u(C_t), \quad u'(\cdot) > 0, \quad u''(\cdot) < 0, \tag{2.12.5}$$

where U stands for lifetime utility, $u(C_t)$ is the instantaneous utility, and C_t is consumption in period t. It is assumed that the individual can save or borrow at an exogenous interest rate (set to zero for simplicity) subject only to the constraint that any outstanding debt must be repaid at the end of the life. The individual's budget constraint is thus given by

$$\sum_{t=1}^{T} C_t \leq \sum_{t=0}^{T} Y_t. \tag{2.12.6}$$

The individual maximizes equation (2.12.5) subject to inequality (2.12.6). The optimal solution is given by

$$C_t = \frac{1}{T} \sum_{t=0}^{T} Y_t. \tag{2.12.7}$$

108 *Economic Growth with Income and Wealth Distribution*

The rational individual would divide the lifetime resources equally among each period of life.

This model predicts that the individual's consumption in a given period is related not only to income in that period, but also the incomes over the remaining periods of the entire lifetime. Friedman dubbed the right-hand side of equation (2.12.7) the permanent income. The difference between current and permanent income is transitory income. The above equation means that consumption is determined by permanent income. This result implies that a temporary rise in income may have little impact on consumption.

2.12.4 The Solow model

We described the Solow model in Section 1.2. The Solow model assumes that the agents regularly set aside some fairly predictable portion $\hat{s}$ of its output for the purpose of capital accumulation, hence

$$\dot{k}(t) = \hat{s}f(k(t)) - (n + \delta_k)k(t).$$

We see that the differential equation for per-worker-capital accumulation in the Solow model is mathematically identical to the capital accumulation equation in the OSG model defined by equation (2.1.11) in Section 2.1

$$\dot{k}(t) = \lambda f(k) - (\xi + n)k(t),$$

if we specify $U = c^\xi s^\lambda$. The Solow model and the OSG model have the same dynamic properties – the system has a unique stable equilibrium. But the OSG model holds that the saving rate is time-dependent; the Solow model predetermines the saving rate.

Historically, the Solow hypothesis is approximately valid for the US economy, while it is hardly acceptable for many other economies. There is some evidence that over the last 150 years savings rates as a percentage of the GNP for the US economy have remained stable while those in many other countries have risen. From the saving rate

$$\bar{s} = \lambda - \frac{\mathcal{B}k^\beta}{A}$$

in the OSG model, we see that the saving rate is time-dependent. In particular, the saving rate is directly related to technological change. We see that a country endowed with wealth tends to have a low saving rate, while a country with high technology but less wealth tends to have a high saving rate. Table 2.12.1, which is based on Maital and Maital (1994), presents data on historical gross savings rates as a percentage of GNP for some industrial economies. Empirical studies show that the savings rates vary over time, except for the US economy. It was observed that national saving as a proportion of GNP or GDP tends to fall in contemporary industrial countries. It is observed that the US and many other OECD countries implemented many tax reforms in the 1980s that were strongly pro-rich. Between 1984 and 1990, top individual tax rates fell by 22 percent in the US, 12 percent in Japan. Since the rich save more of their income than the middle class or poor, and since it is the rich that mainly pay the highest tax rates, low tax rates for the rich should have led to higher personal saving rates. But it is observed that savings rate fell for every income during the 1980s. It is worthwhile citing what Maital and Maital (1994) observe:

Conventional economic theory has been largely unable to explain this decline in saving. Moreover, empirical evidence has long been inconsistent with the predominant models of consumption and saving – the "permanent income" hypothesis and the life-cycle model. Therefore, lacking an empirically well-grounded theory of saving, conventional macroeconomics has little to say, either positive or normative, on a vital economic issue that touches on virtually every important policy question for this decade – intergenerational equity, growth, productivity, inflation, competitive advantage.

Table 2.12.1 Historical gross saving rates as a percentage of the GNP

Country	Pre-World War II	1950–59	1960–84
United States	18.7 (1869–1938)	18.4	18.0
Japan	11.7 (1887–1936)	30.2	32.5
Germany	20.0 (1851–1928)	26.8	23.7
United Kingdom	12.3 (1860–1929)	16.2	18.1

We now show that under certain circumstances the OSG model can explain what the Solow model forecasts. The OSG model endogenously determines saving and consumption. For simplicity, we let $\delta_k = 0$. The OSG's capital accumulation is given by

$$\dot{K}(t) = \lambda F(t) - \xi K(t). \tag{2.12.8}$$

In the OSG model, the APS is given by

$$\bar{s}(t) = \frac{\lambda F(t) + \lambda K(t) - K(t)}{F(t)}.$$

We are interested in when $\bar{s}(t)$ in the OSG model equals the predetermined saving rate $\hat{s}$ in the Solow model, i.e.

$$\frac{\lambda F(t) + \lambda \delta K(t) - \delta K(t)}{F(t)} = \hat{s}. \qquad (2.12.9)$$

If λ is considered as an endogenous variable, the above equation holds if

$$\lambda(t) = \hat{s} + (1 - \hat{s})\delta \frac{K(t)}{F(t) + \delta K(t)} = \hat{s} + \frac{(1 - \hat{s})\delta}{f(k(t))/k(t) + \delta} \; (<1). \qquad (2.12.10)$$

As $\xi(t) + \lambda(t) = 1$, $\xi(t)$ is also a function of $k/f(k)$. If the propensity to save is related to the ratio of capital per capita and output per capita as in equation (2.12.10), then $\bar{s}(t)$ in the OSG model is constant and is equal to the saving rate, $\hat{s}$, in the Solow model. Inserting equation (2.12.10) into equation (2.12.8) yields

$$\dot{K}(t) = \lambda(t)F(t) - (\xi(t) + \lambda(t)\delta_k)K(t) = \lambda(t)(F(t) + \delta K(t)) - K(t)$$
$$= \hat{s}F(t) - \delta_k K(t).$$

Under equation (2.12.10) the evolution of capital in the OSG model is identical to that in the Solow model.

Theorem 2.12.1
Let the production sectors be identical in the OSG model and the Solow model. If the saving rate, $\hat{s}$, in the Solow model and the propensity to save, $\lambda(t)$, in the OSG model satisfy equation (2.12.10), then the OSG model is identical to the Solow model in terms of the saving rate (out of current income), the consumption rate, the interest rate, the wage rate, output, income, consumption, and saving.

The propensity to save, $\lambda(t)$, is not constant. To see how it changes as economic conditions vary, we take the derivative of equation (2.12.10) with respect to t

$$\dot{\lambda} = \frac{(1-\hat{s})(f-kf')}{(f+k)^2}\dot{k} = \frac{(1-\hat{s})w}{(f+k)^2}\dot{k}.$$

The propensity to save rises (falls) as wealth per capita rises (falls).

2.12.5 The Ramsey growth model

We described the Ramsey model in Section 1.3. The dynamical behavior of the Ramsey model is controlled by

$$\dot{k}(t) = w(t) + r(t)k(t) - c(t) - nk(t) = f(t) - c(t) - nk(t),$$
$$\dot{c}(t) = \frac{r(t) - \rho}{\theta}c(t) = \frac{f'(k) - \rho}{\theta}c(t). \tag{2.12.11}$$

If we find some equation of preference change in the OSG model to generate the same behavior as equation (2.12.11), then the two systems should exhibit the same behavior in terms of consumption, capital accumulation and incomes, even though they are built on different assumptions.

We now consider consumption of the OSG model. The consumption per capita in the OSG model is given by

$$c(t) = (1 - \lambda(t))[f(k(t)) + k(t)].$$

Differentiation of this equation with respect to time yields

$$\frac{\dot{c}(t)}{c(t)} = \frac{f' + \delta}{f(k(t)) + \delta k(t)}\dot{k}(t) - \frac{\dot{\lambda}(t)}{1 - \lambda(t)}. \tag{2.12.12}$$

For equations (2.12.11) and (2.12.12) to be equal, it is sufficient for $\lambda(t)$ to evolve according to

$$\dot{\lambda}(t) = \frac{f'(t) + 1}{f(t) + k(t)}\xi(t)\dot{k}(t) - \frac{f'(t) - \rho}{\theta}\xi(t). \tag{2.12.13}$$

The propensity to own wealth, λ, tends to rise (fall) when $\dot{k}$ rises (falls); it tends to rise (fall) when $r < (>)\rho$. We may interpret that the direction of change in λ is influenced by the direction of change in wealth as well as whether the rate of return of wealth is larger or smaller than the rate of time preference. If the wealth is increasing and the rate of time preference is larger than the rate of return, then the propensity to save will definitely rise. If the wealth is falling and the rate of time preference is smaller than the rate of return, the propensity tends to fall. In the other cases, the propensity may either increase or decrease.

Under equation (2.12.13), the consumption per capita in the OSG model evolves in the same way as in the Ramsey model. We now examine the fundamental equation of the OSG, i.e.

$$\dot{k}(t) = \lambda f(k(t)) - (1 - \lambda + n)k(t).$$

By $c = (1 - \lambda)(f + k)$, the above equation can be rewritten as

$$\dot{k}(t) = f(k(t)) - c(t) - nk(t). \qquad (2.12.14)$$

Theorem 2.12.2

Let the production sectors be identical in the OSG model and the Ramsey model. If the propensity to save, $\lambda(t)$, evolves according to equation (2.12.13), then the OSG model generates the same dynamics of the capital-labor ratio, $k(t)$, and per capita consumption, $c(t)$, as the Ramsey model does.

This example illustrates how the Ramsey model is related to the OSG model. We can similarly examine relationships between the two approaches when utility functions are taken on other forms.

Appendix

A.2.1 Economic dynamics with fertility and old age support

This appendix introduces endogenous fertility and old age support into the OLG model introduced in Section 1.4.[37] In the literature, two assumptions about population growth and economic conditions are made; the first is to assume that children are a consumption good and appear in the utility function of the parents; the second is to assume that children are valued as a source of old age support.[38] This assumption is made based on the observation that countries with more developed financial markets or better social security programs tend to have lower population growth rates than those that do not. For instance, in developing countries, children often start contributing to family income while living at home and prior to adulthood. Here, we assume that individuals give a constant fraction of their income to their parents in the form of old age support, and that parents incur a time cost of raising children, which increases with the number of children.

The number of young agents at time t is denoted by $N(t)$ and there are $N(-1)$ agents in the initial old generation. The initial old generation is endowed with an aggregate initial capital stock of $K(0) > 0$. All young agents are identical and they are endowed with one unit of labor when young, and have no other endowments of goods or assets at any date. There is a single good in the economy, which is produced using capital and labor as inputs. For simplicity, it is assumed that individuals care only about old age consumption, denoted by c; their lifetime consumption utility is given by $u(c)$, which is assumed to be increasing in c, and concave. Agents work and raise children when young, and are retired when old. Young agents remit a fraction, μ, of their income to their parents as old age support, and save the rest which is equal to $(1-\mu)$ of the income. Each young agent decides to have $n(t)$ children. A time cost of raising children, $\gamma(n(t))$, satisfies

$$\gamma(0) = 0, \ \gamma' > 0, \ \gamma'' \geq 0.$$

All agents take the wage rate, $w(t)$, at period t as given. The saving, $s(t)$, is given by

$$s(t) = (1-a)w(t)(1-\gamma(n(t))). \qquad (A.2.1.1)$$

Old age consumption is thus given by

$$c(t+1) = r(t+1)s(t) + an(t)w(t+1)(1-\gamma(n(t+1))),$$

where r is the rate of interest. The production is carried out according to the constant returns to scale production function

$$F(t) = F(K(t), (1-\gamma(n(t)))N(t)),$$

where K is the capital stock. The intensive production function is given by $f(k)$, where

$$k \equiv \frac{K}{N(1-\gamma)}.$$

Assume that the production function is of the CES form

$$f(k) = (\alpha k^\rho + \beta)^{1/\rho}, \quad \alpha, \beta > 0, \quad -\infty < \rho < 1.$$

Each unit of the consumption good saved at time t becomes one unit of capital at time $t+1$. The capital is used in production and it depreciates completely in the production process. Hence

$$K(t+1) = s(t)N(t).$$

The labor and capital markets are perfectly competitive. The marginal conditions are

$$\begin{aligned} r(t) &= f'(k(t)) = \alpha k^{\rho-1}(t)[\alpha k^\rho(t) + \beta]^{1/\rho-1}, \\ w(t) &= f(k(t)) - k(t)f'(k(t)) = \beta[\alpha k^\rho(t) + \beta]^{1/\rho-1}, \quad t \geq 0. \end{aligned} \quad (A.2.1.2)$$

The young agent's problem is to maximize $u(c(t+1))$ by choosing $n(t)$ subject to

$$c(t+1) = (1-a)r(t+1)w(t)(1 - \gamma(n(t))) + an(t)w(t+1)(1 - \gamma(n(t+1))).$$

With w and r as given, the problem of optimization has an interior optimum determined by

$$-(1-a)r(t+1)w(t)\gamma'(n(t)) + aw(t+1)(1 - \gamma(n(t+1))) = 0. \quad (A.2.1.3)$$

Substituting equations (A.2.1.2) into equation (A.2.1.3) yields

$$f'(k(t+1)) = \frac{aw(k(t+1))[1 - \gamma(n(t+1))]}{(1-a)w(k(t))\gamma'(n(t))}, \quad (A.2.1.4)$$

which states that the rate of return on capital is equal to the rate of return on children.[39] By the definition, we have

$$K(t+1) = N(t+1)(1 - \gamma(n(t+1)))k(t+1).$$

With this equation and equation (A.2.1.1), we can rewrite $K(t+1) = s(t)N(t)$ as

$$k(t+1) = \frac{(1-a)w(t)(1-\gamma(n(t)))}{[1-\gamma(n(t+1))]n(t)}.$$ (A.2.1.5)

We now specify the cost function as follows:

$$\gamma(n(t)) = cn^2(t).$$

We also introduce a new variable

$$z(t) \equiv \frac{\alpha}{\beta}k^\rho(t).$$

Multiplying both sides of equations (A.2.1.4) and equation (A.2.1.5) by $k(t+1)$ and utilizing (A.2.1.5), we obtain

$$z(t+1) = a\frac{1-cn^2(t)}{2cn^2(t)}.$$ (A.2.1.6)

Applying equation (A.2.1.6) to equation (A.2.1.5) yields

$$1 - cn^2(t+1) = a_0 \frac{(z(t)+1)^{1/\rho-1}}{n^{1-2/\rho}(t)}(1-cn^2(t))^{1-1/\rho},$$ (A.2.1.7)

where

$$a_0 \equiv (1-a)\left(\frac{a}{2\alpha c}\right)^{-1/\rho}.$$

Difference equations (A.2.1.6) and (A.2.1.7) describe the sequence of $\{z(t), n(t)\}$. A fixed point of the system is determined by

$$z = a\frac{1-cn^2}{2cn},$$ (A.2.1.8)

$$1 - cn^2 = a_0\frac{(z+1)^{1/\rho-1}}{n^{1-2/\rho}}(1-cn^2)^{1-1/\rho}.$$ (A.2.1.9)

Proposition A.2.1.1
If $\rho > 0$, then equations (A.2.1.8) and (A.2.1.9) have a unique solution.

The proof is left to the reader. When $\rho > 0$, both equations (A.2.1.8) and (A.2.1.9) define downward-sloping loci, as depicted in Figure A.2.1.1.

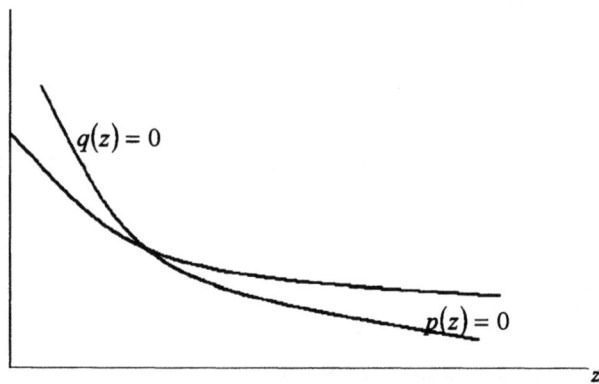

Figure A.2.1.1 The unique fixed point for $\rho > 0$

The linearized system of equations (A.2.1.8) and (A.2.1.9) at a fixed point is

$$J = \begin{bmatrix} 0 & -\dfrac{a}{cn^3} \\ -\dfrac{nz}{a\rho}\dfrac{1-\rho}{1+z} & -\dfrac{z}{a}-\dfrac{1-\rho}{\rho cn^2} \end{bmatrix}.$$

We have

$$\text{Trace}\,J = -\frac{z}{a}-\frac{1-\rho}{\rho cn^2}, \quad \text{Det}\,J = \frac{z}{\rho cn^2}\frac{1-\rho}{1+z}.$$

In the case of $\rho > 0$, $\text{Trace}\,J < 0$ and $\text{Det}\,J < 0$. J has one positive and one negative eigenvalue. In addition, $T < D < 1 + D$. We conclude that the positive eigenvalue is strictly less than one. It can be proved that if $0 < \rho \leq 0.5$, then Trace $J + \text{Det } J < -1$. The steady state is a saddle. When $\rho > 0.5$, the fixed point can be either a sink or a point.

Proposition A.2.1.2[40]

If $\rho > 0$ and sufficiently large (with fixed a, α), then, (i) there is a critical value of c, denoted by c^*, such that for $c > (<) c^*$, the fixed point is a saddle (sink); (ii) at $c = c^*$, a flip bifurcation occurs. Thus, for c in a neighborhood of c^*, periodic solutions of period 2 can be observed.

In the case of $\rho < 0$, the configuration of (A.2.1.8) is the same as in the case of $\rho > 0$; the locus defined by equation (A.2.1.9) has the bell shape, and attains a unique (local) maximum at the value $z = -1/\rho$. As demonstrated in Figure A.2.1.2, there are four possible cases. These cases can be identified as follows.

For Figure A.2.1.2a

a	c	α	ρ	(z_1^*, n_1^*)	(z_2^*, n_2^*)
0.1	0.25	0.5	-0.5	$(0.965, 0.443)$	$(58.592, 0.058)$

For Figure A.2.1.2b

a	c	α	ρ	(z_1^*, n_1^*)	(z_2^*, n_2^*)
0.1	0.25	0.5	-2	$(0.884, 0.463)$	$(4.469, 0.210)$

For Figure A.2.1.2c

a	c	α	ρ	(z_1^*, n_1^*)
0.1	0.25	0.6062	-4	$(1.418, 0.369)$

For Figure A.2.1.2d

a	c	α	ρ
0.1	0.1	0.6	-4

It is straightforward to check the eigenvalues for the above examples. For further examination of the model the reader is referred to Chakrabarti (1999).

118 *Economic Growth with Income and Wealth Distribution*

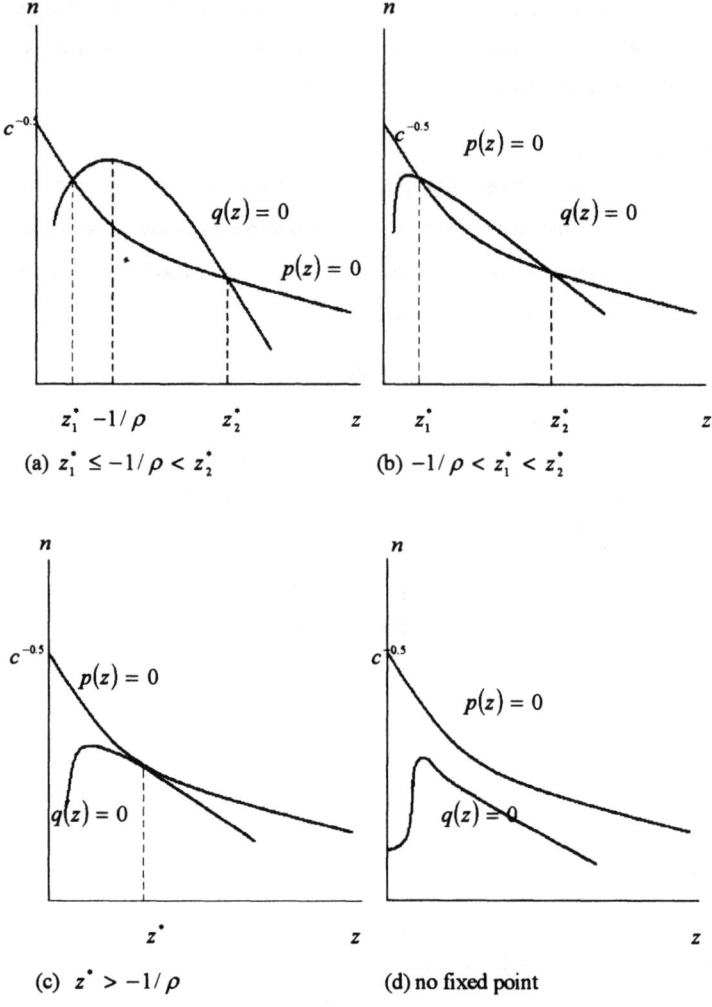

Figure A.2.1.2 Fixed points for $\rho < 0$

3
Growth with Human Capital and Knowledge

In the 1970s, the American economy suffered from the obsolescence of plant and equipment and the inability to compete in international markets in many areas of traditional American strength. As the industries of other nations began to catch up, they developed superior techniques of production and distribution, techniques that directly competed with American industries. Figure 3.0.1 illustrates the dynamics of business productivity for the period 1960–1994 in the US economy.[1] Productivity is measured in output per paid hour in the entire business sector. The slopes are steeper in 1960–1965 and in 1990–94, implying that the growth rates of productivity are higher during these periods, on average. As shown in the figure, during the period of 1975–80 the average annual rate of increase was only 0.7 for the entire business sector.

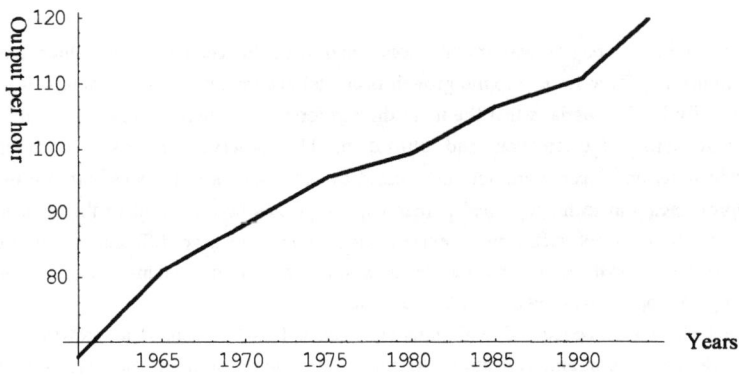

Figure 3.0.1 Indexes of business productivity (1977=100, 1960–94)

120 *Economic Growth with Income and Wealth Distribution*

We also look at the dynamics of disposable personal income (DPI). Figure 3.0.2 shows the DPI per capita for the period 1960–1994 in the US, measured in 1987 dollars.[2] The DPI per capita, in real terms, grew continually between 1960 and 1994. Between 1960 and 1970, real disposable income per capita grew by 36 percent overall, and between 1970 and 1980, the growth rate was 22 percent. The figures show that levels of national average productivity and income are changeable over time.

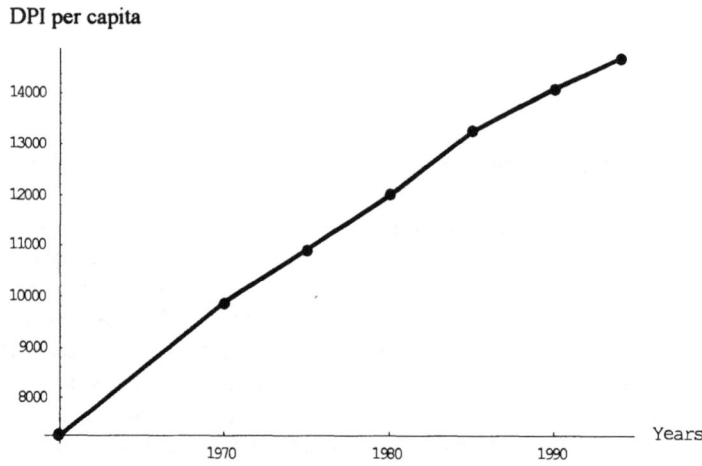

Figure 3.0.2 Disposable personal income (DPI) per capita, 1960–1994

The previous chapter was mainly concerned with the economies in which the main driving force for economic growth is capital accumulation. Nevertheless, it is generally held nowadays that the main driving force of modern economic growth is due to knowledge creation and utilization. The observed increases in labor productivity and income are not only caused by increased capital stocks, but also by improvements in technology and human capital. It has become evident that capital accumulation is not sufficient to explain cross-country income differences. Recent research in growth theory extends the traditional analysis by making technological change or population growth or both endogenous.[3]

This chapter is concerned with interdependence between economic growth and knowledge creation and utilization. Section 3.1 combines the traditional AK growth model with technological change and the OSG approach to consumer behavior. The model generates possible infinite economic growth. Section 3.2 examines

Growth with Human Capital and Knowledge   121

interdependence between education and economic growth. The human capital growth may come from two sources – Arrow's learning by producing and Uzawa's learning through education. We show how path-dependent economic phenomena can be created when two learning sources exhibit different returns to scales. Section 3.3 introduces knowledge utilization and creation into the OSG model. Sections 3.4–3.7 study some models with knowledge utilization and creation under imperfect competition. Section 3.4 studies Romer's growth model with endogenous knowledge under monopolistic competition. Section 3.5 studies endogenous growth based on intentional industrial innovation. The model is proposed by Grossman and Helpman. In this approach, research is treated as an ordinary economic activity that requires the input of resources and responds to profit opportunities. Returns to R&D are possible because of the monopoly rents from imperfectly competitive product markets. Section 3.6 introduces a growth model with a variety of consumer products. The idea is to introduce a variety of consumer goods into the utility function that parallels the treatment of a variety of intermediate products in the production function as in the previous section. Section 3.7 examines a growth model, proposed by Galor and Weil, that captures the historical evolution of population, technology, and output. The economy evolves three regimes that have characterized economic development: from a Malthusian regime (where technological progress is slow and population growth prevents any sustained rise in income per capita) into a post-Malthusian regime (where technological progress rises and population growth absorbs only part of output growth) to a modern growth regime (where population growth is reduced and income growth is sustained).

3.1 The AK-OSG model with learning by doing

The traditional growth models often introduce an exogenously determined time-dependent variable $A(t)$ to production functions $F_t = F(K_t, N_t, A(t))$ to add some exogenous forces for explaining improvement of economic productivity and economic growth. But technological change and knowledge creation take place because economic systems have invested human and other resources for technological improvements. Analytically, this means that we need to introduce some economic mechanism to determine $A(t)$ as a function of human efforts. Before entering fields of technological change, human capital accumulation, and knowledge creation and utilization, we note that since there are so many ways that affect dynamics of knowledge, it is difficult to have a few standard models to cover all possible ways of knowledge creation, diffusion, and utilization. This section introduces a simple model of growth with endogenous human capital accumulation.

Consider a Cobb-Douglas production function with effective labor input

$$F = K^{\alpha}(H^m N)^{\beta}, \quad \alpha + \beta = 1, \quad \alpha, \beta > 0, \quad m \geq 0, \tag{3.1.1}$$

where $H(t)$ is the level of human capital. To be specific, assume that human capital is proportional to the level of capital per worker, so that

$$H(t) = q\frac{K(t)}{N(t)} = qk(t), \tag{3.1.2}$$

where q is the relationship as to how capital and labor are combined to affect the productivity of labor. Substituting $H(t)$ into equation (3.1.1) gives $F(t) = aK(t)$, where $a \equiv q^{1-\alpha}$. This specification of the production function does not exhibit diminishing returns to capital because of $F_{KK} = F_{NN} = 0$. The production function does not satisfy the Inada conditions. In particular, $f'(k) = a$ as k goes from zero to infinity.

In per capita terms $f(t) = ak(t)$ and the growth rates of output-labor and the capital-labor ratio are equal

$$g_y = g_k.$$

Under $F(t) = aK(t)$, the fundamental dynamic equation becomes

$$g_y(t) = g_k(t) \equiv \frac{\dot{k}(t)}{k(t)} = a\lambda - (\xi + n).$$

Thus the rate of growth of output per capita depends positively on $a\lambda$ and negatively on $\xi + n$. As shown in Figure 3.1.1, unless $a\lambda = \xi + n$ there is no convergence to any steady-state value of k. If $a\lambda > (\xi + n)$ capital intensity grows without bound and a higher propensity to hold wealth permanently raises the growth rate. Capital accumulation feeds itself and generates a self-sustained expansion at an increasing growth rate over time.

In this model, the propensity to own wealth has a lasting impact on growth rate. This results from the linearity of the production function with regard to capital. The above formation of human capital through learning by doing is obviously invalid since it implies that without any investment in knowledge-related activities income per capita can grow infinitely. As $c = \xi y = \xi(a+1)k$, we have

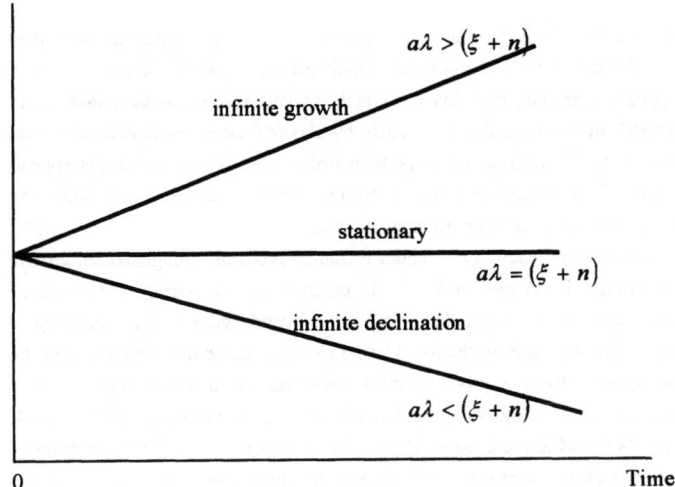

Figure 3.1.1 Sustained growth in the AK-OSG model

$$g_c(t) = g_k(t) = a\lambda - (\xi + n).$$

The growth rate of per capita consumption is equal to that of wealth per capita. Consumption growth does not depend on the stock of capital per capita. If the level of consumption per capita at time 0 is $c(0)$, then consumption per capita at time t is

$$c(t) = c(0)\exp[(a\lambda - \xi - n)t].$$

The saving rate out of the current income is given by

$$\bar{s}(t) = \frac{\dot{K}(t)}{Y(t)} = \frac{a\lambda - \xi - n}{a}.$$

The saving rate out of the current income is also constant. It should be remarked that in the economic literature a model, which is similar to the model proposed in this section, is called *the AK model* (see Bretschger, 1999).

3.2 Growth with capital accumulation and education[4]

Adam Smith held that the large gains in the productivity of labor have their origins in large part in skill, dexterity, and judgment, which are consequences of the division of labor. The opportunities and incentives to which workers respond in their investment in human capital are not considered seriously by classical economists such as Smith, Ricardo, and Marx. The omission was perhaps not as misleading as it might appear, given the role of innovation and education in economic development when the classical economists were constructing their theories.

One of the first seminal attempts to render technical progress endogenous in growth models was initiated by Arrow in 1962. He emphasized one aspect of knowledge accumulation – learning by doing. In 1965 Uzawa introduced a sector specifying in creating knowledge into growth theory. The knowledge sector utilizes labor and the existing stock of knowledge to produce new knowledge, which enhances productivity of the production sector. Another approach is taken by, for instance, Kennedy in 1964, Weisäcker in 1966 and Samuelson in 1965, who took account of the assumption of "inducement through factor prices." In 1981 Schultz emphasized the incentive effects of policy on investment in human capital.[5] There are many other studies on endogenous technical progress.[6] But on the whole theoretical economists had been relatively silent on the topic from the end of the 1970s until the publication of Romer's 1986 paper (Romer, 1986). Since then there has been an increasing number of publications in the literature. In Romer's approach, knowledge is taken as an input in the production function and competitive equilibrium is rendered consistent with increasing aggregate returns owing to externalities. It is assumed that knowledge displays increasing marginal productivity but new knowledge is produced by investment in research technology, which exhibits diminishing returns. Various other issues related to innovation, diffusion of technology, and behavior of economic agents under various institutions have been discussed in the literature. There are also many other models emphasizing different aspects, such as education, trade, R&D policies, entrepreneurship, division of labor, learning through trading, the brain drain, economic geography, dynamic interactions among economic structure, development, and knowledge.[7] The purpose of this section is to introduce a growth model with endogenous human capital accumulation. The model considers Arrow's learning by doing and Uzawa's education as two main sources of human capital accumulation. Another important issue we will address in this section is path-dependent economic development. That an economy's long-term prosperity may depend on initial conditions is nowadays a familiar idea in the growth literature. Many models capture different aspects of this kind of phenomenon in formal models.[8] This section shows that when different sources of learning exhibit increasing and decreasing returns to scale, then the system has multiple equilibrium points and its evolution is characterized as being path-dependent.

3.2.1 The OSG model with endogenous human capital

The economy has one production sector and one education sector. The latter is called the university. We assume a homogeneous and fixed national labor force, N. The labor force is distributed between economic activities, teaching and studying. We select the commodity to serve as numeraire, with all other prices being measured relative to its price. We assume that wage rates are identical among all professions. We introduce

$F(t)$ = output level of the production sector at time t;
$K(t)$ = level of capital stocks of the economy;
$H(t)$ = level of human capital of the population;
$N_i(t)$ and $K_i(t)$ = labor force and capital stocks employed by the production sector;
$N_v(t)$ and N_e = number of teachers and number of students;
$K_e(t)$ = capital stocks employed by the university;
$w(t)$ and $r(t)$ = wage rate and rate of interest.

We first model production and consumption. We assume that production is to combine qualified labor force, $H^m(t)N_i(t)$, and physical capital, $K_i(t)$. Most aspects of our model are the same as the OSG model. The production process is described by

$$F(t) = AK_i^\alpha(t)(H^m(t)N_i(t))^\beta, \quad A, \alpha, \beta > 0, \quad \alpha + \beta = 1.$$

The marginal conditions are given by

$$r(t) = (1-\tau)\alpha A k_i^{-\beta}(t), \quad w(t) = (1-\tau)\beta A H^m(t) k_i^\alpha(t), \qquad (3.2.1)$$

where $k_i \equiv K_i / H^m N_i$ and τ is the tax rate on the product level.

We denote per capita wealth by $k(t)$, where $k(t) \equiv K(t)/N$. Per capita current income is given by

$$y(t) = r(t)k(t) + w(t).$$

The per capita disposable income is given by

$$\hat{y}(t) = y(t) + k(t).$$

The budget constraint is given by

$$c(t) + s(t) = \hat{y}(t).$$

The utility function is given by

$$U(t) = c^{\xi}(t) s^{\lambda}(t), \quad \xi, \lambda > 0, \quad \xi + \lambda = 1.$$

The optimal solution is given by

$$c(t) = \xi \hat{y}(t), \quad s(t) = \lambda \hat{y}(t). \tag{3.2.2}$$

The change in the household's wealth is equal to the savings minus the wealth sold at time t, i.e.

$$\dot{k}(t) = s(\hat{y}(t)) - k(t) = \lambda \hat{y}(t) - k(t). \tag{3.2.3}$$

We now study the behavior of the university. We assume that there are two sources of improving human capital, through education and learning by producing. Arrow (1962) first introduced learning by doing into growth theory; Uzawa (1965) took account of trade-offs between investment in education and capital accumulation.[9] We propose that human capital dynamics is given by

$$\dot{H} = \frac{\upsilon_e K_e^{a_e} (H^m N_v)^{\beta_v} (H^m N_e)^{\beta_e}}{N} + \frac{\upsilon_i F}{NH^{\pi}} - \delta_h H, \tag{3.2.4}$$

where δ_h (> 0) is the depreciation rate of human capital, $\upsilon_e, \upsilon_i, \alpha_e, \beta_v,$ and β_e are nonnegative parameters. The above equation is a synthesis and generalization of Arrow's and Uzawa's ideas about human capital accumulation. The term $\upsilon_e K_e^{a_e} (H^m N_v)^{\beta_v} (H^m N_e)^{\beta_e}$ describes the contribution to human capital improvement through education. Human capital tends to increase with an increase in the number of students. The term divided by N measures the contribution per capita. We take account of learning by doing effects in human capital accumulation by the term $\upsilon_i F / H^{\pi}$. This term implies that the contribution of the production sector to human capital improvement is positively related to its production scale, F, and is dependent on the level of human capital. The term, H^{π_i}, takes account of returns to scale effects in human capital accumulation. The case of $\pi > (<) \, 0$ implies that as human capital is increased it is more difficult (easier) to further improve the level of human capital.

We assume that the students and teachers are paid by government tax income at the same wage rate as that of workers. We assume that the economy has a fixed ratio of the population who are getting education. The number of students is given by $N_e = n_e N$. Assume that the total tax income is used for paying the students, teachers and the capital stocks employed by the university. The government spends $w(t)N_e$ amount of money on students. Obviously, this assumption is strict. A way to relax this assumption without increasing analytical complexity of the model is to assume that each individual spends a given amount of time on education. The time distribution is given by $T_i + T_e = T$, where T is the fixed available time, T_i is the work time, and T_e is the time as a student. The student gets free education but does not receive any wage. It can be seen that the conclusions will not be different in the two cases and the model is still analytically tractable. The budget for paying teachers and the capital stocks of the university is given by

$$w(t)N_v(t) + r(t)K_e(t) = \tau F(t) - w(t)N_e. \tag{3.2.5}$$

The university distributes its total resource $\tau F(t) - w(t)N_e$ to the teachers, $N_v(t)$, and the capital stocks, $K_e(t)$, in such a way that the output of the university, $\upsilon_e K_e^{\alpha_e}(H^m N_v)^{\beta_v}(H^m N_e)^{\beta_e}$, will be maximized. The university's problem is

$$\text{Max } \upsilon_e K_e^{\alpha_e}(H^m N_v)^{\beta_v}(H^m N_e)^{\beta_e}$$

subject to equation (3.2.5). The solution is given by

$$K_e = \frac{\alpha_e(\tau F - wN_e)}{(\alpha_e + \beta_v)r}, \quad N_v = \frac{\beta_v(\tau F - wN_e)}{(\alpha_e + \beta_v)w}. \tag{3.2.6}$$

Labor force and capital stocks are fully employed

$$N_i + N_e + N_v = N, \quad K_i + K_e = K. \tag{3.2.7}$$

We have thus built the model. We now examine properties of the dynamic system.

3.2.2 The dynamics and multiple equilibrium points

From equation (3.2.7), we get $N_i + N_v = N - N_e$. From equations (3.2.1) and (3.2.6), we obtain

$$K_e = \frac{\alpha_e k_i N_i H^m (\tau - (1-\tau)\beta N_e / N_i)}{\alpha \tau_0},$$

$$N_v = \frac{\beta_v (\tau N_i - (1-\tau)\beta N_e)}{\beta \tau_0} \tag{3.2.8}$$

where we use

$$F = N_i H^m f, \quad \tau_0 \equiv (\alpha_e + \beta_v)(1-\tau).$$

From equations (3.2.8) and $N_i + N_v = N - N_e$, we solve

$$N_i = \frac{N - N_e + \beta_v N_e /(\alpha_e + \beta_v)}{\tau_0 \beta + \tau \beta_v} \tau_0 \beta,$$

$$N_v = \frac{\beta_v (\tau N_i - (1-\tau)\beta N_e)}{\tau_0 \beta}. \tag{3.2.9}$$

Hence, given the government policy on education (measured by τ and N_e), and the university's production character (measured by α_e and β_v) we uniquely determine the labor distribution, which is invariant in time. If τ, N_e, α_e, and/or β_v are shifted, then the labor distribution will be changed. The invariance of the labor distribution for the given policy and university production character is due to the assumed Cobb-Douglas functional forms. As shown in the appendix, the invariance is not generally held.

According to the definition of $k_i(t)$, from equations (3.2.8), we have

$$K_e = aK_i, \quad a \equiv \frac{\alpha_e (\tau - (1-\tau)\beta N_e / N_i)}{\alpha \tau_0}.$$

From the above equations and $K_i + K_e = Nk$, we solve

$$K_i(t) = \frac{Nk(t)}{1+a}, \quad K_e(t) = \frac{aNk(t)}{1+a}. \tag{3.2.10}$$

As $k_i = K_i / H^m N_i$, we obtain

$$k_i(t) = n_i \frac{k(t)}{H^m(t)}, \tag{3.2.11}$$

where $n_i \equiv N/N_i(1+a)$. We see that $k_i(t)$ is a function of $k(t)$ and $H(t)$. Summarizing the above discussions, we have the following lemma.

Lemma 3.2.1

For any given levels of wealth and human capital, $k(t)$ and $H(t)$, all the other variables in the system are uniquely determined at any point in time. The values of the variables are given as functions of $k(t)$ and $H(t)$ by the following procedure: N_i and N_v by equations (3.2.9) $\to$ $K_i(t)$ and $K_e(t)$ by equations (3.2.10) $\to$ $k_i(t)$ by equation (3.2.11) $\to$ $f = Ak_i^\alpha$ and $F = N_i H^m f$ $\to$ $r(t)$ and $w(t)$ $\to$ $y = rk + w$ and $\hat{y} = y + k \to c$ and s by equations (3.2.2) $\to$ $U = c^\xi s^\lambda$.

We now show how to determine the two variables, $k(t)$ and $H(t)$, at any point in time. From equations (3.2.3) and (3.2.4), and Lemma 3.2.1, it is not difficult to see that the dynamics of $k(t)$ and $H(t)$ are explicitly given by the following two differential equations:

$$\dot{k}(t) = \lambda^* k^\alpha H^{\beta m} - \xi k,$$
$$\dot{H} = \upsilon_e^* k^{a_e} H^{\beta_v m + \beta_e m} + \upsilon_i^* H^{m - \pi - \alpha m} k^\alpha - \delta_h H, \tag{3.2.12}$$

where

$$\lambda^* \equiv \lambda A (1 - \tau)(\alpha n_i^{-\beta} + \beta n_i^\alpha),$$
$$\upsilon_e^* \equiv \left(\frac{aN}{1+a}\right)^{a_e} \frac{\upsilon_e N_v^{\beta_v} N_e^{\beta_e}}{N}, \quad \upsilon_i^* \equiv \frac{\upsilon_i A n_i^\alpha N_i}{N}.$$

Lemma 3.2.1 guarantees that if we know values of $k(t)$ and $H(t)$, then we can explicitly solve all the other variables as functions of $k(t)$ and $H(t)$. Hence, to examine the dynamic properties of the system, it is sufficient to examine dynamic properties of equations (3.2.12).

A steady state of the system is given by

$$\lambda^* k^\alpha H^{\beta m} = \xi k,$$
$$\upsilon_e^* k^{\alpha_e} H^{\beta_v m + \beta_e m} + \upsilon_i^* H^{m-\pi-\alpha m} k^\alpha = \delta_h H. \tag{3.2.13}$$

From the first equation in equations (3.2.13), we solve $k = (\lambda^*/\xi)^{1/\beta} H^m$. Substituting this equation into the second equation in equations (3.2.13), we get the following equation to determine H:

$$\Phi(H) \equiv \Phi_e(H) + \Phi_i(H) - \delta_h = 0, \tag{3.2.14}$$

where

$$\Phi_e(H) \equiv \left(\frac{\lambda^*}{\xi}\right)^{\alpha_e/\beta} \upsilon_e^* H^{x_e}, \quad \Phi_i(H) \equiv \left(\frac{\lambda^*}{\xi}\right)^{\alpha/\beta} \upsilon_i^* H^{x_i},$$
$$x_e \equiv (\alpha_e + \beta_v + \beta_e)m - 1, \quad x_i \equiv m - \pi - 1.$$

We see that the number of economic equilibrium points is equal to the number of solutions of the equation

$$\Phi(H) = 0, \quad 0 < H < \infty.$$

As shown in Figure 3.2.1, the equation may have no equilibrium point, one equilibrium point, or two equilibrium points. As shown in Figure 3.2.1a, if $x_e < 0$ and $x_i < 0$, the equation monotonically decreases in H and it passes the horizontal axis only once. Figure 3.2.1b depicts the case of $x_e > 0$ and $x_i > 0$; the function monotonically increases in H and it passes the horizontal axis only once. Figure 3.2.1c depicts the case of $x_e > 0$ and $x_i < 0$ ($x_e < 0$ and $x_i > 0$).

In Appendix A.3.1, we precisely check the conditions in Figure 3.2.1. The following proposition shows that the properties of the dynamic system are determined by the two returns to scale parameters, x_e and x_i.

Growth with Human Capital and Knowledge 131

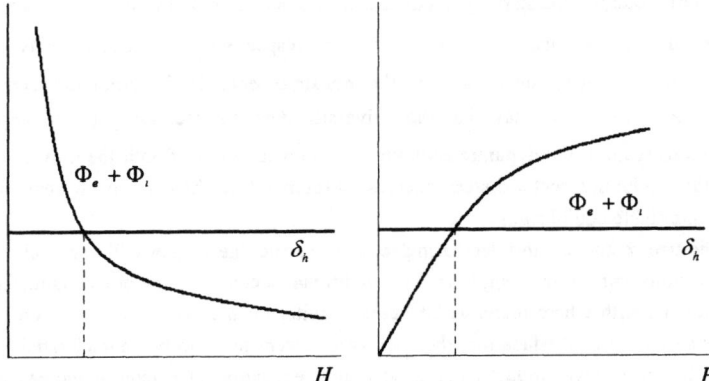

(a) both sectors exhibit decreasing returns (b) both sectors exhibit increasing returns

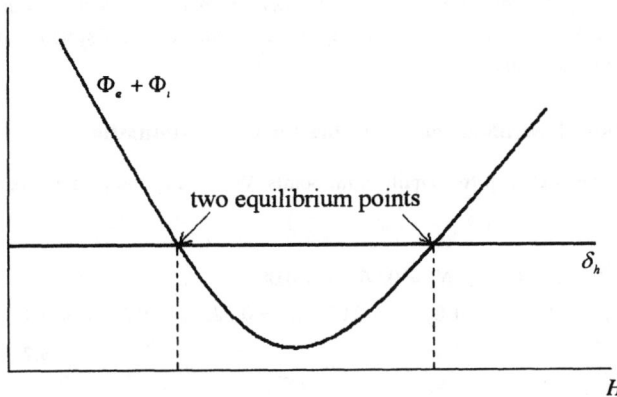

(c) one sector exhibits decreasing returns and the other increasing returns

Figure 3.2.1 The two sectors exhibit different returns to scale effects

Proposition 3.2.1
(1) If $x_e < 0$ and $x_i < 0$, the system has a unique stable equilibrium; (2) If $x_e > 0$ and $x_i > 0$, the system has a unique unstable equilibrium; and (3) If $x_e > 0$ and $x_i < 0$ ($x_e < 0$ and $x_i > 0$), the system has either no equilibrium, one equilibrium or two equilibrium points. When the system has two equilibrium points, the equilibrium with low (high) level of H is stable (unstable).

132 Economic Growth with Income and Wealth Distribution

We only interpret the stability condition, $x_e < 0$ and $x_i < 0$. From the definitions of x_e and x_i, we may interpret x_e and x_i respectively as measurements of returns to scale of the university and the industrial sector in the dynamic system. When $x_e < (>) 0$, we say that the university displays decreasing (increasing) returns to scale in the dynamic economy. We conclude that if both the university and the production sector display decreasing returns, then the dynamic system has a unique stable equilibrium.

If the two sectors exhibit decreasing returns to scale, the system will approach its equilibrium point in the long term. In a traditional society like the one constructed by Adam Smith where increases in human capital mainly come from division of labor and traditional education, the economic system tends to be characterized by stability. In a newly industrializing economy, education may exhibit increasing returns to scale and learning by doing may not be effective in improving human capital. The economy may have multiple equilibrium points. If the society fails to explore increasing returns effects from education, it may not achieve rapid industrialization. We now demonstrate the dynamics of the nonlinear system with multiple equilibrium points.

3.2.3 The path-dependent motion of the system by simulation

We simulate the model with two equilibrium points. We specify the parameters as follows:

$$\alpha = 0.35, \quad N = 1, \quad A = 2, \quad N_e = 0.06, \quad \tau = 0.08, \quad \lambda = 0.7, \quad \alpha_e = 0.7,$$
$$\beta_e = 0.7, \quad \beta_v = 0.7, \quad v_e = 1.8, \quad v_i = 0.02, \quad \delta_h = 0.08, \quad \pi = 0.3, \quad m = 0.8.$$

(3.2.15)

Under the above specifications, we have $x_e = 0.4$ and $x_i = -0.5$. The university exhibits increasing returns to scale and the production sector is characterized by decreasing returns. The system has two equilibrium points

$$(k_1, H_1) = (17.858, 2.226), \quad (k_2, H_2) = (10.401, 19.509).$$

The one with lower levels of human capital and per capita wealth is stable; the other is unstable, also as analytically proved. Figure 3.2.2 depicts the vector field and the steady states of the dynamic system. As shown in Figure 3.2.2, an economy with low level of human capital, even if it was initially rich, tends to converge to the stable equilibrium point with a low standard of living and low level human capital. An economy with a high level of human capital, even if it was initially poor, tends to experience sustained growth. This nonlinear dynamic system has path-dependent features. Here, we can see the significance of cultural value for education. Japanese, Korean, and Chinese-dominated economies like Singapore and Taiwan could have sustained economic growth irrespective of their initial poor conditions in the 1960s, mainly because of their cultural values on education, rather than due to high saving rates.[10] In the 1950s, no one could have foreseen the rapid economic development of East Asia, because few economists recognized the significance of education in economic development and fewer knew the validity of rationalism in classical Confucianism for modern economies.[11] In the literature of economic growth and development published in the 1960s and 1970s, capital accumulation is the main engine of economic development. Economists failed to properly interpret economic evolution of these regions because they did not properly examine the cultural values of education in this region.

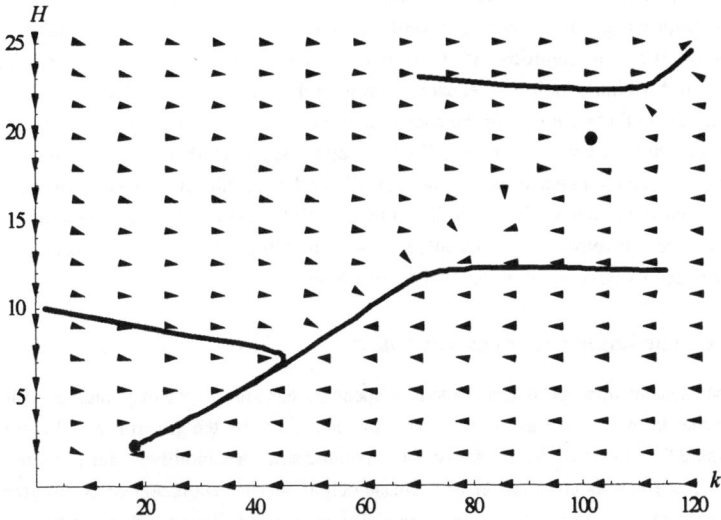

Figure 3.2.2 Path-dependent economic evolution

We simulate three paths of the economy with the initial values

$(k_0, H_0) = (1.5, 10)$, $(k_0, H_0) = (115, 12)$, $(k_0, H_0) = (70, 23)$.

The paths with $(k_0, H_0) = (1.5, 10)$ and $(k_0, H_0) = (115, 12)$ converge to low levels of human capital and per capita wealth. It is interesting to note that the path with $(k_0, H_0) = (115, 12)$ starts with a high level of wealth. But its level of human capital does not improve over time. As decreasing returns dominate this path, its prosperity does not last long. The path with $(k_0, H_0) = (70, 23)$ will grow infinitely because the increasing return to scale dominates the economic evolution. Indeed, this kind of infinite growth will not happen in reality as our model neglects many other significant factors such as endogenous population change, negative externalities such as pollution, and limitations of natural resources.

As far as qualitative features of economic development are concerned, Figure 3.2.2 provides some insights into the difference in economic development in mainland China and Taiwan during the period of 1950 to 1980 – I depict this difference in a book without any mathematical equations.[12] The two areas started economic development with similar economic conditions but different average educational levels. Before the economic reform in 1978 started in mainland China, the living standards and educational achievements in the two Chinese societies had been improving. It is only in recent years that mainland China has begun to explore the opportunities of economic development. Structurally speaking, mainlaind China's political economic system had devalued modern (Western) education so that no sector in the society could have explored the potential benefits of increasing returns offered by Western civilization. Both cultural values and political systems matter in our "neoclassical" model – I call this model neoclassical in the sense that except for the utility function, all the assumptions accepted in this study were developed and accepted in the literature of neoclassical economic growth theory developed in the 1950s and 1960s.

3.2.4 The impact of education policy

In our system, the tax income is totally spent on education. We may thus interpret increases in the tax rate as promotion policy undertaken by the government. We now examine the impact of the tax rate on the economic structure. Intuitively, an increase in the tax rate may either increase or decrease output because education costs resources and may have little impact on human capital improvement. We now show under what conditions an increase in the tax rate may promote the economy. Taking derivatives of equations (3.2.9) with respect to τ, we get the impact on the number of teachers

$$\frac{dN_t}{d\tau} = -\frac{dN_v}{d\tau} = -\left[\frac{1}{1-\tau} + \frac{\alpha\beta_v - \alpha_e\beta}{\tau_0\beta + \tau\beta_v}\right]N_t < 0.$$

As τ is increased, the number of teachers is increased and the number of workers reduced. As the number of students is fixed, an increase in the share of educational expenditure in the total output tends to make some workers shift from the production sector to the university. Taking derivatives of equation (3.2.14) with respect to τ yields

$$-\frac{d\Phi}{dH}\frac{dH}{d\tau} = \left[\left(\frac{\alpha_e}{(1+a)a}\right)\frac{da}{d\tau} - \frac{\alpha_e}{\beta(1-\tau)} - \frac{\beta_v}{N_v}\frac{dN_t}{d\tau}\right]\Phi_e(H)$$
$$+ \left[\frac{\alpha}{\beta(1-\tau)} + \frac{\beta}{N_t}\frac{dN_t}{d\tau} - \frac{\alpha}{1+a}\frac{da}{d\tau}\right]\Phi_t(H),$$

in which

$$\frac{da}{d\tau} = \left[\frac{1}{(1-\tau)^2} - \left(\frac{1}{1-\tau} + \frac{\alpha\beta_v - \alpha_e\beta}{\tau_0\beta + \tau\beta_v}\right)\frac{\beta N_e}{N_t}\right]\frac{\alpha_e}{\alpha(\alpha_e + \beta_v)}.$$

We see that the sign of the right-hand side is ambiguous. It should be noted that (1) if $x_e < 0$ and $x_t < 0$, $d\Phi/dH < 0$; (2) If $x_e > 0$ and $x_t > 0$, $d\Phi/dH > 0$; and (3) If $x_e > 0$ and $x_t < 0$ ($x_e < 0$ and $x_t > 0$), $d\Phi/dH < (>) 0$ at the equilibrium point with low (high) level of H. If the term Φ_t (which is the contribution of learning by doing to human capital) is small, then the sign of the right hand-side is the same as that of

$$\left(\frac{\alpha_e}{(1+a)a}\right)\frac{da}{d\tau} + \left(\frac{\beta_v N_t}{N_v} - \frac{\alpha_e}{\beta}\right)\frac{1}{1-\tau} + \left(\frac{\alpha\beta_v - \alpha_e\beta}{\tau_0\beta + \tau\beta_v}\right)\frac{\beta_v N_t}{N_v}.$$

If N_e is relatively small and τ is low, it is reasonable to consider the above term to be positive. This implies $(d\Phi/dH)dH/d\tau < 0$. We thus conclude that as the tax rate is increased, (1) if $x_e < 0$ and $x_t < 0$, the equilibrium level of human capital will increase; (2) if $x_e > 0$ and $x_t > 0$, the equilibrium level of human capital will decrease; and (3) If $x_e > 0$ and $x_t < 0$ ($x_e < 0$ and $x_t > 0$), the equilibrium level of human capital with low (high) level of H will increase (decrease). By $k = (\lambda^*/\xi)^{1/\beta} H^m$, we get

$$\frac{dk}{d\tau} = \frac{mk}{H}\frac{dH}{d\tau} - \frac{k}{\beta(1-\tau)}.$$

If $dH/d\tau$ is negative, then per capita wealth is reduced as the society spends more resources on education. If the increased ratio $(dH/d\tau)/H$ is positive but low, the impact on per capita wealth is still negative. By equations (3.2.10), we obtain

$$\frac{dK_i}{d\tau} = \left(\frac{1}{k}\frac{dk}{d\tau} - \frac{1}{1+a}\frac{da}{d\tau}\right)K_i,$$

$$\frac{dK_v}{d\tau} = \left(\frac{1}{k}\frac{dk}{d\tau} + \frac{1}{(1+a)a}\frac{da}{d\tau}\right)K_v.$$

From $k_i = n_i k / H^m$, we obtain

$$\frac{dk_i}{d\tau} = -\left[\frac{1}{\beta(1-\tau)} + \frac{1}{N_i}\frac{dN_i}{d\tau} + \frac{1}{(1+a)}\frac{da}{d\tau}\right]k_i.$$

The impact on k_i is ambiguous. From equation (3.2.1) and $F = K^\alpha (N_i H^m)^\beta$, we get the impact on r, w and F.

We may simulate the model again. Here, we are interested in the path-dependent case. We still specify the parameter values as in (3.2.15) except the tax rate, τ. We reduce the resource for education. Let us consider the case that the expenditure on education is reduced from 8 percent of the GDP to 7 percent, that is

$\tau : 0.08 \Rightarrow 0.07.$

Figure 3.2.3 shows the simulation results – the points with larger sizes are the new steady states and the other two points with smaller sizes are the old steady states. The two steady states shift as follows:

(k_1, H_1): $(17.858, 2.226) \Rightarrow (14.758, 1.718),$
(k_2, H_2): $(101.401, 19.509) \Rightarrow (230.783, 53.417).$

We see that the new stable steady state has lower levels of human capital and per capita wealth; but the new unstable steady states have much higher levels of k and

H. It seems promising with the new education policy because the new unstable steady state of higher k and H is much better than the old unstable one. Nevertheless, the economy with the discouraging policy has more chances to live in poverty traps than to perform economic miracles. For instance, if we start from the following three points as in the previous example in Figure 3.2.2:

$$(k_0, H_0) = (1.5, 10), \quad (k_0, H_0) = (115, 12), \quad (k_0, H_0) = (70, 23).$$

As demonstrated in Figure 3.2.3, all the paths with these initial conditions end up in the poverty trap. But in Figure 3.2.2, the path with $(k_0, H_0) = (70, 23)$ exhibits the economic miracle. This example shows that the discouraging policy deprives the society of a development opportunity. The "chance" for development is lost due to the new policy. As shown in Figure 3.2.3, for the economy to experience sustained growth, the economy must have a much higher initial level of human capital than in the case of $\tau = 0.08$. Hence, if the society reduces its investment in education, it will have much less opportunity to experience sustained economic growth, even though heavy investment in education will not guarantee sustainable development of the nonlinear system.

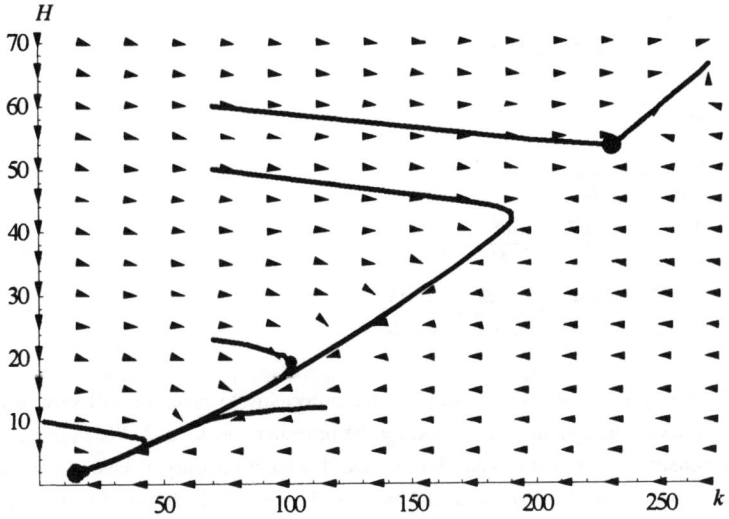

Figure 3.2.3 Path-dependent development as education is discouraged

3.2.5 The impact of the propensity to save

From equations (3.2.9), we see that any change in the preference has no impact on the labor distribution, i.e. $dN_v/d\lambda = 0$ and $dN_i/d\lambda = 0$. Taking derivatives of equation (3.2.14) with respect to λ yields

$$-\frac{d\Phi}{dH}\frac{dH}{d\lambda} = \frac{\alpha_e\Phi_e + \alpha\Phi_i}{\beta\lambda\xi} > 0.$$

The level of human capital is affected by changes in the propensity to save. As the propensity to save is increased, (1) if $x_e < 0$ and $x_i < 0$, the equilibrium level of human capital will increase; (2) if $x_e > 0$ and $x_i > 0$, the equilibrium level of human capital will decrease; and (3) if $x_e > 0$ and $x_i < 0$ ($x_e < 0$ and $x_i > 0$), the equilibrium level of human capital with low (high) level of H will increase (decrease). We thus conclude that in a traditional society where no sector exhibits increasing returns to scale, an increase in the propensity to save will increase human capital. In an economy where its current equilibrium point is located at the higher equilibrium level of H, an increase in the propensity to save will reduce the human capital. It is straightforward to get

$$\frac{1}{K_v}\frac{dK_v}{d\tau} = \frac{1}{k}\frac{dk}{d\tau} = \frac{m}{H}\frac{dH}{d\lambda} + \frac{1}{\lambda\xi},$$

$$\frac{dk_i}{d\lambda} = \frac{k_i}{\beta\xi\lambda} > 0,$$

$$\frac{dr}{d\lambda} = -\beta r\frac{dk_i}{d\lambda},$$

$$\frac{1}{w}\frac{dw}{d\lambda} = \frac{m}{H}\frac{dH}{d\lambda} + \alpha\frac{dk_i}{d\lambda},$$

$$\frac{1}{F}\frac{dF}{d\lambda} = \frac{\beta m}{H}\frac{dH}{d\lambda} + \frac{\alpha}{k}\frac{dk}{d\lambda} + \frac{\beta}{N_i}\frac{dN_i}{d\lambda}.$$

To simulate the impact of change in the propensity to save, we still specify the parameter values as in (3.2.15), except the propensity to save λ. We increase the propensity to save. Let us consider the case that the propensity to save is increased from 0.7 to 0.73, that is, $\lambda: 0.7 \Rightarrow 0.73$. Figure 3.2.4 shows the simulation results – the points with larger sizes are the new steady states and the other two points with smaller sizes are the old steady states. The two steady states shift as follows:

(k_1, H_1): $(17.858, 2.226)$ $\Rightarrow (14.758, 1.718)$,
(k_2, H_2): $(101.401, 19.509) \Rightarrow (230.783, 53.417)$.

We see that the new stable steady state has higher levels of human capital and per capita wealth; but the new unstable steady state has lower levels of k and H. Figure 3.2.4 depicts the impact of change in λ on the dynamics of the system.

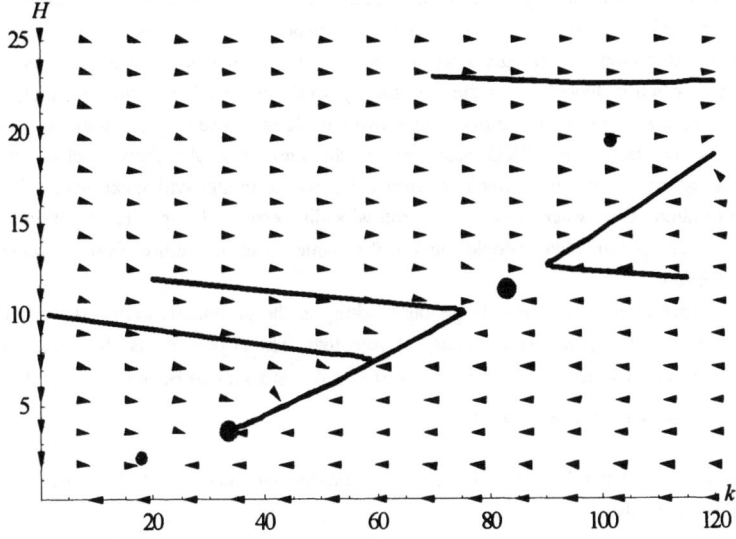

Figure 3.2.4 An increase in the propensity to save

Our simulation results demonstrate the path-dependent characteristics of the nonlinear system. Some of the assumptions should be relaxed. Indeed, our analysis does not rely on the specified production and utility functions.[13] Another direction for extending the model is to introduce the endogenous mechanism of education.[14] It is significant to introduce the impact of leisure or consumption on human capital accumulation.[15]

3.3 Growth with learning by doing and research[16]

Dynamics of occupational choice may influence economic development in different ways.[17] As distribution affects saving, investment, risk bearing, fertility, demand, and production, development processes are connected to distribution. On the other hand, development also affects the structure of occupations. It changes the demand for and supply of different types of labor. For instance, as an economy is industrializing, the labor share in industrial and service sectors tends to increase, while that of the agricultural sector tends to decline. Also more people move from rural areas to cities. This section proposes a dynamic model of the economic system which consists of one production sector and one university. There are two professions, one doing science and the other working in the production sector. The university is supported financially by the government by taxing the production sector. The production sector is the same as in the OSG model developed in Chapter 2. Demand for the commodity, saving, and labor distribution are endogenously determined. A typical household maximizes its utility, which is dependent on the job amenity level, the wealth and the consumption level of the commodity. Knowledge growth is through learning by doing by the production sector and R&D activities by the university. As shown below, the introduction of amenity differences into the dynamic model will make invalid the assumption that wage rates are professionally equal. Temporary equilibrium conditions require that people obtain the same level of utility from different professions.

For convenience, we term the people working in the production sector as workers and those working in the university as scientists. The population is classified into workers and scientists. We define N, $K(t)$, $F(t)$ and $r(t)$ as before. We introduce the following indexes and variables:

i, r – subscript indexes denoting the production sector and the university, respectively;

$N_j(t)$ and $K_j(t)$ – the labor force and capital stocks employed by sector j, $j = i, r$;

$k_j(t)$, $c_j(t)$ and $s_j(t)$ – the capital stocks owned by, the consumption levels of and the total savings made by per person working in sector j; and

$w_j(t)$ – the wage rate of group j.

The production sector
Production is a process of combining labor force, capital, and knowledge. The production function is specified as follows:

$$F(t) = Z(t)^m K_i(t)^\alpha N_i(t)^\beta, \quad \alpha + \beta = 1, \quad \alpha, \beta > 0, \quad m \geq 0, \tag{3.3.1}$$

in which $Z(t)$ is the knowledge stock of the economy and m is the knowledge utilization efficiency parameter. Maximizing the profit by the production sector yields the following conditions:

$$r(t) + \delta_k = \frac{(1-\tau(t))\alpha F(t)}{K_i(t)}, \quad w_i(t) = \frac{(1-\tau(t))\beta F(t)}{N_i(t)}, \tag{3.3.2}$$

in which $\tau(t)$ is the tax rate on the production sector at t. We assume that there is only one resource for the government to get its resource for supporting the university. There is no tax upon property or wage incomes. We may relax this assumption within the framework of this book by introducing heterogeneous tax rates upon production sectors and households' incomes from wages and properties.

We now examine consumer behavior. Let us denote respectively by $y_i(t)$ and $y_r(t)$ the net income per worker and per scientist. The net incomes consist of the wage income and the interest payment, i.e.

$$y_j(t) = r(t)k_j(t) + w_j(t), \quad j = i, r.$$

Our model is concerned with the interplay between workers' occupational decisions and the distribution of income and wealth. Different jobs, such as police officer, university professor, and factory worker, are associated with different social status and amenities. Differences in amenities give rise to compensating wage differentials. We introduce a new approach to take account of these differences in growth theory.

In the past several decades, some newly developed countries have experienced rapid industrialization and urbanization. People have migrated to urban areas, for instance, due to economic opportunities and urban amenities.[18] Many models in economics, regional sciences, and geography have been proposed to explain industrialization with urbanization. Capital accumulation and technological change are treated as the main dynamic forces for structural transformation of economic geography. But it may be argued that dynamic processes of urbanization will be affected by other factors such as infrastructures, land use distribution and environment. Urban areas provide opportunities for employment and a variety of life. Urban and rural areas have different levels of amenities. Different professions may also provide different amenities. Some kinds of work produce more pleasure than others. It is necessary to take account of differences in productivity and amenities in analyzing economic growth. In almost all neoclassical growth models it is assumed that labor (of the same type) will get the same wage. But this might not be true. For instance, a man working in the manufacturing sector might get a higher salary than the wage level he gets if he works in the service sector. Different professions provide varied amenities. An academic professor working in university may get a lower salary than in commercial business. A farmworker may be lowly paid if he moves to a city to enjoy urban amenities. In our model, we will take account of these factors in dealing with labor markets.

As well as the well-discussed issues related to learning by doing, education and R&D activities, we also examine the interdependence between job amenity, knowledge, and economic growth. As far as I know, no theoretical model has been proposed to connect research amenity (in comparison to other jobs' amenities) and economic development within a compact framework. If sophisticated research is boring, a free society may not carry out such research if research results have no profitable markets. In our approach, wage rate is not a single factor that determines choice of profession. People may prefer a profession with low pay but high job amenity level to one with high pay but low job amenity level. It seems that the role of job amenity in affecting professional choice and labor distribution has become increasingly important in post-industrial societies. With many economies facing rapidly improved living conditions and rapid changes of attitudes towards various kinds of jobs, professional choice has become increasingly complicated. It may be argued that how people feel about doing science will strongly affect labor distribution between research and production. If to do science has no advantages in terms of social status and income, then only a few people may want to choose scientific research as a career.

It is assumed that the utility level of typical consumer j, $U_j(t)$, is dependent on the amenity level of his profession, consumption level of the commodity, $c_j(t)$, and his wealth, $s_j(t)$. The utility functions are specified as follows:

$$U_j(t) = A_j c_j(t)^{\xi_j} s_j(t)^{\lambda_j}, \quad \xi_j, \lambda_j > 0, \quad \xi_j + \lambda_j = 1, \quad j = i, r, \qquad (3.3.3)$$

in which the parameters, ξ_j and λ_j, are respectively the propensities to consume the commodity and to own wealth. In equation (3.3.3), A_j is profession j's (fixed) amenity level. It is possible to treat A_j as an endogenous variable by assuming that A_j are functions of the labor distribution, the output of the society, wealth distribution, and the difference in wage rates.

The budget income of individual j is

$$c_j(t) + s_j(t) = \hat{y}_j(t), \quad \hat{y}_j(t) \equiv y_j(t) + k_j(t), \quad j = i, r.$$

Maximization of $U_j(t)$ subject to the budget constrains gives

$$c_j(t) = \xi_j \Omega_j(t), \quad s_j(t) = \lambda_j \Omega_j(t), \quad j = i, r, \tag{3.3.4}$$

where

$$\Omega_j(t) \equiv \rho_j \hat{y}_j(t), \quad \rho_j \equiv \frac{1}{\xi_j + \lambda_j}.$$

The wealth accumulation of individual j is

$$\dot{k}_j(t) = s_j(t) - k_j(t).$$

Substituting s_j in equation (3.3.4) into the above equations yields

$$\dot{k}_j(t) = \lambda_j \Omega_j(t) - k_j(t), \quad j = i, r.$$

The above equations determine the capital accumulation of workers and scientists.

As we assume an identical population and we neglect time and costs involved in professional education and training, different professions should bring the same level of utility. That is, labor market equilibrium requires that the level of utility is the same:

$$U_i(t) = U_r(t).$$

This equation assumes a frictionless labor market. To depict the economy more realistically, it is necessary to consider that the labor market does not function smoothly. As we neglect possible unemployment, immigration due to change in job conditions is given by

$$\dot{N}_i(t) = \Psi(U_i(t) - U_r(t), t),$$

where Ψ is a function of difference of utility levels that workers obtain from the two professions and certain exogenous conditions (measured by parameter t). If we neglect any exogenous factor, the function should have the following properties:

144   *Economic Growth with Income and Wealth Distribution*

$$\Psi > (<) 0 \text{ if } U_i(t) > (<) U_r(t),$$
$$\Psi = 0 \text{ if } U_i(t) = U_r(t).$$

If the two professions provide the same level of utility, the labor market is in steady state if the other conditions in the system are not changed. If to work provides a higher level of utility than does research, then some scientists will give up research and work in factories, and vice versa. If the labor market is governed by this general equation, dynamic analysis will become more complicated as we will be involved in examining a four-dimensional dynamic system. As dynamic analysis has already become complicated, we only examine the special case, $U_i(t) = U_r(t)$, of the general dynamics.

Before closing the model, we examine what conditions will guarantee $U_i(t) = U_r(t)$. Substitution of equations (3.3.4) into the utility functions gives

$$U_j(t) = A_j \xi_j^{\xi_j} \lambda_j^{\lambda_j} \hat{y}_j(t), \quad j = i, r,$$

where we specify $\rho_j = 1$. The utility level is a function of the professional amenity, propensity to consume, and the disposable income. As $\xi_j + \lambda_j = 1$, the term $\xi_j^{\xi_j} \lambda_j^{\lambda_j}$ can be considered as a function of λ_j. In fact

$$\xi_j^{\xi_j} \lambda_j^{\lambda_j} = (1 - \lambda_j)^{1-\lambda_j} \lambda_j^{\lambda_j}.$$

Figure 3.3.1 depicts $\xi_j^{\xi_j} \lambda_j^{\lambda_j}$ for $0 \leq \lambda_j \leq 1$.

We see that the function achieves its minimum 0.5 at $\xi_j = \lambda_j = 0.5$. As λ_j moves away from its minimum, the function increases until it approaches its maximum as λ_j approaches either of its two poles. We see that for fixed A_j and $\hat{y}_j(t)$, consumers enjoy more as they move away from the middle point of the propensity to own wealth. Their utility level is maximized when they either consume or save all their disposable income. This occurs because of the assumed Cobb-Douglas utility function.

As $\hat{y}_j = w_j + (r+1)k_j$, wages tend to be relatively less important in disposable income as wealth is accumulated. This means that in comparison with the wage rate, professional amenity tends to play an increasingly important role in professional choice as wealth is accumulated. This conclusion becomes evident if we make cross-country comparisons. In poor countries where people accumulate little wealth, wage levels play a key role in determining what jobs they choose to do and where they choose to live. As they accumulate more wealth, the more they will weigh working and residential environment when making decisions.

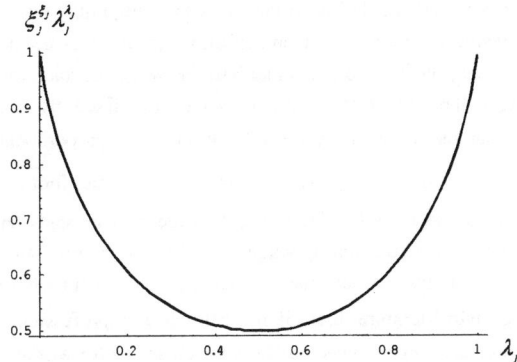

Figure 3.3.1 $\xi_j^{\xi_j} \lambda_j^{\lambda_j}$ **as a function of** λ_j **with** $\xi_j + \lambda_j = 1$

The equilibrium condition, $U_i(t) = U_r(t)$, of the labor market is

$$\frac{\hat{y}_i(t)}{\hat{y}_r(t)} = \frac{A_r \xi_r^{\xi_r} \lambda_r^{\lambda_r}}{A_i \xi_i^{\xi_i} \lambda_i^{\lambda_i}}.$$

If the propensity to own wealth is the same and the professional amenity is equal, $\hat{y}_i(t) = \hat{y}_r(t)$ holds in temporary equilibrium. This is guaranteed by rapid adaptation of the labor market. The condition $\hat{y}_i(t) = \hat{y}_r(t)$ is

$$\frac{w_i(t) - w_r(t)}{k_i(t) - k_r(t)} = -(r(t) + 1) < 0.$$

To maintain the labor market in temporary equilibrium, if the wage rate of the industrial sector is higher than that of the university, the scientist owns more wealth than the worker, and vice versa. As no one can enjoy "professional prestige" or professional benefits, if the worker earns more, the scientist must have more wealth –

no one can have everything in the labor market. In the case of $\lambda_i = \lambda_r$, the ratio of the wage rates is equal to the reciprocal of the ratio of amenity levels of the two professions. If the scientist obtains a higher amenity level than the worker, the scientist should have a lower disposable income than the worker; otherwise, the labor market will not be in equilibrium.

Since we assume that the labor market is balanced through equalizing utility levels among jobs and people are identical in terms of human capital, wage rates may not be equal. In order to close the model, we have to determine how the wages of scientists are determined. We consider the case that scientists' wages are fixed by the government. It is assumed that the scientist's wage rate $w_r(t)$ has a proportional relationship with the worker's wage rate: $w_r(t) = \hat{u} w_s(t)$, $\hat{u} > 0$. This formula assumes a simple relation in the labor market. How scientists are paid depends on factors such as cultural values related to learning, wage rate of workers and actual economic conditions. A labor union, for instance, may play an important role in setting $\hat{u}$. In most models in the growth literature, there is no difference in professional amenity (such as social status) and wage between different professions for workers with similar skills and knowledge.

Some major new knowledge and inventions had far-reaching and prolonged implications, such as Newton's mechanics, Einstein's theory of relativity, the steam engine, electricity, and the computer. Small and nonlasting improvements take place everywhere, serendipitously and intentionally. Innovations may also happen in a drastic, discontinuous fashion or in a slow, continuous manner. The introduction of the first steam engine rapidly triggered a sequence of innovations. The same is true about electricity and the computer. In their seminal article on the theory of general purpose technologies, Bresnahan and Trajtenberg (1995) argued that technologies have a treelike structure, with a few prime movers located at the top and all other technologies radiating out from them. They characterize general purpose technologies by pervasiveness (which means that such a technology can be used in many downstream sectors), technological dynamism (which means that it can support continuous innovational efforts and learning), and innovational complementarities (which exist because productivity of R&D in downstream sectors increases as a consequence of innovation in the general purpose technology, and vice versa). A general purpose technology, such as the computer, has the potential to affect the entire economic system and can lead to far-reaching changes in such social factors as working hours and constraints on family life. An improvement in a general purpose technology can lead to reduction in costs of downstream sectors and the development of improved downstream products.

Economists have recently been concerned with the general purpose of technologies and growth.[19] Like capital, a refined classification of knowledge and technologies tends to lead to new conceptions and modeling strategies. We assume a conventional production function of knowledge in which labor, capital, and technology are combined to create new knowledge in a deterministic way. This is an approximate description of the idea that devoting more resources to research yields more rapidly new knowledge. Since we are concerned with long-run growth without giving attention to economic chaos, modeling the randomness in knowledge creation would add little insight. There does not appear to be certain evidence for supporting any form of how increases in the stock of knowledge affect the creation of new knowledge. We do not require that the creation function for knowledge have constant returns to scale in capital and labor. By constant returns to scale, we mean that if the two inputs are doubled, new inputs can do exactly what the old ones were doing, thereby doubling the amount produced. Constant returns to scale are far stricter for knowledge production than for goods production. It is possible that doubling the number of computers and scientists increases by three times the knowledge creation that existed before – the university's knowledge creation exhibits increasing returns to scale in scientists and capital. It is also possible for the university to have decreasing returns to scale. We thus should allow three possibilities – increasing, constant, decreasing returns to scale in scientists and capital – in the university's knowledge creation.

We propose the following equation for knowledge growth:

$$\dot{Z}(t) = \frac{\tau_i F(t)}{Z(t)^{\varepsilon_i}} + \tau_r Z(t)^{\varepsilon_r} K_r(t)^{\alpha_r} N_r(t)^{\beta_r} - \delta_z Z(t), \qquad (3.3.5)$$

in which δ_z (≥ 0) is the depreciation rate of knowledge, and ε_j, τ_j, ($j = i, r$), α_r and β_r are parameters. We require τ_j, α_r, and β_r to be nonnegative. It should be noted that in equation (3.3.5), we omit the possibility of R&D by private companies.

Like the concept of physical capital, which should have many forms rather than a single one, we have used the concept of knowledge, $Z(t)$, in a highly aggregated sense. Knowledge, like physical capital, is a complexity that has different forms. Knowledge ranges from the highly abstract to the highly applied. At one extreme is abstract knowledge with little applicability. We also have abstract knowledge with broad applicability, such as the general (restricted, special) theory of relativity and the theory of quantum mechanics. At another extreme, we have knowledge about special goods, such as how to write Japanese in a computer. Different types of knowledge play varied roles in economic growth. In order to fully understand these roles, we have to refine economic structures dividing a single production sector into multiple ones and classifying a homogeneous labor force into a heterogeneous one. Progress in any special type of knowledge may have different implications for different production sectors or different people. For instance, an improvement in farming technology enables the agricultural sector to employ fewer people to produce the same amount of products (which would result in unemployment of farmers); but the same technological change has no impact on the industrial sector. Obviously, different types of knowledge may be accumulated through different human activities. The forces underlying the advancement of basic mathematics are different from those behind advance in the designs of cars. The above equation merely describes some possible sources of knowledge creation. It would be ridiculous to think that the growth of knowledge can be written by a single equation. There are various factors underlying the accumulation of knowledge. Curiosity, fame, and pecuniary profits affect growth of knowledge in different ways in different people and in different sectors. The current knowledge stock, preparations for creation, and even pure luck would affect knowledge creation in varied ways.

There are models in which the key to growth is the development of ideas for new goods. To solve the incentive problem of how these ideas get produced, the models rely on monopoly power that is reinforced by patents and copyrights. Baumol (1990) observes that major innovations and advances in knowledge are often brought about by extremely talented individuals. But highly talented individuals often have other pursuits beside making innovations and producing goods. Whether these human resources are concentrated on knowledge-creating activities has significant implications for the accumulation of knowledge. It is thus important for society to provide proper economic incentives and social forces to influence the activities of highly talented individuals. Baumol argues that at various places and times, military conquest, criminal activity, political and religious leadership, philosophical contemplation, financial dealings, and manipulation of the legal system have been attractive to the most talented members of society. These activities often have little or even negative social returns. He pointed out that there has been a strong link between how societies direct the energies of their most able members and whether societies thrive over the long term.

The university is financially supported by the government. The government collects taxes to operate the university. As tax is only enforced on the producers, we have

$$r(t)K_r(t) + w_r(t)N_r(t) = \tau(t)F(t). \qquad (3.3.6)$$

The university pays the rent for the equipment it uses and the scientists' wage it employs; it obtains the research fund from the government. We now design the distribution policy to determine the number of scientists and the amount of equipment.

The number of scientists N_r is determined by the temporary equilibrium condition,

$$U_i(t) = U_r(t),$$

in the labor market. We now have to design a way to determine K_r. In equation (3.3.6), the government may decide on one of the two variables τ or K_r. Here, we consider that the government decides the number of capital stocks of the university in the following way: $K_r = \eta K$, $0 < \eta < 1$, in which η is the policy variable fixed by the government. We assume that η is exogenously given. Hence, in our system the government makes a decision on the two parameters, $\hat{u}$ and η. The tax rate is determined at the level that the balance budget for research is maintained.

By the definition

$$K(t) = k_i(t)N_i(t) + k_r(t)N_r(t).$$

The assumption that the labor force and capital are always fully employed yields the following equations:

$$N_i(t) + N_r(t) = N, \quad K_i(t) + K_r(t) = K(t). \tag{3.3.7}$$

We have thus built the model. We now examine the equilibrium. First, by $\dot{k}_j(t) = \lambda_j \Omega_j - k_j$ and equation (3.3.5), in steady state we have

$$\lambda_j \Omega_j = k_j, \quad \frac{\tau_i F}{Z^{\varepsilon_i}} + \tau_r Z^{\varepsilon_r} K_r^{\alpha_r} N_r^{\beta_r} = \delta_z Z. \tag{3.3.8}$$

Introduce

$$A \equiv \frac{A_r}{A_i}\left(\frac{\xi_r}{\lambda_r}\right)^{\xi_r}\left(\frac{\lambda_i}{\xi_i}\right)^{\xi_i}, \quad x_i \equiv \frac{m}{\beta} - \varepsilon_i - 1, \quad x_r \equiv \frac{\alpha_r m}{\beta} + \varepsilon_r - 1,$$

$$\delta_j \equiv \frac{\xi_j}{\lambda_j} + \delta_k, \quad j = i, r.$$

Then the following proposition holds.

Proposition 3.3.1[20]

If $1 > \alpha + \beta \hat{u} A > \delta_r / \delta_i > \hat{u} A$, then the system has the following properties: (1) If $x_i < 0$ and $x_r < 0$, the system has a unique equilibrium; (2) If $x_i > 0$ and $x_r > 0$, the system has a unique equilibrium; and (3) If $x_i > 0$ and $x_r < 0$ ($x_i < 0$ and $x_r > 0$), the system has either two equilibrium points or no equilibrium.

We will not interpret the behavior of the model as it is similar to that in the previous section.

3.4 Development with monopolistic competition

Since the late 1980s endogenous growth theory has attracted great attention from economists. The "new" endogenous growth pioneered by Romer (1986) and Lucas (1988) has attempted to explain technical change as the outcome of market activity in response to economic incentives. In the new growth theory, technological change does not take place in a predetermined fashion without any social and economic costs. An important development in the new growth theory has been to broaden the definition of capital. It not only includes physical capital, but also research and development, human capital, government-financed infrastructure, and more generally, the institutions needed to protect liberty and property rights. The new growth theory has modeled endogenous knowledge accumulation through many channels, including formal education, on-the-job training, basic scientific research, learning by doing, process innovations, industrial innovations, and product innovations. The crucial assumption that leads to sustainable endogenous growth is the existence of increasing returns to scale in economic production under monopolistic competition.

The concept of monopolistic competition and modeling frameworks associated with a type of imperfect competition have been applied to various problems in macroeconomics, international and interregional economics, economic growth and development. Although this book will not apply this approach to the issues related to wealth and income distribution,[21] because the approach provides some important ideas about modeling human capital accumulation and knowledge creation, we will introduce two models for illustration.[22] Monopolistic competition is characterized as follows:

(i) The products are differentiated. The market consists of many buyers and sellers. Unlike perfectly competitive firms, firms are characterized by significant product differentiation. Consumers view firms' products as imperfect substitutes for each other.
(ii) The number of firms is so large that each firm ignores its strategic interactions with other firms.
(iii) Entry is unrestricted and takes place until the profits of incumbent firms are driven down to zero. Any firm can hire the inputs, such as labor and capital,

needed to compete in the market, and they can release these inputs from employment when they do not need them.

The character of imperfect competition is often emphasized for describing decentralized allocations in the presence of increasing returns. Its competitive feature allows us to avoid the complexity of strategic interactions among firms (as in oligopoly models). The modeling framework with monopolistic competition makes it possible to endogenize entry-exit processes and the range of products supplied in the market through these processes. In determining their prices in the short term, monopolistic competitors behave much like the differentiated product oligopolists. Taking the prices of other firms as given, each firm faces a downward-sloping demand curve – the downward sloping is held because of product differentiation. Each firm maximizes its profit at the point at which its marginal revenue equals marginal cost. In a short-run equilibrium, the price chosen by a firm may exceed the typical firm's average cost at the prevailing output level. This situation will attract new entrants into the industry. As firms enter the monopolistically competitive market, a typical firm's demand curve shifts. At a long-run equilibrium, a typical firm sets the profit-maximizing price equal to the average cost, making zero profit. This section introduces Romer's economic development model with monopolistic competition.

Schumpeter emphasizes market power in explaining the dynamics of innovation. Although Shell (1973) constructs a model with a single monopolist who invests in technological change, the assumption of permanent monopoly is not realistic for dealing with modern industrial competition. Romer (1990) develops a model of economic growth with monopolistic competition. The Romer model revised below is a synthesis of different approaches – the neoclassical growth theory, the model of monopolistic competition in consumption goods formulated by Dixit and Stiglitz (1977), the dynamic framework by Judd (1985), and the model with differentiated inputs in production by Ethier (1982).

The Romer model considers four basic inputs – physical capital, labor, human capital, and an index of the level of technology. Capital, denoted by $K(t)$, is measured in units of consumption goods. Let N stand for the population and the labor force. The number N is assumed to be constant in this model. It can be seen that an exogenous growth rate of the labor force will make the analysis more complicated. The model separates the rival component of knowledge (also called human capital), H, from the nonrival, technological component, $A(t)$. The nonrival knowledge $A(t)$, measured in the number of designs – can grow without bound. It is assumed, for technical reasons, that the total stock, H, of human capital in the population and the fraction supplied to the market are fixed. The economy is composed of three sectors. The research sector produces new knowledge (i.e. new designs) with human capital and the existing stock of knowledge as inputs. An intermediate-goods sector uses the designs from the research sector together with capital to produce producer durables that will be used in final-goods production. A final-goods sector uses labor, human capital, and the set of producer durables. The output of this sector can be either consumed or saved.

The sector that produces producer durables cannot be described by a representative firm. Let there be a distinct firm i for each durable good i. A firm must purchase or produce a design for good i before starting production by converting η units of final output into one durable unit of good i. Once the firm has produced a design for durable i, it obtains an infinitely lived patent on the design. If it manufactures $x(i)$ units of the durable, it rents those durables to final-output firms for a rental rate $p(i)$. Since it is the only seller of durable i, it will face a downward-sloping demand for the good. Neglecting any possible depreciation, we see that the value of one unit of durable i is the present discounted value of the infinite stream of rental income.

Final output $Y(t)$ is produced by combination of physical labor N, human capital devoted to final output H_Y, and physical capital. Here, the physical capital consists of an infinite number of distinct types of producer durables $x(i,t)$, indexed by a continuous variable $i \in [0, \infty)$. It should be noted that only a finite number of these potential inputs (that have already been invented and designed) are available for use at any time t. We adopt the Cobb-Douglas production function for final output

$$Y(t) = H_Y^\alpha N^\beta \int_0^\infty x(i)^{1-\alpha-\beta} di, \quad 1 > \alpha, \beta > 0. \tag{3.4.1}$$

The production function is homogeneous of degree one. Output in the final-goods sector can thus be described in terms of the actions of a single, aggregate, price-taking firm. The specified form of $\int_0^\infty x(i)^{1-\alpha-\beta} dt$ implies that all durables have additively separable effects on output. We omit the possibility of complementarity and of mixtures of types of substitutability among producer durables.

As usual, if we neglect depreciation, capital $K(t)$ evolves according to the following equation:

$$\dot{K}(t) = Y(t) - C(t),$$

where $C(t)$ is aggregate consumption. According to the definitions of η and $x(i,t)$, we have

$$K(t) = \eta \int_0^\infty x(i,t)\,di.$$

To specify the process for the accumulation of new designs, $A(t)$, we assume that research output depends on the amount of human capital devoted to research and on the stock of knowledge available to a person doing research in the following way:

$$\dot{A}(t) = \kappa H_A A(t),$$

where H_A is the total human capital employed in research. As κ and H_A are constant, this specification means that $A(t)$ will grow with a fixed rate of κH_A and will become infinite as time passes. We also have

$$H_A + H_Y = H.$$

We choose price of current output to be unity at any point in time. Let

$r(t)$ = the interest rate on loans denominated in goods;
$p_A(t)$ = the price of new designs;
$w_H(t)$ = the rental rate per unit of human capital.

Because anyone engaged in research can freely take advantage of the entire existing stock of designs in doing research to produce designs, from $\dot{A}(t) = \kappa H_A A(t)$ we should have

$$w_H(t) = p_A(t) \kappa A(t).$$

The final-output firm is faced with a price list $\{p(i): i \in R_+\}$ for all the producer durables, including infinite prices for the durables that have not been invented. The firm maximizes profits in selecting $x(i)$. Given values for H_Y and N, profits for the representative final-output firm are

154 Economic Growth with Income and Wealth Distribution

$$\max_x \int_0^\infty \left[H_Y^\alpha N^\beta x(i)^{1-\alpha-\beta} - p(i)x(i) \right] di.$$

The first-order condition for the above maximization problem is

$$p(i) = (1 - \alpha - \beta) H_Y^\alpha N^\beta x(i)^{-\alpha-\beta}. \tag{3.4.2}$$

The demand curve defined by this equation is what the producer of each specialized durable takes as given in choosing the profit-maximizing price to set. A firm that has already incurred the fixed-cost investment in a design will choose a level of output x to maximize its profit. That is

$$\pi = \max_x p(x)x - r\eta x = \max_x \left[(1-\alpha-\beta) H_Y^\alpha N^\beta x^{1-\alpha-\beta} - r\eta x \right].$$

The flow of rental income is $p(x)x$, the cost equals the interest cost on the ηx units of output needed to produce x durables. In this model, the only sunk cost is the initial expenditure on the design. The monopoly pricing problem defined above is that of a firm with constant marginal cost that faces a constant elasticity demand curve. The resulting monopoly price is a markup over marginal cost, i.e.

$$p^* = \frac{r\eta}{1-\alpha-\beta}. \tag{3.4.3}$$

Each producer of specialized durables charges the monopoly price. Under this pricing strategy, the maximal profit is

$$\pi = (\alpha + \beta) p^* x^*,$$

where x^* is the quantity on the demand curve implied by the price p^*.

The decision to produce a new specialized input depends on a comparison of the discounted stream of net revenue and the cost P_A of the initial investment in a design. Because the market for designs is competitive, the price for designs will equal the present value of the net revenue that a monopoly can extract, i.e.

$$\int_t^\infty e^{-\int_t^\tau r(s)ds} \pi(\tau) d\tau = P_A(t).$$

Assuming P_A to be constant and taking derivatives of the above equations with respect to t, we obtain

$$\pi(t) = r(t)P_A. \tag{3.4.4}$$

This equation states that at any point in time, the instantaneous excess of revenue over marginal cost must be just sufficient to cover the interest cost on the initial investment in a design.

To close the model, we describe the behavior of consumers. Consumers in the Romer model are endowed with fixed quantities of labor and human capital. At the beginning, consumers own the existing durable-goods-producing firms and net revenues of these firms are paid to consumers as dividends. Final-goods firms earn zero profits and own no assets. We specify Ramsey consumers with discounted, constant elasticity preferences

$$U = \int_0^\infty \frac{C^{1-\sigma}}{1-\sigma} e^{-\rho t} \, dt, \ \sigma \in [0, \infty).$$

We have already shown that the intertemporal optimization condition for a consumer faced with a interest rate $r(t)$ is

$$\frac{\dot{C}(t)}{C(t)} = \frac{r(t) - \rho}{\sigma}. \tag{3.4.5}$$

This is the only equation in which consumers' preferences enter the solution of the model.

We now examine the balanced growth equilibrium. The Romer model, like most of the models in the new growth theory, defines a mathematically complicated system. Since such a system is difficult to analyze, one often has to be only concerned with steady states of the model. We now examine the properties of balanced growth equilibrium.

An equilibrium point for the model is paths for prices and quantities such that: (1) consumers make decisions with an interest rate as given; (2) holders of human capital decide whether to work in the research sector or the manufacturing sector with A, P_A, and the wage rate in the manufacturing sector w_A as given; (3) final-goods producers choose labor, human capital, and a list of differentiated durables with prices as given; (4) each firm that owns a design and manufactures a producer durable maximizes profit by setting prices with interest rate and the demand curve as given; (5) firms contemplating entry into the business of producing a durable take prices for designs as given; and (6) the supply of each good is equal to the demand.

We now try to find an equilibrium point at which the variables A, K, and Y grow at constant exponential rates. First, we note

$$\pi = (\alpha + \beta)p^*x^*.$$

By this condition and condition (3.4.4)

$$P_A = \frac{\pi}{r} = \frac{(\alpha + \beta)p^*x^*}{r}.$$

Inserting equation (3.4.2) into the above equation yields

$$P_A = \frac{\alpha + \beta}{r}(1 - \alpha - \beta)H_Y^\alpha N^\beta x^{*1-\alpha-\beta}. \tag{3.4.6}$$

In this model, A is also used as a measure of the number of designs or durables in use at time t. Consequently, at equilibrium

$$K = \eta \int_0^\infty x(i)\,di = \eta A x^*.$$

It is assumed that in the labor market the wages paid to human capital in each sector must be equal. By $w_H = P_A \kappa A$ and the wage for human capital is equal to its marginal product in the final-output sector, i.e.

$$w_Y = \alpha H_Y^{\alpha-1} N^\beta \int_0^\infty x(i)^{1-\alpha-\beta}\,di = \alpha H_Y^{\alpha-1} N^\beta A x^{*1-\alpha-\beta},$$

the condition of $w_H = w_Y$ is given by

$$P_A \kappa = \alpha H_Y^{\alpha-1} N^\beta x^{*1-\alpha-\beta}.$$

Substituting equation (3.4.6) into the above equation solves H_Y as

$$H_Y = \frac{\alpha}{(\alpha + \beta)(1 - \alpha - \beta)} \frac{r}{\kappa}. \tag{3.4.7}$$

For a fixed value of $H_A = H - H_Y$, the implied exponential growth rate for A is κH_A. It is straightforward to check that x^* is constant if r is. The final output is

$$Y^* = H_Y^\alpha N^\beta \int_0^\infty x(i)^{1-\alpha-\beta} di = H_Y^\alpha N^\beta A x^{*1-\alpha-\beta}.$$

Consequently, output Y and capital stock K must grow at the same rate as A if N, H_Y, and x^* are fixed. Denote this rate by g_Y. Since K/Y is a constant, the ratio

$$\frac{C}{Y} = \frac{Y - \dot{K}}{Y} = 1 - g_Y \frac{K}{Y}$$

must be constant. Consequently, the growth rate of C is the same as that of Y. Thus

$$g_Y = \frac{\dot{C}}{C} = \frac{\dot{Y}}{Y} = \frac{\dot{K}}{K} = \frac{\dot{A}}{A} = \kappa H_A.$$

From equation (3.4.7), $H_A = H - H_Y$, and the above equation, we obtain

$$g_Y = \kappa H_A = \kappa H - \Lambda r, \tag{3.4.8}$$

where

$$\Lambda \equiv \frac{\alpha}{(\alpha + \beta)(1 - \alpha - \beta)}.$$

It is necessary to require H_A to be nonnegative. To determine the growth rate g_Y, we use equation (3.4.5), i.e. $g_Y = (r - \rho)/\sigma$. Together with equation (3.4.8), we find

$$g_Y = \frac{\kappa H - \rho\Lambda}{\sigma\Lambda + 1}.\tag{3.4.9}$$

For the integral in the consumer's preferences to be finite, the rate of growth of current utility $(1-\sigma)g_Y$ must be less than the discount rate ρ. Thus, for $\sigma \in [0, 1)$, it is necessary for

$$(1-\sigma)\frac{\kappa H}{\Lambda + 1} < \rho.$$

Equation (3.4.9) is the main result of the Romer model. Because it shows continued positive growth of the main aggregated variables as well as per capita consumption, the model is often cited as the symbol of the new growth theory. The model shows that neither N nor η affects the long-run growth rate. An increase in N increases the demand factor faced by each monopolistic firm and a reduction in η reduces the cost of the monopolist and increases output x^*. In either case, the stream of net revenue generated by a new design rises. Nonetheless, the amount of human capital devoted to research is not affected by the two parameters. It should be remarked that since we consider the system as a whole, a change that increases the return to one activity can raise the return to some other activity that competes with the first activity for resources. An increase in N or reduction in η raises the return to human capital in the two types of activity in this model. For the functional forms used here, these two effects exactly cancel. This explains invariance of the growth rate with respect to these two parameters. As Romer mentioned, this idiosyncratic property will disappear if some functional forms are generalized.

From equation (3.4.9), we immediately see that the growth rate of consumption and income are endogenous only when the total human capital H is exogenously fixed (unlike in the Solow model, the labor force grows at a fixed rate). Since H is fixed and the growth rate of A is equal to a proportion of the component of H (through $\dot{A} = \kappa H_A A$) devoted to research, we see that the Romer model is essentially as "exogenous" as the Solow model. In fact, given the extremely rich literature of the neoclassical growth theory, the key contribution of the new growth theory may be the introduction of monopolistic competition into the neoclassical growth rate, rather than explanation of endogenous economic growth.

3.5 Product variety and growth

As an alternative to the Romer model – in which growth is achieved through the production of an increasing variety of goods – we can use some of the same apparatus to illustrate a similar model proposed by Grossman and Helpman (1991: Chap. 3).[23] The model studies endogenous growth based on intentional industrial innovation. In this approach, research is treated as an ordinary economic activity that requires the input of resources and responds to profit opportunities. Returns to R&D are possible because of the monopoly rents from imperfectly competitive products markets. We will neglect investment in physical and human capital partly because analysis will become too complicated and partly because we are interested in the key ideas in this approach.[24]

Industrial research may be involved either in process innovation to reduce the cost of producing existing goods or product innovation to invent entirely new goods. Product innovation is further classified according to whether the newly invented goods bear a vertical or horizontal relation to existing products. The former provides greater quality but performs similar functions to those of existing goods; the latter increases product variety. This section is concerned with expanding product variety and the next with endogenous quality upgrading. There are unlimited potentials for developing new products and entrepreneurs invest resources to find unique goods. No diminishing returns in the creation of knowledge are assumed. Nevertheless, growth ultimately stops because the economic return to invention may decline as the number of available products increases.

We now study the behavior of consumers. The representative household maximizes utility over an infinite horizon. Intertemporal preferences are described by

$$U(t) = \int_{t}^{\infty} e^{-\rho(\tau - t)} \log(D(\tau)) d\tau, \qquad (3.5.1)$$

where $D(\tau)$ stands for an index of consumption at time τ, and ρ is the subjective discount rate. The natural logarithm of the consumption index measures instantaneous utility at a moment of time. Since we are interested in a variety of goods, the index D should reflect households' tastes for diversity in consumption. We take the product space to be continuous. We represent consumers' preferences over an infinite set of products, indexed by $j \in [0, \infty]$. At any moment only a subset of these varieties is available in the markets. Households can purchase at time t all brands, denoted by the interval $[0, n(t)]$, existing prior to t, where

$n(t)$ is the measure of products invented before time t. The variable n is called the number of available varieties. Following Dixit and Stiglitz (1977), the index D is specified in such a way that it exhibits a constant and equal elasticity of substitution between every pair of goods

$$D = \left[\int_0^n x(j)^\alpha \, dj \right]^{1/\alpha}, \quad 0 < \alpha < 1, \tag{3.5.2}$$

where $x(j)$ denotes consumption of brand j. This specification has found many applications in the contemporary literature of economic growth with high product differentiation. The Dixit-Stiglitz preferences accommodate increasing diversity in consumption and yield aggregate demand functions that have a particular form convenient for analysis. The single parameter α characterizes different tastes for variety. It should be noted that the specification implies that innovative products are in no way superior to older varieties. As shown by Dixit and Stiglitz, with these preferences, the elasticity of substitution between any two products is

$$\varepsilon = \frac{1}{1-\alpha} > 1,$$

and a household spending an amount E (which equals

$$\int_0^n p(j) n(j) \, dj,$$

where $p(j)$ is the price of brand $j \in [0, n]$) maximizes instantaneous utility by purchasing

$$x(j) = \frac{E p(j)^{-\varepsilon}}{\int_0^n p(j')^{1-\varepsilon} \, dj'}. \tag{3.5.3}$$

The demand function features a constant price elasticity of ε and a unitary expenditure elasticity for each product. Ethier (1982) expresses equation (3.5.3) by

$$x(j) = D p(j)^{-\varepsilon} \left[\int_0^n p(j')^{1-\varepsilon} \, dj' \right]^{-1/\alpha}, \quad j \in [0, n], \tag{3.5.4}$$

where we use $D = E/p_D$ and

$$p_D = \left[\int_0^n p(j)^{1-\varepsilon}\, dj\right]^{1/(1-\varepsilon)}$$

Substituting $D = E/p_D$ into equation (3.5.1), we have

$$U(t) = \int_t^\infty e^{-\rho(\tau-t)}\left[\log(E(\tau)) - \log(p_D(\tau))\right]d\tau. \qquad (3.5.5)$$

The weak separability of indirect utility in the level of spending and the price index in equation (3.5.5) simplifies the maximization problem. The household now solves its optimization problem into two stages. The first stage chooses the composition of given levels of spending to maximize instantaneous utility. The second stage optimizes separately the time path of spending. It can be shown that the solution for the latter problem is given by

$$\frac{\dot{E}}{E} = r - \rho. \qquad (3.5.6)$$

Prices can be normalized in such a way that nominal spending remains through time. Consequently, equation (3.5.6) becomes

$$\begin{aligned}E(t) &= 1 \quad \text{for all } t,\\ r(t) &= \rho \quad \text{for all } t.\end{aligned} \qquad (3.5.7)$$

The final decision is to allocate their wealth across available assets according to the conditions given by equation (3.5.3).

We now describe the behavior of producers. The economy is endowed with a single primary factor of production – labor. By an appropriate choice of units, the input-output coefficient is set to one. Producers create blueprints for new goods and manufacture the products previously innovated. The up-front R&D expense can be regarded as a fixed cost in the production cycle of a given commodity. Each known variety of the differentiated product is manufactured by a single, atomistic firm, subject to a common constant-return-to-scale technology. Under these specifications, the unique supplier of variety j maximizes operating profit

$$\pi(j,t) = p(j,t)x(j,t) - w(t)x(j,t), \qquad (3.5.8)$$

where $w(t)$ is the wage rate at time t. Faced with the demand function (3.5.3), the firm maximizes the profit by charging a price $p(j) = w/\alpha$. Henceforth we suppress the time arguments when no confusion arises from doing so. In the momentary equilibrium all varieties are priced equally at p, where $p = w/\alpha$. With symmetric demand and $E = 1$, this pricing strategy yields per brand operating profits of

$$\pi = \frac{1-\alpha}{n}. \qquad (3.5.9)$$

The profits are one component of the return to the owners of firms and are continuously paid to shareholders as dividends. Let $v(t)$ stand for the value of a claim to the infinite stream of profits that accrues to a typical firm operating at time t. In the brief time interval between t and $t + dt$, the total return to the owners of this firm equals $\pi dt + \dot{v} dt$. It is assumed that arbitrage in capital markets ensures equality between this yield and that on a riskless loan. The latter return for an investment of size v is $rvdt$. Thus, the equilibrium in the capital market requires

$$\pi + \dot{v} = rv. \qquad (3.5.10)$$

It is assumed that the stock market value at time t of a firm equals the present discounted value of its profit stream subsequent to t

$$v(t) = \int_t^\infty e^{-[R(\tau) - R(t)]} \pi(\tau) d\tau, \qquad (3.5.11)$$

where $R(t)$ represents the cumulative discount factor applicable to profits earned at time t.

We now describe the technology for product development. An entrepreneur can add incrementally to the set of available products by devoting a given finite amount of labor to R&D for a brief interval of time. Let l denote units of labor devoted to R&D for a time interval of length dt. New products dn produced in the interval are given by $dn = (l/a)dt$. The total cost of such a research venture is

$wldt$ and the effort creates value for the entrepreneur of $v(l/a)dt$. Value maximization by entrepreneurs implies that l will be chosen as large as possible if $v/a > w$ (which cannot arise in general equilibrium because it implies an unbounded demand for labor by research enterprises) and be set to zero if $v/a < w$. Consequently, we have

$$wa \geq v \quad \text{with equality whenever } \dot{n} > 0. \tag{3.5.12}$$

The combination of free entry and constant returns to scale in research means no excess returns for entrepreneurs.

The representative variety of differentiated product bears a price p and aggregate demand $E = 1$. So each firm sells $1/np$ units and demands $1/np$ units of labor. The total demand for labor from n manufactures is equal to $1/p$. Consequently, the labor market equilibrium requires

$$a\dot{n} + \frac{1}{p} = N, \tag{3.5.13}$$

where $a\dot{n}$ is the total employment in R&D. From the above equation we see that $p \geq 1/N$. This completes the specification of the model. We now examine the qualitative properties of the system.

First we are interested in a time interval over which new brands are being developed. During this period, $v = aw$ by equation (3.5.12). Combining this free-entry condition with pricing condition $p = w/\alpha$ and $p \geq 1/N$, we see that R&D is profitable only when the reward for successful research is sufficiently high; that is $dn/dt > 0$ implies $v > v_0$ where $v_0 = \alpha a/N$. Summarizing these discussions and using equation (3.5.13), $v = aw$ and $p = w/\alpha$, we see that the number of varieties evolves according to

$$\dot{n} = \begin{cases} \dfrac{L}{a} - \dfrac{\alpha}{v} & v > v_0, \\ 0 & v \leq v_0. \end{cases} \tag{3.5.14}$$

Next, we obtain an equation for the change in firm value. From equations (3.5.7), (3.5.9), and (3.5.10), we obtain

164 *Economic Growth with Income and Wealth Distribution*

$$\dot{v} = \rho v - \frac{1-\alpha}{n}. \tag{3.5.15}$$

The dynamics are represented by the two differential equations (3.5.14) and (3.5.15). The dynamics are illustrated in Figure 3.5.1.

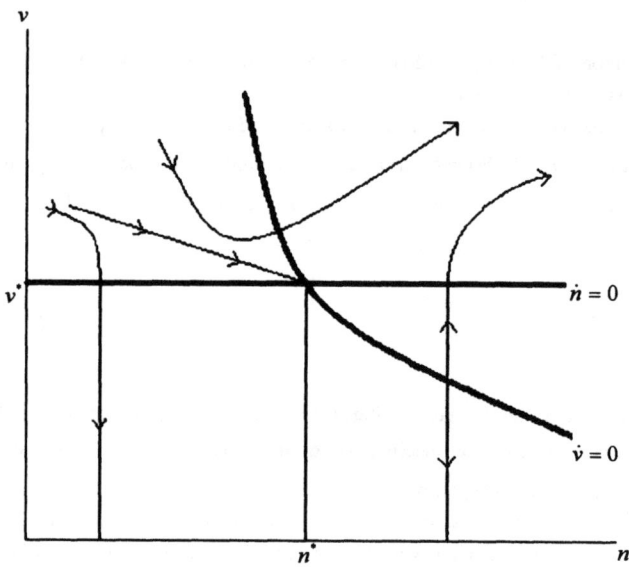

Figure 3.5.1 The dynamics with product variety

The hyperbola shows combinations of n and v for which the value of the typical firm remains constant. The curve is downward sloping. An increase in v raises the opportunity cost of holding shares in the representative firm; then capital markets will expect zero capital gains only if the dividend rate is high; a higher dividend rate requires higher profits and so a smaller set of competing brands. The number of differentiated products is constant on or below the horizontal line $v = v_0$. This occurs because production innovation requires a sufficiently high firm value to justify the large costs of R&D. The system is stationary at the intersection of the horizontal line and the hyperbola and at all points along vv below this point.

3.6 Variety of consumer goods and growth

The previous section is concerned with the growth model of variety of products. This section introduce a growth model with a variety of consumer products. This section is based on Barro and Sala-i-Martin (2004: Chap. 6).[25] The idea is to introduce a variety of consumer goods into the utility function that parallels the treatment of a variety of intermediate products in the production function as in the previous section. We can address these issues with the framework proposed in this book. If we treat variety of consumer goods as a function of knowledge, we can model variety of consumer goods as our utility function is flexible enough to treat variety as an endogenous variable.

Let us assume that the consumers care about variety consumer goods, which is measured by an index for consumer i

$$c_i = \left(\sum_{j=1}^{M} c_{ij}^{\varepsilon} \right)^{1/\varepsilon}, \quad 0 < \varepsilon \leq 1, \tag{3.6.1}$$

where c_{ij} is household i's consumption of goods of type j, M is the number of types available at the current time. The household i's utility is given by

$$U_i = \int_0^{\infty} \left(\frac{c_i^{1-\theta} - 1}{1-\theta} \right) e^{-\rho t} \, dt.$$

To see why the formation of the utility function captures the idea that consumers like variety, suppose that c_{ij} are measured in a common physical unit and the quantities consumed of each type are the same, $c_{ij} = c_i / M$. We have

$$\frac{c_i^{1-\theta} - 1}{1-\theta} = \frac{M^{(1-\varepsilon)(1-\theta)/\varepsilon} c_i^{1-\theta} - 1}{1-\theta}.$$

Hence, the flow of utility rises as M increases for a fixed c_i. This shows a positive relation between consumers' utility and variety.

The invention of a new product – an increase in M – is assumed to cost η units of goods. The inventor retains a perpetual monopoly in the production of the associated nondurable consumer good, C_j. The marginal cost of production of each consumer good is 1, and the producer determines the consumer price, P_j, maximizing the flow of monopoly profit. To determine P_j, we need to know the demand function. Let $a(t)$ stand for assets per person. Then

$$\dot{a}(t) = w(t) + r(t)a(t) - \sum_{j=1}^{M} P_j(t)c_{ij}(t),$$

where w and r are respectively the wage rate and rate of interest. The Hamiltonian associated with consumers' utility maximization is defined by

$$J = \left\{ \frac{\left(\sum_{j=1}^{M} c_{ij}^{\varepsilon}\right)^{(1-\theta)/\varepsilon} - 1}{1-\theta} \right\} e^{-\rho t} + v\left(w + ra - \sum_{j=1}^{M} P_j c_{ij}\right).$$

The first-order condition with respect to c_{ij} yields

$$\frac{c_{ij}}{c_{ik}} = \left(\frac{P_j}{P_k}\right)^{-1/(1-\varepsilon)}, \quad j, k = 1, \ldots, M.$$

This condition enables us to derive the demand function for the jth good

$$c_{ij} = \left\{ \frac{\sum_{k=1}^{M} P_k c_{ik}}{\sum_{k=1}^{M} P_k^{-\alpha/(1-\alpha)}} \right\} P_j^{-1/(1-\varepsilon)}. \tag{3.6.2}$$

We assume that M is sufficiently large so that the producer of good j can neglect the effect of P_j on the households' total spending per variety of good, that is, on the ratio of sums given in equation (3.6.2). Consumer demand then has the constant elasticity $-1/(1-\varepsilon)$ with respect to P_j. Hence, the monopoly producer of good j determines the consumer price with a markup on the unit marginal cost of production, $P_j = 1/\varepsilon$. All prices, denoted by P, are equal. Since the prices of all consumer goods are equal and the goods enter symmetrically into the utility function, the quantities consumed are the same:

$$c_{ij} = \frac{c_i}{M}.$$

For given c_i and M, c_{ij} are determined.

To determine the evolution of c_i, we use the remaining optimization conditions associated with the Hamiltonian. Setting the derivative of J with respect to c_{ij} equal to zero and then substituting $c_{ij} = c_i/M$ for all goods, we find

$$vP = M^{(1-\varepsilon)(1-\theta)/\varepsilon}(c_i)^{-\theta}e^{-\rho t}. \tag{3.6.3}$$

The second condition is associated with the state variable a

$$\dot{v} = -rv. \tag{3.6.4}$$

The two conditions, (3.6.3) and (3.6.4), determine

$$\frac{\dot{c}_i}{c_i} = \frac{1}{\theta}\left\{r - \rho + \left[\frac{(1-\varepsilon)(1-\theta)}{\varepsilon}\right]\frac{\dot{M}}{M}\right\}.$$

Using this equation, we obtain

$$\frac{d(c_i/M)}{dt} = \frac{\dot{M}}{M} - \frac{\dot{c}_i}{c_i} = \frac{1}{\theta}\left\{r - \rho + \left[\frac{\theta + \varepsilon - 1}{\varepsilon}\right]\frac{\dot{M}}{M}\right\}. \tag{3.6.5}$$

We now analyze invention. The net present value, $V(t)$, for an inventor of a new consumer good at time t is

$$V(t) = \int_0^\infty (P_j(\tau) - 1)C_j(\tau)e^{-\bar{r}(\tau,t)(\tau-t)}d\tau,$$

where

$$\bar{r}(\tau,t) \equiv \frac{1}{\tau - t}\int_t^\tau r(\omega)d\omega,$$

is the average interest rate between times t and τ. If the interest rate is constant, then the present-value factor simplifies to $e^{-r(\tau-t)}$. The equation shows that the fixed cost

η for discovering a new good can be recouped only if P_j exceeds the marginal cost of production for at least part of the time after date t.

We assume free entry into the business of being an inventor. This implies that anyone can pay the R&D cost η to secure the present value. If $V(t) > \eta$, then an infinite amount of resources would be channeled into R&D at time t, hence $V(t) > \eta$ cannot hold at equilibrium. If $V(t) < \eta$, then no resources would be devoted at time t to R&D. If r is constant, the free-entry condition is

$$\eta \geq V(t) = \frac{1-\varepsilon}{\varepsilon} \int_t^\infty C_j e^{-r(\tau-t)} d\tau,$$

where we use $P_j = 1/\varepsilon$. The condition holds with equality if $\dot{M} = 0$. In this case, C_j is constant and given by

$$C_j = \frac{C}{M} = \frac{r\eta\varepsilon}{1-\varepsilon}. \tag{3.6.6}$$

If both C_j and population are constant, then c_v/M must also be constant; hence the growth rate of c_i/M must be equal to zero. From equation (3.6.5), we have the following equation:

$$\frac{\dot{C}}{C} = \frac{\dot{M}}{M} = \frac{\varepsilon}{\theta+\varepsilon-1}(r-\rho), \quad \theta + \varepsilon \neq 1. \tag{3.6.7}$$

It is assumed $\theta + \varepsilon > 1$. This assumption guarantees that the growth rate of C is positively proportional to $r - \rho$.

We will not further analyze the behavior of the model because, as shown by Barro and Sala-i-Martin (2004: Chap.4), the model does not provide new insight, given the growth model with a variety of products defined in Section 3.2.

As knowledge and human capital can be created, learned, distributed, and diffused in so many ways, it is reasonable to expect that there are a great number of articles about economic growth with endogenous knowledge. For instance, Zhang constructed an economic growth with knowledge learning by doing, education, and learning by leisure within the Solow framework (Zhang, 1990). Young (1993) constructs a model with invention and bounded learning by doing within a framework of monopolistic competition. Schumpeter's ideas about development and creative destruction have recently been modeled by, for instance, Aghion and Howitt (1992). There are many types of technological changes that improve the quality of current products.[26] As these ideas are extended to regional and international frameworks, the literature has been growing rapidly.

3.7 From Malthusian stagnation to demographic trends of advanced economies

As a concluding section to the chapter, we now introduce a growth model, proposed by Galor and Weil (2000), that captures the historical evolution of population, technology, and output.[27] The economy evolves three regimes that have characterized economic development: from a Malthusian regime (where technological progress is slow and population growth prevents any sustained rise in income per capita) into a post-Malthusian regime (where technological progress rises and population growth absorbs only part of output growth) to a modern growth regime (where population growth is reduced and income growth is sustained). The model is defined with the OLG framework with a single good. The production uses land and efficiency units of labor as inputs. The supply of land is exogenously fixed. The number of efficiency units is endogenous.

The output produced at time t is

$$Y(t) = H^\alpha(t)(A(t)X)^{1-\alpha},$$

where X and $H(t)$ are the quantities of land and efficiency units of labor employed in production at t, $0 < \alpha < 1$, and $A(t) > 0$ is endogenously determined technological level at t. The output per worker at t is

$$y(t) = h^\alpha(t)x^{1-\alpha}(t) \equiv y(h(t), x(t)),$$

where $y_h > 0, y_x > 0$ for any $(h, x) \gg 0$, $h \equiv H/N$ and $x \equiv (AX)/N$, where $N(t)$ is the total labor force at t. Suppose that there are no property rights over land and the return to land is thus zero. The wage per efficiency unit of labor is therefore equal to its average product

$$w(t) = \left(\frac{x(t)}{h(t)}\right)^{1-\alpha} \equiv w(x(t), h(t)). \tag{3.7.1}$$

Each individual born at period $t-1$ lives two periods. In the first period, they consume a fraction of their parents' time. In the second period, they allocate their endowed one unit of time between child-rearing and labor force participation. In each period t a generation that consists of $N(t)$ identical individuals joins the labor force. The utility is represented by

$$u(t) = c^{1-\gamma}(t)[w(t+1)n(t)h(t+1)]^{\gamma}, \quad c(t) \geq \tilde{c} > 0,$$

where $\tilde{c}$ is a subsistence level, $n(t)$ is the number of children of individual t, $h(t+1)$ is the level of human capital of each child, and $w(t+1)$ is the wage per efficiency unit of labor at time $t+1$. The utility function is monotonically increasing and strictly quasi-concave. Let $\tau_0 + \tau e(t+1)$ be the total time for a member of generation t of raising a child with a level of education quality $e(t+1)$. Define potential income as the amount that generation t would earn if they devoted their entire time endowment to labor force participation. That is, potential income is given by $w(t)h(t)$. This income is divided between child-rearing and working. Hence, in the second period of life, the individual faces the budget constraint

$$w(t)h(t)n(t)\{\tau_0 + \tau e(t+1)\} + c(t) \leq w(t)h(t).$$

It is assumed that the level of human capital of members of generation t, $h(t+1)$, is an increasing function of their education $e(t+1)$ and a decreasing function of the rate of progress in the state of technology from period t to $t+1$

$$g(t+1) \equiv (A(t+1) - A(t))/A(t)).$$

That is

$$h(t+1) = h(e(t+1), g(t+1)), \quad h, h_e, h_{ee}, h_{eg} > 0, \quad h_g, h_{ee} < 0, \quad \forall (e, g) \geq 0.$$

It is also assumed that the "erosion effect" is assumed to become higher as a result of technological progress, i.e. $\partial y(h(t), x(t))/\partial g(t) > 0$. It is further assumed that

$$\tau_0 h_e(0, 0) - \tau h(0, 0) < 0.$$

It is straightforward to show that under this assumption, there exists a value of $\tilde{g}$ such that

$$\tau_0 h_e(0, \tilde{g}) - \tau h(0, \tilde{g}) = 0.$$

Denote by $z(t)$ and $\tilde{z}$ the level of potential income and the level of potential income at which the subsistence constraint is just binding; that is, $z(t) = h(t)w(t)$ and $\tilde{z} = \tilde{c}/(1-\gamma)$. By equation (3.7.1), we have

$$z(t) = h^\alpha(t) x^{1-\alpha}(t) = h^\alpha(e(t), g(t)) x^{1-\alpha}(t) \equiv z(e(t), g(t), x(t)). \qquad (3.7.2)$$

Members of generation t choose $n(t)$ and $h(t+1)$ to maximize their intertemporal utility function subject to the budget constraints. It can be proved that the optimal solution is characterized by the following solution:

$$n(t) = \begin{cases} \dfrac{\gamma}{\tau_0 + \tau e(g(t+1))}, & \text{if } z(t) \geq \tilde{z}, \\ \dfrac{1 - \tilde{c}/z(t)}{\tau_0 + \tau e(g(t+1))}, & \text{if } z(t) < \tilde{z}, \end{cases} \qquad (3.7.3)$$

$$\begin{cases} e(t+1) = 0, & \text{if } g(t+1) \leq \tilde{g}, \\ e(t+1) = e(g(t+1)), \ e' > 0 & \text{if } g(t+1) > \tilde{g}, \end{cases} \qquad (3.7.4)$$

where $e(g)$ is an implicit function between e and g, i.e.

$$(\tau_0 + \tau e) h_e(e, g) = \tau h(e, g).$$

It is assumed that $e'' < 0$ for any $g(t) > \tilde{g}$.

We have described the behavior of the producers and consumers. We now describe technological change by the following equation:[28]

$$g(t+1) \equiv \frac{A(t+1) - A(t)}{A(t)} = g(e(t)), \ g(0), \ g' > 0, \ g'' < 0. \qquad (3.7.5)$$

The size of working population at time $t+1$ is determined by

$$N(t+1) = n(t) N(t), \qquad (3.7.6)$$

where N_0 is historically given. Utilizing $x(t) = (A(t)X)/N(t)$, equations (3.7.5) and (3.7.6), we have

$$x(t+1) = \frac{1 + g(t+1)}{n(t)} x(t).$$

Substituting (3.7.3) and (3.7.5) into the above equation yields

$$x(t+1) = \begin{cases} \dfrac{[\tau_0 + \tau e(g(e(t)))][1 + g(e(t))]}{\gamma} x(t), & \text{if } z(t) \geq \tilde{z}, \\ \dfrac{[\tau_0 + \tau e(g(e(t)))][1 + g(e(t))]}{1 - \tilde{c}/z(t)} x(t), & \text{if } z(t) < \tilde{z}. \end{cases} \qquad (3.7.7)$$

The construction of the model is thus completed. The system consists of equations (3.7.2)–(3.7.7). In the dynamical analysis, the economy is divided into two regimes: the subsistence regime characterized by $z(t) \leq \tilde{z}$ and modern regime characterized by $z(t) > \tilde{z}$. Although the analysis is not very complicated, it will take a great deal of space to examine. The reader is encouraged to analyze the behavior of the model, and then to read the analysis by Galor and Weil.

Appendix

A.3.1 Proving Proposition 3.2.1

First, we find conditions such that $\Phi(H) = 0$ has positive solutions. We exclude the case of $x_e = x_i = 0$. It is easy to check that if $x_e > 0$ and $x_i > 0$ (which guarantees $\Phi(0) < 0$, $\Phi(\infty) > 0$ and $\Phi'(H) > 0$ for $H > 0$) or $x_e < 0$ and $x_i < 0$ (which guarantees $\Phi(0) > 0$, $\Phi(\infty) < 0$ and $\Phi'(H) < 0$ for $H > 0$), the system has a unique positive equilibrium point. We now show that in the cases of $x_e > 0$ and $x_i < 0$ (or $x_e < 0$ and $x_i > 0$), the system has two equilibrium points under some additional conditions.

We just prove one case, $x_e > 0$ and $x_i < 0$. The other case can be similarly checked. Since $x_e > 0$ and $x_i < 0$, $\Phi(0) > 0$ and $\Phi(\infty) > 0$. This implies that $\Phi(H) = 0$ has no solution, one solution, or multiple solutions. Since

$$H\Phi' = x_e \Phi_e + x_i \Phi_i,$$

Growth with Human Capital and Knowledge 173

where Φ_e and Φ_i are positive, we see that $\Phi'(H)$ may be either positive or negative, depending upon the values of x_e and x_i. If $\Phi(H) = 0$ has more than two positive solutions, there are at least two positive values of H such that $\Phi'(H) = 0$. Since $dH\Phi'/dH > 0$ strictly holds for $H > 0$, it is impossible for $\Phi'(H) = 0$ to have more than one solution. Accordingly, $\Phi(H) = 0$ has no, one or two solutions. A necessary and sufficient condition for the existence of two equilibrium points is that there exists a value of H^* such that $\Phi(H^*) < 0$. It should be noted that it is straightforward to show that as the parameters vary, the system may experience bifurcations from a single equilibrium point to two equilibrium points. Although the bifurcation analysis for this model is not difficult and it is not difficult to simulate the conditions,[29] the analysis is tedious and provides few new insights. We omit this issue.

The stability conditions are confirmed by calculating the two eigenvalues.

4
Growth with Heterogeneous Households

One dominant view on the interplay between growth and inequality holds that income inequality promotes saving and therefore promotes development. This opinion is closely related to the view that saving is the engine of growth. Lewis (1954: 156–57) expounds this view as follows:

> We are interested not in the people in general, but only say in the 10 percent of them with the largest incomes. ... The remaining 90 percent of the people never manage to save a significant fraction of their incomes. ... Saving increases relatively to the national income because the incomes of the savers increase relatively to the national income. The central fact of economic development is that the distribution of income is altered in favour of the saving class.

Nevertheless, this view has been called into question by the combination in the high-performing East Asian economies of relatively equal distributions of income with rates of growth in per capita income (and with savings rates) that were among the world's highest.[1]

Some economists maintain that inequality normally increases in earlier phases of modern economic growth, then reduces, and increases again later on. This implies that a country seeking economic advancement will first experience growth with increasing inequality. Kuznets (1955) conjectured that something like this may well have happened during the course of economic development in currently advanced economies. Williamson and Lindert (1980) studied the dynamics of income inequality in the US. They showed that Kuznets' hypothesis does hold for the US economy. Income and wealth inequality increased with the beginning of America's modern economic growth in the early 19th century. Inequality tended to be reduced with the advent of mature capitalist development in the 20th century. In the interim, the US economy experienced extensive inequality for seven decades. The wage structure around 1816 was quite narrow. The difference in the nominal pay for common labor and skilled workers such as engineers, teachers, carpenters, and mechanics rose rapidly between 1816 and 1856. A slight decline in later 19th-century pay ratios was followed by another abrupt increase in difference between the 1890s and 1914. The advantages gained by the skilled groups were maintained and even reinforced through 1916. The US enjoyed the longest period of shared prosperity in history from the 1940s into the 1970s. During this period, a worker with even limited formal education could earn a middle-class income if he was willing to work hard. However, since the energy price shocks of the 1970s, the American economy began to experience slower growth in productivity and output, and a rise in long-term joblessness. Perhaps the most serious problem has been the widening income gap between the poor and the rich, associated with the slowdown in economic growth. The recent prosperity in the US is enjoyed by the rich; most Americans have not benefited from it.[2] Since the late 1970s, the US has experienced substantial rises in wage inequality. By 1993, it reached a peak not seen since the end of the Great Depression. The Census Bureau estimates that the Gini coefficient of family income inequality rose from 0.365 to 0.425 or about 16 percent between 1979 and 1996.

Figure 4.0.1 shows the wage inequality for the years 1979, 1989, and 1996.[3] The wage ratio is the ratio of a worker in the 90th percentile of the wage distribution to that of a worker in the 10th percentile of the distribution. For men, the ratio increased from 3.67 in 1979 to 4.23 in 1989 and to 4.45 by 1996. For women, the ratio increased from 2.71 in 1979 to 3.85 in 1989 and then to 4.02 by 1996. The figure unambiguously shows that earnings inequality jumped among men. The situation among women is more complicated. We see that the level of inequality among women workers was below that of men. It has been observed that in some economies the relative supply of college-educated workers has increased noticeably and the wage ratio between college graduates and high-school graduates has risen substantially.[4] For instance, Autor et al. (1998) show that in the US, the ratio of college equivalents (defined as the number of workers with a college degree plus 0.5 of the number of workers with some college education) to noncollege equivalents (defined as the complementary set of workers) increased at an average rate of 3.05 percent between 1970 and 1995, up from an average rate of 2.35 percent between 1940 and 1970. In the meantime, the ratio between the average weekly wages of college and high-school graduates went up by more than 25 percent during the period 1970–1995, whilst it fell by 0.11 percent a year on average during the previous period. Moreover, wage inequality also increased sharply within educational and age groups.[5]

Wealth ownership seems to be concentrated in the hands of a small (and ever smaller) minority of the population in the US. Enlarged wealth distribution tends to strengthen social conflicts in democratic society since those who have wealth tend not only to maintain that wealth but also to accumulate more, while those who own little tend to acquire less wealth (Keister, 2000).[6] According to Keister, wealth inequality has become more concentrated in the 1980s and 1990s than in the 1960s in the US. It was estimated that the top 1 percent of wealth owners enjoyed two-thirds of all increases in household financial wealth, while the bottom 80 percent actually owned less real financial wealth in 1998 than in 1983. It appears that the US has surpassed all industrial societies in family wealth inequality.[7]

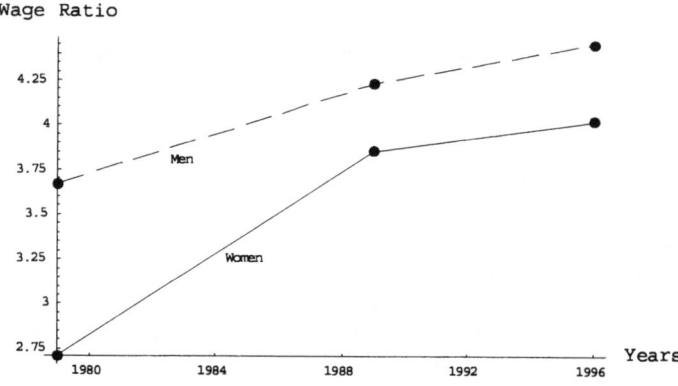

Figure 4.0.1 Enlarged wage differences in the US, 1979–96

Irrespective of widely observed changes of inequalities in income and wealth in different societies, economics still lacks proper theories for examining dynamics of income and wealth distribution over time and space. Atkinson and Bourguignon[8] describe the current situation as follows:

No unified theory of income distribution actually exists. Even though several titles of books and articles announce quite ambitiously the state of such a "theory of income distribution", they typically refer to only one part of what actually be covered by such a theory: the determination of wages in the labor market, factor shares, the accumulation of wealth, etc. Rather than a unified theory, the literature thus offers a series of building blocks with which distribution issues are to be studied. Because of the natural complexity of the subject, however, no serious attempt at integrating them has really been made.

As shown in this book, the OSG modeling framework enables us to make, at least, one serious attempt at integrating different ideas.

Chapter 4 introduces heterogeneous households into one-sector growth economies. We emphasize interdependence of growth and income and wealth distribution among various households. Section 4.1 examines a dynamic interdependence of two groups with different productivity and preferences within the OSG framework. Section 4.2 studies the OSG model with any number of types of households. After writing the economic dynamics, we simulate the model with three groups of households. Section 4.3 introduces knowledge creation and utilization to the two-group model. Section 4.4 illustrates a widely used approach to issues related to growth with inequality. The model is proposed by Moav. It demonstrates persistence of inequality. In this model, the evolution of income within each dynasty in society is governed by a dynamical system that generates a poverty trap equilibrium point along with a high-income equilibrium point. Section 4.5 is concerned with interactions between human capital accumulation, economic growth, and inequality. In Section 4.6, we discuss issues related to how to aggregate labor input of heterogeneous labors.

4.1 The OSG model of two-type households

In reality, there are no two identical products or inputs. Economic approaches, which can only deal with a perfect world with a single identical product and identical people, tend to be ineffective for providing insights into reality. For instance, the Ramsey approach to consumers does not provide an effective way to deal with economic dynamics with heterogeneous households, not to mention to study economies of multiple regions and countries with heterogeneous households. Nevertheless, macroeconomic analysis relies on proper aggregation and the aggregation rests upon intrinsic similarities. As argued by Lancaster (1966), it is important to distinguish goods or labor force according to their characteristics. For human capital distributions, the distinction is accomplished by viewing a laborer as a vector of characteristics or skill. We may classify the population into m categories or classes and assume that there are n distinct characteristics. A class is defined as a group of persons who are each perfect substitutes for all others in the class. This section examines a dynamic interdependence of two groups with different productivity and preferences, following the framework proposed in Section 2.1.

4.1.1 The OSG model of two-type households

The production aspects of the economic system under consideration are similar to the OSG model in Section 2.1. Let there be two groups of consumers, indexed by j, in the economy. Each type of consumer has a fixed number of the population, denoted by N_j. The aggregated labor force, N, is given by

$$N = z_1 N_1 + z_2 N_2,$$

where z_j are the level of human capital of group j, $j = 1, 2$. We assume z_j to be fixed.

We now study the behavior of producers. Let $K(t)$ denote the capital stock at time t and N the flow of labor services used at t for production. We use the conventional production function to describe a relationship between inputs and output. The rate of interest and the wage rate are determined by the markets. Hence, for any individual firm r and w_j are given at each point in time. The production sector chooses the two variables, K and N, to maximize its profit. Denote by δ_k ($0 \leq \delta_k < 1$) the depreciation rate of physical capital. The marginal conditions are given by

$$r(t) + \delta_k = f'(k(t)),$$
$$w_j(t) = z_j w(t), \quad w(t) \equiv f(k(t)) - k(t) f'(k(t)). \tag{4.1.1}$$

The ratio of wage rates is equal to the ratio of the human capital levels between the two groups.

We now describe the behavior of consumers. Each consumer of group j obtains the current income

$$y_j(t) = r(t) k_j(t) + w_j(t), \quad j = 1, 2, \tag{4.1.2}$$

from the interest payment, rk_j, and the wage payment, w_j. The disposable income is given by

$$\hat{y}_j(t) = y_j(t) + k_j(t). \tag{4.1.3}$$

The budget constraints are given by

$$c_j(t) + s_j(t) = \hat{y}_j(t) = rk_j(t) + w_j(t) + k_j(t). \tag{4.1.4}$$

We assume that the utility level, $U(t)$, that the consumers obtain is dependent on the consumption level of the commodity, $c_j(t)$, and the saving, $s_j(t)$. The utility level of group j, $U_j(t)$, is specified as follows:

$$U_j(t) = c_j^{\xi_j}(t)s_j^{\lambda_j}(t), \quad \xi_j, \lambda_j > 0, \quad \xi_j + \lambda_j = 1, \quad j = 1, 2,$$

where ξ_j and λ_j are respectively group j's propensities to consume and to hold wealth. Here, for simplicity, we specify the utility function with the Cobb-Douglas form. It would provide more insights if we take some other forms of utility functions. Maximizing U_j subject to the budget constraints (4.1.4) yields

$$c_j(t) = \xi_j \hat{y}_j(t), \quad s_j(t) = \lambda_j \hat{y}_j(t). \tag{4.1.5}$$

According to the definitions of $s_j(t)$, group j's wealth accumulation is given by

$$\dot{k}_j = s_j - k_j.$$

Substituting $s_j(t)$ in equations (4.1.5) into the above equation yields

$$\dot{k}_j(t) = \lambda_j y_j(t) - \xi_j k_j(t). \tag{4.1.6}$$

As output is either consumed or saved, the sum of net savings and consumption equals output. That is

$$C(t) + S(t) - K(t) + \delta_k K(t) = F(t),$$

where $C(t)$ is the sum of consumption and $S(t) - K(t) + \delta_k K(t)$ is the sum of net savings of the two groups

$$C(t) = \sum_j c_j(t) N_j, \quad S(t) - \delta K(t) = \sum_j (s_j(t) - \delta k_j(t)) N_j,$$

where $\delta \equiv 1 - \delta_k$. It can be shown that the above equation is redundant. We have thus built the dynamic model. The dynamics consists of two-dimensional differential equations for k_1 and k_2. In order to analyze properties of the dynamic system, it is necessary to express the dynamics in terms of the two variables at any point in time. From the definitions of k_j and K, we have

$$n_1 k_1 + n_2 k_2 = k,$$

where $n_j \equiv N_j/N$ and $k \equiv K/N$. From equations (4.1.1) and (4.1.2) and the definitions of $y_j(t)$, we see that the dynamics of the system are given by the two-dimensional dynamic system (4.1.6) with two variables $k_1(t)$ and $k_2(t)$. It is straightforward to show that all the other variables are uniquely determined as functions of $k_1(t)$ and $k_2(t)$ at any point in time.

4.1.2 Equilibrium and stability

We now rewrite the dynamics in terms of per capita. Substituting equations (4.1.1) into equations (4.1.2) yields

$$y_j(t) = z_j f(k(t)) + (k_j(t) - z_j k(t))f'(k(t)) - \delta_k k_j(t).$$

From the above equations and equations (4.1.6), we have

$$\dot{k}_j(t) = \lambda_j \Omega_j(k_1(t), k_2(t)) - \lambda_j \bar{\delta}_j k_j(t), \quad j = 1, 2, \tag{4.1.7}$$

where

$$\Omega_j(k_1, k_2) \equiv z_j f(k) + (k_j - z_j k)f'(k), \quad \bar{\delta}_j \equiv \delta_k + \frac{\xi_j}{\lambda_j}.$$

First, we show that the system has a unique nontrivial equilibrium point. At equilibrium

$$\Omega_j(k_1, k_1) = \bar{\delta}_j k_j.$$

Substitute $\Omega_j = z_j f(k) + (k_j - z_j k)f'(k)$ into these equations:

$$\left(\frac{f(k) - kf'(k)}{\bar{\delta}_j - f'(k)}\right) z_j = k_j. \tag{4.1.8}$$

As f is strictly concave, $f(k) - kf'(k) > 0$ for $k > 0$. For $k_j > 0$, we thus should require $\bar{\delta}_j - f'(k) > 0$, $j = 1, 2$. Define

$$\bar{k} \equiv \max_j\{k: f'(k) = \delta_j\}.$$

Because $f''(k) < 0$

$$\lim_{k \to 0} f'(0) = \infty, \quad \lim_{k \to +\infty} f'(0) = 0,$$

we see that $\bar{k}$ is uniquely defined. Obviously

$$\delta_j - f'(k) > 0 \text{ for } k > \bar{k}, \quad j = 1, 2,$$
$$\delta_j - f'(k) < 0 \text{ for some } j \text{ if } k < \bar{k}.$$

We should require $k > \bar{k}$.

Multiplying the two sides of each equation by n_j and then adding the two equations in equations (4.1.8) yields

$$\left(\frac{n_1 z_1}{\delta_1 - f'(k)} + \frac{n_2 z_2}{\delta_2 - f'(k)}\right)\left(\frac{f(k)}{k} - f'(k)\right) = 1, \quad k > \bar{k}, \quad (4.1.9)$$

where we use $n_1 k_1 + n_2 k_2 = k$. We now show that this equation has a unique solution for $k > \bar{k}$. Introduce

$$\Phi(k) \equiv \left(\frac{n_1 z_1}{\delta_1 - f'(k)} + \frac{n_2 z_2}{\delta_2 - f'(k)}\right)\left(\frac{f(k)}{k} - f'(k)\right) - 1.$$

As $\Phi(k) \to +\infty$ as $k \to \bar{k}$ from the right and $\Phi(+\infty) \to -1$, we conclude that $\Phi(k) = 0$ has at least one solution for $k \in (\bar{k}, +\infty)$. Here, we use

$$\frac{f(k)}{k} \to 0 \text{ as } k \to \infty,$$
$$\lim_{k \to \infty} \frac{f(k)}{k} = \frac{\lim_{k \to \infty} f'(k)}{\lim_{k \to \infty} 1} = 0.$$

We calculate

$$\Phi' = \left[\frac{n_1 z_1}{(\delta_1 - f'(k))^2} + \frac{n_2 z_2}{(\delta_2 - f'(k))^2}\right]\left(\frac{f(k)}{k} - f'(k)\right)f''(k)$$
$$- \left(\frac{n_1 z_1}{\delta_1 - f'(k)} + \frac{n_2 z_2}{\delta_2 - f'(k)}\right)\frac{\Delta(k)}{k^2}.$$

We see that if

$$\Delta(k) \equiv f - kf' + k^2 f'' \geq 0,$$

then $\Phi'(k) \leq 0$ for $k \in (\bar{k}, +\infty)$. It should be noted that even if the term $f - kf' + k^2 f''$ is negative, $\Phi'(k) \leq 0$ may hold. Hence, if

$$\Delta(k) \geq 0, \quad k \in (\bar{k}, +\infty), \tag{4.1.10}$$

the equation $\Phi(k) = 0$ has a unique solution. It is straightforward to check that if F takes on the Cobb-Douglas form, then (4.1.10) holds. If the production function takes on the CES form

$$f = A(ak^\sigma + 1)^{1/\rho},$$

where $\sigma < 1$, a and A are positive, we calculate

$$\Delta(k) = \left(\frac{1 + (\sigma - 1)^2 ak^\sigma}{ak^\sigma + 1}\right) f > 0.$$

For any positive solution k^* $(> \bar{k})$, we solve k_1 and k_2 by equations (4.1.8). We get r and w_j by equations (4.1.1), y_j by equations (4.1.2), $\hat{y}_j$ by equations (4.1.3), and c_j and s_j by equations (4.1.5).

For illustration, we examine the case when $f(k) = k^\alpha$, where $0 < \alpha < 1$. By definition

$$\bar{k} \equiv \max_i \left\{\left(\frac{\delta_i}{\alpha}\right)^{1/(\alpha-1)}, \quad i = 1, 2\right\}.$$

As

$$\Delta(k) = (1-\alpha)^2 k^\alpha > 0,$$

the system has a unique nontrivial equilibrium, $k \in (\bar{k}, +\infty)$. In summary, we get the following proposition.

Proposition 4.1.1
The dynamic system has at least one equilibrium point. If

$$\Delta(k) \geq 0, \quad k \in (\bar{k}, +\infty),$$

the system has a unique stable equilibrium point.

The stability part is proved in Appendix A.4.2.
It should be noted that from equations (4.1.8) we obtain

$$\frac{k_1}{z_1} - \frac{k_2}{z_2} = \frac{(\lambda_1 - \lambda_2)(f - kf')}{\lambda_1 \lambda_2 (\delta_1 - f')(\delta_2 - f')}.$$

Noting that $f - kf'$ and $\delta_j - f'$ are positive, we see that the sign of $k_1/z_1 - k_2/z_2$ is the same as that of $\lambda_1 - \lambda_2$. If one group's propensity to save is higher than the other group, then the wealth per qualified capita of the former is more than that of the latter. The differences in wealth per qualified capita are determined by the differences in propensities to save among different groups. It should be noted that the sign of $k_1 - k_2$ is not determined solely by $\lambda_1 - \lambda_2$. For instance, if $\lambda_1 - \lambda_2 > 0$ and $z_2 - z_1 > 0$, $k_1 - k_2 < 0$ is possible. From equations (4.1.8), we have

$$k_1 - k_2 = \left(\frac{\lambda_1 z_1 - \lambda_2 z_2}{\lambda_1 \lambda_2} - (z_1 - z_2)(1 + f' - \delta_k) \right) \frac{(f - kf')}{(\delta_1 - f')(\delta_2 - f')}.$$

At equilibrium, we have $\hat{y}_j = k_j / \lambda_j$. From equations (4.1.8), we have

$$\hat{y}_1 - \hat{y}_2$$
$$= ((z_1 - z_2)(1 + \delta_k) - (z_1 \lambda_2 - z_2 \lambda_1)(1 + f')) \frac{(f - kf')}{(\delta_k + \xi_2 - f')(\delta_k + \xi_1 - \lambda_1 f')}.$$

We can obtain explicit conclusions about the signs of differences in the key variables only when one group does not have a lower level of the propensity to save and lower level of human capital than the other group. That is $\lambda_1 \geq \lambda_2$ and $z_1 \geq z_2$. Otherwise, the relative economic conditions of the two groups tend to be ambiguous.

4.1.3 Different levels of human capital

We now examine impact of changes in human capital and preference. We assume that $\Delta(k) \geq 0$ for any $k \in (\bar{k}, +\infty)$. There is a unique equilibrium point under presumed $\Delta(k) \geq 0$. Taking derivatives of $\Phi(k) = 0$ with respect to z_1 yields

$$-\Phi' \frac{dk}{dz_1} = (\lambda_1 - \lambda_2) \frac{n_2 z_1 z_2}{\lambda_1 \lambda_2 (\delta_1 - f')(\delta_2 - f')} \left(\frac{f}{k} - f' \right) < 0,$$

where $\Phi' < 0$ is given by equation (4.1.9). We see that the sign of dk/dz_1 is the same as that of $\lambda_1 - \lambda_2$. As group 1's human capital is increased, k is increased (decreased) if group 1's propensity is higher (lower) than group 2's. If $\lambda_1 = \lambda_2$, then k is not affected. By equations (4.1.8), we obtain

$$\frac{dk_1}{dz_1} = \frac{k_1}{z_1} + \left(\frac{f}{k} - \delta_1 \right) \frac{k^2 f'' z_1}{(\delta_1 - f')^2} \frac{dk}{dz_1},$$

$$\frac{dk_2}{dz_1} = \left(\frac{f}{k} - \delta_2 \right) \frac{k^2 f'' z_2}{(\delta_2 - f')^2} \frac{dk}{dz_1}.$$

As shown in Appendix A.4.2, if $\lambda_1 > (<) \lambda_2$, then

$$\frac{f}{k} - \delta_2 < (>) 0, \quad \frac{f}{k} - \delta_1 > (<) 0.$$

If $\lambda_1 = \lambda_2$, $f/k - \delta_j = 0$. From these results, the following lemma follows.

Lemma 4.1.1

As group 1's human capital is increased: (i) if group 1's propensity to save is higher than group 2's (i.e., $\lambda_1 > \lambda_2$), change in group 1's wealth per capita is ambiguous and group 2's wealth per capita increases; (ii) if $\lambda_1 = \lambda_2$, then group 1's wealth per capita increases but group 2's wealth per capita is not affected; and (iii) if $\lambda_1 < \lambda_2$, change in group 1's wealth per capita is ambiguous and group 2's wealth per capita increases.

We directly get the impact on s_j by $s_j = k_j$. By (4.1.1), $y_j = c_j = \xi_j k_j / \lambda_j$, we get

$$\frac{dr}{dz_1} = f'' \frac{dk}{dz_1},$$

$$\frac{dw_1}{dz_1} = -z_1 kf'' \frac{dk}{dz_1} + \frac{w_1}{z_1},$$

$$\frac{dw_2}{dz_1} = -z_2 kf'' \frac{dk}{dz_1},$$

$$\frac{1}{y_j}\frac{dy_j}{dz_1} = \frac{1}{c_j}\frac{dc_j}{dz_1} = \frac{1}{k_j}\frac{dk_j}{dz_1}.$$

From Lemma 4.1.1, as group 1's human capital is improved, in the case of $\lambda_1 > (<) \lambda_2$, the rate of interest decreases (increases); the change direction in group 2's wage rate is the opposite to that of the rate of interest.

4.1.4 Preference differences

We now study the impact of change in group 1's propensity to save on the equilibrium structure. Taking the derivative of $\Phi(k) = 0$ with respect to λ_1 yields

$$-\Phi'\frac{dk}{d\lambda_1} = \left(\frac{n_1 z_1 \xi_1}{(\delta_1 - f')^2 \lambda_1^2}\right)\left(\frac{f}{k} - f'\right) > 0.$$

As group 1's propensity to save is increased, k is increased. By equation (4.1.8), we obtain

$$\frac{1}{k_1}\frac{dk_1}{d\lambda_1} = \frac{1}{s_1}\frac{ds_1}{d\lambda_1} = \left(\frac{f - \delta_1 k}{\delta_1 - f'}\right)f''\frac{dk}{d\lambda_1} + \frac{\xi_1}{(\delta_1 - f')\lambda_1^2},$$

$$\frac{1}{k_2}\frac{dk_2}{d\lambda_1} = \frac{1}{s_2}\frac{ds_2}{d\lambda_1} = \left(\frac{f - \delta_2 k}{\delta_2 - f'}\right)f''\frac{dk}{d\lambda_1}.$$

Lemma 4.1.2

As group 1's propensity to save is increased: (i) if group 1's propensity to save is higher than group 2's (i.e., $\lambda_1 > \lambda_2$), change in group 1's wealth per capita is ambiguous and group 2's wealth per capita increases; (ii) if $\lambda_1 = \lambda_2$, then group 1's wealth per capita increases but group 2's wealth per capita is not affected; and (iii) if $\lambda_1 < \lambda_2$, change in group 1's wealth per capita is increased and group 2's wealth per capita is decreased.

By (4.1.1), $y_j = c_j = \xi_j k_j / \lambda_j$, we get

$$\frac{dr}{d\lambda_1} = f'' \frac{dk}{d\lambda_1} < 0,$$

$$\frac{dw_j}{d\lambda_1} = -z_j kf'' \frac{dk}{d\lambda_1} > 0,$$

$$\frac{1}{y_1}\frac{dy_1}{d\lambda_1} = \frac{1}{c_1}\frac{dc_1}{d\lambda_1} = \frac{1}{k_1}\frac{dk_1}{d\lambda_1} - \frac{1}{\lambda_1},$$

$$\frac{1}{y_2}\frac{dy_2}{d\lambda_1} = \frac{1}{c_2}\frac{dc_2}{d\lambda_1} = \frac{1}{k_2}\frac{dk_2}{d\lambda_1}.$$

As group 1's propensity to save is increased, the rate of interest declines; each group's wage rate increases. The direction of changes in group 2's current income and consumption level is the same as that in group 2's per capita wealth.

4.2 The OSG model with heterogeneous groups

It is straightforward to extend the two-group model of the previous section to multiple groups of consumers. We may generally assume that the population is N_0 and the population can be classified into M groups, indexed by j, according to their preferences, wealth, human capital, and social status. We have $N_0 \geq M$.[9] Two extreme cases are $M = N_0$ and $M = 1$. Let the number of group j be N_j. The aggregated labor force, N, is given by

$$N_0 = \sum_{j=1}^{M} z_j N_j,$$

where z_j are the level of human capital or the work time of group j. The neoclassical production function is

$$F(t) = F(K(t), N).$$

Let K, r, w_j, and δ_k ($0 \leq \delta_k < 1$) be defined as before. The marginal conditions are given by

$$r(t) + \delta_k = f'(k(t)),$$
$$w_j(t) = z_j w(t), \quad w(t) \equiv f(k(t)) - k(t)f'(k(t)),$$

where $k \equiv K/N$. The per capita disposable income of group j is

$$\hat{y}_j(t) = y_j(t) + k_j(t), \quad j = 1, 2, \cdots, M,$$

where

$$y_j(t) = r(t)k_j(t) + w_j(t).$$

The budget constraint is given by

$$c_j(t) + s_j(t) = \hat{y}_j(t).$$

Consumer j maximizes the utility level

$$U_j(t) = c_j^{\xi_j}(t) s_j^{\lambda_j}(t), \quad \xi_j, \lambda_j > 0, \quad j = 1, 2, \cdots, M,$$

subject to the budget constraint. The optimal solution is

$$c_j(t) = \xi_j \hat{y}_j(t), \quad s_j(t) = \lambda_j \hat{y}_j(t).$$

As in equations (4.1.7), group j's wealth accumulation is given by

$$\dot{k}_j(t) = \lambda_j \Omega_j(k_1(t), \cdots, k_M(t)) - \lambda_j \delta_j k_j(t), \quad j = 1, \cdots, M, \tag{4.2.1}$$

where

$$\Omega_j(k_1(t), \cdots, k_M(t)) \equiv z_j f(k) + (k_j - z_j k) f'(k), \quad \bar{\delta}_j \equiv \delta_k + \frac{\xi_j}{\lambda_j}.$$

As in equations (4.1.8), an equilibrium point is determined by

$$\left(\frac{f(k) - kf'(k)}{\bar{\delta}_j - f'(k)} \right) z_j = k_j. \qquad (4.2.2)$$

Multiplying the two sides of each equation by n_j and then adding the M equations yields

$$\left(\sum_{j=1}^{M} \frac{n_j z_j}{\bar{\delta}_j - f'(k)} \right) \left(\frac{f(k)}{k} - f'(k) \right) = 1, \quad k > \bar{k}.$$

Introduce

$$\bar{k} \equiv \max_j \{ k : f'(k) = \bar{\delta}_j \}, \quad \Delta(k) \equiv f - kf' + k^2 f'' \geq 0.$$

We can prove the following proposition as Proposition 4.1.1.

Proposition 4.2.1

The dynamic system has at least one equilibrium point. If $\Delta(k) \geq 0$, $k \in (\bar{k}, +\infty)$, the system has a unique equilibrium point.

As in the case of $M = 2$, when

$$f(k) = k^\alpha, \quad 0 < \alpha < 1$$

or

$$f = A(ak^\sigma + 1)^{1/\rho},$$

where $\sigma < 1$, a and A are positive, the dynamic system has a unique equilibrium point. We omit analyzing stability properties of the equilibrium point. For illustration, we simulate the model when $M = 3$. The aggregated labor force N is

$$N = \sum_{j=1}^{3} z_j N_j,$$

where z_j is the level of human capital of group j, $j = 1, 2, 3$. Suppose that the production function takes the Cobb-Douglas form. The production function and marginal conditions are

$$F = AK^\alpha N^\beta, \quad r = \frac{\alpha F}{K}, \quad w_j = \frac{\beta z_j F}{N},$$

where A is the total productivity. Let $K_j(t)$ and $Y_j(t)$ be respectively the capital stocks owned by group j and the current income level of group j. The total capital, $K(t)$, and total current income, $Y(t)$, are

$$K(t) = \sum_{1}^{3} K_j(t), \quad Y(t) = \sum_{1}^{3} Y_j(t),$$

where $K_j(t) = k_j(t)N_j$ and $Y_j(t) = y_j(t)N_j$. The consumer behavior is described by

$$c_j(t) = \xi_j \hat{y}_j(t), \quad s_j(t) = \lambda_j \hat{y}_j(t).$$

To simulate the model, we specify the groups' human capital and preferences as follows:

$$\begin{pmatrix} z_1 \\ z_2 \\ z_3 \end{pmatrix} = \begin{pmatrix} 3 \\ 1 \\ 0.5 \end{pmatrix}, \begin{pmatrix} \lambda_1 \\ \lambda_2 \\ \lambda_3 \end{pmatrix} = \begin{pmatrix} 0.8 \\ 0.65 \\ 0.50 \end{pmatrix}, \begin{pmatrix} N_1 \\ N_2 \\ N_3 \end{pmatrix} = \begin{pmatrix} 1 \\ 5 \\ 10 \end{pmatrix}.$$

Group 1 is the rich class – with the highest level of human capital and highest propensity to own wealth. The population share of the rich in the total population is only 1/16 percent. Group 2 is the middle class – with the middle level of human capital and "middle propensity" to own wealth. The population of this group is

5/16 percent. Group 3 has the lowest level of human capital and the lowest propensity to own wealth. This group has the largest share in the total population. We specify the rest of the parameters as follows:

$$\alpha = 0.25, \quad A = 1.3, \quad \delta_k = 0.05.$$

The three eigenvalues are given by

$$\rho_1 = -0.449554, \quad \rho_2 = -0.29414, \quad \rho_3 = -0.160935.$$

The equilibrium point is stable. The motion of the total income, consumption, wealth, the wage rates, the rate of interest, the individual incomes, and individual consumption levels are illustrated in Figure 4.2.1. The dynamics approach the long-term equilibrium point. It is important to note that the difference in consumption levels between the rich and the poor is quite large in the long term because of the differences in human capital and the propensity to save.

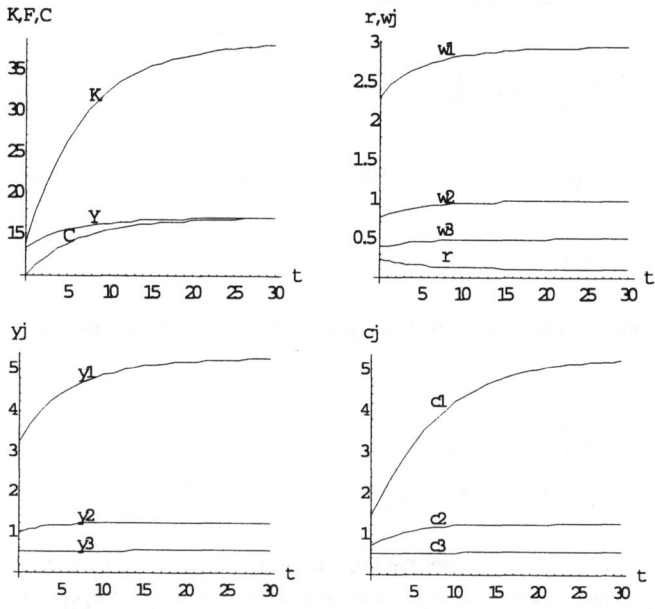

Figure 4.2.1 The time-dependent paths of the key variables

As the dynamic system has a unique equilibrium point, we may examine the impact of changes in the parameters. We allow some parameters to change. For instance, we consider that group 3 which has the lowest level of human capital and lowest level of propensity to save improves the level of human capital and increases the propensity to save in the following way:

$$z_3: 0.5 \Rightarrow 0.7; \quad \lambda_3: 0.5 \Rightarrow 0.65.$$

We simulate the dynamics again. We calculate the three eigenvalues as

$$\rho_1 = -0.305305, \quad \rho_2 = -0.292974, \quad \rho_3 = -0.159902.$$

The unique equilibrium point is stable. We depict the dynamics in Figure 4.2.2 with the same initial conditions as in Figure 4.2.1. We observe that as group 3 improves its human capital and increases its propensity to save, the aggregated wealth, K, total consumption, C, and total current income, Y are increased over time. The wage rates of the three groups are increased. The rate of interest declines. In particular, group 3's per capita current income and consumption are improved greatly. In our competitive economy where capital accumulation is the only engine of economic growth, an improvement in any group's human capital or propensity to save will benefit the group itself as well as other groups. If we allow the possibility of unemployment as in the Keynesian economy, this conclusion will not always hold.

4.3 Growth with knowledge and multiple groups

The production aspects of the economic system under consideration are similar to the model in Section 2.1. The output and the rate of interest are denoted respectively by $F(t)$ and $r(t)$. The population is classified into two groups, indexed respectively by group 1 and group 2. The variables N_j, $K_j(t)$, $C_j(t)$, $S_j(t)$, and $w_j(t)$ are defined as in Section 4.1. We assume that the labor and capital are always fully employed. The total capital stock $K(t)$ and the total qualified labor force $N^*(t)$ are given by

$$K_1(t) + K_2(t) = K(t), \quad N^*(t) = N_1^*(t) + N_2^*(t),$$

where

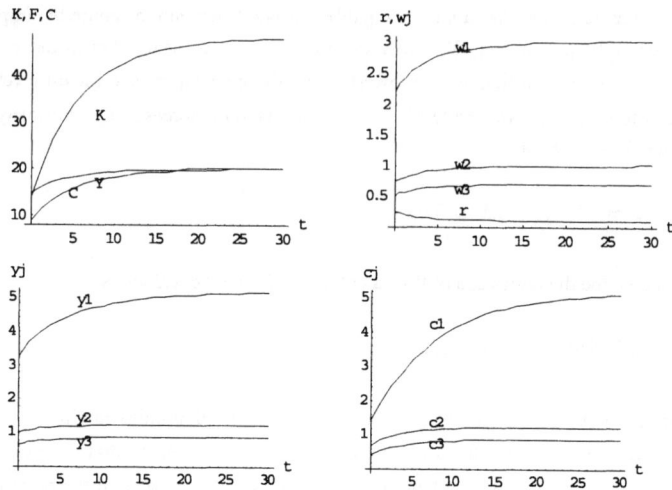

Figure 4.2.2 The poorest group improves human capital and increases the propensity to save

$$N_j^*(t) \equiv Z(t)^{m_j} N_j$$

and m_j (≥ 0) is group j's efficiency of knowledge utilization. The parameters, m_j, distinguish the difference in productivity of the two groups. The production function is

$$F(t) = K^\alpha N^{*\beta},$$

where $\alpha + \beta = 1$. The marginal conditions are given by

$$r + \delta_k = \frac{\alpha F}{K}, \quad w_j = \frac{\beta Z^{m_j} F}{N^*}, \quad j = 1, 2.$$

The current incomes, Y_j, are given by $Y_j = rK_j + w_j N_j$. The incomes per capita are given by

$$y_j = rk_j + w_j,$$

where

$$y_j \equiv \frac{Y_j}{N_j}, \quad k_j \equiv \frac{K_j}{N_j}, \quad n \equiv \frac{N_1}{N_2}.$$

Specify the utility functions as $U_j = C_j^{\xi_j} S_j^{\lambda_j}$, where $\xi_j + \lambda_j = 1$. Group j's consumption and savings are

$$C_j(t) = \xi_j \hat{Y}_j(t), \quad S_j(t) = \lambda_j \hat{Y}_j(t),$$

where $\hat{Y}_j \equiv Y_j + K_j$. Group j's capital accumulation is

$$\dot{K}_j(t) = Y_j(t) - \xi_j K_j(t). \tag{4.3.1}$$

For simplicity, we only take account of learning by doing in knowledge accumulation. We propose the following possible dynamics of knowledge:

$$\dot{Z} = \frac{\tau_1 N_1^* F}{N^* Z^{\varepsilon_1}} + \frac{\tau_2 N_2^* F}{N^* Z^{\varepsilon_2}} - \delta_z Z, \tag{4.3.2}$$

in which $\tau_j \, (\geq 0), \varepsilon_j$, and $\delta_z \, (> 0)$ are parameters. Here, we interpret $\tau_j N_j^* F / N^* Z^{\varepsilon_j}$ as group j's contribution to knowledge accumulation through learning by doing. The term F/N^* is equal to production scale per unity of the qualified labor force. We assume that the contribution to knowledge creation of group j is positively and linearly related to the group's total production scale, $N_j^* F/N^*$. The parameters, ε_j, in $1/Z^{\varepsilon_j}$ measure returns to scale in the knowledge accumulation by group j. We interpret τ_j as a measurement of the knowledge accumulation efficiency of group j.

We have thus built the model with endogenous capital and knowledge and wealth distribution between the two groups. The dynamics consist of equations (4.3.1) and (4.3.2). We now express the dynamics in terms of $K_j(t)$ and $Z(t)$. Using the definition of N^*, $F = K^{\alpha} N^{*\beta}$, and

$$Y_j = \left(\frac{\alpha K_j}{K} + \frac{\beta N_j Z^{m_j}}{N^*} \right) F - \delta_k K_j,$$

we express equations (4.3.1) and (4.3.2) as

$$\dot{K}_j = \lambda_j \left\{ \left(\frac{\alpha K_j}{K} + \frac{\beta N_j Z^{m_j}}{N^*} \right) K^\alpha N^{*\beta} - \delta_j K_j \right\},$$

$$\dot{Z} = \left(\tau_1 N_1 Z^{m_1 - \varepsilon_1} + \tau_2 N_2 Z^{m_2 - \varepsilon_2} \right) \frac{K^\alpha}{N^{*\alpha}} - \delta_z Z, \qquad (4.3.3)$$

where $\delta_j \equiv \xi_j / \lambda_j + \delta_k$. This is a three-dimensional dynamic system. We may analyze dynamic properties when the two groups have the same preference structure, i.e. $\lambda_1 = \lambda_2$. This special case has already been examined by Zhang (1999: Section 5.4). Introduce

$$x_j \equiv m_j - \varepsilon_j - 1, \quad j = 1, 2.$$

According to Zhang's analysis, the following proposition holds.

Proposition 4.3.1
Assume $\lambda_1 = \lambda_2$. Then
If $x_1 < 0$ and $x_2 < 0$, the system has a unique stable equilibrium point;
If $x_1 > 0$ and $x_2 > 0$, the system has a unique unstable equilibrium point;
If $x_1 > 0$ and $x_2 < 0$ ($x_1 < 0$ and $x_2 > 0$), the system has either one equilibrium point, two equilibrium points or no equilibrium point. When it has two equilibrium points, the one with low values of K and Z is stable; the other one is unstable.

As the two parameters x_j determine the properties of the system, to interpret the above proposition, we only need to interpret the parameters, x_j. As m_j is the knowledge utilization efficiency parameter and ε_j is returns to scale in the knowledge accumulation, we may interpret $m_j - \varepsilon_j - 1$ as measurement of returns to scale in the whole system. We may thus make the following interpretations of the parameters. We say that the knowledge utilization and creation of group j exhibit increasing (decreasing) return to scale in the dynamic system when $x_j < (>) 0$. We can thus interpret Proposition 4.3.1 as follows: if the knowledge utilization and creation of the two groups exhibit decreasing (increasing) returns to scale in the system, the system has a unique stable (unstable) equilibrium; and if the knowledge utilization and creation of one group exhibit decreasing returns to scale in the system and the other one exhibits increasing return to scale, the system has two equilibrium points. The one with higher values of K and Z is unstable, and the other one is stable. The behavior of the dynamic system with multiple equilibrium points is similar to that illustrated in Section 3.2. We will not further examine the behavior of the system.

4.4 Persistence of inequality with poverty traps

This section illustrates another widely used approach to issues related to growth with inequality. We introduce a growth model proposed by Moav to demonstrate persistence of inequality.[10] In this model, the evolution of income within each dynasty in society is governed by a dynamical system that generates a poverty trap equilibrium point along with a high-income equilibrium. Poor dynasties, those with income at the threshold level, converge to a low-income steady state, whereas dynasties with income above the threshold converge to a high-income steady state.

Consider a small open overlapping-generations economy that operates in a one-good world. The economic activity extends over infinite discrete time in a competitive environment. In each period the economy produces a single homogeneous product that can be used either for consumption or for investment. Production occurs within a period according to a concave, constant-returns-to-scale technology. The output produced at time t uses capital, $K(t)$, and human capital efficiency units, $H(t)$, as follows: $Y(t) = F(K(t), H(t))$, where investment in physical and human capital is made one period in advance. Assume that the world capital rate of return remains constant, denoted by R. Unrestricted international capital movements yield

$$F_K(K(t), H(t)) = R. \qquad (4.4.1)$$

From the properties of the production function, we obtain that the wage per unit of human capital, w, is uniquely determined given the rate of return to capital, R, and is therefore constant over time.[11] Individuals live in two periods. Individuals, within as well as across generations, are identical in their preferences and their technology of human capital formation. They may differ in their initial wealth, inherited from their parents. Individuals cannot borrow in order to finance investment in human capital. An individual born in period t allocates her second life period income, $I_i(t+1)$, between household consumption, $c_i(t+1)$, and a bequest to the offspring, $b_i(t+1)$. The budget constraint is given by

$$I_i(t+1) = c_i(t+1) + b_i(t+1). \qquad (4.4.2)$$

Preferences are defined by the utility function

$$U_i(t) = (1-\beta)\log c_i(t+1) + \beta\log\{\bar{\theta} + b_i(t+1)\},$$

where $\beta \in (0, 1)$ and $\bar{\theta} > 0$. The optimal transfer of individual i born in period t is given by

$$b_i(t+1) = b(I_i(t+1)) = \begin{cases} 0 & \text{if } I_i(t+1) \le \theta, \\ \beta(I_i(t+1) - \theta) & \text{if } I_i(t+1) > \theta, \end{cases} \quad (4.4.3)$$

where $\theta \equiv \bar{\theta}(1-\beta)/\beta$.

We now discuss the formation of human capital. In the first period of their lives in period t, individuals devote their entire time to the acquisition of human capital. Individuals acquire one efficiency unit of labor – basic skills. The level of human capital of an individual i, $h_i(t+1)$, is an increasing concave function of real resources invested in education, $e_i(t)$:

$$h_i(t+1) = h(e_i(t)) = \begin{cases} 1 + \gamma e_i(t) & \text{if } e_i(t) < \bar{e}, \\ 1 + \gamma\bar{e} & \text{if } e_i(t) \ge \bar{e}. \end{cases} \quad (4.4.4)$$

It is assumed that the marginal return to human capital, for $e_i(t) < \bar{e}$, is larger than the marginal return to physical capital, $w\gamma > R$. We require that the income level below which individuals choose a zero bequest, θ, is larger than the wage rate, w, $\theta > w$. We also assume that the return to physical capital, R, is sufficiently low, i.e. $\beta R < 1$. In summary, we assume

$$\theta > w > \frac{R}{\gamma}, \quad \beta R < 1. \quad (4.4.5)$$

Under the above constraints, the second life period income, $I_i(t+1)$, is uniquely determined by the first life period bequest, $b_i(t)$:

$$I_i(t+1) = I(b_i(t)) = \begin{cases} w(1+\gamma b_i(t)) & \text{if } b_i(t) \le \bar{e}, \\ w(1+\gamma b_i(t)) + R(b_i(t)-\bar{e}) & \text{if } b_i(t) \ge \bar{e}. \end{cases} \quad (4.4.6)$$

From equations (4.4.3) and (4.4.6), the evolution of income within a dynasty is uniquely determined by

$$I_i(t+1) = \varphi(I_i(t)) = \begin{cases} w & \text{if } \beta(I_i(t) - \theta) < 0, \\ w(1 + \gamma\beta(I_i(t) - \theta)) & \text{if } \beta(I_i(t) - \theta) \in [0, \bar{e}], \\ w(1 + \bar{\gamma e}) + R(\beta(I_i(t) - \theta) - \bar{e}) & \text{if } \beta(I_i(t) - \theta) > \bar{e}, \end{cases}$$

(4.4.7)

where $I_i(0)$ is given. We have $I_i(t) \geq w$ for all t. Under constraints (4.4.5), from equation (4.4.7) we conclude that there exists a low income, locally stable, poverty trap steady state $\bar{I} = w$ because

$$I_i(t+1) = \varphi(I_i(t)) = w, \text{ for all } I_i(t) \in [w, \theta].$$

It is assumed that the return to human capital, γw, and its potential magnitude, $\bar{e}$, are sufficiently large, such that an individual who receives a bequest $b_i(t) = \bar{e}$ will transfer her offspring a higher bequest, $b_i(t+1) > b_i(t) = \bar{e}$. This assumption is expressed as

$$\beta[w(1 + \gamma\bar{e}) - \theta] > \bar{e}. \quad (4.4.8)$$

It assures a range of income, above the poverty trap range of income, in which

$$I_i(t+1) > I_i(t).$$

From constraints (4.4.5), we see that there is a higher income steady state $\tilde{I}$, than the poverty trap, which is determined by

$$\tilde{I} = \frac{w(\bar{\gamma e} + 1) - R(\beta\theta + \bar{e})}{1 - \beta R}.$$

This steady state is locally stable.
In the dynamic economy, there exists an income threshold

$$\hat{I}, \bar{I} < \hat{I} < \tilde{I}.$$

198 *Economic Growth with Income and Wealth Distribution*

From equations (4.4.7), the threshold is given by

$$\hat{I} = \frac{\gamma\beta\theta - 1}{\gamma\beta w - 1} w. \qquad (4.4.9)$$

This equilibrium point is locally unstable. It can be seen that dynasties with income below the threshold ($I_0(t) < \hat{I}$) converge to the poverty trap income level, and dynasties with income above the threshold ($I_0(t) > \hat{I}$) converge to the high income steady state.

In summary, the dynamical system

$$I_,(t+1) = \phi(I_,(t)),$$

which is depicted in Figure 4.4.1, generates three steady states: (i) a poverty trap; (ii) a high income steady state and; (iii) a threshold income. The dynasties with initial income below the threshold level converge to a low income steady state; the dynasties with income above the threshold level converge to a high income steady state.

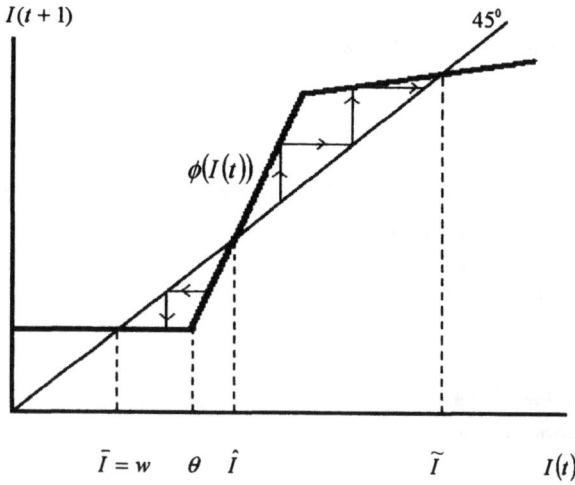

Figure 4.4.1 Multiple steady states and persistent income inequality

4.5 A growth model with human capital and income distribution

We are now concerned with interactions between human capital accumulation, economic growth, and inequality.[12] In the economy, a competitive final goods sector produces one homogeneous output using human capital and a variety of intermediate inputs with the following production function:

$$Y(t) = \sum_{i=1}^{D(t)} n^{1-\delta}(i, t) H^{\delta}(t),$$

where $D(t)$ is the number of different intermediate goods used in production, $n(i, t)$ is the quantity of the ith intermediate good employed, and H is the skilled adjusted stock of labor in the economy. The intermediate goods sector is competitive, and each intermediate good requires one unit of capital, k, to transform a new technology into a new intermediate good. The symmetric use of inputs implies $n(i, t) = n(t)$. Hence, the production function becomes

$$Y(t) = D(t) n^{1-\delta}(t) H^{\delta}(t).$$

There are two types of workers, skilled and unskilled. The skill-adjusted stock of labor is given by

$$H(t) = \left(\frac{D(t-1)}{D(t)} U^{-\alpha} + S_p^{-\alpha}(t) \right)^{1/\alpha}, \quad 0 > \alpha > -1, \qquad (4.5.1)$$

where $S_p(t)$ denotes skilled labor employed in production and $U(t)$ unskilled labor. The elasticity of substitution, $1/(1+\alpha)$, falls in the interval $(1, \infty)$. Here, the rate of technological change is measured by $D(t)/D(t-1)$. The above information takes account of the hypothesis that the greater the speed of technological change, the relatively more productive skilled labor becomes, compared to unskilled labor. Let $w(t)$, $w_s(t)$, and $w_u(t)$ stand for, respectively, the relative wage of skilled to unskilled labor, the wage of the skilled and the wage of the unskilled labor. Perfect competition in labor markets yields

$$w(t) \equiv \frac{w_s(t)}{w_u(t)} = \left(\frac{U(t)}{S_p(t)}\right)^{1+\alpha} \frac{D(t)}{D(t-1)}. \tag{4.5.2}$$

Agents live two periods; work when young and consume only when old. Let $S(t)$ be the total number of skilled labor. We normalize the total population of each generation

$$S(t) + U(t) = 1.$$

The skilled workers can be employed either in production, $S_p(t)$, or research, $S_r(t)$. When new technologies are introduced, agents must learn to work with these technologies to become skilled labor. Hence, at the start of their working lives, agents have to decide whether to invest in education or to remain unskilled. We assume that agents differ in their abilities to learn, μ, and that their abilities are distributed uniformly, $\mu \in [0, 1]$. Education is instantaneous and the cost of education is equal to $c(t)w_u(t)/\mu$. It is assumed that the direct cost of education, $c(t)w_u(t)$, is a decreasing function of the number of agents being educated, i.e. $c(t) = c(S(t))$, $c' < 0$. We specify

$$c(t) = \rho S^{-\sigma}(t).$$

Assume that an income tax, τ, is imposed only on skilled wages. The income of a skilled worker born at t is

$$Y_s(t) = (1-\tau)w_s(t) - \frac{\rho S^{-\sigma} w_u(t)}{\mu}. \tag{4.5.3}$$

Agents choose to invest in skills if the income in (4.5.3) exceeds that of remaining unskilled

$$Y_u(t) = w_u(t).$$

The equality between these two expressions gives the level of ability of the agent that is indifferent between investing in education and working as unskilled

$$\tilde{\mu}(t) = \frac{\rho S^{-\sigma}(t)}{(1-\tau)w(t) - 1}.$$

Substituting the uniform ability distribution, that is

$$S(t) = 1 - \tilde{\mu}(t)$$

into the above condition yields the following inverse labor supply equation:

$$w(t) = \frac{1}{1-\tau}\left(1 + \frac{\rho S^{-\sigma}(t)}{1-S(t)}\right). \tag{4.5.4}$$

From equation (4.5.4), we conclude that externalities in education, σ, generate a U-shaped relationship between the relative wage and the supply of skilled labor. The greater the externality, the more prolonged the initial decline of the relative wage. Increases in the direct cost of education, ρ, or in the differential tax on skilled labor, τ, require a higher wage for each level of skilled labor supply.

We take account of two ways of technological change, learning by doing (LBD) and costly investment in research and development (R&D). LBD takes place as skilled workers serendipitously discover new types of intermediate goods during the production process. This source of technological change is given by

$$\frac{D(t)}{D(t-1)} = 1 + \gamma S(t-1).$$

Research which is undertaken only by the government is financed by a public entity that raises revenues through tax collection, τ. When $S_r(t)$ researchers are employed, the economy produces technological blueprints according to

$$\frac{D(t)}{D(t-1)} = (1 + \beta S(t-1))\beta S_r(t-1).$$

As skilled workers are fully employed

$$S_p(t) + S_r(t) = S(t).$$

The budget constraint of the government is

$$\tau w_s(t) S(t) = w_s(t) S_r(t).$$

These two conditions yield

$$S_r(t) = \tau S(t), \quad S_p(t) = (1-\tau)S(t).$$

We assume that technological change takes place either via LBD or R&D, but not both in one period. It is not difficult to show that utilizing the equations above, we can express the inverse relative labor demands under the "LBD regime" and "R&D regime" as follows:

$$w(t)\big|_{LBD} = (1 + \gamma S(t-1))\left(\frac{1-S(t)}{S(t)}\right)^{1+\alpha}, \qquad (4.5.5)$$

$$w(t)\big|_{R\&D} = \tilde{\tau}(1 + \gamma S(t-1))S(t-1)\left(\frac{1-S(t)}{S(t)}\right)^{1+\alpha}, \qquad (4.5.6)$$

where $\tilde{\tau} = \beta\tau/(1-\tau)^{1+\alpha}$. General equilibrium in the goods and factor markets is attained by equating the labor supply, expressed in equation (4.5.4), to the labor demand conditions (4.5.5) and (4.5.6). That is

$$\Phi(S(t)) = \begin{cases} 1 + \gamma S(t-1), & \text{for LBD}, \\ \tilde{\tau}(1 + \gamma S(t-1))S(t-1), & \text{for R \& D}, \end{cases} \qquad (4.5.7)$$

where

$$\Phi(S(t)) \equiv \frac{1}{1-\tau}\left(1 + \frac{\rho S^{-\sigma}(t)}{1-S(t)}\right)\left(\frac{S(t)}{1-S(t)}\right)^{1+\alpha}$$

The evolution of the economy is governed by the one-dimensional difference equation (4.5.7). It is straightforward to see that for any given level of $S(t)$, all the other variables are uniquely determined. In steady state

$$S(t-1) = S(t) = S^*,$$

the steady growth rate is given by

$$\frac{Y(t) - Y(t-1)}{Y(t)} = \frac{D(t) - D(t-1)}{D(t)} = \begin{cases} \gamma S^*, & \text{for LBD}, \\ \beta\tau(1 + \gamma S^*)S^* - 1, & \text{for R \& D}. \end{cases}$$

We now analyze the behavior of equation (4.5.7). To simplify the analysis, in the remainder of this section we impose $1+\alpha > \sigma$, which means that the education externality is not strong given the elasticity of substitution between the two types of labor. Under this requirement, we have $d\Phi/dS(t) > 0$ for $S(t) \in [0,1]$. This also leads to

$$\frac{dS(t)}{dS(t-1)} > 0.$$

It can be shown that $\Phi(S(t))$ is first concave and then convex, $\Phi(0) = 0$ and $\Phi(1) = \infty$. Figure 4.5.1 depicts the functions of (4.5.7). We see that there are three possible equilibrium points: a low-growth trap in the LBD phase and a pair of equilibrium points in the intermediate and advanced development phase. If these equilibrium points exist, it can be shown that the LBD equilibrium point will be stable, while in the R&D phase, the first equilibrium point will be unstable and the second one stable. Checking of these properties is left to the reader as exercises. Economic interpretations refer to the original article.

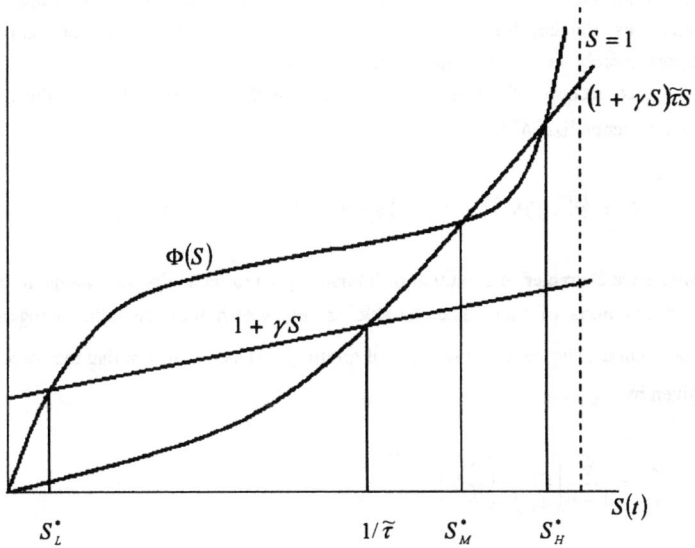

Figure 4.5.1 Three possible equilibrium points and their stability

4.6 On modeling group differences

The OSG models in this chapter are based on a linear form of qualified labor force given by $N_1 + zN_2$. This form implies a perfect substitution between the two groups. The description is oversimplified if we consider that one group is unskilled and the other skilled. We now mention a few other directions in aggregating labor force.

First, let us consider a case that human capital is changeable. If we use the same formation of aggregating labor input, a general description of $N^*(t)$ should be given by

$$N^*(t) = z_1(t)N_1 + z_2(t)N_2,$$

where $z_j(t)$ are group j's level of human capital at time t. People learn through different sources. They may improve skills by producing. Learning by doing is a source of skill or knowledge accumulation. Schools and universities are established to improve human capital. Through formal education, people learn more about nature, man, and society. Another possible source of learning, which has recently been introduced into formal growth theory by the author, is learning by playing. In different stages of economic development, people learn different things in leisure activities. Clubs and parties not only connect people but also enable men to skillfully manage situations. Reading for leisure is an obvious sources of information and knowledge. Sports merely for fun can improve health as well as skills for jobs.

To take account of substitution of workers with different skills, introduce another way to generalize $N^*(t)$

$$N^*(t) = \left\{ v(z_1(t)N_1)^{-\sigma} + (1-v)(z_2(t)N_2)^{-\sigma} \right\}^{-1/\sigma}, \quad -1 < \sigma \neq 0,$$

where we characterize evolution of human capital or technological change in terms of two functions of time. The variable, $z_j(t)$, which may be either exogenous or endogenous, augments the services of group j. It can be shown that the wage ratio is given by

$$\frac{w_1}{w_2} = \frac{v}{1-v} \left(\frac{z_1}{z_2} \right)^{-\sigma} \left(\frac{N_1}{N_2} \right)^{-(1+\sigma)}$$

If we nest $N^*(t)$ and $K(t)$ in the Cobb-Douglas production function, the parameter σ determines the elasticity of substitution between the two groups in the economy. It is known that the elasticity of substitution between the two groups of labor is dependent on the value of the parameter σ [13]

$$\left.\begin{array}{l} -<\sigma<0 \\ \sigma=0 \\ 0<\sigma<\infty \end{array}\right\} \Rightarrow \text{The elasticity of substitution} \begin{cases} >1, \\ =1, \\ <1. \end{cases}$$

The income and wealth distribution is not only related to preference and work time. It is related to many other factors. For instance, Becker et al. (2005) explore the implications for risk-taking behavior and the equilibrium distribution of income by assuming that the desire for status positions is a powerful motive and that it raises the marginal utility of consumption. They consider the case in which status positions are sold in a hedonic market. They show that such a complete hedonic market in status positions can be perfectly replicated by a simpler arrangement with a "status good" and a social norm that assigns higher status to those that consume more of this good. The main result is that for a wide range of initial conditions the equilibrium distribution over income, status, and consumption is the same, that this allocation requires inequality of income and consumption, and that this allocation coincides with the optimum of a utilitarian planner. Another important issue is related to impact of taxation. For instance, Lucas (1990) employs an infinite-horizon, representative agent, endogenous growth model and examines the impact of eliminating the tax on income and raising the lost revenue through a higher labor tax. He found out that the tax reform leads to a 32 percent increase in capital stock, and that the welfare benefit from the tax reform is equivalent to 6 percent of aggregation consumption.[14] Ioannides and Loury (2004) survey the theoretical and empirical literature to examine the use by different social groups of informal sources of information provided by friends, relatives, and acquaintances during job search and its consequences for the job market. They also examine the role of network structure and size, the resource endowments of contacts, and nature of the links between contacts to explain differences in the effects of job information networks. In doing so, they provide an economic perspective on such sociological concepts as strong versus weak ties, inbreeding, distance from structural holes, etc. They distinguish between models of exogenous job information networks, that is where individuals obtain job-related information through a given social structure, and endogenous job information networks, which are social networks that result from individuals' uncoordinated actions. They pay special attention to such issues as physical and social proximity and sharing of information and outline a model that integrates job information networks, where interactions occur in business cycle frequencies, with the dynamics of human capital formation, which include the joint effects of parental, community, and neighborhood human capital, and are set in life cycle frequencies, for the purpose of organizing suggestions for future research and examining earned income inequality. Calvó-Armengol and Jackson (2004) develop a model where agents obtain information about job opportunities through an explicitly modeled network of social contacts. They show that employment is positively correlated across time and agents. Moreover, unemployment exhibits duration dependence: the probability of obtaining a job decreases with the length of time that an agent has been unemployed. They also examine inequality between two groups. If staying in the labor market is costly and one group starts with a worse employment status, then that group's drop-out rate will be higher and their employment prospects will be persistently below that of the other group.[15]

Appendix

A.4.1 Proving Proposition 4.1.1

The Jacobian matrix at equilibrium is

$$J = \begin{bmatrix} \lambda_1 a_{11} & \lambda_1 a_{12} \\ \lambda_2 a_{21} & \lambda_2 a_{22} \end{bmatrix},$$

where

$$a_{11} = \frac{n_1}{n_2} a_{12} - (f - kf')\frac{z_1}{k_1},$$

$$a_{22} = \frac{n_2}{n_1} a_{21} - (f - kf')\frac{z_2}{k_2},$$

$$a_{12} = (k_1 - z_1 k) n_2 f'',$$

$$a_{21} = (k_2 - z_2 k) n_1 f''. \tag{A.4.1.1}$$

The two eigenvalues, $\rho_{1,2}$, are determined by

$$M(\rho) \equiv \rho^2 - \text{Trace}(J)\rho + \text{Det}(J) = 0,$$

where

$$\text{Trace}(J) = \lambda_1 a_{11} + \lambda_2 a_{22},$$
$$\text{Det}(J) = \lambda_1 \lambda_2 (a_{11} a_{22} - a_{12} a_{21}). \tag{A.4.1.2}$$

Growth with Heterogeneous Households 207

We solve $\rho_{1,2}$ as

$$\rho_{1,2} = \frac{\text{Trace}(J) \pm \sqrt{\text{Trace}(J)^2 - 4\text{Det}(J)}}{2}.$$

From the definitions of k, k_j, and n_j, we have

$$(k_1 - z_1 k)n_1 + (k_2 - z_2 k)n_2 = 0. \tag{A.4.1.3}$$

Hence, $(k_1 - z_1 k)$ and $(k_2 - z_2 k)$ have the opposite sign. From this equation, we also have: $a_{12} a_{21} < 0$. From equations (4.1.8) we have

$$k_j - z_j k = \left(\frac{f - k\delta_j}{\delta_j - f'}\right) z_j,$$

where $\delta_j - f' > 0$. We see that if $\delta_2 > \delta_1$, $k_2 - z_2 k$ (and $f - k\delta_2$) must be negative. As $\delta_j = 1/\lambda_j - \delta > 0$, $\delta_2 > \delta_1$ means $\lambda_1 > \lambda_2$. In the remainder of the proof, we require $\lambda_1 > \lambda_2$. We can similarly prove the case of $\lambda_1 \leq \lambda_2$.

Under $\lambda_1 > \lambda_2$, we have

$$\frac{k_2}{k} - z_2 < 0, \quad \frac{f}{k} - \delta_2 < 0,$$

$$\frac{k_1}{k} - z_1 > 0, \quad \frac{f}{k} - \delta_1 > 0, \quad a_{12} < 0, \quad a_{21} > 0. \tag{A.4.1.4}$$

From equations (A.4.1.1) and (A.4.1.2), we have

$$\frac{n_1}{n_2} a_{12} + \frac{n_2}{n_1} a_{21} = 0. \tag{A.4.1.5}$$

From equations (A.4.1.1) and (A.4.1.2), we calculate

$$\text{Det}(J) = \left[(f - kf') + \left(\frac{k_1}{z_1} - \frac{k_2}{z_2}\right)\frac{n_2}{n_1} a_{21}\right] \frac{z_1 z_2}{k_1 k_2} \lambda_1 \lambda_2 (f - kf') > 0,$$

where we use equation (A.4.1.4), $f - kf' > 0$, $a_{21} > 0$ and $k_1/z_1 - k_2/z_2$. From equations (A.4.1.1) and (A.4.1.3), we have

$$\text{Trace}(J) = (\lambda_1 - \lambda_2)\frac{n_1}{n_2}a_{12} - \left(\frac{z_1\lambda_1}{k_1} + \frac{z_2\lambda_2}{k_2}\right)(f - kf') < 0,$$

where we use inequalities (A.4.1.3) and equation (A.4.1.4). As $\text{Trace}(J) < 0$ and $\text{Det}(J) > 0$, we see that the equilibrium point is stable.

5
Multi-Sector Growth Economies

There are many kinds of commodities and services that we use and consume in our daily life: food, housing, clothing, cars, computers, air-conditioners, services from doctors or teachers or retailers, and entertainment by visiting museums or watching the performance of artists and sportsmen. Even in a simple food category, we may list thousands of kinds of food, depending on our likes. In modern times, this list has grown explosively. Evidently, it is impossible to analyze economic issues at national and regional levels without aggregation. In an aggregated sense, there are three types of commodities (and services): some are capital goods like TVs, clothing and machines; some are consumption goods such as vegetables, milk and meat; and the others are services. So far, we have mainly been concentrating on economies with a single commodity. This chapter broadens our analysis to multiple sector economies.

To explain the economic mechanism of the division of labor and competitive equilibrium in the labor market, the one-sector model is not sufficient to provide insights into dynamic processes of the division of the labor and interdependence between division of labor, knowledge, and efficiency. It is necessary to extend one-sector economies to multi-sector economies. It may be argued that the main task of developmental economics is to explain how structural changes occur in economic systems.[1] Since the pioneering works of Leontief, numerous theoretical studies on economic structure and dynamics have been published.[2] In the past two decades, analysts have become increasingly aware of the need to improve the specification of household behavior in the input-output models. There are some multi-sector growth models which are concerned with capital accumulation in the neoclassical growth literature (see the appendix to this chapter). Pasinetti (1993) readdressed issues related to structural dynamics.[3] He studies the role of technical progress in evolution; one of the problems of his approach is that, like most recent growth models with endogenous knowledge, capital accumulation is neglected. It is well observed that changes in the absolute levels of macroeconomic variables such as gross national product, total consumption, and total investment are associated with changes in composition in industrializing processes of many economies. Though the input-output system has proved to be very effective for analyzing economic structure with complicated linkages among various sectors in multiregional or multinational systems, it is argued that it is often analytically difficult to introduce endogenous behavior of households in an effective way in this framework. But the role of consumption demand in industrial revolutions and its importance to growth and structural change have been recognized by economists. It has been argued that the Engel effects not only cause a shift in the industrial origin of production, but also induce high levels of productivity and output. Nevertheless, theoretical analysis of this role has been rather limited in dynamic theory. Many of multisector economic growth models have omitted a consideration of the role of consumption demand structure. For instance, in Uzawa's two-sector growth model and its extensions the economic structure is not designed to confront issues of demand, since only one consumption sector is postulated. Although the role of consumption demand is explicitly recognized in the neo-Keynesian literature, the level of aggregation in most of these models is such that there is little scope for changes in the composition of consumption to influence the pattern of growth and structural change.

This chapter deals with multi-sector growth economies with a homogeneous household. Section 5.1 introduces the Uzawa two-sector growth model. Section 5.2 re-examines the economic issues in the Uzawa model with the utility function proposed in this study. Different from the Uzawa model in which consumer behavior is treated in the same way as in the Solow model, our model determines the consumer's decision on saving and consumption with the assumption of utility maximization. Section 5.3 examines the interdependence between economic growth and economic structure with labor supply and consumer durables. Section 5.4 introduces endogenous knowledge into the growth model with economic structure. We identify conditions for existence of multiple equilibrium points and examine stability conditions of different equilibrium points.

5.1 The Uzawa two-sector model

The Solow model does not describe consumer behavior with a rational assumption – a proportion of his income is used for saving and the rest is for consumption. Since there is no rational rule to determine consumer choice, it is difficult to analyze consumer behavior when the consumer is faced with a choice of multiple consumption goods. Perhaps because of this obstacle, the Solow model was not successfully extended to cases where consumers have multiple goods and services to choose from. Uzawa (1961) made an extension of Solow's one-sector economy by a breakdown of the productive system into two sectors using capital and labor, one of which produces capital goods, the other consumption goods. According to this model, output of the capital sector goes entirely to investment and that of the consumption sector entirely to consumption. This assumption avoids the problem of modeling consumers' choice among goods and services in growth theory. Again, there is a single commodity for consumers. As capital goods are not consumed, Uzawa's extension appears to be a mathematical exercise with few new behavioral insights, as argued by Solow after Uzawa published the work.

In Uzawa's two-sector growth model, it is assumed that consumption and capital goods are different commodities, which are produced in two distinct sectors. Labor is homogeneous and labor grows at an exogenously given exponential rate, n. There is only one malleable capital good, which can be used as an input in both sectors in the economy. Capital depreciates at a constant exponential rate, δ_k, which is independent of the manner of use. The production functions are given by

$$Y_j = F_j(K_j, N_j), \quad j = 1, 2,$$

where Y_j are the output of sector j, K_j and N_j are respectively the capital and labor used in sector j, F_j the production functions, the subscripts 1 and 2 denoting the capital goods sector and the consumption good sector. Assume F_j to be neoclassical. We have $y_j = f_j(k_j)$, where

$$y_j \equiv \frac{Y_j}{N_j}, \quad k_j \equiv \frac{K_j}{N_j}, \quad f_j' > 0, \quad f_j'' < 0, \quad j = 1, 2.$$

It is assumed that the usual static efficiency conditions of pure competition hold at any time. This requirement means that the wages, w_j, and the wage-rental ratio, w_j^*, in the two sectors are equal:

$$w = w_1 = w_2, \quad w^* = w_1^* = w_2^*.$$

We have

$$w^* = \frac{f_j}{f_j'} - k_j.$$

As full employment of labor and capital is assumed, we have

$$K_1 + K_2 = K, \quad N_1 + N_2 = N,$$

which can be rewritten in the form of

$$n_1 k_1 + n_2 k_2 = k,$$

where $n_j \equiv N_j / N$, $j = 1, 2$.

The gross saving propensities – both average and marginal – from wage incomes and profits are nonnegative constants denoted respectively by s_w and s_r. Thus, if the two propensities are equal (to s), the consumption is equal to a constant fraction $1 - s$ of the gross national product. If we denote the rental rate of the two sectors by r, then the total gross savings in the economy is equal to $s_r rK + s_w wN$.

As the investment in the economy comes from the production of new capital and savings is always equal to investment, we have

$$P_1 Y_1 = s_r rK + s_w wN,$$

where $P_1(t)$ is the price of new capital. As $F_{1K}(t) = r(t)/P_1(t)$, the above equation becomes

$$n_1 f_1(k_1) = f_1'(s_r k + s_w w^*).$$

As $\dot{K} = Y_1 - \delta_k K$, we have

$$\dot{k} = f_1'(s_r k + s_w w^*) - (n + \delta_k) k. \qquad (5.1.1)$$

Under certain conditions, the dynamic system is causal. If we assume that the conditions are satisfied, then the right-hand side of equation (5.1.1) can be written as a function of k

$$\dot{k}(t) = H(k) = kh(k).$$

The functional form of h is based on Burmeister and Dobell (1970). Let us denote the extended Jacobian by J and define two numbers a and b as

$$a = \max\left\{ \lim_{k_j \to 0} \left(\frac{f_j}{f_j'} - k_j \right), \ j = 1, 2 \right\},$$

$$b = \min\left\{\lim_{k_j \to 0}\left(\frac{f_j}{f_j'} - k_j\right), \ j = 1, 2\right\}.$$

Then the following theorems hold.

Theorem 5.1.1
Let k^* be any root of $h = 0$. If $s_w/(n + \delta_k)$ is not larger than $k/f_1(k_1)$ or $s_r/(n + \delta_k)$ is not less than $k/f_1(k_1)$, then the equilibrium point is locally stable.

Theorem 5.1.2
If any of the following conditions are satisfied for all $a < w^* < b$, then it is proved that any equilibrium of the dynamic system is unique and stable: (i) s_r is not less than s_w, while k_1 is not larger than k_2; (ii) the wage elasticity of capital intensity $(w^*/k)dk/dw^*$ is not less than unity; (iii) the substitution elasticity of the consumption sector is not less than unity; (iv) $s_r = 1$ and $J > 0$; (v) $s_w = 0$ and $J > 0$, in which all functions and variables are evaluated at the equilibrium of the system.

It should be mentioned that even if all the conditions (i)–(v) are violated, it is still possible to find a unique and balanced growth path, and unstable balanced growth paths may exist.

Certain features of the two-sector model cannot be observed in the Solow one-sector model. For instance, in the two-sector model the existence of a positive unique equilibrium point cannot always be asserted. The capital-labor ratio may permanently oscillate around an unstable equilibrium. Numerous extensions and generalizations of the Uzawa model have been performed.[4] Technological changes have been introduced into the system. It was demonstrated that the labor supply might be treated as a function of the real wage rate without significantly altering the structure of the two-sector model. There are studies based on the assumption that capital cannot be shifted between sectors. This assumption means that once a machine is installed in a particular sector, it must remain in that sector for its lifetime. There are also some studies which replace the smooth neoclassical production functions by fixed coefficient production functions. The model is modified so that labor is divided into two classes: capitalists who derive their income solely from the ownership of capital, and workers who receive both wage income and returns from capital ownership.

5.2 A two-sector growth model with endogenous saving

Solow's one-sector growth model and Uzawa's two-sector growth model have played the role of the key models in the neoclassical growth theory. These two models and their various extensions and generalizations are fundamental for the development of new economic growth theories as well. Since Uzawa proposed the model in 1961, many works have been published to extend and generalize the model from the 1960s till today.[5] But all these studies follow the Ramsey approach to consumer behavior. This section proposes another approach to consumer behavior to reexamine the basic issues addressed by the two-sector growth model within the OSG framework.

5.2.1 The model

As in the traditional two-sector growth model, it is assumed that consumption and capital goods are different commodities, which are produced in two distinct sectors. Labor is homogeneous and grows at an exogenously given exponential rate, n, which is assumed to be zero in this section. The assumption of zero population growth rate does not affect our analysis in the sense that we can get similar results with a constant growth rate (because the two sectors exhibit constant returns to scale). Capital depreciates at a constant exponential rate, δ_k, which is independent of the manner of use. The production functions are given by

$$F_j(K_j(t), N_j(t)), \quad j = i, s,$$

where F_j are the output of sector j, K_j and N_j are respectively the capital and labor used in sector j, F_j the production functions, the subscripts i and s denoting the capital goods sector and the consumption goods sector. Assume F_j to be neoclassical. We have

$$f_j(t) = f_j(k_j(t)), \quad f_j(t) \equiv \frac{F_j(t)}{N_j(t)}, \quad k_j(t) \equiv \frac{K_j(t)}{N_j(t)}, \quad j = i, s.$$

The functions, f_j, have the following properties:

(i) $f_j(0) = 0$;

(ii) f_j are increasing, strictly concave on R^+, and C^2 on R^{++}; $f_j'(k_j) > 0$ and $f_j''(k) < 0$; and

(iii) $\lim_{k_j \to 0} f_j'(k_j) = \infty$ and $\lim_{k_j \to +\infty} f_j'(k_j) = 0$.

Markets are competitive; thus labor and capital earn their marginal products, and firms earn zero profits. We assume that the capital goods serve as a medium of exchange and is taken as numeraire. The price of consumption goods is denoted by $p(t)$. The rate of interest, $r(t)$, and wage rate, $w(t)$, are determined by the markets. Hence, for any individual firm $r(t)$ and $w(t)$ are given at each point in time. The production sector chooses the two variables, $K_j(t)$ and $N_j(t)$, to maximize its profit. The marginal conditions are given by

$$r + \delta_k = f_i'(k_i) = p f_s'(k_s),$$
$$w(t) = f_i(k_i) - k_i f_i'(k_i) = p(t)[f_s(k_s) - k_s f_s'(k_s)]. \qquad (5.2.1)$$

The total capital stock, $K(t)$, is allocated to the two sectors. As full employment of labor and capital is assumed, we have

$$K_i(t) + K_s(t) = K(t), \quad N_i(t) + N_s(t) = N.$$

We rewrite the above equations as

$$n_i(t)k_i(t) + n_s(t)k_s(t) = k(t), \quad n_i(t) + n_s(t) = 1, \qquad (5.2.2)$$

where

$$k(t) = \frac{K(t)}{N}, \quad n_j(t) = \frac{N_j(t)}{N}, \quad j = i, s.$$

First define group j's per capita current income, $y(t)$, from the interest payment, $r(t)k(t)$, and the wage payment, $w(t)$, is defined by

$$y(t) = r(t)k(t) + w(t).$$

The per capita disposable income is defined as the sum of the current income and the wealth available for purchasing consumption goods and saving:

$$\hat{y}(t) = y(t) + k(t) = (1 + r(t))k(t) + w(t).$$

The disposable income is used for saving and consumption. At each point in time, a consumer would distribute the total available budget among saving, $s(t)$, and consumption of goods, $c(t)$. The budget constraint is given by

$$p(t)c(t) + s(t) = \hat{y}(t). \tag{5.2.3}$$

In our model, at each point in time, consumers have two variables to decide on. A consumer decides how much to consume and to save. Equation (5.2.3) means that the consumption and saving exhaust the consumers' disposable income. We assume that the utility level, $U(t)$, that the representative household obtains is dependent on the consumption level, $c(t)$, and savings, $s(t)$. The utility function is specified as follows:

$$U(t) = c^{\xi}(t)s^{\lambda}(t), \quad \xi, \; \lambda > 0, \; \xi + \lambda = 1,$$

where ξ and λ are respectively the representative household's propensity to consume consumer goods and to save. Maximizing U_j subject to the budget constraints (5.2.3) yields

$$p(t)c(t) = \xi \hat{y}(t), \quad s(t) = \lambda \hat{y}(t). \tag{5.2.4}$$

According to the definition of $s(t)$, the representative household's wealth changes according to the following differential equation:

$$\dot{k}(t) = s(t) - k(t).$$

Substituting $s(t)$ in the equations (5.2.4) into the above equation yields

$$\dot{k}(t) = \lambda \hat{y}(t) - k(t). \tag{5.2.5}$$

The output of the consumer goods sector is consumed by the households. That is

$$c(t)N = F_s(t).$$

As output of the capital goods sector is equal to the depreciation of capital stock and the net savings, we have

$$S(t) - K(t) + \delta_k K(t) = F_i(t), \tag{5.2.6}$$

where $S(t) - K(t) + \delta_k K(t)$ is the sum of the net saving and depreciation. It is straightforward to show that this equation can be derived from the other equations in the system. We have thus built the dynamic model.

5.2.2 The motion of the economic system

We show that the motion of the system is determined by a differential equation. First, from

$$r(t) + \delta_k = f_i'(k_i) = p f_s'(k_s)$$

in (5.2.1), we get

$$p = \frac{f_i'(k_i)}{f_s'(k_s)}.$$

Substituting this equation into $f_i(k_i) - k_i f_i'(k_i) = p(f_s(k_s) - k_s f_s'(k_s))$ in equations (5.2.1) yields

$$\Psi_i(k_i) \equiv \frac{f_i(k_i)}{f_i'(k_i)} - k_i = \frac{f_s(k_s)}{f_s'(k_s)} - k_s \equiv \Psi_s(k_s). \tag{5.2.7}$$

From the properties of $f_i(k_i)$, we can show that the function, $\Psi_i(k_i)$, has the following properties:

$$\Psi_i(0) = 0, \ \Psi_i(k_i) > 0 \ \text{for} \ k_i > 0, \ \Psi_i'(k_i) = -\frac{f_i(k_i) f_i''(k_i)}{f_i'^2(k_i)} \geq 0.$$

The function $\Psi_s(k_s)$ has the same properties in k_s. We see that for any given $k_s \geq 0$, equation (5.2.7) determines $k_i \geq 0$ as a unique function of k_s, denoted by $k_i = \Omega(k_s)$.

We have $\Omega(0) = 0$ and $\Omega' > 0$. From equations (5.2.2), we solve the labor distribution as functions of k, k_s, and k_i as follows:

218 Economic Growth with Income and Wealth Distribution

$$n_i = \frac{k - k_s}{k_i - k_s}, \quad n_s = \frac{k_i - k}{k_i - k_s}. \tag{5.2.8}$$

The labor distribution is uniquely determined by k and k_s. According to the definitions of S, K, s, and k, we have

$$S(t) - \bar{\delta}K(t) = (s(t) - \delta k(t))N,$$

where $\bar{\delta} \equiv 1 - \delta_k$. From this equation, equation (5.2.6), and $s = \lambda \hat{y}$, we obtain

$$\hat{y} = \frac{n_i f_i(k_i) + \bar{\delta} k}{\lambda}. \tag{5.2.9}$$

From $pc = \xi \hat{y}$, $c = n_s f_s$, and $p = f_i' / f_s'$, we get

$$\hat{y} = \frac{n_s f_s f_i'}{\xi f_s'}.$$

From the above equation and equation (5.2.9), we have

$$f_i + \bar{\delta} k = \lambda n_s f^* f_i' + n_s f_i,$$

where we use $n_i + n_s = 1$ and $f^*(k_s) = f_s / \xi f_s'$. Substituting n_s in equations (5.2.8) into the above equation yields

$$k = \frac{\lambda k_i f^* f_i' + k_s f_i}{\bar{\delta} k_i - \bar{\delta} k_s + \lambda f^* f_i' + f_i} \equiv \Lambda(k_s). \tag{5.2.10}$$

This equation guarantees that for any given $k_s(t)$, $k(t)$ is uniquely determined. Substituting equation (5.2.10) into equation (5.2.5) yields

$$\frac{d\Lambda}{dk_s} \dot{k}_s = \lambda f_i(\Omega(k_s)) \frac{\Lambda(k_s) - k_s}{\Omega(k_s) - k_s} - \delta_k \Lambda(k_s), \tag{5.2.11}$$

where we use equations (5.2.8) and (5.2.9) and $k_i = \Omega(k_s)$ and

$$\frac{d\Lambda}{dk_s} = \frac{\lambda k_i f''_i f'_i + \lambda \Omega' f^*\left(f'_i + k_i f''_i\right) + f'_i + k_i f''_i \Omega'}{\delta k_i - \delta k_s + \lambda f^* f'_i + f_i}$$
$$- \frac{\left(\lambda k_i f^* f'_i + k_s f_i\right)\left(\delta \Omega' - \delta + \lambda f''_i f'_i + \lambda \Omega' f^* f''_i + f'_i \Omega'\right)}{\left(\delta k_i - \delta k_s + \lambda f^* f'_i + f_i\right)^2},$$

where

$$f''(k_s) = \frac{1 - f_s f''_s / f_s'^2}{\xi} > 0.$$

It is straightforward to analyze dynamic properties of (5.2.11). But since it is difficult to interpret results, we further specify production functions for illustration.

5.2.3 The dynamics with the Cobb-Douglas production functions

For explicit interpretation, we specify production functions in the Cobb-Douglas form

$$f_j(k_j) = A_j k_j^{\alpha_j}, \quad A_j > 0, \quad 0 < \alpha_j < 1, \quad j = i, s. \tag{5.2.12}$$

We now analyze dynamic properties of the system with production functions (5.2.12). From equations (5.2.7), we directly obtain $k_s = \alpha k_i$, where

$$\alpha \equiv \frac{\beta_i \alpha_s}{\beta_s \alpha_i}, \quad \beta_j \equiv 1 - \alpha_j, \quad j = i, s.$$

The capital intensity of the consumer goods sector is proportional to that of the capital goods sector. By $k_s = \alpha k_i$ and $\beta_s f_s = \beta_s p f_s$, we solve

$$p(t) = \frac{\beta_i A_i}{\beta_s \alpha^{\alpha_s} A_s} k_i(t)^{\alpha_i - \alpha_s}. \tag{5.2.13}$$

The price of consumer goods is positively related to the technological level of the capital goods sector but negatively related to that of the consumer goods sector. The price is positively or negatively related to the capital intensity of the capital goods sector, depending on the sign of $\alpha_i - \alpha_s$. If $\alpha_i = \alpha_s$, then the price is constant, $p = A_i / A_s$. In the remainder of this section, we require $\alpha_i \neq \alpha_s$. If the equality holds, then labor distribution is invariant in time. The analysis of case $\alpha_i = \alpha_s$ is straightforward. Corresponding to equations (5.2.8), we have

$$n_i = \frac{\alpha k_i - k}{(\alpha - 1)k_i}, \quad n_s = \frac{k - k_i}{(\alpha - 1)k_i}. \tag{5.2.14}$$

The labor distribution between the two sectors is uniquely determined by k and k_i. By equation (5.2.10), we solve

$$k = \frac{k_i}{A_0\left(1 + Ak_i^{\beta_i}\right)}, \tag{5.2.15}$$

where

$$A_0 \equiv \frac{1 + \beta_i \lambda / \beta_s \xi}{\alpha + \beta_i \lambda / \beta_s \xi}, \quad A \equiv \frac{(1-\alpha)\delta / A_i}{1 + \beta_i \lambda / \beta_s \xi}.$$

By equations (5.2.14) and (5.2.15) and according to the definitions of A and A_0, we find

$$n_i = \frac{\beta_i \lambda / \beta_s \xi - \alpha \delta k_i^{\beta_i} / A_i}{\alpha + \beta_i \lambda / \beta_s \xi} = 1 - \frac{\alpha + \alpha \delta k_i^{\beta_i} / A_i}{\alpha + \beta_i \lambda / \beta_s \xi}.$$

Hence, for $n_i(t)$ to satisfy $1 > n_i(t) > 0$, it is sufficient to have

$$k_i(t) < \left(\frac{A_i \beta_i \lambda}{\alpha \delta \beta_s \xi}\right)^{1/\beta_i} \tag{5.2.16}$$

Under $f_j = A_j k_j^{\alpha_j}$, equation (5.2.11) becomes

$$\phi(k_i)\dot{k}_i = (\alpha A_0 - 1)\alpha_0 - (\delta_k - \alpha \alpha_0 A_0 A)k_i^{\beta_i}, \tag{5.2.17}$$

where

$$\phi(k_i) \equiv \left[\frac{1 + \alpha_i A k_i^{\beta_i}}{1 + A k_i^{\beta_i}}\right] k_i^{-\alpha_i} \geq 0, \quad \alpha_0 \equiv \frac{A_i}{(\alpha - 1)}.$$

We see that the differential equation (5.2.17) involves a single variable, $k_i(t)$. With proper initial conditions satisfying (5.2.16), the equation has a unique solution. The following lemma shows that for any meaningful solution of equation (5.2.17), all the other variables in the system are uniquely determined. Hence, it would be sufficient for us to examine equation (5.2.17) in order to understand the dynamic properties of the entire economic system.

Lemma 5.2.1
The dynamics of the two-sector model with the Cobb-Douglas production functions follow equation (5.2.17). For any given positive value of $k_i(t)$ at any point in time, the other variables are uniquely determined by the following procedure: $k(t)$ by equation (5.2.15) $\to$ $k_s(t) = \alpha k_i(t)$ $\to$ $n_i(t)$ and $n_s(t)$ by equations (5.2.14) $\to r(t)$ and $w(t)$ by equations (5.2.1) $\to$ $f_j(t), j = i, s$ by equations (5.2.12) $\to p(t)$ by equation (5.2.13) $\to N_j(t) = n_j(t)N \to K_j(t) = k_j(t)N_j(t) \to F_j(t) = f_j(t)N_j(t) \to$ $\hat{y}(t)$ by equation (5.2.12) $\to$ $c(t)$ and $s(t)$ by equations (5.2.4).

Once we determine $k_i(t)$, we solve all the other variables. The unique equilibrium of equation (5.2.17) is given by

$$k_i^* = \left[\frac{(\alpha A_0 - 1)\alpha_0}{\delta_k - \alpha_0 \alpha A A_0}\right]^{1/\beta_i} \tag{5.2.18}$$

To demonstrate k_i to be a positive solution, we examine two terms $(\alpha A_0 - 1)\alpha_0$ and $(\delta_k - \alpha \alpha_0 A_0 A)$. It should be noted that α may be either larger or smaller than unity. In the case of $\alpha > (<) 1$, according to their definitions, $\alpha_0 > (<) 0$, $A < (>) 0$, and $A_0 < (>) 1$. We conclude

$$\delta_k - \alpha \alpha_0 A_0 A > 0, \quad (\alpha A_0 - 1)\alpha_0 = \frac{\beta_i \lambda A_i / \beta_s \xi}{\alpha + \beta_i \lambda / \beta_s \xi} > 0.$$

This guarantees a unique positive solution as well as stability of the equilibrium. The system is stable because

222   *Economic Growth with Income and Wealth Distribution*

$$\left.\frac{d\dot{k}_i}{dk_i}\right|_{k_i = k_i^*} = -\frac{(\delta_k - \alpha\alpha_0 A_0 A)\beta_i}{k_i^{*\alpha_i}\phi(k_i^*)} < 0.$$

We now show that for $k_i^* > 0$, $0 < n_i^* < 1$. By (5.2.14), (5.2.15), and (5.2.18), we have

$$n_i^* = \frac{\alpha k_i - k}{(\alpha - 1)k_i} = \frac{(\alpha A_0 - 1)}{(\alpha - 1)A_0} \frac{\delta_k}{(\delta_k + \delta/(1 + \beta_i\lambda/\beta_s\xi))}.$$

As

$$0 < \frac{\delta_k}{(\delta_k + \delta/(1 + \beta_i\lambda/\beta_s\xi))} < 1, \quad 0 < \frac{(\alpha A_0 - 1)}{(\alpha - 1)A_0} = \frac{\beta_i\lambda/\beta_s\xi}{1 + \beta_i\lambda/\beta_s\xi} < 1,$$

we guarantee $0 < n_i^* < 1$.

Theorem 5.2.1
The dynamic system has a unique stable equilibrium.

5.2.4 Simulate the model

It is straightforward to examine the impact of changes in parameter values on the equilibrium structure by standard comparative statics analysis as we guaranteed the existence of a unique equilibrium point. We now simulate the model for illustrating dynamic processes. First, we specify the parameter values as follows:

$$\alpha_i = 0.40, \quad \alpha_s = 0.35, \quad \delta_k = 0.05, \quad \lambda = 0.65, \quad A_i = 1.1, \quad A_s = 0.9. \qquad (5.2.19)$$

We note that the productivity of the capital goods sector is higher than that of the consumption goods sector. We simulate the motion of the economic system over 15 years with $k_i(0) = 2.2$. The equilibrium value of k_i^* is 3.033. Figure 5.2.1a shows the growth of the per worker input in the two sectors and per capita wealth. These variables experience dramatic growth during the study period. Figure 5.2.1b shows the growth of the per worker output levels of the two sectors. The two sectors exhibit positive growth rates. Figure 5.2.1c describes the motion of the labor distribution and the output ratio between the two sectors. It can be seen that the ratio falls steadily over the study period. The labor participation rate in the capital goods sector of the total labor force also declines steadily over the study period. The consumption goods sector

Multi-Sector Growth Economies 223

absorbs more and more labor force. Figure 5.2.1d shows how the price, the real wage rate, and the rate of interest change over time. The price of consumption goods (in comparison to capital goods) changes slowly over the period. The real wage rate increases; the rate of interest falls during the study period. Figure 5.2.1e demonstrates the current income per capita and consumption per capita. Figure 5.2.1f depicts the dynamics of the shares of the two sectors in the GNP. The share of the capital goods sector, $y_i \equiv F_i/(F_i + pF_s)$, falls, and that of consumption goods sector, $y_s \equiv pF_s/(F_i + pF_s)$, rises.

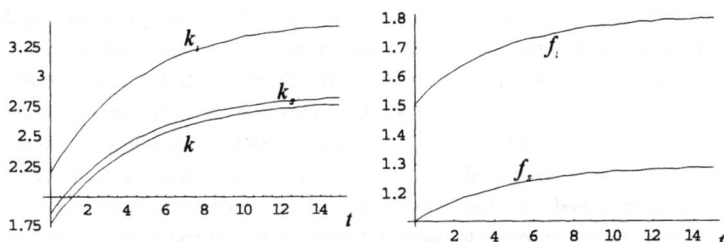
(a) per-worker inputs and per capita wealth (b) the output levels of the two sectors

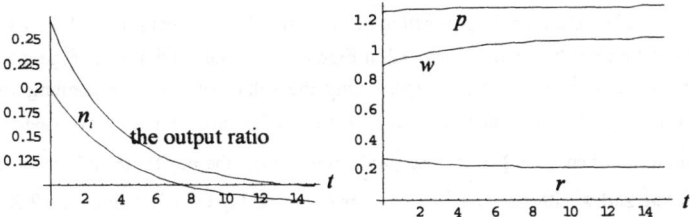
(c) the labor distribution and output ratio (d) the price, rate of interest, and wage rate

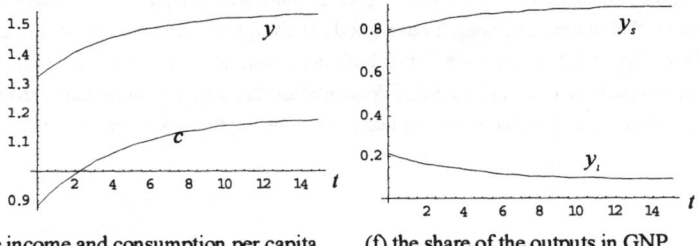
(e) the income and consumption per capita (f) the share of the outputs in GNP

Figure 5.2.1 Simulating the two-sector model

5.2.5 Comparative dynamic analysis by simulation

We now examine the impact of changes on dynamic processes of the system. First, we examine the case that all the parameters, except λ, are the same as in (5.2.19). We increase the propensity to save from 0.65 to 0.70. The simulation results are demonstrated in Figure 5.2.2. The solid lines in Figure 5.2.2 are the same as in Figure 5.2.1, representing the values of the corresponding variables when $\lambda = 0.65$; the dashed lines in Figure 5.2.2 represent the new values of the variables when $\lambda = 0.70$. As the propensity to save increases, the capital intensities of the two sectors and wealth per capita increase as shown in Figure 5.2.2a. Figure 5.2.2b shows that the per worker output levels of the two sectors increase. The labor participation ratio in the capital goods sector and the output ratio of the capital goods sector and the consumption goods sector increase, as illustrated in Figure 5.2.2c. Figure 5.2.2d shows that the price of consumption goods increases slightly, the wage rate increases, and the rate of interest falls. From Figure 5.2.2e, we observe that the current income increases from over the simulation period and the consumption level falls at the initial stage of the simulation period and then rises. Figure 5.2.2f demonstrates that the share of output of the capital goods sector in the GNP increases, and that of the consumption goods sector falls.

We now examine the case that all the parameters, except A_i, are the same as in (5.2.19). We increase the productivity of the capital goods sector from 1.1 to 1.4. The simulation results are demonstrated in Figure 5.2.3. The solid lines in Figure 5.2.3 are the same as in Figure 5.2.1, representing the values of the corresponding variables when $A_i = 1.1$; the dashed lines in Figure 5.2.3 represent the new values of the variables when $A_i = 1.4$. As the productivity rises, the capital intensities of the two sectors and wealth per capita increase as shown in Figure 5.2.3a. Figure 5.2.3b shows that the per worker output levels of the two sectors rise. The labor participation ratio in the capital goods sector and the output ratio of the capital goods sector and the consumption goods sector become higher, as illustrated in Figure 5.2.3c. Figure 5.2.3d shows that the price of consumption goods, the wage rate, and the rate of interest rise. From Figure 5.2.3e, we observe that both the current income and consumption rise as the productivity rises. Figure 5.2.3f demonstrates that the share of output of the capital goods sector in the GNP rises, and that of the consumption goods sector falls.

Multi-Sector Growth Economies 225

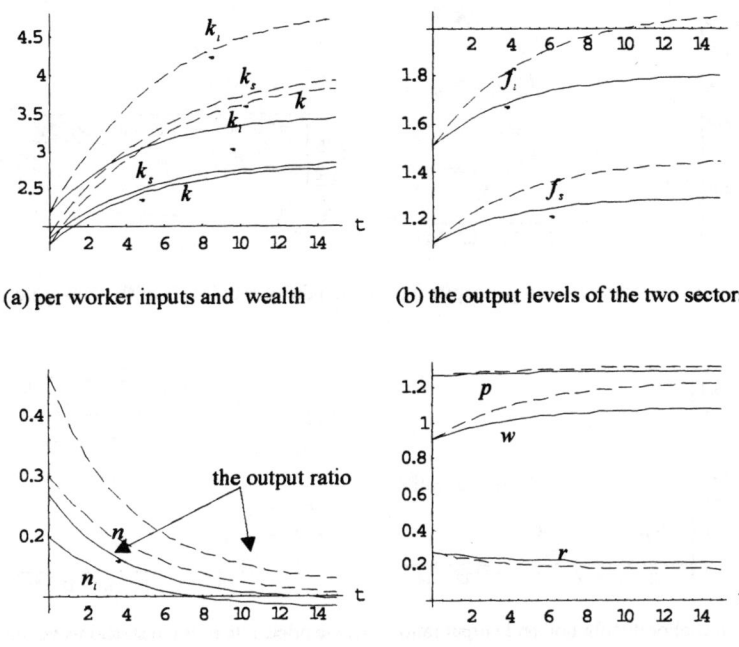

(a) per worker inputs and wealth

(b) the output levels of the two sectors

(c) the labor distribution and output ratio

(d) the price, rate of interest, and wage rate

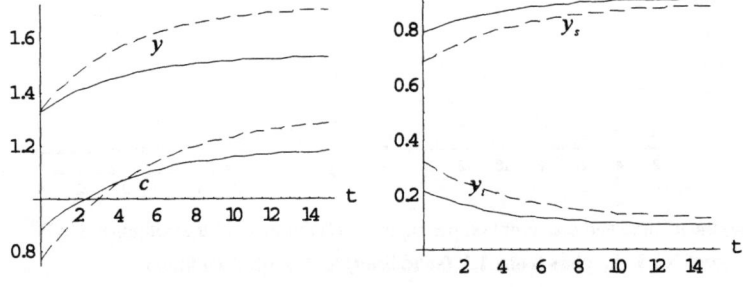

(e) the income and consumption per capita

(f) the share of the outputs in GNP

Figure 5.2.2 λ rises from 0.65 (solid lines) to 0.70 (dashed lines)

226 *Economic Growth with Income and Wealth Distribution*

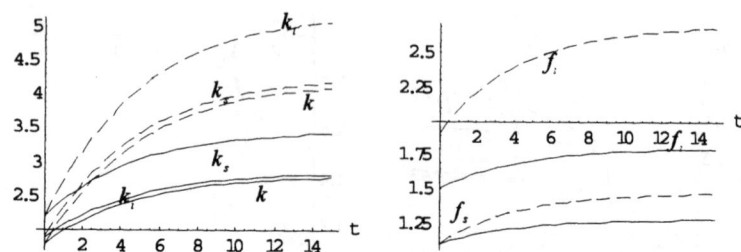

(a) per worker inputs and per capita wealth (b) the output levels of the two sectors

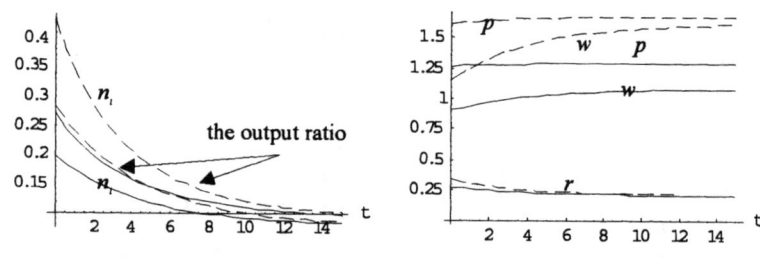

(c) the labor distribution and output ratio (d) the price, rate of interest, and wage rate

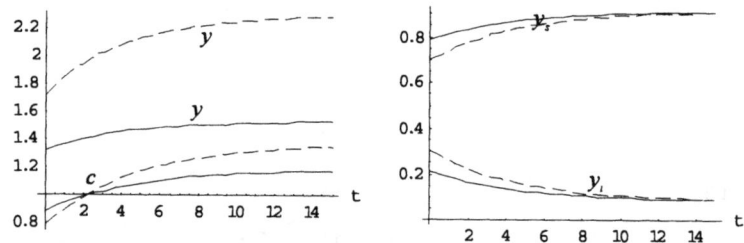

(e) the income and consumption per capita (f) the share of the outputs in GNP

Figure 5.2.3 A_i rises from 1.1 (solid lines) to 1.4 (dashed lines)

5.3 A two-sector growth model with labor supply and consumer durables

As pointed out by Greenwood and Hercowiz (1991), the stock of household capital actually exceeds market capital. Benhabib et al. (1991) estimated that the output of the household sector may be as much as half that of the market sector. Hence, proper introduction of household capital, called consumer durables in this section, in growth theory is essential. The purpose of this section is to introduce consumer durables and endogenous time into economic growth theory.

5.3.1 The model with endogenous leisure and consumer durables

The model is an extension of the model in the previous section. Let $N(t)$ denote the flow of labor services used at time t for production. The total labor force, $N(t)$, is given by $N(t) = T(t)N_0$, where $T(t)$ is the work time of a representative household and N_0 is the total labor force. The production functions are given by

$$F_j(K_j(t), N_j(t)), \quad j = i, s,$$

where F_j is the output of sector j, K_j and N_j are respectively the capital and labor used in sector j, and the subscripts 1 and 2 denote the capital goods sector and the consumption goods sector. The marginal conditions are given by

$$r + \delta_k = f_i'(k_i) = pf_s'(k_s),$$
$$w(t) = f_i(k_i) - k_i f_i'(k_i) = p(t)[f_s(k_s) - k_s f_s'(k_s)]. \quad (5.3.1)$$

The total capital stock, $K(t)$, is allocated to the two sectors and households. As full employment of labor and capital is assumed, we have

$$K_i(t) + K_s(t) + K_h(t) = K(t),$$
$$N_i(t) + N_s(t) = N(t),$$

where $K_h(t)$ is consumer durables. We rewrite the above equations as

$$n_i(t)k_i(t) + n_s(t)k_s(t) + k_h(t) = k(t), \quad n_i(t) + n_s(t) = 1, \quad (5.3.2)$$

where

$$k(t) \equiv \frac{K(t)}{N(t)}, \quad k_h(t) \equiv \frac{K_h(t)}{N(t)}, \quad n_j(t) \equiv \frac{N_j(t)}{N(t)}, \quad j = i, s.$$

Let $\bar{k}(t)(\equiv K(t)/N_0)$ stand for per capita wealth. According to the definitions of $k(t)$ and $\bar{k}(t)$, we have

$$\bar{k}(t) = k(t)T(t).$$

The current income is given by

$$y(t) = r(t)\bar{k}(t) + w(t)T(t).$$

The per capita disposable income is given by

$$\hat{y}(t) = y(t) + \bar{k}(t).$$

The disposable income is used for saving and consumption. At each point in time, a consumer would distribute the total available budget among saving, $s(t)$, consumer durables, $k_h(t)$, and consumption of goods, $c(t)$. The budget constraint is given by

$$p(t)c(t) + (r(t) + \delta_k)k_h(t) + s(t) = \hat{y}(t) = r(t)\bar{k}(t) + w(t)T(t) + \bar{k}(t).$$

Denote by $T_h(t)$ the leisure time at time t and the (fixed) available time for work and leisure by T_0. The time constraint is expressed by

$$T(t) + T_h(t) = T_0.$$

Substituting this function into the budget constraint yields

$$wT_h + pc + (r + \delta_k)k_h + s = \bar{y} \equiv r\bar{k} + wT_0 + \bar{k}. \qquad (5.3.3)$$

In our model, at each point in time, consumers have three variables to decide upon. We assume that the utility level, $U(t)$, that the consumer obtains is dependent on the leisure time, $T_h(t)$, consumer durables, $k_h(t)$, the consumption level of consumption goods, $c(t)$, and the saving, $s(t)$, as follows:

$$U(t) = T_h^\sigma(t) k_h^\eta(t) c^\xi(t) s^\lambda(t), \quad \sigma, \eta, \xi, \lambda > 0, \quad \sigma + \eta + \xi + \lambda = 1,$$

where σ is the propensity to use leisure time, η is the propensity to use consumer durables, ξ is the propensity to consume consumption goods, and λ is the propensity to own wealth. For consumers, wage rate, $w(t)$, the price, $p(t)$, and rate of interest, $r(t)$, are given in the markets and the wealth $\bar{k}(t)$ is predetermined before decision. Maximizing $U(t)$ subject to the budget constraint (5.3.3) yields

$$w(t)T_h(t) = \sigma\bar{y}(t), \ (r(t) + \delta_k)\bar{k}_h(t) = \eta\bar{y}(t), \ p(t)c(t) = \xi\bar{y}(t), \ s(t) = \lambda\bar{y}(t).$$
(5.3.4)

We now find the dynamics of capital accumulation. According to the definition of $s(t)$, the change in the household's wealth is given by

$$\dot{\bar{k}}(t) = s(t) - \bar{k}(t) = \lambda\bar{y}(t) - \bar{k}(t).$$
(5.3.5)

The output of the consumer goods sector is consumed by the households. That is

$$c(t)N_0 = F_s(t).$$
(5.3.6)

As output of the capital goods sector is equal to the depreciation of capital stock and the net savings, we have

$$S(t) - K(t) + \delta_k K(t) = F_i(t),$$
(5.3.7)

where $S - K + \delta_k K = (s - \delta\bar{k})N_0$ (where $\delta = 1 - \delta_k$) is the sum of the net savings and depreciation. It is straightforward to show that this equation can be derived from the other equations in the system. We have thus built the dynamic model.

5.3.2 The dynamics with the Cobb-Douglas production functions

We now examine the behavior of the dynamic system when the production functions are specified with the following Cobb-Douglas form:

$$F_j(t) = A_j K_j^{\alpha_j}(t) N_j^{\beta_j}(t), \ \alpha_j + \beta_j = 1, \ \alpha_j, \beta_j > 0, \ j = i, s.$$

The appendix shows the dynamics of the system for general production functions. We rewrite these functions in terms of capital intensities:

$$f_j(t) = A_j k_j^{\alpha_j}(t).$$

We now show that the motion of the system is determined by a one-dimensional differential equation. First, from $r(t) + \delta_k = f_i'(k_i) = pf_s'(k_s)$ in equations (5.3.1), we get

$$p = \frac{\alpha_i A_i k_i^{-\beta_i}}{\alpha_s A_s k_s^{-\beta_s}}.$$

Substituting this equation into $f_i(k_i) - k_i f_i'(k_i) = p(f_s(k_s) - k_s f_s'(k_s))$ in equations (5.3.1) yields

$$k_s = \overline{\alpha} k_i, \tag{5.3.8}$$

where $\overline{\alpha} \equiv \alpha_s \beta_i / \alpha_i \beta_s > 0$. There is a linear relationship between the capital intensities of the two sectors. Hence, the price can be expressed as a function of $k_i(t)$:

$$p = \frac{\overline{\alpha}^{\beta_s} \alpha_i A_i k_i^{\beta_s - \beta_i}}{\alpha_s A_s}. \tag{5.3.9}$$

From $pc = \xi \overline{y}$ and $(r + \delta_k) k_h = \eta \overline{y}$ in equations (5.3.4), we get

$$\frac{pc}{(r + \delta_k) k_h} = \frac{\xi}{\eta}.$$

Substituting $r + \delta_k = pf_s'(k_s)$ from equations (5.3.1) and $c = Tn_s f_s$ from equation (5.3.6) into this equation, we get

$$k_h = \overline{\eta} n_s k_s T, \tag{5.3.10}$$

where we use equations (5.3.8) and $\overline{\eta} \equiv \overline{\alpha} \eta / \alpha_s \xi > 0$. Insert equation (5.3.10) into the first equation in equations (5.3.2)

$$n_i + (\overline{\alpha} + \overline{\eta} T) n_s = \frac{k}{k_i}, \tag{5.3.11}$$

where we use equation (5.3.8). From equation (5.3.11) and $n_i + n_s = 1$, we solve the labor distribution as functions of k and k_i as follows:

$$n_i = \frac{k - (\overline{\alpha} + \overline{\eta}T)k_i}{(1 - \overline{\alpha} - \overline{\eta}T)k_i}, \quad n_s = \frac{k_i - k}{(1 - \overline{\alpha} - \overline{\eta}T)k_i}. \tag{5.3.12}$$

The labor distribution is uniquely determined by $k(t)$, $k_i(t)$, and $T(t)$ at any point in time. From $S - \delta K = (s - \delta \bar{k})N_0$, equation (5.3.7), and $s = \lambda \bar{y}$, we obtain

$$\bar{y} = \frac{n_i f_i(k_i) + \delta k}{\lambda} T, \tag{5.3.13}$$

where we use $\bar{k}(t) = k(t)T(t)$. From $pc = \xi \bar{y}$, $c = Tn_s f_s$, and $p = f_i' / f_s'$, we get

$$\bar{y} = \frac{n_s T f_s f_i'}{\xi f_s'}.$$

From this equation and equation (5.3.13), we have

$$\frac{\delta k}{f_i} = \overline{\lambda} - (1 + \overline{\lambda})n_i, \tag{5.3.14}$$

where we use $n_i + n_s = 1$ and

$$\overline{\lambda} \equiv \frac{\lambda \alpha_i \overline{\alpha}}{\alpha_s \xi} > 0.$$

Substituting $r = \alpha_i A_i k_i^{-\beta_i} - \delta_k$ and $w = \beta_i A_i k_i^{\alpha_i}$ into $\bar{y} = r\bar{k} + wT_0 + \bar{k}$, we get

$$\bar{y} = (\alpha_i A_i k_i^{-\beta_i} + \delta)kT + \beta_i A_i T_0 k_i^{\alpha_i}, \tag{5.3.15}$$

where we use $\bar{k} = kT$. Substituting equation (5.3.15) into $wT_h = \sigma \bar{y}$, we have

$$T = \frac{(1 - \sigma)\beta_i A_i T_0 k_i}{(\alpha_i A_i + \delta k_i^{\beta_i})\sigma k + \beta_i A_i k_i}, \tag{5.3.16}$$

where we use $w = \beta_i A_i k_i^{\alpha_i}$ and $T_h = T_0 - T$. From the above equation, we uniquely determine T as a function of k_i and k.

Substitute n_i in equations (5.3.12) into equation (5.3.14):

$$\left(\frac{(1-\bar{\alpha})\delta}{f_i} + \frac{1+\bar{\lambda}}{k_i}\right)k - (\bar{\lambda} + \bar{\alpha}) = \left(1 + \frac{\delta k}{f_i}\right)\bar{\eta}T. \qquad (5.3.17)$$

As $\bar{\alpha} > 0$ and $\bar{\lambda} > 0$ and the right-hand side of the above equation has to be positive, it is necessary to require

$$\frac{(1-\bar{\alpha})\delta}{f_i} + \frac{1+\bar{\lambda}}{k_i} > 0. \qquad (5.3.18)$$

Insert equation (5.3.16) into equation (5.3.17):

$$\tilde{f}_0(k_i)k^2 - \tilde{f}_1(k_i)k - \tilde{f}_2(k_i) = 0, \qquad (5.3.19)$$

where

$$\tilde{f}_0(k_i) \equiv \left(\frac{(1-\bar{\alpha})\delta}{f_i} + \frac{1+\bar{\lambda}}{k_i}\right)\left(\alpha_i A_i + \delta k_i^{\beta_i}\right)\sigma,$$

$$\tilde{f}_1(k_i) \equiv (\bar{\lambda} + \bar{\alpha})\left(\alpha_i A_i + \delta k_i^{\beta_i}\right)\sigma + \left((1-\sigma)\bar{\eta}T_0 - 1 + \bar{\alpha}\right)\delta\beta_i k_i^{\beta_i} - (1+\bar{\lambda})\beta_i A_i,$$

$$\tilde{f}_2(k_i) \equiv (\bar{\lambda} + \bar{\alpha} + (1-\sigma)\bar{\eta}T_0)\beta_i A_i k_i > 0, \quad \forall k_i > 0.$$

Under condition (5.3.18), we always have $\tilde{f}_0(k_i) > 0$. Hence, under condition (5.3.18), equation (5.3.19) has a unique solution for any given $k_i > 0$ as follows:

$$k(t) = \phi(k_i) \equiv \frac{\tilde{f}_1 + \sqrt{\tilde{f}_1^2 + 4\tilde{f}_0 \tilde{f}_2}}{2\tilde{f}_0}. \qquad (5.3.20)$$

Substitute this equation into equation (5.3.16):

$$T(t) = \tilde{\phi}(k_i) = \frac{(1-\sigma)\beta_i A_i T_0 k_i}{(\alpha_i A_i + \delta k_i^{\beta_i})\sigma\phi(k_i) + \beta_i A_i k_i}. \qquad (5.3.21)$$

We have $\bar{k} = Tk = \bar{\phi}(k_i)\phi(k_i)$. Substituting $\bar{k} = \bar{\phi}\phi$, equations (5.3.15), (5.3.20), and (5.3.21) into equation (5.3.5), we have

$$\dot{k}_i = \frac{(\lambda\alpha_i A_i k_i^{-\beta_i} + \lambda\delta - 1)\bar{\phi}(k_i)\phi(k_i) + \lambda\beta_i A_i T_0 k_i^{\alpha_i}}{\bar{\phi}'(k_i)\phi(k_i) + \bar{\phi}(k_i)\phi'(k_i)}. \qquad (5.3.22)$$

The right-hand side of equation (5.3.22) contains a single variable $k_i(t)$. The one-dimensional differential equation determines the motion of $k_i(t)$ for proper initial condition, $k_i(0)$.

Lemma 5.3.1
The dynamics of the two-sector model with the Cobb-Douglas production functions are given by the one-dimensional differential equation (5.3.22) with $k_i(t)$ as the variable. For any given positive value of $k_i(t)$ at any point in time, the other variables are uniquely determined by the following procedure: $k(t)$ by equation (5.3.20) → $k_s(t) = \bar{\alpha}k_i(t)$ → $T(t)$ by equation (5.3.21) → $n_i(t)$ and $n_s(t)$ by equations (5.3.12) → $r(t)$ and $w(t)$ by equations (5.3.1) → $f_j(t) = A_j k_j^{\alpha_j}$ → $p(t)$ by equation (5.3.9) → $k_h(t)$ by equation (5.3.10) → $N_j(t) = n_j(t)N$ → $K_j(t) = k_j(t)N_j(t)$ → $F_j(t) = f_j(t)N_j(t)$ → $\bar{y}(t)$ by equation (5.3.3) → $c(t)$ and $s(t)$ by equations (5.3.4).

Although it is straightforward to analyze the behavior of the one-dimensional differential equation, it is difficult to explicitly interpret results. Following the computing procedure given in Lemma 5.3.1, we simulate the model to illustrate motion of the system.

5.3.3 Simulate the model

It is straightforward to examine the impact of changes in parameter values on the equilibrium structure by standard comparative statics analysis as we guaranteed the existence of a unique equilibrium point. We now simulate the model in order to illustrate dynamic processes. First, we specify the parameter values as follows:

$$\alpha_i = 0.32, \quad \alpha_s = 0.34, \quad \delta_k = 0.03, \quad A_i = 1.3, \quad A_s = 1.1, \quad N = 1,$$
$$T_0 = 1, \quad \lambda = 0.82, \quad \sigma = 0.12, \quad \eta = 0.03. \qquad (5.3.23)$$

We note that the productivity of the capital goods sector is higher than that of the consumption goods sector. By (5.3.22), an equilibrium point is given by

$$(\lambda \alpha_i A_i k_i^{-\beta_i} + \lambda \delta - 1)\bar{\phi}(k_i)\phi(k_i) + \lambda \beta_i A_i T_0 k_i^{\alpha_i} = 0.$$

As demonstrated in Figure 5.3.1, the equation has a unique equilibrium point.

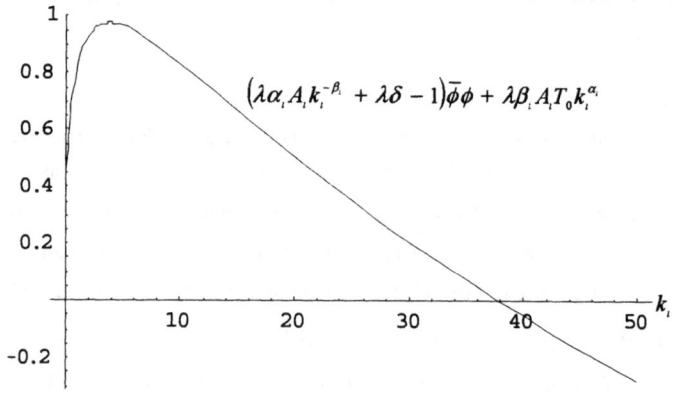

Figure 5.3.1 The existence of a unique equilibrium point

Following the procedure given by Lemma 5.3.1, we calculate the equilibrium values of the variables as follows:

$k_i = 37.896$, $k_s = 36.255$, $k = 49.990$, $n_i = 0.590$, $n_s = 0.410$,
$F_i = 4.639$, $F_s = 3.729$, $r = 0.013$, $w = 3.016$, $p = 1.225$,
$\bar{y} = 17.794$, $T = 0.292$, $\bar{k} = 14.591$, $c = 0.436$, $k_h = 12.767$, $s = 14.591$.

The GDP is given by

$$y_0 = F_i + pF_s = 1.346.$$

The share of the capital goods sector in the GDP is given by $F_i / y_0 = 0.594$.

Multi-Sector Growth Economies 235

We simulate the motion of the economic system over 50 years with $k_i(0) = 50$. Figure 5.3.2 depicts the motion of the key variables over the period. We choose 50 years because further simulation demonstrates that the system achieves the equilibrium point by the end of the period.

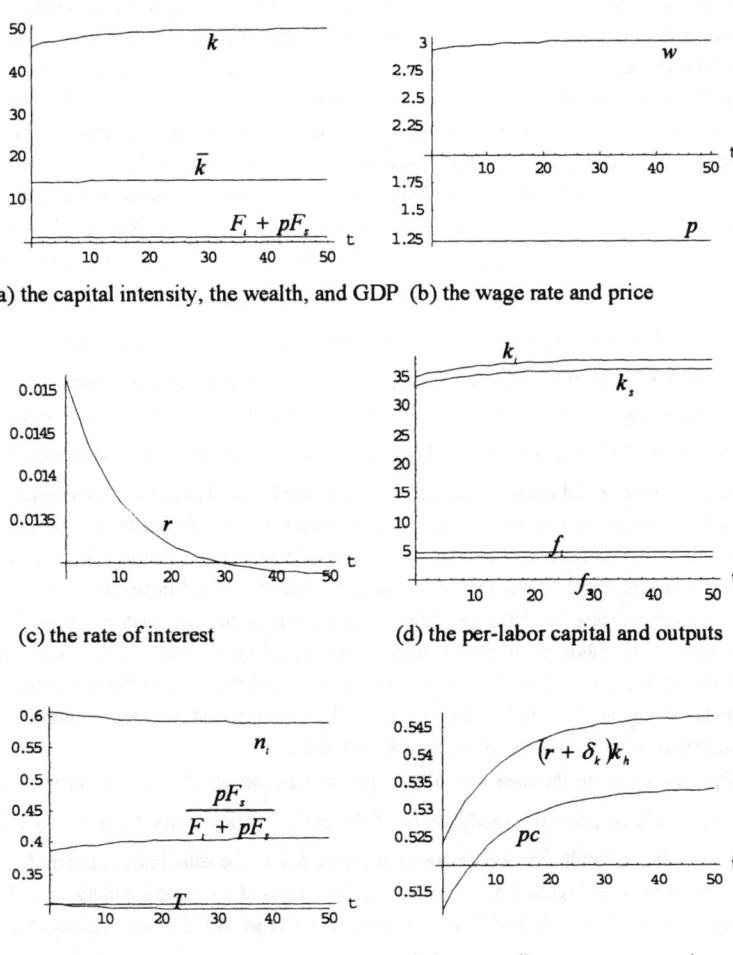

(a) the capital intensity, the wealth, and GDP
(b) the wage rate and price
(c) the rate of interest
(d) the per-labor capital and outputs
(e) the labor distribution, output share, and work time
(f) the expenditures on consumption goods and consumer durables

Figure 5.3.2 The motion of the variables over 50 years

Figure 5.3.2a shows the growth of the per capita wealth, the capital intensity per unit of labor, and the GDP over time. These variables experience nonnegative growth during the study period. Figure 5.3.2b shows the changes of the price and wage rate. The wage rate rises and the price changes slightly as time passes. Figure 5.3.2c depicts the motion of the rate of interest. The rate falls as time passes. Figure 5.3.2d describes the motion of the capital intensities of the two sectors and the per labor output levels of the two sectors. These variables experience positive growth. Figure 5.3.2e shows the labor distribution between the two sectors, the share of the consumption goods sector in the GDP, and the work time. We see that the labor force shifts to the consumption goods sector. The share of the consumption goods sector rises over time. The work time declines. Figure 5.3.2f shows how the expenditures on the consumption goods and the consumer durables change. The expenditures on the two goods rise over time.

We now examine the impact of changes on the dynamic processes of the system. First, we examine the case that all the parameters, except the propensities, are the same as in (5.3.23). We increase the propensity to save from 0.82 to 0.84. As $\sigma + \xi + \eta + \lambda = 1$ has to be satisfied, we reduce the values of σ, ξ, and η each by 0.01. The simulation results are demonstrated in Figure 5.3.3. The solid lines in Figure 5.3.3 are the same as in Figure 5.3.2, representing the values of the corresponding variables when $\lambda = 0.82$; the dashed lines in Figure 5.3.2 represent the new values of the variables when $\lambda = 0.84$. As the propensity to save increases, the wealth and the per labor capital intensity are increased. The change has little impact on the GDP. Figure 5.3.3b shows that the price is not much affected by the specified changes in the preference. The wage rate increases over time. In Figure 5.3.3c, we see that the rate of interest falls. Figure 5.3.3d shows that the capital intensities of the two sectors are increased and the per labor output levels of the two sectors are slightly increased. The labor participation ratio in the capital goods sector is increased, as illustrated in Figure 5.3.3e. The work time increases and the share of the consumption goods sector in the GDP falls. Figure 5.3.3f shows that the expenditures on consumption goods and consumer durables are reduced.

We now examine the case that all the parameters, except A_i, are the same as in (5.3.23). We increase the productivity of the capital goods sector from 1.3 to 1.5. The simulation results are demonstrated in Figure 5.3.4. The solid lines in Figure 5.3.4 are the same as in Figure 5.3.2, representing the values of the corresponding variables when $A_i = 1.3$; the dashed lines in Figure 5.3.4 represent the new values of the variables when $A_i = 1.5$. As the productivity rises, the total wealth and the GDP rise. As shown in Figure 5.3.4b, the wage rate rises and the price falls. Figure 5.3.4c shows that the rate of interest rises initially but is not affected in the long term.

Multi-Sector Growth Economies 237

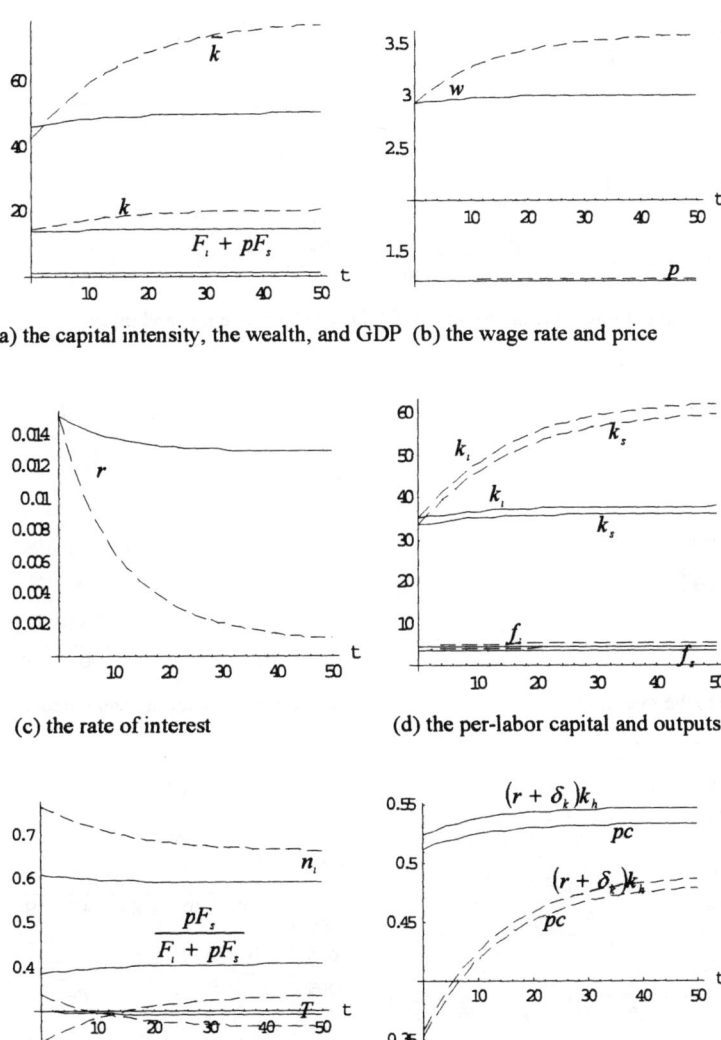

(a) the capital intensity, the wealth, and GDP

(b) the wage rate and price

(c) the rate of interest

(d) the per-labor capital and outputs

(e) the labor distribution, output share, and work time

(f) the expenditures on consumption goods and consumer durables

Figure 5.3.3 λ rises from 0.82 (solid lines) to 0.84 (dashed lines)

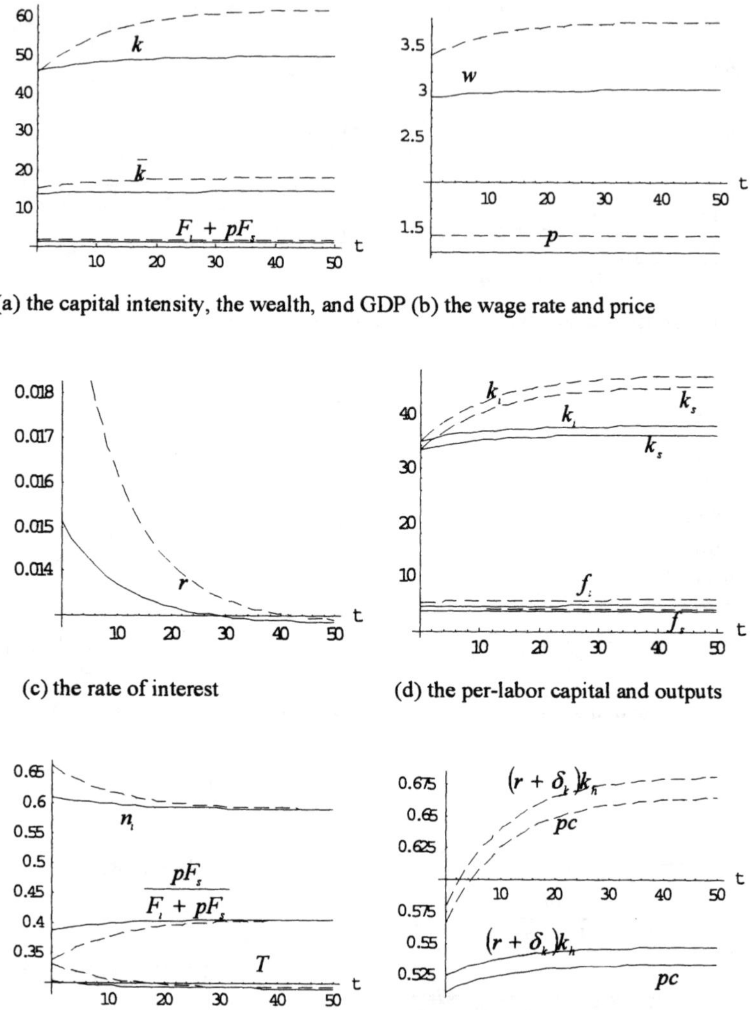

238 Economic Growth with Income and Wealth Distribution

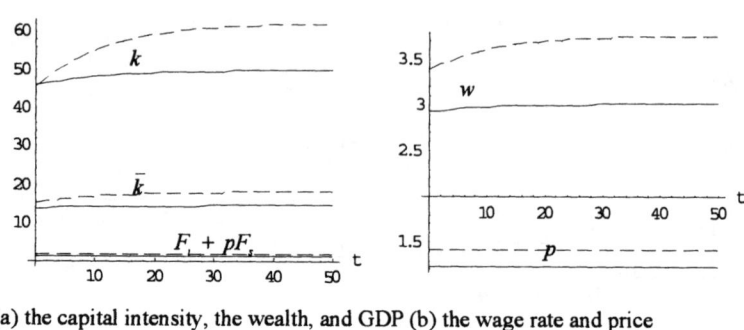

(a) the capital intensity, the wealth, and GDP (b) the wage rate and price

(c) the rate of interest (d) the per-labor capital and outputs

(e) the labor distribution, output share, work time (f) the expenditures on consumption goods and consumer durables

Figure 5.3.4 As A_i rises from 1.3 (solid lines) to 1.5 (dashed lines)

5.4 Knowledge accumulation and economic structure

This section introduces endogenous knowledge into the two-sector model proposed in Section 5.2. The economic structure and the economic variables are the same as in Section 5.2. Let us denote the knowledge stock at time t by $Z(t)$. We specify the following production functions:

$$F_j(t) = A_j Z^{m_j} K_j^{\alpha_j} N_j^{\beta_j}, \quad \alpha_j + \beta_j = 1, \quad \alpha_j, \beta_j > 0,$$

where m_j (≥ 0) is sector j's efficiency of knowledge utilization. We thus have

$$r + \delta_k = \frac{\alpha_i f_i}{k_i} = \frac{\alpha_s p f_s}{k_s}, \quad w = \beta_i f_i = \beta_s p f_s, \quad f_j = A_j Z^{m_j} k_j^{\alpha_j}. \tag{5.4.1}$$

As full employment of labor and capital is assumed, we have

$$K_i(t) + K_s(t) = K(t), \quad N_i(t) + N_s(t) = N(t),$$

which can be rewritten in the form of

$$n_i(t) k_i(t) + n_s(t) k_s(t) = k(t), \quad n_i(t) + n_s(t) = 1, \tag{5.4.2}$$

where

$$k(t) = \frac{K(t)}{N(t)}, \quad n_j(t) = \frac{N_j(t)}{N(t)}, \quad j = i, s.$$

The current income, $Y(t)$, is given by

$$Y(t) = r(t)K(t) + w(t)N = F_i(t) + p(t)F_s(t).$$

The consumer problem is defined by

Maximize $U(t) = C(t)^\xi S(t)^\lambda$, $\xi + \lambda = 1$, $\xi, \lambda > 0$,

s.t.: $p(t)C(t) + S(t) = \hat{Y}(t) \equiv Y(t) + K(t).$

The optimal solution is

$$C(t) = \frac{\xi \hat{Y}(t)}{p(t)}, \quad S(t) = \lambda \hat{Y}(t). \tag{5.4.3}$$

The wealth accumulation is given by

$$\dot{K}(t) = \lambda \hat{Y}(t) - K(t) = \lambda Y(t) - \xi K(t). \tag{5.4.4}$$

As consumption goods cannot be saved, we have

$$C(t) = F_s(t). \tag{5.4.5}$$

It is assumed that knowledge accumulation is through learning by doing. We propose the following equation for knowledge growth:

$$\dot{Z}(t) = \frac{\tau_i F_i(t)}{Z(t)^{\varepsilon_i}} + \frac{\tau_s F_s(t)}{Z(t)^{\varepsilon_s}} - \delta_z Z(t), \tag{5.4.6}$$

in which δ_z (≥ 0) is the depreciation rate of knowledge, and ε_j and τ_j ($j = i, s$) are parameters. We require τ_j nonnegative. The term, $\tau_j F_j(t)/Z(t)^{\varepsilon_j}$, is sector j's contribution to knowledge accumulation through learning by doing.

First, we describe the dynamics in terms of two variables. Substituting $k(t) = K(t)/N(t)$ into equation (5.4.4) yields

$$\dot{k}(t) = \lambda \hat{y}(t) - k(t) = \lambda y(t) - \xi k(t), \tag{5.4.7}$$

where

$$\hat{y}(t) = \frac{\hat{Y}(t)}{N} = y(t) + k(t), \quad y(t) \equiv \frac{Y(t)}{N} = n_i(t) f_i(k_i) + n_s(t) f_s(k_s).$$

By equations (5.4.3) we have

$$c(t) = \frac{\xi \hat{y}(t)}{p(t)}, \quad s(t) = \lambda \hat{y}(t),$$

where $c(t) \equiv C(t)/N$ and $s(t) \equiv S(t)/N$. From these equations and $S - \delta K = F_i$ and $C = F_s$, we have

$$\lambda \hat{y} - \delta k = n_i f_i(k_i), \quad \xi \hat{y} = p n_s f_s(k_s). \tag{5.4.8}$$

By equations (5.4.1), we have

$$k_s(t) = \alpha k_i(t),$$

where $\alpha \equiv \alpha_s \beta_i / \alpha_i \beta_s$.

By $k_s = \alpha k_i$ and $\beta_i f_i = \beta_s p f_s$, we solve

$$p(t) = \frac{\beta_i A_i}{\beta_s \alpha^{\alpha_s} A_s} Z(t)^m k_i(t)^{\alpha_i - \alpha_s}, \tag{5.4.9}$$

where $m \equiv m_i - m_s$. If $\alpha_i = \alpha_s$, then the price is given by $p = A_i Z^m / A_s$. In this study, we require $\alpha_i \neq \alpha_s$. Corresponding to equations (5.4.2) and $k_s(t) = \alpha k_i(t)$, we have

$$n_i = \frac{\alpha k_i - k}{(\alpha - 1)k_i}, \quad n_s = \frac{k - k_i}{(\alpha - 1)k_i}. \tag{5.4.10}$$

Corresponding to equation (5.2.10), we have

$$k = \frac{k_i}{A_0 \left(1 + A k_i^{\beta_i} Z^{-m_i}\right)}, \tag{5.4.11}$$

where

$$A_0 \equiv \frac{1 + \beta_i \lambda / \beta_s \xi}{\alpha + \beta_i \lambda / \beta_s \xi}, \quad A \equiv \frac{(1 - \alpha) \delta / A_i}{1 + \beta_i \lambda / \beta_s \xi}.$$

It is straightforward to show that for any positive $k(t) > 0$ and $Z(t) > 0$, $k_i(t)$ is uniquely determined as a function of $k(t)$ and $Z(t)$. We denote this function by

$$k_i(t) = \varphi(k(t), Z(t)).$$

242 Economic Growth with Income and Wealth Distribution

By equations (5.4.10) and (5.4.11) and according to the definitions of A and A_0, we find

$$n_i = 1 - \frac{\alpha + \alpha\delta Z^{-m_i}k_i^{\beta_i}/A_i}{\alpha + \beta_i\lambda/\beta_s\xi}.$$

Hence, for $n_i(t)$ to satisfy $1 > n_i(t) > 0$, it is sufficient to have

$$\varphi < \left(\frac{A_i\beta_i\lambda}{\alpha\delta\beta_s\xi}\right)^{1/\beta_i} Z^{m_i/\beta_i}.$$

Substituting $\lambda\hat{y} = n_i f_i(k_i) + \delta k$ into equation (5.4.7) yields

$$\dot{k}(t) = \Phi_k(k, Z) \equiv \frac{\alpha\varphi(k, Z) - k}{\alpha - 1} A_i Z^{m_i} \varphi(k, Z)^\beta - \delta k(t),$$

where we use equations (5.4.10) and (5.4.11).

We now represent knowledge evolution equation (5.4.6) as a function of $k(t)$ and $Z(t)$. By equations (5.4.10), $k_s = \alpha k_i$, $k_i = \varphi$, equation (5.4.6) can be rewritten as

$$\dot{Z}(t) = \Phi_Z(k, Z)$$
$$\equiv \tau_i^* \frac{(\alpha\varphi(k, Z) - k)Z^{m_i - \varepsilon_i}}{\varphi(k, Z)^{\beta_i}} + \tau_s^* \frac{(k - \varphi(k, Z))Z^{m_s - \varepsilon_s}}{\varphi(k, Z)^{\beta_s}} - \delta_z Z(t),$$

where

$$\tau_i^* \equiv \frac{\tau_i A_i}{(\alpha - 1)N}, \quad \tau_s^* \equiv \frac{\tau_s \alpha^{\alpha_s} A_s}{(\alpha - 1)N}.$$

Lemma 5.4.1
The dynamics of the two-sector growth model with endogenous knowledge follow

$$\dot{k}(t) = \Phi_k(k, Z), \quad \dot{Z}(t) = \Phi_Z(k, Z).$$

For given values of $k(t)$ and $Z(t)$ at any point in time, the other variables are determined by the following procedure: $k_i(t) = \varphi(k, Z) \rightarrow k_s(t) = \alpha k_i(t) \rightarrow n_i(t)$ and $n_s(t)$ by equations (5.4.10) $\rightarrow r(t)$, $w(t)$, and $f_j(t)$, $j = i, s$ by equations (5.4.1) $\rightarrow p(t)$ by equation (5.4.9) $\rightarrow N_j(t) = n_j(t)N \rightarrow K_j(t) = k_j(t)N_j(t) \rightarrow F_j(t) = f_j(t)N_j(t) \rightarrow Y(t) = F_i(t) + p(t)F_s(t) \rightarrow \hat{Y}(t) = Y(t) + \delta K(t) \rightarrow C(t) = \xi \hat{Y}(t) \rightarrow S(t) = \lambda \hat{Y}(t)$.

Hence, once we determine $k(t)$ and $Z(t)$, we solve all the variables. It can be shown that the system may have either a unique or two equilibrium points. Since the analysis is complicated and we can get few new insights,[6] we omit any further examination of the model.

5.5 Conclusions

This section examines a few two-sector growth models. Obviously, the number of sectors should not be limited to two.[7] As mentioned in the introduction, Uzawa's two-sector model has been generalized and extended in many directions. It is not difficult to generalize our models along these lines. It is straightforward to develop the models in discrete time. We may analyze behavior of the models with other forms of production or utility functions.[8]

Appendix

A.5.1 The dynamics with general production functions

The appendix shows the dynamics of the system with general production functions. We show that the motion of the system is determined by a differential equation. First, from $r(t) + \delta_k = f_i'(k_i) = pf_s'(k_s)$ in equations (5.3.1), we get $p = f_i'(k_i)/f_s'(k_s)$. Substituting this equation into

$$f_i(k_i) - k_i f_i'(k_i) = p(f_s(k_s) - k_s f_s'(k_s)),$$

in equations (5.3.1) yields

$$\Psi_i(k_i) \equiv \frac{f_i(k_i)}{f_i'(k_i)} - k_i = \frac{f_s(k_s)}{f_s'(k_s)} - k_s \equiv \Psi_s(k_s). \quad (A.5.1.1)$$

From the properties of $f_i(k_i)$, we can show that the function $\Psi_i(k_i)$ has the following properties:

$$\Psi_i(0) = 0, \ \Psi_i(k_i) > 0 \text{ for } k_i > 0, \ \Psi_i'(k_i) = -\frac{f_i(k_i)f_i''(k_i)}{f_i'^2(k_i)} \geq 0.$$

The function $\Psi_s(k_s)$ has the same properties in k_s. We see that for any given $k_s(t) \geq 0$, the equation (A.5.1.1) determines $k_i(t) \geq 0$ as a unique function of $k_s(t)$, denoted by $k_s(t) = \Omega(k_i(t))$. We have $\Omega(0) = 0$ and $\Omega' > 0$.

First, from $r(t) + \delta_k = f_i'(k_i) = pf_s'(k_s)$ in (5.3.1), we get

$$p = \frac{f_i'(k_i)}{f_s'(\Omega(k_i))}. \tag{A.5.1.2}$$

The price can be expressed as a function of $k_i(t)$.

From $pc = \xi \bar{y}$ and $(r + \delta_k)k_h = \eta \bar{y}$ in (5.3.4), we get

$$\frac{pc}{(r + \delta_k)k_h} = \frac{\xi}{\eta}.$$

Substituting $r + \delta_k = pf_s'(k_s)$ from (5.3.1) and $c = Tn_s f_s$ from (5.3.6) into this equation, we get

$$k_h = \frac{\eta T n_s f_s(k_s)}{\xi f_s'(k_s)}. \tag{A.5.1.3}$$

Substitute (A.5.1.3) into $n_i k_i + n_s k_s + k_h = k$

$$n_i k_i + \left(k_s + \frac{\eta T f_s}{\xi f_s'}\right) n_s = k.$$

From this equation and $n_i + n_s = 1$, we determine the labor distribution as functions of T, k, and k_i:

$$n_i = \frac{k_s + \eta T f_s / \xi f_s' - k}{k_s + \eta T f_s / \xi f_s' - k_i}, \quad n_s = \frac{k - k_i}{k_s + \eta T f_s / \xi f_s' - k_i}. \tag{A.5.1.4}$$

The labor distribution is uniquely determined by $k(t)$, $k_i(t)$, and $T(t)$ at any point in time. Equation (5.3.13) still holds. That is

$$\bar{y} = \frac{n_i f_i(k_i) + \delta k}{\lambda} T. \tag{A.5.1.5}$$

From $pc = \xi \bar{y}$, $c = T n_s f_s$, and $p = f_i' / f_s'$, we get

$$\bar{y} = \frac{n_s T f_s f_i'}{\xi f_s'}.$$

From this equation and equations (A.5.1.4), we have

$$\frac{\delta k}{f_i} = \hat{f}(k_i) - (\hat{f}(k_i) + 1)n_i, \tag{A.5.1.6}$$

where we use $n_i + n_s = 1$ and $\hat{f}(k_i) \equiv \lambda f_s f_i' / \xi f_s'$. Substitute $r = f_i' - \delta_k$ and $w = f_i - k_i f_i'$ into $\bar{y} = r\bar{k} + wT_0 + \bar{k}$

$$\bar{y} = (f_i' + \delta)kT + (f_i - k_i f_i')T_0. \tag{A.5.1.7}$$

where we use $\bar{k} = kT$. Substitute equation (A.5.1.7) into $wT_h = \sigma \bar{y}$:

$$T = \frac{(1 - \sigma)T_0}{1 + (f_i' + \delta)\sigma k / (f_i - k_i f_i')}. \tag{A.5.1.8}$$

From the above equation, we uniquely determine T as a function of k_i and k. Substitute n_i in equations (A.5.1.4) into equation (A.5.1.6):

$$\left(k_i + (\hat{f} + 1)\frac{f_i}{\delta} - k_s - \frac{\eta T f_s}{\xi f_s'}\right)\frac{\delta k}{f_i} = (k_s + k_i \hat{f}) + \frac{\eta T f_s}{\xi f_s'}.$$

246 Economic Growth with Income and Wealth Distribution

Inserting equation (A.5.1.6) into the above equation, we obtain the following relation between $k_i(t)$ and $k(t)$:

$$\tilde{f}_0(k_i)k^2 - \tilde{f}_1(k_i)k - \tilde{f}_2(k_i) = 0,$$

where $\tilde{f}_j(k_i)$ are functions of $k_i(t)$. We omit their expressions because they are tedious. Under proper conditions, the equation has a unique solution for any given $k_i > 0$ as follows:

$$k(t) = \phi(k_i) \equiv \frac{\tilde{f}_1 + \sqrt{\tilde{f}_1^2 + 4\tilde{f}_0\tilde{f}_2}}{2\tilde{f}_0}. \qquad (A.5.1.9)$$

Substituting this equation into equation (A.5.1.8), we get T as a function of $k_i(t)$, expressed as

$$T(t) = \tilde{\phi}(k_i).$$

We have

$$\bar{k} = Tk = \bar{\phi}(k_i)\phi(k_i).$$

Substituting $\bar{k} = \bar{\phi}\phi$, equations (A.5.1.7), (A.5.1.8), and (A.5.1.9) into equation (5.3.5), we have

$$\dot{k}_i = \frac{(f_i'(k_i) + \lambda\delta - 1)\bar{\phi}(k_i)\phi(k_i) + (f_i(k_i) - k_i f_i'(k_i))\lambda T_0}{\bar{\phi}'(k_i)\phi(k_i) + \bar{\phi}(k_i)\phi'(k_i)}. \qquad (A.5.1.10)$$

The right-hand side of equation (A.5.1.10) contains a single variable $k_i(t)$. The one-dimensional differential equation determines the motion of $k_i(t)$ for proper initial condition, $k_i(0)$.

Lemma A.5.1
The dynamics of the two-sector model are given by the one-dimensional differential equation (A.5.1.1) with $k_i(t)$ as the variable. For any given positive value of $k_i(t)$ at any point in time, the other variables are uniquely determined by the following

procedure: $k(t)$ by equation (A.5.1.9) $\to$ $k_s(t) = \Omega(k_i)$ $\to$ $T(t)$ by equation (A.5.1.8) $\to$ $n_i(t)$ and $n_s(t)$ by equations (A.5.1.4) $\to$ $r(t)$ and $w(t)$ by equations (5.3.1) $\to$ $f_j(t) = f_j(k_j)$ $\to$ $p(t)$ by equation (A.5.1.2) $\to$ $k_h(t)$ by equation (A.5.1.3) $\to$ $N_j(t) = n_j(t)N$ $\to$ $K_j(t) = k_j(t)N_j(t)$ $\to$ $F_j(t) = f_j(t)N_j(t)$ $\to$ $\bar{y}(t)$ by equation (A.5.1.5) $\to$ $c(t)$ and $s(t)$ by equations (5.3.4).

6
Multiple Sectors and Heterogeneous Households

The Walrasian system is a beautiful theory. Nevertheless, its success is mainly limited to short-run economic phenomena. It is important to introduce endogenous wealth accumulation, population growth, and knowledge creation and utilization into this structurally beautiful system. As pointed out in Chapter 1, the traditional growth theories are not effective in analyzing economic systems with heterogeneous households and economic structures. The previous chapter studied one-sector group models of heterogeneous groups. It is a natural step to combine the main ideas of the previous two chapters to examine economic dynamics with multiple sectors and heterogeneous households. This chapter examines multi-sector growth models with homogeneous population.

This chapter shows that by extending the multi-sector models and growth models with heterogeneous households in the previous two chapters, we can generalize the traditional static Walrasian system to a dynamic model with endogenous wealth accumulation. First, I propose a two-sector two-group growth model to provide some insights into dynamics of wealth and income distribution in a competitive economy with capital accumulation as the main engine of economic dynamics. It should be noted that the economic issues and the analytical framework of this model are similar to these of the two-sector two-class model proposed by Stiglitz (1967a).[1] The Stiglitz model classifies the productive system into two sectors using capital and labor, one of which produces capital goods, the other consumption goods. We consider our model as an extension of Stiglitz's two-sector two-class model with the spirit of Leontief's input-output system. The remainder of this chapter is organized as follows. Section 6.1 defines the two-sector two-group model. Section 6.2 analyzes the behavior of the model when the production functions take on the Cobb-Douglas form. Section 6.3 simulates the model analyzed in Section 6.2. Section 6.4 concludes the chapter. The appendix analyzes the dynamic properties of the model with general production functions.

6.1 The two-sector two-group model

The model is a combination of the basic models in the previous two chapters. Labor is homogeneous and labor grows at an exogenously given exponential rate n $(=0)$. There is only one malleable capital good. Capital goods can be used as an input in both sectors in the economy. Capital depreciates at a constant exponential rate, δ_k, which is independent of the manner of use. The two sectors use a single grade of labor and a single type of capital goods. The two inputs are smoothly substitutable for each other in each sector and are freely transferable from one sector to the other. Both exogenously determined labor supply and irrevocably existing capital stock are inelastically offered for employment. Both sectors use neoclassical technology with the standard Inada conditions. The production functions are given by

$$F_j(K_j(t), N_j(t)), \quad j = i, s,$$

where F_j are the output of sector j, K_j and N_j are respectively the capital and labor used in sector j, and the subscripts i and s denote respectively the capital goods sector and the consumer goods sector. Assume the production functions, F_j, to be neoclassical. We have

$$f_j(t) = f_j(k_j(t)), \quad f_j(t) \equiv \frac{F_j(t)}{N_j(t)}, \quad k_j(t) \equiv \frac{K_j(t)}{N_j(t)}, \quad j = i, s.$$

The production functions, f_j, have the following properties:

(i) $f_j(0) = 0$;

(ii) f_j are increasing, strictly concave on R^+, and C^2 on R^{++}; $f_j'(k_j) > 0$ and $f_j''(k_j) < 0$; and

(iii) $\lim_{k_j \to 0} f_j'(k_j) = \infty$ and $\lim_{k_j \to +\infty} f_j'(k_j) = 0$.

Let N stand for the total flow of labor services employed at time t for production. We assume that labor is always fully employed. We measure N as follows:

$$N = \sum_{j=1}^{2} h_j \overline{N}_j, \tag{6.1.1}$$

where h_j are the levels of human capital of group j, $j = 1, 2$.

Markets are competitive; thus labor and capital earn their marginal products, and firms earn zero profits. We assume that the capital goods serve as a medium of exchange and are taken as numeraire. The price of consumption goods is denoted by $p(t)$. The rate of interest, $r(t)$, and wage rate, $w(t)$, of per unit qualified labor force are determined by the markets. Hence, for any individual firm, $r(t)$ and $w(t)$ are given at each point in time. The production sector chooses the two variables, $K_j(t)$ and $N_j(t)$, to maximize its profit. The marginal conditions are given by

$$r + \delta_k = f_i'(k_i) = p f_s'(k_s),$$
$$w(t) = f_i(k_i) - k_i f_i'(k_i) = p(t)[f_s(k_s) - k_s f_s'(k_s)]. \quad (6.1.2)$$

The wage rate of group j is given by

$$w_j(t) = h_j w(t), \quad j = 1, 2.$$

Total capital stock, $K(t)$, is allocated to the two sectors. As full employment of labor and capital is assumed, we have

$$K_i(t) + K_s(t) + \sum_{j=1}^{2} \tilde{K}_j = K(t), \quad N_i(t) + N_s(t) = N, \quad (6.1.3)$$

where $\tilde{K}_j(t)$ is the level of consumer durables of group j, $j = 1, 2$. We rewrite the above equations as

$$n_i(t)k_i(t) + n_s(t)k_s(t) + \sum_j^2 \tilde{n}_j \tilde{k}_j(t) = k(t), \quad n_i(t) + n_s(t) = 1, \quad (6.1.4)$$

where

$$k(t) \equiv \frac{K(t)}{N}, \quad n_q(t) \equiv \frac{N_q(t)}{N}, \quad q = i, s, \quad \tilde{k}_j(t) \equiv \frac{\tilde{K}_j(t)}{\tilde{N}_j}, \quad \tilde{n}_j \equiv \frac{\overline{N}_j}{N}, \quad j = 1, 2.$$

Let $\bar{k}_j(t)$ denote per capita wealth of group j at t. According to the definitions, we have

$$K(t) = \sum_{j=1}^{2} \bar{k}_j(t) \bar{N}_j. \qquad (6.1.5)$$

Group j's per capita current income, $y_j(t)$, from the interest payment, $r(t)\bar{k}_j(t)$, and the wage payment, $w_j(t)$, is defined by

$$y_j(t) = r(t)\bar{k}_j(t) + w_j(t).$$

The per capita disposable income of consumer j is defined as the sum of the current income and the wealth available for purchasing consumption goods and saving:

$$\hat{y}_j(t) = y_j(t) + \bar{k}_j(t) = (1 + r(t))\bar{k}_j(t) + w_j(t), \quad j = 1, 2. \qquad (6.1.6)$$

The disposable income is used for saving and consumption. At each point in time, a consumer would distribute the total available budget among saving, $s_j(t)$, consumer durables, $\tilde{k}_j(t)$, and consumption goods, $c_j(t)$. The budget constraints are given by

$$p(t)c_j(t) + (r(t) + \delta_k)\tilde{k}_j(t) + s_j(t) = \hat{y}_j(t). \qquad (6.1.7)$$

The total disposable income, $\hat{y}_j$, is distributed among consuming consumption goods, pc_j, utilizing consumer durables, $(r + \delta_k)\tilde{k}_j$, and saving, s_j. In our approach, at each point in time, consumers have three variables to decide upon. A consumer decides how much to consume, how much to utilize consumer durables, and how much to save. Equation (6.1.7) means that consumption and saving exhaust consumers' disposable personal incomes. We assume that the utility level, $U_j(t)$, that the consumer of group j obtains is dependent on the level of consumption goods, $c_j(t)$, the level of consumer durables, $\tilde{k}_j(t)$, and the level of saving, $s_j(t)$. The utility level, $U_j(t)$, of group j is specified as follows:

$$U_j(t) = c_j^{\xi_j}(t)\tilde{k}_j^{\eta_j}(t)s_j^{\lambda_j}(t), \quad \xi_j, \eta_j, \lambda_j > 0, \quad \xi_j + \mu_j + \lambda_j = 1, \quad j = 1, 2, \qquad (6.1.8)$$

where ξ_j, η_j, and λ_j are respectively group j's propensities to consume consumption goods, to utilize consumer durables, and to own wealth.[2] Here, for simplicity, we specify the utility function with the Cobb-Douglas form. It would provide more insights if we take some other forms of utility function. Maximizing U_j subject to budget constraints (6.1.7) yields

$$p(t)c_j(t) = \xi_j \hat{y}_j(t), \quad (r(t) + \delta_k)\widetilde{k}_j(t) = \eta_j \hat{y}_j(t), \quad s_j(t) = \lambda_j \hat{y}_j(t). \quad (6.1.9)$$

According to the definitions of $s_j(t)$, the wealth accumulation of group j is given by

$$\dot{\bar{k}}_j(t) = s_j(t) - \bar{k}_j(t). \quad (6.1.10)$$

The output of the consumer goods sector is consumed by the households. That is

$$\sum_{j=1}^{2} c_j(t)\overline{N}_j = F_s(t). \quad (6.1.11)$$

As output of the capital goods sector is equal to the depreciation of capital stock and the net savings, we have

$$\sum_{j=1}^{2} s_j(t)\overline{N}_j - K(t) + \delta_k K(t) = F_i(t). \quad (6.1.12)$$

It is straightforward to show that this equation can be derived from the other equations in the system. It can be shown that equation (6.1.12) is redundant. We have thus built the dynamic model. We will show that the dynamics consist of two-dimensional differential equations.

6.2 Dynamics with the Cobb-Douglas production functions

As it is difficult to analyze behavior of the dynamic system with general production functions, for explicit interpretation we specify production functions in the Cobb-Douglas form

$$f_j(k_j) = A_j k_j^{\alpha_j}, \quad A_j > 0, \quad 0 < \alpha_j < 1, \quad j = i, s. \quad (6.2.1)$$

From equations (6.2.1) and (6.1.2), we directly obtain

$$k_s(t) = \alpha k_i(t),$$

where

$$\alpha \equiv \frac{\beta_i \alpha_s}{\beta_s \alpha_i}, \quad \beta_j \equiv 1 - \alpha_j, \quad j = i, s.$$

The capital intensity of the consumer goods sector is proportional to that of the capital goods sector. By $k_s = \alpha k_i$ and $\beta_i f_i = \beta_s p f_s$, we solve

$$p(t) = \frac{\beta_i A_i}{\beta_s \alpha^{\alpha_s} A_s} k_i(t)^{\alpha_i - \alpha_s}. \tag{6.2.2}$$

The price of consumer goods is positively related to the technological level of the capital goods sector but negatively related to that of the consumer goods sector. The price is positively or negatively related to the capital intensity of the capital goods sector, depending on the sign of $\alpha_i - \alpha_s$. If $\alpha_i = \alpha_s$, then the price is constant, $p = A_i / A_s$. In the remainder of this section, we require $\alpha_i > \alpha_s$. If the equality holds, then labor distribution is invariant in time. The analysis of $\alpha_i \leq \alpha_s$ is similar. The condition $\alpha_i > \alpha_s$ (which implies $\alpha < 1$) guarantees $k_s(t) < k_i(t)$ for any t. According to the definitions, we can rewrite equations (6.1.11) and (6.1.12) as

$$\sum_{j=1}^{2} \tilde{n}_j c_j = n_s f_s, \quad \sum_{j=1}^{2} \tilde{n}_j s_j - \delta k = n_i f_i. \tag{6.2.3}$$

Substitute $pc_j = \xi_j \hat{y}_j$ and $s_j = \lambda_j \hat{y}_j$ into equations (6.2.3):

$$\begin{bmatrix} \xi_1 \tilde{n}_1 & \xi_2 \tilde{n}_2 \\ \lambda_1 \tilde{n}_1 & \lambda_2 \tilde{n}_2 \end{bmatrix} \begin{bmatrix} \hat{y}_1 \\ \hat{y}_2 \end{bmatrix} = \begin{bmatrix} pn_s f_s \\ n_i f_i + \delta k \end{bmatrix}.$$

We solve the above linear equations as

$$\hat{y}_1 = \frac{\beta_i \lambda_2 n_s f_s - (n_i f_i + \delta k)\beta_s \xi_2}{\lambda \beta_s \tilde{n}_1}, \quad \hat{y}_2 = \frac{\beta_s \xi_1 (n_i f_i + \delta k) - \beta_i \lambda_1 n_s f_s}{\lambda \beta_s \tilde{n}_2}, \tag{6.2.4}$$

where we use $pf_s = \beta_s f_i / \beta_i$ and $\lambda \equiv \xi_1 \lambda_2 - \xi_2 \lambda_1$ ($\neq 0$ assumed). Substituting equations (6.2.4) and $r + \delta_k = f_i'(k_i)$ into $(r + \delta_k)\bar{k}_j = \eta_j \hat{y}_j$, we solve

$$\tilde{k}_1 = (\bar{\xi}_2 n_s f_i - n_i f_i - \delta k)\xi_2 \tilde{\lambda}_1 k_i^\beta, \quad \tilde{k}_2 = (n_i f_i + \delta k - \bar{\xi}_1 n_s f_i)\xi_1 \tilde{\lambda}_2 k_i^\beta, \quad (6.2.5)$$

where

$$\tilde{\lambda}_j \equiv \frac{\eta_j}{\lambda \tilde{n}_j \alpha_i A_i}, \quad \bar{\xi}_j \equiv \frac{\lambda_j \beta_i}{\xi_j \beta_s}, \quad j = 1, 2.$$

Substitute equations (6.2.5) into equations (6.1.4):

$$\psi_i(k_i)n_i + \psi_s(k_i)n_s = k, \qquad (6.2.6)$$

where

$$\psi_i(k_i) \equiv \frac{1 - A_i \tilde{n}_1 \xi_2 \tilde{\lambda}_1 + A_i \tilde{n}_2 \xi_1 \tilde{\lambda}_2}{1 + \delta \tilde{n}_1 \xi_2 \tilde{\lambda}_1 k_i^\beta - \delta \tilde{n}_2 \xi_1 \tilde{\lambda}_2 k_i^\beta} k_i,$$

$$\psi_s(k_i) \equiv \frac{\alpha + A_i \bar{\xi}_2 \tilde{n}_1 \xi_2 \tilde{\lambda}_1 - A_i \bar{\xi}_1 \tilde{n}_2 \xi_1 \tilde{\lambda}_2}{1 + \delta \tilde{n}_1 \xi_2 \tilde{\lambda}_1 k_i^\beta - \delta \tilde{n}_2 \xi_1 \tilde{\lambda}_2 k_i^\beta} k_i.$$

Solve equation (6.2.6) and $n_i + n_s = 1$,

$$n_i = \frac{\psi_s(k_i) - k}{\psi_s(k_i) - \psi_i(k_i)}, \quad n_s = \frac{k - \psi_i(k_i)}{\psi_s(k_i) - \psi_i(k_i)}. \qquad (6.2.7)$$

The labor distribution between the two sectors is uniquely determined by k and k_i. Insert $s_j = \lambda_j \hat{y}_j$ into the second equation in equations (6.2.3):

$$\sum_{j=1}^{2} \tilde{n}_j \lambda_j \hat{y}_j - \delta k = A_i k_i^{\alpha_i} n_i. \qquad (6.2.8)$$

Substituting equations (6.1.6) into equation (6.2.8) yields

$$\sum_{j=1}^{2}\tilde{n}_{j}\lambda_{j}(1+r)\bar{k}_{j} + \sum_{j=1}^{2}\tilde{n}_{j}\lambda_{j}w_{j} - \delta k = A_{i}k_{i}^{\alpha_{i}}n_{i}.$$

Insert $r = \alpha_{i}A_{i}k_{i}^{-\beta_{i}} - \delta_{k}$ and $w_{j} = h_{j}\beta_{i}A_{i}k_{i}^{\alpha_{i}}$ into the above equation:

$$\sum_{j=1}^{2}\tilde{n}_{j}\lambda_{j}\left(\alpha_{i}A_{i}k_{i}^{-\beta_{i}} + \delta\right)\bar{k}_{j} + \beta_{i}A_{i}k_{i}^{\alpha_{i}}\sum_{j=1}^{2}\tilde{n}_{j}\lambda_{j}h_{j} - \delta k = A_{i}k_{i}^{\alpha_{i}}n_{i}. \tag{6.2.9}$$

Insert n_i in equations (6.2.7) into equation (6.2.9)

$$\sum_{j=1}^{2}\tilde{n}_{j}\lambda_{j}\left(\alpha_{i}A_{i}k_{i}^{-\beta_{i}} + \delta\right)\bar{k}_{j} + \left(\beta_{i}A_{i}\sum_{j=1}^{2}\tilde{n}_{j}\lambda_{j}h_{j} - \frac{A_{i}\psi_{s}(t)}{\psi_{s}(t) - \psi_{i}(t)}\right)k_{i}^{\alpha_{i}}$$
$$= \left(\delta - \frac{A_{i}k_{i}^{\alpha_{i}}(t)}{\psi_{s}(t) - \psi_{i}(t)}\right)k. \tag{6.2.10}$$

According to the definitions, we can rewrite equation (6.1.5) as

$$k(t) = \sum_{j=1}^{2}\tilde{n}_{j}\bar{k}_{j}(t). \tag{6.2.11}$$

Substitute equation (6.2.11) into equation (6.2.10):

$$\bar{k}_{1} = \Lambda(k_{i},\bar{k}_{2}) \equiv \frac{\psi(k_{i}) - \psi_{2}(k_{i})\bar{k}_{2}}{\psi_{1}(k_{i})}, \tag{6.2.12}$$

where

$$\psi(k_{i}) \equiv \left(\frac{A_{i}\psi_{s}(k_{i})}{\psi_{s}(k_{i}) - \psi_{i}(k_{i})} - \beta_{i}A_{i}\sum_{j=1}^{2}\tilde{n}_{j}\lambda_{j}h_{j}\right)k_{i}^{\alpha_{i}},$$

$$\psi_{1}(k_{i}) \equiv \left(\frac{A_{i}k_{i}^{\alpha_{i}}(k_{i})}{\psi_{s}(k_{i}) - \psi_{i}(k_{i})} + \lambda_{j}\alpha_{i}A_{i}k_{i}^{-\beta_{i}} + \lambda_{j}\delta - \delta\right)\tilde{n}_{1},$$

$$\psi_{2}(k_{i}) \equiv \left(\frac{A_{i}k_{i}^{\alpha_{i}}(k_{i})}{\psi_{s}(k_{i}) - \psi_{i}(k_{i})} + \lambda_{j}\alpha_{i}A_{i}k_{i}^{-\beta_{i}} + \lambda_{j}\delta - \delta\right)\tilde{n}_{2}.$$

256 Economic Growth with Income and Wealth Distribution

We see that $\bar{k}_1(t)$ is a function of $k_i(t)$ and $\bar{k}_2(t)$. By equations (6.2.11) and (6.2.12), we solve $k(t)$ as a function of $k_i(t)$ and $\bar{k}_2(t)$:

$$k = \Lambda_0(k_i, \bar{k}_2) \equiv \tilde{n}_1 \Lambda(k_i, \bar{k}_2) + \tilde{n}_2 \bar{k}_2.$$

By equations (6.2.7), we see that the labor distribution $n_i(t)$ and $n_s(t)$ are also uniquely determined as functions of $k_i(t)$ and $\bar{k}_2(t)$. According to equations (6.2.5), we can explicitly express $\hat{y}_j(t)$ as functions of $k_i(t)$ and $\bar{k}_2(t)$ as

$$\hat{y}_j = \Lambda_j(k_i, \bar{k}_2).$$

We omit giving explicit expressions as it is straightforward and the expressions are tedious.

Insert $s_j = \lambda_j \Lambda_j(k_i, \bar{k}_2)$ into equation (6.1.10):

$$\dot{\bar{k}}_j = \lambda_j \Lambda_j(k_i, \bar{k}_2) - \bar{k}_j, \quad j = 1, 2. \tag{6.2.13}$$

Taking derivatives of equation (6.2.12) with respect to t yields

$$\dot{\bar{k}}_1 = \left(\frac{\psi' - \bar{k}_2 \psi_2' - \Lambda \psi_1'}{\psi_1} \right) \dot{k}_i - \frac{\psi_2}{\psi_1} \dot{\bar{k}}_2. \tag{6.2.14}$$

Equations (6.2.13)–(6.2.14) contain three variables, $\bar{k}_1$, $\bar{k}_2$, and k_i. Nevertheless, the original dynamic system is two-dimensional. To express the dynamics in a two-dimensional differential equations system, we substitute equations (6.2.14) and (6.2.12) into equations (6.2.13) to eliminate $\bar{k}_1(t)$:

$$\dot{k}_i = \frac{\lambda_1 \psi_1(k_i) \Lambda_1(k_i, \bar{k}_2) - \psi_1(k_i) \Lambda(k_i, \bar{k}_2) + (\lambda_2 \Lambda_2(k_i, \bar{k}_2) - \bar{k}_2) \psi_2(k_i)}{\psi'(k_i) - \bar{k}_2 \psi_2'(k_i) - \Lambda \psi_1'(k_i)},$$

$$\dot{\bar{k}}_2 = \lambda_2 \Lambda_2(k_i, \bar{k}_2) - \bar{k}_2. \tag{6.2.15}$$

The two-dimensional differential equations (6.2.15) contain two variables, k_1 and $\bar{k}_2$.

Lemma 6.2.1
The dynamics of the economic system are governed by the two-dimensional differential equations (6.2.15) with $k_1(t)$ and $\bar{k}_2(t)$ as the variables. Moreover, all the other variables can be determined as functions of $k_1(t)$ and $\bar{k}_2(t)$ at any point in time by the following procedure: $\bar{k}_1(t)$ by equation (6.2.12) → $k_s(t) = \alpha k_i(t)$ → $k(t)$ by equation (6.2.11) → $p(t)$ by equation (6.2.2) → $n_i(t)$ and $n_s(t)$ by equations (6.2.7) → $r(t)$ and $w(t)$ by equations (6.1.2) → $w_j(t) = h_j w(t)$, $j = 1, 2$ → $\hat{y}_j(t)$ by equations (6.1.6) → $c_j(t)$ and $s_j(t)$ by equations (6.1.9) → $N_i(t) = n_i(t)N$ and $N_s(t) = n_s(t)N_s$ → $K(t) = k(t)N$ → $K_i(t) = k_i(t)N_i(t)$ and $K_s(t) = k_s(t)N_s(t)$ → $F_i(K_i(t), N_i(t))$ and $F_s(K_s(t), N_s(t))$ → $U_j(t)$ by (6.1.8).

We now simulate the model to illustrate the dynamic behavior of the system.

6.3 Simulating the model

This section simulates the model of the previous section. In this section, the depreciation rate is fixed at $\delta_k = 0.07$. We specify the production functions, the population structure, and preferences as follows:

$$\begin{pmatrix} A_i \\ A_s \end{pmatrix} = \begin{pmatrix} 0.7 \\ 0.9 \end{pmatrix}, \begin{pmatrix} \alpha_i \\ \alpha_s \end{pmatrix} = \begin{pmatrix} 0.34 \\ 0.32 \end{pmatrix}, \begin{pmatrix} \bar{N}_1 \\ \bar{N}_2 \end{pmatrix} = \begin{pmatrix} 1 \\ 5 \end{pmatrix}, \begin{pmatrix} h_1 \\ h_2 \end{pmatrix} = \begin{pmatrix} 9 \\ 2 \end{pmatrix},$$
$$\begin{pmatrix} \lambda_1 \\ \lambda_2 \end{pmatrix} = \begin{pmatrix} 0.87 \\ 0.75 \end{pmatrix}, \begin{pmatrix} \eta_1 \\ \eta_2 \end{pmatrix} = \begin{pmatrix} 0.05 \\ 0.12 \end{pmatrix}. \quad (6.3.1)$$

The capital goods sector's technological parameter A_i is higher than that of the consumer goods sector. Group 1's level of human capital and propensity to save are both higher than group 2's. The population share of group 1 is only about 16.7 percent. Before demonstrating motion of the system over time, we show that the system has a (unique) equilibrium point. At equilibrium, according to equations (6.2.15), the following equations hold:

$$\lambda_1 \psi_1(k_i) \Lambda_1(k_i, \bar{k}_2) - \psi_1(k_i) \Lambda(k_i, \bar{k}_2) + (\lambda_2 \Lambda_2(k_i, \bar{k}_2) - \bar{k}_2) \psi_2(k_i) = 0,$$
$$\lambda_2 \Lambda_2(k_i, \bar{k}_2) - \bar{k}_2 = 0.$$

The simulation demonstrates the existence of a unique equilibrium point for the given parameters. The equilibrium values of the variables are as follows:

$r = 0.072$, $p = 0.789$, $k = 5.417$, $K = 93.431$, $Y = F_i + pF_s = 17.001$,

$$\begin{pmatrix} n_i \\ n_s \end{pmatrix} = \begin{pmatrix} 0.377 \\ 0.623 \end{pmatrix}, \begin{pmatrix} k_i \\ k_s \end{pmatrix} = \begin{pmatrix} 2.177 \\ 1.988 \end{pmatrix}, \begin{pmatrix} N_i \\ N_s \end{pmatrix} = \begin{pmatrix} 7.172 \\ 11.828 \end{pmatrix},$$

$$\begin{pmatrix} K_i \\ K_s \end{pmatrix} = \begin{pmatrix} 148.30 \\ 848.37 \end{pmatrix}, \begin{pmatrix} F_i \\ F_s \end{pmatrix} = \begin{pmatrix} 6.640 \\ 13.264 \end{pmatrix},$$

$$\begin{pmatrix} w_1 \\ w_2 \end{pmatrix} = \begin{pmatrix} 5.417 \\ 1.204 \end{pmatrix}, \begin{pmatrix} \bar{k}_1 \\ \bar{k}_2 \end{pmatrix} = \begin{pmatrix} 70.362 \\ 4.614 \end{pmatrix}, \begin{pmatrix} \hat{y}_1 \\ \hat{y}_2 \end{pmatrix} = \begin{pmatrix} 80.873 \\ 6.152 \end{pmatrix},$$

$$\begin{pmatrix} \tilde{k}_1 \\ \tilde{k}_2 \end{pmatrix} = \begin{pmatrix} 28.389 \\ 5.183 \end{pmatrix}, \begin{pmatrix} c_1 \\ c_2 \end{pmatrix} = \begin{pmatrix} 8.198 \\ 1.013 \end{pmatrix}.$$

We see that most of the labor force is employed by the consumer goods sector at the equilibrium point. As $\alpha < 1$, the capital intensity of the capital goods sector is higher than that of the consumer goods sector. The GDP share of the capital goods sector is much lower than that of the consumer goods sector. Group 1's wage rate is higher than that of group 2. Group 1's per capita wealth is much higher than that of group 2; and group 1's consumption levels of consumer goods and consumer durables are higher than group 2's in terms of per capita. The relative economic position of group 1 in the national economy is illustrated as follows:

$$\frac{\bar{N}_1}{\sum_j \bar{N}_j} = 0.167, \quad \frac{\bar{k}_1 \bar{N}_1}{K} = 0.75.3, \quad \frac{y_1 \bar{N}_1}{\sum_j c_j \bar{N}_j} = 0.87.2, \quad \frac{\tilde{k}_1 \bar{N}_1}{\sum_j \tilde{k}_j \bar{N}_j} = 0.523,$$

$$\frac{c_1 \bar{N}_1}{\sum_j c_j \bar{N}_j} = 0.618.$$

Group 1's population share is only 16.7 percent; but its shares of national wealth and current income are respectively 75.3 percent and 87.2 percent; its shares in consumption of national consumer durables and consumer goods are respectively 52.3 percent and 61.8 percent. The inequality results from differences in levels of human capital and preferences. Evidently, it is important to examine effects of changes in these parameters. Before carrying out comparative statics analysis by simulation, we illustrate the motion of the economy with the initial conditions, $k_1(0) = 2.75$ and $\bar{k}_2(0) = 26$ as in Figure 6.3.1.

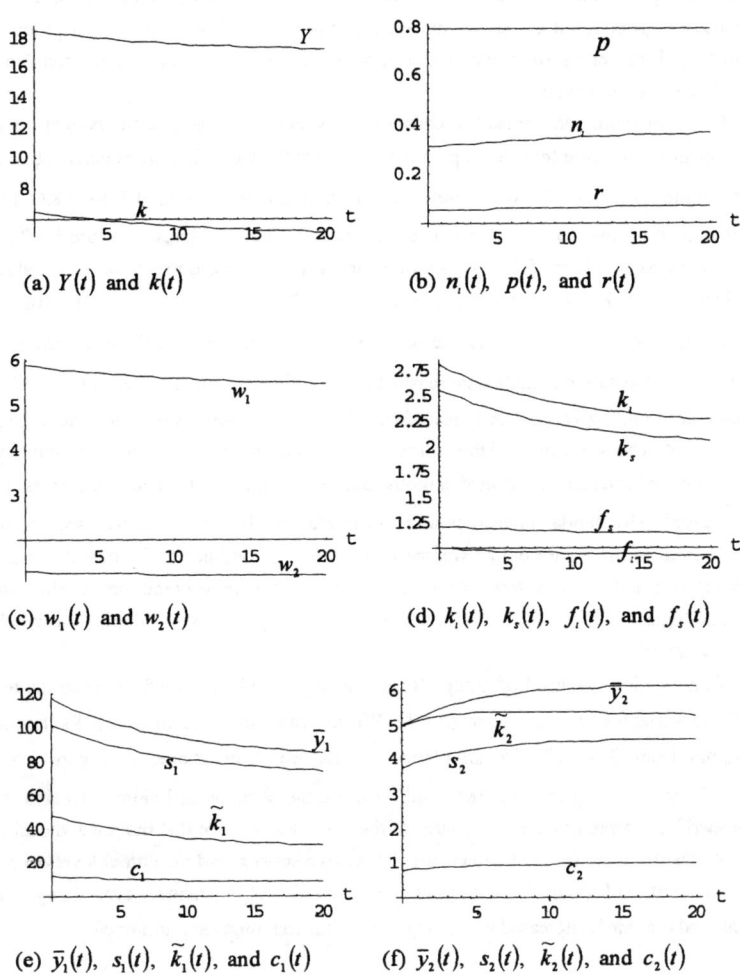

(a) $Y(t)$ and $k(t)$

(b) $n_1(t)$, $p(t)$, and $r(t)$

(c) $w_1(t)$ and $w_2(t)$

(d) $k_i(t)$, $k_s(t)$, $f_i(t)$, and $f_s(t)$

(e) $\bar{y}_1(t)$, $s_1(t)$, $\tilde{k}_1(t)$, and $c_1(t)$

(f) $\bar{y}_2(t)$, $s_2(t)$, $\tilde{k}_2(t)$, and $c_2(t)$

Figure 6.3.1 The motion of the system

All the variables approach their equilibrium values in the long term. We see that the current national income and the capital stock of per labor input decline over time. The share of the labor force of the capital goods sector increases and the rate of interest increases. The price remains almost constant. Group 1's wage rate declines and group 2's wage rate changes slightly. The capital intensities of the two sectors decline and the levels of outputs in terms of per labor inputs decline slightly. The living conditions of group 1 measured in terms of consumption levels of consumer goods and consumer durables decline; the living conditions of group 2 measured in terms of consumption levels of consumer goods and consumer durables are improved.

We now examine the impact of changes on dynamic processes of the system. First, we examine the case that all the parameters, except the technology parameter, A_1, are the same as in (6.3.1). We increase the technology level from 0.7 to 0.82. The simulation results are demonstrated in Figure 6.3.2. The solid lines in Figure 6.3.2 are the same as in Figure 6.3.1, representing the values of the corresponding variables when $A_1 = 0.7$; the dashed lines in Figure 6.3.2 represent the new values of the variables when $A_1 = 0.82$. As the technology level of the capital goods sector is improved, the national income increases and $k(t)$ declines initially below the level of the corresponding variable and rises above it after a few periods of time. The price is increased. The share of the labor force in the capital goods sector increases initially. The rate of interest is changed slightly due to change in A_1. The wage rates are increased. The capital intensities and the production levels of the two sectors are increased. From Figure 6.3.2e we see that the living conditions of group 2 initially deteriorate but after a few years the living conditions become better after the technological change. Figure 6.3.2f shows that group 2 benefits during the whole study period.

We now allow the level of group 1's human capital to be changed and keep the rest of the variables constant as in (6.3.1). We increase the level of group 1's human capital from 9 to 10. The simulation results are demonstrated in Figure 6.3.3. Similarly as in Figure 6.3.2, the solid lines are the same as in Figure 6.3.1 and the dashed lines represent the new values of the variables. We see that the price, the labor force distribution, the capital intensities of the two sectors, and the output levels of per labor input, and group 2's living conditions are almost unchanged, even though the national income is increased and group 2's living conditions are improved.

Multiple Sectors and Heterogeneous Households

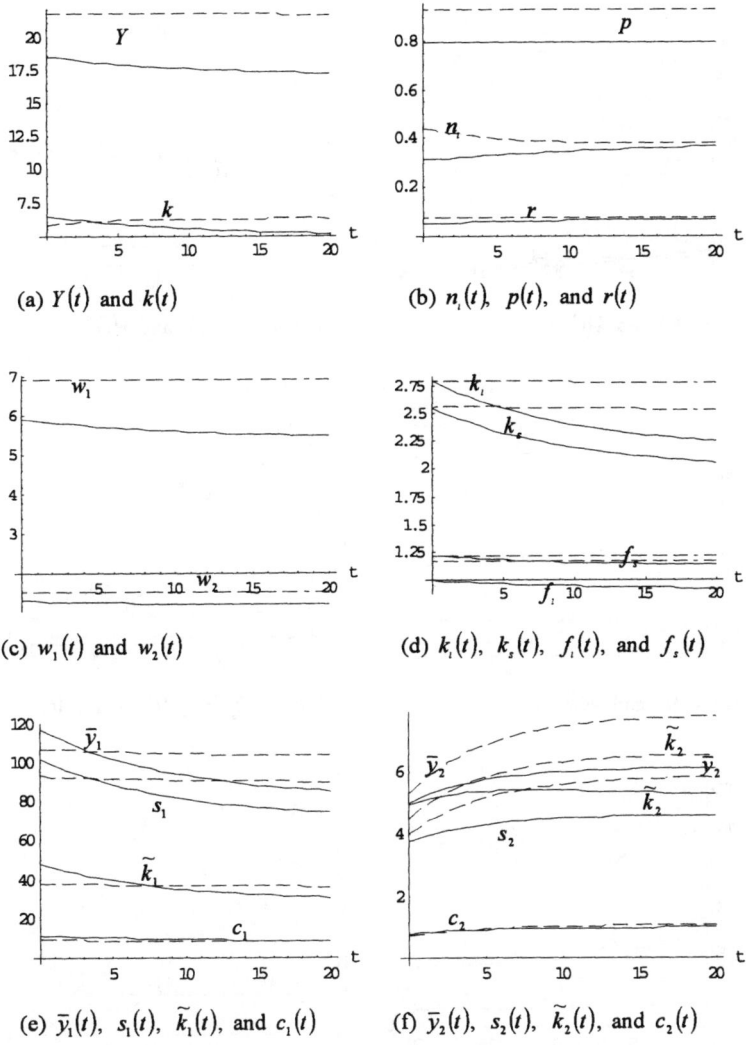

(a) $Y(t)$ and $k(t)$

(b) $n_i(t)$, $p(t)$, and $r(t)$

(c) $w_1(t)$ and $w_2(t)$

(d) $k_i(t)$, $k_s(t)$, $f_i(t)$, and $f_s(t)$

(e) $\bar{y}_1(t)$, $s_1(t)$, $\tilde{k}_1(t)$, and $c_1(t)$

(f) $\bar{y}_2(t)$, $s_2(t)$, $\tilde{k}_2(t)$, and $c_2(t)$

Figure 6.3.2 As A_1 rises from 0.7 (solid lines) to 0.82 (dashed lines)

262 *Economic Growth with Income and Wealth Distribution*

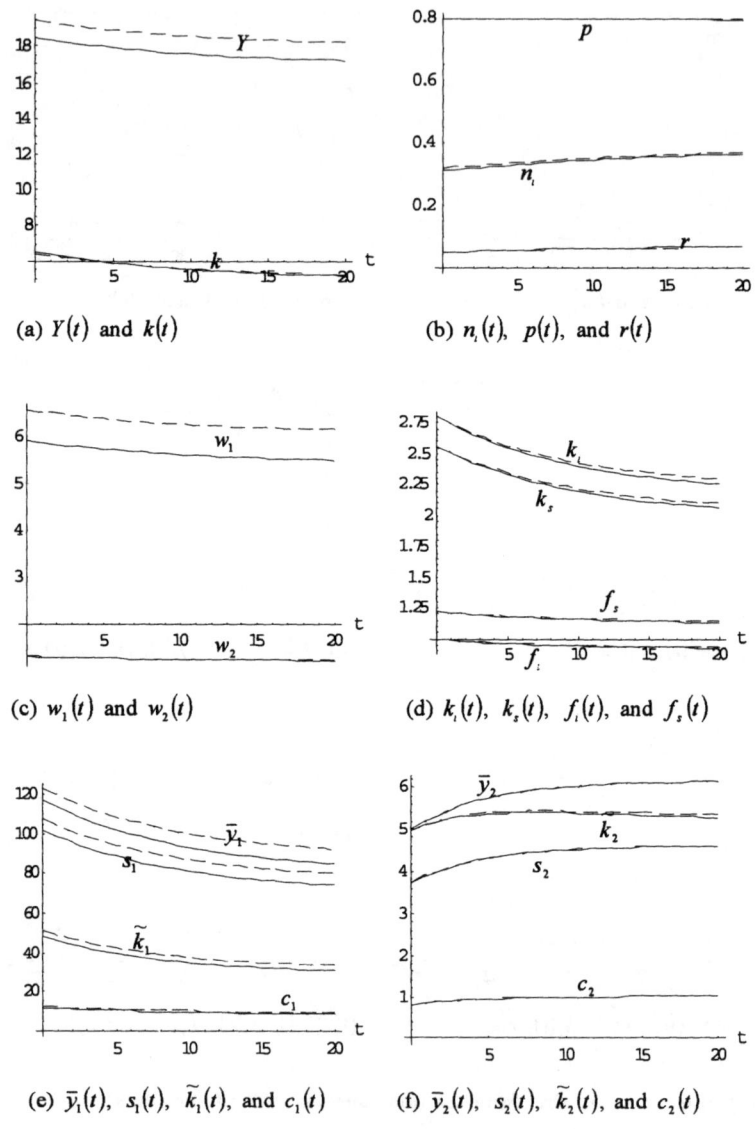

Figure 6.3.3 As h_1 rises from 9 (solid lines) to 10 (dashed lines)

Figure 6.3.4 provides the impact of change in group 1's human capital. We increase the level of group 1's human capital from 2 to 3.5. It is important to observe that in the case of group 2's human capital improvement, both groups benefit. This is different from the case when group 1's level of human capital is increased. The improvement of human capital of the rich class only benefits the rich class; but the improvement of human capital of the poor class benefits all in the economy.

Figure 6.3.5 examines the impact of change in group 1's population. We increase group 1's population from 1 to 1.5. It can be seen that the national income increases as a consequence of the increase in the population. The price and the rate of interest are slightly affected by the change in the population. The share of the labor force of the capital goods sector increases. The wage rates of the two groups are slightly increased. The capital intensities of the two sectors and the output levels of the two sectors in terms of per labor input are increased. The living conditions of group 1 in per capita terms deteriorate; group 2's level of consumer durables is increased. Group 2 benefits from group 1's population growth.

Figure 6.3.6 summarizes the impact of change in group 2's population. We increase group 2's population from 5 to 6. It can be seen that the effects are similar to those caused by the change in group 1's population with regard to Y, r, p, w_1, w_2, and k. But the capital intensities of the two sectors and the output levels of the two sectors in terms of per labor input are increased as N_1 rises, while these variables fall as N_2 rises.

In Figure 6.3.7, we give the impact of change in group 1's preference. We specify the preference change as follows: let λ_1 increase from 0.87 to 0.89 and both η_1 and ξ_1 be reduced by 0.01. We see that group 1 does not benefit from the preference change in terms of consumption levels of consumer durables and consumer goods, but group 2 benefits.

In Figure 6.3.8, we give the impact of change in group 2's preference. We specify the preference change as follows: let λ_1 increase from 0.75 to 0.79 and both η_2 and ξ_2 be reduced by 0.02. In the contrast to the case when group 1 increases the propensity to save, when group 2 increases the propensity to save, the group which changes the preference benefits and the other group is harmed.

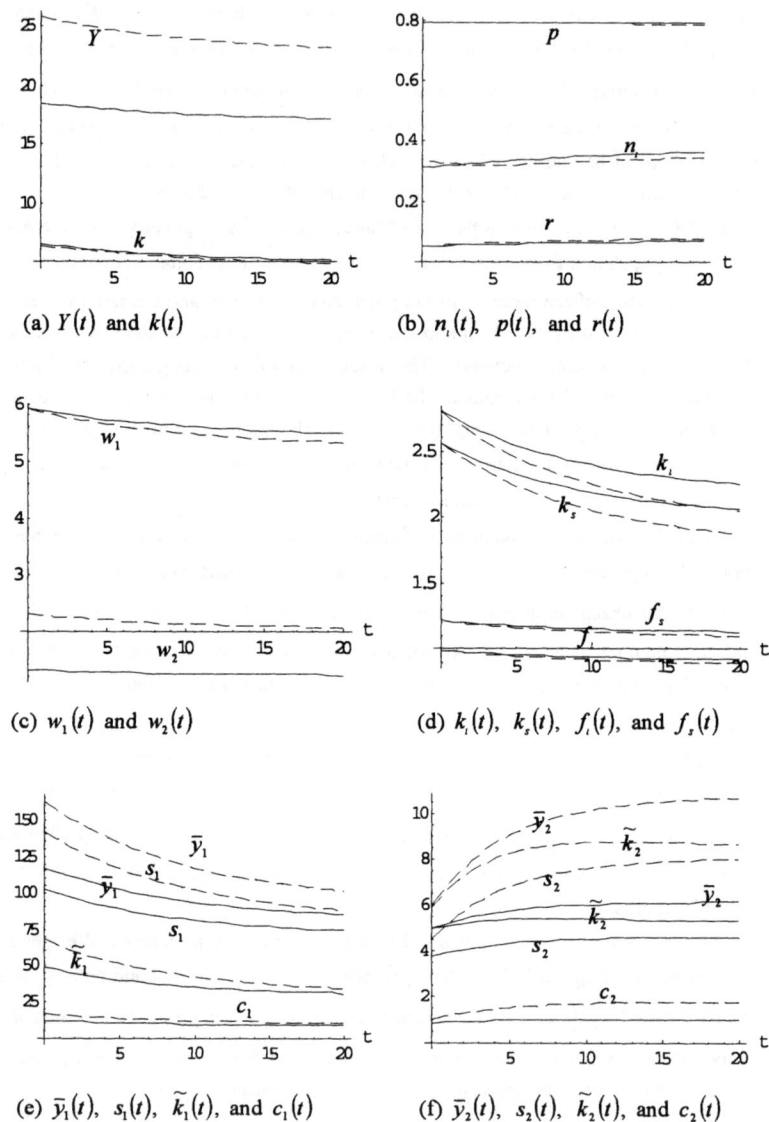

(a) $Y(t)$ and $k(t)$

(b) $n_i(t)$, $p(t)$, and $r(t)$

(c) $w_1(t)$ and $w_2(t)$

(d) $k_i(t)$, $k_s(t)$, $f_i(t)$, and $f_s(t)$

(e) $\bar{y}_1(t)$, $s_1(t)$, $\tilde{k}_1(t)$, and $c_1(t)$

(f) $\bar{y}_2(t)$, $s_2(t)$, $\tilde{k}_2(t)$, and $c_2(t)$

Figure 6.3.4 As h_2 rises from 2 (solid lines) to 3.5 (dashed lines)

Multiple Sectors and Heterogeneous Households 265

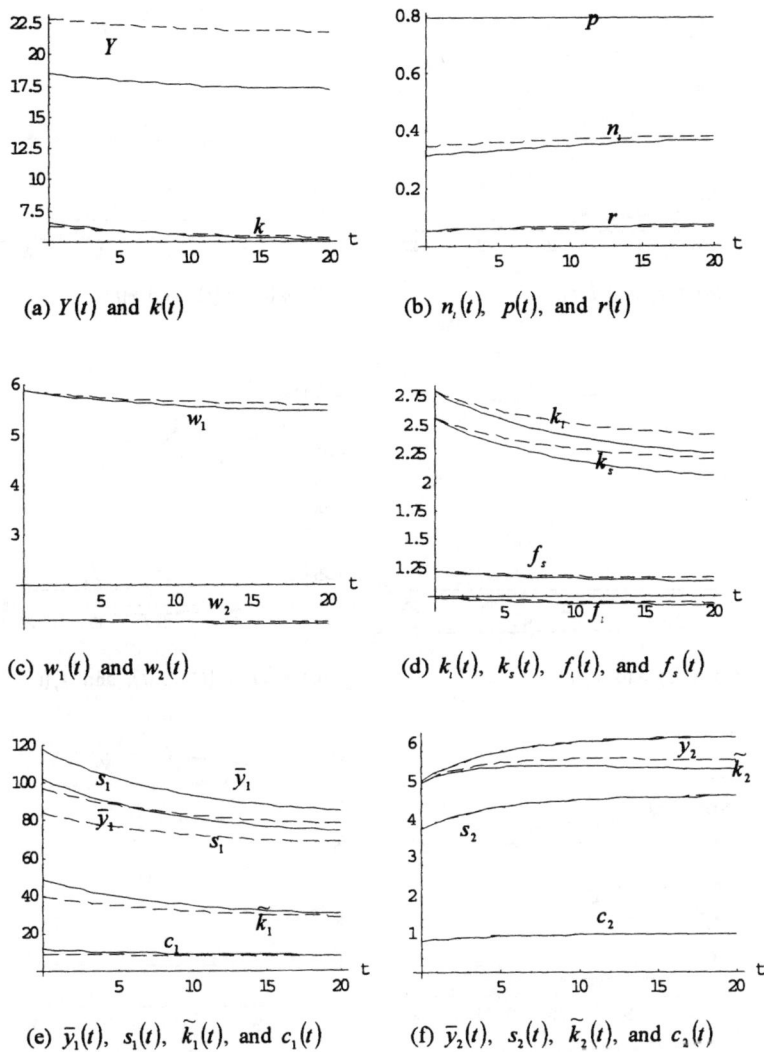

Figure 6.3.5 As N_1 rises from 1 (solid lines) to 1.5 (dashed lines)

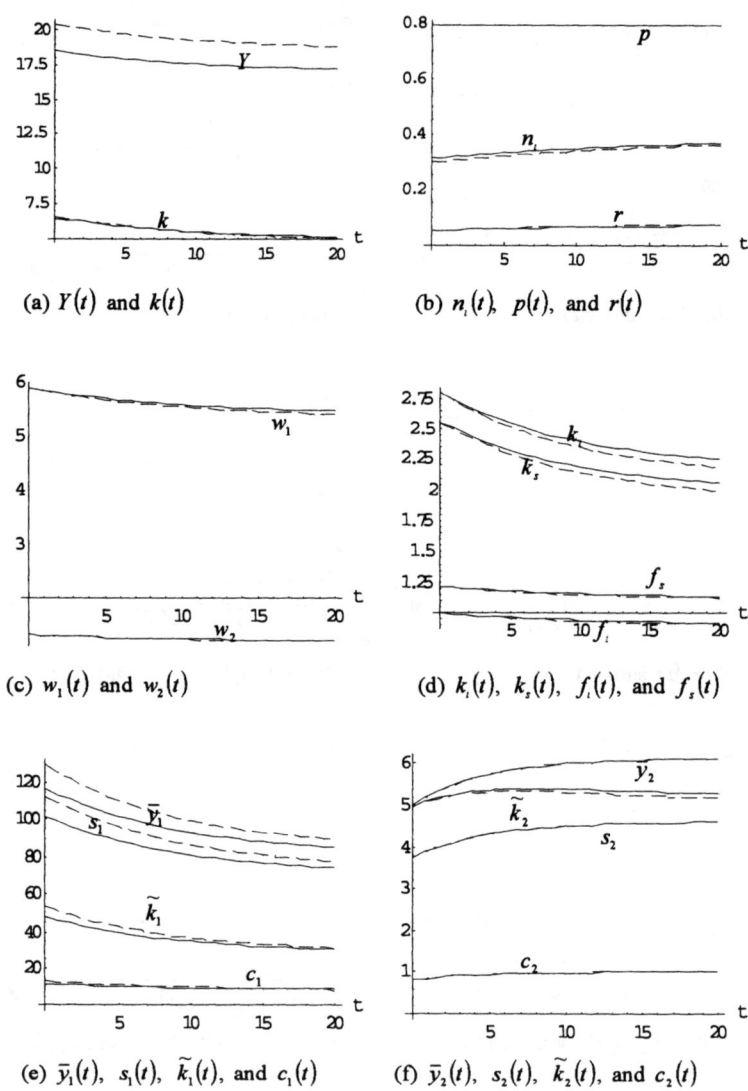

(a) $Y(t)$ and $k(t)$

(b) $n_i(t)$, $p(t)$, and $r(t)$

(c) $w_1(t)$ and $w_2(t)$

(d) $k_i(t)$, $k_s(t)$, $f_i(t)$, and $f_s(t)$

(e) $\bar{y}_1(t)$, $s_1(t)$, $\tilde{k}_1(t)$, and $c_1(t)$

(f) $\bar{y}_2(t)$, $s_2(t)$, $\tilde{k}_2(t)$, and $c_2(t)$

Figure 6.3.6 As N_2 rises from 5 (solid lines) to 6 (dashed lines)

Multiple Sectors and Heterogeneous Households 267

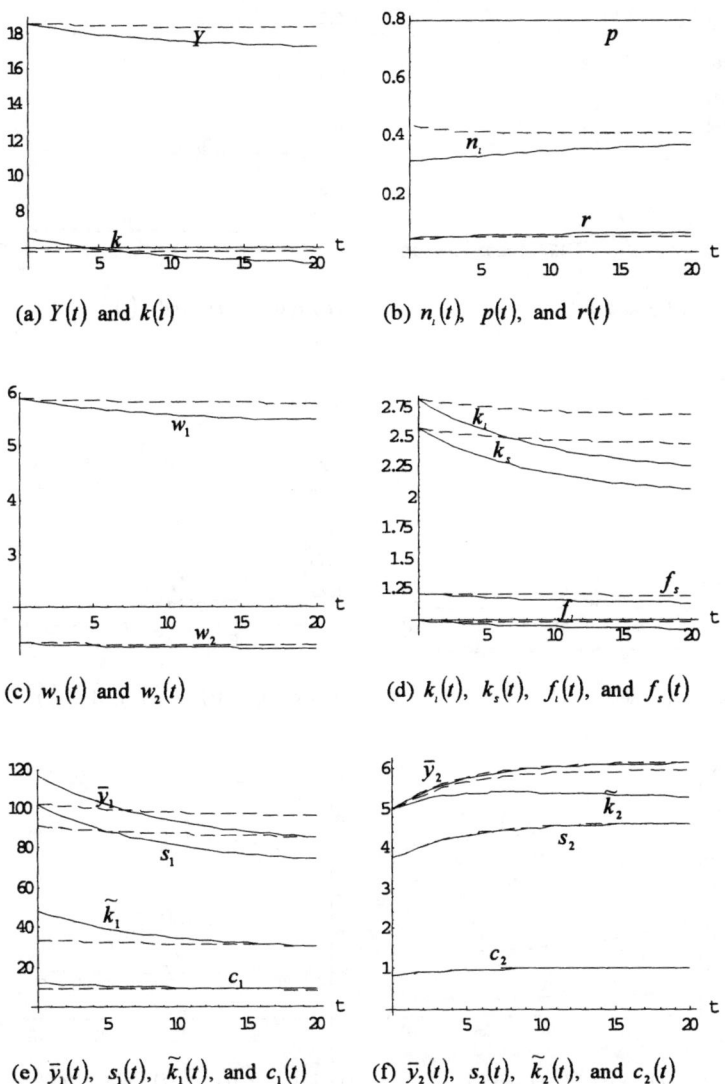

Figure 6.3.7 As λ_1 rises from 0.87 (solid lines) to 0.89 (dashed lines)

268 *Economic Growth with Income and Wealth Distribution*

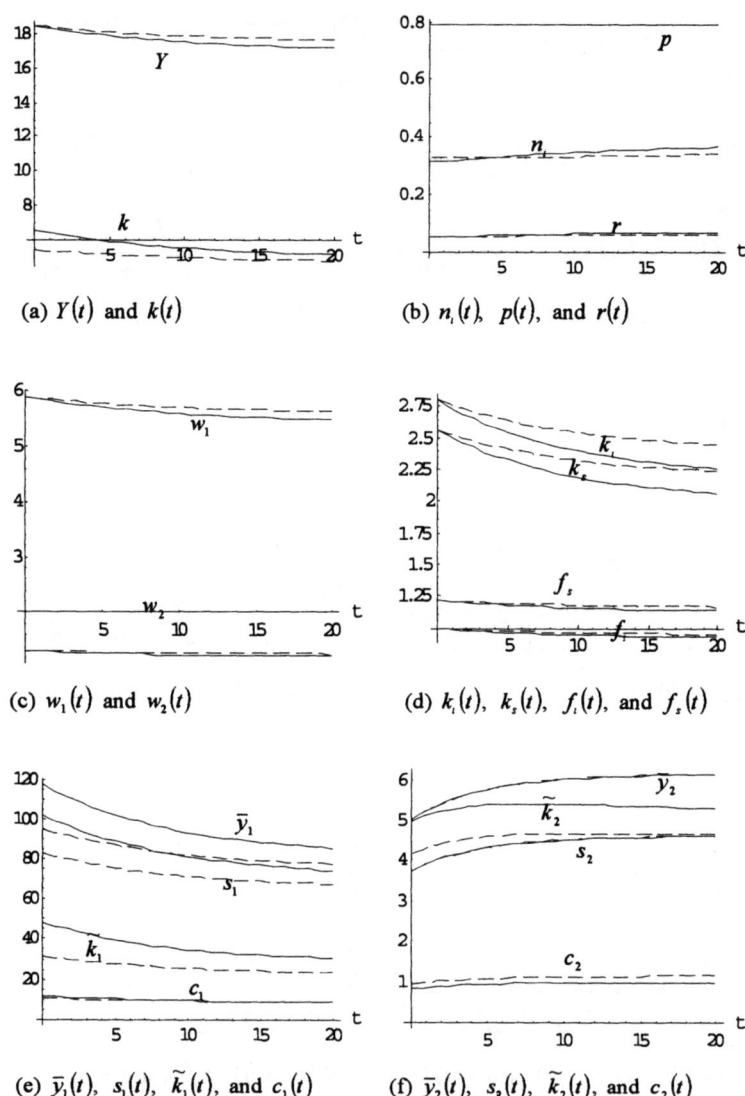

Figure 6.3.8 As λ_2 rises from 0.75 (solid lines) to 0.79 (dashed lines)

6.4 Further discussions

This chapter assumes that only absolute income and consumption matter. Nevertheless, there is considerable evidence that relative income and consumption may affect both individual well-being and behavior. Veblen (1898) introduces the term "conspicuous consumption" to refer to expenditure in goods that signal the consumer's position in society. Duesenberry (1949) emphasizes the importance of relative standing in determining consumption and saving patterns over time.[3] Based on a large number of survey-based psychological studies, Easterlin (1974, 1975) demonstrates that subjective happiness increases with income in a given country and in a given year, but also that average happiness in a given country seems to be roughly constant over time, even though average income increases. Furthermore, people also seem to be about equally as happy in different countries with different incomes. It has recently been observed that relative wealth, relative consumption, or/and relative social status play an important role in individuals' economic behavior.[4] Becker and Murphy (1992) introduce the cost of combining specified workers, based on the assumption that the cost of coordinating a group of complementary specified workers grows as the number of specialists increases.[5] They examine how specification and the division of labor depend on coordination costs, and also on the amount and the extent of knowledge. They explore implications of these relations for economic development, industrial organization, and activities of workers.

There are many ways to incorporate relative standing into the utility function.[6] We may use some kind of ratio comparison utility function expressed as follows:

$$U_j(s_j(t), c_j(t), \bar{s}(t), \bar{c}(t)),$$

where $s_j(t)$ and $c_j(t)$ are an individual's saving and vector of goods and services consumption and $\bar{s}(t)$ and $\bar{c}(t)$ are the average values of the corresponding variables in society. We may also use some kind of additive comparison utility function as

$$U_j(s_j(t) - \bar{s}(t), c_j(t) - \bar{c}(t)).$$

It should be remarked that it is important to examine how attitudes toward social status will affect properties of the utility function and thus social evolution. If social status gaps are too large, people in some classes might care little about social status. If one believes in a philosophy and society is full of corruption, one may even have a negative attitude to social status. What is important here is that our analytical framework allows us to examine different possibilities in a consistent manner.

Another important issue is about taste change.[7] In any basic course in microeconomics, concepts of normal, inferior, and luxury goods will be introduced. A freshman in social sciences is taught that for different people the same goods or service can be either normal or inferior, also as a man's income and wealth are increased, some goods which are once normal may become inferior. Yet the freshman has not been taught that no well-accepted theory of economic growth can easily analyze this kind of normal change as endogenous processes of economic evolution. The reader might have already seen that neither the Solow model nor the Ramsey approach can deal with the preference change properly. It is not difficult to see that the well-accepted Dixit-Stiglitz utility function cannot properly deal with the issues associated with preference change.

For illustration, we now point out possible ways to take account of a household's preference change due to changes in income. Let there be n kinds of goods and services. The household's utility function is given, for instance, by

$$U(t) = s^{\lambda(t)}(t)\prod_{j=1}^{n} c_j^{\xi_j(t)}(t),$$

where $c_j(t)$ is the consumption level of goods j, $s(t)$ and the preference parameters are defined similarly as in, for instance, formula (6.1.8). The budget constraint is given by

$$\sum_{j=1}^{n} p_j(t)c_j(t) + s(t) = \hat{y}(t),$$

where $\hat{y}(t)$ is the disposable income. The optimal solution is

$$s(t) = \lambda(t)\hat{y}(t), \quad c_j(t) = \frac{\xi_j(t)\hat{y}(t)}{p_j(t)}, \quad j = 1, \cdots, n.$$

Here, we consider that the propensities are influenced by the household's disposable income (and/or wage and wealth), his age, and other factors like relative social status in the following way:

$$\lambda(t) = \lambda(\hat{y}(t), t), \quad \xi_j(t) = \xi_j(\hat{y}(t), t), \quad j = 1, \cdots, n.$$

For instance, if good 1 is an inferior good, and the others are normal, we may specify the preference change as follows:

$\xi_1(t) = \xi_{10} - \xi_{11}\hat{y}(t)$, $\xi_1(t) \geq 0$,

where ξ_{10} and ξ_{11} are constant and the rest of the parameters are kept constant. The preference change may be nonlinear. Anyway, this example just illustrates how to introduce preference change into our analytical framework.[8] The significance of our analytical framework is that it enables us to examine many economic issues in a consistent manner.

Appendix

A.6.1 The two-sector multi-group model with general production functions

We now analyze the dynamics when the production functions take on general forms. First, we show that the motion of the system is determined by two-dimensional differential equations. From

$$r(t) + \delta_k = f_i'(k_i) = pf_s'(k_s)$$

in equations (6.1.1), we get

$$p = \frac{f_i'(k_i)}{f_s'(k_s)}.$$

Substituting this equation into $f_i(k_i) - k_i f_i'(k_i) = p(f_s(k_s) - k_s f_s'(k_s))$ in equations (6.1.1) yields

$$\Psi_i(k_i) \equiv \frac{f_i(k_i)}{f_i'(k_i)} - k_i = \frac{f_s(k_s)}{f_s'(k_s)} - k_s \equiv \Psi_s(k_s). \qquad (A.6.1.1)$$

From the properties of $f_i(k_i)$, we can show that the function $\Psi_i(k_i)$ has the following properties:

$$\Psi_i(0) = 0, \ \Psi_i(k_i) > 0 \text{ for } k_i > 0, \ \Psi_i'(k_i) = -\frac{f_i(k_i) f_i''(k_i)}{f_i'^2(k_i)} \geq 0.$$

The function, $\Psi_s(k_s)$, has the same properties in k_s. We see that for any given $k_s \geq 0$, equation (A.6.1.1) determines $k_i \geq 0$ as a unique function of k_i, denoted by $k_s = \Omega(k_i)$. We have $\Omega(0) = 0$ and $\Omega' > 0$. From equations (6.1.3), we solve the labor distribution as functions of k, k_s, and k_i as follows:

$$n_i = \frac{k - k_s}{k_i - k_s}, \quad n_s = \frac{k_i - k}{k_i - k_s}. \tag{A.6.1.2}$$

The labor distribution is uniquely determined by k and k_s. We should require that $k_i(t) - k_s(t)$ does not switch the sign of $k_i(0) - k_s(0)$ for any t; otherwise, for some $t > 0$, $0 < n_i(t), n_s(t) < 1$ would not hold. We assume $k_i(t) > k_s(t)$ for any positive t. For $0 < n_i(t), n_s(t) < 1$, we should require

$$k_i(t) > k(t) > \Omega(k_i(t)).$$

Insert $p(t)c_j = \xi_j \hat{y}_j$ and equations (6.1.4) into equation (6.1.9):

$$(1 + r(t))\sum_{j=1}^{2} \overline{k}_j(t)\xi_j \overline{N}_j + w(t)\sum_{j=1}^{2} h_j \xi_j \overline{N}_j = p(t)F_s(t), \tag{A.6.1.3}$$

where we use $w_j = h_j w$. Substitute r and w in equations (6.1.2) into the above equation:

$$\overline{\Omega}_0(k_i)\sum_{j=1}^{2} \overline{n}_j \overline{k}_j + \overline{\Omega}(k_i) - (k_i - k)f_s^*(k_i) = 0, \tag{A.6.1.4}$$

where we use $F_s = f_s n_s N$ and equations (A.6.1.2) and

$$f_s^*(k_i) \equiv \frac{f_s(\Omega)f_i'(k_i)}{f_i'(\Omega)},$$

where

$$\overline{\Omega}_0(k_i) \equiv (k_i - \Omega(k_i))(f'(k_i) + \delta),$$

Multiple Sectors and Heterogeneous Households 273

$$\overline{\Omega}(k_i) \equiv (k_i - \Omega(k_i))(f_i(k_i) - k_i f_i'(k_i)) \frac{\sum h_j \xi_j \overline{N}_j}{N},$$

$$\overline{n}_j \equiv \frac{\xi_j \overline{N}_j}{N}.$$

Substituting equation (6.2.3) into equation (A.6.1.4), we solve

$$\overline{k}_1 = \Lambda(k_i, \overline{k}_2) \equiv \frac{k_i f_s^*(k_i) - \overline{\Omega}(k_i) - (\overline{\Omega}_0(k_i)\overline{n}_2 + f_s^*(k_i)\overline{N}_2/N)\overline{k}_2}{\overline{\Omega}_0(k_i)\overline{n}_1 + f_s(\Omega)f_i'(k_i)\overline{N}_1/f_s''(k_i)N}, \qquad \text{(A.6.1.5)}$$

where

$$f_s^{*'}(k_i) = \frac{f_i'(k_i)f_s'(\Omega)\Omega' + f_s(\Omega)f_i''(k_i)}{f_s'(\Omega)} - \frac{f_s(\Omega)f_i'(k_i)f_s''(\Omega)\Omega'}{f_s'^2(\Omega)}.$$

Insert $s_j = \lambda_j \hat{y}_j$ and equations (6.1.4) into equations (6.1.8):

$$\dot{\overline{k}}_j = (\lambda_j r - \xi_j)\overline{k}_j + \lambda_j w_j.$$

Substitute equation (A.6.1.5) and r and w_j in equations (6.1.2) and (6.1.3) into the above equations:

$$\dot{\overline{k}}_1 = \Lambda_1(k_i, \overline{k}_2) \equiv (f_i'(k_i) - \delta_1)\lambda_1 \Lambda(k_i, \overline{k}_2) + \lambda_1 h_1 (f_i(k_i) - k_i f_i'(k_i)),$$
$$\dot{\overline{k}}_2 = \Lambda_2(k_i, \overline{k}_2) \equiv (f_i'(k_i) - \delta_2)\lambda_2 \overline{k}_2 + \lambda_2 h_2 (f_i(k_i) - k_i f_i'(k_i)), \qquad \text{(A.6.1.6)}$$

where $\delta_j \equiv \delta_k + \xi_j/\lambda_j$. The above two differential equations contain three variables, $\overline{k}_1, \overline{k}_2$, and k_i. Equation (A.6.1.5) relates $\overline{k}_1$ to $\overline{k}_2$ and k_i. Take derivatives of equation (A.6.1.5) with respect to t:

$$\dot{\overline{k}}_1 = \Lambda_i(k_i, \overline{k}_2)\dot{k}_i - \frac{(\overline{\Omega}_0 \overline{n}_2 + f_s^*(k_i)\overline{N}_2/N)}{\overline{\Omega}_0 \overline{n}_1 + f_s^*(k_i)\overline{N}_1/N} \Lambda_2(k_i, \overline{k}_2), \qquad \text{(A.6.1.7)}$$

where

$$\Lambda_1(k_1, \bar{k}_2)$$
$$\equiv \frac{f_s^* + k_1 f_s'' \Omega' - \overline{\Omega}_0' - (\overline{\Omega}_0' \bar{n}_2 + f_s'' \Omega' \overline{N}_2 / N) \bar{k}_2 - (\overline{\Omega}_0' \bar{n}_1 + f_s'' \Omega' \overline{N}_1 / N)}{\overline{\Omega}_0 \bar{n}_1 + f_s^* \overline{N}_1 / N},$$

$$\overline{\Omega}_0' = (1 - \Omega')(f' + \delta) + (k_1 - \Omega)f'',$$

$$\overline{\Omega}'(k_1) = [(1 - \Omega')(f - k_1 f') - (k_1 - \Omega)k_1 f''] \frac{\sum_j h_j \xi_j \overline{N}_j}{N}.$$

Substituting equation (A.6.1.7) into the dynamic system (A.6.1.6), we obtain

$$\dot{k}_1 = \frac{\Lambda_1(k_1, \bar{k}_2)}{\Lambda_1(k_1, \bar{k}_2)} + \frac{(\overline{\Omega}_0' \bar{n}_2 + f_s^* \overline{N}_2 / N)}{\overline{\Omega}_0 \bar{n}_1 + f_s^* \overline{N}_1 / N} \frac{\Lambda_2(k_1, \bar{k}_2)}{\Lambda_1(k_1, \bar{k}_2)},$$

$$\dot{\bar{k}}_2 = \Lambda_2(k_1, \bar{k}_2).$$

The two differential equations contain two variables. With proper initial conditions $k_1(0)$ and $\bar{k}_2(0)$, the above equations determine values of $k_1(t)$ and $\bar{k}_2(t)$ over time.

7
Multi-Region Growth Economies

When one contrasts spatial inequality of economic geography between, for instance, Los Angeles and Boston, one may think of differences in cultural, geographical, and economic factors between the two regions. Regional differences in income and wealth distribution are evident. Nevertheless, there is no proper theoretical framework for studying regional growth and development with income and wealth distribution. Although the neoclassical growth models are the main analytical tool for theoretical economists to explore the complexity of economic growth with capital accumulation, the predication from neoclassical growth theory that the free movements of goods and factors of production and their ensuing price convergence will lead to the spatial convergence of income is not empirically confirmed in general. As shown before, the traditional neoclassical growth theory does not have a proper behavioral mechanism for the behavior of households. This is perhaps the main reason that the neoclassical growth theory has been almost silent on spatial issues of economic growth.

From theoretical perspectives, income and wealth inequality across geography is far more difficult to model than it is to analyze growth of heterogeneous households without spatial dimension. As mentioned before, the Solow and Ramsey models are the two key models in the neoclassical growth theory. The neoclassical growth theory characterized by the Solow model had an important influence on the development of regional growth theory. It is shown that a two-region neoclassical growth model under certain conditions has an equilibrium point at which regional growth rates are equalized.[1] The neoclassical regional growth theory is based on the Solow tradition. It is well known that the long-term growth rate in the Solow model is exogenously determined. In particular, the steady-state growth rate of per capita income is equal to the rate of exogenous technological change or population growth rate in these models. In order to allow for different regional growth paths, differences in the rate of regional technological change should be assumed. The neoclassical growth theory assumes that the market mechanism works so perfectly that any disparity in regional wages tends to disappear. Differences in productivity growth are considered to be due to interregional misallocation of resources. Disparity in productivity growth will eventually vanish as the misallocation is progressively corrected and regional growth rates approach the steady state. Only a few attempts have been made to apply the Ramsey approach to growth with interregional interactions, even though the Ramsey approach has been applied to international issues. To explain regional differences, international trade theories are not very helpful as most of dynamic international trade models (in which people are assumed to be immobile between countries) do not have rational mechanisms for explaining regional mobility of people.[2] This chapter introduces a dynamic analytical framework that integrates growth, geography, and income and wealth distribution in an explicit interregional context.

There is an increasingly expanding web of linkages and interconnections among states, societies, and organizations that make up contemporary world economic systems. Irrespective of the significance of understanding regional economic phenomena, regional economic theory is a relatively neglected area of economic analysis. It is argued that analytical difficulties associated with modeling dynamics of interregional economic interactions are a main obstacle to progress in regional economics. Isard (1956) assures:

> the general theory of location and space-economy is conceived as embracing the total spatial array of economic activities, with attention paid to the geographical distribution of inputs and outputs and the geographical variations in prices and costs.

The necessity of establishing dynamic regional theories has been recognized. Nevertheless, the traditional equilibrium economics and neoclassical growth theory, which have formed the two mainstreams of theoretical economics, fail to explain the complexity of economic geography. Although regional scientists and regional economists have proposed various kinds of regional dynamic models,[3] the current models do not integrate the spatial factor satisfactorily from the theoretical point of view.

Regional location, interaction, economic structure, and dynamic processes of various social and economic activities under different institutions are the main concerns of regional science. Regional economic analysis is to analyze regional location, regional demand and supply, prices of goods, services, distribution of immobile factors such as land and amenities among various activities, and interregional (monetary, material, and information) flows.[4] It may be argued that two modeling frameworks are important in dealing with multiregional economic issues. The first is the interregional input–output analysis.[5] Although the input–output systems have proved effective at analyzing economic structure with complicated linkages among various sectors in multiregional or multinational systems, it is analytically difficult to introduce the endogenous behavior of households. The second is the equilibrium approach. But equilibrium economics has failed to provide significant insights into the complexity of economic geography.[6] Scotchmer and Thisse (1992) argue

> integrating space and competition demands at the same time a certain dose of abnegation (abandon the familiar model of perfect competition) and of imagination (invent a new model of competition).

In this chapter regional economics refers to the study of economic phenomena that occur within and among regions. Natural endowment differences in, for instance, climate and natural resources, lead to regional divergences in lifestyle, consumption structure, and productivity. Regional factors such as climates, accessibility, infrastructures, land and natural resources, and regional cultures, affect economic geography in different ways. Issues arise due to the importance of nontraded goods (such as climate, land) and services (which are consumed simultaneously as they are produced) in analyzing the movements of product factors, such as labor and capital within a country. For instance, workers will move to the location at which they can achieve higher utility. Factor mobility will equalize utility levels across regions, but not necessarily wage rates. Wages tend to be higher in locations where the cost of nontraded goods is higher to compensate workers for the higher cost of living. It is significant to examine how these endowments affect wages, rents, and service prices. From studies on regional economies with regional differences of wages and land rent, it is discerned that it is difficult to analyze spatial economic phenomena with natural endowment differences even when we purposefully limit the investigation to static economies.

Our concern is limited to economic interactions among regions within the country but not among countries. In regional economics factors such as people and capital are free to move; while in international economics some factors (such as labor) may not be allowed to move beyond the national boundary. Differences in degrees of mobility of factors and goods within a country and between countries suggests that international trade theory may be invalid for addressing issues related to patterns of interregional trade and income distribution. At this initial stage, I distinguish international and regional economics mainly by whether or not people are free to move among the areas under consideration.[7]

This chapter will develop a few interregional models which explicitly include three spatial factors: land, amenities, and services.[8] A regional analysis must treat services differently from commodity goods since many services provided by schools, hospitals, and restaurants must be consumed where they are supplied. The spatial character of services implies that service prices will be spatially varied. Amenities such as climatic conditions and historical buildings are location-dependent and have an important impact upon residential location. This chapter is organized as follows. Section 7.1 develops a multi-region model with leisure, amenity, and capital accumulation as endogenous variables. As it is difficult to explicitly analyze behavior of the model, we simulate the system. Section 7.2 introduces a two-region model and each region has two production sectors. Both capital and knowledge are endogenous variables in the model. We demonstrate possible path-dependent regional economic evolution and carry out comparative statics analyses with regard to some parameters. Section 7.3 discusses some issues about regional economic development with capital and knowledge.

7.1 Leisure, amenity, and capital accumulation

This section analyzes a perfectly competitive economy with regional differentials in living conditions and productivity. The productivity advantages of one region may be offset to some extent by the higher wages that must be paid in a system where people are free to choose where they work and live. Higher wages are often associated with some kinds of disamenities (such as noise, pollutants, and densely populated neighborhood) and high living costs. Labor force, capital, and knowledge are main inputs of economic production. Labor and capital are easily mobile between regions in industrialized economies. As capital mobility becomes high and costs associated with capital movement among regions become low, it is reasonable to assume that capital movement equalizes rate of interest between regions within a national economy. But there are different principles for analyzing temporary equilibrium conditions for labor movement in a dynamic regional framework. For example, in the theoretical literature on regional economics two principles have been proposed to analyze labor movement. One is that labor movement, if costs associated with professional or locational changes are neglected, equalizes wage rates between regions. This assumption is limited in a freely competitive national labor market if various regions provide different levels of amenity (such as regional cultures, climates, and pollution) and have different technologies. The other is that free movement of people equalizes utility levels, which they may obtain in different regions. Although this assumption is reasonable for analyzing issues related to movement of people between regions, the traditional approaches to consumer behavior in economic theory often make it analytically intractable to properly model migration with regional differences in lifestyles and wage rates. One reason is that it is difficult to examine issues related to ownership of resources and capital in a dynamic interregional economy. If wage rates and lifestyle (including saving behavior) are interregionally different and people may freely move within the economy, how to calculate each individual's wealth and income in a dynamic multiregional economy over time is not an easy matter.

This section deals with one of most challenging questions for dynamic economic geography with the environment – to model multiregional economic growth with endogenous capital accumulation under assumptions of profit maximization, utility maximization, and perfect competition. Traditional growth theories – which have no spatial dimension – have not been successfully extended to multiregional dynamics mainly because they do not have economic mechanisms for properly dealing with spatial issues.[9] To make an initial attempt to synthesize ideas in location theory, urban economics, economic geography, equilibrium theory, and neoclassical growth theory, we construct a dynamic model to describe interactions between capital accumulation, the regional distribution of capital and labor, the division of labor, the capital distribution in each region, and land rents within the analytical framework in the previous chapters.

This section treats endogenous amenity as a significant factor of regional dynamics. First, we build the model and show that the dynamics of the J- region national economy can be described by J- dimensional differential equations. Then, we simulate the national economy with three regions. It is demonstrated that when the production functions take on the Cobb-Douglas form and the parameters are properly specified, the national dynamics has a unique equilibrium point. Our comparative statics analysis also provides some important insights. For instance, if environmental improvement occurs in the technologically advanced region, the national output rises; but if environmental improvement occurs in the technologically less advanced region, the national output falls. As a region improves its technology, the other two regions' aggregated output levels fall not only in relative terms, but also in absolute values. This implies that if any region has a high rate of technological change and the other regions remain technologically stationary, then the economic activities tend to be concentrated in the technologically advancing region. We also show positive support for the empirical findings on wage determination by Combes et al. that individual skills account for a large fraction of existing spatial wage disparities with strong evidence of spatial sorting by skills, and endowments only appear to play a small role.

7.1.1 The model with time, amenity, and capital accumulation

We now build a dynamic one-commodity and multiple-region trade model to examine interdependence between regional trades and national growth. We analyze trade issues within the framework of an interregional macroeconomic growth model with perfect capital mobility. This model is influenced by the neoclassical trade theory with capital accumulation.[10] In describing economic production, we follow the neoclassical trade framework. It is assumed that the regions produce a homogeneous commodity. Most aspects of production sectors in our model are similar to the neoclassical one-sector growth model. It is assumed that there is only one (durable) good in the national economy.

The system consists of multiple regions, indexed by $j = 1, ..., J$. Perfect competition is assumed to prevail in good markets both within each region and between the regions, and commodities are traded without any barriers such as transport costs or tariffs. The labor markets are perfectly competitive within each region and among regions. Let prices be measured in terms of the commodity and the price of the commodity be unity.[11] We denote wage and interest rates by $w_j(t)$ and $r_j(t)$, respectively, in the j th region. The interest rate is identical throughout the national economy, that is $r(t) = r_j(t)$. We assume a homogeneous population.[12] A person is free to choose his residential location. We assume that any person chooses the same region where he works and lives. Each region has fixed land. Land quality, climates, and environment are homogeneous within each region, but they may vary among the regions. We neglect transportation cost of commodities between and within regions. As becomes evident later on, although it is conceptually not difficult to introduce a transportation cost function and to provide balance conditions for demand and supply and for price equalization conditions with transportation cost,[13] the problem will become analytically too complicated. The assumption of zero transportation cost of commodities implies price equality for the commodity among regions. As amenity and land are immobile, wage rates and land rent may not be equal among regions.

Let $T_j(t)$ stand for the work time of a representative household of region j, and $\overline{N}_j(t)$ the population of region j. Let $N_j(t)$ stand for the flow of labor services used at time t for production in region j. We measure $N_j(t)$ as follows:

$$N_j(t) = \overline{N}_j(t) T_j(t), \quad j = 1, \cdots, J.$$

We introduce

$\overline{N}$ – the given population of the economy;

L_j – the given (residential) area of region j;

$K(t)$ – the total capital stocks of the economy at time t;

$F_j(t)$ – the output levels of region j's production sector at time t;

$K_j(t)$ – the level of capital stocks employed by region j's production sector;

$c_j(t)$ and $s_j(t)$ – per capita consumption level of commodity and savings made per capita in region j;

$l_j(t)$ – the lot size per capita in region j;

$R_j(t)$ – the land rent in region j.

We describe the behavior of producers. We assume that there are only two productive factors, capital, $K_j(t)$, and labor, $N_j(t)$. The production functions are given by

$$F_j(K_j(t), N_j(t)), \quad j = 1, \cdots, J,$$

where F_j is the output of region j. Assume F_j to be neoclassical. We have

$$f_j(t) = f_j(k_j(t)), \quad f_j(t) \equiv \frac{F_j(t)}{N_j(t)}, \quad k_j(t) \equiv \frac{K_j(t)}{N_j(t)}.$$

Markets are competitive; thus labor and capital earn their marginal products, and firms earn zero profits. The rate of interest, $r(t)$, and wage rates, $w_j(t)$, are determined by the markets. Hence, for any individual firm, $r(t)$ and $w_j(t)$, are given at each point in time. The production sector chooses the two variables, $K_j(t)$ and $N_j(t)$, to maximize its profit. The marginal conditions are given by

$$r + \delta_{kj} = f_j'(k_j), \quad w_j(t) = f_j(k_j) - k_j f_j'(k_j), \qquad (7.1.1)$$

where δ_{kj} is the depreciation rate of physical capital in region j.

We now study the behavior of consumers. Each worker may get income from landownership, wealth ownership, and wages. In order to define incomes, it is necessary to determine landownership structure. It can be seen that land properties may be distributed in multiple ways under various institutions. To simplify the model, we accept the assumption of absent landownership which means that the income of land rent is spent outside the economic system. A possible case is that the land is owned by the government, people can rent the land in the competitive market, and the government uses the income for military or other public purposes. We may assume that each worker owns $L_j / \overline{N}$ amount of land in region j and it is impossible to sell land but it is free to rent one's own land to others. Under this assumption, the land revenue $\bar{r}$ per worker is given as follows:

$$\bar{r}(t) = \frac{1}{N} \sum_{j=1}^{J} L_j R_j.$$

Hence, each worker receives the land revenue $\bar{r}$ irrespective of his dwelling region.[14]

Let $\bar{k}_j(t)$ stand for the per capita wealth in region j. Region j's per capita current income, $y_j(t)$, from the interest payment, $r(t)\bar{k}_j(t)$, and the wage payment, $w_j(t)T_j(t)$, is given by

$$y_j(t) = r(t)\bar{k}_j(t) + w_j(t)T_j(t).$$

The per capita disposable income of consumer j is defined as the sum of the current income and the wealth available for purchasing consumption goods and saving:

$$\hat{y}_j(t) = y_j(t) + \bar{k}_j(t) = (1 + r(t))\bar{k}_j(t) + w_j(t)T_j(t), \quad j = 1, \cdots, J.$$

At t a consumer distributes the total available budget among housing, $l_j(t)$, saving, $s_j(t)$, and consumption of goods, $c_j(t)$. The budget constraint is given by

$$R_j l_j + c_j + s_j = \hat{y}_j = r\bar{k}_j + w_j T_j + \bar{k}_j, \quad j = 1, \cdots, J. \tag{7.1.2}$$

Consumers have four variables to decide upon. A consumer decides how much to spend on housing, how long to work, how much to consume, and how much to save.

Denote by $\tilde{T}_j(t)$ the leisure time at time t and T_0 the (fixed) available time for work and leisure. The time constraint is expressed by

$$T_j(t) + \tilde{T}_j(t) = T_0, \quad j = 1, \cdots, J. \tag{7.1.3}$$

Substituting equations (7.1.3) into the budget constraints yields

$$w_j(t)\tilde{T}_j(t) + R_j(t)l_j(t) + c_j(t) + s_j(t) = \bar{y}_j(t) \equiv (1 + r(t))\bar{k}_j(t) + w_j(t)T_0. \tag{7.1.4}$$

We assume that the utility level, $U_j(t)$, that the consumers obtain is dependent on the leisure time, $\tilde{T}_j(t)$, the lot size, $l_j(t)$, the consumption level of the commodity,

$c_j(t)$, and the saving, $s_j(t)$. The utility level of the consumer in region j, $U_j(t)$, is specified as follows:

$$U_j(t) = \theta_j(t)\widetilde{T}_j^\sigma(t) l_j^\eta(t) c_j^\xi(t) s_j^\lambda(t), \quad \sigma, \eta, \xi, \lambda > 0, \quad \sigma + \eta + \xi + \lambda = 1, \quad (7.1.5)$$

in which σ, η, ξ, and λ are a person's elasticity of utility with regard to leisure time, lot size, commodity, and saving. We call σ, η, ξ, and λ propensities to use leisure time, to consume lot size, to consume goods, and to hold wealth (save), respectively. In formula (7.1.5), $\theta_j(t)$ is called region j's amenity level. Amenities are affected by infrastructures, regional cultures, and climates.[15] In this study, we assume that amenity is affected by production and consumption activities. We specify θ_j as follows:

$$\theta_j(t) = \overline{\theta}_j F_j^a(t) N_j^b(t), \quad j = 1, \cdots, J,$$

where $\overline{\theta}_j$ (> 0), a and b are parameters. We do not specify signs of a and b as economic activities and population may have either positive or negative effects on regional attractiveness. Regional amenities are given to individuals. As $F_j = f_j N_j$, we can rewrite the above equations as follows:

$$\theta_j(t) = \overline{\theta}_j f_j^a(t) N_j^{a+b}(t), \quad j = 1, \cdots, J.$$

It should be remarked that there are a number of potentially important spatial influences, such as public goods, amenities, and different externalities, transportation costs that may challenge the validity of competitive equilibrium theory for explaining a regionally heterogeneous economy. For instance, one difficult factor is the so-called capitalization, which implies that the price of land is interdependent with local amenities, economic agents' densities, transportation costs, and other local variables or parameters. Although the significance of capitalization has been noticed by locational theorists, it may be said that we still have no compact framework within which we can satisfactorily explain the issue. The seminal paper on compensating regional variation in wages and rents by Roback (1982) has caused a wide interest among regional and urban economists to theoretically investigate how the value of locational attributes is capitalized into wages and services.[16] Since the publication of Roback's work, many empirical and theoretical studies have also shown that between urban areas wages may capitalize differences in amenity levels or living costs.[17] Our model discusses the issue within a perfectly competitive equilibrium framework.

Maximizing $U_j(t)$ subject to budget constraints (7.1.4) yields

$$w_j(t)\widetilde{T}_j(t) = \sigma \bar{y}_j(t), \quad l_j(t)R_j(t) = \eta \bar{y}_j(t), \quad c_j(t) = \xi \bar{y}_j(t), \quad s_j(t) = \lambda \bar{y}_j(t).$$
(7.1.6)

According to the definitions of $s_j(t)$, the wealth accumulation of households is

$$\dot{\bar{k}}_j(t) = s_j(t) - \bar{k}_j(t).$$
(7.1.7)

As households are assumed to be freely mobile among the regions, people should obtain the same level of utility, irrespective of in which region they live, i.e.

$$U_j(t) = U_m(t), \quad j, m = 1, \cdots, J.$$
(7.1.8)

We neglect possible costs of migration. In reality, even to move house in a small town has costs. Although it is not difficult to introduce migration costs into the model, it will become far more difficult to explicitly get analytical results. In this study, instead of wage equalization (which is often used as the equilibrium mechanism of population distribution), we assume that consumers obtain the same level of utility in different regions as the equilibrium mechanism of population distribution among the regions. Although the condition of utility equalization is often used in the literature of urban economics,[18] the assumption of utility equalization is rarely used in the literature of economic dynamics as the temporary equilibrium condition of population distribution. It is argued that this assumption is more reasonable than the assumption of wage equalization. It is well observed that wage rates vary over regions. Wage disparities may be caused by many factors, such as spatial differences in the skill composition of the workforce, in nonhuman endowments (such as climate and infrastructures), and in local interactions. Many empirical studies are carried out to study regional wage disparities in different countries.[19] As shown later on, as the utility level at each point in time in each region is related to regional wealth distribution, regional amenity levels, lands, and regional technological levels, wage disparity is determined by all regional factors such as resource endowments and technological levels. In general, wage rates among regions should not converge if regional differences in amenity and technology differ.[20]

The total capital stock employed by the production sectors is equal to the total wealth owned by all the regions. That is

$$K(t) = \sum_{j=1}^{J} K_j(t) = \sum_{j=1}^{J} \bar{k}_j(t) \bar{N}_j(t). \qquad (7.1.9)$$

The national production is equal to the national consumption and national net saving

$$C(t) + S(t) - K(t) + \sum_{j=1}^{J} \delta_{kj} K_j(t) = F(t), \qquad (7.1.10)$$

where

$$C(t) \equiv \sum_{j=1}^{J} c_j(t) N_j(t), \quad S(t) \equiv \sum_{j=1}^{J} s_j(t) N_j(t), \quad F(t) \equiv \sum_{j=1}^{J} F_j(t).$$

The assumption that labor force and land are fully employed is represented by

$$\sum_{j=1}^{J} \bar{N}_j(t) = \bar{N}, \quad l_j(t) \bar{N}_j(t) = L_j, \quad j = 1, \cdots, J. \qquad (7.1.11)$$

We have thus built the model which explains the endogenous capital accumulation and regional capital and labor distribution in the national economy in which all the markets are perfectly competitive and product, capital, and labor are freely mobile.

Finally, we describe trade balances among regions. First, we calculate

$$F_j - (R_j l_j + c_j + s_j - \bar{k}_j) \bar{N}_j - \delta_{kj} K_j = r(K_j - \bar{k}_j \bar{N}_j),$$

where we use

$$R_j l_j + c_j + s_j = r \bar{k}_j + w_j T_j + \bar{k}_j, \quad F_j = (r + \delta_{kj}) K_j + w_j N_j, \quad N_j = T_j \bar{N}_j.$$

That is

$$F_j = (R_j l_j + c_j + s_j - \bar{k}_j) \bar{N}_j + \delta_{kj} K_j + r(K_j - \bar{k}_j \bar{N}_j).$$

The regional output is used up for housing, $R_j l_j \bar{N}_j$, consumption, $c_j \bar{N}_j$, net saving, $(s_j - c_j) \bar{N}_j$, the payment for the depreciation of capital employed by the economy, $\delta_{kj} K_j$, and the region's interest payment for the capital owned by the other regions, $r(K_j - \bar{k}_j \bar{N}_j)$. If $K_j - \bar{k}_j \bar{N}_j > (<) 0$, we say that region j is in trade deficit (trade surplus). If $K_j - \bar{k}_j \bar{N}_j = 0$, region j is in trade balance. We introduce variables to measure trade balances

$$E_j(t) \equiv \bar{k}_j(t)\bar{N}_j(t) - K_j(t). \tag{7.1.12}$$

If $E_j(t) > (=, <) 0$, we say that region j's trade is in surplus (balance, deficit). We now examine the behavior of the system.

7.1.2 Simulate the three-region economy

We first show that the dynamics of the national economy can be expressed as J-dimensional differential equations for any number of regions. The following lemma is proved in Appendix A.7.1.

Lemma 7.1.1

The dynamics of the national economy is given by the following J-dimensional differential equations with $k_1(t)$ and $\bar{k}_j(t)$, $j = 2, \cdots, J$, as the variables

$$\dot{k}_1 = \frac{\Lambda_1(k_1, \{\bar{k}_j\}) - \sum_{j=2}^{J}\Lambda_j(k_1, \{\bar{k}_j\})\partial\Lambda/\partial\bar{k}_j}{\partial\Lambda/\partial k_1},$$

$$\dot{\bar{k}}_j = \Lambda_j(k_1, \bar{k}_j) \equiv (\lambda \tilde{f}(k_1) - 1)\bar{k}_j + \lambda T_0 \bar{\phi}_j(k_1), \quad j = 2, \cdots, J, \tag{7.1.13}$$

in which $\bar{\phi}_j(k_1)$, $\Lambda_j(k_1, \{\bar{k}_j\})$ and $\Lambda(k_1, \{\bar{k}_j\})$ are functions of the variables, $k_1(t)$ and $\bar{k}_j(t)$ which are defined in the Appendix. For any given positive values of $k_1(t)$ and $\bar{k}_j(t)$ at any point in time, the other variables are uniquely determined by the following procedure: $\bar{y}_1(t)$ by equation (A.7.1.11) $\to$ $\bar{k}_1(t)$ by equation (A.7.1.13) $\to$ $k_j(t), j = 2, \cdots, J$ by equations (A.7.1.2) $\to$ $f_j = f_j(k_j)$ $\to$ $r(t)$ and $w_j(t)$ by equations (7.1.1) $\to$ $\bar{y}_j(t)$ by equations (A.7.1.9) $\to$ $n_j(t), j = 2, \cdots, J$, by equations (A.7.1.4) $\to$ $T_j(t)$ by equations (A.7.1.6) $\to$ $\tilde{T}_j(t) = T_0 - T_j(t)$ $\to$

$$N_1(t) = \frac{\overline{N}}{1/T_1(t) + \sum_{j=2}^{J} n_j(t)/T_j(t)}$$

$\rightarrow N_j(t) = n_j(t)N_1(t) \rightarrow \overline{N}_j(t) = N_j(t)/T_j(t) \rightarrow l_j(t) = L_j/\overline{N}_j(t) \rightarrow R_j(t) = \eta \overline{y}_j(t)/l_j(t) \rightarrow c_j(t)$ and $s_j(t)$ by equations (7.1.5) $\rightarrow F_j(t) = N_j(t)f_j(t)$.

Although we may analyze the behavior of the J-dimensional differential equations, it is difficult to explicitly interpret results. For illustration, we specify the production functions as follows:

$$F_j(t) = A_j K_j^{\alpha_j}(t) N_j^{\beta_j}(t), \quad \alpha_j + \beta_j = 1, \quad \alpha_j, \beta_j > 0, \quad j = 1, \cdots, J,$$

where A_j is region j's productivity. From $f_j = A_j k_j^{\alpha_j}$, and equations (A.7.1.1) and (A.7.1.2), we have

$$k_j = \phi_j(k_1) \equiv \left(\frac{\alpha_1 A_1 k_1^{-\beta_1} - \delta_j}{\alpha_j A_j}\right)^{-1/\beta_j}, \quad j = 2, \cdots, J.$$

By equations (A.7.1.3) and (A.7.1.7)

$$\overline{\phi}_j = A_j \beta_j \phi_j^{\alpha_j}(k_1),$$
$$\overline{y}_j = \widetilde{f}(k_1)\overline{k}_j + T_0 A_j \beta_j \phi_j^{\alpha_j}(k_1), \quad j = 1, \cdots, J, \tag{7.1.14}$$

in which we use $\phi_1(k_1) = k_1$, $\widetilde{f}(k_1) = \alpha_1 A_1 k_1^{-\beta_1} + \delta_1$ and $\delta_1 \equiv 1 - \delta_{k1}$. According to their definitions and equations (7.1.13)

$$g_j(k_1) = \widetilde{\theta}_j \left(\frac{f_j(\phi_j(k_1))}{f_1(k_1)}\right)^{a\widetilde{\eta}} \left(\frac{\overline{\phi}_1(k_1)}{\overline{\phi}_j(k_1)}\right)^{\sigma \widetilde{\eta}}, \quad \widetilde{\theta}_j = \left(\frac{\theta_j L_j^\eta}{\theta_1 L_1^\eta}\right)^{\widetilde{\eta}}, \quad \widetilde{\eta} = \frac{1}{\eta - a - b},$$

$$\widetilde{g}_j(k_1) = \left(1 + \frac{\sigma \widetilde{f}(k_1)\phi_j(k_1)}{\overline{\phi}_j(k_1)}\right), \quad j = 1, \cdots, J,$$

$$\hat{f}(k_1) = T_0 \overline{\phi}_1(k_1) + (1 - \sigma) T_0 k_1 \widetilde{f}(k_1) \widetilde{g}_1^{-1}(k_1) > 0,$$

$$\overline{f}(k_1, \{\overline{k}(t)\}) \equiv \widetilde{f}(k_1) \widetilde{g}_1^{-1}(k_1) \sum_{j=2}^{J} g_j(k_1) \overline{y}_j^\eta ((1 - \sigma) T_0 \phi_j(k_1) - \widetilde{g}_j(k_1)\overline{k}_j), \tag{7.1.15}$$

in which

$$\{\bar{k}(t)\} \equiv (\bar{k}_2(t), \cdots, \bar{k}_J(t)).$$

To simulate the model, we now have to find solutions to the following equation with $\bar{y}_1$ as the variable and $\hat{f}$ and $\tilde{f}$ as parameters:

$$\bar{y}_1^{1+\bar{\eta}}(t) - \hat{f}(t)\bar{y}_1^{\bar{\eta}}(t) - \tilde{f}(t) = 0. \qquad (7.1.16)$$

For any positive value of $\bar{\eta} = (1-\eta)/(\eta - a - b)$, it is impossible to explicitly solve the above equation. We specify values of the parameters as follows:

$$\eta = \frac{1}{12}, \quad a = -\frac{11}{24}, \quad b = \frac{1}{12}. \qquad (7.1.17)$$

The specification $\eta = 1/12$ implies that a typical household spends about 8.3 percent of the "potential income" $\bar{y}_j(t)$ on housing. The negative sign of a implies that as a region has more economic activities, it becomes less attractive as a residential place; the positive sign of b means that as more people choose to live in a region, it becomes more attractive, with all the other conditions given. Indeed, the parameter specification is strict in the sense that either a and/or b take the opposite signs to the specified signs. Under (7.1.15), we have $\bar{\eta} = 2$.

In the remainder of this study, we limit our study to specification (7.1.17). With $\bar{\eta} = 2$, we solve equation (7.1.16) as follows:

$$\bar{y}_1(k_1, \{\bar{k}_j(t)\}) = \Lambda_0(k_1, \{\bar{k}(t)\}) = \frac{\hat{f}}{3} + \frac{\sqrt[3]{2}\hat{f}^2}{3\tilde{F}} + \frac{\tilde{F}}{3\sqrt[3]{2}}, \qquad (7.1.18)$$

where

$$\tilde{F}(k_1, \{\bar{k}_j(t)\}) \equiv \left[2\hat{f}^3 + 27\tilde{f} + \sqrt{27\tilde{f}(4\hat{f}^3 + 27\tilde{f})}\right]^{1/3}.$$

From equation (A.7.1.13), we solve

$$\bar{k}_1(t) = \Lambda(k_1, \{\bar{k}\}) = \frac{\Lambda_0(k_1, \{\bar{k}\}) - T_0\bar{\phi}_1(k_1)}{\tilde{f}(k_1)}. \tag{7.1.19}$$

According to the above analysis and equations (A.7.1.11) and (A.7.1.12), we have

$$\dot{\bar{k}}_1 = \Lambda_1(k_1, \{\bar{k}_j\}) \equiv \lambda\Lambda_0(k_1, \{\bar{k}_j\}) - \Lambda(k_1, \{\bar{k}(t)\}), \tag{7.1.20}$$

$$\dot{\bar{k}}_j = \Lambda_j(k_1, \bar{k}_j) \equiv (\lambda\tilde{f}(k_1) - 1)\bar{k}_j + \lambda T_0\bar{\phi}_j(k_1), \quad j = 2, \cdots, J, \tag{7.1.21}$$

where $\bar{\lambda} \equiv 1 - \lambda + \lambda\delta_{k1}$. Taking derivatives of equation (7.1.18) with respect to t yields

$$\dot{\bar{k}}_1 = \frac{\partial\Lambda}{\partial k_1}\dot{k}_1 + \sum_{j=2}^{J}\Lambda_j\frac{\partial\Lambda}{\partial\bar{k}_j}. \tag{7.1.22}$$

Equaling two sides of equations (7.1.19) and (7.1.21) yields

$$\dot{k}_1 = \frac{\Lambda_1(k_1, \{\bar{k}_j\}) - \sum_{j=2}^{J}\Lambda_j(k_1, \{\bar{k}_j\})\partial\Lambda/\partial\bar{k}_j}{\partial\Lambda/\partial k_1}. \tag{7.1.23}$$

The J-dimensional differential equations (7.1.23) and (7.1.21) contain J variables, $k_1(t)$ and $\{\bar{k}(t)\}$. With proper initial conditions, the system determines the values of these variables at any point in time. Following Lemma 7.1.1, we can determine all the other variables in the national economic system. In the remainder of the section, we are concerned with a three-region economy, that is, $J = 3$.

An equilibrium point is given by setting $\dot{k}_1 = 0$ and $\dot{k}_j = 0$ in equations (7.1.20) and (7.1.21). That is

$$(\lambda\tilde{f}(k_1) - 1)\left(\frac{\hat{f}}{3} + \frac{\sqrt[3]{2}\hat{f}^2}{3\tilde{F}} + \frac{\tilde{F}}{3\sqrt[3]{2}}\right) + T_0A_1\beta_1k_1^{\alpha_1} = 0,$$

$$(\lambda\tilde{f}(k_1) - 1)\bar{k}_j + \lambda T_0\bar{\phi}_j(k_1) = 0, \quad j = 2, 3, \tag{7.1.24}$$

where we use $\bar{\phi}_1 = A_1\beta_{1j}k_1^{\alpha_1}$, and equations (7.1.18) and (7.1.19).

From equations (7.1.24), we solve

$$\bar{k}_j = \frac{\lambda T_0 \bar{\phi}_j(k_1)}{1 - \lambda \bar{f}(k_1)}, \quad j = 2, 3. \tag{7.1.25}$$

We thus can express $\bar{k}_2$ and $\bar{k}_3$ as functions of k_1 at an equilibrium point. Substituting equations (7.1.25) into equations (7.1.14) and (7.1.15), we can express $\bar{y}_2, \bar{y}_3$ and $\bar{f}$ as functions of k_1 at an equilibrium point. We see that all the functions in the system can be expressed as functions of k_1. We omit the explicit expressions as they are straightforward but tedious. It should be noted that under equations (7.1.25) and (A.7.1.6), we have

$$T_j = (1-\sigma)T_0 - \frac{\lambda \sigma T_0 \tilde{f}(k_1)}{1 - \lambda \tilde{f}(k_1)}, \quad j = 1, 2, 3.$$

The above equations imply that there is no difference in the work time among the regions. This property is due to the specified form of the Cobb-Douglas functions.

By equation (7.1.14), we see that an equilibrium value of k_1 is a positive solution of the following equation:

$$\Omega(k_1) \equiv \left(\lambda \tilde{f}(k_1) - 1\right)\left(\frac{\hat{f}(k_1)}{3} + \frac{\sqrt[3]{2}\hat{f}^2(k_1)}{3\tilde{F}(k_1)} + \frac{\tilde{F}(k_1)}{3\sqrt[3]{2}}\right) + T_0 A_1 \beta_1 k_1^{\alpha_1} = 0. \tag{7.1.26}$$

Equation (7.1.26) determines an equilibrium value of k_1 and equations (7.1.25) determine the corresponding equilibrium values of $\bar{k}_j$, $j = 2, 3$, for each k_1.

To simulate the model, we specify the parameter values as follows:

$$\begin{pmatrix} A_1 \\ A_2 \\ A_3 \end{pmatrix} = \begin{pmatrix} 1.5 \\ 1.2 \\ 1 \end{pmatrix}, \begin{pmatrix} \bar{\theta}_1 \\ \bar{\theta}_2 \\ \bar{\theta}_3 \end{pmatrix} = \begin{pmatrix} 4 \\ 3.8 \\ 4.3 \end{pmatrix}, \begin{pmatrix} \eta \\ \sigma \\ \lambda \end{pmatrix} = \begin{pmatrix} 1/12 \\ 2/12 \\ 7/12 \end{pmatrix}, \begin{pmatrix} L_1 \\ L_2 \\ L_3 \end{pmatrix} = \begin{pmatrix} 3 \\ 4 \\ 3.5 \end{pmatrix}, \begin{pmatrix} \alpha_1 \\ \alpha_2 \\ \alpha_3 \end{pmatrix} = \begin{pmatrix} 0.3 \\ 0.3 \\ 0.3 \end{pmatrix},$$

$$\begin{pmatrix} \delta_{k1} \\ \delta_{k2} \\ \delta_{k3} \end{pmatrix} = \begin{pmatrix} 0.15 \\ 0.14 \\ 0.13 \end{pmatrix}, \tag{7.1.27}$$

and $N = 10$ and $T_0 = 1$. As the sum of the propensities is equal to 1, we have $\xi = 1/6$. Region 1 has the highest level of productivity. Region 2's level of productivity is second, next to region 1's. We term region 1 as the advanced region, region 2 the middle region, and region 3 the less advanced region. We now show that the dynamic system has a unique equilibrium point.

We plot the function $\Omega(k_1)$ in Figure 7.1.1. The equation $\Omega(k_1) = 0$ has a unique meaningful positive solution $k_1 = 4.057$.

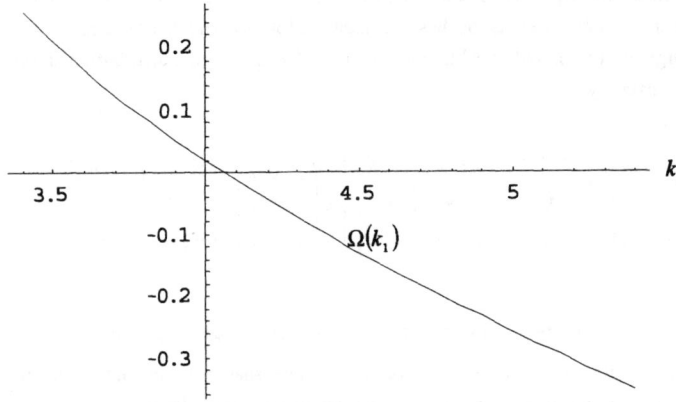

Figure 7.1.1 The existence of positive solutions of $\Omega(k_1) = 0$

From $k_1 = 4.057$ and equations (7.1.25), we get the equilibrium values of $\bar{k}_2$ and $\bar{k}_3$. Following Lemma 7.1.1, we get the equilibrium values of all the other variables. We list the simulation results as follows:

$$F = 10.32, \ K = 17.64, \ r = 0.019, \ T\left(=T_j\right) = 0.589,$$

$$\begin{pmatrix} f_1 \\ f_2 \\ f_3 \end{pmatrix} = \begin{pmatrix} 2.283 \\ 1.620 \\ 1.219 \end{pmatrix}, \ \begin{pmatrix} k_1 \\ k_2 \\ k_3 \end{pmatrix} = \begin{pmatrix} 4.06 \\ 2.72 \\ 1.94 \end{pmatrix}, \ \begin{pmatrix} \bar{N}_1 \\ \bar{N}_2 \\ \bar{N}_3 \end{pmatrix} = \begin{pmatrix} 3.90 \\ 2.95 \\ 3.15 \end{pmatrix}, \ \begin{pmatrix} F_1 \\ F_2 \\ F_3 \end{pmatrix} = \begin{pmatrix} 5.244 \\ 2.817 \\ 2.268 \end{pmatrix},$$

$$\begin{pmatrix} C_1 \\ C_2 \\ C_3 \end{pmatrix} = \begin{pmatrix} 2.560 \\ 1.375 \\ 1.105 \end{pmatrix}, \ \begin{pmatrix} \bar{k}_1 \\ \bar{k}_2 \\ \bar{k}_3 \end{pmatrix} = \begin{pmatrix} 2.30 \\ 1.63 \\ 1.23 \end{pmatrix}, \ \begin{pmatrix} w_1 \\ w_2 \\ w_3 \end{pmatrix} = \begin{pmatrix} 1.60 \\ 1.13 \\ 0.85 \end{pmatrix}, \ \begin{pmatrix} c_1 \\ c_2 \\ c_3 \end{pmatrix} = \begin{pmatrix} 0.66 \\ 0.47 \\ 0.35 \end{pmatrix},$$

$$\begin{pmatrix} l_1 \\ l_2 \\ l_3 \end{pmatrix} = \begin{pmatrix} 0.770 \\ 1.355 \\ 1.111 \end{pmatrix}, \begin{pmatrix} R_1 \\ R_2 \\ R_3 \end{pmatrix} = \begin{pmatrix} 0.427 \\ 0.172 \\ 0.158 \end{pmatrix}.$$

We see that the per capita levels of wealth and consumption and wage rate in the advanced region are higher than the corresponding variables in the middle and less advanced regions. But the lot size of the middle region is the largest in the nation and the land rent in the region is next to the lowest level in the less advanced region. A household in the advanced region has the smallest lot size and the land rent in the region is highest. The output, wealth, population, and wage income distribution among regions are given by

$$\begin{pmatrix} \hat{F}_1 \\ \hat{F}_2 \\ \hat{F}_3 \end{pmatrix} = \begin{pmatrix} 50.8\% \\ 27.3\% \\ 21.9\% \end{pmatrix}, \begin{pmatrix} \hat{K}_1 \\ \hat{K}_2 \\ \hat{K}_3 \end{pmatrix} = \begin{pmatrix} 52.8\% \\ 26.8\% \\ 20.4\% \end{pmatrix}, \begin{pmatrix} \hat{N}_1 \\ \hat{N}_2 \\ \hat{N}_3 \end{pmatrix} = \begin{pmatrix} 39.0\% \\ 29.5\% \\ 31.5\% \end{pmatrix}, \begin{pmatrix} \hat{W}_1 \\ \hat{W}_2 \\ \hat{W}_3 \end{pmatrix} = \begin{pmatrix} 50.8\% \\ 27.3\% \\ 21.9\% \end{pmatrix},$$

where a variable x_j with circumflex, $\hat{x}_j$, denotes region j's share of the corresponding variable in the national economy. The shares of the output, capital stocks, population, and wage income of the advanced regions in the national economy are respectively 50.8 percent, 52.8 percent, 39.9 percent, and 50.8 percent. The less advanced region's corresponding shares are respectively 21.9 percent, 20.4 percent, 31.5 percent, and 21.9 percent. The region's share of the population is much higher than its share of the national output, because of its relatively low productivity and high amenity level in the national economy.

We calculate the regional trade balances at equilibrium as follows:

$$\begin{pmatrix} E_1 \\ E_2 \\ E_3 \end{pmatrix} = \begin{pmatrix} -0.358 \\ 0.089 \\ 0.271 \end{pmatrix}.$$

The advanced region is in trade deficit and the middle and less advanced regions are in trade surplus.

7.1.3 Parameter changes and regional economic structures

First, we examine the case that all the parameters, except region 1's productivity, A_1, are the same as in (7.1.27). We increase the productivity level, A_1, from 1.5 to 1.7.

Multi-Region Growth Economies 293

The simulation results are summarized in (7.1.28), in which a variable $\overline{\Delta x}_j$ stands for the change rate of the equilibrium value of the variable x_j in percentage due to the change in the parameter value from A_{10} (= 1.5 in this case) to A_1 (= 1.7). That is

$$\overline{\Delta x}_j \equiv \frac{x_j(A_1) - x_j(A_{10})}{|x_j(A_{10})|} \times 100,$$

where $x_j(A_1)$ stands for the equilibrium value of the variable x_j with the parameter value A_1 and $x_j(A_{10})$ stands for the value of the variable x_j with the parameter value A_{10}. We will use the symbol $\overline{\Delta}$ with the same meaning when we analyze other parameters.

We see that as the advanced region's productivity is improved, the national output is increased and the rate of interest is increased. As the productivity is improved, the work time is reduced. The per-work-time output level of the advanced region rises; the levels of per-work-time output of the other two regions fall. Some people migrate from the middle and less advanced regions to the advanced region. The per capita wealth, wage rate, and consumption level are increased in the advanced region; the per capita wealth and consumption levels and wage rates of the other regions are reduced. The lot size of the advanced region falls and the land rent rises due to the immigration; the lot sizes of the other regions rise and the land rents fall due to emigration. The share of national product of the advanced region is further increased and the other two regions' shares are reduced. The trade balance of the advanced region deteriorates and the other two regions' trade balances improve.

$A_1: 1.5 \Rightarrow 1.7 \Rightarrow \overline{\Delta F} = 11.72, \ \overline{\Delta K} = 11.92, \ \overline{\Delta T} = -0.07, \ \overline{\Delta r} = 3.81,$

$$\begin{pmatrix} \overline{\Delta f_1} \\ \overline{\Delta f_2} \\ \overline{\Delta f_3} \end{pmatrix} = \begin{pmatrix} 19.36 \\ -0.17 \\ -0.16 \end{pmatrix}, \ \begin{pmatrix} \Delta k_1 \\ \Delta k_2 \\ \Delta k_3 \end{pmatrix} = \begin{pmatrix} 18.86 \\ -0.57 \\ -0.54 \end{pmatrix}, \ \begin{pmatrix} \overline{\Delta N_1} \\ \overline{\Delta N_2} \\ \overline{\Delta N_3} \end{pmatrix} = \begin{pmatrix} 7.01 \\ -4.49 \\ -4.48 \end{pmatrix}, \ \begin{pmatrix} \overline{\Delta F_1} \\ \overline{\Delta F_2} \\ \overline{\Delta F_3} \end{pmatrix} = \begin{pmatrix} 27.65 \\ -4.72 \\ -4.90 \end{pmatrix},$$

$$\begin{pmatrix} \overline{\Delta k_1} \\ \overline{\Delta k_2} \\ \overline{\Delta k_3} \end{pmatrix} = \begin{pmatrix} 19.48 \\ -0.07 \\ -0.06 \end{pmatrix}, \ \begin{pmatrix} \overline{\Delta w_1} \\ \overline{\Delta w_2} \\ \overline{\Delta w_3} \end{pmatrix} = \begin{pmatrix} 19.36 \\ -0.17 \\ -0.16 \end{pmatrix}, \ \begin{pmatrix} \overline{\Delta c_1} \\ \overline{\Delta c_2} \\ \overline{\Delta c_3} \end{pmatrix} = \begin{pmatrix} 19.48 \\ -0.07 \\ -0.06 \end{pmatrix}, \ \begin{pmatrix} \overline{\Delta l_1} \\ \overline{\Delta l_2} \\ \overline{\Delta l_3} \end{pmatrix} = \begin{pmatrix} -6.56 \\ 4.70 \\ 4.69 \end{pmatrix},$$

$$\begin{pmatrix} \overline{\Delta R_1} \\ \overline{\Delta R_2} \\ \overline{\Delta R_3} \end{pmatrix} = \begin{pmatrix} 27.87 \\ -4.56 \\ -4.54 \end{pmatrix}, \ \begin{pmatrix} \overline{\Delta \hat{F}_1} \\ \overline{\Delta \hat{F}_2} \\ \overline{\Delta \hat{F}_3} \end{pmatrix} = \begin{pmatrix} 14.25 \\ -14.72 \\ -14.71 \end{pmatrix}, \ \begin{pmatrix} \overline{\Delta E_1} \\ \overline{\Delta E_2} \\ \overline{\Delta E_3} \end{pmatrix} = \begin{pmatrix} -7.99 \\ 25.13 \\ 2.47 \end{pmatrix}. \quad (7.1.28)$$

294 Economic Growth with Income and Wealth Distribution

We summarize the effects of change in the middle region's productivity in (7.1.29). The productivity level, A_2, rises from 1.2 to 1.4. As the middle region's productivity is improved, the national output is increased. The per-work-time output levels of all the regions rise. But different from the previous case when the advanced region improves its productivity, the rate of interest falls as the middle region improves its productivity. The per-work-time output levels of all the regions rise. Some people migrate from the advanced and less advanced regions to the middle region. The per capita wealth levels, wage rates, and consumption levels are increased in all the regions. The lot size of the middle region falls and the land rent rises due to the immigration; the lot sizes of the other regions rise and the land rent falls due to emigration. The share of national product of the middle region is increased and the other two regions' shares are reduced. The trade balances of the advanced region deteriorates and the advanced and middle regions' trade balances improve.

$$A_2: 1.2 \Rightarrow 1.4 \Rightarrow \overline{\Delta F} = 7.169, \ \overline{\Delta K} = 7.107, \ \overline{\Delta T} = 0.024, \ \overline{\Delta r} = -1.252,$$

$$\begin{pmatrix} \overline{\Delta f_1} \\ \overline{\Delta f_2} \\ \overline{\Delta f_3} \end{pmatrix} = \begin{pmatrix} 0.06 \\ 24.71 \\ 0.05 \end{pmatrix}, \begin{pmatrix} \Delta k_1 \\ \Delta k_2 \\ \Delta k_3 \end{pmatrix} = \begin{pmatrix} 0.20 \\ 24.87 \\ 0.18 \end{pmatrix}, \begin{pmatrix} \overline{\Delta N_1} \\ \overline{\Delta N_2} \\ \overline{\Delta N_3} \end{pmatrix} = \begin{pmatrix} -4.25 \\ 10.15 \\ -4.25 \end{pmatrix}, \begin{pmatrix} \overline{\Delta F_1} \\ \overline{\Delta F_2} \\ \overline{\Delta F_3} \end{pmatrix} = \begin{pmatrix} -4.17 \\ 37.40 \\ -1.18 \end{pmatrix},$$

$$\begin{pmatrix} \overline{\Delta k_1} \\ \overline{\Delta k_2} \\ \overline{\Delta k_3} \end{pmatrix} = \begin{pmatrix} 0.03 \\ 24.66 \\ 0.02 \end{pmatrix}, \begin{pmatrix} \overline{\Delta w_1} \\ \overline{\Delta w_2} \\ \overline{\Delta w_3} \end{pmatrix} = \begin{pmatrix} 0.06 \\ 24.71 \\ 0.05 \end{pmatrix}, \begin{pmatrix} \overline{\Delta c_1} \\ \overline{\Delta c_2} \\ \overline{\Delta c_3} \end{pmatrix} = \begin{pmatrix} 0.03 \\ 24.66 \\ 0.02 \end{pmatrix}, \begin{pmatrix} \overline{\Delta l_1} \\ \overline{\Delta l_2} \\ \overline{\Delta l_3} \end{pmatrix} = \begin{pmatrix} 4.44 \\ -9.22 \\ 4.44 \end{pmatrix},$$

$$\begin{pmatrix} \overline{\Delta R_1} \\ \overline{\Delta R_2} \\ \overline{\Delta R_3} \end{pmatrix} = \begin{pmatrix} -4.22 \\ 37.32 \\ -4.23 \end{pmatrix}, \begin{pmatrix} \overline{\Delta \hat{F}_1} \\ \overline{\Delta \hat{F}_2} \\ \overline{\Delta \hat{F}_3} \end{pmatrix} = \begin{pmatrix} -10.58 \\ 28.20 \\ -10.59 \end{pmatrix}, \begin{pmatrix} \overline{\Delta E_1} \\ \overline{\Delta E_2} \\ \overline{\Delta E_3} \end{pmatrix} = \begin{pmatrix} 0.70 \\ 23.21 \\ -6.56 \end{pmatrix}. \quad (7.1.29)$$

We summarize the effects of change in the less advanced region's productivity in (7.1.30). As the less advanced region's productivity is improved, the national output is increased and the rate of interest falls. The per-work-time output levels, wage rates, per capita wealth levels, and consumption levels in all the regions rise. Some people migrate from the advanced and middle regions to the less advanced region. The lot size of the less advanced region falls and the land rent rises due to the immigration; the lot sizes of the other regions rise and the land rents fall due to emigration. The share of national product of the less advanced region is increased and the other two regions' shares are reduced. The trade balances of the advanced and middle regions deteriorate and the less advanced region's trade balance improves.

$$A_3: 1 \Rightarrow 1.2 \Rightarrow \overline{\Delta F} = 5.98, \ \overline{\Delta K} = 5.75, \ \overline{\Delta T} = 0.09, \ \overline{\Delta r} = -4.80,$$

$$\begin{pmatrix}\overline{\Delta f_1}\\ \overline{\Delta f_2}\\ \overline{\Delta f_3}\end{pmatrix}=\begin{pmatrix}0.23\\ 0.22\\ 30.02\end{pmatrix},\begin{pmatrix}\overline{\Delta k_1}\\ \overline{\Delta k_2}\\ \overline{\Delta k_3}\end{pmatrix}=\begin{pmatrix}0.77\\ 0.73\\ 30.64\end{pmatrix},\begin{pmatrix}\overline{\Delta N_1}\\ \overline{\Delta N_2}\\ \overline{\Delta N_3}\end{pmatrix}=\begin{pmatrix}-5.37\\ -5.37\\ 11.68\end{pmatrix},\begin{pmatrix}\overline{\Delta F_1}\\ \overline{\Delta F_2}\\ \overline{\Delta F_3}\end{pmatrix}=\begin{pmatrix}-5.06\\ -5.08\\ 45.33\end{pmatrix},$$

$$\begin{pmatrix}\overline{\Delta k_1}\\ \overline{\Delta k_2}\\ \overline{\Delta k_3}\end{pmatrix}=\begin{pmatrix}0.10\\ 0.09\\ 29.85\end{pmatrix},\begin{pmatrix}\overline{\Delta w_1}\\ \overline{\Delta w_2}\\ \overline{\Delta w_3}\end{pmatrix}=\begin{pmatrix}0.23\\ 0.22\\ 30.02\end{pmatrix},\begin{pmatrix}\overline{\Delta c_1}\\ \overline{\Delta c_2}\\ \overline{\Delta c_3}\end{pmatrix}=\begin{pmatrix}0.10\\ 0.09\\ 29.85\end{pmatrix},\begin{pmatrix}\overline{\Delta l_1}\\ \overline{\Delta l_2}\\ \overline{\Delta l_3}\end{pmatrix}=\begin{pmatrix}5.67\\ 5.68\\ -10.47\end{pmatrix},$$

$$\begin{pmatrix}\overline{\Delta R_1}\\ \overline{\Delta R_2}\\ \overline{\Delta R_3}\end{pmatrix}=\begin{pmatrix}-5.27\\ -5.29\\ 45.01\end{pmatrix},\begin{pmatrix}\overline{\Delta \hat{F}_1}\\ \overline{\Delta \hat{F}_2}\\ \overline{\Delta \hat{F}_3}\end{pmatrix}=\begin{pmatrix}-10.41\\ -10.44\\ 37.13\end{pmatrix},\begin{pmatrix}\overline{\Delta E_1}\\ \overline{\Delta E_2}\\ \overline{\Delta E_3}\end{pmatrix}=\begin{pmatrix}-13.44\\ -42.68\\ 31.51\end{pmatrix}. \qquad (7.1.30)$$

We observe that as a region improves its technology, its land rent increases and the land rents in the other regions fall. The region's trade balance is improved and the other two regions' trade balances deteriorate. It is important to note that as a region improves its technology, the other two regions' aggregated output levels fall not only in relative terms, but also in absolute values. This implies that if any region has a high rate of technological change and the other regions remain technologically stationary, then the economic activities tend to be concentrated in the technologically advancing region. Also we observe that as a region improves its technology, the other two regions' total output falls but all the individual households in the other two regions benefit in terms of consumption of goods, housing, and wealth. If we introduce some mechanism for endogenous technological changes, our analytical framework may be more powerful than contemporary theoretical approaches in explaining agglomeration.[21] The topic of endogenous technological change is too complicated to be studied in detail here.

We summarize the effects of change in the advanced region's amenity parameter, $\overline{\theta}_1$, in (7.1.31). As the advanced region's amenity parameter is increased, the national output is increased and the rate of interest rises. The per-work-time output levels of all the regions decline. Some people migrate from the middle and less advanced regions to the advanced region. The per capita wealth, wage rates, and consumption levels in all the regions are reduced. The lot size of the advanced region falls and the land rent rises; the lot sizes of the other regions rise and the land rents fall. The share of national product of the advanced region is increased and the other two regions' shares are reduced. The trade balances of the advanced and less advanced regions deteriorate and the middle region's trade balance improves.

$$\overline{\theta}_1: 4 \Rightarrow 4.2 \Rightarrow \overline{\Delta F} = 1.18, \ \overline{\Delta K} = 1.24, \ \overline{\Delta T} = -0.03, \ \overline{\Delta r} = 1.40,$$

296   *Economic Growth with Income and Wealth Distribution*

$$\begin{pmatrix} \overline{\Delta f_1} \\ \overline{\Delta f_2} \\ \overline{\Delta f_3} \end{pmatrix} = \begin{pmatrix} -0.07 \\ -0.06 \\ -0.06 \end{pmatrix}, \begin{pmatrix} \overline{\Delta k_1} \\ \overline{\Delta k_2} \\ \overline{\Delta k_3} \end{pmatrix} = \begin{pmatrix} -0.22 \\ -0.21 \\ -0.20 \end{pmatrix}, \begin{pmatrix} \overline{\Delta N_1} \\ \overline{\Delta N_2} \\ \overline{\Delta N_3} \end{pmatrix} = \begin{pmatrix} 6.56 \\ -4.19 \\ -4.19 \end{pmatrix}, \begin{pmatrix} \overline{\Delta F_1} \\ \overline{\Delta F_2} \\ \overline{\Delta F_3} \end{pmatrix} = \begin{pmatrix} 6.46 \\ -4.28 \\ -4.28 \end{pmatrix},$$

$$\begin{pmatrix} \overline{\Delta \bar{k}_1} \\ \overline{\Delta \bar{k}_2} \\ \overline{\Delta \bar{k}_3} \end{pmatrix} = \begin{pmatrix} -0.03 \\ -0.03 \\ -0.02 \end{pmatrix}, \begin{pmatrix} \overline{\Delta w_1} \\ \overline{\Delta w_2} \\ \overline{\Delta w_3} \end{pmatrix} = \begin{pmatrix} -0.07 \\ -0.06 \\ -0.06 \end{pmatrix}, \begin{pmatrix} \overline{\Delta c_1} \\ \overline{\Delta c_2} \\ \overline{\Delta c_3} \end{pmatrix} = \begin{pmatrix} -0.03 \\ -0.03 \\ -0.02 \end{pmatrix}, \begin{pmatrix} \overline{\Delta l_1} \\ \overline{\Delta l_2} \\ \overline{\Delta l_3} \end{pmatrix} = \begin{pmatrix} -6.16 \\ 4.38 \\ 4.38 \end{pmatrix},$$

$$\begin{pmatrix} \overline{\Delta R_1} \\ \overline{\Delta R_2} \\ \overline{\Delta R_3} \end{pmatrix} = \begin{pmatrix} 6.53 \\ -4.22 \\ -4.22 \end{pmatrix}, \begin{pmatrix} \overline{\Delta \hat{F}_1} \\ \overline{\Delta \hat{F}_2} \\ \overline{\Delta \hat{F}_3} \end{pmatrix} = \begin{pmatrix} 5.22 \\ -5.40 \\ -5.39 \end{pmatrix}, \begin{pmatrix} \overline{\Delta E_1} \\ \overline{\Delta E_2} \\ \overline{\Delta E_3} \end{pmatrix} = \begin{pmatrix} -0.41 \\ 6.77 \\ -1.62 \end{pmatrix}. \quad (7.1.31)$$

The effects of change in the middle region's amenity parameter, $\bar{\theta}_2$, are given in (7.1.32). As the middle region's amenity parameter is increased, the national output is reduced and the rate of interest falls. The per-work-time output levels and wage rates of all the regions rise. Some people migrate from the advanced and less advanced regions to the middle region. The lot size of the middle region falls and the land rent rises; the lot sizes of the other regions rise and the land rents fall. The share of national product of the middle region is increased and the other two regions' shares are reduced. The trade balances of the advanced and middle regions improve and the less advanced region's trade balance deteriorates. The results for change in the less advanced region's amenity parameter are similar to this case.

$$\bar{\theta}_2 : 3.8 \Rightarrow 4 \Rightarrow \overline{\Delta F} = -0.23, \ \overline{\Delta K} = -0.25, \ \overline{\Delta T} = 0.01, \ \overline{\Delta r} = -0.37,$$

$$\begin{pmatrix} \overline{\Delta f_1} \\ \overline{\Delta f_2} \\ \overline{\Delta f_3} \end{pmatrix} = \begin{pmatrix} 0.02 \\ 0.02 \\ 0.02 \end{pmatrix}, \begin{pmatrix} \overline{\Delta k_1} \\ \overline{\Delta k_2} \\ \overline{\Delta k_3} \end{pmatrix} = \begin{pmatrix} 0.06 \\ 0.06 \\ 0.05 \end{pmatrix}, \begin{pmatrix} \overline{\Delta N_1} \\ \overline{\Delta N_2} \\ \overline{\Delta N_3} \end{pmatrix} = \begin{pmatrix} -3.38 \\ 8.06 \\ -3.38 \end{pmatrix}, \begin{pmatrix} \overline{\Delta F_1} \\ \overline{\Delta F_2} \\ \overline{\Delta F_3} \end{pmatrix} = \begin{pmatrix} -3.35 \\ 8.10 \\ -3.36 \end{pmatrix},$$

$$\begin{pmatrix} \overline{\Delta \bar{k}_1} \\ \overline{\Delta \bar{k}_2} \\ \overline{\Delta \bar{k}_3} \end{pmatrix} = \begin{pmatrix} 0.01 \\ 0.01 \\ 0.01 \end{pmatrix}, \begin{pmatrix} \overline{\Delta w_1} \\ \overline{\Delta w_2} \\ \overline{\Delta w_3} \end{pmatrix} = \begin{pmatrix} 0.02 \\ 0.02 \\ 0.02 \end{pmatrix}, \begin{pmatrix} \overline{\Delta c_1} \\ \overline{\Delta c_2} \\ \overline{\Delta c_3} \end{pmatrix} = \begin{pmatrix} 0.01 \\ 0.01 \\ 0.01 \end{pmatrix}, \begin{pmatrix} \overline{\Delta l_1} \\ \overline{\Delta l_2} \\ \overline{\Delta l_3} \end{pmatrix} = \begin{pmatrix} 3.49 \\ -7.46 \\ 3.50 \end{pmatrix},$$

$$\begin{pmatrix} \overline{\Delta R_1} \\ \overline{\Delta R_2} \\ \overline{\Delta R_3} \end{pmatrix} = \begin{pmatrix} -3.37 \\ 8.07 \\ -3.37 \end{pmatrix}, \begin{pmatrix} \overline{\Delta \hat{F}_1} \\ \overline{\Delta \hat{F}_2} \\ \overline{\Delta \hat{F}_3} \end{pmatrix} = \begin{pmatrix} -3.13 \\ 8.34 \\ -3.13 \end{pmatrix}, \begin{pmatrix} \overline{\Delta E_1} \\ \overline{\Delta E_2} \\ \overline{\Delta E_3} \end{pmatrix} = \begin{pmatrix} 1.91 \\ 4.80 \\ -4.06 \end{pmatrix}. \quad (7.1.32)$$

We conclude that if amenity improvement occurs in the technologically advanced region, then the national output rises; but if environmental improvement occurs in the technologically less advanced region, the national output falls. This hints at the possibility that if the central government improves a technologically less advanced region, the national output may fall. This issue will be studied in the future, as this study does not include any government intervention. Environmental improvement may either improve or worsen the region's trade balance. It is important to note that environmental improvement has weak but symmetrical impact on the regions' wage rate.

We now examine change in the preference. As our results are based on the assumption of $\eta = 1/12$, we can change σ, ξ and λ. As $\eta + \sigma + \xi + \lambda = 1$, any preference change is subject to $\sigma + \xi + \lambda = 11/12$. We now reduce the propensity to save and increase the propensity to consume as specified in (7.1.33). The effects of change in the nation's preference are provided in (7.1.33). As the propensity to save is reduced, the national output is decreased and the rate of interest rises. The per-work-time output levels, wage rates, consumption levels, and per capita wealth in all the regions are reduced. Some people migrate from the middle and less advanced regions to the advanced region. The lot size of the less advanced region falls; the lot sizes of the other regions rise. The land rents in all the regions fall. The share of national product of the advanced region falls and the other two regions' shares rise. The trade balance of the advanced region improves; the trade balances of the other two regions deteriorate.

$$(\rho, \lambda, \xi): \left(\frac{2}{12}, \frac{7}{12}, \frac{2}{12}\right) \Rightarrow \left(\frac{2.25}{12}, \frac{6.6}{12}, \frac{2.25}{12}\right) \Rightarrow$$

$$\overline{\Delta F} = -9.40, \quad \overline{\Delta K} = -19.33, \quad \overline{\Delta T} = -3.13, \quad \overline{\Delta r} = 111.33,$$

$$\begin{pmatrix}\overline{\Delta f_1}\\ \overline{\Delta f_2}\\ \overline{\Delta f_3}\end{pmatrix} = \begin{pmatrix}-4.90\\ -4.62\\ -4.41\end{pmatrix}, \begin{pmatrix}\Delta k_1\\ \Delta k_2\\ \Delta k_3\end{pmatrix} = \begin{pmatrix}-15.41\\ -14.65\\ -13.97\end{pmatrix}, \begin{pmatrix}\overline{\Delta N_1}\\ \overline{\Delta N_2}\\ \overline{\Delta N_3}\end{pmatrix} = \begin{pmatrix}-11.43\\ 12.71\\ 2.23\end{pmatrix}, \begin{pmatrix}\overline{\Delta F_1}\\ \overline{\Delta F_2}\\ \overline{\Delta F_3}\end{pmatrix} = \begin{pmatrix}-18.40\\ 4.11\\ -5.34\end{pmatrix},$$

$$\begin{pmatrix}\overline{\Delta k_1}\\ \overline{\Delta k_2}\\ \overline{\Delta k_3}\end{pmatrix} = \begin{pmatrix}-17.97\\ -17.76\\ -17.56\end{pmatrix}, \begin{pmatrix}\overline{\Delta w_1}\\ \overline{\Delta w_2}\\ \overline{\Delta w_3}\end{pmatrix} = \begin{pmatrix}-4.90\\ -4.64\\ -4.41\end{pmatrix}, \begin{pmatrix}\overline{\Delta c_1}\\ \overline{\Delta c_2}\\ \overline{\Delta c_3}\end{pmatrix} = \begin{pmatrix}-0.62\\ -0.36\\ -0.12\end{pmatrix}, \begin{pmatrix}\overline{\Delta l_1}\\ \overline{\Delta l_2}\\ \overline{\Delta l_3}\end{pmatrix} = \begin{pmatrix}12.90\\ -11.28\\ -2.18\end{pmatrix},$$

$$\begin{pmatrix}\overline{\Delta R_1}\\ \overline{\Delta R_2}\\ \overline{\Delta R_3}\end{pmatrix} = \begin{pmatrix}-21.76\\ -0.17\\ -9.24\end{pmatrix}, \begin{pmatrix}\overline{\Delta \hat{F_1}}\\ \overline{\Delta \hat{F_2}}\\ \overline{\Delta \hat{F_3}}\end{pmatrix} = \begin{pmatrix}-9.94\\ 14.91\\ 4.47\end{pmatrix}, \begin{pmatrix}\overline{\Delta E_1}\\ \overline{\Delta E_2}\\ \overline{\Delta E_3}\end{pmatrix} = \begin{pmatrix}29.22\\ -33.50\\ -27.84\end{pmatrix}. \quad (7.1.33)$$

We now allow the advanced region's residential land to be enlarged. The effects of change are given in (7.1.34). As the advanced region's residential area is enlarged, the

298 Economic Growth with Income and Wealth Distribution

national output is increased and the rate of interest rises. The per capita output levels and wage rates of all the regions are reduced. Some people migrate from the middle and less advanced regions to the advanced region. The per capita wealth and consumption levels are all slightly affected. The lot sizes in all the regions rise. The land rents in all the regions fall. The share of national product of the advanced region is increased and the other two regions' shares are reduced. The trade balances of the advanced and less advanced regions deteriorate and the middle region's trade balance improves.

$$L_1: 3 \Rightarrow 3.3 \Rightarrow \overline{\Delta F} = 0.19, \ \overline{\Delta K} = 0.20, \ \overline{\Delta T} = -0.004, \ \overline{\Delta r} = 0.22,$$

$$\begin{pmatrix} \overline{\Delta f_1} \\ \overline{\Delta f_2} \\ \overline{\Delta f_3} \end{pmatrix} = \begin{pmatrix} -0.01 \\ -0.01 \\ -0.01 \end{pmatrix}, \ \begin{pmatrix} \overline{\Delta k_1} \\ \overline{\Delta k_2} \\ \overline{\Delta k_3} \end{pmatrix} = \begin{pmatrix} -0.04 \\ -0.03 \\ -0.03 \end{pmatrix}, \ \begin{pmatrix} \overline{\Delta N_1} \\ \overline{\Delta N_2} \\ \overline{\Delta N_3} \end{pmatrix} = \begin{pmatrix} 1.06 \\ -0.68 \\ -0.68 \end{pmatrix}, \ \begin{pmatrix} \overline{\Delta F_1} \\ \overline{\Delta F_2} \\ \overline{\Delta F_3} \end{pmatrix} = \begin{pmatrix} 1.04 \\ -0.69 \\ -0.69 \end{pmatrix},$$

$$\begin{pmatrix} \overline{\Delta \bar{k}_1} \\ \overline{\Delta \bar{k}_2} \\ \overline{\Delta \bar{k}_3} \end{pmatrix} = \begin{pmatrix} 0.00 \\ 0.00 \\ 0.00 \end{pmatrix}, \ \begin{pmatrix} \overline{\Delta w_1} \\ \overline{\Delta w_2} \\ \overline{\Delta w_3} \end{pmatrix} = \begin{pmatrix} -0.01 \\ -0.01 \\ -0.01 \end{pmatrix}, \ \begin{pmatrix} \overline{\Delta c_1} \\ \overline{\Delta c_2} \\ \overline{\Delta c_3} \end{pmatrix} = \begin{pmatrix} 0.00 \\ 0.00 \\ 0.00 \end{pmatrix}, \ \begin{pmatrix} \overline{\Delta l_1} \\ \overline{\Delta l_2} \\ \overline{\Delta l_3} \end{pmatrix} = \begin{pmatrix} 8.85 \\ 0.68 \\ 0.68 \end{pmatrix},$$

$$\begin{pmatrix} \overline{\Delta R_1} \\ \overline{\Delta R_2} \\ \overline{\Delta R_3} \end{pmatrix} = \begin{pmatrix} -8.13 \\ -0.68 \\ -0.68 \end{pmatrix}, \ \begin{pmatrix} \overline{\Delta \hat{F}_1} \\ \overline{\Delta \hat{F}_2} \\ \overline{\Delta \hat{F}_3} \end{pmatrix} = \begin{pmatrix} 0.85 \\ -0.88 \\ -0.88 \end{pmatrix}, \ \begin{pmatrix} \overline{\Delta E_1} \\ \overline{\Delta E_2} \\ \overline{\Delta E_3} \end{pmatrix} = \begin{pmatrix} -0.11 \\ 1.18 \\ -0.24 \end{pmatrix}. \quad (7.1.34)$$

We now allow the middle region's residential area to be enlarged. The effects of change are given in (7.1.35). The national output is reduced and the rate of interest falls. Some people migrate from the advanced and less advanced regions to the middle region.

$$L_2: 4 \Rightarrow 4.2 \Rightarrow \overline{\Delta F} = -0.02, \ \overline{\Delta K} = -0.02, \ \overline{\Delta T} = 0.00, \ \overline{\Delta r} = -0.03,$$

$$\begin{pmatrix} \overline{\Delta f_1} \\ \overline{\Delta f_2} \\ \overline{\Delta f_3} \end{pmatrix} = \begin{pmatrix} 0.00 \\ 0.00 \\ 0.00 \end{pmatrix}, \ \begin{pmatrix} \overline{\Delta k_1} \\ \overline{\Delta k_2} \\ \overline{\Delta k_3} \end{pmatrix} = \begin{pmatrix} 0.00 \\ 0.00 \\ 0.00 \end{pmatrix}, \ \begin{pmatrix} \overline{\Delta N_1} \\ \overline{\Delta N_2} \\ \overline{\Delta N_3} \end{pmatrix} = \begin{pmatrix} -0.26 \\ 0.63 \\ -0.26 \end{pmatrix}, \ \begin{pmatrix} \overline{\Delta F_1} \\ \overline{\Delta F_2} \\ \overline{\Delta F_3} \end{pmatrix} = \begin{pmatrix} -0.26 \\ 0.63 \\ -0.26 \end{pmatrix},$$

$$\begin{pmatrix} \overline{\Delta \bar{k}_1} \\ \overline{\Delta \bar{k}_2} \\ \overline{\Delta \bar{k}_3} \end{pmatrix} = \begin{pmatrix} 0.00 \\ 0.00 \\ 0.00 \end{pmatrix}, \ \begin{pmatrix} \overline{\Delta w_1} \\ \overline{\Delta w_2} \\ \overline{\Delta w_3} \end{pmatrix} = \begin{pmatrix} 0.00 \\ 0.00 \\ 0.00 \end{pmatrix}, \ \begin{pmatrix} \overline{\Delta c_1} \\ \overline{\Delta c_2} \\ \overline{\Delta c_3} \end{pmatrix} = \begin{pmatrix} 0.00 \\ 0.00 \\ 0.00 \end{pmatrix}, \ \begin{pmatrix} \overline{\Delta l_1} \\ \overline{\Delta l_2} \\ \overline{\Delta l_3} \end{pmatrix} = \begin{pmatrix} 0.26 \\ 4.34 \\ 0.26 \end{pmatrix},$$

$$\begin{pmatrix} \overline{\Delta R_1} \\ \overline{\Delta R_2} \\ \overline{\Delta R_3} \end{pmatrix} = \begin{pmatrix} -0.26 \\ -4.16 \\ -0.26 \end{pmatrix}, \ \begin{pmatrix} \overline{\Delta \hat{F}_1} \\ \overline{\Delta \hat{F}_2} \\ \overline{\Delta \hat{F}_3} \end{pmatrix} = \begin{pmatrix} -0.24 \\ 0.65 \\ -0.24 \end{pmatrix}, \ \begin{pmatrix} \overline{\Delta E_1} \\ \overline{\Delta E_2} \\ \overline{\Delta E_3} \end{pmatrix} = \begin{pmatrix} 0.14 \\ 0.39 \\ -0.32 \end{pmatrix}. \quad (7.1.35)$$

Our model demonstrates divergence of wages rates among regions in the long term. From our simulation result, we see that although wage rates are affected by changes in regional differences in technology, land, and amenity, the wage disparity is mostly strongly affected by change in regional technology. This also implies that as far as neoclassical economics is concerned, if technological differences among regions are not large, wage rates may tend to converge as the other factors weakly affect the differences. It is interesting to note that from the empirical study on wage determination with a large panel of French workers, Combes et al. (2004) have found that individual skills account for a large fraction of existing spatial wage disparities with strong evidence of spatial sorting by skills, and endowments only appear to play a small role. As far as relations between wage disparity and endowments are concerned, our model gives similar results. It remains to prove whether this character of economic development can be observed under more general conditions.

7.2 Regional economic structure with endogenous knowledge

Industrialization, urbanization, population growth, and migration drive economic geography to materialize differently over time. In modern times, global as well as national economic geographies have dramatically changed in association with sectoral adjustments from agriculture to manufacturing and from manufacturing to services. Economic growth of multiregional systems is one of the main issues in regional economics and regional sciences. Some economists were cognizant of the causes of spatial differences in long-run growth rates and the causes of productivity improvements such as innovation, economies of scales, and learning-by-doing. But these later causes violate the assumptions of perfect competition and constant returns to scale; it is difficult to formally take these causes into account when modeling regional growth. There are some contemporary studies of increasing returns; most of those works deal with economies of increasing returns under imperfect competition. Agglomeration economies are associated with increasing returns from specification, from the higher rate of technological change and spillover effects, and from the higher rate of human capital accumulation. Myrdal (1957) brings about ideas of circular and cumulative causation to examine multiregional growth. The cumulative causation theory treats increasing returns to scale as the main source of regional growth. Kaldor (1966) argues how export-led regional growth impulses may set off self-reinforcing growth processes through agglomeration economies and the achievement of successively higher market thresholds.[22] It is held that linkages between growing and lagging regions may not be equally beneficial.

It is observed that there are substantial differences in labor productivity among the manufacturing sectors of the various regions of the US. Moomaw (1983) reviews the literature on the study of the existence of spatial differentials in labor productivity and possible implications of these differentials for regional and urban development. Another early study carried out by Verdoorn demonstrates that manufacturing industry is subject to substantial economies of scale.[23] It is argued that faster growing regions will experience a greater growth of productivity than the more slowly growing regions. Rapidly growing regional competitiveness is increased in the manner of cumulative causation. McCombie (1988) examines the causes of regional disparities in growth and unemployment within the neoclassical growth framework. One of the causes of disparities in regional productivity growth is the eradication of an initial interregional misallocation of resources. McCombie also analyzes the impact of a progressive reduction in the degree of intraregional misallocation of resources on productivity growth and emphasizes the role of the spatial diffusion of innovations in regional productivity.

In examining agglomeration economies, Krugman (1989, 1991) develops a few models of economic geography. He tries to incorporate regional aspects such as factor mobility, transport costs, and the interaction of agglomeration advantages and costs. Abel-Rahman (1988) explains urban agglomeration and regional equilibrium on the basis of the Dixit-Stiglitz approach of monopolistic competition to determine equilibrium city size. The model uses the concept of product differentiation as an important factor in the formation of large cities. The supply side is characterized by monopolistic competition and decreasing average cost at the firm level. For the demand side, product variety is presented as a key factor in consumer agglomeration. Consumers buy differentiated products available in the local market. Consumer agglomeration in a particular area enlarges the equilibrium number of firms selling differentiated products, which raises utility in the Dixit-Stiglitz manner and at the same time augments the city's radius and raises rents at any given location. The equilibrium is achieved by the interactive forces of product diversity gains, consumer agglomeration and changes in transport costs and rents. Abel-Rahman shows that in a system of two cities with no trade, at equilibrium all workers may not concentrate in the city with more product variety as is argued by Krugman (1979). This shows the importance of spatial consideration in regional trade models. Applying the frameworks proposed by Ethier in trade theory and in growth theory, Rivera-Batiz proposes a model that endogenizes agglomeration economies from both the production and consumption sides. It is assumed that an increase in city size enlarges the variety of consumer services locally available, shifting upwards household utility, and is associated with an agglomeration of industrial producers that raises the derived demand for local business, allowing increased specialization among them.[24] The increased number of producer or business services available in the city improves the productivity of the industrial base of that city and results in endogenous external economies of scale.

Modern developed economies are knowledge-based in the sense that knowledge creation and utilization play the key role in the rise and decline of national economies. In knowledge-based economies, knowledge creation and utilization also play the key role in the rise or decline of regions. Changes in technology and productivity are the key variables in explaining regional economic phenomena. Although natural resources, regional amenity and infrastructures are not highly mobile, the population and the skills and available human capital associated with people are mobile and flexible. It has been observed that regions that become important loci of invention stand to gain enormous economic and political influence.[25] The development of major loci of invention tends to be associated with high qualitative level of human capital resources and infrastructure with long-lasting effects on industry, services, competitiveness, and migration. The development of an innovative region is usually accompanied by the creation of radically new economic activities, markets, and technological applications. Highly skilled individuals and labor tend to be attracted to regions with good inventive infrastructures.

The neo-Ricardian notation of landlocked comparative advantage is not sufficient to explain phenomena associated with constructed advantages with knowledge (Varga, 1998). The approach of spatial economy by Nelson and Winter (1982) dispenses with the neoclassical conventions of continuous production and exogenous technological progress. In this approach the technological progress occurs from processes of economic search and selection. Economic search occurs when firms are induced by declining profits to seek new technologies. Firms which succeed in finding efficient technologies will expand; while those which are not so successful will contract. The processes of search and selection together comprise the economic sources of increasing technological efficiency of the aggregate economy through time. Influenced by recent works in international trade theory, Englmann and Walz (1995) propose a spatial model of economic growth with endogenous technological change in the two regions.[26] They examine the determinants of regions' growth rates in the presence of factor mobility. In this approach, regional specification patterns arise from the interaction of transport costs in combination with economies of scale and a given regional endowment with an immobile factor. They analyze the long-run effects of a variety of regional policy instruments. They show that under certain circumstances various policies would not achieve their intended targets. For instance, a regional policy which provides subsidies to traditional goods producers and is supposed to reduce regional gaps in income actually enlarges the gap due to returns to scale economies. A political instrument of making investment in interregional transport infrastructure in the less advanced region may reduce the region's location advantage either by decreasing the available number of immobile workers for production in the industrial sector or by increasing price competition in the less advanced region. The impact of certain regional policies is situation-dependent. The regional policy with a good will may turn out to be the opposite. This also implies that regional policy makers should be fully aware of each region's advantages and disadvantages and each region's special situation in order to be able to implement sensible policies in an effective way. Simply providing the less developed region with good conditions may not have the positive impact in the presence of mobile factors of productions, footloose industries, and nonconstant returns to scale.

7.2.1 The regional model with economic structure

For simplicity, we consider an economy which consists of two regions, indexed by 1 and 2, respectively. The system produces two commodities, indexed by 1 and 2, respectively. Each region is assumed to produce only one commodity. Each region has two production sectors: industry and services. Services are produced by combining knowledge, labor and land. Industrial production is regionally specified. Region j produces commodity j. It is assumed that each region's product is homogeneous. We assume a homogeneous and fixed national labor force, N. We neglect any cost for migration and professional changes. We assume perfect competition in all markets.

Each region has fixed land. The land is distributed between the service sector and housing by perfect competition. We select commodity 1 to serve as numeraire, with all the other prices being measured relative to its price. The assumption of zero transportation cost of commodities implies price equality for any commodities between the two regions. As amenity and land are immobile, wage rates and land rent are not necessarily equal between the two regions.

We introduce

i, s – subscript index for industry and services, respectively;

N and L_j – the fixed total population and region j's territory size, $j = 1, 2$;

$F_{ij}(t)$ and $F_{sj}(t)$ – the output levels of region j's industrial and service sectors at time t, $j = 1, 2$;

$N_{ij}(t)$ and $N_{sj}(t)$ – the labor force employed by region j's industrial and service sectors;

$N_j(t)$ – region j's population;

$L_{sj}(t)$ and $L_{hj}(t)$ – the land size used by the service sector and for housing in region j;

$Z(t)$ – the knowledge stock of the national economy;

$p(t)$ and $p_j(t)$ – price of commodity 2 and price of services in region j; and

$w_j(t)$ and $R_j(t)$ – region j's wage rate and land rent in region j.

First, we describe the behavior of the production sectors in the system. We assume that service production is to combine knowledge, labor and land. We specify the production functions of the service sectors as follows:

$$F_{sj} = Z^{m_{sj}} L_{sj}^{\alpha} N_{sj}^{\beta}, \quad \alpha, \beta > 0, \quad \alpha + \beta = 1, \quad m_{sj} \geq 0, \quad j = 1, 2. \tag{7.2.1}$$

We only use labor and knowledge as input factors. It should be noted that to introduce other factors such as capital may cause great analytical difficulties. We use the variable, $Z(t)$, to measure, in an aggregated sense, stock of knowledge in the society at time t. In this section, knowledge is treated as a public good in the sense that utilization of knowledge by any agent in the system will not affect that by any other. We assume that knowledge utilization efficiency varies spatially and professionally. The parameter, m_{sj}, describes knowledge utilization efficiency. We call m_{sj} the knowledge utilization efficiency parameter of region j's service sector. There are obviously limitations to knowledge as public goods in modeling the innovation and imitation processes. But to model the complexity of private and public characteristics of knowledge, it is necessary to further disaggregate the knowledge variable into multiple components. This will result in high-dimensional dynamic problems.

The marginal conditions of service production are given by

$$R_j = \frac{\alpha p_j F_{sj}}{L_{sj}}, \quad w_j = \frac{\beta p_j F_{sj}}{N_{sj}}, \quad j = 1, 2. \tag{7.2.2}$$

We specify the two regions' industrial production functions as follows:

$$F_{ij} = Z^{m_{ij}} N_{ij}, \quad m_{ij} \geq 0, \quad j = 1, 2, \tag{7.2.3}$$

where m_{ij} is the knowledge utilization efficiency parameter of region j's industrial sector.

The marginal conditions are given by

$$w_1 = Z^{m_{i1}}, \quad w_2 = pZ^{m_{i2}}. \tag{7.2.4}$$

We now examine the behavior of consumers. We assume that a household's utility in a given region is dependent on the amenity level, per household consumption levels of industrial commodities and housing conditions. We measure housing conditions by lot size. The utility function is specified as follows:

$$U_j(t) = \frac{A_j C_{sj}^\gamma C_{1j}^{\xi_1} C_{2j}^{\xi_2} L_{hj}^\eta}{N_j}, \quad j=1, 2, \quad \gamma, \xi_1, \xi_2, \eta > 0,$$

$$\gamma + \xi_1 + \xi_2 + \eta = 1, \tag{7.2.5}$$

in which $C_{sj}(t)$, $C_{1j}(t)$, and $C_{2j}(t)$ are respectively region j's consumption levels of services, commodity 1, and commodity 2 at time t. In (7.2.5), A_j denotes region j's amenity level. Amenity is an aggregated measure of regional living conditions such as infrastructure status, regional culture, and climate. Some locational amenities such as pollution level, residential density, and transportation congestion may be dependent on economic agents' activities, while other locational amenities such as climate, transport structure, and historical buildings, may not be strongly affected by economic agents' activities, at least in the short term. Accordingly, in a strict sense, it is necessary to classify amenities into endogenous and exogenous categories when we deal with dynamics of economic geography. Which kinds of amenities should be classified as endogenous or exogenous also depends upon the timescale of the analysis and the economic system under consideration.

The assumption that utility level is identical over space at any point in time is represented by

$$U_1(t) = U_2(t). \tag{7.2.6}$$

The consumer problem is defined by

$$\max U_j$$
$$\text{s.t.}: p_j C_{sj} + C_{1j} + p C_{2j} + R_j L_{hj} = w_j N_j.$$

We have the following optimal solutions:

$$C_{sj} = \frac{\gamma w_j N_j}{p_j}, \quad C_{1j} = \xi_1 w_j N_j, \quad C_{2j} = \frac{\xi_2 w_j N_j}{p}, \quad L_{hj} = \frac{\eta w_j N_j}{R_j}, \quad j=1, 2. \tag{7.2.7}$$

The balances of demand for and supply of commodities are given by

$$C_{j1} + C_{j2} = F_{ij}, \quad C_{sj} = F_{sj}, \quad j=1, 2. \tag{7.2.8}$$

The assumption that labor force and land are fully employed is represented by

$$N_{ij}(t) + N_{sj}(t) = N_j(t), \quad N_1(t) + N_2(t) = N, \quad L_{sj}(t) + L_{hj}(t) = L_j, \quad j = 1, 2. \tag{7.2.9}$$

We model knowledge accumulation as follows:

$$\dot{Z} = \sum_{j=1}^{2} \left(\frac{\tau_{sj} F_{sj}}{Z^{\varepsilon_{sj}}} + \frac{\tau_{ij} F_{ij}}{Z^{\varepsilon_{ij}}} \right) - \delta_z Z, \tag{7.2.10}$$

in which δ_z is the fixed depreciation rate of knowledge, and τ_{sj} (≥ 0), τ_{ij} (≥ 0), ε_{sj} and ε_{ij}, $j = 1, 2$, are parameters.

We only take account of learning by doing effects in knowledge accumulation. The term $\tau_{i1} F_{i1} / Z^{\varepsilon_{i1}}$ for instance, implies that the contribution of region 1's industrial sector to knowledge is positively related to its production scale, F_{i1}, and is dependent on the current level of knowledge stocks. The term $Z^{\varepsilon_{i1}}$ takes account of returns to scale effects in knowledge accumulation. The case of $\varepsilon_{i1} > (<) 0$ implies increasing (decreasing) returns to scale in knowledge accumulation. The other three terms in equation (7.2.10) can be similarly interpreted. Knowledge accumulation may be affected by many factors in different ways. The above specification takes account of one source of knowledge accumulation. We omit possible effects of R&D activities on knowledge accumulation.

We have built the multiregional growth model with endogenous knowledge accumulation and economic structure. The system has 30 variables, N_{sj}, N_{ij}, L_{hj}, L_{sj}, F_{sj}, F_{ij}, C_{sj}, C_{1j}, C_{2j}, U_j, N_j, w_j, p_j, R_j ($j = 1, 2$), p and Z. It contains the same number of independent equations. We now examine the properties of the dynamic system.

7.2.2 The equilibrium structure and stability

This section is concerned with the conditions for existence of equilibrium points and for stability. First, we show that for any given knowledge stock, $Z(t)$, the division of labor and economic geography is uniquely determined as functions of the knowledge stock at any point in time. The following proposition, which is proved in the appendix, shows how, for any given $Z(t)$, to calculate the rest of the variables in the dynamic interregional economic system.

Proposition 7.2.1

For any given level of knowledge, $Z(t)$, all the other variables in the system are uniquely determined at any point in time. The values of the variables are given as functions of $Z(t)$ by the following procedure: p by equation (A.7.2.14) → N_j, $j = 1, 2$, by equations (A.7.2.5) → N_{sj} and N_{ij} by equations (A.7.2.1) → w_j by equations (A.7.2.7) → R_j by equations (A.7.2.8) → L_{hj} and L_{sj} by equations (A.7.2.9) → p_j by equations (A.7.2.10) → F_{sj} by equations (7.2.1) → $C_{sj} = F_{sj}$ → L_{ij} by equations (7.2.3) → $C_{11} = \xi_1 w_1 N_1$ → C_{12} by equations (A.7.2.6) → U_j by formula (7.2.5).

The above proposition guarantees that if we can find knowledge $Z(t)$, then we can explicitly solve all the other variables as functions of $Z(t)$ in the system at any point in time. Hence, to examine the dynamic properties of the system, it is sufficient to examine the dynamic properties of equation (7.2.10). By the procedure given in Proposition 7.2.1 we can represent $N_{sj}(t)$ and $N_{ij}(t)$ as functions of $Z(t)$ as follows:

$$N_{s1} = \gamma\beta\xi_1 ANZ^m\Psi, \quad N_{i1} = (1 - \gamma\beta)\xi_1 ANZ^m\Psi,$$
$$N_{s2} = \gamma\xi_2\beta N\Psi, \quad N_{i2} = (1 - \gamma\beta)\xi_2 N\Psi,$$

in which

$$A \equiv \left\{\left(\frac{\xi_2 L_1}{\xi_1 L_2}\right)^{\eta+\alpha\gamma} \frac{A_1}{A_2}\right\}^{\frac{1}{1-\gamma\beta}}, \quad \Psi(Z) \equiv \frac{1}{\xi_2 + \xi_1 AZ^m},$$

$$m \equiv -\frac{m_s\gamma}{1-\gamma\beta}, \quad m_s \equiv m_{s2} - m_{s1}.$$

Substituting these into the production functions (7.2.1) and (7.2.3), we get F_{ij} and F_{sj} as functions of Z. Substituting $F_{ij}(t)$ and $F_{sj}(t)$ into equation (7.2.10), we determine knowledge accumulation dynamics $Z(t)$, as follows:

$$\dot{Z} = \sum_{j=1}^{2}\{\Omega_{sj}(Z) + \Omega_{ij}(Z)\}Z - \delta_z Z, \qquad (7.2.11)$$

where

$$\Omega_{s1} = \tau_{s1}(\beta\xi_1\xi_2 AN)^\beta L_{s1}^\alpha Z^{x_{s1}}\Psi^\beta, \quad \Omega_{i1} = v_1 Z^{x_{i1}}\Psi,$$
$$\Omega_{s2} = \tau_{s2}(\gamma\beta\xi_2 N)^\beta L_{s2}^\alpha Z^{x_{s2}}\Psi^\beta, \quad \Omega_{i2} = v_2 Z^{x_{i2}}\Psi, \quad (7.2.12)$$

in which

$$v_1 \equiv (1-\gamma\beta)\tau_{i1}\xi_1 AN > 0, \quad v_2 \equiv (1-\gamma\beta)\tau_{i2}\xi_2 N > 0,$$
$$x_{s1} \equiv m_{s1} - m - \varepsilon_{s1} - 1, \quad x_{s2} \equiv m_{s2} - \varepsilon_{s2} - 1,$$
$$x_{i1} \equiv m_{i1} - m - \varepsilon_{i1} - 1, \quad x_{i2} \equiv m_{i2} - \varepsilon_{i2} - 1.$$

For simplicity of discussion, we make the following assumption.

Assumption 7.2.1
In the remainder of this chapter, we require $\tau_{s1} = \tau_{s2} = 0$.

This requirement implies $\Omega_{s1} = \Omega_{s2} = 0$. The service sectors make no contribution to knowledge accumulation. From the functional forms of Ω_{sj} and Ω_{ij} in equations (7.2.11) and (7.2.12) we see that the omission of service sectors' creativity does not affect the essential conclusions of our model. If we do not make this omission, we have to discuss more cases of different combinations of the parameters. As these discussions will provide little new insight, we limit our analysis to the case of $\Omega_{s1} = \Omega_{s2} = 0$.

First, we note that the dynamic properties of the system are determined by the combination of the parameters, x_{i1}, x_{i2}, and m. The three parameters may be either positive or negative. As

$$m = -\frac{m_{s2} - m_{s1}}{1-\gamma\beta}\gamma,$$

we see that if region 1's service sector utilizes knowledge more (less) effectively than region 2's service sector, i.e. $m_{s1} > m_{s2}$ ($m_{s1} < m_{s2}$), then $m > 0$ ($m < 0$); if the two regions' knowledge utilization efficiency is equal, then $m = 0$. From $x_{i2} = m_{i2} - \varepsilon_{i2} - 1$, if region 2's industrial sector is effective in knowledge utilization (i.e. m_{i2} being large) and its contribution to knowledge exhibits increasing returns to scale (i.e. $m_{i2} < 0$), then x_{i2} may be positive; if region 2's industrial sector is not effective in knowledge utilization and its contribution to knowledge exhibits decreasing returns to scale, then $x_{i2} < 0$. We can similarly discuss the sign of $x_{i1} = m_{i1} - m - \varepsilon_{i1} - 1$. We say that when $x_{ij} > (<) 0$, region j's industrial sector exhibits increasing (decreasing) returns to scale effects in knowledge accumulation.

We thus conclude that the parameters x_{ij} and m may be either positive or negative, depending upon various combinations of knowledge utilization efficiency and creativity of different economic sectors in the two regions. The following proposition shows that the properties of the one-dimensional differential equation, (7.2.11), are dependent on how these knowledge parameters are combined.

Proposition 7.2.2
(1) If $x_{i1} > 0$, $x_{i2} > 0$ and $m < 0$, the system has a unique unstable equilibrium; (2) if $x_{i1} < 0$, $x_{i2} < 0$ and $m > 0$, the system has a unique stable equilibrium; and (3) in each of the other six combinations of $x_{i1} < 0$ or $x_{i1} > 0$, $x_{i2} < 0$ or $x_{i2} > 0$ and $m < 0$ or $m > 0$, the system has either no equilibrium or multiple ones.

The above proposition is proved in the Appendix. We interpreted the meanings of x_{i1}, x_{i2} and m. From these discussions we can directly interpret the conditions in the above proposition as implying that if the two regions exhibit increasing (decreasing) scale effects in knowledge accumulation, the system has an unstable (stable) unique equilibrium; if one region exhibits increasing scale effects in knowledge accumulation but the other region decreasing ones, the system has two equilibrium points.

It can be seen that for given parameter values, we can explicitly determine the properties of the dynamic system. For simplicity, we were only concerned with the cases that none of the parameters, x_{i1}, x_{i2} and m, is equal to zero. It is not difficult to discuss the cases that one or two of the three parameters are equal to zero. The following corollary, summarizing the properties of the dynamic system in the case of $m = 0$, is proved in Appendix A.7.2.

Corollary 7.2.1
If $m = 0$, we have (1) if $x_{ij} > 0$, $j = 1, 2$, the system has a unique unstable equilibrium; (2) if $x_{ij} < 0$, $j = 1, 2$, the system has a unique stable equilibrium; and (3) if $x_{i1} < 0$ and $x_{i2} > 0$ (or $x_{i1} > 0$ and $x_{i2} < 0$), the system has two equilibrium points – the one with the higher value of knowledge is unstable and the other is stable.

In the remainder of this section, we will examine the impact of some parameter changes on the equilibrium structure of the system.

7.2.3 The creativity and the regional economic structure

This section is concerned with the impact of changes in knowledge accumulation efficiency parameters, τ_{ij}, $j=1,2$, of the industrial sector in region j on the system.

First, from equation (A.7.2.2) we get the impact of changes in τ_{ij} on Z as follows:

$$-\Phi^{*\prime} \frac{dZ}{d\tau_{ij}} = \frac{\Phi_j}{\tau_{ij}} > 0, \quad j=1,2, \tag{7.2.13}$$

where $\Phi^{*\prime}$ is defined in (A.7.2.3). The sign of $\Phi^{*\prime}$ may be either positive or negative, depending on the parameter values of x_{ij}. In the case of $m = 0$, we directly have the following three cases: (i) if $x_{ij} > 0$, $j=1,2$, $\Phi^{*\prime} > 0$ at the unique equilibrium point; (ii) if $x_{ij} < 0$, $j=1,2$, $\Phi^{*\prime} < 0$ at the unique equilibrium point; (iii) if $x_{i1} < 0$ and $x_{i2} > 0$ (or $x_{i1} > 0$ and $x_{i2} < 0$), $\Phi^{*\prime} > (<) 0$ at the equilibrium point with the high (low) value of Z. We conclude that the sign of $\Phi^\prime$ is dependent on whether the industrial sectors exhibit increasing or decreasing returns. In case (i), we have $dZ/d\tau_{ij} < 0$. In case (ii), we have $dZ/d\tau_{ij} > 0$. In case (iii), we have $dZ/d\tau_{ij} < (>) 0$ at the equilibrium with high (low) values of Z. We see that an improvement in knowledge accumulation efficiency may either increase or decrease the equilibrium value of knowledge. For instance, in case (ii) which means that the two industrial sectors exhibit decreasing returns, an improvement in knowledge accumulation efficiency of any region's industrial sector increases the equilibrium level of knowledge. In case (i), the impact in changes of knowledge accumulation efficiency is the opposite of that in the case of stability. The effects of changes in the parameters on the system are dependent upon the stability conditions. To explain how the new equilibrium given by equation (7.2.13) is achieved through a dynamic process, we have to examine all the relations connecting the 30 variables in the system. We omit the explanation of equation (7.2.13) in detail.

From equation (A.7.2.14) we directly have

$$\frac{Z}{p} \frac{dp}{d\tau_{ij}} = (m - m_i) \frac{dZ}{d\tau_{ij}}, \tag{7.2.14}$$

in which $m \geq 0$. In the remainder of this section, we assume: $x_{ij} < 0$, $j = 1, 2$. We have: $dZ/d\tau_{ij} > 0$. If $m_i < 0$, i.e. $m_{i1} > m_{i2}$, the price of commodity 2 is increased. This implies that when region 1's two sectors utilize knowledge more effectively than the two sectors in region 2, then an increase in knowledge increases the price level of commodity 2. In the case of $m_i > 0$, from equation (7.2.14) $dp/d\tau_{ij}$ may be either positive or negative.

Taking derivatives of equations (A.7.2.5) and (A.7.2.1) with respect to τ_{ij} yields

$$\frac{Z}{N_1}\frac{dN_1}{d\tau_{ij}} = m\xi_2 \frac{dZ}{d\tau_{ij}} > 0,$$

$$\frac{dN_2}{d\tau_{ij}} = -\frac{dN_1}{d\tau_{ij}} < 0,$$

$$\frac{1}{N_{sk}}\frac{dN_{sk}}{d\tau_{ij}} = \frac{1}{N_{ik}}\frac{dN_{ik}}{d\tau_{ij}} = \frac{1}{N_k}\frac{dN_k}{d\tau_{ij}}, \quad k = 1, 2.$$

The direction of migration due to the improvement in productivity is only determined by the sign of $m_{s1} - m_{s2}$. As we are only concerned with the case of $m_{s1} > m_{s2}$, we see that some of region 2's population migrate to region 1. If the knowledge utilization efficiency in the two regions' service sectors is identical, then improved productivity has no impact on the labor distribution. The labor employed by the two sectors in each region will be increased or decreased if the region's total employment is increased or decreased.

By equations (A.7.2.7), we get the impact on the wage rates of the two regions as

$$\frac{Z}{w_1}\frac{dw_1}{d\tau_{ij}} = m_{i1}\frac{dZ}{d\tau_{ij}} > 0,$$

$$\frac{Z}{w_2}\frac{dw_2}{d\tau_{ij}} = (m + m_{i1})\frac{dZ}{d\tau_{ij}} > 0.$$

An improvement in knowledge accumulation efficiency increases the wage rates in the two regions. From equations (A.7.2.8) we get the impact on the land rent as follows:

$$\frac{Z}{R_1}\frac{dR_1}{d\tau_{ij}} = (m_{i1} + m\xi_2)\frac{dZ}{d\tau_{ij}} > 0,$$

$$\frac{Z}{R_2}\frac{dR_2}{d\tau_y} = \left(m + m_{t1} - m\xi_2\frac{N_1}{N_2}\right)\frac{dZ}{d\tau_y} > 0.$$

We see that region 1's land rent is increased. If $N_1/N_2 \le 1$, then region 2's land rent is increased. But if the population of region 2 is larger than region 1, then it is possible for region 2's land rent to decline as more people move from region 2 to region 1. We see that in the case that region 2 employs more workers, the sign of $dR_2/d\tau_y$ may be either positive or negative. From equations (A.7.2.10), we get the effects of changes in τ_y on the prices of services as follows:

$$\frac{Z}{p_1}\frac{dp_1}{d\tau_y} = (m_{t1} + \alpha m\xi_2 - m_{s1})\frac{dZ}{d\tau_y},$$

$$\frac{Z}{p_2}\frac{dp_2}{d\tau_y} = \left(m + m_{t1} - m_{s2} - \alpha m\xi_2\frac{N_1}{N_2}\right)\frac{dZ}{d\tau_y} > 0.$$

We see that as knowledge accumulation efficiency is improved, the prices of services may be either increasing or decreasing. From the above discussion, it is easy to get the impact of changes in τ_y upon all the 30 variables in the system. It can be seen that the effects are sensitive to how different values of the parameters are combined.

As we have explicitly solved the equilibrium problem, it is straightforward to examine the effects of changes in any parameter in the system as we did for τ_y. For instance, by taking derivatives of equation (A.7.2.2) with respect to A_2, we get

$$-\Phi^*\frac{dZ}{dA_2} = \frac{\xi_1 AZ^m - \Phi_1}{(1-\gamma\beta)A_2}, \tag{7.2.15}$$

where $\Phi^{*\prime} < 1$ and $\Phi_1 > 0$. An improvement in region 2's amenity may either increase or decrease the equilibrium level of knowledge. If the term, Φ_1, associated with creativity of the industrial sector in region 1 is larger than the term, $\xi_1 AZ^m$, then dZ/dA_2 is negative. This can be interpreted as that when region 1's industrial sector has a high contribution to knowledge accumulation, then an increase in region 2's living conditions may reduce the long-run equilibrium level of knowledge. An improvement in region 2's amenity causes a change in region 1's equilibrium utility level. This will result in reallocation of the labor force. As knowledge utilization and creativity are spatially different, the reallocation of the labor force will cause shifts in the equilibrium structure.

There are two points. One is that if we take derivatives of the equilibrium condition for knowledge accumulation with respect to region 1's amenity, A_1, then we can show that the sign of dZ/dA_1 is identical to that of $\Phi_1 - \xi_1 A Z^m$. The other is that if we are concerned with the case that the system has an unstable unique equilibrium, i.e. $x_{ij} > 0$, $j = 1, 2$, and $m \leq 0$, then $dZ/dA_2 < 0$, which is opposite to the case that the system has a unique stable equilibrium.

By equation (A.7.2.14), we have

$$\frac{Z}{p}\frac{dp}{dA_2} = -\frac{Z}{(1-\gamma\beta)A_2} + (m - m_i)\frac{dZ}{dA_2}.$$

To see how the price of commodity 2 is changed by changes in A_2, we first look at the balance condition (7.2.6). As region 2's amenity is changed, the balance condition (7.2.6) is disturbed. Therefore, migration between the two regions will be necessary for the system to achieve a new equilibrium (because we assume the existence of a unique stable equilibrium). As the employment distribution is changed, demand conditions (7.2.7) will be disturbed, which will result in adjustment of the price variables. As the prices and demand conditions are changed, the production scales will be shifted toward the new equilibrium point. All of these changes further shift the balance condition (7.2.6). The process will thus be repeated until the system achieves the new equilibrium point. The shift in the price of commodity 2 is given by equation (7.2.15). The new price level may become either higher or lower than the old one.

From equations (A.7.2.5) we get the impact on N_j as follows:

$$\frac{\Psi}{\xi_1 A N_2 Z^m}\frac{dN_2}{dA_2} = \frac{1}{(1-\gamma\beta)A_2} - \frac{m}{Z}\frac{dZ}{dA_2},$$

$$\frac{dN_1}{dA_2} = -\frac{dN_2}{dA_2}.$$

If the knowledge utilization efficiency of the two service sectors is equal, i.e. $m = 0$, then an improvement in region 2's amenities attracts more people from region 1 to region 2. But in the case that $m > 0$ and dZ/dA_2 is large, an improvement in region 2's amenities may not increase region 2's population. Hence, the direction of migration is also dependent on the characteristics of knowledge utilization in the two regions. We may easily prove the effects of changes in A_2 on the other variables in the system. As little new insight can be gained, we omit further examination.

7.3 On regional dynamics with capital and knowledge

The application of the utility function in Section 7.1 enables us to determine saving and consumption with utility optimization without leading to a higher dimensional dynamic system as with the traditional Ramsey approach. The dynamics of an n-region national economy is controlled by an n-dimensional differential equations system. We also simulated the model with the Cobb-Douglas production functions and demonstrated effects of changes in the parameters.[27] The model proposed in Section 7.1 is structurally general in the sense that if we allow all the regions to have the same character, then the model becomes a one-sector growth model; if we allow people to be interregionally immobile, the model becomes a multi-country trade model with capital accumulation. An obvious extension of this model is to introduce agglomeration and other scale-related factors to the production side. It is well known that the one-sector growth model has been generalized and extended in many directions. It is not difficult to generalize our model along these lines. It is straightforward to develop the model in discrete time. We may analyze the behavior of the model with other forms of production or utility functions. There are multiple production sectors and households are not homogeneous. Any extension will cause some analytical difficulties because of the complexity of regional dynamics. Moreover, it is known that issues related to tax competition among regions has increasingly caused great interest in economic geography.[28] We can extend the dynamic equilibrium framework proposed in this study to deal with these issues.

In the last decade, many models have been proposed to deal with economic inequality over space in association with agglomeration. It is interesting to cite from Krugman's comments (Fujita and Krugman, 2004: 143):

[to explain plainly the new economic geography] requires some funny assumptions both about consumer behavior and about the technology of production; but it has the virtue of producing in the end a picture of an economy in which there are increasing returns, in which one need not get into the fascinating but messy issues posed by realistic oligopoly.

It takes a long time to digest "funny assumptions", not to mention to follow sophisticated mathematics and computing skills, in order to understand what is happening in the contemporary mainstream(s) of economic theory. Since assumptions in each model are "funny" in their own way, the models in the current literature cannot be closely connected to each other.

Appendices

A.7.1 Proving Lemma 7.1.1

We now prove Lemma 7.1.1. First, from equations (7.1.1) we obtain

$$f_j'(k_j) = f_1'(k_1) - \delta_j, \quad j = 2, \cdots, J, \qquad (A.7.1.1)$$

where $\delta_j \equiv \delta_{k1} - \delta_{kj}$. If $f_1'(k_1) - \delta_j > 0$ for all $j = 2, \cdots, J$ and given $k_1(t) > 0$, then the equations determine unique relations between k_j and k_1, denoted by

$$k_j = \phi_j(k_1), \quad j = 1, \cdots, J, \qquad (A.7.1.2)$$

where $\phi_1(k_1) = k_1$. From equations (A.7.1.1), we have

$$f_j''(k_j)\frac{dk_j}{dk_1} = f_1''(k_1), \quad j = 2, \cdots, J.$$

As $f_j''(k_j) \leq 0, j = 1, \cdots, J$, we see that $dk_j / dk_1 \geq 0, j = 2, \cdots, J$. That is, $\phi_j'(k_1) \geq 0$. Hence, for any given $k_1(t) > 0$, we determine $k_j(t), j = 2, \cdots, J$ as unique functions of $k_1(t)$. From equations (7.1.1), we determine the wage rates as functions of $k_1(t)$ as follows:

$$w_j(t) = \overline{\phi}_j(k_1) \equiv f_j(\phi_j(k_1)) - \phi_j(k_1)f_j'(\phi_j(k_1)) > 0, \quad j = 1, \cdots, J. \qquad (A.7.1.3)$$

Substitute equations (7.1.4) and $c_j = \xi \hat{y}_j$ and $s_j = \lambda \hat{y}_j$ in equations (7.1.5) and $l_j = L_j / \overline{N}_j$ from equations (7.1.11) into the utility functions:

$$U_j(t) = \overline{\theta}_j f_j^a w_j^{-\sigma} L_j^\eta \sigma^\sigma \xi^\xi \lambda^\lambda \overline{N}_j^{a+b-\eta} \overline{y}_j^{1-\eta}, \quad j = 1, \cdots, J.$$

Inserting the above equations into equations (7.1.8), we get

$$n_j(t) = g_j(k_1)\left(\frac{\overline{y}_j}{\overline{y}_1}\right)^{\overline{\eta}}, \quad j = 2, \cdots, J, \qquad (A.7.1.4)$$

where $\overline{\overline{\eta}} \equiv (1-\eta)\widetilde{\eta}$ and

$$n_j(t) \equiv \frac{\overline{N}_j(t)}{\overline{N}_1(t)}, \quad g_j(k_1) \equiv \widetilde{\theta}_j \left(\frac{f_j(\phi_j(k_1))}{f_1(k_1)}\right)^{a\widetilde{\eta}} \left(\frac{\overline{\phi}_1(k_1)}{\overline{\phi}_j(k_1)}\right)^{\sigma\widetilde{\eta}},$$

$$\widetilde{\theta}_j \equiv \left(\frac{\overline{\theta}_j L_j^{\eta}}{\overline{\theta}_1 L_1^{\eta}}\right)^{\widetilde{\eta}}, \quad \widetilde{\eta} \equiv \frac{1}{\eta - a - b}.$$

We can rewrite equation (7.1.9) as

$$\sum_{j=1}^{J} k_j(t) T_j(t) \overline{N}_j(t) = \sum_{j=1}^{J} \overline{k}_j(t) \overline{N}_j(t).$$

Insert equation (7.1.8) into the above equation:

$$\overline{k}_1(t) = T_1 k_1 + \sum_{j=2}^{J} n_j \left(T_j \phi_j(k_1) - \overline{k}_j\right). \tag{A.7.1.5}$$

From $w_j \widetilde{T}_j = \sigma \overline{y}_j$, $T_j + \widetilde{T}_j = T_0$, and $\overline{y}_j = (1 + r(t))\overline{k}_j + w_j T_0$, we solve

$$T_j = (1-\sigma)T_0 - \frac{\sigma \widetilde{f}(k_1)\overline{k}_j}{\overline{\phi}_j(k_1)}, \tag{A.7.1.6}$$

in which we use $r(t) = f_1'(k_1) - \delta_{k1}$ and $\widetilde{f}(k_1) \equiv f_1'(k_1) + \delta_1$, where $\delta_1 \equiv 1 - \delta_{k1}$. Substitute equations (A.7.1.6) into equations (A.7.1.5):

$$\overline{k}_1(t) = (1-\sigma)T_0 k_1 \widetilde{g}_1^{-1}(k_1) + \widetilde{g}_1^{-1}(k_1) \sum_{j=2}^{J} n_j \left((1-\sigma)T_0 \phi_j(k_1) - \widetilde{g}_j(k_1)\overline{k}_j\right), \tag{A.7.1.7}$$

where

$$\widetilde{g}_j(k_1) \equiv \left(1 + \frac{\sigma \widetilde{f}(k_1)\phi_j(k_1)}{\overline{\phi}_j(k_1)}\right), \quad j = 1, \cdots, J.$$

Insert equations (A.7.1.4) into equation (A.7.1.7):

$$\bar{k}_1(t) = (1-\sigma)T_0 k_1 \tilde{g}_1^{-1}(k_1) + \frac{\tilde{g}_1^{-1}(k_1)}{\bar{y}_1^{\bar{\eta}}} \sum_{j=2}^{J} g_j(k_1) \bar{y}_j^{\bar{\eta}} \left((1-\sigma)T_0 \phi_j(k_1) - \tilde{g}_j(k_1) \bar{k}_j \right),$$
(A.7.1.8)

From equations (7.1.1) and (7.1.4), we obtain

$$\bar{y}_j(t) = \tilde{f}(k_1)\bar{k}_j + T_0 \bar{\phi}_j(k_1), \quad j = 1, \cdots, J.$$
(A.7.1.9)

It should be noted that $\bar{y}_j(t)$ are only dependent on region 1's capital intensity, k_1, and region j's per capita wealth, $\bar{k}_j$. Solve equation (A.7.1.9) for $j = 1$ with regard to $\bar{k}_1$:

$$\bar{k}_1 = \frac{\bar{y}_1 - T_0 \bar{\phi}_1(k_1)}{\tilde{f}(k_1)}.$$
(A.7.1.10)

Equaling both right-hand sides of equations (A.7.1.8) and (A.7.1.10), we have

$$y_1^{1+\bar{\eta}} - \hat{f}(k_1)\hat{y}_1^{\bar{\eta}} - \bar{f}(k_1, \{\bar{k}(t)\}) = 0,$$
(A.7.1.11)

where

$$\hat{f}(k_1) \equiv T_0 \bar{\phi}_1(k_1) + (1-\sigma)T_0 k_1 \tilde{f}(k_1) \tilde{g}_1^{-1}(k_1) > 0,$$

$$\bar{f}(k_1, \{\bar{k}(t)\}) \equiv \tilde{f}(k_1) \tilde{g}_1^{-1}(k_1) \sum_{j=2}^{J} g_j(k_1) \bar{y}_j^{\bar{\eta}} \left((1-\sigma)T_0 \phi_j(k_1) - \tilde{g}_j(k_1) \bar{k}_j \right),$$

in which $\{\bar{k}(t)\} \equiv (\bar{k}_2(t), \cdots, \bar{k}_J(t))$. It should be noted that the functions $\hat{f}$ and $\bar{f}$ are only dependent on J variables, $k_1(t)$ and $\{\bar{k}(t)\}$. This is important as it will allow us to express the dynamics in a J-dimensional differential equations system. We assume that equation (A.7.1.11) has a (at least one) positive solution, denoted as

$$\bar{y}_1 = \Lambda_0(k_1, \{\bar{k}(t)\}).$$
(A.7.1.12)

This equation is crucial for finding out explicit expressions of the dynamics. In general, equation (A.7.1.10) may have multiple solutions for any given positive $k_1(t)$

and $\{\bar{k}(t)\}$, depending on the parameter value of $\bar{\eta}$. By equation (A.7.1.12), we express $\hat{y}_1$ as a function of k_1 and $\{\bar{k}(t)\}$. Substitute equation (A.7.1.12) into equation (A.7.1.10):

$$\dot{k}_1(t) = \Lambda(k_1, \{\bar{k}\}) \equiv \frac{\Lambda_0(k_1, \{\bar{k}\}) - T_0\bar{\phi}_1(k_1)}{\tilde{f}(k_1)}. \tag{A.7.1.13}$$

Substitute $s_j = \bar{\lambda}\bar{y}_j$ from equations (7.1.6) into equations (7.1.7):

$$\dot{\bar{k}}_j = \bar{\lambda}\bar{y}_j - \bar{k}_j.$$

Substitute equations (A.7.1.9) and (A.7.1.13) into the above equations:

$$\dot{\bar{k}}_1 = \Lambda_1(k_1, \{\bar{k}_j\}) \equiv \lambda\Lambda_0(k_1, \{\bar{k}_j\}) - \Lambda(k_1, \{\bar{k}(t)\}), \tag{A.7.1.14}$$

$$\dot{\bar{k}}_j = \Lambda_j(k_1, \bar{k}_j) \equiv (\lambda\tilde{f}(k_1) - 1)\bar{k}_j + \lambda T_0\bar{\phi}_j(k_1), \quad j = 2, \cdots, J, \tag{A.7.1.15}$$

where $\bar{\lambda} \equiv 1 - \lambda + \lambda\delta_{k1}$.

Taking derivatives of equation (A.7.1.13) with respect to t yields

$$\dot{\bar{k}}_1 = \frac{\partial\Lambda}{\partial k_1}\dot{k}_1 + \sum_{j=2}^{J}\Lambda_j\frac{\partial\Lambda}{\partial\bar{k}_j}, \tag{A.7.1.16}$$

where we use equations (A.7.1.14). We do not explicitly calculate partial derivatives as it is straightforward but the expressions are tedious. Equating both right-hand sides of equations (A.7.1.14) and (A.7.1.16), we solve

$$\dot{k}_1 = \frac{\Lambda_1(k_1, \{\bar{k}_j\}) - \sum_{j=2}^{J}\Lambda_j(k_1, \{\bar{k}_j\})\partial\Lambda/\partial\bar{k}_j}{\partial\Lambda/\partial k_1}.$$

We see that $\dot{k}_1$ is a function of $k_1(t)$ and $\{\bar{k}(t)\}$. From equations (A.7.1.15), $\dot{\bar{k}}_j$ are functions of $k_1(t)$ and $\bar{k}_j(t)$ for $j = 2, \cdots, J$. In summary, we obtain Lemma 7.1.1.

A.7.2 Proving Proposition 7.2.1

From $C_{sj} = F_{sj}$ together with equations (7.2.2)

$$N_{ij} + N_{sj} = N_j, \quad C_{sj} = \frac{\gamma w_j N_j}{p_j},$$

we have

$$N_{sj} = \gamma \beta N_j, \quad N_{ij} = (1 - \gamma \beta)N_j, \quad j = 1, 2. \tag{A.7.2.1}$$

Substituting C_{ij} in equations (7.2.7) into $C_{j1} + C_{j2} = F_{ij}$ in equations (7.2.8) together with equations (7.2.3) and (7.2.4) yields

$$N_1 + Z^{m_i} N_2 = \frac{N_{i1}}{\xi_1}, \quad N_1 + Z^{m_i} N_2 = \frac{pZ^{m_i} N_{i2}}{\xi_2}, \tag{A.7.2.2}$$

where $m_i \equiv m_{i2} - m_{i1}$. As the left-hand sides of the two equations in equations (A.7.2.2) are identical, we have

$$\frac{N_{i1}}{N_{i2}} = \frac{\xi_1 pZ^{m_i}}{\xi_2}. \tag{A.7.2.3}$$

The ratio of employment in the two industrial sectors depends upon the difference in knowledge utilization efficiency and in marginal utility of the two industrial commodities. Substituting N_{ij} in equation (A.7.2.1) into equation (A.7.2.3) yields

$$\frac{N_1}{N_2} = \frac{\xi_1 pZ^{m_i}}{\xi_2}. \tag{A.7.2.4}$$

The ratio of employment between the two regions is related to the preference parameters, level of knowledge, and knowledge utilization parameters. By the above equation and $N_1 + N_2 = N$, we get

$$N_1 = \xi_1 ANZ^m \Psi(Z), \quad N_2 = \xi_2 N\Psi(Z). \tag{A.7.2.5}$$

By equations (A.7.2.1) and (A.7.2.5), we solved the labor distribution, N_{sj}, N_{ij} and N_j, as functions of p and Z. We determine F_{ij} as functions of p and Z by substituting N_{ij} in equations (A.7.2.1) into equations (7.2.3). Region 1's consumption of commodity 1 is given by: $C_{11} = \xi_1 w_1 N_1$. From $C_{11} + C_{12} = F_{i1}$, we get

$$C_{12} = F_{i1} - C_{11} = \xi_0 F_{i1}, \tag{A.7.2.6}$$

in which $\xi_0 \equiv 1 - \xi_1/(1-\gamma\beta) > 0$. By equations (7.2.4), $C_{12} = \xi_1 w_2 N_2$ and equations (A.7.2.6), we have

$$w_1 = Z^{m_1}, \quad w_2 = \frac{(1-\beta)\xi_0 A Z^{m+m_1}}{\xi_2}. \tag{A.7.2.7}$$

From equations (7.2.2) we get $L_{sj} = \alpha w_j N_{sj} / \beta R_j$. Substituting this and $L_{hj} = \eta w_j N_j / R_j$ and equations (A.7.2.1) into the last equation in equations (7.2.9), we obtain

$$R_j = \frac{(\eta + \alpha\gamma)w_j N_j}{L_j}, \quad j = 1, 2. \tag{A.7.2.8}$$

By equations (A.7.2.8) and (A.7.2.5) and

$$L_{hj} = \frac{\eta w_j N_j}{R_j}, \quad L_{sj} = \frac{\alpha w_j N_{sj}}{\beta R_j},$$

we get

$$L_{hj} = \frac{\eta L_j}{\eta + \alpha\gamma}, \quad L_{sj} = \frac{\alpha\gamma L_j}{\eta + \alpha\gamma}. \tag{A.7.2.9}$$

From L_{sj} and N_{sj}, we determine F_{sj}. We obtain C_{sj} as functions of Z by $C_{sj} = F_{sj}$. Utilizing $C_{sj} = \gamma w_j N_j / p_j$ in equations (7.2.7), we get

$$p_j = \frac{\gamma w_j N_j}{F_{sj}}, \quad j = 1, 2. \tag{A.7.2.10}$$

We have thus shown that the 28 variables, N_{sj}, N_{ij}, L_{hj}, L_{sj}, F_{sj}, F_{ij}, C_{sj}, C_{1j}, C_{2j}, U_j, N_j, w_j, p_j, R_j ($j = 1, 2$), are determined as functions of p and Z. We now show that commodity 2's price can be determined as a function of Z.

Substituting equations (7.2.7) into equation (7.2.6) yields

$$\frac{w_1}{w_2} = \left(\frac{p_1}{p_2}\right)^\gamma \left(\frac{R_1}{R_2}\right)^\eta \frac{A_2}{A_1}. \tag{A.7.2.11}$$

The equation gives a relation between the wage rates, amenity, service prices, and land rents in the two regions.

From equations (7.2.4) we have

$$\frac{w_1}{w_2} = \frac{1}{pZ^{m_i}}. \tag{A.7.2.12}$$

By equations (A.7.2.4), (A.7.2.12), and (A.7.2.8), we have

$$\frac{R_1}{R_2} = \frac{\xi_2 L_2}{\xi_1 L_1}.$$

From equations (A.7.2.10), (7.2.1) and (A.7.2.1), we have

$$\frac{p_1}{p_2} = \left(\frac{w_1}{w_2}\right)^\beta \left(\frac{R_1}{R_2}\right)^\alpha Z^{m_*}, \tag{A.7.2.13}$$

where w_1/w_2 is given in equation (A.7.2.12). Substituting equations (A.7.2.12) and (A.7.2.13) into (A.7.2.11) yields

$$p = AZ^{m-m_i}. \tag{A.7.2.14}$$

A.7.3 Proving Proposition 7.2.2

In the case of $\Omega_{s1} = \Omega_{s2} = 0$, the knowledge accumulation is given by

$$\dot{Z} = \{\Phi_1(Z) + \Phi_2(Z)\}Z\Psi(Z) - \delta_z Z \equiv \Phi(Z), \tag{A.7.3.1}$$

where $\Phi_j = v_j Z^{x_{ij}}$, $j = 1, 2$. We now examine properties of equation (A.7.3.1). Equilibrium is given as a solution of the following equation:

$$\Phi^*(Z) \equiv \Phi_1(Z) + \Phi_2(Z) - \xi_1 A Z^m - \xi_2 \delta_z = 0. \tag{A.7.3.2}$$

Our problem is to study whether or not $\Phi^*(Z) = 0$ has a positive solution.

In the case of $x_{i1} > 0$, $x_{i2} > 0$ and $m < 0$, we have: $\Phi^*(0) < 0$, $\Phi^*(+\infty) > 0$, $\Phi^{*'}(Z) > 0$ for $0 < Z < +\infty$. Accordingly, there is a unique positive Z such that $\Phi^*(Z) = 0$. The stability is determined by the sign of $\Phi(Z)$ at the equilibrium. If $\Phi > 0$, the system is unstable; if $\Phi' < 0$, it is stable; and if $\Phi' = 0$, it is neutral. Taking derivatives of Φ with respect to Z yields

$$\Phi' = x_{i1}\Psi\Phi_1 + x_{i2}\Psi\Phi_2 - (\Phi_1 + \Phi_2)\xi_1 mA\Psi^2 Z^{m-1}, \tag{A.7.3.3}$$

which is evaluated at the equilibrium point. We thus conclude the system has a unique unstable equilibrium point in this case.

In the case of $x_{i1} < 0$, $x_{i2} < 0$ and $m > 0$, we have: $\Phi^*(0) > 0$, $\Phi^*(+\infty) < 0$, $\Phi^{*'}(Z) < 0$ for $0 < Z < +\infty$. We see that the system has a unique stable equilibrium in this case.

There are six other possible combinations of $x_{i1} < 0$ or $x_{i1} > 0$, $x_{i2} < 0$ or $x_{i2} > 0$ and $m < 0$ or $m > 0$. It can be checked that if the system has equilibrium, it must have multiple ones. For instance, in the case of $x_{i1} < 0$, $x_{i2} > 0$ and $m < 0$, because $\Phi^*(0) < 0$ and $\Phi^*(+\infty) < 0$ are held, the equation, $\Phi^*(Z) = 0$, has either no solution or multiple ones. Similarly, we can check the other five cases. We can directly check the stability of each equilibrium point by equation (A.7.3.3). Summarizing the above discussion, we have proved Proposition 7.2.2.

We now check Corollary 7.2.1. As in cases (i) and (ii) in Proposition 7.2.2, we can show that (i) if $x_{ij} > 0$, $j = 1, 2$, then the system has a unique unstable equilibrium; (ii) if $x_{ij} < 0$, $j = 1, 2$, then the system has a unique stable equilibrium. We now show that if $x_{i1} < 0$ and $x_{i2} > 0$ (or $x_{i1} > 0$ and $x_{i2} < 0$), the system has two equilibrium points – the one with the higher value of knowledge is unstable and the other is stable.

It is sufficient to check the case of $x_{i1} > 0$ and $x_{i2} < 0$ as the case $x_{i1} < 0$ and $x_{i2} > 0$ can be similarly proved. As $\Phi^*(0) > 0$ and $\Phi^*(+\infty) > 0$, the system has either no equilibrium or multiple ones. From $\Phi^* = (x_{i1}\Phi_1 + x_{i2}\Phi_2)/Z$, we see that $\Phi^{*'} = 0$ has a unique positive solution, denoted by Z_0. This implies that $\Phi^*(Z) = 0$ cannot have more than two solutions. When the system has two equilibrium points, the stability of each equilibrium point is determined by the sign of Φ'. If $Z < Z_0$, then $\Phi' < 0$. If $Z > Z_0$, $\Phi > 0$. We have thus proved the corollary.

8
Multi-Country Growth Economies

It is important to examine the possible effects of trade upon personal income distribution in a globalizing world economy.[1] In 1997, *Forbes* magazine counted 170 billionaires. Microsoft's Bill Gates had $40 billion, the investor Warren Buffet, $21 billion, the Dupont family $14 billion, the Rockefeller family $7 billion. At the same time, in 1995 the average American family was worth $45,600. Real wage rates for most Americans have not increased much over the last 20 years. It is held that the rise in inequality between the rich and the poor and the decline of real wages of the less skilled in the US is closely related to international trade with low-wage countries.[2] Nevertheless, some economists argue that the role of foreign trade in enlarged inequality is negligible. Keller (2004) examines the extent of international technology diffusion and the channels through which technology spreads.[3] It is shown that productivity differences explain much of the variation in incomes across countries, and technology plays a key role in determining productivity. The pattern of worldwide technical change is determined largely by international technology diffusion because a few rich countries account for most of the world's creation of new technology. Cross-country income convergence turns on whether technology diffusion is global or local. There is no indication that international diffusion is inevitable or automatic, but rather, domestic technology investments are necessary. Winter et al. (2004) have recently examined the impact of trade policy reform on poverty in developing countries. It is demonstrated that there is no simple generalizable conclusion about the relationship between trade liberalization and poverty. In the long run and on average, trade liberalization is likely to be strongly poverty alleviating, and there is no convincing evidence that it will generally increase overall poverty or vulnerability. But there is evidence that the poor may be less well placed in the short run to protect themselves against adverse effects and take advantage of favorable opportunities.

In extensively and intensively connected world markets, workers are confronted with increasing competition from other countries and capital owners can move their wealth easily to wherever returns appear likely to be the highest. Yet, modern technology tends to diminish the demand and therefore the wages for low-skilled workers, while pushing up the demand for highly educated specialists. As globalization is deepening, it is important to provide analytical frameworks for analyzing global economic interactions. For instance, a frequently discussed question is related to the dynamics of income and wealth distribution within each economy as well as among economies. It is important to examine how a developing economy like India or China may affect different economies and different people in a special economy as its technology is improved or population is enlarged; or how the global trade patterns may be affected as technologies are further improved or propensities to save are increased in developed economies like the US or Japan.

This chapter is concerned with economic development with economic interactions among multiple countries. Section 8.1 introduces the Ricardian trade theory. In Section 8.2, we review the Heckscher-Ohlin theory. Section 8.3 develops a two-country growth model with capital accumulation within the OSG framework. Section 8.4 extends the model of the previous section to the case that the world consists of multiple countries and each country has any number of types of households. Section 8.5 examines interactions of capital and knowledge within a two-country modeling framework. Section 8.6 discusses trade and income and wealth distribution.

8.1 The Ricardian trade theory

Adam Smith (1776) held that a country could gain from free trade. He pointed out that if one country has an absolute advantage over the other in one production and the other country has an absolute advantage over the first in another production, both countries gain from trading. But Smith failed to create a convincing economic theory of international trade. It is generally agreed that David Ricardo is the creator of the classical theory of international trade, even though many concrete ideas about trade existed before his *Principles*.[4] The theories of comparative advantage and the gains from trade are usually connected with his name. The theory of comparative advantage or the theory of comparative costs is one of oldest theories of economics. In this theory the crucial variable used to explain international trade patterns is technology. The theory holds that a difference in comparative costs of production is the necessary condition for the existence of international trade. But this difference reflects a difference in techniques of production. According to this theory, technological differences between countries determine the international division of labor and consumption and trade patterns. It holds that trade is beneficial to all participating countries. This conclusion is against the viewpoint about trade held by the doctrine of mercantilism. In mercantilism it is argued that the regulation and planning of economic activity are efficient means of fostering goals of nations.

In order to illustrate the theory of comparative advantage, we consider an example constructed by Ricardo. We assume that the world consists of two countries (for instance, England and Portugal). There are two commodities (cloth and wine) and a single factor (labor) of production. Technologies of the two countries are fixed. Let us assume that the unit cost of production of each commodity (expressed in terms of labor) is constant. We consider a case in which each country is superior to the other one in production of one (and only one) commodity. For instance, England produces cloth at lower unit cost than Portugal and Portugal makes wine at lower unit cost than England. In this situation, international exchanges of commodities will occur under free trade conditions. It benefits both England and Portugal if the former is specified in the production of cloth and the latter in wine. This case is easy to understand. The Ricardian theory also shows that even if one country is superior to the other in the production of two commodities, free international trade may still benefit the two countries. We may consider the following example to illustrate the point.

Let us assume that the unit costs of production of cloth and wine in terms of labor are respectively 4 and 8 in England; while they are 6 and 10 in Portugal. That is, England is superior to Portugal in the production of both commodities. It seems that there is no scope for international trade since England is superior in everything. But the theory predicts a different conclusion. It argues that the condition for international trade to take place is the existence of a difference between the comparative costs. Here, we define comparative costs as the ratio between the unit costs of the two commodities in the same countries. In our example comparative costs are $4/8 = 0.5$ and $6/10 = 0.6$ in England and Portugal respectively. It is straightforward to see that England has a relatively greater advantage in the production of cloth than wine: the ratio of production costs of cloth between England and Portugal is $4/6$; the ratio of production costs of wine is $8/10$. It can also be seen that Portugal has a relatively smaller disadvantage in the production of wine. The Ricardian model predicts that if the terms of trade are greater than 0.5 and smaller than 0.6, British cloth will be exchanged for Portuguese wine to the benefit of the two countries. For instance, if we fix the trade terms at 0.55 which means that 0.55 units of wine exchanges for one unit of cloth, then in the free trade system in England one unit of cloth exchanges for 0.55 units of wine (rather than 0.5 as in the isolated system) and in Portugal 0.55 (rather than 0.6) units of wine exchanges for one unit of cloth. The model thus concludes that international trade is beneficial to both countries. It is easy to check that the terms of trade must be strictly located between the two comparative costs (i.e. between 0.5 and 0.6 in our example). We can check directly that if the terms of trade were equal to either comparative cost, the concerned country would have no economic incentive to trade; if the terms of trade were outside the interval between the comparative costs, then some countries will suffer a loss by engaging in international trade.

This theory may be represented in different ways. For instance, we may interpret the theory of comparative costs in terms of optimization. We base the following example on Gandolfo (1994). We consider a simple case in which the world economy consists of two countries and produces commodities. Here, we consider the benefits from international trade in terms of an increase in the quantity (rather than utility) of goods which can be obtained from the given amount of labor. Our optimal problem is to maximize each country's real income under constraints of the fixed labor and technology. We use p_x and p_y to denote the absolute prices of goods x and y (expressed in terms of some external unit of measurement, for instance, gold). Under the assumptions of free trade, perfect competition and zero transportation cost, the domestic price ratio is equal between the two countries. The exchange ratio of the two goods, p_x/p_y, is taken as given. Let x_j and y_j denote respectively country j's outputs of goods x and y and N_j stand for country j's fixed labor force. Country j's optimal problem is defined by

$$\text{Max } Y_j = \left(\frac{p_x}{p_y}\right) x_j + y_j,$$

subject to $a_{1j} x_j + a_{2j} y_j \leq N_j, \quad x_j, y_j \geq 0, \quad j = 1, 2,$ \hfill (8.1.1)

in which Y_j is country j's real national income measured in terms of good y and a_{1j} and a_{2j} are respectively country j's unit costs of production of goods x and y. The optimal problems defined by problem (8.1.1) can find an easy graphic solution. It is shown that international trade and international specification occur as a consequence of the maximization of the real national income of each country considered separately.

One of the attractive features of the Ricardian model is that its modeling structure allows virtually all the results obtained for the simple two-commodity and two-country case to be extended to many countries and many commodities, even though some new features appear in high dimensions.[5] For example, when the global economy consists of many commodities but only two countries, commodities can be ranked by comparative costs in a chain of decreasing relative labor costs

$$\frac{a_{21}}{a_{11}} > \frac{a_{22}}{a_{12}} > \cdots > \frac{a_{2j}}{a_{1j}} > \cdots > \frac{a_{2n}}{a_{1n}},$$ \hfill (8.1.2)

in which a_{ij} is country i's labor requirement per unit output in sector j, $i = 1, 2$, $j = 1, 2, \ldots, n$. Demand conditions determine where the chain is broken. The comparative unit costs ensure that country 1 must export all commodities to the left of the break and import all those to the right, with at most one commodity produced in common.

This theory assumes that production costs are independent of factor prices and the composition of output. The model throws no light on issues related to the internal distribution of income since it assumes either a single mobile factor or multiple mobile factors which are used in equal proportions in all sectors. From this theory we can only determine the limits within which the terms of trade must lie. Since it lacks consideration of demand sides, the theory cannot determine how and at what value the terms of trade are determined within the limits. This is a serious limitation of this theory because a trade theory should be able to explain the causes and directions of trade but also determine the terms of trade.

8.2 The neoclassical theory and the Heckscher-Ohlin theory

The Ricardian theory failed to determine the terms of trade, even though it can be used to determine the limits in which the terms of trade must lie. It was recognized long ago that in order to determine the terms of trade, it is necessary to build trade theory which not only takes account of the productive side but also the demand side.[6] The neoclassical theory holds that the determinants of trade patterns are to be found simultaneously in the differences between the technologies, the factor endowments, and the tastes of different countries.[7] Preference accounts for the existence of international trade even if technologies and factor endowments were completely identical between countries.

The Marshallian offer curve has often been used to analyze problems such as the existence of equilibrium, the stability of equilibrium, the gains from trade, optimum tariffs and so on within static frameworks. For illustration, we show how Mill solved the trade equilibrium problem and how this problem can be solved with help of modern analytical tools. Mill introduced the equation of international demand, according to which the terms of trade are determined so as to equate the value of exports and the value of imports. Mill (1848: 596) argued: "the exports and imports between the two countries (or, if we suppose more than two, between each country and the world) must in the aggregate pay for each other, and must therefore be exchanged for one another at such values as will be compatible with the equation of the international demand." Mill initiated the theory of reciprocal demand which is one of the earliest examples of general equilibrium analysis in trade theory. In Chapter 18, book 3 of his *Principles*, he showed the existence of trade equilibrium, using a simplified model and explicitly solving equations in the model numerically. He assumed that there exists only one factor of production and production is subjected to constant returns to scale and requires on the demand side as follows (Mill, 1848: 598):

Let us therefore assume, that the influence of cheapness on demand conforms to some simple law, common to both countries and to both commodities. As the simplest and most convenient, let us suppose that in both countries any given increase of cheapness produces an exactly proportional increase of consumption; or, in other words, that the value expended in the commodity, the cost incurred for the sake of obtaining it, is always the same, whether that cost affords a greater or a smaller quantity of the commodity.

As a numerical example, consider that the world economy consists of Germany and England and the economic system has two goods, cloth and linen. Let us assume that in Germany 10 yards of cloth was exchanged for 20 yards of linen and that England wants to sell 1,000,000 yards of cloth to Germany. If Germany wants 800,000 yards of cloth, this is equal to 1,600,000 yards of linen at German exchange ratio. Since German expended value in cloth is constant, England will receive 1,600,000 yards of linen in exchange for 1,000,000 yards of cloth, replacing German supply of cloth entirely. Under the assumption mentioned above and some additional requirements, Mill explicitly solved the international exchange ratio of two commodities in terms of coefficients of production in two countries and by so doing showed the existence of trade equilibrium. Chipman pointed out that the case analyzed by Mill can be treated as a problem of nonlinear programming and the existence of trade equilibrium can be proved by the existence theorem of a solution of nonlinear programming.[8]

We now use analytical methods to prove the existence of trade equilibrium as showed by Mill.[9] This example also illustrates the difference between the Ricardian theory and the neoclassical theory. Let subscript indexes 1 and 2 represent respectively Germany and England. We denote the amount of cloth and linen produced by country j respectively y_{jc} and y_{jl} which are nonnegative. If we denote the total amount of cloth (linen) produced in country j when the country is completely specified in producing cloth (linen) by a_{jc} (a_{jl}), the possible sets of y_{jc} and y_{jl} are given by

$$\frac{y_{jc}}{a_{jc}} + \frac{y_{jl}}{a_{jl}} \leq 1, \quad y_{jc}, y_{jl} \geq 0, \quad j = 1, 2. \tag{8.2.1}$$

The above two equations mean that the demand for labor does not exceed the supply in each country. We denote respectively the prices of cloth and linen by p_c and p_l. At equilibrium country j's production structure (y_{jc}, y_{jl}) should maximize

$$\frac{p_c y_{jc}}{p_l} + y_{jl}.$$

Multiplying inequalities (8.2.1) by a_{jc} ($j = 1, 2$) and adding the two equations, we get

$$y_c + \frac{a_{1c}}{a_{1l}} y_{1l} + \frac{a_{2c}}{a_{2l}} y_{2l} \leq a_c,$$

where

$$y_c \equiv y_{1c} + y_{2c}, \quad a_c \equiv a_{1c} + a_{2c}.$$

If we assume that Germany has the comparative advantage in linen, i.e. $a_{1c}/a_{1l} < a_{2c}/a_{2l}$, from the above inequality we get

$$\frac{y_c}{a_{1c}} + \frac{y_l}{a_{1l}} \leq \frac{a_c}{a_{1c}}, \tag{8.2.2}$$

where $y_l \equiv y_{1l} + y_{2l}$. Similarly multiplying inequalities (8.2.1) by a_{jl}, we get

$$\frac{y_c}{a_{2c}} + \frac{y_l}{a_{2l}} \leq \frac{a_l}{a_{2l}}, \tag{8.2.3}$$

where $a_l \equiv a_{1l} + a_{2l}$.

In order to describe the demand, let x_c (≥ 0), x_l (≥ 0) and R (≥ 0) respectively stand for the demand for cloth, demand for linen, and income measured in terms of the factor of production. Maximizing the following utility $U = x_c x_l$, subject to the budget constraint

$$p_c x_c + p_l x_l = R$$

yields the demand functions

$$x_c = \frac{R}{2p_c}, \quad x_l = \frac{R}{2p_l},$$

which satisfy Mill's assumption. Since the two countries have an identical preference structure but different incomes, we have that country j's demand for cloth and linen, X_{jc} and X_{jl}, are given by

$$X_{jc} = \frac{R_j}{2p_c}, \quad X_{jl} = \frac{R_j}{2p_l}, \quad j = 1, 2, \qquad (8.2.4)$$

where R_j is country j's income. Since demands for commodities cannot exceed supplies at the equilibrium of free international trade, we have

$$X_c \leq y_{1c} + y_{2c}, \quad X_l \leq y_{1l} + y_{2l}, \qquad (8.2.5)$$

where $X_c \equiv X_{1c} + X_{2c}$ and $X_l \equiv X_{1l} + X_{2l}$. Introduce the world utility function as

$$U = \log X_c + \log X_l.$$

We maximize this U subject to inequalities (8.2.1) and (8.2.5). The Lagrangean is given by

$$\log X_c + \log X_l + p_c(y_{1c} + y_{2c} - X_c) + p_l(y_{1l} + y_{2l} - X_l)$$
$$+ \sum_{j=1}^{2} w_j \left(\frac{y_{jc}}{a_{jc}} + \frac{y_{jl}}{a_{jl}} - 1 \right).$$

It is shown that the Lagrangean has a strictly positive saddle point at which inequalities (8.2.1) and (8.2.5) are satisfied with equality at the saddle point. In fact, this saddle point is an equilibrium point of free international trade, with p_c/p_l, w_1/p_l and w_2/p_l respectively satisfying the price of cloth and the price of factor of production in Germany and in England. Since the world total income is equal to

$$p_c X_c + p_l X_1 = w_1 + w_2,$$

we have $R_j = w_j$. By conditions (8.2.4) we get X_{jc} and X_{jl} which is an optimal solution of the problem that country j maximizes its utility subject to its budget constraint with the given world prices.

The Ricardian and Heckscher-Ohlin models are two basic models of trade and production. They provide the pillars upon which much of the pure theory of international trade rests. The Heckscher-Ohlin theory emphasizes the differences between the factor endowments of different countries and differences between commodities in the intensities with which they use these factors. The basic model deals with a long-term general equilibrium in which the two factors are both mobile between sectors and the cause of trade is different countries having different relative factor endowments. This theory deals with the impact of trade on factor use and factor rewards. The theory is different from the Ricardian model which isolates differences in technology between countries as the basis for trade. In the Heckscher-Ohlin theory costs of production are endogenous in the sense that they are different in the trade and autarky situations, even when all countries have access to the same technology for producing each good. This model has been a main stream of international trade theory. According to Ethier (1974), this theory has four "core proportions." In the simple case of two-commodity and a two-country world economy, we have these four propositions (which are of course held under certain conditions) as follows: (1) factor-price equalization theorem by Lerner (1952) and Samuelson (1948, 1949), stating that free trade in final goods alone brings about complete international equalization of factor prices; (2) Stolper-Samuelson theory by Stolper and Samuelson (1941), saying that an increase in the relative price of one commodity raises the real return of the factor used intensively in producing that commodity and lowers the real return of the other factor; (3) Rybczynski theorem by Rybczynski (1955), stating that if commodity prices are held fixed, an increase in the endowment of one factor causes a more than proportionate increase in the output of the commodity which uses that factor relatively intensively and an absolute decline in the output of the other commodity; and (4) Heckscher-Ohlin theorem by Heckscher (1919) and Ohlin (1933), stating that a country tends to have a bias towards producing and exporting the commodity which uses intensively the factor with which it is relatively well-endowed.

The Heckscher-Ohlin theory provides simple and intuitive insights into the relationships between commodity prices and factor prices, factor supplies and factor rewards, and factor endowments and the pattern of production and trade. Although the Heckscher-Ohlin model was the dominant framework for analyzing trade in the 1960s, it had neither succeeded in supplanting the Ricardian model nor had been replaced by the specific-factor trade models. Each theory has been refined. Each theory is limited to a range of questions. It is argued that as far as general ideas are concerned, the Heckscher-Ohlin theory may be considered as a special case of the neoclassical theory mentioned before as it accepts all the logical promises of neoclassical methodology.[10] The Heckscher-Ohlin theory may be seen as a special case of the neoclassical trade theory in which production technology and preferences are internationally identical. This loss of generality has long been held necessary in order to construct a clear picture of international trade patterns and division of labor and consumption. This book shows that it is possible to construct a compact trade theory without loss of the generality characterized by the neoclassical trade theory.

Ricardo's initial discussion of the concept of comparative advantage is limited to the case when factors of production are immobile internationally. His arguments about gains from trade between England and Portugal are valid only if English labor and/or Portuguese technology (or climate) are prevented from moving across national boundaries. The Heckscher-Ohlin theory is similarly limited to the study of how movements of commodities can substitute for international movements of productive factors. It is obvious that if technologies are everywhere identical and if production is sufficiently diversified, factor prices become equalized between countries. But if production functions differ between countries, no presumption as to factor equalization remains. Most of the early contributions to trade theory deal with goods trade only and ignore the international mobility of factors of production. For a long period of time since Ricardo, the classical mobility assumption had been well accepted. This assumption states that all final goods are tradable between countries whereas primary inputs are nontradable, though they are fully mobile between different sectors of the domestic economy. In reality, this classical assumption is invalid in many circumstances. For instance, many kinds of final "goods," services, are not traded and capitals are fully mobile between countries as well as within domestic economies. A great deal of work on trade theory has been concerned with examining the consequences of departures from these assumptions. There is an extensive literature on various aspects of international factor mobility.[11]

8.3 A two-country trade model with capital accumulation

Most of the pure theory of international trade emerged from Ricardo's *Principles*. The simple example of the exchange of cloth and wine between England and Portugal gives us a beautiful illustration of the concept of comparative advantage. The further development of the subject by Mill, Marshall, and Edgeworth remained largely within the bounds set by Ricardo. Since then, much attention has been focused on the determination of the terms of trade by reciprocal demand within frameworks of many goods, countries and factors under various forms of intervention. As mentioned by Findlay (1984), one topic that was almost entirely absent from the pure theory of international trade was any consideration of the connection between economic growth and international trade in the classical literature of economic theory. Almost all of the trade models developed before the 1960s are static in the sense that the supplies of factors of production are given and do not vary over time; the classical Ricardian theory of comparative advantage and the Heckscher-Ohlin theory are static since labor and capital stocks (or land) are assumed to be given and constant over time. Although Marshall held that it is important to study international trade in order to be clear about the causes which determine the economic progresses of nations, it has only been in the last three or four decades that trade theory has made some systematic treatment of capital accumulation or technological changes in the context of international economics.

The consideration of endogenous capital or technological change in trade theory was influenced by the development of neoclassical growth theory with capital accumulation and growth theory with endogenous knowledge. This order of development of economic theory is reasonable as it is only after we are able to explain how national economies operate that we can effectively model international economies. When economists had no compact framework to explain national economies, it is hard to imagine how international economies could be analyzed. A national economy may be perceived as a special case of the global economy in the sense that the global economy is national when it consists of identical multiple national economies.

Trade models with capital movements are originated by MacDougall (1960) and Kemp (1961), even though these models were limited to static and one-commodity frameworks. A dynamic model, which takes account of accumulating capital stocks and of growing population within the Heckscher-Ohlin type of model, was initially developed by Oniki and Uzawa and others, in terms of the two-country, two-good, two-factor model of trade. The Oniki-Uzawa model is developed within the framework of neoclassical growth theory. The model is primarily concerned with the process of world capital accumulation and distribution with demands and supplies as fast processes. The two-sector growth model has often been applied to analyze the interdependence between trade patterns and economic growth. These models are used to study the dynamics of capital accumulation and the various balance of payments accounts. There are different sets of assumptions made about the structure of trade. For instance, in the trade models by Oniki and Uzawa (1965) and Johnson (1971), free trade in both consumption and investment goods is allowed. This framework was extended by Zhang.[12] An alternative specification of trade structure in the growth framework allows for the existence of international financial markets and for free trade in consumption goods and securities, but not in investment goods.[13] This framework emphasizes the interaction of foreign borrowing, debt service, and domestic capital accumulation. The two-sector neoclassical growth theory was also applied to analyzing small open economies.[14]

Eaton (1987) proposed a dynamic two-sector, three-factor model of international trade. The dynamic specification of the model is based on Samuelson's overlapping generations model. The dynamic model at each point in time t proposed by Eaton is identical to the three-factor, two-commodity model examined in a static context by Jones (1971), Samuelson (1971), and Mussa (1974). The model tries to extend the Heckscher-Ohlin theory to include endowments of factors as endogenous variables. In this model land and capital serve not only as factors of production but also as assets which individuals use to transfer income from working periods to retirement. The model shows that changes in the terms of trade and in the endowments of fixed factors do not necessarily have the same effects on factor prices and on the composition of output as they do in a static framework. Some results obtained from the specific-factors model about the relationships between commodity prices and factor prices, factor endowments and factor rewards, and factor endowments and the pattern of production are not held in the dynamic model. For instance, a permanent increase in the relative price of one commodity does not necessarily lower the steady-state income of the factor specific to the industry producing the other commodity.

Obstfeld examines the saving behavior of a small economy facing a certain world real interest rate.[15] Obstfeld (1981) proposes a dynamic Heckscher-Ohlin model with internationally mobile capital and overlapping generations of infinitely lived agents. The model focuses on the effects of government debt and spending shocks. Devereux and Shi (1991) develop a trade model which includes intertemporal consumption-saving decisions with the use of recursive preferences. These preferences make it possible to analyze heterogeneity in a representative-agent infinite horizon model with well-defined steady states. The key factors driving the steady state are the convergence of national rates of time preference with one another and the monotonic relationship between consumption and the real interest rate at the steady state. This implies that each country's share of total world output depends only on its degree of impatience and not on country-specific factors. The model concludes that the more patient country has a higher steady-state consumption level and will be a steady-state external creditor.

We now suggest a dynamic one-commodity and multi-country trade model to examine interdependence between trades and global growth. We analyze trade issues within the framework of a simple international macroeconomic growth model with perfect capital mobility. Irrespective of analytical difficulties involved in analyzing two-country, dynamic-optimization models with capital accumulation, many efforts have been made to examine the impact of saving, technology, and various policies upon trade patterns within this framework. For instance, Frenkel and Razin (1987) use a two-country and two-period model to analyze the effects of various fiscal policies, even though their model ignores capital accumulation. In Ikeda and Ono (1992), an optimal multi-country model is constructed to analyze dynamic trade patterns, even though the model ignores capital growth by assuming a constant capital supply.[16] We now model international trade within the OSG framework. We show that our analytical framework greatly reduces difficulties involved in the dynamic analysis of traditional two-country trade models with endogenous capital accumulation.

8.3.1 The trade model

In describing economic production, we follow the neoclassical trade framework. It is assumed that the countries produce a homogeneous commodity. Most aspects of production sectors in our model are similar to the neoclassical one-sector growth model. The system consists of two countries, indexed by $j = 1, 2$. Only one good is produced in the system. Perfect competition is assumed to prevail in good markets both within each country and between the countries and commodities are traded without any barriers such as transport costs or tariffs. We assume that there is no migration between the countries and the labor markets are perfectly competitive within each country. Each country has a fixed labor force, N_j, ($j = 1, 2$). Let prices be measured in terms of the commodity and the price of the commodity be unity. We denote wage and interest rates by $w_j(t)$ and $r_j(t)$, respectively, in the j th country. In the free trade system, the interest rate is the same throughout the world economy, i.e. $r(t) = r_j(t)$.

First, we describe the behavior of the production sections. We use production functions to describe the physical facts of a given technology. Let $K_j(t)$ stand for the capital stocks owned by country j. Let $E(t)$ stand for the capital stocks which are employed by country 1 but owned by country 2. When $E(t) > (<) 0$, country 1 (2) uses country 2's (1's) capital. The production functions are specified as follows:

$$F_1(t) = A_1 (K_1(t) + E(t))^{\alpha_1} N_1^{\beta_1}, \quad F_2(t) = A_2 (K_2(t) - E(t))^{\alpha_2} N_2^{\beta_2},$$

where $\alpha_j + \beta_j = 1, j = 1, 2$. Markets are competitive; thus labor and capital earn their marginal products, and firms earn zero profits. The rate of interest, $r(t)$, and wage rates, $w_j(t)$, are determined by the markets. The marginal conditions are given by

$$r + \delta_k = \alpha_1 A_1 (K_1(t) + E(t))^{-\beta_1} N_1^{\beta_1} = \alpha_2 A_2 (K_2(t) - E(t))^{-\beta_2} N_2^{\beta_2},$$
$$w_1(t) = \beta_1 A_1 (K_1(t) + E(t))^{\alpha_1} N_1^{-\alpha_1}, \quad w_2(t) = \beta_2 A_2 (K_2(t) - E(t))^{\alpha_2} N_2^{-\alpha_2}, \quad (8.3.1)$$

where δ_k is the depreciation rate of physical capital. We assume that the depreciation rate is identical between the economies.

We now describe the behavior of consumers. Let $k_j(t)$ stand for the per capita wealth in country j. That is, $k_j = K_j / N_j$. A consumer of country j obtains the current income

$$y_j(t) = r(t)k_j(t) + w_j(t), \quad j = 1, 2, \tag{8.3.2}$$

from the interest payment, rk_j, and the wage payment, w_j. The disposable income is given by

$$\hat{y}_j(t) = y_j(t) + k_j(t). \tag{8.3.3}$$

The disposable income is used for saving and consumption. At each point in time, a consumer distributes the total available budget among saving, $s_j(t)$, and consumption of goods, $c_j(t)$. The budget constraint is given by

$$c_j(t) + s_j(t) = \hat{y}_j(t) = rk_j(t) + w_j(t) + k_j(t). \tag{8.3.4}$$

We assume that utility level, $U(t)$, that the consumers obtain is dependent on $c_j(t)$ and $s_j(t)$. The utility function is specified as follows:

$$U_j(t) = c_j^{\xi_j}(t) s_j^{\lambda_j}(t), \quad \xi_j, \lambda_j > 0, \quad \xi_j + \lambda_j = 1,$$

Maximizing U_j subject to the budget constraints (8.3.4) yields

$$c_j(t) = \xi_j \hat{y}_j(t), \quad s_j(t) = \lambda_j \hat{y}_j(t). \tag{8.3.5}$$

According to the definitions of $s_j(t)$, the wealth accumulation of the typical household in country j is given by

$$\dot{k}_j(t) = s_j(t) - k_j(t). \tag{8.3.6}$$

The total capital stocks employed by the production sectors is equal to the total wealth owned by all the countries. That is

$$K(t) = \sum_{j=1}^{2} k_j(t) N_j. \tag{8.3.7}$$

The world production is equal to the world consumption and world net saving. That is

$$C(t) - S(t) - K(t) + \sum_{j=1}^{2} \delta_{kj} K_j(t) = F(t),$$

where

$$C(t) \equiv \sum_{j=1}^{2} c_j(t) N_j, \quad S(t) \equiv \sum_{j=1}^{2} s_j(t) N_j, \quad F(t) \equiv \sum_{j=1}^{2} F_j(t).$$

We have thus built the model which explains the endogenous accumulation of capital and the international distribution of capital in the world economy in which the domestic markets of each country are perfectly competitive, international product and capital markets are freely mobile, and labor is internationally immobile. We now examine the properties of the system.

8.3.2 Behavior of the dynamic system

From the condition that the world economy has an equal interest rate throughout, we get

$$\frac{\alpha_1 F_1}{K_1 + E} = \frac{\alpha_2 F_2}{K_2 - E}.$$

From this equation and equations (8.3.1), we obtain

$$K_2 - E = \upsilon (K_1 + E)^\theta, \tag{8.3.8}$$

in which

$$\upsilon \equiv \left(\frac{\alpha_2}{\alpha_1}\right)^{1/\beta_2} \frac{N_2}{N_1^\theta}, \quad \theta \equiv \frac{\beta_1}{\beta_2} < 1.$$

In the remainder of this section, for convenience of discussion we require $\theta \leq 1$, i.e. $\beta_1 \leq \beta_2$. This requirement will not affect our discussion.

Introducing $x \equiv K_1 + E$, we may rewrite equation (8.3.8) as follows:

$$\Phi(x) \equiv x + vx^\theta - K = 0, \quad 0 < x < K. \tag{8.3.9}$$

We now show that for any positive $K > 0$, the equation $\Phi(x) = 0$ has a unique positive solution.

It is easy to check that the function Φ has the following properties:

$$\Phi(0) < 0, \quad \Phi(K) > 0, \quad \frac{d\Phi}{dx} > 0$$

for all x. This implies that equation (8.3.9) has a unique positive solution

$$x = \Lambda(K) > 0.$$

For instance, in the case of $\theta = 1$, we have $\Lambda(K) = K/(1+v)$. In the case of $\theta = 1/2$, we have

$$x = \left\{ \left(\frac{v^2}{4} + K \right)^{1/2} - \frac{v}{2} \right\}^2.$$

We thus solve E as a unique function of K_j as follows:

$$E = \Lambda(K) - K_1. \tag{8.3.10}$$

Substituting equation (8.3.10) and r in equations (8.3.1) into equations (8.3.2) yields

$$Y_j(K_1, K_2) = g_j(K_1, K_2), \quad j = 1, 2, \tag{8.3.11}$$

where $Y_j = y_j N_j$ and

$$g_1(K_1, K_2) \equiv \frac{\alpha_1 K_1 + \beta_1 \Lambda}{\Lambda^{\beta_1}} N_1^{\beta_1} - \delta_k K_1,$$

$$g_2(K_1, K_2) \equiv \frac{\alpha_2 K_2 + \beta_2 K - \beta_2 \Lambda}{(K-\Lambda)^{\beta_2}} N_2^{\beta_1} - \delta_k K_2.$$

From equations (8.3.6), we have

$$\dot{K}_j = \lambda_j Y_j - \xi_j K_j, \quad j = 1, 2. \tag{8.3.12}$$

At equilibrium, we have

$$\lambda_j Y_j = \xi_j K_j, \quad j = 1, 2. \tag{8.3.13}$$

From equations (8.3.11) and (8.3.13), we solve K_j as functions of K as follows:

$$K_1 = \frac{\beta_1 \Lambda}{\phi_1(\Lambda)}, \quad K_2 = \frac{\beta_2 \Lambda^\theta}{\phi_2(\Lambda)}, \tag{8.3.14}$$

in which

$$\phi_1(\Lambda) \equiv \frac{\delta_1 \Lambda^{\beta_1}}{\lambda_1 N_1^{\beta_1}} - \alpha_1, \quad \phi_2(\Lambda) \equiv \frac{\delta_2 v^{\beta_2} \Lambda^{\beta_1}}{\lambda_2 N_2^{\beta_2}} - \alpha_2, \tag{8.3.15}$$

where $\delta_j \equiv \xi_j + (1 - \delta_k)\lambda_j$. As $K_j \geq 0$, $j = 1, 2$, it is necessary to require $\phi_j \geq 0$. Define

$$\Lambda_0 \equiv \min\{\Lambda | \phi_j(\Lambda) = 0, \Lambda > 0, j = 1, 2\}. \tag{8.3.16}$$

It is obvious that such a positive Λ_0 exists. As ϕ_j are increasing in Λ, Λ is meaningful only when $\Lambda > \Lambda_0$.

To guarantee $K \geq K_j$, $j = 1, 2$, where $K = \Lambda + v\Lambda^\theta$, we introduce

$$\Lambda_1 \equiv \max\{\Lambda | \frac{\beta_1}{\phi_1(\Lambda)} = 1 + v\Lambda^{\theta-1}, \frac{\beta_2 v \Lambda^{\theta-1}}{\phi_2(\Lambda)} = 1 + v\Lambda^{\theta-1}, \Lambda > \Lambda_0\}. \tag{8.3.17}$$

It is easy to show the existence of such a positive Λ_1. Adding the two equations in equations (8.3.14) yields

$$\Phi^*(\Lambda) \equiv \frac{\beta_1}{\phi_1(\Lambda)} + \frac{\beta_2 v\Lambda^{\theta-1}}{\phi_2(\Lambda)} - 1 - v\Lambda^{\theta-1} = 0, \qquad (8.3.18)$$

where we use $K = K_1 + K_2$ and $K = \Lambda + v\Lambda^\theta$. As $\Phi^*(\Lambda_0) > 0$ and $\Phi^*(\Lambda_1) < 0$, we see that there is at least one positive Λ, $\Lambda_0 < \Lambda < \Lambda_1$, such that $\Phi^*(\Lambda) = 0$. From equations (8.3.10) and (8.3.14), we have

$$E = \left\{1 - \frac{\beta_1}{\phi_1(\Lambda)}\right\}\Lambda.$$

The sign of $1 - \beta_1/\phi_1(\Lambda)$ determines the direction of trade flow. As we cannot explicitly solve equation (8.3.18), it is not easy to explicitly interpret the economic meanings of the sign.

We have thus shown how to explicitly solve the equilibrium problem. The procedure is as follows: Λ by equation (8.3.18) $\to K_j$ by equations (8.3.14) $\to K = K_1 + K_2$ $\to Y_j$ by equations (8.3.11) $\to E$ by equation (8.3.10) $\to F_1 = A_1(K_1 + E)^{\beta_1} N_1^{\beta_1} \to$ $F_2 = A_2(K_2 - E)^{\beta_2} N_2^{\beta_2} \to r$ and w_j by equations (8.3.10) $\to C_j$ and S_j by equations (8.3.16).

We provide the conditions for the uniqueness of equilibrium and for stability. Summarizing the above discussion, we have the following lemma.

Lemma 8.3.1
The dynamic system has at least one equilibrium point. In the case of $\theta = 1$, the system has a unique solution. In the case of $\theta < 1$, if $\Lambda_1 \leq \Lambda_2$, where Λ_2 is the solution of $1 - \theta = 1/\phi_2(\Lambda)$, the system has a unique equilibrium point. The stability condition is explicitly given by (A.5.1.8) in Appendix A.8.3.

As it is not easy to generally interpret the above conclusions, we will examine some special cases to illustrate the results.

8.3.3 Some special cases

We now examine the trade patterns when the parameters are taken on some special values. In this section, we assume $N_1 = N_2$.

Case 1 The identical production function

First, we are concerned with the case that the two countries have an identical production function, i.e., $\theta = 1$. From Appendix A.5.1, the system has a unique equilibrium point. From the definitions of $\phi_1(\Lambda)$ and $\phi_2(\Lambda)$ in equations (8.3.15), we see that if $\delta_1/\lambda_1 > \delta_2/\lambda_2$, i.e. $\xi_1/\lambda_1 > \xi_2/\lambda_2$, then $\phi_1(\Lambda) > \phi_2(\Lambda)$, for any $\Lambda > \Lambda_0$. We require $\xi_1/\lambda_1 > \xi_2/\lambda_2$ in the following discussion.

On the other hand, in the case of $\theta = 1$ and $N_1 = N_2$, we can rewrite equation (8.3.18) as

$$\frac{1}{\phi_1(\Lambda)} + \frac{1}{\phi_2(\Lambda)} = \frac{2}{\beta}, \qquad (8.3.19)$$

where we use $\upsilon = 1$ and $\beta = \beta_1 = \beta_2$. From $\phi_1(\Lambda) > \phi_2(\Lambda)$ and equation (8.3.19), we have

$$\frac{2}{\phi_1(\Lambda)} < \frac{1}{\phi_1(\Lambda)} + \frac{1}{\phi_2(\Lambda)} = \frac{2}{\beta}.$$

Hence, we have $1/\phi_1(\Lambda) < 1$. As $K_1 = \beta_1 \Lambda / \phi_1(\Lambda)$, we have $K_1/\Lambda < 1$. With $\Lambda = K_1 + E$, we conclude that $E > 0$. In the case of $\theta = 1$ and $\upsilon = 1$, $\Lambda(K) = K/2$, i.e. $K_1 + E = K/2$. This implies that $K_1 < K_2$. As $S_j = \delta_k K_j$ at equilibrium, we have $S_1 < S_2$. From equation (8.3.8), we get $F_1 = F_2$ and $w_1 = w_2$. We have

$$Y_1 - Y_2 = -2rE < 0.$$

We conclude that $Y_1 - Y_2$ is less than zero. It is easy to check that

$$C_1 - C_2 = \left(K_1 - \frac{\delta_2/\lambda_2 \, p_2}{\delta_1/\lambda_1 \, p_1} K_2\right)\frac{\delta_1}{\lambda_1 p_1} - \delta_k(K_1 - K_2) < 0,$$

where we use

$$\frac{\delta_2/\lambda_2 \, p_2}{\delta_1/\lambda_1 \, p_1} < 1, \quad \frac{\delta_1}{\lambda_1 p_1} > \delta_k.$$

Summarizing the above discussion, we have the following corollary.

Corollary 8.3.1
Let $\theta = 1$, $N_1 = N_2$ and $\xi_1/\lambda_1 > \xi_2/\lambda_2$. Then, the system has a unique equilibrium point at which $E > 0$, $K_1 < K_2$, $S_1 < S_2$, $F_1 = F_2$, $w_1 = w_2$, $Y_1 < Y_2$ and $C_1 < C_2$.

The condition, $\xi_1/\lambda_1 > \xi_2/\lambda_2$, implies that country 1 has a lower propensity to hold wealth than country 2. The difference in the preferences determines that country 1 employs country 2's capital in production even though the two countries have identical production function and labor force.

Case 2 The identical preference
Let the two countries have an identical utility function, i.e. $\xi_1 = \xi_2$ and $\lambda_1 = \lambda_2$. We require $\theta < 1$, i.e. $\beta_1 < \beta_2$ and $\alpha_2 < \alpha_1$. From the definition of υ and equations (8.3.15), we have

$$\phi_2(\Lambda) = \frac{\alpha_2 \phi_1(\Lambda)}{\alpha_1},$$

for any $\Lambda > \Lambda_0$. Using this relation and equation (8.3.18), we have

$$1 + \upsilon\Lambda^{\theta-1} = \frac{\beta_1}{\phi_1(\Lambda)} + \frac{\beta_2 \upsilon\Lambda^{\theta-1}}{\phi_2(\Lambda)} = \left\{1 + \frac{\alpha_1\beta_2\upsilon\Lambda^{\theta-1}}{\alpha_2\beta_1\phi_2(\Lambda)}\right\}\frac{\beta_1}{\phi_1(\Lambda)}$$

$$> \left(1 + \upsilon\Lambda^{\theta-1}\right)\frac{\beta_1}{\phi_1(\Lambda)}. \qquad (8.3.20)$$

From (8.3.20), we directly have

$$\phi_1(\Lambda) > \beta_1.$$

We thus have $K_1/\Lambda > 1$, that is

$$E < 0.$$

Country 1's capital is employed by country 2.

Corollary 8.3.2

Let $\theta < 1$ and $\xi_1/\lambda_1 = \xi_2/\lambda_2$. Then, the system has a unique equilibrium point at which $E > 0$.

As $\theta < 1$ implies that the marginal productivity of capital in country 1 is higher than that in country 2, the conclusion is reasonable under the condition that the two countries have identical preference and labor force.

Similarly, we may examine other cases. For instance, it is easy to check that if $\theta < 1$ and $\xi_1/\lambda_1 > \xi_2/\lambda_2$, then $E < 0$. But it is difficult to determine the sign of E in the case of $\theta > 1$ and $\xi_1/\lambda_1 > \xi_2/\lambda_2$. The above discussion implies that trade patterns are determined by combinations of preferences and production functions of various countries. It is difficult to obtain general explicit conclusions even when we use simple production and utility functions.

8.4 A multi-country trade model with heterogeneous households

This section extends the model in the previous section to heterogeneous households in each country. The system consists of multiple countries, indexed by $j = 1, ..., J$. Only one good is produced in the system. Perfect competition is assumed to prevail in goods markets both within each country and between the countries, and commodities are traded without any barriers such as transport costs or tariffs. We assume that there is no migration between the countries and the labor markets are perfectly competitive within each country. Let prices be measured in terms of the commodity and the price of the commodity be unity. We assume that the population of country j can be classified into Q_j groups, indexed by q, according to their preferences, wealth, human capital, and social status. The total number of types of households Q in the world economy is given by

$$Q = \sum_{j=1}^{J} Q_j.$$

A group q in country j is indexed by (j, q). We introduce

$$Q^* \equiv \{(j, q) | j = 1, \cdots, J, \ q = 1, \cdots, Q_j\}.$$

8.4.1 The trade model with heterogeneous households

Let the number of group q in country j be N_{jq}. The aggregated labor force N_j of country j is given by

$$N_j = \sum_{q=1}^{Q_j} h_{jq} N_{jq}, \qquad (8.4.1)$$

where h_{jq} are the level of human capital of group q in country j. In this initial stage, we assume human capital to be constant. We denote wage and interest rates by $w_{jq}(t)$ and $r_j(t)$, respectively, in the jth country. In the free trade system, the interest rate is equal throughout the world economy, i.e., $r(t) = r_j(t)$.

We now describe the behavior of the production sections. We use production functions to describe the physical facts of a given technology. We assume that there are only two productive factors, capital, $K_j(t)$, and labor, N_j, at each point in time t. The production functions are given by

$$F_j(K_j(t), N_j), \quad j = 1, \cdots, J,$$

where F_j are the output of country j. Assume F_j to be neoclassical. We have

$$f_j(t) = f_j(k_j(t)), \quad f_j(t) \equiv \frac{F_j(t)}{N_j}, \quad k_j(t) \equiv \frac{K_j(t)}{N_j}.$$

Markets are competitive; thus labor and capital earn their marginal products, and firms earn zero profits. The rate of interest, $r(t)$, and wage rates, $w_{jq}(t)$, are determined by the markets. The marginal conditions are given by

$$r + \delta_{kj} = f_j'(k_j), \quad w_{jq}(t) = h_{jq}(f_j(k_j) - k_j f_j'(k_j)), \quad (j, q) \in Q^*, \qquad (8.4.2)$$

where δ_{kj} is the depreciation rate of physical capital in country j.

Consumers make decisions on choice of consumption levels of services and commodities as well as on how much to save. Let $\bar{k}_{jq}(t)$ stand for the per capita wealth of group q in country j. A consumer q of country j obtains the current income

$$y_{jq}(t) = r(t)\bar{k}_{jq}(t) + w_{jq}(t), \ (j, q) \in Q^*, \tag{8.4.3}$$

from the interest payment, $r\bar{k}_{jq}$, and the wage payment, w_{jq}. The disposable income is

$$\hat{y}_{jq}(t) = y_{jq}(t) + \bar{k}_{jq}(t). \tag{8.4.4}$$

The disposable income is used for saving and consumption. At each point in time, a consumer distributes the total available budget among saving, $s_{jq}(t)$, and consumption of goods, $c_{jq}(t)$. The budget constraints are given by

$$c_{jq}(t) + s_{jq}(t) = \hat{y}_{jq}(t) = r\bar{k}_{jq}(t) + w_{jq}(t) + \bar{k}_{jq}(t). \tag{8.4.5}$$

Consumers have two variables to decide upon. A consumer decides how much to consume and to save. Equations (8.4.5) mean that consumption and savings exhaust the consumer's disposable income.

We assume that utility levels, $U_{jq}(t)$, that the consumers obtain are dependent on $c_{jq}(t)$ and $s_{jq}(t)$. The utility level of consumer (j, q) is specified as follows:

$$U_{jq}(t) = c_{jq}^{\xi_{jq}}(t) s_{jq}^{\lambda_{jq}}(t), \ \xi_{jq}, \lambda_{jq} > 0, \ \xi_{jq} + \lambda_{jq} = 1$$

where ξ_{jq} and λ_{jq} are respectively (j, q)'s propensities to consume and to hold wealth. Maximizing U_j subject to the budget constraints (8.4.4) yields

$$c_{jq}(t) = \xi_{jq}\hat{y}_{jq}(t), \ s_{jq}(t) = \lambda_{jq}\hat{y}_{jq}(t), \ (j, q) \in Q^*. \tag{8.4.6}$$

According to the definitions of $s_{jq}(t)$, (j, q)'s wealth accumulation is given by

$$\dot{\bar{k}}_{jq}(t) = s_{jq}(t) - \bar{k}_{jq}(t), \ (j, q) \in Q^*. \tag{8.4.7}$$

The total capital stocks employed by the production sectors is equal to the total wealth owned by all the countries. That is

$$K(t) = \sum_{j=1}^{J} K_j(t) = \sum_{j=1}^{J}\sum_{q=1}^{Q_j} \bar{k}_{jq}(t) N_{jq}. \qquad (8.4.8)$$

The world production is equal to the world consumption and world net saving. That is

$$C(t) + S(t) - K(t) + \sum_{j=1}^{J} \delta_{kj} K_j(t) = F(t),$$

where

$$C(t) \equiv \sum_{j=1}^{J}\sum_{q=1}^{Q_j} c_{jq}(t) N_{jq}, \quad S(t) \equiv \sum_{j=1}^{J}\sum_{q=1}^{Q_j} s_{jq}(t) N_{jq}, \quad F(t) \equiv \sum_{j=1}^{J} F_j(t).$$

We have thus built the model, which explains the endogenous capital accumulation, labor supply and international distribution of capital in the world economy.

We now examine trade balances among countries. First, we calculate

$$F_j - \sum_{q=1}^{Q_j}\left(c_{jq} + s_{jq} - \bar{k}_{jq}\right) N_{jq} - \delta_{kj} K_j = r\left(K_j - \sum_{q=1}^{Q_j} \bar{k}_{jq} N_{jq}\right),$$

where we use

$$c_{jq} + s_{jq} = r\bar{k}_{jq} + w_{jq} + \bar{k}_{jq}, \quad F_j = (r + \delta_{kj}) K_j + \sum_{q=1}^{Q_j} w_{jq} N_{jq}.$$

That is

$$F_j = \sum_{q=1}^{Q_j}\left(c_{jq} + s_{jq} - \bar{k}_{jq}\right) N_{jq} + \delta_{kj} K_j + r\left(K_j - \sum_{q=1}^{Q_j} \bar{k}_{jq} N_{jq}\right). \qquad (8.4.9)$$

The national output is used for the consumption, $\sum_{q=1}^{Q_j} c_{jq} N_{jq}$, the net saving, $\sum_{q=1}^{Q_j} (s_{jq} - \bar{k}_{jq}) N_{jq}$, the payment for the depreciation of capital employed by the economy, $\delta_{kj} K_j$, and the payment for the net foreign capital employed by the economy

$$r\left(K_j - \sum_{q=1}^{Q_j} \bar{k}_{jq} N_{jq}\right).$$

If

$$K_j - \sum_{q=1}^{Q_j} \bar{k}_{jq} N_{jq} > (<) 0,$$

we say that country j is in trade deficit (trade surplus). If

$$K_j - \sum_{q=1}^{Q_j} \bar{k}_{jq} N_{jq} = 0,$$

we see that country j is in trade balance. We introduce variables to measure trade balances:

$$E_j(t) \equiv \sum_{q=1}^{Q_j} \bar{k}_{jq} N_{jq} - K_j, \quad \tilde{E}_j(t) \equiv \left(\sum_{q=1}^{Q_j} \bar{k}_{jq} N_{jq} - K_j\right) r(t).$$

We now examine the properties of the system.

8.4.2 The world economic dynamics

We show that the dynamics of the world economy can be expressed as J-dimensional differential equations. First, from equations (8.4.1) we obtain

$$f_j'(k_j) = f_1'(k_1) - \delta_j, \quad j = 2, \cdots, J, \tag{8.4.10}$$

where $\delta_j \equiv \delta_{k1} - \delta_{kj}$. If $f_1'(k_1) - \delta_j > 0$ for all $j = 2, \cdots, J$ and given $k_1(t) > 0$, then the equations determine unique relations between k_j and k_1, denoted by

$$k_j = \phi_j(k_1), \quad j = 1, \cdots, J, \tag{8.4.11}$$

where $\phi_1(k_1) = k_1$. From equations (8.4.10), we have

$$f_j''(k_j)\frac{dk_j}{dk_1} = f_1''(k_1), \quad j = 2, \cdots, J.$$

As $f_j''(k_j) \leq 0$, $j = 1, \cdots, J$, we see that $dk_j/dk_1 \geq 0$, $j = 2, \cdots, J$. That is, $\phi_j'(k_1) \geq 0$. Hence, for any given $k_1(t) > 0$, we uniquely determine $k_j(t)$, $j = 2, \cdots, J$ as unique functions of $k_1(t)$.

From equations (8.4.1), we determine the wage rates as functions of $k_1(t)$ as follows:

$$w_{jq}(t) = \bar{\phi}_{jq}(k_1) \equiv h_{jq}\left(f_j(\phi_j(k_1)) - \phi_j(k_1)f_j'(\phi_j(k_1))\right), \quad (j, q) \in Q^*. \tag{8.4.12}$$

We can rewrite equation (8.4.8) as

$$\sum_{j=1}^{J} k_j(t) N_j = \sum_{j=1}^{J} \sum_{q=1}^{Q_j} \bar{k}_{jq}(t) N_{jq}.$$

Insert equation (8.4.9) into the above equation:

$$\bar{k}_{11}(t) = \Lambda(k_1, \{\bar{k}(t)\}) \equiv \sum_{j=1}^{J} n_j \phi_j(k_1) - \sum_{j=2}^{J} \sum_{q=1}^{Q_j} n_{jq} \bar{k}_{jq}(t) - \sum_{q=2}^{Q_1} n_{1q} \bar{k}_{1q}(t), \tag{8.4.13}$$

in which

$$n_j \equiv \frac{N_j}{N_{11}}, \quad n_{jq} \equiv \frac{N_{jq}}{N_{11}}, \quad \{\bar{k}(t)\} \equiv \left(\bar{k}_{12}(t), \cdots, \bar{k}_{1Q_1}(t), \cdots, \bar{k}_{JQ_J}(t)\right).$$

We see that group $(1, 1)$'s per capita wealth $k_{11}(t)$ can be expressed as a unique function of country 1's capital intensity and all the other groups' per capita wealth $\{\bar{k}(t)\}$ at any point in time.

From equations (8.4.2) and (8.4.3), we obtain

$$\hat{y}_{jq}(t) = (f_1'(k_1) + 1 - \delta_{k1})\bar{k}_{jq} + \bar{\phi}_{jq}(k_1), \tag{8.4.14}$$

where we apply equations (8.4.10) and $r(t) = f_1'(k_1) - \delta_{k1}$. Insert $s_{jq}(t) = \lambda_{jq}\hat{y}_{jq}(t)$ in equations (8.4.6) into (8.4.7):

$$\dot{\bar{k}}_{jq} = \lambda_{jq}\hat{y}_{jq} - \bar{k}_{jq}.$$

Substitute equations (8.4.12) into the above equations:

$$\dot{\bar{k}}_{jq} = \Lambda_{jq}(k_1, \bar{k}_{jq}) \equiv (\lambda_{jq}f_1'(k_1) - \bar{\lambda}_{jq})\bar{k}_{jq} + \lambda_{jq}\bar{\phi}_{jq}(k_1), \ (j, q) \in Q^*, \quad (8.4.15)$$

where $\bar{\lambda}_{jq} \equiv 1 - \lambda_{jq} + \lambda_{jq}\delta_{k1}$.

Taking derivatives of equation (8.4.13) with respect to t yields

$$\dot{\bar{k}}_{11}(t) = \dot{k}_1 \sum_{j=1}^{J} n_j\phi_j'(k_1) - \sum_{j=2}^{J}\sum_{q=1}^{Q_j} n_{jq}\dot{\bar{k}}_{jq}(t) - \sum_{q=2}^{Q_j} n_{1q}\dot{\bar{k}}_{1q}(t). \quad (8.4.16)$$

Equating equation (8.4.16) and $\dot{\bar{k}}_{11} = \Lambda_1(k_1, \bar{k}_{11})$ in equations (8.4.15), we have

$$\dot{k}_1 \sum_{j=1}^{J} n_j\phi_j'(k_1) = \sum_{j=2}^{J}\sum_{q=1}^{Q_j} n_{jq}\dot{\bar{k}}_{jq}(t) + \sum_{q=2}^{Q_j} n_{1q}\dot{\bar{k}}_{1q}(t) + (\lambda_{11}f_1'(k_1) - \bar{\lambda}_{11})\bar{k}_{11} + \lambda_{11}\bar{\phi}_{11}(k_1).$$

Substituting equations (8.4.13) and (8.4.15) into the above equation yields

$$\dot{k}_1 = \frac{\Lambda_6(k_1, \bar{k}_{jq}) + \lambda_{11}\bar{\phi}_{11}(k_1)}{\sum_{j=1}^{J} n_j\phi_j'(k_1)}, \quad (8.4.17)$$

where

$$\Lambda_6 \equiv \sum_{j=2}^{J}\sum_{q=1}^{Q_j} n_{jq}\Lambda_{jq}(k_1, \bar{k}_{jq}) + \sum_{q=2}^{Q_j} n_{1q}\Lambda_{jq}(k_1, \bar{k}_{jq}) + (\lambda_{11}f_1'(k_1) - \bar{\lambda}_{11})\Lambda(k_1, \{\bar{k}(t)\}).$$

We see that $\dot{k}_1$ is a function of $k_1(t)$ and $\{\bar{k}(t)\}$. From equations (8.4.15), we see that $\{\dot{\bar{k}}(t)\}$ are functions of $k_1(t)$ and $\{\bar{k}(t)\}$. We obtain the following lemma.

Lemma 8.4.1
The dynamics of the global economy are described by the differential equation (8.4.17) and the following $(Q - 1)$ differential equations:

$$\dot{\bar{k}}_{jq} = \Lambda_{jq}(k_1, \bar{k}_{jq}) \equiv (\lambda_{jq} f_1'(k_1) - \bar{\lambda}_{jq})\bar{k}_{jq} + \lambda_{jq}\bar{\phi}_{jq}(k_1),$$
$$(j, q) \in Q^*, \quad (j, q) \neq (1, 1),$$

with $k_1(t)$ and $\{\bar{k}\}$ as the variables. For any given positive values of $k_1(t)$ and $\{\bar{k}\}$ at any point in time, the other variables are uniquely determined by the following procedure: $\bar{k}_{11}(t)$ by equation (8.4.13) $\to$ $k_j(t)$, $j = 2, \cdots, J$ by equations (8.4.11) $\to$ $f_j = f_j(k_j)$ $\to$ $r(t)$ and $w_j(t)$ by equations (8.4.2) $\to$ $\hat{y}_j(t)$ by equations (8.4.14) $\to$ $c_j(t)$ and $s_j(t)$ by equations (8.4.6) $\to$ $F_j(t) = N_j f_j(t)$.

Although we may analyze the behavior of the J-dimensional differential equations, it is difficult to explicitly interpret results. Following the computing procedure given in Lemma 8.4.1, we simulate the model to illustrate motion of the system.

8.4.3 The three-country two-group economy

For illustration, we will follow the procedure given in Lemma 8.4.1 to simulate motion of the trade system. We will consider the case that the world consists of three countries and each country has two groups. We specify the production functions as follows:

$$F_j(t) = A_j K_j^{\alpha_j}(t) N_j^{\beta_j}, \quad \alpha_j + \beta_j = 1, \quad \alpha_j, \beta_j > 0,$$

where A_j are country j's productivity and α_j are positive parameters. From $f_j = A_j k_j^{\alpha_j}$, and equations (8.4.10)–(8.4.12), we have

$$k_j = \phi_j(k_1) \equiv \left(\frac{\alpha_1 A_1 k_1^{-\beta_1} - \delta_j}{\alpha_j A_j}\right)^{-1/\beta_j}, \quad j = 2, \cdots, J,$$

$$\bar{\phi}_{jq}(k_1) = A_j \beta_j h_{jq} \phi_j^{\alpha_j}(k_1), \quad (j, q) \in Q^*. \tag{8.4.18}$$

An equilibrium point is given by setting $\dot{k}_1 = 0$ and $\{\dot{\bar{k}}\} = 0$ in equations (8.4.15) and (8.4.17). That is

$$(\lambda_{11} f_1'(k_1) - \bar{\lambda}_{11})\bar{k}_{11} + \lambda_{11}\bar{\phi}_{11}(k_1) = 0, \tag{8.4.19}$$

$$(\lambda_{jq} f_1'(k_1) - \bar{\lambda}_{jq})\bar{k}_{jq} + \lambda_{jq}\bar{\phi}_{jq}(k_1) = 0, \quad (j, q) \in Q^*, \quad (j, q) \neq (1, 1). \tag{8.4.20}$$

Solve equations (8.4.20)

$$\bar{k}_{jq} = \frac{-\lambda_{jq}\bar{\phi}_{jq}(k_1)}{\lambda_{jq}f_1'(k_1) - \bar{\lambda}_{jq}}, \quad (j, q) \in Q^*, \quad (j, q) \neq (1, 1). \tag{8.4.21}$$

Insert equations (8.4.13) into equation (8.4.19):

$$\sum_{j=1}^{J} n_j \phi_j(k_1) - \sum_{j=2}^{J}\sum_{q=1}^{Q_j} n_{jq}\bar{k}_{jq} - \sum_{q=2}^{Q_1} n_{1q}\bar{k}_{1q} + \frac{\lambda_{11}\bar{\phi}_{11}(k_1)}{\lambda_{11}f_1'(k_1) - \bar{\lambda}_{11}} = 0. \tag{8.4.22}$$

Substitute equations (8.4.21) into equation (8.4.22):

$$\Omega(k_1) \equiv \sum_{j=1}^{J} n_j \phi_j(k_1) + \sum_{j=1}^{J}\sum_{q=1}^{Q_j} \frac{n_{jq}\lambda_{jq}\bar{\phi}_{jq}(k_1)}{\lambda_{jq}f_1'(k_1) - \bar{\lambda}_{jq}} = 0. \tag{8.4.23}$$

Equation (8.4.23) determines k_1 and equations (8.4.21) determine $\bar{k}_{jq}$.

To simulate the model, we specify the parameter values as follows:

$$\begin{pmatrix} A_1 \\ A_2 \\ A_3 \\ \alpha_1 \\ \alpha_2 \\ \alpha_3 \end{pmatrix} = \begin{pmatrix} 4 \\ 2 \\ 1 \\ 1/3 \\ 0.3 \\ 1/3 \end{pmatrix}, \begin{pmatrix} N_{11} \\ N_{12} \\ N_{21} \\ N_{22} \\ N_{31} \\ N_{32} \end{pmatrix} = \begin{pmatrix} 2 \\ 4 \\ 2 \\ 8 \\ 1 \\ 20 \end{pmatrix}, \begin{pmatrix} h_{11} \\ h_{12} \\ h_{21} \\ h_{22} \\ h_{31} \\ h_{32} \end{pmatrix} = \begin{pmatrix} 12 \\ 5 \\ 7 \\ 3 \\ 5 \\ 1 \end{pmatrix}, \begin{pmatrix} \lambda_{11} \\ \lambda_{12} \\ \lambda_{21} \\ \lambda_{22} \\ \lambda_{31} \\ \lambda_{32} \end{pmatrix} = \begin{pmatrix} 0.87 \\ 0.78 \\ 0.80 \\ 0.74 \\ 0.75 \\ 0.65 \end{pmatrix}, \begin{pmatrix} \delta_{k1} \\ \delta_{k2} \\ \delta_{k3} \end{pmatrix} = \begin{pmatrix} 0.07 \\ 0.06 \\ 0.05 \end{pmatrix}. \tag{8.4.24}$$

For convenience of interpretation, we call countries 1, 2, and 3 respectively the developed economy, the industrializing economy, and the developing economy. Groups $(j, 1)$ and $(j, 2)$ in country j are called the rich group (RG) and the poor group (PP) respectively. The level of the total productivity of the developed economy is the highest; the second is the industrializing economy; and the lowest is the developing economy. The developed economy's RG has the highest level of human capital and highest propensity to save. Its population is the same as that of the industrializing economy's RG. The developing economy's PP has the lowest level of human capital and the largest number of the population. We now show that the dynamic system has a unique equilibrium point.

We plot the function $\Omega(k_1)$ defined in equation (8.4.23) as in Figure 8.4.1. The equation $\Omega(k_1) = 0$ has multiple positive solutions

$$k_1 = 3.49, \ k_1 = 6.09, \ k_1 = 6.51, \ k_1 = 8.47, \ k_1 = 10.41, \ k_1 = 57.77. \quad (8.4.25)$$

It can be shown that only the equilibrium point, $k_1 = 57.71$, is meaningful; the rest are not meaningful in the sense that at any of these points, per capita wealth of some group(s) becomes negative. Hence, the equation, $\Omega(k_1) = 0$, has a unique meaningful solution $k_1 = 57.71$.

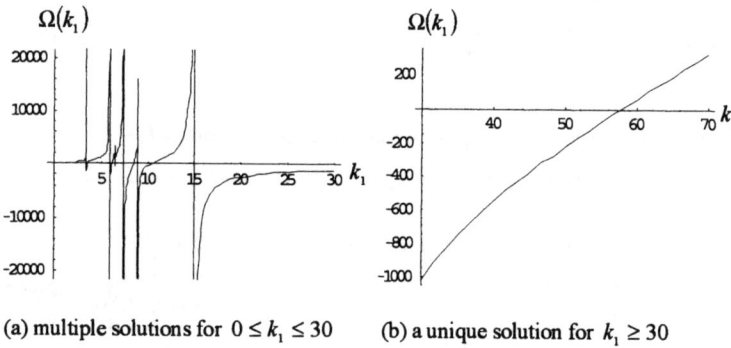

(a) multiple solutions for $0 \leq k_1 \leq 30$ (b) a unique solution for $k_1 \geq 30$

Figure 8.4.1 The existence of positive solutions of $\Omega(k_1) = 0$

By equations (8.4.13), (8.4.18), and (8.4.21), we solve the equilibrium values of k_j and $\bar{k}_j$. Following Lemma 8.4.1, we get the equilibrium values of all the other variables. We list the simulation results as follows:

$r = 0.0193$,

$$\begin{pmatrix} f_1 \\ f_2 \\ f_3 \end{pmatrix} = \begin{pmatrix} 15.46 \\ 4.32 \\ 1.75 \end{pmatrix}, \ \begin{pmatrix} k_1 \\ k_2 \\ k_3 \end{pmatrix} = \begin{pmatrix} 57.71 \\ 13.06 \\ 5.33 \end{pmatrix}, \ \begin{pmatrix} F_1 \\ F_2 \\ F_3 \end{pmatrix} = \begin{pmatrix} 680.12 \\ 164.30 \\ 43.66 \end{pmatrix}, \ \begin{pmatrix} C_1 \\ C_2 \\ C_3 \end{pmatrix} = \begin{pmatrix} 505.20 \\ 126.27 \\ 31.29 \end{pmatrix},$$

$$\begin{pmatrix}\bar{K}_1\\\bar{K}_2\\\bar{K}_3\end{pmatrix}=\begin{pmatrix}1684.77\\417.52\\66.45\end{pmatrix},$$

$$\begin{pmatrix}\bar{k}_{11}\\\bar{k}_{12}\\\bar{k}_{21}\\\bar{k}_{22}\\\bar{k}_{31}\\\bar{k}_{32}\end{pmatrix}=\begin{pmatrix}950.12\\196.09\\95.99\\28.19\\18.80\\2.33\end{pmatrix},\begin{pmatrix}w_{11}\\w_{12}\\w_{21}\\w_{22}\\w_{31}\\w_{32}\end{pmatrix}=\begin{pmatrix}123.66\\51.53\\21.19\\9.08\\5.82\\1.16\end{pmatrix},\begin{pmatrix}c_{11}\\c_{12}\\c_{21}\\c_{22}\\c_{31}\\c_{32}\end{pmatrix}=\begin{pmatrix}141.96\\55.31\\23.81\\9.83\\6.50\\1.24\end{pmatrix},\begin{pmatrix}C_{11}\\C_{12}\\C_{21}\\C_{22}\\C_{31}\\C_{32}\end{pmatrix}=\begin{pmatrix}283.97\\221.23\\47.61\\78.66\\6.50\\24.79\end{pmatrix},$$

(8.4.26)

where

$$C_{jq}\equiv c_{jq}N_{jq},\ C_j\equiv C_{j1}+C_{j2},\ \bar{K}_{jq}\equiv\bar{k}_{jq}N_{jq},\ \bar{K}_j\equiv\bar{K}_{j1}+\bar{K}_{j2}.$$

We see that the per capita levels of wealth and consumption and wage rate of the RG of the developed economy are much higher than the corresponding variables in the other economies. A representative household from the RG of the developed economy holds more than 400 times wealth and consumes more than 100 times than a representative household from the PP of the developing economy. Also the wage rate differences are over 100 times between the poorest and the richest. The developed economy's output level of per-unit human capital is about nine times higher than that in the developing economy.

The income and wealth distribution of the world economy is given by

$$\begin{pmatrix}\hat{N}_1\\\hat{N}_2\\\hat{N}_3\end{pmatrix}=\begin{pmatrix}16.21\%\\27.03\%\\56.76\%\end{pmatrix},\begin{pmatrix}\hat{F}_1\\\hat{F}_2\\\hat{F}_3\end{pmatrix}=\begin{pmatrix}76.58\%\\18.50\%\\4.92\%\end{pmatrix},\begin{pmatrix}\hat{W}_1\\\hat{W}_2\\\hat{W}_3\end{pmatrix}=\begin{pmatrix}80.01\%\\18.44\%\\1.52\%\end{pmatrix},$$

$$\begin{pmatrix}\hat{C}_1\\\hat{C}_2\\\hat{C}_3\end{pmatrix}=\begin{pmatrix}75.88\%\\19.25\%\\4.87\%\end{pmatrix},\begin{pmatrix}\hat{\bar{K}}_1\\\hat{\bar{K}}_2\\\hat{\bar{K}}_3\end{pmatrix}=\begin{pmatrix}84.73\%\\13.18\%\\2.10\%\end{pmatrix},$$

where a variable x_j with circumflex, $\hat{x}_j$, denotes country j's share of the corresponding variable in the world economy. The developed economy's share of the population is 16.21 percent; the industrializing economy 27.03 percent; and the developing economy 56.76 percent. Irrespective of its small population size, the global shares of the output, wage income, consumption, and wealth of the developed economy are respectively 76.58 percent, 80.01 percent, 75.88 percent and 84.73 percent. The developing economy's global shares of the output, wage income, consumption and wealth are respectively only 4.92 percent, 1.52 percent, 4.87 percent, and 2.1 percent. We calculate the national trade balances at equilibrium as follows:

$$\begin{pmatrix} E_1 \\ E_2 \\ E_3 \end{pmatrix} = \begin{pmatrix} 145.65 \\ -78.93 \\ -66.72 \end{pmatrix}, \begin{pmatrix} \tilde{E}_1 \\ \tilde{E}_2 \\ \tilde{E}_3 \end{pmatrix} = \begin{pmatrix} 2.81 \\ -1.52 \\ -1.29 \end{pmatrix}.$$

The developed economy is in trade surplus and the industrializing and developing economies are in trade deficit.

We have just examined the equilibrium structure of the global economy. It is important to follow the motion of the global economy when it starts from a state far away from the equilibrium point. As we have shown by Lemma 8.4.1 how to follow dynamic processes, it is straightforward to simulate the motion. We simulate the model with the parameter values specified as in (8.4.24) and the following initial conditions:

$$k_1(t) = 70, \ \bar{k}_{12}(0) = 150, \ \bar{k}_{21}(0) = 70, \ \bar{k}_{22}(0) = 20, \ \bar{k}_{31}(0) = 10, \ \bar{k}_{32}(0) = 1.$$

The simulation results are plotted in Figure 8.4.2. We observe that the variables approach their equilibrium values in the long term. It can be seen that from different positions, we may observe various patterns of global economy growth over time.

8.4.4 Comparative dynamic analysis

It is important to examine questions such as how a developing economy like India or China may affect the global economy as its technology is improved or its population enlarged; or how the global trade patterns may be affected as technologies are further improved in developed economies like the US or Japan. This section examines the impact of changes in some parameters on dynamic processes of the global economic system.

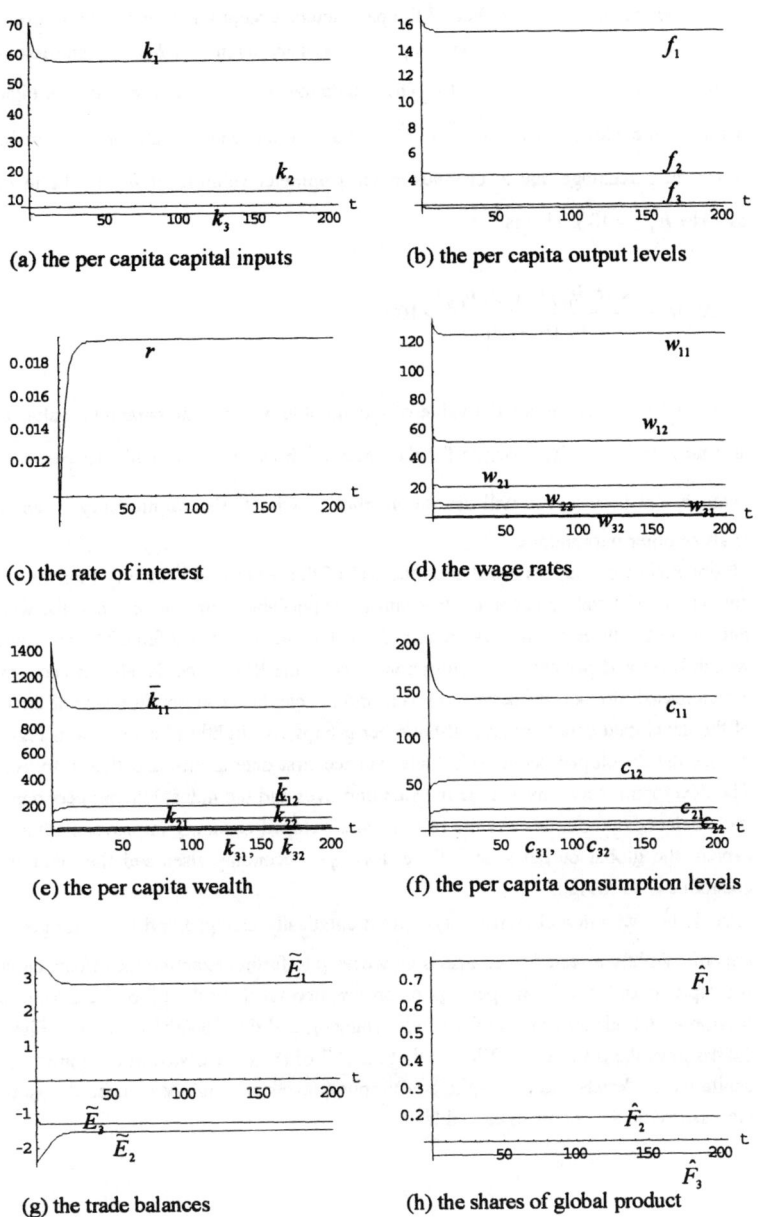

(a) the per capita capital inputs
(b) the per capita output levels
(c) the rate of interest
(d) the wage rates
(e) the per capita wealth
(f) the per capita consumption levels
(g) the trade balances
(h) the shares of global product

Figure 8.4.2 The motion of the global economy

First, we examine the case that all the parameters, except the human capital level of the RG of the developed economy, h_{11}, are the same as in (8.4.24). We increase the human capital level from 12 to 13. The simulation results are demonstrated in Figure 8.4.3. In the plots, a variable, $\overline{\Delta}x_j(t)$, stands for the change rate of the variable, $x_j(t)$, in percentage due to changes in the parameter value from h_{110} ($=12$ in this case) to h_{11} ($=13$). That is

$$\overline{\Delta}x_j(t) \equiv \frac{x_j(t;\,h_{11}) - x_j(t;\,h_{110})}{|x_j(t;\,h_{110})|} \times 100,$$

where $x_j(t;\,h_{11})$ stands for the value of the variable x_j with the parameter value h_{11} at time t and $x_j(t;\,h_{110})$ stands for the value of the variable x_j with the parameter value h_{110} at time t. We will use the symbol $\overline{\Delta}$ with the same meaning when we analyze other parameters.

From Figure 8.4.3a, we see that as the RG of the developed economy improves its human capital level, the capital-labor ratios, the per-labor output levels, and the wage rates in all the three economies are increased. The rate of interest falls. The per capita wealth level and per capita consumption level of the RG of the developed economy are increased; the per capita wealth levels and per capita consumption levels of the PP of the developed economy and all the other groups are slightly affected. From Figure 8.4.3g, the developed economy's trade balance first deteriorates and then improves. The developing economy's trade balance improves and the industrializing economy's trade balance deteriorates. As the RG of the developed economy improves its human capital, the global output share of the developed economy rises and the other two economies' shares fall.

As $(1,1)$'s wealth and consumption are dramatically changed and the other groups are only slightly affected in comparison, we need to further examine the effects on the per capita wealth levels and per capita consumption levels of the PP of the developed economy and all the groups of the industrializing and developing economies. Figure 8.4.4 shows the differences. We see that the RG of the industrializing economy's per capita wealth levels and per capita consumption levels are slightly reduced due to the increase in the RG's human capital level.

Multi-Country Growth Economies 357

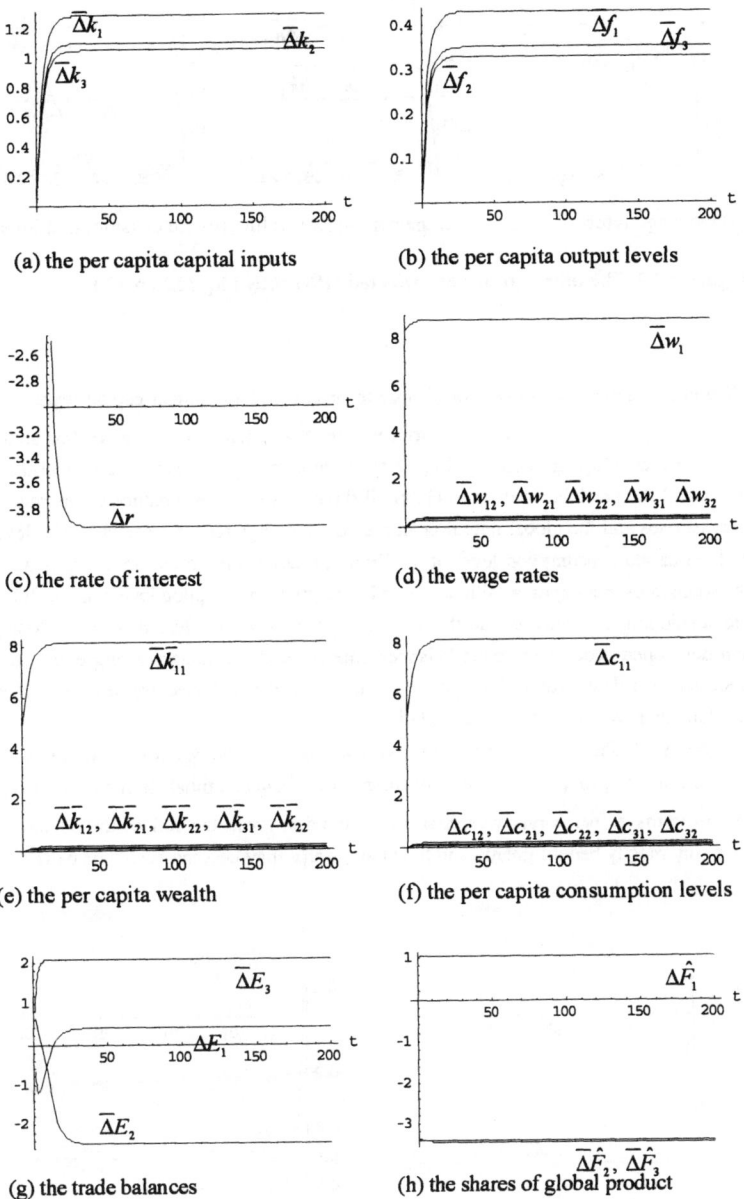

Figure 8.4.3 Group $(1,1)$ improves its human capital ($h_{11} : 12 \Rightarrow 13$)

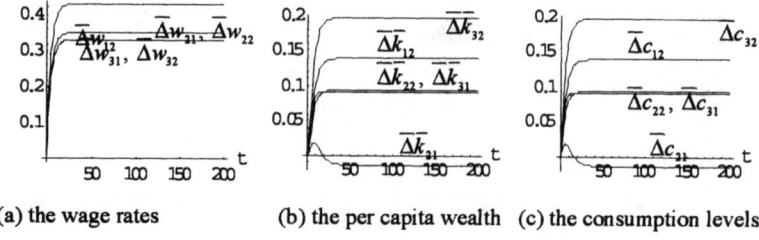

(a) the wage rates (b) the per capita wealth (c) the consumption levels

Figure 8.4.4 The other groups are affected differently ($h_{11}: 12 \Rightarrow 13$)

We now examine the effects of change in group $(3, 2)$'s human capital level. The effects are plotted in Figure 8.4.5. From Figures 8.4.5a and 8.4.5b, we see that as the PP of the developing economy improves its human capital level, the capital-labor ratios and the per-labor output levels in all three economies are reduced. The rate of interest rises and the global output is increased. The wage rate, per capita wealth level and per capita consumption level of the PP of the developing economy are increased; the wage rates, per capita wealth levels and per capita consumption levels of the RG of the developing economy and all the other groups are slightly affected. The developing and developed economies' trade balances improve and the industrializing economy's trade balance deteriorates. The global output share of the developing economy rises and the other two economies' shares fall.

Figure 8.4.6 shows the differences. We see that all these groups' wage rates are reduced due to group $(3, 2)$'s improvement in its human capital. It should be noted that in terms of per capita wealth and consumption level, the RG of the developed economy mostly benefit greatly and the other groups may become even worse off.

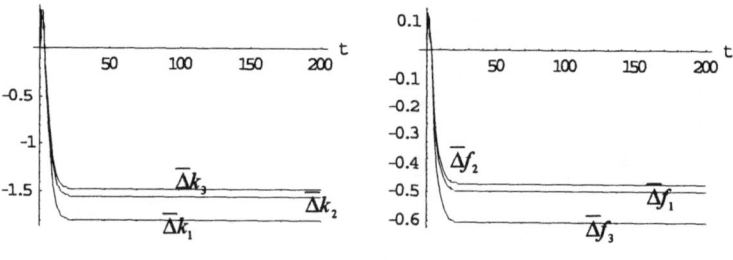

(a) the per capita capital inputs (b) the per capita output levels

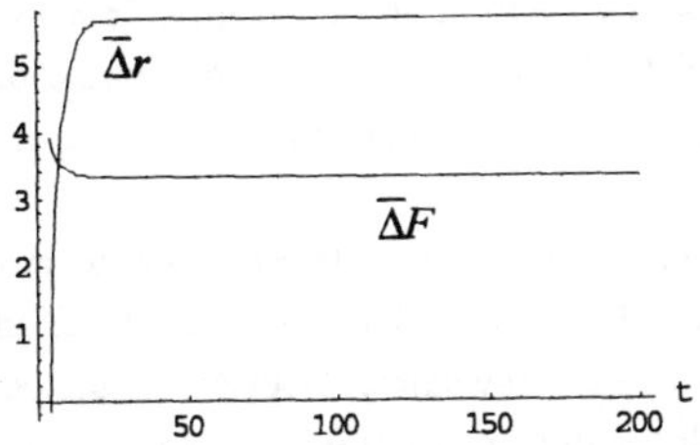

Multi-Country Growth Economies

(c) the rate of interest and the world output

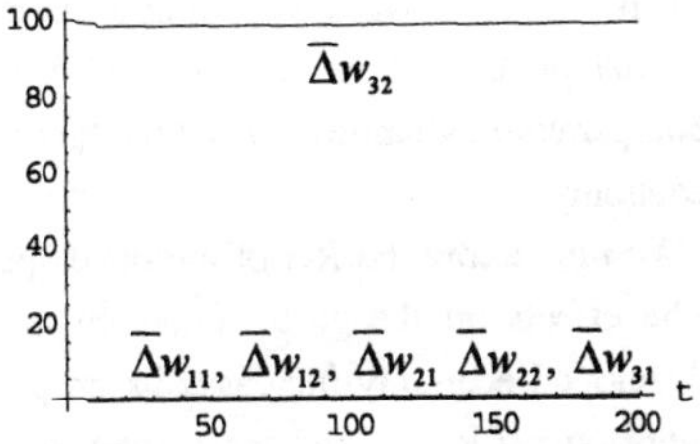

(d) the wage rates

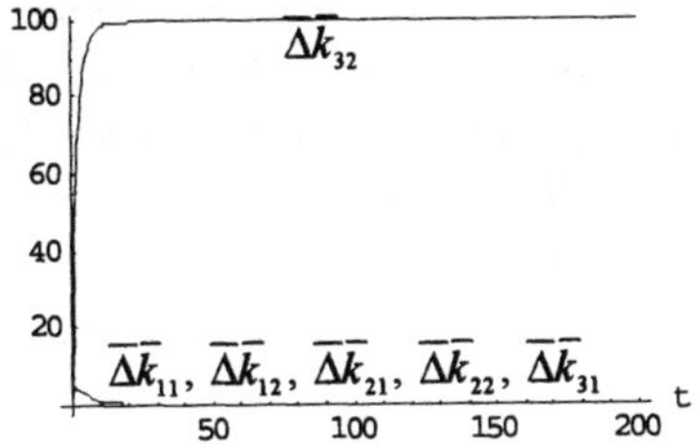

(e) the per capita wealth

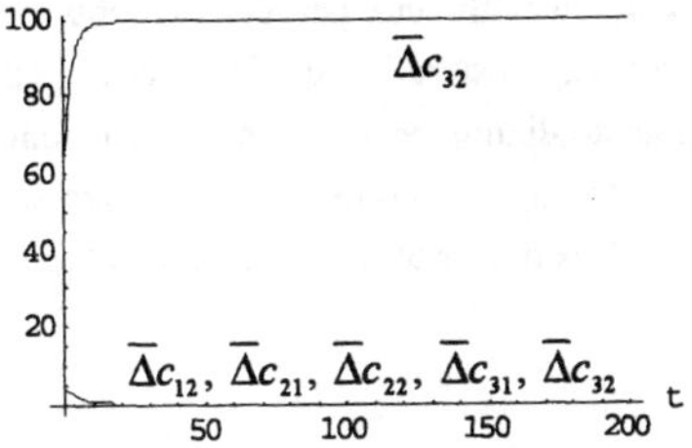

(f) the per capita consumption levels

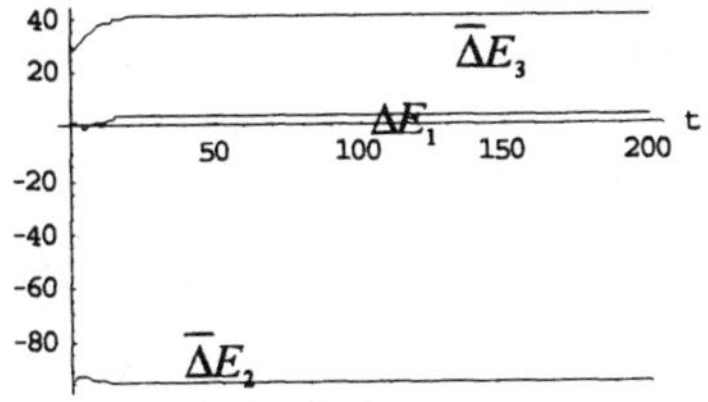

(g) the trade balances

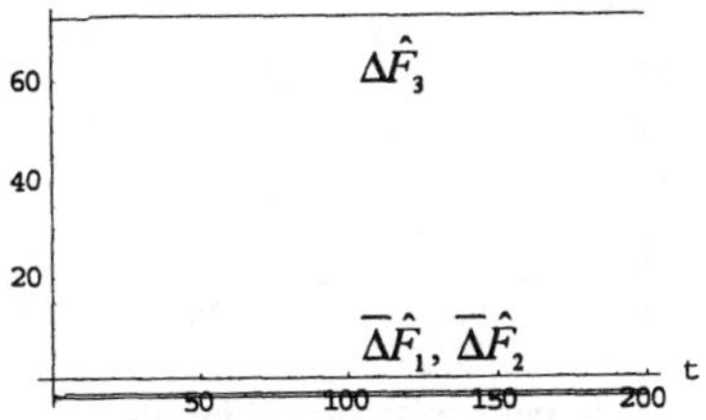

(h) the shares of global product

Figure 8.4.5 Group (3, 2) improves its human capital ($h_{32} : 1 \Rightarrow 2$)

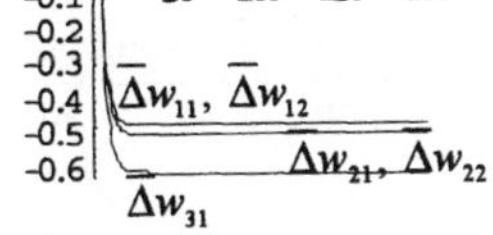

(a) the wage rates

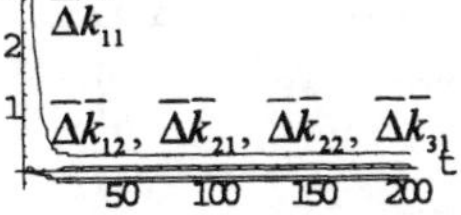

(b) the per capita wealth

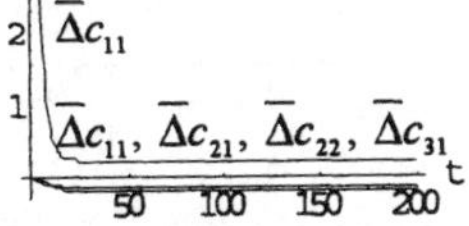

(c) the consumption level

Figure 8.4.6 The other groups are affected differently ($h_{32} : 1 \Rightarrow 2$)

It is straightforward to examine the effects of change in any other group's human capital on the global economy. Because of the limit of space, we concentrate our comparative dynamic analysis on the richest group and the poorest group of the global economy.

We now allow the RG of the developed economy to increase its propensity to save. The effects on the global economy are plotted in Figure 8.4.7. As the RG of the developed economy increases its propensity to save, the capital-labor ratios, the per-labor output levels, and the wage rates in all the three economies are increased. The rate of interest falls. The per capita wealth levels and per capita consumption levels of all the groups (except the RG of the industrializing economy) are increased; the per capita wealth and per capita consumption level of the RG of the industrializing economy are reduced. The developed economy's trade balance deteriorates. The industrializing economy's trade balance first improves and then deteriorates. The developing economy's trade balance improves. The global output share of the developed economy rises and the other two economies' shares fall.

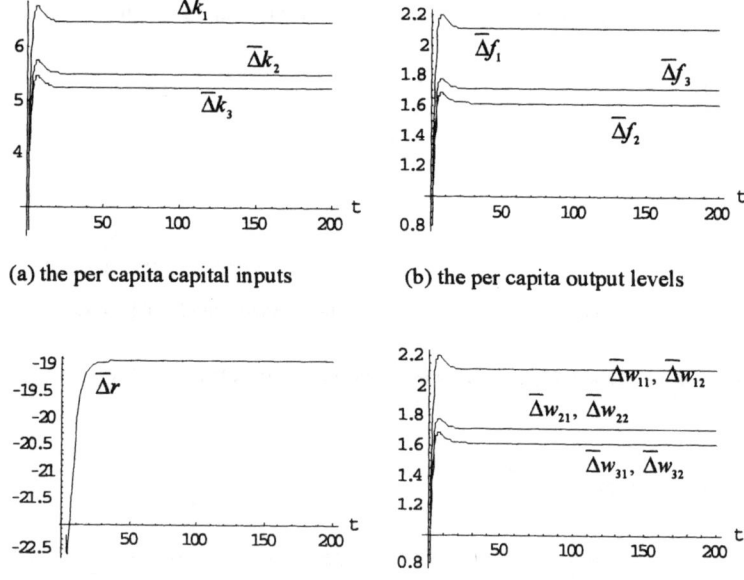

(a) the per capita capital inputs

(b) the per capita output levels

(c) the rate of interest

(d) the wage rates

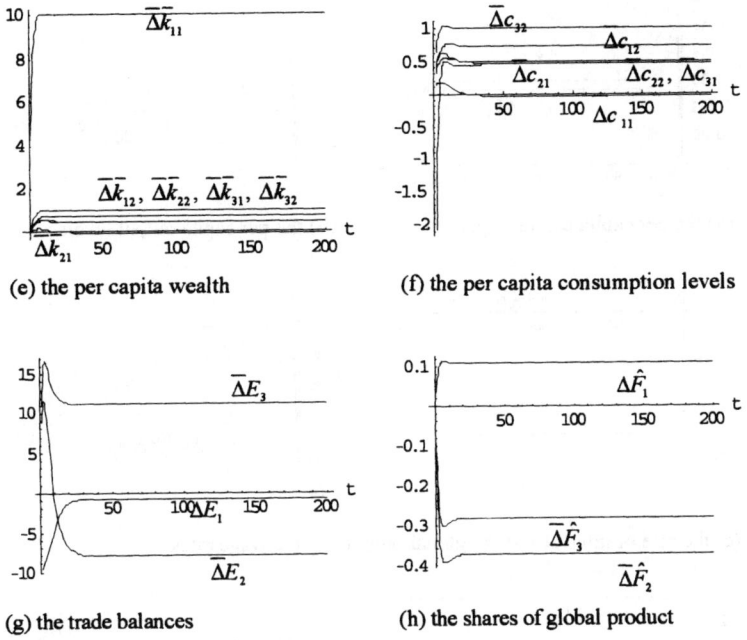

Figure 8.4.7 Group $(1, 1)$ increases its propensity to save ($\lambda_{11}: 0.87 \Rightarrow 0.88$)

The effects of an increase in group $(3, 2)$'s propensity to save on the global economy are plotted in Figure 8.4.8. As the PP of the developing economy increases its propensity to save, the capital-labor ratios, the per-labor output levels, and the wage rates in all three economies are increased. The rate of interest falls and the global output rises. The per capita wealth level and per capita consumption level of the PP of the developing economy are increased; the per capita wealth and per capita consumption levels of the other groups are only slightly affected. The developing economy's trade balance improves. The industrializing and developed economies' trade balances deteriorate.

362 *Economic Growth with Income and Wealth Distribution*

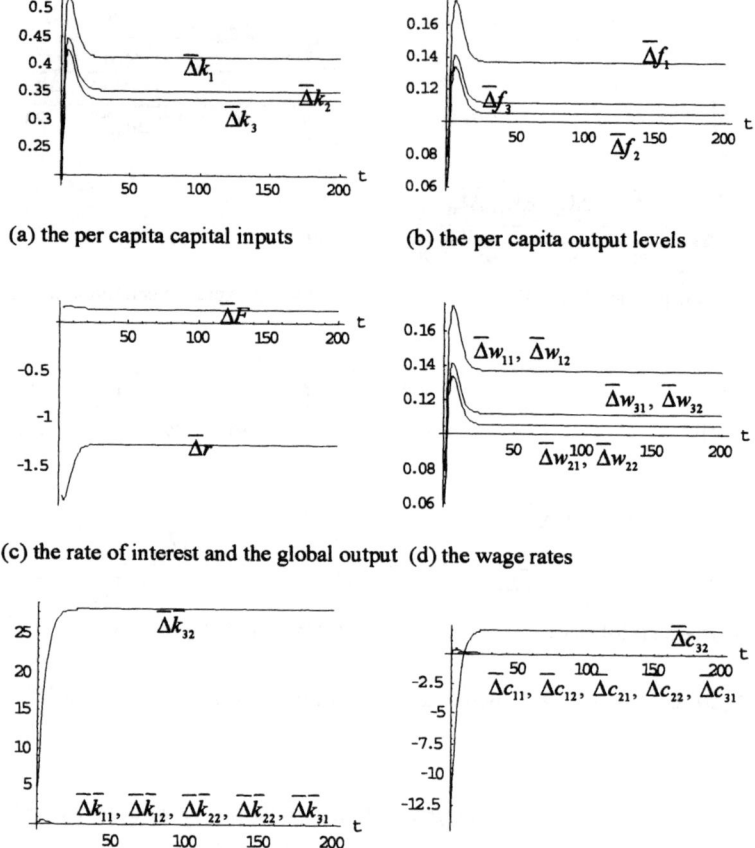

(a) the per capita capital inputs

(b) the per capita output levels

(c) the rate of interest and the global output

(d) the wage rates

(e) the per capita wealth

(f) the per capita consumption levels

(g) the trade balances

(h) the shares of global product

Figure 8.4.8 Group (3, 2) increases its propensity to save ($\lambda_{32} : 0.65 \Rightarrow 0.7$)

We now allow the RG of the developed economy to increase its population. The effects on the global economy are plotted in Figure 8.4.9. As the RG of the developed economy increases its population, the capital-labor ratios, the per-labor output levels, and the wage rates in all three economies are increased. The rate of interest falls and the global output rises. The per capita wealth level and per capita consumption level of the RG of the developed economy are reduced; the per capita wealth level and per capita consumption level of the RG of the industrializing economy are slightly reduced; the per capita wealth levels of all the other groups are increased. The developed economy's trade balance initially deteriorates and then improves. The industrializing economy's trade balance initially improves and then deteriorates. The developing economy's trade balance improves. The global output share of the developed economy rises and the other two economies' shares fall. It should be noted that as the RG of the developed economy increases its population, all the other groups benefit.

We now allow the PP of the developing economy to increase its population. The effects on the global economy are plotted in Figure 8.4.10. As the PP of the developing economy increases its population, the capital-labor ratios, the per-labor output levels, and the wage rates in all three economies are reduced. The rate of interest rises and the global output rises. The per capita wealth levels and per capita consumption levels of the RG of the developed economy are increased; the per capita wealth level and per capita consumption level of the RG of the industrializing economy are slightly increased; the per capita wealth levels of all the other groups are reduced. The developed and industrializing economies' trade balances improve. The developing economy's trade balance deteriorates. The global output share of the developing economy rises and the other two economies' shares fall.

8.5 International trade with capital and technology[17]

Ricardo's doctrine of comparative costs presupposed that countries differed from one another in the productivity of labor in producing commodities. Although the Ricardian theory is not concerned with how technology itself may be affected by trade, the theory studies the consequence of technological differences between countries. Marshall was concerned with trade and increasing returns. Issues related to gains from trade and other social welfare were well raised even in the classical tradition. For instance, Marshall discussed terms of trade effects, arguing that with increasing returns to scale a country may improve its terms of trade by expanding demand for its imports.

364 Economic Growth with Income and Wealth Distribution

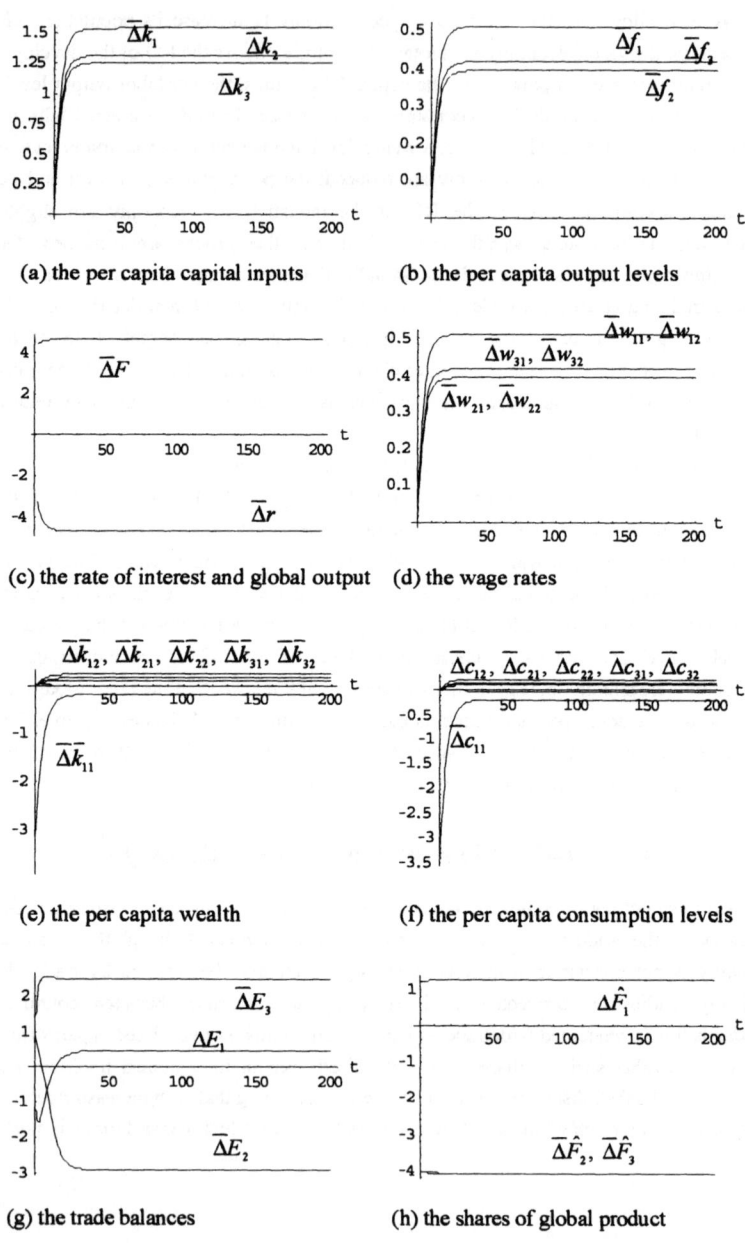

(a) the per capita capital inputs

(b) the per capita output levels

(c) the rate of interest and global output

(d) the wage rates

(e) the per capita wealth

(f) the per capita consumption levels

(g) the trade balances

(h) the shares of global product

Figure 8.4.9 Group $(1,1)$'s population is increased ($N_{11}: 2 \Rightarrow 2.2$)

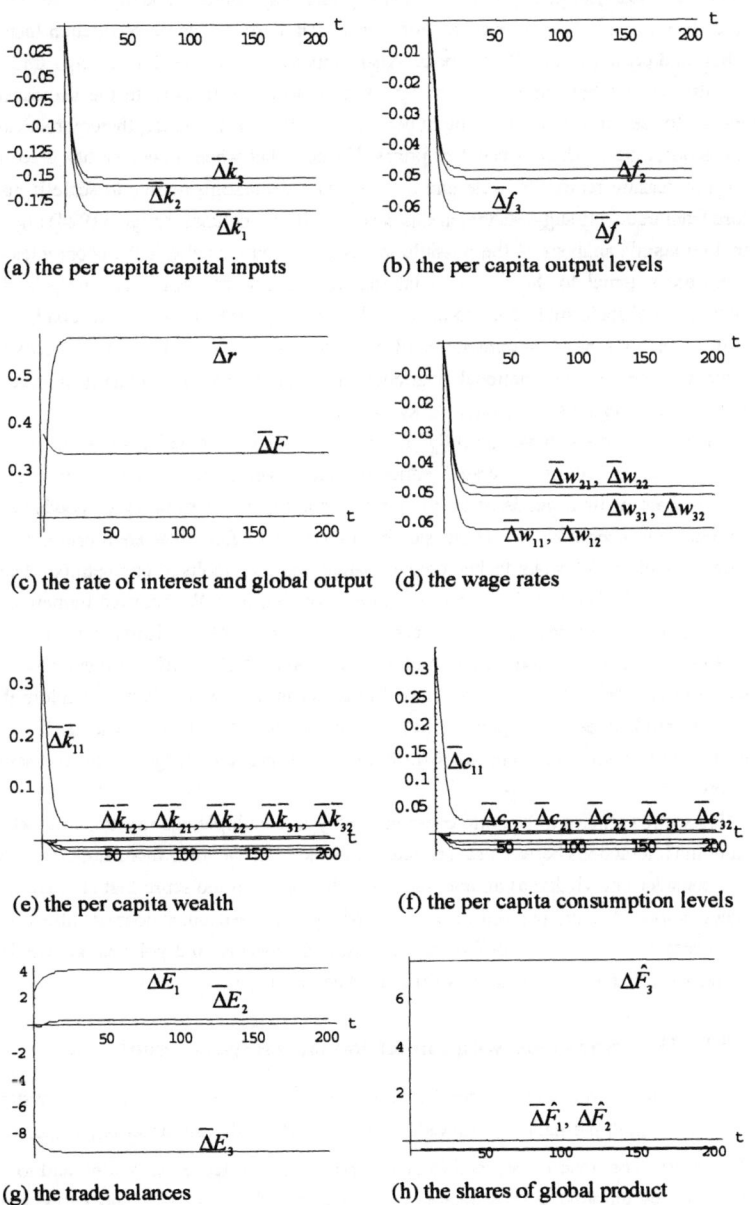

Figure 8.4.10 Group $(3, 2)$'s population is increased ($N_{32} : 20 \Rightarrow 22$)

Graham (1923) argues that economies of scale may cause a country to lose from trade. For instance, consider an economy in which there is a single production factor, labor, and equal prices of both goods. Also suppose that as a result of foreign trade a country shifts labor from the increasing returns to scale industry to the decreasing returns to scale industry. Then output per man falls in both industries, thereby reducing gross domestic product at constant prices. He held that when a country has a sector with increasing returns to scale and a sector with decreasing returns to scale it may lose from trade. He suggests that in this case a tariff is beneficial. Knight (1924) argues that Graham's analysis of the possible losses from trade is valid if the economies of scale are external to the firm and internal to the industry; but it is wrong if the economies of scale are internal to the firm. Ethier (1979, 1982) explores the conditions under which Graham's arguments hold: they depend on the nature of the increasing returns which are either national or international and the pattern of change in relative prices due to the transition from autarky to trade.

Trade economists have recently developed different trade models in which endogenous growth is generated either by the development of new varieties of intermediate or final goods or by the improvement of an existing set of goods with endogenous technologies. These studies attempted to formalize equilibrium trade patterns with endogenous technological change and monopolistic competition. They often link trade theory with increasing-returns growth theory. Within such frameworks the dynamic interdependence between trade patterns, R&D efforts, and various economic policies are connected. With the development of models with endogenous long-run growth, economists now have formal techniques with which to explore the relationship between trade policy and long-run growth either with knowledge or with capital, but in most of them not with both capital and knowledge within the same framework.

This section studies a dynamic one-commodity and multiple-country trade model to examine interactions between saving rates, trade, knowledge utilization, and creativity. We consider knowledge as an international public good in the sense that all countries access knowledge and the utilization of knowledge by one country does not affect that by others. Due to cultural differences, educational systems, and policies, knowledge utilization efficiency and creativity differ between countries.

8.5.1 The trade model with capital and knowledge accumulation

The economic production is similar to that in the previous chapters. The system consists of multiple nations, indexed by $j = 1, ..., J$. Only one good is produced in the system. The good is assumed to be composed of homogeneous quality, and to be produced by employing three factors of production – labor, capital, and knowledge. Market conditions are similar to those in the trade models in Chapters 2–4. Each country has a fixed labor force, N_j, $j = 1, \cdots, J$. Let prices be measured in terms of the commodity and the price of the commodity be unity. We denote by $w_j(t)$ and $r_j(t)$ respectively the wage and interest rate in the jth country. In the free trade system, the interest rate is equal in all countries

$$r(t) = r_j(t), \quad j = 1, \cdots, J.$$

We specify the production functions as follows:

$$F_j(t) = Z^{m_j}(K_j + E_j)^\alpha N_j^\beta, \quad \alpha + \beta = 1, \quad \alpha, \beta > 0, \quad m_j \geq 0, \quad j = 1, ..., J,$$
(8.5.1)

in which $Z \, (> 0)$ is the world knowledge stock at time t, $K_j(t)$ are the capital stocks owned by country j, and $E_j(t) > (<) \, 0$ are foreign capital stocks (home capital stocks located abroad). Here, we call m_j country j's knowledge utilization efficiency parameter. If we interpret $Z^{m_j/\beta} N_j$ as country j's human capital or qualified labor force, we see that the production function is a neoclassical one and homogeneous of degree one with the inputs. As cultures, political systems and educational and training systems vary between countries, m_j are different. Equation (8.5.1) implies that if the labor force and capital stocks employed by two countries are identical, then the difference in output between the two countries is only determined by the difference between their knowledge utilization efficiency.

According to the definitions of E_j, we have

$$\sum_{j=1}^{J} E_j = 0.$$
(8.5.2)

The marginal conditions are given by

$$r_j + \delta_k = \frac{\alpha F_j}{K_j + E_j}, \quad w_j = \frac{\beta F_j}{N_j},$$

where δ_k is the depreciation rate of capital. For simplicity, we assume that the savings rate, s_j, $j = 1, ..., J$, is constant. The capital accumulation of country j is given by

368 Economic Growth with Income and Wealth Distribution

$$\dot{K}_j = s_j F_j - \delta_k K_j. \tag{8.5.3}$$

We propose the following possible dynamics of knowledge

$$\dot{Z} = \sum_{j=1}^{J} \frac{\tau_j F_j}{Z^{\varepsilon_j}} - \delta_z Z, \tag{8.5.4}$$

in which τ_j (≥ 0) and ε_j ($j = 1, ..., J$), and δ_z (≥ 0) are parameters. We have thus built the model which explains the endogenous accumulation of capital and knowledge and the international distribution of capital under the assumptions of perfect competition and international immobility of the labor force. We now examine the properties of the system.

8.5.2 The dynamics of the trade system

We now show that the dynamics of the trade system can be represented by two different equations of the world capital and knowledge. From equation (8.5.2), we have

$$\frac{(K_1 + E_1)N_j}{(K_j + E_j)N_1} = Z^{-q_j}, \quad j = 2, ..., J, \tag{8.5.5}$$

where

$$q_j \equiv \frac{m_j - m_1}{\beta}.$$

Substituting equations (8.5.5) into equations (8.5.1) yields

$$F_j = n_j Z^{q_j} F_1, \quad j = 2, ..., J, \tag{8.5.6}$$

in which $n_j \equiv N_j / N_1$. From equations (8.5.5), we directly obtain the following lemma.

Lemma 8.5.1

At any point in time, the ratio of the capital stocks employed per capita and that of the incomes between any two countries in the trade system are determined only by the difference in the knowledge utilization efficiency parameters between the two countries.

Define the world capital stock by $K = \sum_j K_j$. Utilizing $\sum_j E_j = 0$ and equation (8.5.5), we have

$$K_1 + E_1 = K - \sum_{j \neq 1}(K_j + E_j) = K - (K_1 + E_1)\left(\frac{H_0}{N_1} - 1\right), \quad (8.5.7)$$

where

$$H_0 \equiv \sum_{j \neq 1} N_j Z^{q_j}. \quad (8.5.8)$$

From equations (8.5.1), (8.5.5), and (8.5.7), we have

$$K_1 + E_1 = \frac{N_1 K}{H_0}, \quad F_1 = N_1 Z^{m_1}\left(\frac{K}{H_0}\right)^\alpha. \quad (8.5.9)$$

From equations (8.5.5), (8.5.6) and (8.5.9), we can explicitly express $K_j + E_j$ and F_j as functions of K and Z. Hence, we can rewrite dynamics (8.5.3) and (8.5.4) in terms of K and Z as follows:

$$\dot{K} = H_k(Z)K^\alpha - \delta_k K,$$
$$\dot{Z} = H_z(Z)K^\alpha - \delta_z Z,$$

where

$$H_k(Z) \equiv \frac{\sum_j s_j N_j Z^{q_j}}{H_0^\alpha} Z^{m_1}, \quad H_z(Z) \equiv \frac{\sum_j H_j(Z)}{H_0^\alpha},$$

$$H_j \equiv \tau_j N_j Z^{q_j + m_1 - \varepsilon_j}, \quad j = 1, ..., J.$$

Equilibrium of the system is determined by

$$K = \left(\frac{H_k}{\delta_k}\right)^{1/\beta}, \quad H_{\scriptscriptstyle=}(Z)K^{\alpha} = \delta_{\scriptscriptstyle=}Z. \tag{8.5.10}$$

Substituting K in equations (8.5.10) into the right-hand side equation in equations (8.5.10), we see that the equilibrium problem is to find a positive Z such that

$$\Phi(Z) \equiv \left(\frac{H_k}{\delta_k}\right)^{\alpha/\beta} \frac{H_{\scriptscriptstyle=}}{Z} - \delta_{\scriptscriptstyle=} = \Phi_0(Z)\sum_j \Phi_j(Z) - \delta_{\scriptscriptstyle=} = 0, \tag{8.5.11}$$

in which

$$\Phi_0(Z) \equiv \left(\frac{\sum_j s_j \phi_j(Z)}{\sum_j \phi_j(Z)}\right)^{\alpha/\beta}, \quad \phi_j(Z) \equiv N_j Z^{m_j/\beta},$$

$$\Phi_j(Z) \equiv \left(\frac{1}{\delta}\right)^{\alpha/\beta} \tau_j N_j Z^{x_j}, \quad x_j \equiv \frac{m_j}{\beta} - \varepsilon_j - 1, \quad j = 1, \cdots, J. \tag{8.5.12}$$

As m_j is country j's knowledge utilization efficiency and ε_j is country j's returns to scale effect of knowledge in knowledge accumulation, we may interpret x_j as measurement of return to scale effect of knowledge in the whole system. We may thus make the following interpretations of the parameters. We say that country j's knowledge utilization and creation exhibit increasing (decreasing) returns to scale effect in the dynamic system when $x_j > (<) 0$.

When $x_j = 0$ for all j, we have $\Phi_0(Z) = \delta_{\scriptscriptstyle=}$, i.e.

$$\sum_j (s_j - \delta_{\scriptscriptstyle=}^{\beta/\alpha}) \phi_j(Z) = 0.$$

As $\phi_j > 0$, $\Phi(Z) = 0$ has infinite positive solutions in the case of $s_j = \delta_{\scriptscriptstyle=}^{\beta/\alpha}$ for all j. If $s_j > \delta_{\scriptscriptstyle=}^{\beta/\alpha}$ for all j or $s_j < \delta_{\scriptscriptstyle=}^{\beta/\alpha}$ for all j, it has no solution. If $s_j < \delta_{\scriptscriptstyle=}^{\beta/\alpha}$ for some of j and $s_j > \delta_{\scriptscriptstyle=}^{\beta/\alpha}$ for the others, then it may have solutions. In the remainder of this section, we omit the case of $x_j = 0$ for all j.

We can check directly that when $x_j > (<) 0$ for all j, $\Phi(Z) = 0$ has at least one solution. To check the uniqueness, we take derivatives of equation (8.5.11) with respect to Z:

$$\frac{Z}{\Phi_0}\Phi' = \sum_j x_j \Phi_j + \alpha_0(Z) \sum_{j=1}^{J-1} \sum_{k>j}^{J} M_{jk} \phi_k(Z) \phi_j(Z), \tag{8.5.13}$$

where Φ' is the derivative of Φ with respect to Z and

$$\alpha_0(Z) \equiv \left(\frac{\sum_j \Phi_j(Z)}{\sum_j s_j \phi_j(Z) \sum_j \phi_j(Z)} \right) \frac{\alpha}{\beta^2} > 0, \quad M_{jk} \equiv (m_k - m_j)(s_j - s_k). \tag{8.5.14}$$

From equation (8.5.13), we see that when $x_j < (>) 0$ and $M_{jk} < (>) 0$ for all j and k ($j = 1, ..., J - 1$, $k = j + 1, ..., J$), then $\Phi'(Z) < (>) 0$ for all positive $Z > 0$. Accordingly, we conclude that when $x_j < (>) 0$ and $M_{jk} < (>) 0$ for all j and k, there is a unique equilibrium point. If $M_{jk} < 0$ for some of j and k and $M_{jk} > 0$ for the other j and k, then Φ' may be either positive or negative, i.e. $\Phi(Z) = 0$ may have multiple solutions.

When $x_j < 0$ for some j and $x_j > 0$ for the other j, $\Phi(Z) > 0$ and $\Phi(\infty) > 0$. Accordingly, a necessary and sufficient condition for the existence of equilibrium points is that there exists a positive number Z_0 such that $\Phi(Z_0) \leq 0$. Moreover, if $\Phi(Z_0) < 0$, the system must have multiple equilibrium points. When the trade system has multiple equilibrium points, we cannot compare the trade system with the autarky system. Hence, the remainder of this study limits our discussion to those cases in which the system has a unique equilibrium.

Proposition 8.5.1
In the free trade system, we have: (i) when $x_j < 0$ for all j and $M_{jk} \leq 0$ for all j ($= 1, ..., J - 1$) and all k ($j < k \leq J$), the system has a unique stable equilibrium point; and (ii) when $x_j > 0$ for all j and $M_{jk} \geq 0$ for all j ($= 1, ..., J - 1$) and all k ($j < k \leq J$), the system has a unique unstable equilibrium point.

We may check the stability conditions by directly calculating the eigenvalues. We have just interpreted conditions $x_j > 0$ or $x_j < 0$. The conditions $(m_k - m_j)(s_j - s_k) < (>) 0$ simply mean that when country j's saving rate is higher than that in country k, country j's knowledge utilization efficiency is higher (lower) than that of country k. Hence, the above proposition can be interpreted as follows: (i) if all the countries' knowledge utilization efficiencies are low, all the countries exhibit decreasing returns, and the difference in the savings rates between any two countries has the same sign as that in the knowledge utilization efficiency parameters between the two countries, then the system has a unique stable equilibrium point; (ii) if the countries' knowledge utilization efficiency is high, all the countries exhibit increasing returns, and the difference in the savings rates between any two countries has the opposite sign to that in the knowledge utilization efficiency parameters between the two countries, then the system has a unique unstable equilibrium point.

It is should be mentioned that the requirements in Proposition 8.5.1 are strict. If we relax any of them, then the system may have multiple equilibrium points.

8.5.3 The global economy in the autarky system

In order to explain the impact of free trade, we examine an international system in which people have freedom in exchange of ideas, but there is neither trade nor migration among countries. That is, $E_j = 0$ for all j and r_j are not globally identical. The $(n+1)$-dimensional dynamics are defined by equations (8.5.3) and (8.5.4). Equilibrium is defined by

$$K_j^* = \left(\frac{s_j}{\delta_k}\right)^{1/\beta} N_j Z^{*m_j/\beta} = \frac{s_j^{\alpha/\beta} \phi_j(Z^*)}{\delta_k^{1/\beta}},$$

$$\Phi^*(Z^*) \equiv \sum_j s_j^{\alpha/\beta} \Phi_j(Z^*) - \delta_z = 0, \qquad (8.5.15)$$

in which Φ_j and x_j are defined in equations (8.5.12). In the remainder of this section, superscript * stands for values of variables or functions in the autarky system.

Our task is to find whether $\Phi^* = 0$ has a positive solution. We may directly check that if $x_j \geq 0$ for all j (i.e. $\Phi^*(0) < 0$, $\Phi^*(\infty) > 0$, and $\Phi^{*'}(Z^*) > 0$ for $Z^* > 0$) or $x_j \leq 0$ for all j (i.e. $\Phi^*(0) > 0$, $\Phi^*(\infty) < 0$, and $\Phi^{*'}(Z^*) < 0$ for $Z^* > 0$), the system has a unique positive equilibrium point. For any of the remaining $2^J - 2$ combinations of $x_j > 0$ or $x_j < 0$ for all j, the system has either two equilibrium points or none. We prove the case of $x_1 > 0$ and $x_j < 0$, $j = 2, \cdots, J$. The other cases can be checked in the same way. Since $x_1 > 0$, $x_j < 0$, $\Phi^*(0) > 0$ and $\Phi^*(\infty) > 0$. This means that $\Phi^* = 0$ has either no solution or multiple solutions. As

$$Z^* \Phi^{*\prime} = \sum_j x_j \Phi_j,$$

$\Phi^{*\prime}$ may be either positive or negative, depending upon the parameter values. If $\Phi^* = 0$ has more than two solutions, there are at least two values of Z^* such that $\Phi^* = 0$. Since $d(Z^* \Phi^{*\prime})/dZ^* > 0$ holds for $Z^* > 0$, it is impossible for $\Phi^* = 0$ to have multiple solutions. The necessary and sufficient condition for the existence of two equilibrium points is that there exists a value of Z_0^* such that $\Phi^*(Z_0^*) < 0$.

Proposition 8.5.2
We omit the case of $x_j = 0$ for all j.
If $x_j \leq 0$ for all j, then there is a unique equilibrium.
If $x_j \geq 0$ for all j, then there is a unique equilibrium.
For any of the remaining ($2^J - 2$) combinations of $x_j > 0$ or $x_j < 0$ for all j, the system has either two equilibrium points or none.

It is important to note that if the conditions for the existence of a unique equilibrium point for the trade system are satisfied, then the autarky system has a unique equilibrium point, too. Hence, we can compare the equilibrium points in the two systems. We do not determine the stability conditions for the general case, though we can prove the case of $J = 2$. It can be easily checked that in the case of $J = 2$, (i) if $x_j < 0$, $j = 1, 2$, the unique equilibrium point is stable; (ii) if $x_j > 0$, $j = 1, 2$, the unique equilibrium point is unstable; and (iii) if $x_1 < 0$ and $x_2 > 0$ ($x_1 > 0$ and $x_2 < 0$), the equilibrium point with higher values of K and Z is unstable, and the other one is stable.

8.5.4 Comparing the autarky and trade systems

This section examines the following two cases (a) when $x_j < 0$ and $M_{jk} \leq 0$ and (b) $x_j > 0$ and $M_{jk} \geq 0$ for all $j (= 1, \cdots, I-1)$ and all k ($j < k \leq J$), in which the

374 *Economic Growth with Income and Wealth Distribution*

two economic systems have a unique equilibrium point. From equations (8.5.11) and (8.5.15), we have

$$\left(\frac{\sum_j s_j \phi_j(Z)}{\sum_j \phi_j(Z)}\right)^{\alpha/\beta} \sum_j \Phi_j(Z) = \sum_j s_j^{\alpha/\beta} \Phi_j(Z^*), \qquad (8.5.16)$$

in which Z^* and Z are the equilibrium values of the autarky and trade systems, respectively and ϕ_j are positive functions of Z. From (8.5.16), we see that it is not easy to generally determine whether $Z > Z^*$ or $Z < Z^*$. But we may consider a special case in which τ_1 is large and τ_j ($j = 2, \cdots, J$) are small (e.g. $\tau_j = 0$). This implies that only country 1 makes an important contribution to world knowledge growth. The other countries may effectively utilize knowledge, but not make an important contribution to knowledge growth. Under this requirement, equation (8.5.16) can be approximately written as

$$\left(\frac{\sum_j s_j \phi_j(Z)}{\sum_j \phi_j(Z)}\right)^{\alpha/\beta} \Phi_1(Z) = s_1^{\alpha/\beta} \Phi_1(Z^*). \qquad (8.5.17)$$

We have

$$\Phi_1(Z) < \Phi_1(Z^*), \text{ if } s_1 = s_m,$$
$$\Phi_1(Z) > \Phi_1(Z^*), \text{ if } s_1 = s_M, \qquad (8.5.18)$$

where

$$s_m \equiv \min\{s_j, j = 1, \cdots, J\}, \quad s_M \equiv \max\{s_j, j = 1, ..., J\}.$$

By the definition of Φ_1, equation (8.5.18) can be rewritten as follows:

$$Z^{x_1} < Z^{*x_1}, \text{ if } s_1 = s_m;$$
$$Z^{x_1} > Z^{*x_1}, \text{ if } s_1 = s_M.$$

We have the following conclusions:

(i) if $x_1 > 0$ and $s_1 = s_m$, then $Z < Z^*$;

(ii) if $x_1 > 0$ and $s_1 = s_M$, then $Z > Z^*$;

(iii) if $x_1 < 0$ and $s_1 = s_m$, then $Z > Z^*$; and

(iv) if $x_1 < 0$ and $s_1 = s_M$, then $Z < Z^*$.

We see that even in the extreme case that only one country makes an important contribution to knowledge growth, trade may either reduce or increase world knowledge in the long term, depending on the combinations of the saving rates and the knowledge utilization efficiency parameters.

By equations (8.5.10) and (8.5.15), we have

$$\frac{K}{K^*} = \frac{\left(\sum_j \phi_j\right)^{1/\beta}}{\left(\sum_j N_j Z^{*m_j/\beta}\right)^{\alpha/\beta} \sum_j s_j^{\alpha/\beta} \phi_j^*} < \frac{\sum_j \phi_j}{\sum_j s_j^{\alpha/\beta} \phi_j^*},$$

in which ϕ_j^* is the value of $\phi_j(Z)$ evaluated at Z^* and $K^* (= \sum_j K_j^*)$ is the world capital stock in the autarky system. Hence, if

$$\frac{Z}{Z^*} = s_j^{\alpha/m_j} < 1, \text{ for all } j, \qquad (8.5.19)$$

then $K/K^* < 1$. That is, when trade greatly reduces the knowledge stock, then the world capital stock is reduced in the long term. It can be seen that equation (8.5.19) may be valid only in cases (i) and (ii) when $Z < Z^*$. In cases (ii) and (iii), it is much too difficult to explicitly judge the impact of trade upon capital accumulation.

From equations (8.5.6), (8.5.10), and (8.5.15), the impact upon the income of the jth country is given by

$$\frac{F_j}{F_j^*} = \left(\frac{Z}{Z^*}\right)^{m_j/\beta} \frac{\left(\sum_k s_k^{\alpha/\beta} \phi_k^* / s_j\right)^{\alpha/\beta}}{\sum_k \phi_k}.$$

We see that F_j / F_j^* is determined by combinations of the saving rates and the knowledge utilization efficiency parameters. In particular, when $x_1 < 0$ and $s_1 = s_M$, $F_1 < F_1^*$, where we use

376 *Economic Growth with Income and Wealth Distribution*

$$\frac{Z}{Z^*} < 1, \quad \left(\sum_k \frac{s_k^{\alpha/\beta} \phi_k}{s_1} \right)^{\alpha/\beta} < \sum_k \phi_k.$$

It is difficult to make general judgments about the impact of trade upon the income distribution between countries. We will not interpret the above conclusions in detail as the conditions are clearly given by different combinations of the saving rates, s_j, and the knowledge utilization efficiency parameters m_j.

8.6 On trade and income and wealth distribution

It can be seen that the OSG framework provides a useful framework for analyzing different issues related to growth, trade, and distribution. It is possible to introduce the ideas about multiple sectors, heterogeneous groups, multiple regions in each country, research, education, and human capital proposed in the previous chapters into the trade models in this chapter. One important issue is not addressed in this book. This is related to unemployment. As this book is concentrating on long-run mechanisms of growth and distribution, we simplify monetary and labor markets.

The impact of increasing returns to scale on international trade has been one of the main topics in international trade theory. A host of trade problems such as trade patterns, gains from trade, commercial policy, transaction corporations, and direct foreign investment have been examined within economic systems with increasing returns. Increasing returns to scale are a characteristic feature of many economic activities. It may come from population dynamics, knowledge creation and utilization, and institutional changes. But the history of economic analysis shows that it is not an easy matter to formally model nonconstant return to scales within a competitive framework. In fact most of formal theories are developed under the assumption of constant returns to scale. The assumption that technology exhibits constant returns to scale had been accepted in most general equilibrium models. Some years ago Chipman (1965b) pointed out two reasons for this omission. The first is that economies of scale tend to be ignored in theoretical models not so much on empirical grounds as for the simple reason that it is difficult to build a trade theory with increasing returns. This is indeed a poor reason; but no theoretical trade economist could avoid being criticized for neglecting one of the principal sources of international trade simply for this reason. The second reason given by Chipman is that the presence of increasing returns in production leads to multiple equilibrium points. The existence of multiple trade patterns introduces an intrinsic arbitrariness into the determination of the international pattern of specification and trade. It is known that if there are equilibrium points, comparative static analysis becomes invalid. It should be noted that trade economists have proposed many theoretical trade models with increasing returns.

They have overcome the theoretical difficulties involved in building such models and they have recently accepted the existence of multiple equilibria and instability as economists naturally accepted the existence of a unique equilibrium and stability in the 1960s and 1970s.

Economists recognized a long time ago that economies of scale provide an alternative to differences in technology or factor endowments as an explanation of international trade. But increasing returns as a cause of trade have received relatively little attention from formal trade theory. Ohlin (1933) points out that economies of scale serve as one explanation of foreign trade patterns. Since then, many trade theorists emphasize the role of monopolistic competition in differentiated products. In particular, there exist early attempts to extend trade theory on the basis of Chamberlin's *Monopolistic Competition* (Chamberlin, 1933). Explicit general-equilibrium analysis of trade based on external economies was initiated with Matthews (1949). Kemp and Negishi (1970) made an important contribution to the literature, showing that gains from trade are guaranteed if free trade leads to an expansion (noncontraction) of all increasing returns industries and nonexpansion of all decreasing returns industries. Eaton and Panagariya (1979) refine the Kemp-Negishi result. They proved that there are gains from trade as long as there exists an industry such that all industries with stronger degree of increasing returns (to weaker decreasing returns) do not contract in the move to free trade, and all industries with weaker increasing returns (or stronger decreasing returns) do not expand. In order to take account of the relative importance of increases and decreases in the increasing returns to scale sectors, Markusen and Melvin (1984) define a weighted average rule which applies under the assumption of a convex production possibilities frontier and the absence of factor market distortions. But this rule is not valid when increasing returns lead to nonconvex production possibilities. Helpman and Krugman (1985) provide a rule that applies if aggregate factor usage is fixed between equilibrium points. Grinols (1992) develops a rule which applies to more general cases and does not require a convex production possibility frontier or fixed factor usage between equilibrium points. He develops a sufficient condition for gains from trade when some increasing returns industries expand and others contract. His conclusions do not depend on the restrictions that the production frontier must be convex, changes must satisfy a pre-specified hierarchical pattern, or that total factor supplies must be fixed between equilibrium points. Krugman (1989, 1990) develops a trade model with a single scarce factor of production, labor, on the basis of the assumptions that scale economies are internal to firms and the market structure is one of Chamberlian monopolistic competition. His treatment of monopolistic competition is influenced by the model by Dixit and Stiglitz (1977). He produces trade between identical economies where comparative advantage is not the cause of trade, whether that comparative advantage comes from Ricardian or Heckscher-Ohlin factors. It is shown that trade may be a way of extending the market and allowing exploitation of scarce economies, with the effects of trade being similar to industrial, urban, or regional agglomeration. This trade model is better suited to explain intraindustry trade (i.e. trade in similar products) between advanced countries.

Much of the early attention in the literature of modeling two-way trade with increasing returns was placed on trade at the final product level, rather than trade in intermediate products. Ethier (1979, 1982) emphasizes that returns to specification and two-way trade in intermediate products imply external returns to scale that spill over between economies. It is argued that the spillover effects associated with international scale economies are an immediate result of the global and regional integration of industries subject to external static or dynamic scale effects. In Francois (1994),[18] a dual model of trade under international returns economies is developed and applied to examine foreign investment, labor migration, and commercial policy. It is demonstrated that spillover effects associated with international scale economies are an immediate result of global and regional integration of industries, and have important implications for commercial policy. As far as economic modeling is concerned, the models with increasing returns mentioned above were limited to static frameworks. These works did not provide much indication as to what are the dynamic effects of international trade on growth, technological progress, and welfare.

It is not an easy matter to mathematically model dynamics of trade with increasing returns. Theoretical economists engaged in trade theory did not show any possibility of formally explaining international trade based on increasing returns in a comprehensive framework. In fact, one of the main obstacles to formally model economies with nonconstant returns is the problem of market structure. It is generally believed that increasing returns are inconsistent with perfect competition. Faced with increasing significance of endogenous technological changes in affecting trading patterns among economists, economists have recently produced the new trade theory. This theory produces many clear and simple mathematical models and provides insights into international trade based on increasing returns. These models explain trade in the presence of increasing returns and imperfect competition. The new trade theory is influenced by the developments in the theory of growth with endogenous knowledge and industrial organization. It highlights the roles of knowledge accumulation and international dissemination in explaining how trade structure and trade policy affect rates of growth. Specification and rationalization at the immediate product level, along with related effects of trade, market integration, learning by doing, technical innovation, and other external returns have recently emerged as central issues in the theory.

The new trade theory with endogenous knowledge has two main differences from the traditional trade theory. The first is that it is developed mainly under the assumption of imperfect competition. Although the significance of imperfect competition for the pure theory of international trade has been recognized and there are a number of macroeconomic models with imperfect competition as a crucial feature,[19] most of these models are developed within a static framework with fixed factors of production. As in the Dixit-Stiglitz model, many of these trade models assume monopolistic competition in which each good is produced by a separate firm and labor is the only factor of production. The second main difference between the traditional trade theory and the new trade theory is that most of the formal models in the new trade theory omit explicit treatment of physical capital. This lack of endogenous physical capital is not due to the fact that new trade theorists do not recognize the significance of physical accumulation. We mentioned that one of the reasons that traditional trade theorists did not make formal modeling of trade based on increasing returns is that they did not have some analytical frameworks to formally examine issues. It is for a similar reason that trade in the presence of possible physical capital accumulation is not formally examined in the formal modeling of the new trade theory with endogenous knowledge. If endogenous physical capital accumulation is introduced into trade models in the new trade theory, it will be difficult to make models tractable.

There are some models which deal with technology transfer via direct foreign investment in the theoretical literature on growth and international capital movements.[20] For instance, Findlay (1978) builds an international growth model under the assumption about technology transfer that the rate of technological change in a less developed country will be an increasing function of the amount of foreign capital operating in the less developed country and the extent to which the technology in the advanced country exceeds that in the less developed one. Wang (1990) proposes a dynamic two-country model to examine the interactions among growth, technological change, and international capital movements. It includes capital accumulation and treats human capital as a country-specific variable. Perfect capital mobility links the two countries and human capital plays an important role in determining the effective rate of return for physical capital and affects the direction and magnitude of international capital movements. Rivera-Batiz and Romer (1991) develop a dynamic model with specification driven by R&D. Their model examines the effects of economic integration on economic growth rates. It demonstrates that to the extent that economic integration and other commercial policy changes increase the global resource or activity base over which external economies are generated, such integration may induce globally positive level and growth effects. Matsuyama (1991b) develops a dynamic model to examine economic development under external economies and learning-by-doing effects. It is shown that free trade may lower the growth rate of low-income countries while accelerating the rate for high-income countries. These dynamic models exhibit instabilities and multiple equilibrium points. Hence, history as reflected in initial factor allocations, technology choices, and sectoral efficiency may be critical to global economic development.

Another important topic we did not discuss is the political economy of trade policy. In a democratic society, there are pressure groups for or against some form of trade protection through lobbying efforts. As a country's population is heterogeneous in terms of factor ownership, trade policy changes may have asymmetric effects on individual households and/or nations and generate asymmetric pressure on policy. In political competition, candidates may seek to win elections by standing for certain trade policies. Many models have been proposed for studying interactions among trade and politics.[21] For instance, Das (2001) analyzes the political economy of trade in the context of a small open economy. In this approach, trade policy is set according to the median voter's preference. In the long run, both trade policy and distribution of wealth and income are endogenous. Like many dynamic trade models, the assumption of a small open economy is strict. It is possible to introduce the ideas of this approach into our analytical framework in which interplays of multiple countries and multiple groups within each economy can be analyzed. Dynamic game theory may be involved in analyzing these issues. It is also important to take account of trade costs when examining trade patterns and income and wealth distribution. For instance, Anderson and Wincoop (2004) show that total trade costs in rich countries are large. The ad valorem tax equivalent may be about 170 percent. Poor countries face even higher trade costs. There is a lot of variation across countries and across goods within countries. Yang and Maskus (2001) deal with the role of intellectual property rights (IPRs) in encouraging firms in developed countries to innovate and in helping developing countries gain access to knowledge on the global frontier. Their model analyzes the effects of Southern IPRs on incentives of Northern firms to innovate and to license state-of-the-art technologies to the South.[22]

Appendix

A.8.1 Equilibrium and stability conditions in the two-country economy

The appendix provides the conditions for the existence of a unique equilibrium and for stability of the two-country free trade system. Taking derivatives of the function $\Phi^*(\Lambda)$ with respect to Λ yields

$$\Phi^{*\prime} = -\frac{\beta_1 \phi_1'}{\phi_1^2} + \frac{(\theta-1)\beta_2 \upsilon \Lambda^{\theta-2}}{\phi_2} - \frac{\beta_2 \upsilon \Lambda^{\theta-1} \phi_2'}{\phi_2^2} - (\theta-1)\upsilon \Lambda^{\theta-2}, \qquad \text{(A.8.1.1)}$$

in which

$$\phi_1' = \frac{\beta_1 \delta_1 \Lambda^{\beta_1-1}}{\lambda_1 N_1^{\beta_1}} > 0, \quad \phi_1' \equiv \frac{\beta_2 \delta_2 \upsilon^{\beta_2} \Lambda^{\beta_1-1}}{\lambda_2 N_2^{\beta_2}} > 0. \qquad \text{(A.8.1.2)}$$

If $\Phi'' < 0$ for any $\Lambda > \Lambda_0$, then $\Phi^* = 0$ has a unique solution. From equation (A.8.1.1), we see that in the case of $\theta = 1$, the system has a unique equilibrium. If $\Phi'' > 0$, the equation may have multiple solutions.

Using $\phi_2 = \Lambda \phi_2' / \beta_2 - \alpha_2$ and $\theta = \beta_1 / \beta_2$, we have

$$\Phi^{*\prime} = -\frac{\beta_1 \phi_1'}{\phi_1^2} + \frac{\theta - 1 + (\beta_2 - \beta_1)\Lambda\phi_2' - \beta_2\Lambda\phi_2'/\phi_2}{\phi_2} v\Lambda^{\theta-2}. \qquad (A.8.1.3)$$

From this equation, we see that if $\beta_2 - \beta_1 < \beta_2 / \phi_2$, then $\Phi'' < 0$. This implies that if the equation has any solution in the domain (Λ_0, Λ_2), then $\Phi^* = 0$ has a unique solution in the domain. But if the inequality is not held, $\Phi^{*\prime}$ may be positive.

We now examine the stability of the equilibrium points. From equations (5.3.11) and (5.3.12), we calculate

$$\frac{\partial Y_1}{\partial K_1} = \frac{\alpha_1 + \beta_1 \Lambda'}{\alpha_1 K_1 + \beta_1 \Lambda} g_1 - \frac{\beta_1 \Lambda'}{\Lambda} g_1,$$

$$\frac{\partial Y_2}{\partial K_2} = \frac{1 - \beta_2 \Lambda'}{\alpha_2 K_2 + \beta_2 K - \beta_2 \Lambda} g_2 - \frac{\beta_2(1 - \Lambda')}{K - \Lambda} g_2,$$

$$\frac{\partial Y_1}{\partial K_2} = \frac{\partial Y_1}{\partial K_1} - \frac{\alpha_1 g_1}{\alpha_1 K_1 + \beta_1 \Lambda},$$

$$\frac{\partial Y_2}{\partial K_1} = \frac{\partial Y_2}{\partial K_2} - \frac{\alpha_2 g_2}{\alpha_2 K_2 + \beta_2 K - \beta_2 \Lambda}, \qquad (A.8.1.4)$$

in which $\Lambda' \equiv d\Lambda / dK$. From $\Lambda + v\Lambda^\theta = K$, we see that $\Lambda' < 1$. Two eigenvalues, f_1 and f_2, are given by

$$f_{1,2} = \frac{\eta_1}{2} \pm \eta_2^{1/2}, \qquad (A.8.1.5)$$

where

$$\eta_1 \equiv \lambda_1 \frac{\partial Y_1}{\partial K_1} + \lambda_2 \frac{\partial Y_2}{\partial K_2} - \delta_1 - \delta_2,$$

$$\eta_2 \equiv \frac{\eta_1^2}{4} + \lambda_1 \lambda_2 \frac{\partial Y_1}{\partial K_2} \frac{\partial Y_2}{\partial K_1}. \qquad (A.8.1.6)$$

If $\eta_1 < 0$ and $4\eta_2 \leq \eta_1^2$, then the equilibrium point is stable. By equations (A.8.1.4) and (A.8.1.5), we have

$$\lambda_1 \frac{\partial Y_1}{\partial K_1} - \delta_1 = \frac{\alpha_1 \Lambda' K_1 (\Lambda - K_1) - \Lambda^2}{(\alpha_1 K_1 + \beta_1 \Lambda) K_1 \Lambda} \lambda_1 \beta_1 g_1,$$

$$\lambda_2 \frac{\partial Y_2}{\partial K_2} - \delta_2 = \beta_2 g_2 \lambda_2 \frac{(K_2 - \Lambda' K_2 - K + \Lambda)(K - \Lambda) - (\alpha_2 K_2 + \beta_2 K - \beta_2 \Lambda)(1 - \Lambda') K_2}{(\alpha_2 K_2 + \beta_2 K - \beta_2 \Lambda)(K - \Lambda) K_2}. \quad (A.8.1.7)$$

As Λ and $\Lambda - K_1$ are, respectively, the capital stock and foreign capital employed by country 1, we see that it is reasonable to have

$$\alpha_1 \Lambda' K_1 (\Lambda - K_1) - \Lambda^2 > 0.$$

This implies $\lambda_1 \partial Y_1 / \partial K_1 - \delta_1 < 0$. Similarly, we may have $\lambda_2 \partial Y_2 / \partial K_2 - \delta_2 < 0$. Accordingly, it is acceptable to have $\eta_1 < 0$. The condition $4\eta_2 \leq \eta_1^2$ can be rewritten as follows:

$$\left(\frac{\partial Y_1}{\partial K_1} + \delta_k - \frac{\alpha_1 g_1}{\alpha_1 K_1 + \beta_1 \Lambda} \right)\left(\frac{\partial Y_2}{\partial K_2} + \delta_k - \frac{\alpha_2 g_2}{\alpha_2 K_2 + \beta_2 K - \beta_2 \Lambda} \right)$$

$$\leq \left(\frac{\partial Y_1}{\partial K_1} - \frac{\delta_1}{\lambda_1} \right)\left(\frac{\partial Y_2}{\partial K_2} - \frac{\delta_2}{\lambda_2} \right). \quad (A.8.1.8)$$

It is difficult to explicitly interpret this condition.

9
Endless Complexity

Economic growth with income and wealth distribution is a complex topic. It can be examined from many perspectives. The growth theory developed in this book addresses some important aspects of economic growth with income and wealth distribution, mainly under perfect competition, but neglects many others. For instance, population, resources and environment are essential determinants of economic growth. We almost omit them on purpose because a proper treatment of these factors would greatly lengthen the book. From the economic structural point of view, our theoretical framework includes some well-established economic systems such as the Arrow-Debreu equilibrium model, the Solow model, the Uzawa two-sector model, the Kaldor-Pasinetti two-group model, the Arrow learning-by-doing model, the Ricardian model by Pasinetti and Samuelson, and the Oniki-Uzawa trade model, as special cases. We can now treat different ideas in growth theory within a single theoretical framework. The usefulness of our framework lies not only in that it unifies some theories, but also in that it can explain, in a compact way, many economic phenomena which cannot be explained by the traditional theories.

This book covers a large area of economics with a few assumptions. Our main purpose is to construct a theoretical framework, which would permit valid generalizations from one special modeling structure to another, and would deepen our understanding of economic evolution as an organic whole. It is easy to extend and generalize most of the models in this book. This book actualizes a general vision about economic evolution. Our investigation is quite limited in scope if one considers obviously possible extensions of the framework proposed in this book and available modern analytical methods and the modern computer, as well as innovative ideas in different schools of economics. We now conclude this book, mentioning some possible extensions.

Democracy and distributional justice
It is a matter of fact that human beings are unequal in almost every way. They are different in shape, size, sex, genetic endowments, abilities, sense of humor, ear for

music, intelligence, social sensitivity, health, longevity, strength, athletic prowess, and so on. Nevertheless, it is a basic tenet of democracy that humans are of equal worth. This value should be reflected in the economic, social, and political structures of democratic society. In the minds of many, equality has come to be identified with justice and fairness. In *Politics* (Book V), Aristotle asks

> Now justice is recognized universally as some sort of equality. Justice involves assignment of things to persons. Equals are entitled to equal things. But here we are met by the important question: equal and unequal in what?

This is not an easy problem. In modern times, the economic reality of many democratic societies is characterized by inequality. Thoreau asserted[1]

> It is a mistake to suppose that, in a country where the usual evidences of civilisation exist, the condition of a very large body of the inhabitants may not be as degraded as that of savages. I refer to the degraded poor, not, now, to the degraded rich.

Modern democracy means political equality of all adult citizens within the regime: all people are equal as persons before the law, and each is possessed of the political rights, permissions, and duties. Everyone is a first-class citizen in a democracy. Nevertheless, democracy does not mean that all people must be socially and economically equal. Within democratic regimes, there are inequalities in wealth and power. It is often believed that even when democracy brings greater inequalities, it increases the absolute income of the poor. This study offers almost no discussion on issues of distributive justice. As defined by Roemer (1996: 1), the theory of distributive justice is about

> how a society or group should allocate its scarce resources or product among individuals with competing needs or claims.

The word "justice" actually can be used in a wide variety of ways, so that it tends to be interpreted with a great degree of latitude when referring to concrete phenomena. Modern (mainstream) economics has little to offer about the dynamics of inequalities and poverty. Roemer (1996: 3) says: "I do not, however, believe that the economist's way of thinking has produced, or will ever produce, important new insights into what distributive justice is. The key new concepts in the last thirty years in the theory of distributive justice – primary goods, functionings and capacity, responsibility in its various forms, procedural versus outcome justice, midfare – have all come from the philosophical way of thinking."[2] As analytical economics lacks proper dynamic frameworks for addressing distributive issues, it can be seen why modern economics does not make essential contributions to the theory of distributive justice. Nevertheless, given the knowledge stocks of classical philosophical thought, one might also wonder about any meaningful contributions from "the philosophical way of thinking" in modern times. It can be seen that as our analytical framework allows us to model growth and income and wealth distribution, it is possible that the economic theory proposed in this study may provide some new insights into interdependence between justice and distribution.

Scale effects of endogenous population
From the literature of classical economics we know at least four input factors which may exhibit increasing or decreasing returns to scale effects in economic dynamics: infrastructures (of transportation and communication systems), institutions, knowledge, and population. This book introduced endogenous knowledge and capital. Nevertheless, we did not discuss implications of population growth of heterogeneous households. For instance, it is not difficult to see that the impact of trade upon the long-run welfare of the world may be complicated in economic systems with endogenous population. If we allow the world population to be affected by economic conditions, trade between countries is perhaps economically harmful to the world in the long term under certain circumstances.

Networks and infrastructures
In order to take infrastructure structures for transportation and communication into account, it is necessary to explicitly take account of space. Channels, roads, railways, and airline systems, which may be effectively treated as parameters in short-term analyses, determine the mobility and the costs associated with movements of people and goods. In a long-term analysis, it is necessary to examine decision-making processes involved in construction and maintenance of infrastructures.

Knowledge and human capital
There are so many ways of knowledge creation and diffusion that no single book can provide a comprehensive study about interdependence of knowledge and economic dynamics. For instance, perhaps no theoretical model is proposed to connect research amenity (in comparison to other jobs' amenities) and international trade within a compact framework. If sophisticated research is "boring", a free society may not carry out sophisticated research when the research results have no immediate profitable markets. It is obvious that some professions are associated with more pleasures or less sufferings than others. People may get different levels of job amenity in doing science and working in a manufacturing factory. Wage rate is not a single factor that determines choice of profession. People may prefer a profession with low pay but high

job amenity level to one with high pay but low job amenity level. It seems that the role of job amenity in affecting professional choice and labor distribution has increasingly become important in post-industrial societies. As many economies are experiencing rapid improvement in living conditions and rapid changes of attitudes towards various kinds of jobs, professional choice has increasingly become complicated. It may be argued that how people feel about doing science will strongly affect labor distribution between research and production.

Variety of capital, people and natural resources
It is not difficult to relax the assumption of a single kind of capital. The introduction of multiple capital goods will cause analytical difficulties. It should be noted that the traditional neoclassical growth theory did not succeed in dealing with growth issues with multiple capital goods in the sense that consumer behavior was not properly modeled. Although we developed multi-group trade models, our classification of the labor force was simplified. Different kinds of labor force may enter production functions in different ways. We neglected issues related to natural resources and the environment. The issues related to trade, resources and capital accumulation should be further examined.

Preference structures
Utility functions may be in various forms. We may also introduce preference change. For instance, when we write a utility function in the form of

$$U(t) = C(t)^{\xi(t)} S(t)^{\lambda(t)},$$

we may introduce endogenous preference changes by allowing ξ and λ to be changeable in the long term.[3]

Government policy
Governments may intervene in economic systems in different ways. It is important to examine the impact of various government interventions on income and wealth distribution over time and space. For instance, economic issues related to regional integration and block formation are currently important in trade theory. Various possible taxes on imports and exports are important for analyzing trade flows and global economic growth. It is well known that tax structures also have important implications for growth and income and wealth distribution.

Unemployed production factors
We assumed that production factors such as labor force, capital, and land are always fully employed. These assumptions should be relaxed. In particular, one of the central

topics in growth theory is related to the dynamics of unemployment of the labor force. Many possible factors for unemployment have been proposed in the literature of economics.[4]

Conditions of capital mobility and people migration

We assumed that perfect competition of the international capital market makes the interest rates identical across the world economy. But due to factors such as transaction costs, risks, and institutions, rates of interest may not be equalized among nations. It is necessary to specify some principles of capital mobility among nations. How migration is endogenously determined is a complicated issue. There are many possibilities of migration patterns; some of them might be important in analyzing trade patterns. We may also introduce international tourism (i.e. the utilization of the service sectors by foreigners) into our modeling framework.

Dynamics of monetary variables

Except in one model, we assume that trade takes place in the form of barter; in other words, money is treated as a veil, which has no impact on the underlying variables but serves as a reference unit, the *numeraire*. This book is not concerned with important issues such as the balance-of-payments adjustment processes under fixed or varying exchange rates. This omission of monetary aspects does not mean that we consider it unimportant to integrate monetary economics with our approach. We assumed that monetary variables are fast in the sense that their values are determined by their marginal values at any point in time. In reality, monetary variables may seldom be adjusted so quickly. We may generally denote monetary dynamics in the following general form:

$$\dot{p} = \varepsilon G(p, K),$$

where p is a vector of monetary variables such as money, exchange rates, and prices of goods and ε is the adjustment speed vector. Different theories can be applied to specify functional forms of $G(p, K, Z)$.

Spatial structures and urbanization

This book does not deal with spatial economic structures. Although the author has made some preliminary but original contributions by applying the analytical framework proposed in this study, further extensions should be carried out. Again, our analytical framework enables us to deal with many dynamic issues of spatial economies, which cannot be effectively examined by the Ramsey and Solow approaches.

388 *Economic Growth with Income and Wealth Distribution*

We only briefly mentioned a few possible ways of extending our study. The list can be easily refined and continued. For instance, we do not mention issues related to information, gender difference, organization, market structure, family structure, and expectations.[5]

This book has endeavored to make some contributions to the theory of economic growth and income and wealth distribution. The number of questions raised is much more than the number of questions fully answered. More challenges are left for research in the future. I quote from the final words of my previous book, *Capital and Knowledge*, to conclude this book (Zhang, 1999: 406):

Over-simplification in scientific economics tends to result in misleading conclusions; over-complication tends to lead to uselessness. This book is concerned with economic issues as broad as possible but not so broad that we cannot scientifically analyze them. A rich idea does not live alone. A rich theory is like the central grand square from which multiple roads start to lead to remote places. It will take much longer space to explore possible implications of the ideas represented in this book. Anyhow, the economist never completes his work.

Notes

Preface

1. A comprehensive survey of the literature on the theoretical study of growth and income distribution by the 1970s is given by Sahota (1978).
2. The framework is established with a series of books by this author. The basic vision, the framework, and the "raw" ideas are already systematically represented in Zhang (1996d). A recent refinement and extension of the approach for national economies is given by Zhang (2005a).

1 Growth and Distribution

1. Further explanations of the neoclassical growth theory are based on, for instance, Burmeister and Dobell (1970) and Zhang (1990).
2. See, for instance, Pasinetti (1974), Kaldor (1966), Sato, (1966), and Marglin (1984).
3. This section is based on Section 7.3 in Jehle and Reny (1998). We also refer to the theory of Arrow and Hahn (1971) and Mas-Colell et al. (1995).
4. This means that for all distinct $y^1, y^2 \in Y^j$ and all $t \in (0,1)$, there exists $\bar{y} \in Y^j$ such that $\bar{y} \geq ty^1 + (1-t)y^2$ and equality does not hold.
5. The proof is based on Section 7.3 in Jehle and Reny (1998).
6. See Arrow and Hahn (1971) and Takayama (1996).
7. From Zhang (1999: 402–3).
8. This way of interpreting various schools of economics is acceptable, at least for convenience of organizing our thought about economic evolution.
9. Solow (1956) and Swan (1956). Actually, the Solow model is often called the Solow-Swan model because Swan's work is similar to Solow's seminal paper. We now describe the Solow model.
10. The description of the behavior of producers and production sectors follows the traditional approach (e.g., Burmeister and Dobell, 1970; Azariadis, 1993; Zhang, 1999).
11. The proof is based on, for instance, Burmeister and Dobell (1970), or Zhang (2005a, Chap. 3).
12. Refer to Takayama (1985) and Romer (1996) in detail.
13. Restrictions on the structure of preference in the Ramsey approach are well recognized. The central difficult question is to create a more effective approach. A well-adapted way to relax the assumptions of additive utility function and constant rate of time preference is to make the discounting parameter an endogenous variable (see, for instance, Uzawa, 1968; Boyer, 1978; Epstein and Hynes, 1983; Shi and Epstein, 1993; Das, 2003). This approach is not very fruitful. It is not easy to introduce meaningful changes in the discounting rate. Also a growth model with endogenous discount rate tends to be analytically intractable.

14 A comprehensive survey on time discounting and time preference is given by Frederick et al. (2002). It is observed that there is a growing list of anomalies for the discounted utility model – patterns of choice that are inconsistent with the model's theoretical predictions. Scholars have also proposed different models to replace the discounted utility model; nevertheless no one has been successful in the replacement. As observed by Frederick et al., when this model "eventually became entrenched as the dominant theoretical framework for modeling intertemporal framework for modeling interremporal choice, it was due largely to its simplicity and its resemblance to the familiar compound interest formula, and not as a result of empirical research demonstrating validity." This book is based on an alternative utility approach to handle intertemporal choice problems without reference to the compound interest formula.

15 See, for instance, Samuelson and Modigliani (1966), Pasinetti (1974), and Salvadori (1991).

16 This approach has not had much influence upon the development of growth theory. One reason is that like the Solow model, it does not have a proper behavioral mechanism for the behavior of households. The lack of behavioral mechanism makes it almost impossible to be further extended and generalized.

17 Sato (1966). See also Appendix A.5.1 in Zhang (1999). A contemporary extension in discrete time is given by Böhm and Kaas (2000).

18 Sorger (2002a). Some further contemporary extensions and generalizations of the Ramsey model of heterogeneous households are given in, for instance, Nishimura and Shimomura (2002), Ghiglino and Sorger (2002), Sorger (2000), and Glachant and Vellutini (2002).

19 Caselli and Ventura (2000). The model is a generalization of the models by Stiglitz (1969), Chatterjee (1994), Bertola (1993), Alesina and Rodrik (1994), and Persson and Tabellini (1994).

20 This assumption makes the approach technically tractable but economically less attractive. The representative consumer is a fictional consumer whose utility maximization problem when facing aggregate resource constraints generates the economy's aggregate demand functions. The assumption of the identical discounting rate allows consumer heterogeneity to be represented by a single consumer. See also a recent study by Gollier and Zeckhauser (2005) on issues related to aggregation of heterogeneous time preference by the Ramsey approach.

21 This assumption is in contrast to what the growth model of heterogeneous households by Becker (1980) tries to prove. See also Becker and Tsyganov (2002).

22 It is possible to consider that some of β_j's are negative.

23 The studies, for instance, by Rader (1981) and Jouini and Napp (2006) also hold that there is no reason to believe that different consumers have identical time preferences for utility streams. It should be remarked that Becker (1992) first observed that if individuals have heterogeneous constant rates of impatience, the representative agent will not in general use a constant rate to discount the future.

24 In principle, it may be many periods. Nevertheless, if a man lives more than two periods, complicated analytical problems will arise and the model may become analytically intractable.

25 The model was initially proposed by Samuelson (1958) and Diamond (1965). The model here is based on Blanchard (1985) and Section 3.8 in Barro and Sala-I-Martin (2004). Some of extensions of the model are based on de la Croix and Michel (2002). For extensions of the model, see also Azariadis (1993) and Azariadis and Lambertini (2003).

26 As mentioned in Azaridias (1993), each period should last over 30 years if one really wants to use analytical results to provide direct insights into reality. The length of over 30 years is generally considered too long for discussing changes, for instance, in prices, government policy, knowledge, capital, or unemployment. Nevertheless, theoretical economists have accepted the framework mainly because it makes many growth problems analytically tractable.

27 The importance of timescales and changeable speeds for constructing general economic theory is examined by Zhang (2002). Zhang (1991, 2005b, 2006a) provides modern mathematical foundations for analyzing nonlinear dynamic systems. As far as the history of analytical economics is concerned, nonlinear dynamic economic analysis is a great step over Samuelson's *Foundation of Economic Analysis*.

28 See Schumpeter (1954), Blaug (1985), and Negishi (1989).

29 A recent refinement and extensions of the approach for national economies are given by Zhang (2005a). The theory provides an integrated approach to the theory of national economic growth and development (Zhang, 1999), international trade theory (Zhang, 2000), urban economics (Zhang, 2002a), and interregional economics (Zhang, 2003a) with heterogeneous households and economic structure over time.

2 One-Sector Growth (OSG) Economies with Capital Accumulation

1 As rational economics predicts, the acceptance of an alternative approach to a dominant idea like discounted utility in theoretical economics may take years or decades. Keynes (1936) says

> the difficulty lies, not in the new ideas, but in escaping the old ones, which ramify ... into every corner of our minds.

2 Most contents of this chapter are abstracted from Chaps. 2–4 in Zhang (2005a). Further explanations and the proofs are based on Zhang (2005a).

3 See Chiang (1984), Mas-Colell et al. (1995), and Simon and Blume (1994).

4 See Zhang (1991, 2005b).

5 See Chap. 2 in Zhang (2005a) for the cases that the production function is taken in the CES form and the Leontief form.

6 This section is based on Zhang (2005c).

7 This section provides a typical way of changing the continuous version to the discrete version. Most of our models in this book are developed in continuous time. The reader is encouraged to change them into the discrete version. For mathematical reference, see Zhang's recent book which deals with the modern theory of discrete dynamical systems and its applications to economics (Zhang, 2006a).

8   Becker (1965). Becker's works are mainly static. There are many growth models with leisure as an endogenous variable. For instance, Barro and Sala-I-Martin (2004) propose a one-sector growth model with endogenous time within the Ramsey framework. Nevertheless, as demonstrated by Barro and Sala-I-Martin, a growth model even with simple utility and production functions becomes complicated. A comprehensive literature review on time in economic theory is provided by Zamagni and Agliardi (2004).

9   See, for instance, Benhabib and Perli (1994), Ladrón-de-Guevara et al. (1997, 1999), Jones and Manuelli (1995), Turnovsky (1999), Greenwood and Hercowitz (1991), Rupert et al. (2000), and Campbell and Ludvigson (2001).

10 It should be noted that as the growth model of leisure time with the Ramsey utility function examined by Barro and Sala-I-Martin (2004, Section 9.3) has a unique saddle equilibrium point, its stability properties are different from our model. How to maintain the dynamic path of the Ramsey model near to the new saddle equilibrium after disturbances is not well addressed in the traditional literature. As our system has a unique stable equilibrium, we can carry out our comparative statics analysis with regard to any parameter.

11 There are numerous models on growth with government spending. Barro (1990) builds a growth model with government spending and income taxation where government activity enters directly into production as a public intermediate input. King and Rebelo (1993) compute the growth and welfare effects of income taxes in a two-sector growth model. Rebelo (1991) develops a number of basic endogenous growth models and explores the impact of various government policies on balanced growth paths. Glomm and Ravikumar (1994, 1997) examine growth and government's investments. Davis (2003) examines the relations between growth of government and the division of labor. See also Shleifer and Vishny (1993), Tataru (1999), Krusell and Rios-Rull (1999), Song (2002), Barreto (2002), Waller et al. (2002), and Dixit (2003) for possible directions of extending my analytical framework.

12 This model is examined in detail in Chap. 4 in Zhang (2005a). A model, which discusses similar issues to this model but is developed within the traditional optimal growth framework, is proposed by Guo (2004). See also Devereux et al. (1996, 2000), Chang et al. (1998a, b), Bajo-Rubio (2000), Zhang (2000jx), and Chatterjee et al. (2003).

13 Different methods of taxation in different analytical frameworks are given in Jha (1998).

14 See Rosenzweig and Stark (1997), Gray (1998), Chiappori et al. (2002) and Suen et al. (2003) for further literature on the subject. It should be noted that lifetime is also an endogenous variable in the recent literature (e.g. Ehrlich and Lui, 1991; Chakraborty, 2004).

15 The proofs in this section are referred to Chap. 4 in Zhang (2005a). The model is a simplified version of the growth model with housing and location proposed by Zhang (1996c). As pointed out by Greenwood and Hercowitz (1991), the stock of household capital actually exceeds market capital. Benhabib et al. (1991) estimate that the output of the household sector may be as much as half that of the market sector and that labor hours in the home sector are almost as great as in the market sector. Hence, proper introduction of household capital in growth theory is essential.

16 Home production needs time (see Gomme et al., 2001). It is thus necessary to combine this model with the model in Section 4.2. The task is conceptually straightforward and analytically easy. See further literature on home production and leisure time, for instance, by Blundell et al. (1994), McGrattan et al. (1997), Chiappori (1997), Chiappori and Ekeland (1999), Kimmel and Kniesner (1998), Rupert et al. (2000), Seckin (2001), Hazan and Maoz (2002), Vendrik (2003), and Dressing (2002, 2004). I should point out that the main character of my economic theory was designed in such a way that any individual model itself is a whole but can be integrated into any other model in an enlarged whole.

17 This section is mainly based on Zhang (1996a). A similar model with the Ramsey approach is proposed by Bovenberg and Smulders (1996).

18 This section is based on Chap. 4 in Zhang (2005a). Refer to Zhang (1999) for extending the model in this section to include endogenous technological change.

19 See Gruver (1976), Kennedy (1994), Cropper (1976), Mäler (1974, 2000), Ayong Le Kama (2001), Gerlagh and van der Zwaan (2002), and Wirl (2004).

20 See Fisher and Peterson (1976) and Stephens (1976).

21 This assumption may be relaxed along the lines suggested by Smith (1972) and Clarke and Reed (1994).

22 Our population dynamics are influenced by Haavelmo (1954), Niehans (1963), and Pitchford (1974).

23 Haavelmo (1954). It should be remarked that economic growth with endogenous population has recently been modeled with microfoundations in numerous works (see Becker et al., 1990; Galor and Weil, 2000; Galor, 2000; Boucekkine et al., 2002). In Appendix A.2.1 to this chapter, we provide another approach to economic growth with endogenous population. This section is based on Chap. 4 in Zhang (2005a).

24 More simulation results are given in Zhang (2005a).

25 See Tobin (1965). Outside money is the part of money stock which is issued by the government.

26 See Galor and Ryder (1989), Tirole (1985), Matsuyama (1991a, 2004), von Thadden (1999), Benhabib et al. (2001), Rey (2001), Evans and Honkaponja (2003), and Amato and Laubach (2004).

27 Here, we consider that the conduct of monetary policy takes precedence over all fiscal matters. Gale (1983: Chap. 2) provides a discussion of how to resolve the coordination problem between monetary and fiscal measures in a similar context.

28 The proof is given in Chap. 4 in Zhang (2005a).

29 The substitution of capital for fiat money in reaction to an increase in anticipated inflation is called the Tobin effect, as described in Tobin (1965). See also Champ and Freeman (2001).

30 Refer to, for instance, Obstfeld and Rogoff (1995, 1998), Lane (2001), Koomann (2002), Benigno and Benigno (2003), and Galí and Monacelli (2005), for the open economic literature. It can be seen that the model here can be generalized and extended in different directions. Nevertheless, this book will not deal with open economies when we study international trade. We try to treat every economy as a part of the integrated whole. As shown later on, as we can develop a global economy model of any number of economies, it is not necessary, at least technically, to be concerned with small open economies.

31 We assume a homogeneous population of size 1 and full employment of the production factors at any point in time.
32 We will specify production and utility functions to further demonstrate these properties.
33 It should be noted that the costs due to depreciation are paid by producers.
34 As trade will affect an economy's preference and technology, validity of this comparison is limited.
35 Our following discussion on the relationship between the preference structure and utility function is based on Barten and Böhm (1982).
36 This section is referred to Froyen (1999: 282–6).
37 The model is proposed by Chakrabarti (1999). See also Ren and Rangazas (2003) and Cardia and Michel (2004) for similar issues.
38 The first approach is accepted by, for instance, Barro and Becker (1989), Becker et al. (1990), and Galor and Weil (1996); the second approach by, for instance, Raut and Srinivasan (1994). Chakrabarti tried to combine the two ideas in one framework.
39 The rate of return on children $\gamma'(n(t))$ is given by equation (A.2.1.3), which equals the right-hand side of equation (A.2.1.4).
40 The proof of this proposition is based on Chakrabarti (1999).

3 Growth with Human Capital and Knowledge

1 The figure is based on Hughes and Cain (1998: 561).
2 The figure is based on Hughes and Cain (1998: 591).
3 Samuelson (2004) provides an introduction to how knowledge is modeled in economic contexts and the role played by the concepts of knowledge and common knowledge in economic analysis.
4 This section is based on Zhang (2005d).
5 See Arrow (1962), Uzawa (1965), Kennedy (1964), Weizsäcker (1966), Samuelson (1965), and Schultz (1981).
6 Works, for instance, by Sato and Tsutsui (1984) and Nelson and Winter (1982) are examples along this line.
7 See, for example, Dollar (1986), Krugman (1991), Rauch (1991), Stokey (1991), and Nardini (2001).
8 There is a great deal of literature on economic growth with bifurcations and chaos (for instance, Day, 1984; Hommes, 1991, 1998; Zhang, 1990, 1991; Azariadis, 1993; Boldrin et al., 2001; Matsuyama, 1991b, 2001; Shone, 2002). I have recently provided comprehensive reviews on applications of contemporary theories of differential and difference equations to economics (Zhang, 2005b, 2006a).
9 It should be remarked that learning by doing has been introduced into growth theory in different ways. For instance, Chari and Hopenhayn (1991), Parente (1994), and Stokey (1988) study learning by doing as a force for sustained growth; Brezis et al. (1993), Krusell and Rios-Rull (1996), and Jovanovic and Nyarko (1996) show that learning by doing can give rise to overtaking; Karp and Lee (2001) examined learning by doing and the choice of technology; and Liso et al. (2001) examine the implications of learning by doing for division of labor.

10 Over the years, I have systematically studied the modern economic developments of Confucian regions, Japan, Singapore, Hong Kong, and mainland China, from the perspectives of philosophy, historical conditions, and international relations, not to mention modern nonlinear economics (Zhang, 1998a, 2001, 2002c, 2003b, c, 2006b).
11 Among well-known East Asian thinkers, perhaps only Fukuzawa Yukichi (1835–1901) is exceptional.
12 See Zhang (2003c) and Zhang (1998a).
13 Zhang (2005c) also examined the case that the utility and production functions are taken in general forms.
14 See, for instance, Becker (1975), Heckman (1976), Heckman et al. (1996), Blinder and Weiss (1976), Weiss and Gronau (1981), Trostel (1993), Turrini (1998), Grossmann (2001), Blankenau and Simpson (2004), Gong et al. (2004), and Banerjee (2004). A recent article by Chen (2005) addresses growth, distribution, and internal structures of educational institutions under some institutional constraints. This is also an interesting direction for examining implications of education for distribution and growth.
15 The importance of consumption or leisure on human capital is important, but rarely introduced into formal economic theory. Zhang (2001, 2005a) explicitly introduces the impact of leisure and consumption upon human capital accumulation into growth theory. Empirical studies are now also conducted to examine the impact of leisure activities on learning. For instance, using detailed time data for Germany, Fahr (2005) identified a positive correlation between the level of schooling and time investments in informal education. The study also identifies an important determinant of labor market success (other than formal degrees) – that is the specific use of leisure time by successful workers. Fahr emphasizes the necessity for research on the educational character of certain leisure activities.
16 The model in this section is initially proposed in Zhang (1996b). Here, we provide a more refined vision. The proofs are given in Chap. 9 in Zhang (2005a).
17 Banerjee and Newman (1993), for instance, address issues related to development and occupational choice by focusing on the interplay between agents' occupational decisions and the distribution of wealth. Their study is restricted to capital market imperfections and the situation in which poor agents choose working for a wage over self-employment and wealthy agents' become entrepreneurs who monitor workers.
18 See, for instance, Banerjee and Newman (1993) on relationships between job amenity and occupational choice.
19 A review on related ideas is given by Helpman (1998).
20 See Chap. 9 in Zhang (2005a).
21 In fact, as it is difficult to introduce endogenous wealth accumulation into the approach, the models based on this approach provides few insights into issues related to income and wealth distribution.
22 We base the approach on Grossman and Helpman (1991), Aghion and Howitt (1998), and Chap. 9 in Zhang (2005a). It should be noted that it is not difficult to introduce imperfect competition in the new growth theory into the approach proposed in this book. I have concentrated my analysis on perfect competition .
23 See also Judd (1985).

24 Further discussions about human capital and human capital accumulation are given in Grossman and Helpman (1991).
25 The model is developed under the influence of Spence (1976) and Grossman and Helpman (1991).
26 See Barro and Sala-I-Martin (2004) and Grossman and Helpman (1991).
27 This section shows how to construct a discrete dynamical system which explains very complicated economic phenomena.
28 It should be noted that Galor and Weil (2000) also discuss implications of introducing $N(t)$ into the technological progress function g.
29 See Iooss and Joseph (1980), Hale and Koçak (1991), Kuznetsov (1998), and Zhang (2005b).

4 Growth with Heterogeneous Households

1 See Chapter VIII in Meier and Rauch (2000).
2 See Chasin (1997).
3 The figure is based on Table 9.1 in Schmitt (2000: 159).
4 See Aghion (2002).
5 See Katz and Autor (2000). A recent survey article on inequality and technical change is given by Acemoglu (2002). A related issue is about differences in saving behavior of different households. Recent literature about this issue is found in Dynan et al. (2004).
6 When we examine society as an organic whole, "ownership" means not only economic benefits and social status, it also confers direct or indirect political influence, for instance through lobbying, private funding of research and policy institutes, and campaign financing (see, for instance, Domhoff, 1990; Lindbeck et al., 1999; Forteza, 2001; Zak and Feng, 2003).
7 See Greenberg (1986) and Wolff (1996).
8 Atkinson and Bourguignon (2000: 5).
9 In the general equilibrium theory, the number of households is equal to the number of types of households. It can be seen that the analytical framework proposed in this book can include the general equilibrium theory, as far as economic relations among variables are concerned, as a special case where capital and other stock variables are not changeable (or in stationary state).
10 This section is based on Moav (2002). See also some other approaches by, for instance, Galor and Zeira (1993), Benabou (1996), Durlauf (1996), Piketty (1997), Aghion and Bolton (1997), and Glomm and Ravikumar (1998) to issues related to development and distribution. Multi-group growth models with endogenous savings can be found in the literature of economic growth. Foley and Michi (1999), Matsuyama (2000), Duranton (2000), Franke (2000), Acemoglu (2002), Aghion et al. (2002), Laslier and Picard (2002), Davis (2003), and Duménil and Lévy (2003) provide some interesting insights into evolution of inequality due to institutional frictions. A literature review on ethic diversity and economic growth by Alesina and Ferrara (2005) also provides some interesting topics for further research.

11 As $R = f'(k)$, where $k \equiv K/H$, $f \equiv F(k,1)$, we have $k = g(R)$. Hence, k is constant. As $w = f - Rk$, w is constant.
12 The model is based on Eicher and García-Peñalosa (2001). See also, for instance, Aghion (2002) and Eeckhout and Jovanovic (2002) for similar approaches.
13 See Chap. 5 in Zhang (2005a).
14 See also, for instance, Chari and Christiano (1994), Aiyagari (1995), Laitner (1995), Jones et al. (1997), Imrohoroglu (1998), Milesi-Ferretti and Roubini (1998), Bénabou (2002), and Abel (2005) for impact of taxation on different groups of households.
15 These ideas are important for explaining wealth accumulation. It should be noted that these ideas can be introduced into the growth theory based on the OSG framework, with some new modeling methods. A fruitful approach seems to apply some methods and concepts in logit models which are widely used in research on transportation and operations research. This topic is beyond the scope of this book.

5 Multi-Sector Growth Economies

1 See, for instance, Rostow (1960), Kuznets (1963, 1966), and Lewis (1955).
2 Leontief (1941), Sraffa (1960), Nikaido (1968), Morishima (1964, 1969), and Pasinetti (1981).
3 It is also interesting to observe different roles of different sectors in processes of industrialization (see, for instance, Harris and Todaro, 1970; Kaiyama, 1973; Matsuyama, 1992; Echevarria, 1997; Laitner, 2000; Eswaran and Kotwal, 2002; Wang and Xie, 2004).
4 For instance, Corden (1966), Diamond (1965), Drandakis (1963), Stiglitz (1967a), Takayama (1965), Azariadis (1993), and Ortigueira and Santos (2002) within a continuous framework. There are numerous discrete two-sector models, for instance, Galor (1992), Nishimura and Yano (1995), Ralf (2001), and Song (2003).
5 See, for instance, Drandakis (1963), Diamond (1965), Weizsäcker (1966), Corden (1966), Stiglitz (1967a), Gram (1976), Mino (1996), Benhabib et al. (2000), Drugeon and Venditti (2001), and Duczynski (2002).
6 See Chap. 3 for behavior of the dynamic system with multiple equilibrium points.
7 See some growth multi-sector models in Zhang (2005a, 2005e). It should be noted that issues related to sectoral development and economic growth are not yet fully examined. As different sectors exhibit various returns to scale and people have various (changeable) preferences for various goods, the issues are important. As my framework is designed in such a way that multiple sectors and multiple groups are integrated within a compact framework, these issues can be examined.
8 See also for growth models with multiple sectors and increasing returns to scale, for instance, Mulligan and Sala-I-Martin (1993), Benhabib and Farmer (1994), Baierl et al. (1998), Drugeon and Venditti (2001), and Boldrin et al. (2001). It is also interesting to take account of the portfolio approach in deciding distribution of components of wealth (e.g. Knapp and Nourzad, 1994) and/or to take account of demand complementarities (e.g. Oulton, 1993, Ciccone and Matsuyama, 1999).

6 Multiple Sectors and Heterogeneous Households

1. We do not represent the Stiglitz model as it is a simple combination of Sato's two-class growth model mentioned in Chap. 4 and Uzawa's two-sector model described in Chap. 5.
2. It is also interesting to introduce consumer externality into our modeling framework to examine interdependence among households' preferences and economic structure. Refer to the concept of consumer externality in Friedman and Grilo (2005).
3. For recent literature on implications of social status, see Weiss and Fershtman (1998), Holländer (2001), and Brekke and Howarth (2004).
4. See Frank (1985), Oswald (1997), and Alpizar et al. (2005) for the recent literature.
5. See also Sattinger (1993) and Teulings (1995).
6. There are many models with utility functions which are affected by an individual's relative standing in society. See, for instance, Ng (1987), Robson (1992), Carroll et al. (1997), Akerlof (1997), Corneo and Jeanne (1997), Clark and Oswald (1998), Knell (1999), and Ljungquist and Uhlig (2000).
7. More discussions on this issue are based on Zhang (2005a).
8. Preference changes brought about by changes in economic conditions are important, but seldom discussed in trade models. For instance, as one country's economic conditions improve or deteriorate, its preference for different countries' goods may vary. It is important to examine effects of the preference change on trade patterns and production structures.

7 Multi-Region Growth Economies

1. Borts and Stein (1964) and Siebert (1969).
2. There are some theoretical international trade models which allow for immigration (e.g. Tang and Wälde, 2001; Zak et al., 2002; Giannetti, 2003).
3. See, for instance, Richardson (1977), Henderson (1985, 2003), Arnott (1996a, b), Fujita et al. (1999), Walz (1999), Murata (2002), and Henderson et al. (2003).
4. Isard (1960).
5. Leontief (1936, 1941) and Isard (1953).
6. See, for instance, Alonso (1964), Beckmann (1968), Greenhut et al. (1997), Krugman (1991), Rauch (1991), Fujita (1989), Brito and Pereira (2002), and Tabuchi and Thisse (2002).
7. The distinction between interregional and international economics should not be strict as factor mobility is an endogenous variable of dynamic economics as well as in long-term perspectives.
8. It is difficult to provide a comprehensive review on the literature of studies of regional and interregional dynamics. As both national growth and international dynamic theories can be extended to regional or international contexts, the variety of regional models is reasonably great. In particular, the recent attention of economics on economic geography has made the literature very complicated.
9. The Arrow-Debreu equilibrium theory explicitly neglects economic geography. Most dynamic interregional economic models have been developed in the discrete

framework (mainly the OLG framework), technically because the discrete framework enables model builders to discard issues related to capital accumulation.

10 See, for instance, Oniki and Uzawa (1965), Deardorff (1973), Ruffin (1979), Findlay (1984), Eaton (1987), Brecher et al. (2002), Sorger (2002b), and Zhang (2006c).

11 Empirical studies on price convergence on commodities are found in, for instance, Isard (1977), Baffes (1991), Milikovic (1999), Fielding and Shields (2003), and Bukenya and Labys (2005). As so many factors, such as time of transportation, exogenous shocks, information, and expectations, affect price convergence, it is to be expected that the empirical studies do not provide converging conclusions on issues related to commodity price convergence.

12 The author has also analyzed the system of heterogeneous households. As the system is already too complicated, we have concentrated on the homogeneous population. The next chapter on international trade theory will introduce the model with heterogeneous households. It can be seen that it is straightforward to introduce heterogeneous households into the interregional framework.

13 See, for instance, Takayama and Judge (1971), Batten (1982), and Roy and Johansson (1993).

14 The author tried to solve the case when the land income is distributed equally among the households. The dynamics are more complicated than the system obtained below.

15 See, for instance, Kanemoto (1980), Diamond and Tolley (1981), Blomquist et al. (1988), Andersson et al. (2003). It should be remarked that concept of amenity has recently been introduced into the Ramsey growth model (e.g. Gerlagh and Keyzer, 2004). See, for instance, Kostiuk (1990) and Lanfranchi et al. (2002) for issues related to costs associated with job shifts.

16 For similar issues, see also Fujita (1988), Tabuchi (1998), Tabuchi and Yoshida (2000), Berliant et al. (2002), and Glazer et al. (2003).

17 See, for instance, Sivitanidou and Wheaton (1992), Simon and Love (1990), Bell (1991), Voith (1991), and Brueckner and Zenou (1999).

18 See, for instance, Fujita (1989).

19 For instance, Glaeser and Maré (2001), Duranton and Monastiriotis (2002), and Combes et al. (2004).

20 Accurately, the Solow model or other neoclassical approaches should have nothing to say theoretically about convergence or divergence among nations or regions, simply because these theoretical models have not been logically extended to multiregional or multi-country economies. Yet economists often use the neoclassical growth theory to discuss issues related to convergence or divergence. One may wonder how a theory without spatial contents can address spatial issues (see, for instance, Barro and Sala-I-Martin, 2004).

21 For instance, Krugman (1991), Fujita et al. (1999), Martin and Ottaviano (2001), Fujita and Thisse (2002a), and Nocco (2005). It should be noted that the currently well-accepted approach to economic geography often applies the iceberg transport cost functions for studying agglomeration. As pointed out by McCann (2005: 315–16): "The properties of the Krugman iceberg model, which are quite different to the Samuelson iceberg model, imply that the delivered prices of goods increase exponentially with the distance shipped. On the other hand, all of the available

evidence suggests that delivered prices tend to be concave rather than convex with distance. As such, the treatment of geography and space in these types of new economic geography models is very particular, and is based on assumptions which would be regarded as untenable in most other spatial models." Also as mentioned by McCann, empirical studies do not convince us of the validity of the assumption well accepted in the new economic geography. Indeed, transportation costs are one factor for spatial agglomeration – the degree of the importance is difficult to empirically judge.

22   For related topics in the recent literature, see Dixon and Thirlwall (1975), Black and Henderson (1999), Ottaviano and Thisse (2002), Fujita and Thisse (2002a, b), Bertinelli and Black (2004), and Burbidge and Cuff (2005).
23   The study is based on McCombie (1988). See also Carlino and Mills (1996), Rey and Montouri (1999), and Webber et al. (2005) for recent literature on regional income issues in the US economy.
24   See Ethier (1982), Romer (1987), and Rivera-Batiz (1988).
25   Suarez-Villa (1993).
26   Yamamoto (2005) has recently developed a two-sector model for similar issues. The model shows the existence of multiple equilibrium points and thus path-dependent properties of regional evolution. Different from the approach accepted in this section, those works are based on the assumption of monopolistic competition. As regional phenomena are highly aggregated, the assumption of monopolistic competition for interregional modeling might not be so practically valid as it appears. With regard to empirical observations, Sedgley and Elmslie (2004) conduct an insightful research on the US regions.
27   The model of this section is a generalization of the two-region growth model proposed by Zhang (1998b). Some other two-region models with the approach are given in Zhang (2003a). Also refer to Lucas (2004) for regional development with learning. It should be remarked that the role of governments in regional economic development is important (see Hockman et al., 1995). Moreover, each region may consist of multiple cities. It is significant to take account of urban structures (Fujita, 1989; Zhang, 2002a; Lucas and Rossi-Hansberg, 2002).
28   For instance, Andersson and Forslid (2003), Baldwin and Krugman (2004), Bayindir-Upmann and Ziad (2005), and Borck and Pflüger (2006).

8 Multi-Country Growth Economies

1   This issue is addressed within an overlapping-generations 2×2 modeling framework by Fisher (1992).
2   See Nahuis (2003: Chap. 2), which surveys some empirical studies on possible causes for the decrease in the relative wage of low-skilled workers in the US in the 1980s. For trade and wage inequalities for developing economies, see Marjit and Acharyya (2003).
3   Other channels of enlarged inequalities are modeled by, for instance, Krugman and Venables (1995), Manasse and Turrini (2001).
4   Ricardo (1817) and Morishima (1989).
5   For instance, Jones and Neary (1984).

6   See, for instance, Negishi (1972), Dixit and Norman (1980) and Jones (1979).
7   Mill (1848) and Marshall (1890).
8   Chipman (1965a) and Negishi (1972).
9   This example is from Negishi (1972).
10 See, for instance, Gandolfo (1994).
11 See, for instance, Jones and Kenen (1984), Ethier and Svensson (1986), Bhagwati (1991), and Wong (1995). It should be noted that a trade model based on the Solow approach (which deals with similar questions as the model in this section) is proposed by Sorger (2002b). It is important to examine possible poverty traps due to capital mobility (see Vellutini, 2003, for the Ramsey approach, and Zhang, 2005a, for further study with the OSG approach).
12 See Zhang (1995, 1998b, 2003a).
13 See, for instance, Fischer and Frenkel (1972).
14 See Bardhan (1965), Ryder (1967), and Bruce (1977).
15 See also Section 2.10 for a small open economy described within the OSG framework.
16 Ikeda and Ono (1992). See also, for instance, Jensen (1994), Valdés (1999), Jensen and Wong (1998), Maurer (1998), and Nishimura and Shimomura (2002) for various extensions.
17 This section is based on Zhang (1992a). It is straightforward to introduce education into the model, based on the model with education in Chap. 2. See also Nakajima (2003) for taking account of learning by doing, and Kim and Kim (2000) for modeling gains from trade and education.
18 See also Ni (1999) and Aloi et al. (2000).
19 See, for instance, Dixit and Stiglitz (1977), Helpman and Krugman (1985), and Dixon and Rankin (1994).
20 For instance, Findlay (1978), Wang (1990) and Wang and Blomström (1992).
21 Issues about relations between political games and trade are also discussed in, for instance, Hillman (1982), Mayer and Riezman, (1987, 1990), Grossman and Helpman (1994), Levy (1997), and Das (2001). Another interesting approach from the perspective of interactions between capitalists and workers is given by Krawczyk and Shimomura (2003).
22 Trade models in the new growth theory are so many that even a proper review will take up a great deal of space.

9 Endless Complexity

1   Thoreau (1817–62, 1910: 31). An excellent introduction to traditional theories of value and distribution from perspectives of ideology and economic theory is given by Dobb (1973).
2   One might also ask whether all these new philosophical and social concepts can provide any meaningful insights into social reality without help of economic analysis. It seems to me that no meaningful new insights into justice can be obtained within a static framework.
3   See Zhang (2005a) for some types of preference changes.

4   Zhang (2005a) provides various reasons for unemployment and also developments of some growth models with unemployment in the OSG framework.
5   It should be noted that most of these issues have been analyzed, yet only in very brief ways, within the analytical framework of this book by the author over the years. My main concerns had been concentrated on the fundamental work of constructing a framework of perfect competition, which will enable us to analyze economic complexity from various aspects but in a consistent manner – I often liken this vision to the *I Ching*.

Bibliography

Abel, A.B., 2005. 'Optimal Taxation when Consumers Have Endogenous Benchmark Levels of Consumption', Review of Economic Studies, Vol. 72, pp. 21–42.

Abel, A.B. and B.S. Bernanke, 1998. *Macroeconomics*, 3rd edn. New York: Addison-Wesley.

Abel-Rahman, H.M., 1988. 'Product Differentiation, Monopolistic Competition and City Size', Regional Science and Urban Economics, Vol. 18, pp. 69–86.

Acemoglu, D., 2002. 'Technical Change, Inequality, and the Labor Market', Journal of Economic Literature, Vol. 40, pp. 7–72.

Aghion, P., 2002. 'Schumpeterian Growth Theory and the Dynamics of Income Inequality', Econometrica, Vol. 70, pp. 855–82.

Aghion, P. and P. Bolton, 1997. 'A Theory of Trickle-Down Growth and Development', Review of Economic Studies, Vol. 64, pp. 151–72.

Aghion, P. and P. Howitt, 1992. 'A Model of Growth through Creative Destruction', Econometrica, Vol. 60, pp. 323–51.

Aghion, P. and P. Howitt, 1998. *Endogenous Growth Theory*. Cambridge, Mass.: The MIT Press.

Aghion, P., P. Howitt and G.L. Violante, 2002. 'General Purpose Technology and Wage Inequality', Journal of Economic Growth, Vol. 7, pp. 315–45.

Aiyagari, R., 1995. 'Optimal Capital Income Taxation with Incomplete Markets, Borrowing Constraints, and Constant Discounting', Journal of Political Economy, Vol. 103, pp. 1158–75.

Akerlof, G.A., 1997. 'Social Distance and Social Decisions', Econometrica, Vol. 65, pp. 1005–27.

Alesina, A. and E.L. Ferrara, 2005. 'Ethnic Diversity and Economic Performance', Journal of Economic Literature, Vol. 43, pp. 762–800.

Alesina, A. and D. Rodrik, 1994. 'Distributive Politics and Economic Growth', Quarterly Journal of Economics, Vol. 109, pp. 465–90.

Aloi, M., H.D. Dixon and T. Lloyd-Braga, 2000. 'Endogenous Fluctuations in an Open Economy with Increasing Returns to Scale', Journal of Economic Dynamics & Control, Vol. 24, pp. 97–125.

Alonso, W., 1964. *Location and Land Use*. Cambridge, Mass.: Harvard University Press.

Alpizar, F., F. Carlsson and O. Johansson-Stenman, 2005. 'How Much Do We Care About Absolute versus Relative Income and Consumption?', Journal of Economic Behavior & Organization, Vol. 56, pp. 405–21.

Amato, J.D. and T. Laubach, 2004. 'Implications of Habit Formation for Optimal Monetary Policy', Journal of Monetary Economics, Vol. 51, pp. 305–25.

Andersson, Å.E., B. Johansson, and W.P. Anderson, eds., 2003. *The Economics of Disappearing Distance*. Aldershot, Hampshire: Ashgate.

Anderson, J.E. and E. van Wincoop, 2004. 'Trade Costs', Journal of Economic Literature, Vol. 42, pp. 691–751.

Andersson, F. and R. Forslid, 2003. 'Tax Competition and Economic Geography', Journal of Public Economic Theory, Vol. 5, pp. 279–303.
Arnott, R., ed., 1996a. *Regional and Urban Economics*, Part 1. Amsterdam: Harwood Academic Publishers.
Arnott, R., ed., 1996b. *Regional and Urban Economics*, Part 2. Amsterdam: Harwood Academic Publishers.
Arrow, K.J., 1962. 'The Economic Implications of Learning by Doing', Review of Economic Studies, Vol. 29, pp. 155–73.
Arrow, K.J. and F.H. Hahn, 1971. *General Competitive Analysis*. San Francisco: Holden-Day, Inc.
Atkinson, A.B., 1975. *The Economics of Inequality*. Oxford: Clarendon Press.
Atkinson, A.B. and F. Bourguignon, eds., 2000. *Handbook of Income Distribution*, Vol.1. Amsterdam: Elsevier.
Autor, D., L. Latz, and A. Krueger, 1998. 'Computing Inequality: Have Computers Changed the Labor Market? ', Quarterly Journal of Economics, Vol. 113, pp. 1169–214.
Ayong Le Kama, A.D., 2001. 'Sustainable Growth, Renewable Resources and Pollution', Journal of Economic Dynamics and Control, Vol. 25, pp. 1911–18.
Azariadis, C., 1993. *Intertemporal Macroeconomics*. Oxford: Blackwell.
Azariadis, C. and L. Lambertini, 2003. 'Endogenous Debt Constraints in Lifecycle Economies', Review of Economic Studies, Vol. 70, pp. 461–87.
Baffes, J., 1991. 'Some Further Evidence on the Law of One Price: the Law of One Price Still Holds', American Journal of Agricultural Economics, Vol. 73, pp. 124–73.
Baierl, G., K. Nishimura, and M. Yano, 1998. 'The Role of Capital Depreciation in Multi-Sectoral Models', Journal of Economic Behavior & Organization, Vol. 33, pp. 467–79.
Bajo-Rubio, O., 2000. 'A Further Generalization of the Solow Growth Model: the Role of the Public Sector', Economics Letters, Vol. 68, pp. 79–84.
Baldwin, R.E. and P. Krugman, 2004. 'Agglomeration, Integration and Tax Harmonization', European Economic Review, Vol. 48, pp. 1–23.
Banerjee, A.V., 2004. 'Educational Policy and the Economics of the Family', Journal of Development Economics, Vol. 74, pp. 3–32.
Banerjee, A.V. and A.F. Newman, 1993. 'Occupational Choice and the Process of Development', Journal of Political Economy, Vol. 101, pp. 274–98.
Bardhan, P.K., 1965. 'Optimum Capital Accumulation and International Trade', Review of Economic Studies, Vol. 32, pp. 241–4.
Barreto, R.A., 2002. 'Endogenous Corruption in a Neoclassical Growth Model', European Economic Review, Vol. 44, pp. 35–60.
Barro, R., 1990. 'Government Spending in a Simple Model of Endogenous Growth', Journal of Political Economy, Vol. 98, pp. S103–25.
Barro, R., 1991. 'Economic Growth in a Cross Section of Countries', Quarterly Journal of Economics, Vol. 106, pp. 407–43.
Barro, R. and G.S. Becker, 1989. 'Fertility Choice in a Model of Economic Growth', Econometrica, Vol. 57, pp. 481–501.
Barro, R. and X. Sala-I-Martin. 2004. *Economic Growth*. New York: McGraw-Hill, Inc.

Barten, A.P. and V. Böhm, 1982. 'Consumer Theory', in *Handbook of Mathematical Economics* II. Ed. by K.J. Arrow and M. D. Intriligator. Amsterdam: North-Holland Publishing Company.

Batten, D.F., 1982. 'The Interregional Linkages between National and Regional Input–Output Models', International Regional Science Review, Vol. 7, pp. 53–67.

Baumol, W., 1990. 'Entrepreneurship: Productive, Unproductive, and Destructive', Journal of Political Economy, Vol. 98, pp. 893–921.

Bayindir-Upmann, T. and A. Ziad, 2005. 'Existence of Equilibria in a Basic Tax Competition Model', Regional Science and Urban Economics, Vol. 35, pp. 1–22.

Becker, G. S., 1965. 'A Theory of Allocation of Time', Economic Journal, Vol. 75, pp. 493–517.

Becker, G. S., 1975. *Human Capital*. New York: National Bureau of Economic Research.

Becker, G. S., 1981. *A Treatise on the Family*. Cambridge, Mass.: Harvard University Press.

Becker, G. S. and K. Murphy, 1992. 'The Division of Labor, Coordination Costs, and Knowledge', Quarterly Journal of Economics, Vol. 107, pp. 1137–60.

Becker, G. S., K. Murphy and R. Tamura, 1990. 'Human Capital, Fertility and Economic Growth', Journal of Political Economy, Vol. 98, pp. 512–37.

Becker, G.S., K.M. Murphy and I. Werning, 2005. 'The Equilibrium Distribution of Income and the Market for Status', Journal of Political Economy, Vol. 113, pp. 282–310.

Becker, R.A., 1980. 'On the Long-Run Steady State in a Simple Dynamic Model of Equilibrium with Heterogeneous Households', Quarterly Journal of Economics, Vol. 95, pp. 375–82.

Becker, R.A., 1992. 'Cooperative Capital Accumulation Games and the Core', in *Economic Theory and International Trade: Essays in Memoriam, J. Trout Rader*. Ed. by W. Neuefeind and R.G. Riezman. Berlin: Springer-Verlag.

Becker, R.A. and E.N. Tsyganov, 2002. 'Ramsey Equilibrium in a Two-sector Model with Heterogeneous Households', Journal of Economic Theory, Vol. 105, pp. 188–225.

Beckmann, M.J., 1968. *Location Theory*. New York: Harper & Brothers.

Bell, C., 1991. 'Regional Heterogeneity, Migration, and Shadow Prices', Journal of Public Economics, Vol. 46, pp. 1–27.

Bénabou, R., 1996. 'Equity and Efficiency in Human Capital Investment: the Local Connection', Review of Economic Studies, Vol. 63, pp. 267–74.

Bénabou, R., 2002. 'Tax and Education Policy in a Heterogeneous-Agent Economy: What Levels of Redistribution Maximize Growth and Efficiency?', Econometrica, Vol. 70, pp. 481–517.

Benhabib, J. and R.E. Farmer, 1994. 'Indeterminancy and Increasing Returns', Journal of Economic Theory, Vol. 63, pp. 19–41.

Benhabib, J., Q.L. Meng and K. Nishimura, 2000. 'Indeterminacy under Constant Returns to Scale in Multisector Economy', Econometrica, Vol. 68, pp. 1541–8.

Benhabib, J. and R. Perli, 1994. 'Uniqueness and Indeterminacy: on the Dynamics of Endogenous Growth', Journal of Economic Theory, Vol. 63, pp. 113–42.

Benhabib, J., R. Rogerson and R. Wright, 1991. 'Homework in Macroeconomics: Household Production and Aggregate Fluctuations', Journal of Political Economy, Vol. 99, pp. 1166–87.

Benhabib, J., S. Schmitt-Grohé and M. Uribe, 2001. 'The Perils of Taylor Rules', Journal of Economic Theory, Vol. 96, pp. 40–69.

Benigno, G. and P. Benigno, 2003. 'Price Stability in Open Economies', Review of Economic Studies, Vol. 70, pp. 743–64.
Berliant, M., S.K. Peng and P. Wang, 2002. 'Production Externalities and Urban Configuration', Journal of Economic Theory, Vol. 104, pp. 275–303.
Bertinelli, L. and D. Black, 2004. 'Urbanization and Growth', Journal of Urban Economics, Vol. 56, pp. 80–96.
Bertola, G., 1993. 'Factor Shares and Savings in Endogenous Growth', American Economic Review, Vol. 83, pp. 1184–98.
Bhagwati, J.N., ed., 1991. *International Trade – Selected Readings*, 2nd edn. Cambridge, Mass.: The MIT Press.
Black, D. and V. Henderson, 1999. 'A Theory of Urban Growth', Journal of Political Economy, Vol. 107, pp. 252–84.
Blanchard, O., 1985. 'Debt, Deficits, and Finite Horizons', Journal of Political Economy, Vol. 93, pp. 223–47.
Blankenau, W.F. and N.B. Simpson, 2004. 'Public Education Expenditures and Growth', Journal of Development Economics, Vol. 73, pp. 583–605.
Blaug, M., 1985. *Economic Theory in Retrospect*, 4th edn. Cambridge: Cambridge University Press.
Blinder, A. and Y. Weiss, 1976. 'Human Capital and Labor Supply: a Synthesis', Journal of Political Economy, Vol. 84, pp. 449–72.
Blomquist, G.C., M.C. Berger and J.C. Hoehn, 1988. 'New Estimates of Quality of Life in Urban Areas', American Economic Review, Vol. 78, pp. 89–107.
Blundell, R., M. Browning and C. Meghir, 1994. 'Consumer Demand and the Life Cycle Allocation of Household Expenditures', Review of Economic Studies, Vol. 61, pp. 57–80.
Böhm, V. and L. Kaas, 2000. 'Differential Savings, Factor Shares, and Endogenous Growth Cycles', Journal of Economic Dynamics & Control, Vol. 24, pp. 965–80.
Boldrin, M., K. Nishimura, T. Shigoka and M. Yano, 2001. 'Chaotic Equilibrium Dynamics in Endogenous Growth Models', Journal of Economics, Vol. 96, pp. 107–31.
Borck, R. and M. Pflüger, 2006. 'Agglomeration and Tax Competition', European Economic Review (in press).
Borts, G.H. and J.L. Stein, 1964. *Economic Growth in a Free Market*. New York: Columbia University Press.
Boucekkine, R., D. de la Croix and O. Lisandro, 2002. 'Vintage Human Capital, Demographic Trend, and Endogenous Growth', Journal of Economic Theory, Vol. 104, pp. 340–75.
Bovenberg, A.L. and S.A. Smulders, 1996. 'Transitional Impacts of Environmental Policy in an Endogenous Growth Model', International Economic Review, Vol. 37, pp. 861–93.
Boyer, M., 1978. 'A Habit Forming Optimal Growth Model', International Economic Review, Vol. 19, pp. 585–609.
Brecher, R.A., Z.Q. Chen and E.U. Choudhri, 2002. 'Absolute and Comparative Advantage, Reconsidered: the Pattern of International Trade with Optimal Saving', Review of International Economics, Vol. 10, pp. 645–56.
Brekke, K.A. and R.B. Howarth, 2004. *Affluence, Well-being and Environment Quality*. Cheltenham: Edward Elgar.

Bresnahan, T.F. and M. Trajtenberg, 1995. 'General Purpose Technologies: 'Engines of Growth'? ', Journal of Econometrics, Vol. 65, pp. 83–108.
Bretschger, L., 1999. *Growth Theory and Sustainable Development*. Cheltenham: Edward Elgar.
Brezis, E.S., P.R. Krugman and D. Tsiddon, 1993. 'Leapfrogging in International Competition: a Theory of Cycles in National Technological Leadership', American Economic Review, Vol. 83, pp. 1211–19.
Brito, P.M.B. and A.M. Pereira, 2002. 'Housing and Endogenous Long-Term Growth', Journal of Urban Economics, Vol. 51, pp. 246–71.
Bruce, N., 1977. 'The Effects of Trade Taxes in a Two-Sector Model of Capital Accumulation', Journal of International Economics, Vol. 7, pp. 283–94.
Brueckner, J.K. and Y. Zenou, 1999. 'Harris-Todaro Models with a Land Market', Regional Science and Urban Economics, Vol. 29, pp. 317–39.
Bukenya, J.O. and W.C. Labys, 2005. 'Price Convergence on World Commodity Markets: Fact or Fiction? ', International Regional Science Review, Vol. 28, pp. 302–29.
Burbidge, J. and K. Cuff, 2005. 'Capital Tax Competition and Returns to Scale', Regional Science and Urban Economics, Vol. 35, pp. 353–73.
Burmeister, E. and A.R. Dobell, 1970. *Mathematical Theories of Economic Growth*. London: Collier Macmillan Publishers.
Calvó-Armengol, A. and M.O. Jackson, 2004. 'The Effects of Social Networks on Employment and Inequality', American Economic Review, Vol. 94, pp. 426–54.
Campbell, J.Y. and S. Ludvigson, 2001. 'Elasticities of Substitution in Real Business Cycle Model with Home Production', Journal of Money, Credit, and Banking, Vol. 33, pp. 847–75.
Cardia, E. and P. Michel, 2004. 'Altruism, Intergenerational Transfers of Time and Bequests', Journal of Economic Dynamics & Control, Vol. 28, pp. 1681–701.
Carlino, J. and L. Mills, 1996. 'Convergence and the US States: a Time-Series Analysis', Journal of Regional Science, Vol. 36, pp. 597–616.
Carroll, C., J. Overland and D. Weil, 1997. 'Comparison Utility in a Growth Model', Journal of Economic Growth, Vol. 2, pp. 229–67.
Caselli, F. and J. Ventura, 2000. 'A Representative Consumer Theory of Distribution', American Economic Review, Vol. 90, pp. 909–26.
Cass, D., 1965. 'Optimum Growth in an Aggregative Model of Capital Accumulation', Review of Economic Studies, Vol. 32, pp. 233–40.
Chakrabarti, R., 1999. 'Endogenous Fertility and Growth in a Model with Old Age Support', Economic Theory, Vol. 13, pp. 393–416.
Chakraborty, S., 2004. 'Endogenous Lifetime and Economic Growth', Journal of Economic Theory, Vol. 116, pp. 119–37.
Chamberlin, E., 1933. *The Theory of Monopolistic Competition*. Cambridge: Harvard University Press.
Champ, B. and S. Freeman, 2001. *Modeling Monetary Economies*. Cambridge: Cambridge University Press.
Chang, W.Y., H.F. Tsai and W.F. Liu, 1998a. 'Effects of Government Spending on the Current Account with Endogenous Time Preference', Southern Economic Journal, Vol. 64, pp. 728–40.

Chang, W.Y., H.F. Tsai and W.F. Liu, 1998b. 'Government Spending and Capital Accumulation with Endogenous Time Preference', Canadian Journal of Economics, Vol. 31, pp. 624–45.

Chari, V.V. and L.J. Christiano, 1994. 'Optimal Fiscal Policy in a Business Cycle Model', Journal of Political Economy, Vol. 102, pp. 617–52.

Chari, V.V. and H. Hopenhayn, 1991. 'Vintage Human Capital, Growth, and the Diffusion of New Technology', Journal of Political Economy, Vol. 99, pp. 1142–65.

Chasin, B.H., 1997. *Inequality and Violence in the United States: Casualties of Capitalism.* New Jersey: Humanities Press.

Chatterjee, S., 1994. 'Transitional Dynamics and the Distribution of Wealth in a Neoclassical Growth Model', Journal of Public Economics, Vol. 54, pp. 97–119.

Chatterjee, S., G. Sakoulis and S.J. Turnovsky, 2003. 'Unilateral Capital Transfers, Public Investment, and Economic Growth', European Economic Review, Vol. 47, pp. 1077–103.

Chen, H.J., 2005. 'Educational Systems, Growth and Income Distribution: a Quantitative Study', Journal of Development Economics, Vol. 76, pp. 325–53.

Chiang, A.C., 1984. *Fundamental Methods of Mathematical Economics.* London: McGraw-Hill Book Company.

Chiappori, P.A., 1997. 'Introducing Household Production in Collective Models of Labor Supply', Journal of Political Economy, Vol. 105, pp. 191–209.

Chiappori, P.A. and I. Ekeland, 1999. 'Aggregation and Market Demand: an Exterior Differential Calculus Viewpoint', Econometrica, Vol. 67, pp. 1435–57.

Chiappori, P.A., B. Fortin and G. Lacroix, 2002. 'Marriage Market, Divorce Legislation, and Household Labor Supply', Journal of Political Economy, Vol. 110, pp. 37–72.

Chipman, J.S., 1965a. 'A Survey of the Theory of International Trade, Part 1', Econometrica, Vol. 33, pp. 477–519.

Chipman, J.S., 1965b. 'A Survey of the Theory of International Trade, Part 2', Econometrica, Vol. 33, pp. 685–760.

Ciccone, A. and K. Matsuyama, 1999. 'Efficiency and Equilibrium with Dynamic Increasing Aggregate Returns Due to Demand Complementarities', Econometrica, Vol. 67, pp. 499–524.

Clark, A.E. and A.J. Oswald, 1998. 'Comparison-Concave Utility and Following Behavior in Social and Economic Settings', Journal of Public Economics, Vol. 70, pp. 133–55.

Clarke, H.R. and W.J. Reed, 1994. 'Consumption/pollution Trade offs in an Environment Vulnerable to Pollution-Related Catastrophic Collapse', Journal of Economic Dynamics and Control, Vol. 18, pp. 991–1010.

Combes, P.G., G. Duranton and L. Gobillon, 2004. 'Spatial Wage Disparities: Sorting Matters!', CEPR Discussion Paper, 4220.

Corden, W.M., 1966. 'The Two Sector Growth Model with Fixed Coefficients', Review of Economic Studies, Vol. 33, pp. 253–63.

Corneo, G. and O. Jeanne, 1997. 'Conspicuous Consumption, Snobbism and Conformism', Journal of Public Economics, Vol. 66, pp. 44–71.

Cropper, M.L., 1976. 'Regulating Activities with Catastrophic Environmental Effects', Journal of Environmental Economics and Management, Vol. 3, pp. 1–15.

Das, S.P., 2001. 'Endogenous Distribution and the Political Economy of Trade Policy', European Journal of Political Economy, Vol. 17, pp. 465–91.

Das, M., 2003. 'Optimal Growth with Decreasing Marginal Impatience', Journal of Economic Dynamics & Control, Vol. 27, pp. 1881–91.

Davis, L.S., 2003. 'The Division of Labor and the Growth of Government', Journal of Economic Dynamics & Control, Vol. 27, pp. 1217–35.

Day, R.H., 1984. *Complex Economic Dynamics*. Cambridge, Mass.: The MIT Press.

Deardorff, A.V., 1973. 'The Gains from Trade in and out of Steady State Growth', Oxford Economic Papers, Vol. 25, pp. 173–91.

Debreu, G., 1959. *Theory of Value*. New York: John Wiley & Sons, Inc.

De la Croix, D. and P. Michel, 2002. *A Theory of Economic Growth: Dynamics and Policy in Overlapping Generations*. Cambridge: Cambridge University Press.

Devereux, M.B., A.C. Head and B.J. Lapham, 1996. 'Monopolistic Competition, Increasing Returns, and the Effects of Government Spending', Journal of Money, Credit, and Banking, Vol. 28, pp. 233–54.

Devereux, M.B., A.C. Head and B.J. Lapham, 2000. 'Government Spending and Welfare with Returns to Specification', Scandinavian Journal of Economics, Vol. 102, pp. 547–61.

Devereux, M.B. and S. Shi, 1991. 'Capital Accumulation and the Current Account in a Two-Country Model', Journal of International Economics, Vol. 30, pp. 1–25.

Diamond, P.A., 1965. 'Disembodied Technical Change in a Two-Sector Model', Review of Economic Studies, Vol. 32, pp. 161–8.

Diamond, D.B. and G.S. Tolley, eds., 1981. *The Economics of Urban Amenities*. New York: Academic Press.

Dixit, A., 2003. 'On Modes of Economic Governance', Econometrica, Vol. 71, pp. 449–81.

Dixit, A. and V. Norman, 1980. *Theory of International Trade*. Cambridge: Cambridge University Press.

Dixit, A. and J.E. Stiglitz, 1977. 'Monopolistic Competition and Optimum Product Diversity', American Economic Review, Vol. 67, pp. 297–308.

Dixon, H.D. and N. Rankin, 1994. 'Imperfect Competition and Macroeconomics: a Survey', Oxford Economic Papers, Vol. 46, pp. 171–99.

Dixon, R.J. and A.P. Thirlwall, 1975. 'A Model of Regional Growth Rate Differences on Kaldorian Lines', Oxford Economic Papers, Vol. 2, pp. 201–14.

Dobb, M., 1973. *Theories of Value and Distribution since Adam Smith*. Cambridge: Cambridge University Press.

Dollar, D., 1986. 'Technological Innovation, Capital Mobility, and the Product Cycle in the North-South Trade', American Economic Review, Vol. 76, pp. 177–90.

Domhoff, G.W., 1990. *The Power Elite and the State: How Policy Is Made in America*. New York: Aldine de Gruyter.

Drandakis, E., 1963. 'Factor Substitution in the Two-Sector Growth Model', Review of Economic Studies, Vol. 30, pp. 105–18.

Dressing, M., 2002. 'Labor Supply, the Family and Poverty: the S-shaped Labor Supply Curve', Journal of Economic Behavior & Organization, Vol. 49, pp. 433–58.

Dressing, M., 2004. 'Implications for Minimum-Wage Policies of an S-Shaped-Supply Curve', Journal of Economic Behavior & Organization, Vol. 53, pp. 543–68.

Drugeon, J.P. and A. Venditti, 2001. 'Intersectoral External Effects, Multiplicities & Indeterminacies', Journal of Economic Dynamics & Control, Vol. 25, pp. 765–87.

Duczynski, P., 2002. 'Adjustment Costs in a Two-Capital Growth Model', Journal of Economic Dynamics & Control, Vol. 26, pp. 837–50.

Duesenberry, J.S., 1949. *Income, Savings, and the Theory of Consumer Behavior*. Cambridge, Mass.: Harvard University Press.

Duménil, G. and D. Lévy, 2003. 'Technology and Distribution: Historical Trajectories à la Marx', Journal of Economic Behavior & Organization, Vol. 52, pp. 201–33.

Duranton, G., 2000. 'Growth and Imperfect Competition on Factor Markets: Increasing Returns and Distribution', European Economic Review, Vol. 44, pp. 255–80.

Duranton, G. and V. Monastiriotis, 2002. 'Mind the Gaps: the Evolution of Regional Earnings Inequalities in the UK 1982–1997', Journal of Regional Science, Vol. 42, pp. 219–56.

Durlauf, S.N., 1996. 'On the Convergence and Divergence of Growth Rates', Economic Journal, Vol. 106, pp. 1016–18.

Dynan, K.E., J. Skinner and S.P. Zeldes, 2004. 'Do the Rich Save More?', Journal of Political Economy, Vol. 112, pp. 397–444.

Easterlin, R.A., 1974. 'Does Economic Growth Enhance the Human Lot?' in *Nations and Households in Economic Growth*. Ed. by P.A. David et al. Palo Alto: Stanford University Press.

Easterlin, R.A., 1975. 'An Economic Framework for Fertility Analysis', Studies in Family Planning, Vol. 6, pp. 54–63.

Eaton, J., 1987. 'A Dynamic Specific-Factors Model of International Trade', Review of Economic Studies, Vol. 54, pp. 325–38.

Eaton, J. and A. Panagariya, 1979. 'Gains from Trade under Variable Returns to Scale, Commodity Taxation, Tariffs and Factor Market Distortions', Journal of International Economics, Vol. 9, pp. 481–502.

Echevarria, C., 1997. 'Changes in Sectoral Composition Associated with Economic Growth', International Economic Review, Vol. 38, pp. 431–52.

Eeckhout, J. and B. Jovanovic, 2002. 'Knowledge Spillovers and Inequality', American Economic Review, Vol. 92, pp. 1290–307.

Ehrlich, I. and F.T. Lui, 1991. 'Intergenerational Trade, Longevity and Economic Growth', Journal of Political Economy, Vol. 99, pp. 1029–59.

Eicher, T.S. and C. García-Peñalosa, 2001. 'Inequality and Growth: the Dual Role of Human Capital in Development', Journal of Development Economics, Vol. 66, pp. 173–97.

Englmann, F.C. and U. Walz, 1995. 'Industrial Centers and Regional Growth in the Presence of Local Inputs', Journal of Regional Science, Vol. 35, pp. 3–27.

Epstein, L.G. and J.A. Hynes, 1983. 'The Rate of Time Preference and Dynamic Economic Analysis', Journal of Political Economy, Vol. 91, pp. 611–35.

Eswaran, M. and A. Kotwal, 2002. 'The Role of the Service Sector in the Process of Industrialiation', Journal of Development Economics, Vol. 68, pp. 401–20.

Ethier, W.J., 1974. 'Some of the Theorems of International Trade with Many Goods and Factors', Journal of International Economics, Vol. 4, pp. 199–206.

Ethier, W.J., 1979. 'Internationally Decreasing Costs and World Trade', Journal of International Economics, Vol. 9, pp. 1–24.

Ethier, W.J., 1982. 'National and International Returns to Scale in the Modern Theory of International Trade', American Economic Review, Vol. 72, 389–405.

Ethier, W.J. and L.E.O. Svensson, 1986. 'The Theorems of International Trade with Factor Mobility', Journal of International Economics, Vol. 20, pp. 21–42.

Evans, G. and S. Honkaponja, 2003. 'Expectations and the Stability Problem for Optimal Monetary Policies', Review of Economic Studies, Vol. 70, pp. 807–24.

Fahr, R., 2005. 'Loafing or Learning – the Demand for Informal Education', European Economic Review, Vol. 49, pp. 75–98.

Fielding, D. and K. Shields, 2003. 'A Nation Divided? Price and Output Dynamics in English Regions', Economic Modelling, Vol. 20, pp. 651–77.

Findlay, R., 1978. 'Relative Backwardness, Direct Foreign Investment and Transfer of Technology', Quarterly Journal of Economics, Vol. 92, pp. 1–16.

Findlay, R., 1984. 'Growth and Development in Trade Models', in *Handbook of International Economics*. Ed. by R.W. Jones and R.B. Kenen. Amsterdam: North-Holland.

Fischer, S. and J.A. Frenkel, 1972. 'Investment, the Two-Sector Model and Trade in Debt and Capital Goods', Journal of International Economics, Vol. 2, pp. 211–33.

Fisher, A.C. and F.A. Peterson, 1976. 'The Environment in Economics: a Survey', Journal of Economic Literature, Vol. 14, pp. 1–33.

Fisher, E.O., 1992. 'Sustained Growth in the Model of Overlapping Generations', Journal of Economic Theory, Vol. 58, pp. 77–92.

Fisher, E.O., 1999. 'On Exchange Rates and Economic Growth', Journal of Economic Dynamics and Control, Vol. 23, pp. 851–72.

Fisher, I., 1912. *Elementary Principles of Economics*. New York: Macmillan.

Foley, D. and D. Michi, 1999. *Growth and Distribution*. Cambridge, Mass.: Harvard University Press.

Forster, B.A., 1973. 'Optimal Consumption Planning in a Polluted Environment', Economic Record, Vol. 49, pp. 534–45.

Forteza, A., 2001. 'Multiple Equilibria in Government Transfer Policy', European Journal of Political Economy, Vol. 17, pp. 531–55.

Francois, J.F., 1994. 'Global Production and Trade: Factor Migration and Commercial Policy with International Scale Economies', International Economic Review, Vol. 35, pp. 565–81.

Frank, R.H., 1985. *Choosing the Right Pond: Human Behavior and the Quest for Status*. New York: Oxford University Press.

Franke, R., 2000. 'An Integration of Schumpeterian and Classical Theories of Growth and Distribution', Structural Change and Economic Dynamics, Vol. 11, pp. 317–36.

Frederick, S., G. Loewenstein and T. O'Donoghue, 2002. 'Time Discontinuing and Time Preference: a Critical Review', Journal of Economic Literature, Vol. 40, pp. 351–401.

Frenkel, J.A. and A. Razin, 1987. *Fiscal Policy and the World Economy*. Cambridge, Mass.: MIT Press.

Friedman, J.W. and I. Grilo, 2005. 'A Market with a Social Consumption Externality', Japanese Economic Review, Vol. 56, pp. 251–72.

Friedman, M., 1956. 'The Quantity Theory of Money: a Restatement, *Studies in the Quantity Theory of Money*. Ed. by M. Friedman. Chicago: University of Chicago Press.

Friedman, M., 1957. *A Theory of the Consumption Function*. Princeton, NJ: Princeton University Press.

Froyen, R. T., 1999. *Macroeconomics: Theories and Policies*, 6th edn. Singapore: Prentice Hall International Inc.

Fujita, M., 1988. 'A Monopolistic Competition Model of Spatial Agglomeration', Regional Science and Urban Economics, Vol. 18, pp. 87–124.

Fujita, M., 1989. *Urban Economic Theory – Land Use and City Size*. Cambridge: Cambridge University Press.

Fujita, M. and P. Krugman, 2004. 'The New Economic Geography: Past, Present and the Future', Papers in Regional Science, Vol. 83, pp. 139–64.

Fujita, M., P. Krugman and A. J. Venables, 1999. *The Spatial Economy*. Cambridge, Mass.: MIT Press.

Fujita, M. and J.F. Thisse, 2002a. *Economics of Agglomeration: Cities, Industrial Location, and Regional Growth*. Cambridge: Cambridge University Press.

Fujita, M. and J.F. Thisse, 2002b. 'Does Geographical Agglomeration Foster Economic Growth? And Who Gains and Loses from It?', Japanese Economic Review, Vol. 54, pp. 121–45.

Gale, D., 1983. *Money: In Disequilibrium*. Cambridge: Cambridge University Press.

Galí, J. and T. Monacelli, 2005. 'Monetary Policy and Exchange Rate Volatility in a Small Open Economy', Review of Economic Studies, Vol. 72, pp. 707–34.

Galor, O., 1992. 'Two-Sector Overlapping-generations Model: a Global Characterization of the Dynamical System', Econometrica, Vol. 60, pp. 1351–86.

Galor, O., 2000. 'Income Distribution and the Process of Development', European Economic Review, Vol. 44, pp. 704–12.

Galor, O. and H.E. Ryder, 1989. 'Existence, Uniqueness, and Stability of Equilibrium in an Overlapping-Generations Model with Productive Capital', Journal of Economic Theory, Vol. 49, pp. 360–75.

Galor, O. and D. Weil, 1996. 'Gender Gap, Fertility, and Growth', American Economic Review, Vol. 86, pp. 374–87.

Galor, O. and D. Weil, 2000. 'Population, Technology, and Growth: from Malthusian Stagnation to the Demographic Transition and Beyond', American Economic Review, Vol. 90, pp. 806–28.

Galor, O. and J. Zeira, 1993. 'Income Distribution and Macroeconomics', Review of Economic Studies, Vol. 60, pp. 35–52.

Gandolfo, G., 1994. *International Economics I – the Pure Theory of International Trade*, 2nd edn. Berlin: Springer-Verlag.

Gerlagh, R. and M.A. Keyzer, 2004. 'Path-Dependent in a Ramsey Model with Resource Amenities and Limited Regeneration', Journal of Economic Dynamics & Control, Vol. 28, pp. 1159–84.

Gerlagh, R. and B.C.C. van der Zwaan, 2002. 'Long-Term Substitutability between Environmental and Man-Made Goods', Journal of Environmental and Economic Management, Vol. 44, pp. 329–45.

Ghiglino, C. and G. Sorger, 2002. 'Poverty Traps, Indeterminacy, and the Wealth Distribution', Journal of Economic Theory, Vol. 105, pp. 120–39.

Giannetti, M., 2003. 'On the Mechanics of Migration Decisions: Skill Complementarities and Endogenous Price Differentials', Journal of Development Economics, Vol. 71, pp. 329–49.

Glachant, J. and C. Vellutini, 2002. 'Quantifying the Relationship between Wealth Distribution and Aggregate Growth in the Ramsey Model', Economics Letters, Vol. 74, pp. 273–41.

Glaeser, E.L. and D.C. Maré, 2001. 'Cities and Skills', Journal of Labor Economics, Vol. 19, pp. 316–42.

Glazer, A., M. Granstein and P. Ranjan, 2003. 'Consumption Variety and Urban Agglomeration', Regional Science and Urban Economics, Vol. 33, pp. 653–61.

Glomm, G. and B. Ravikumar, 1994. 'Public Investment in Infrastructure in a Simple Growth Model', Journal of Economic Dynamics & Control, Vol. 18, pp. 1173–87.

Glomm, G. and B. Ravikumar, 1997. 'Productive Government Expenditures and Long-Run Growth', Journal of Economic Dynamics & Control, Vol. 21, pp. 183–204.

Glomm, G. and B. Ravikumar, 1998. 'Increasing Returns, Human Capital, and the Kuznets Curve', Journal of Development Economics, Vol. 55, pp. 353–67.

Gollier, C. and R. Zeckhauser, 2005. 'Aggregation of Heterogeneous Time Preference', Journal of Political Economy, Vol. 113, pp. 878–95.

Gomme, P., F.E. Kydland and P. Rupert, 2001. 'Home Production Meets Time to Build', Journal of Political Economy, Vol. 109, pp. 1115–31.

Gong, G., A. Greiner and W. Semmler, 2004. 'The Uzawa-Lucas Model without Scale Effects: Theory and Empirical Evidence', Structural Change and Economic Dynamics, Vol. 15, pp. 401–20.

Graham, F.D., 1923. 'Some Aspects of Protection Further Considered', Quarterly Journal of Economics, Vol. 37, pp. 199–227.

Gram, H.G., 1976. 'Two-Sector Models in the Theory of Capital and Growth', American Economic Review, Vol. 66, pp. 891–903.

Gray, J.S., 1998. 'Divorce-Law Changes, Household Bargaining, and Married Women's Labor Supply', American Economic Review, Vol. 88, pp. 628–42.

Greenberg, E.S., 1986. *The American Political System – a Radical Approach*. Boston: Little, Brown and Company.

Greenhut, M.L., G. Norman and C.S. Hung, 1987. *The Economics of Imperfect Competition – a Spatial Approach*. Cambridge: Cambridge University Press.

Greenwood, J. and Z. Hercowitz, 1991. 'The Allocation of Capital and Time over the Business Cycle', Journal of Political Economy, Vol. 99, pp. 1188–214.

Grinols, E.L., 1992. 'Increasing Returns and the Gains From Trade', International Economic Review, Vol. 32, pp. 973–84.

Grossman, G.M. and E. Helpman, 1991. *Innovation and Growth in the Global Economy*. Cambridge, Mass.: The MIT Press.

Grossman, G.M. and E. Helpman, 1994. 'Protection for Sale', American Economic Review, Vol. 84, pp. 833–50.

Grossmann, V., 2001. *Inequality, Economic Growth, and Technological Change*. New York: Physica-Verlag.

Gruver, G.W., 1976. 'Optimal Investment in Pollution Control Capital in a Neoclassical Growth Context', Journal of Environmental Economics and Management, Vol. 3, pp. 165–77.

Guo, J.T., 2004. 'Increasing Returns, Capital Utilization, and the Effects of Government Spending', Journal of Economic Dynamics & Control, Vol. 28, pp. 1059–78.
Haavelmo, T., 1954. *A Study in the Theory of Economic Evolution.* Amsterdam: North-Holland.
Hale, J. and H. Koçak, 1991. *Dynamics and Bifurcations.* Berlin: Springer-Verlag.
Harris, J.R. and M.P. Todaro, 1970. 'Migration, Unemployment and Development: a Two-Sector Analysis', American Economic Review, Vol. 60, pp. 126–42.
Hazan, M. and Y.D. Maoz, 2002. 'Women's Labor Force Participation and the Dynamics of Tradition', Economics Letters, Vol. 75, pp. 193–8.
Heckman, J.J., 1976. 'A Life-Cycle Model of Earnings, Learning, and Consumption', Journal of Political Economy, Vol. 84, pp. S11–44.
Heckman, J.J., A. Layner-Farrar and P. Todd, 1996. 'Human Capital Pricing Equations with an Application to Estimating the Effect of School Quality on Earnings', Review of Economics and Statistics, Vol. 78, pp. 562–610.
Heckscher, E., 1919. 'The Effect of Foreign Trade on the Distribution of Income', Ekonomisk Tidskrift, pp. 497–512.
Helpman, E., ed., 1998. *General Purpose Technologies and Economic Growth.* Cambridge, Mass.: The MIT Press.
Helpman, E. and P. R. Krugman, 1985. *Market Structure and Foreign Trade.* Cambridge, Mass.: MIT Press.
Henderson, J.V., 1985. *Economic Theories and Cities*, 2nd edn. New York: Academic Press.
Henderson, J. V., 2003. 'The Urbanization Process and Economic Growth: the So-What Question', Journal of Economic Growth, Vol. 8, pp. 47–71.
Henderson, J. V., A. Kuncoro and M. Turner, 2003. 'Industrial Development in Cities', Journal of Political Economy, Vol. 103, pp. 1067–90.
Hillman, A.L., 1982. 'Declining Industries and Political-Support Protectionist Motives', American Economic Review, Vol. 72, pp. 1180–7.
Hockman, O., D. Pines and J.F. Thisse, 1995. 'On the Optimal Structure of Local Governments', American Economic Review, Vol. 85, pp. 1224–40.
Holländer, H., 2001. 'On the Validity of Utility Statements: Standard Theory Versus Duesenberry's', Journal of Economic Behavior & Organization, Vol. 45, pp. 227–49.
Hommes, C.H., 1991. *Chaotic Dynamics in Economic Models: Some Simple Case-Studies.* Groningen: Wolters-Noordhoff.
Hommes, C.H., 1998. 'On the Consistency of Backward-Looking Expectations: the Case of the Cobweb', Journal of Economic Behavior & Organization, Vol. 33, pp. 333–62.
Hughes, J. and L.P. Cain, 1998. *American Economic History.* New York: Addison-Wesley.
Ikeda, S. and Y. Ono, 1992. 'Macroeconomic Dynamics in a Multi-Country Economy – a Dynamic Optimization Approach', International Economic Review, Vol. 33, pp. 629–44.
Imrohoroglu, S., 1998. 'A Quantitative Analysis of Capital Income Taxation', International Economic Review, Vol. 39, pp. 307–28.
Ioannides, Y.M. and L.D. Loury, 2004. 'Job Information Network, Neighborhood Effects, and Inequality', Journal of Economic Literature, Vol. 42, 1056–93.
Iooss, G. and D.D. Joseph, 1980. *Elementary Stability and Bifurcation Theory.* New York: Springer-Verlag.

Isard, W., 1953. 'Some Empirical Results and Problems of Regional Input–Output Analysis', in *Studies in the Structure of the American Economy*. Ed. by W. Leontief et al. New York: Oxford University Press.
Isard, W., 1956. *Location and Space Economy*. Cambridge, Mass.: MIT Press.
Isard, W., 1960. *Methods of Regional Analysis*. Cambridge, Mass.: MIT Press.
Isard, W., 1977. 'How Far Can We Push the "Law of One Price"?', American Economic Review, Vol. 67, pp. 942–8.
Jehle, G.A. and P.J. Reny, 1998. *Advanced Microeconomic Theory*. New York: Addison-Wesley.
Jellah, M. and Y. Zenou, 2000. 'A Dynamic Efficiency Wage Model with Learning by Doing', Economic Letters, Vol. 66, pp. 99–105.
Jensen, B.S., 1994. *The Dynamic Systems of Basic Economic Growth Models*. Dordrecht: Kluwer Academic.
Jensen, B.S. and K.Y. Wong, eds., 1998, *Dynamics, Economic Growth, and International Trade*. Ann Arbor: The University of Michigan Press.
Jha, R., 1998. *Modern Public Economics*. London: Routledge.
Johnson, H.G., 1971. 'Trade and Growth: a Geometric Exposition', Journal of International Economics, Vol. 1, pp. 83–101.
Jones, L.E. and R.E. Manuelli, 1995. 'Growth and the Effects of Inflation', Journal of Economic Dynamics and Control, Vol. 19, pp. 1405–28.
Jones, L.E., R.E. Manuelli and P.E. Rossi, 1997. 'On the Optimal Taxation of Capital Income', Journal of Economic Theory, Vol. 73, pp. 93–117.
Jones, R.W., 1971. 'A Three-Factor Model in Theory, Trade and History', in *Trade, Balance of Payments and Growth*. Ed. by J.N. Bhagwati et al. Amsterdam: North-Holland.
Jones, R.W., 1979. *International Trade: Essays in Theory*. Amsterdam: North-Holland Publishing Company.
Jones, R.W. and P.B. Kenen, eds., 1984, *Handbook of International Economics – International Trade*. Amsterdam: North-Holland.
Jones, R.W. and J.P. Neary, 1984. 'The Positive Theory of International Trade', in *Handbook of International Economics – International Trade*. Ed. R.W. Jones and P.B. Kenen. Amsterdam: North-Holland.
Jouini, E. and C. Napp, 2006. 'Heterogeneous Beliefs and Asset Pricing in Discrete Time: an Analysis of Pessimism and Doubt', Journal of Economic Dynamics and Control (in press).
Jovanovic, B. and Y. Nyarko, 1996. 'Learning by Doing and the Choice of Technology', Econometrica, Vol. 64, pp. 1299–310.
Judd, K.L., 1985. 'On the Performance of Patents', Econometrica, Vol. 53, pp. 567–86.
Kaiyama, M., 1973. 'On the Growth Model of a Dual Economy', Economic Studies Quarterly, Vol. 24, pp. 1–15.
Kaldor, N., 1955. 'Alternative Theories of Distribution', Review of Economic Studies, Vol. 23, pp. 83–100.
Kaldor, N., 1966. 'Marginal Productivity and the Macro-Economic Theories of Distribution', Review of Economic Studies, Vol. 33, pp. 309–19.
Kanemoto, Y., 1980. *Theories of Urban Externalities*. Amsterdam: North-Holland.
Karp, L. and H. Lee, 2001. 'Learning by Doing and the Choice of Technology: the Role of Patience', Journal of Economic Theory, Vol. 100, pp. 73–92.

Katz, L. and D. Autor, 2000. 'Changes in the Wage Structure and Earnings Inequality', in *The Handbook of Labor Economics*, Vol. 3. Ed. by O. Ashenfelter and D. Card. Amsterdam: Elsevier.

Keister, L.A., 2000. *Wealth in America: Trends in Wealth Inequality*. Cambridge: Cambridge University Press.

Keller, W., 2004. 'International Technological Diffusion', Journal of Economic Literature, Vol. 42, pp. 752–82.

Kemp, M.C., 1961. 'Foreign Investment and National Advantage', Economic Record, Vol. 28, pp. 56–62.

Kemp, M.C. and T. Negishi, 1970. 'Variable Returns to Scale, Commodity Taxes, Factor Market Distortions, and Implications for Trade Gains', Swedish Journal of Economics, Vol. 72, pp. 1–11.

Kennedy, C., 1964. 'Induced Bias in Innovation and the Theory of Distribution', Economic Journal, Vol. 74, Sep.

Kennedy, P.W., 1994. 'Equilibrium Pollution Taxes in Open Economies with Imperfect Competition', Journal of Environmental Economics and Management, Vol. 27, pp. 49–63.

Keynes, J.M., 1936. *The General Theory of Employment, Interest Rate and Money*. New York: Harcourt, Brace.

Kim, S.J. and Y.J. Kim, 2000. 'Growth Gains from Trade and Education', Journal of International Economics, Vol. 50, pp. 519–45.

Kimmel, J. and T.J. Kniesner, 1998. 'New Evidence on Labor Supply: Employment versus Hours Elasticities by Sex and Martial Status', Journal of Monetary Economics, Vol. 42, pp. 289–302.

King, R.G. and S. Rebelo, 1993. 'Transitional Dynamics and Economic Growth in the Neoclassical Model', American Economic Review, Vol. 83, pp. 908–31.

Knapp, D.J. and F. Nourzad, 1994. 'The Substitutability of Equities and Consumption Durable Goods: a Portfolio-Choice Approach', Southern Economic Journal, Vol. 60, pp. 612–21.

Knell, M., 1999. 'Social Comparisons, Inequality, and Growth', Journal of Institutional and Theoretical Economics, Vol. 155, pp. 664–95.

Knight, F.H., 1924. 'Some Fallacies in the Interpretation of Social Costs', Quarterly Journal of Economics, Vol. 38, pp. 582–606.

Koomann, R., 2002. 'Monetary Policy Rules in the Open Economy: Effects on Welfare and Business Cycles', Journal of Monetary Economics, Vol. 49, pp. 899–1015.

Koopmans, T.C., 1965. *On the Concept of Optimal Economic Growth*. Amsterdam: North-Holland.

Kostiuk, P.F., 1990. 'Compensating Differentials for Shift Work', Journal of Political Economy, Vol. 98, pp. 1055–75.

Krawczyk, J.B. and K. Shimomura, 2003. 'Why Countries with the Same Technology and Preferences Can Have Different Growth Rates', Journal of Economic Dynamics & Control, Vol. 27, pp. 1899–916.

Krugman, P., 1979. 'A Model of Innovation, Technology Transfer and the World Distribution of Income', Journal of Political Economy, Vol. 87, pp. 253–66.

Krugman, P., 1989. 'Increasing Returns, Monopolistic Competition, and International Trade', Journal of International Economics, Vol. 9, pp. 469–79.
Krugman, P., 1990. *Rethinking International Trade*. Cambridge, Mass.: The MIT Press.
Krugman, P., 1991. 'Increasing Returns and Economic Geography', Journal of Political Economy, Vol. 99, pp. 183–99.
Krugman, P. and A.J. Venables, 1995. 'Globalization and the Inequality of Nations', Quarterly Journal of Economics, Vol. 110, pp. 857–80.
Krusell, P. and J.V. Rios-Rull, 1996. 'Vested Interests in a Positive Theory of Stagnation and Growth', Review of Economic Studies, Vol. 63, pp. 301–29.
Krusell, P. and J.V. Rios-Rull, 1999. 'On the Size of U.S. Government: Political Economy in the Neoclassical Growth Model', American Economic Review, Vol. 89, pp. 1156–81.
Kuhn, T.S., 1977. *The Structure of Scientific Revolutions*. Chicago: The University of Chicago Press.
Kuznets, S., 1955. 'Economic Growth and Income Inequality', American Economic Review, Vol. 45, pp. 1–28.
Kuznets, S., 1963. 'Quantitative Aspects of the Economic Growth of Nations', Economic Development and Cultural Change, Vol. 11, pp. 1–80.
Kuznets, S., 1966. *Modern Economic Growth*. London: Yale University Press.
Kuznets, S., 1973. 'Modern Economic Growth – Findings and Reflections', American Economic Review, Vol. 63, pp. 247–58.
Kuznetsov, Y.A., 1998. *Elements of Applied Bifurcation Theory*. Berlin: Springer.
Ladrón-de-Guevara, A., S. Ortigueira and M.S. Santos, 1997. 'Equilibrium Dynamics in Two-Sector Models of Endogenous Growth', Journal of Economic Dynamics and Control, Vol. 21, pp. 115–43.
Ladrón-de-Guevara, A., S. Ortigueira and M.S. Santos, 1999. 'A Two Sector Model of Endogenous Growth with Leisure', Review of Economic Studies, Vol. 66, pp. 609–31.
Laitner, J., 1995. 'Quantitative Evaluations of Efficient Tax Policies for Lucas Supply-Side Models', Oxford Economic Papers, Vol. 47, pp. 471–92.
Laitner, J., 2000. 'Structural Change and Economic Growth', Review of Economic Studies, Vol. 67, pp. 545–61.
Lancaster, K.J., 1966. 'A New Approach to Consumer Theory,' Journal of Political Economy, Vol. 74, pp. 132–57.
Lancaster, K. J., 1971. *Consumer Demand*. New York: Columbia University Press.
Lane, P.R., 2001. 'The New Open Economy Macroeconomics: a Survey', Journal of International Economics, Vol. 54, pp. 235–66.
Lanfranchi, J., H. Ohlsson and A. Skalli, 2002. 'Compensating Wage Differentials and Shift Work Preferences', Economics Letters, Vol. 74, pp. 393–8.
Laslier, J.F. and N. Picard, 2002. 'Distributive Politics and Electoral Competition', Journal of Economic Theory, Vol. 103, pp. 106–30.
Leontief, W.W., 1936. 'Quantitative Input–Output Relations in the Economic System of the United States', Review of Economics and Statistics, Vol. 8, pp. 105–25.
Leontief, W.W., 1941. *The Structure of American Economy, 1919–1939*. New York: Oxford University Press.

Lerner, A.P., 1952. 'Factor Prices and International Trade', Economica, Vol. 19, pp. 1–15.

Levy, P.I., 1997. 'A Political-Economic Analysis of Free-Trade Agreements', American Economic Review, Vol. 87, pp. 506–19.

Lewis, W.A., 1954. 'Economic Development with Unlimited Supplies of Labour', The Manchester School, Vol. 22, pp. 139–91.

Lewis, W.A., 1955. *The Theory of Economic Growth*. London: Allen & Unwin.

Lindbeck, A., S. Nyberg and J.W. Weibull, 1999. 'Social Norms and Economic Incentives in the Welfare State', Quarterly Journal of Economics, Vol. 114, pp. 1–35.

Liso, N.D., G. Filatrella and N. Weaver, 2001. 'On Endogenous Growth and Increasing Returns: Modeling Learning-by-Doing and the Division of Labor', Journal of Economic Behavior & Organization, Vol. 46, pp. 39–55.

Ljungquist, L. and H. Uhlig, 2000. 'Tax Policy and Aggregate Demand Management under Catching up with the Joneses', American Economic Review, Vol. 90, pp. 356–66.

Lucas, R.E., 1988. 'On the Mechanics of Economic Development', Journal of Monetary Economics, Vol. 22, pp. 3–42.

Lucas, R.E., 1990. 'Supply-Side Economics: an Analytical Review', Oxford Economic Papers, Vol. 42, pp. 293–316.

Lucas R.E., 2004. 'Earnings and Rural-Urban Migration', Journal of Political Economy, Vol. 112, pp. S29–59.

Lucas, R.E. and E. Rossi-Hansberg, 2002. 'On the Internal Structure of Cities', Econometrica, Vol. 70, pp. 1445–76.

MacDougall, G.D.A., 1960. 'The Benefits and Costs of Private Investment from Abroad: a Theoretical Approach', Economic Record, Vol. 27, pp. 13–15.

Maital, S. and S.L. Maital, 1994. 'Is the Future What It Used To Be? A Behavioral Theory of the Decline of Saving in the West', Journal of Socio-Economics, Vol. 23, pp. 1–32.

Mäler, K.G., 1974. *Environmental Economics – a Theoretical Inquiry*. Baltimore: Johns Hopkins University.

Mäler, K.G., 2000. 'Development, Ecological Resources and Their Management: a Study of Complex Dynamic Systems, Joseph Schumpeter Lecture', European Economic Review, Vol. 44, pp. 645–65.

Manasse, P. and A. Turrini, 2001. 'Trade, Wages, and "Superstars"', Journal of International Economics, Vol. 54, pp. 97–117.

Marglin, S.A., 1984. *Growth, Distribution, and Prices*. Cambridge: Harvard University Press.

Marjit, S. and R. Acharyya, 2003. *International Trade, Wage Inequality and the Developing Economy*. Heidelberg: Physica-Verlag.

Markusen, J.R. and J.R. Melvin, 1984. 'The Gains from Trade Theorem with Increasing Returns to Scale', in *Monopolistic Competition and International Trade*. Ed. by H. Kierzkowski. Oxford: Clarendon Press.

Marshall, A., 1890. *Principles of Economics*, 1990. London: Macmillan.

Martin, P. and G. Ottaviano, 2001. 'Growth and Agglomeration', International Economic Review, Vol. 42, pp. 947–68.

Mas-Colell, A., M.D. Whinston and J.R. Green, 1995. *Microeconomic Theory*. New York: Oxford University Press.

Matsuyama, K., 1991a. 'Endogenous Price Fluctuations in an Optimizing Model of a Monetary Economy', Econometrica, Vol. 59, pp. 1617–31.

Matsuyama, K., 1991b. 'Increasing Returns, Industrialization, and Indeterminacy of Equilibrium', Quarterly Journal of Economics, Vol. 106, pp. 617–50.

Matsuyama, K., 1992. 'Agricultural Productivity, Comparative Advantage, and Economic Growth', Journal of Economic Theory, Vol. 58, pp. 317–34.

Matsuyama, K., 2000. 'Endogenous Inequality', Review of Economic Studies, Vol. 67, pp. 743–59.

Matsuyama, K., 2001. 'Growing through Cycles in an Infinitely Lived Agent Economy', Journal of Economic Theory, Vol. 100, pp. 220–34.

Matsuyama, K., 2004. 'Financial Market Globalization, Symmetry-Breaking and Endogenous Inequality of Nations', Econometrica, Vol. 72, pp. 853–84.

Matthews, R.C.O., 1949. 'Reciprocal Demand and Increasing Returns', Review of Economic Studies, Vol. 37, pp. 149–58.

Maurer, R., 1998. *Economic Growth and International Trade with Capital Goods – Theories and Empirical Goods.* Tübingen: Mohr Siebeck.

Mayer, W. and R.G. Riezman, 1987. 'Endogenous Choice of Trade Policy Instruments', Journal of International Economics, Vol. 23, pp. 377–81.

Mayer, W. and R.G. Riezman, 1990. 'Voter Preferences for Trade Policy Instruments', Economics and Politics, Vol. 2, pp. 259–73.

McCann, P., 2005. 'Transport Costs and New Economic Geography', Journal of Economic Geography, Vol. 5, pp. 305–18.

McCombie, J.S.L., 1988. 'A Synoptic View of Regional Growth and Unemployment: I – Neoclassical Theory', Urban Studies, Vol. 25, pp. 267–81.

McGrattan, E., E. Rogerson and R. Wright, 1997. 'An Equilibrium Model of the Business Cycle with Household Production and Fiscal Policy', International Economic Review, Vol. 38, pp. 267–90.

Meier, G.M. and J.E. Rauch, 2000. *Leading Issues in Economic Development.* Oxford: Oxford University Press.

Milesi-Ferretti, G.M. and N. Roubini, 1998. 'Growth Effects of Income and Consumption Taxes', Journal of Money, Credit and Banking, Vol. 30, pp. 721–44.

Milikovic, D., 1999. 'The Law of One Price in International Trade: a Critical Review', Review of Agricultural Economics, Vol. 21, pp. 126–39.

Mill, J.S., 1848. *Principles of Political Economy.* 1970. London: Penguin.

Mino, K., 1996. 'Analysis of a Two-Sector Model of Endogenous Growth with Capital Income Taxation', International Economic Review, Vol. 37, pp. 227–51.

Moav, O., 2002. 'Income Distribution and Macroeconomics: the Persistence of Inequality in a Convex Technology Framework', Economics Letters, Vol. 75, pp. 187–92.

Modigliani, F., 1966. 'The Life Cycle Hypothesis of Saving, the Demand for Wealth and the Supply of Capital', Social Research, Vol. 33, pp. 160–217.

Moomaw, R.L., 1983. 'Spatial Productivity Variations in Manufacturing: a Critical Survey of Cross-Sectional Analyses', International Regional Science Review, Vol. 8, pp. 1–22.

Morishima, M., 1964. *Equilibrium, Stability, and Growth.* Oxford: Clarendon Press.

Morishima, M., 1969. *Theory of Economic Growth*. Oxford: Clarendon Press.
Morishima, M., 1989. *Ricardo's Economics – a General Equilibrium Theory of Distribution and Growth*. Cambridge: Cambridge University Press.
Mulligan, C.B. and X. Sala-I-Martin, 1993. 'Transitional Dynamics in Two-Sector Models of Endogenous Growth', Quarterly Journal of Economics, Vol. 108, pp. 739–73.
Murata, Y., 2002. 'Rural-urban Interdependence and Industrialization', Journal of Development Economics, Vol. 68, pp. 1–34.
Mussa, M., 1974. 'Tariffs and the Distribution of Income: the Importance of Factor Specificity, Substitutability, and Intensity in the Short and Long Run', Journal of Political Economy, Vol. 82, pp. 1191–203.
Myrdal, G., 1957. *Rich Lands and Poor*. New York: Harper and Row.
Nahuis, R., 2003. *Knowledge, Inequality and Growth in the New Economy*. Cheltenham: Edward Elgar.
Nakajima, T., 2003. 'Catch-up in Turn in a Multi-Country International Trade Model with Learning-by-Doing and Invention', Journal of Development Economics, Vol. 72, pp. 117–38.
Nardini, F., 2001. *Technical Progress and Economic Growth: Business Cycles and Stabilization Policies*. Berlin: Springer.
Negishi, T., 1972. *General Equilibrium and International Trade*. Amsterdam: North-Holland Publishing Company.
Negishi, T., 1989. *History of Economic Theory*. Amsterdam: North-Holland.
Nelson, R.R. and S.G. Winter, 1982. *An Evolutionary Theory of Economic Change*. Cambridge, Mass.: Harvard University Press.
Ng, Y.K., 1987. 'Relative Income Effects and the Appropriate Level of Public Expenditure', Oxford Economic Papers, Vol. 39, pp. 293–300.
Ni, S., 1999. 'National Debt, Savings, and Real Interest Rates in a Neoclassical Model with Endogenous Labor-Supply and Knowledge-Based Growth', Canadian Journal of Economics, Vol. 32, pp. 1227–44.
Niehans, J., 1963. 'Economic Growth with Two Endogenous Factors', Quarterly Journal of Economics, Vol. 77, pp. 349–71.
Nikaido, H., 1968. *Convex Structures and Economic Theory*. New York: Academic Press.
Nishimura, K. and K. Shimomura, 2002. 'Trade and Indeterminacy in a Dynamic General Equilibrium Model', Journal of Economic Theory, Vol. 105, pp. 244–60.
Nishimura, K. and M. Yano, 1995. 'Nonlinear Dynamics and Chaos in Optimal Growth: an Example', Econometrica, Vol. 63, pp. 981–1001.
Nocco, A., 2005. 'The Rise and Fall of Regional Inequalities with Technological Differences and Knowledge Spillovers', Regional Science and Urban Economics, Vol. 35, pp. 542–69.
Obstfeld, M., 1981. 'Capital Mobility and Devaluation in an Optimizing Model with Rational Expectations', American Economic Review, Vol. 71, pp. 217–21.
Obstfeld, M. and K. Rogoff, 1995. 'Exchange Rate Dynamics Redux', Journal of Political Economy, Vol. 103, pp. 624–60.
Obstfeld, M. and K. Rogoff, 1998. *Foundations of International Macroeconomics*. Cambridge, Mass.: MIT Press.
Ohlin, B., 1933. *Interregional and International Trade*. Cambridge: Harvard University Press.

Oniki, H. and H. Uzawa, 1965. 'Patterns of Trade and Investment in a Dynamic Model of International Trade', Review of Economic Studies, Vol. 32, pp. 15–38.

Ortigueira, S. and M.S. Santos, 2002. 'Equilibrium Dynamics in a Two-Sector Model with Taxes', Journal of Economic Theory, Vol. 105, pp. 99–119.

Oswald, A.J., 1997. 'Happiness and Economic Performance', Economic Journal, Vol. 107, pp. 1815–31.

Ottaviano, G.I.P. and J.F. Thisse, 2002. 'Integration, Agglomeration and the Political Economics of Factor Mobility', Journal of Public Economics, Vol. 83, pp. 429–56.

Oulton, N., 1993. 'Widening the Human Stomach: the Effects of New Consumer Goods on Economic Growth and Leisure', Oxford Economic Papers, Vol. 45, pp. 364–86.

Parente, S., 1994. 'Technology Adoption, Learning-by-Doing, and Economic Growth', Journal of Economic Theory, Vol. 63, pp. 349–69.

Pasinetti, L.L., 1974. *Growth and Income Distribution – Essays in Economic Theory*. Cambridge: Cambridge University Press.

Pasinetti, L.L., 1981. *Structural Change and Economic Growth – a Theoretical Essay on the Dynamics of the Wealth of Nations*. Cambridge: Cambridge University Press.

Pasinetti, L.L., 1993. *Structural Economic Dynamics – a Theory of the Economic Consequences of Human Learning*. Cambridge: Cambridge University Press.

Persson, T. and G. Tabellini, 1994. 'Is Inequality Harmful for Growth? ', American Economic Review, Vol. 84, pp. 600–21.

Piketty, T., 1997. 'The Dynamics of the Wealth Distribution and the Interest Rate with Credit Rationing', Review of Economic Studies, Vol. 64, pp. 173–89.

Pitchford, J.D., 1974. *Population in Economic Growth*. Amsterdam: North-Holland Publishing Company.

Plourde, G.C., 1972. 'A Model of Waste Accumulation and Disposal', Canadian Journal of Economics, Vol. 5, pp. 119–25.

Rader, T., 1963. 'The Existence of a Utility Function to Represent Preferences', Review of Economic Studies, Vol. 30, pp. 229–32.

Rader, T., 1981. 'Utility over Time: the Homothetic Case', Journal of Economic Theory, Vol. 25, pp. 219–36.

Ralf, K., 2001. 'Do Complementary Factors Lead to Economic Fluctuations? ', Economics Letters, Vol. 71, pp. 97–103.

Ramsey, F., 1928. 'A Mathematical Theory of Saving', Economic Journal, Vol. 38, pp. 543–59.

Rauch, J.E., 1991. 'Comparative Advantage, Geographic Advantage and the Volume of Trade', Economic Journal, Vol. 101, pp. 1230–44.

Raut, L.K. and T.N. Srinivasan, 1994. 'Dynamics of Endogenous Growth', Economic Theory, Vol. 4, pp. 770–90.

Rebelo, S., 1991. 'Long-Run Policy Analysis and Long-Run Growth', Journal of Political Economy, Vol. 99, pp. 500–21.

Ren, L.Q. and P. Rangazas, 2003. 'Retirement Saving and Development Traps', Journal of Development Economics, Vol. 70, pp. 119–32.

Rey, H., 2001. 'International Trade and Currency Exchange', Review of Economic Studies, Vol. 68, pp. 443–64.

Rey, S.J. and B.D. Montouri, 1999. 'US Regional Income Convergence: a Spatial Econometric Perspective', Regional Studies, Vol. 33, pp. 143–56.

Ricardo, D., 1817. *The Principles of Political Economy and Taxation*, 3rd edn., 1965. London: Everyman's Library.

Richardson, H. W., 1977. *Regional Growth Theory*. London: Macmillan.

Rivera-Batiz, F., 1988. 'Increasing Returns, Monopolistic Competition, and Agglomeration Economies in Competition and Production', Regional Science and Urban Economics, Vol. 18, pp. 125–53.

Rivera-Batiz, L.A. and P.M. Romer, 1991. 'Economic Integration and Endogenous Growth', Quarterly Journal of Economics, Vol. 106, pp. 531–56.

Roback, J., 1982. 'Wages, Rents and Quality of Life', Journal of Political Economy, Vol. 90, pp. 1257–78.

Robson, A.J., 1992. 'Status, the Distribution of Wealth, Private and Social Attitudes to Risk', Econometrica, Vol. 60, pp. 837–57.

Roemer, J.E., 1996. *Theories of Distributive Justice*. Chicago: The University of Chicago Press.

Romer, D., 1996. *Advanced Macroeconomics*. New York: The McGraw-Hill Companies.

Romer, P.M., 1986. 'Increasing Returns and Long-Run Growth', Journal of Political Economy, Vol. 94, pp. 1002–37.

Romer, P.M., 1987. 'Growth Based on Increasing Returns due to Specialization', American Economic Review, Vol. 77, pp. 56–62.

Romer, P.M., 1990. 'Endogenous Technological Change', Journal of Political Economy, Vol. 98, pp. S71–102.

Rosenzweig, M.R. and O. Stark, eds., 1997. *Handbook of Population and Family Economics*, in two volumes. Amsterdam: Elsevier.

Rostow, W.W., 1960. *Stages of Economic Growth*. Cambridge: Cambridge University Press.

Roy, J.R. and B. Johansson, 1993. 'A Model of Trade Flows in Differentiated Goods', Annals of Regional Science, Vol. 27, pp. 95–115.

Ruffin, R.J., 1979. 'Growth and the Long-Run Theory of International Capital Movements', American Economic Review, Vol. 69, pp. 832–42.

Rupert, P., R. Rogerson, and R. Wright, 2000. 'Homework in Labor Economics: Household Production and Intertemporal Substitution', Journal of Monetary Economics, Vol. 46, pp. 557–79.

Rybczynski, T.M., 1955. 'Factor Endowments and Relative Commodity Prices', Economica, Vol. 22, pp. 336–41.

Ryder, H.E., 1967. 'Optimal Accumulation and Trade in an Open Economy of Moderate Size', in *Essays on the Theory of Optimal Growth*. Ed. by K. Shell. Cambridge, Mass.: MIT Press.

Sahota, G.S., 1978. 'Theories of Personal Income Distribution', Journal of Economic Literature, Vol. 16, pp. 1–55.

Salvadori, N., 1991. 'Post-Keynesian Theory of Distribution in the Long Run', in *Nicholas Kaldor and Mainstream Economics – Confrontation or Convergence?*. Ed. by E.J. Nell and W. Semmler. London: Macmillan.

Samuelson, L., 2004. 'Modeling Knowledge in Economic Analysis', Journal of Economic Literature, Vol. 42, pp. 367–403.

Samuelson, P.A., 1937. 'A Note on Measurement of Utility', Review of Economic Studies, Vol. 4, pp. 155–61.
Samuelson, P.A., 1948. 'International Trade and Equalisation of Factor Prices', Economic Journal, Vol. 58, pp. 163–84.
Samuelson, P.A., 1949. 'International Factor-Price Equalisation Once Again', Economic Journal, Vol. 59, pp. 181–97.
Samuelson, P.A., 1958. 'An Exact Consumption Loan Model of Interest with or without the Social Contrivance of Money', Journal of Political Economy, Vol. 66, pp. 467–82.
Samuelson, P.A., 1965. 'A Theory of Induced Innovation along Kennedy-Weizsäcker Lines', Review of Economics and Statistics, Vol. 18, pp. 343–56.
Samuelson, P.A., 1971. 'Ohlin Was Right', Swedish Journal of Economics, Vol. 73, pp. 365–84.
Samuelson, P.A. and F. Modigliani, 1966. 'The Pasinetti Paradox in Neo-Classical and More General Models', Review of Economic Studies, Vol. 33, pp. 269–301.
Sato, K., 1966. 'The Neoclassical Theorem and Distribution of Income and Wealth', Review of Economic Studies, Vol. 33, pp. 331–6.
Sato, R. and S. Tsutsui, 1984. 'Technical Progress, the Schumpeterian Hypothesis and Market Structure', Journal of Economics, Vol. S4, pp. 1–37.
Sattinger, M., 1993. 'Assignment Models of the Distribution of Earnings', Journal of Economic Literature, Vol. 31, 831–80.
Schmitt, J., 2000. 'Inequality and Globalization: Some Evidence from the United States', in *The Ends of Globalization: Bringing Society Back*. Ed. by D. Kalb, M. V. D. Land, R. Staring, B.V. Steenbergen and N. Wilterdink. Lanham: Rowman & Littlefield.
Schultz, T.W., 1981. *Investing in People – the Economics of Population Quality*. Berkeley: University of California Press.
Schumpeter, J.A., 1954. *History of Economic Analysis*. New York: Oxford University Press.
Scotchmer, S. and J.F. Thisse, 1992. 'Space and Competition – a Puzzle', Annals of Regional Science, Vol. 26, pp. 269–86.
Seckin, A., 2001. 'Consumption-Leisure Choice with Habit Formation', Economics Letters, Vol. 70, pp. 115–20.
Sedgley, N. and B. Elmslie, 2004. 'The Geographical Concentration of Knowledge: Scale, Agglomeration, and Congestion in Innovation across U.S. States', International Regional Science Review, Vol. 27, pp. 111–37.
Shell, K., 1973. 'Incentive Activity, Industrial Organization and Economic Growth', in *Models of Economic Growth*. Ed. by J.M. Mirrlees and N.H. Stern. New York: Wiley.
Shi, S. and L.G. Epstein, 1993. 'Habits and Time Preference', International Economic Review, Vol. 34, pp. 61–84.
Shleifer, A. and R.W. Vishny, 1993. 'Corruption', Quarterly Journal of Economics, Vol. 108, pp. 599–617.
Shone, R., 2002. *Economic Dynamics – Phase Diagrams and Their Economic Application*. Cambridge: Cambridge University Press.
Siebert, H., 1969. *Regional Growth – Theory and Policy*. Scranton: International Textbook Company.

Simon, C.P. and L. Blume, 1994. *Mathematics for Economics*. New York: W.W. Norton & Company.

Simon, J.L. and D.O. Love, 1990. 'City Size, Prices, and Efficiency for Individual Goods and Services', Annals of Regional Science, Vol. 24, pp. 163–75.

Sivitanidou, R. and W.C. Wheaton, 1992. 'Wage and Rent Capitalization in the Commercial Real Estate Market', Journal of Urban Economics, Vol. 31, pp. 206–29.

Smith, A., 1776. *An Inquiry into the Nature and Causes of the Wealth of Nations*, edited by E. Cannan, 1976. Chicago: The University of Chicago Press.

Smith, V.K., 1972. 'Dynamics of Waste Accumulation: Disposal versus Recycling', Quarterly Journal of Economics, Vol. 86, pp. 601–16.

Solow, R., 1956. 'A Contribution to the Theory of Growth', Quarterly Journal of Economics, Vol. 70, pp. 65–94.

Solow, R., 1999. 'Neoclassical Growth Theory', in *Handbook of Macroeconomics*, Vol. 1. Ed. by J.B. Taylor and M. Woodford. Amsterdam: Elsevier.

Solow, R., 2000. *Growth Theory – an Exposition*. New York: Oxford University Press.

Song, E.Y., 2002. 'Taxation, Human Capital and Growth', Journal of Economic Dynamics & Control, Vol. 26, pp. 205–16.

Song, X.C., 2003. 'A Two-Sector Adaptive Economizing Model of Economic Growth', Journal of Economic Behavior & Organization, Vol. 52, pp. 585–94.

Sorger, G., 2000. 'Income and Wealth Distribution in a Simple Model of Growth', Economic Theory, Vol. 16, pp. 23–42.

Sorger, G., 2002a. 'On the Long-Run Distribution of Capital in the Ramsey Model', Journal of Economic Theory, Vol. 105, pp. 226–43.

Sorger, G., 2002b. 'On the Multi-Region Version of the Solow-Swan Model', Japanese Economic Review, Vol. 54, pp. 146–64.

Spence, M., 1976. 'Product Selection, Fixed Costs, and Monopolistic Competition', Review of Economic Studies, Vol. 43, pp. 217–35.

Sraffa, P., 1960. *Production of Commodities by Means of Commodities: Prelude to a Critique of Economic Theory*. Cambridge: Cambridge University Press.

Stephens, J.K., 1976. 'A Relatively Optimistic Analysis of Growth and Pollution in a Neoclassical Framework', Journal of Environmental Economics and Management, Vol. 3, pp. 85–96.

Stiglitz, J.E., 1967a. 'A Two Sector Two Class Model of Economic Growth', Review of Economic Studies, Vol. 34, pp. 227–38.

Stiglitz, J.E., 1967b. 'Distribution of Income and Wealth among Individuals', Econometrica, Vol. 37, pp. 382–97.

Stiglitz, J.E., 1969. 'Allocation of Heterogeneous Capital Goods in a Two-Sector Economy', International Economic Review, Vol. 10, pp. 373–90.

Stokey, N.L., 1988. 'Learning-by-Doing and the Introduction of New Goods', Journal of Political Economy, Vol. 96, pp. 701–17.

Stokey, N.L., 1991. 'The Volume and Composition of Trade between Rich and Poor Countries', Review of Economic Studies, Vol. 58, pp. 63–80.

Stolper, W. and P.A. Samuelson, 1941. 'Protection and Real Wages', Review of Economic Studies, Vol. 9, pp. 58–73.

Suarez-Villa, L., 1993. 'The Dynamics of Regional Invention and Innovation: Innovative Capacity and Regional Change in the Twentieth Century', Geographical Analysis, Vol. 25, pp. 147–64.
Suen, W., W. Chan and J. Zhang, 2003. 'Marital Transfer and Intra-Household Allocation: a Nash-Bargaining Analysis', Journal of Economic Behavior & Organization, Vol. 52, pp. 133–46.
Swan, T.W., 1956. 'Economic Growth and Capital Accumulation', Economic Record, Vol. 32, pp. 334–61.
Tabuchi, T., 1998. 'Urban Agglomeration and Dispersion: a Synthesis of Alonso and Krugman', Journal of Urban Economics, Vol. 44, pp. 333–51.
Tabuchi, T. and J.F. Thisse, 2002. 'Taste Heterogeneity, Labor Mobility and Economic Geography', Journal of Development Economics, Vol. 69, pp. 155–77.
Tabuchi, T. and A. Yoshida, 2000. 'Separating Urban Agglomeration Economies in Consumption and Production', Journal of Urban Economics, Vol. 48, pp. 70–84.
Takayama, A., 1965. 'On a Two-Sector Model of Economic Growth with Technological Progress', Review of Economic Studies, Vol. 32, pp. 251–62.
Takayama, A., 1985. *Mathematical Economics*. Cambridge: Cambridge University Press.
Takayama, A., 1996. *Mathematical Economics*, 2nd, edn. New York: Cambridge University Press.
Takayama, T. and G.G. Judge, 1971. *Spatial and Temporal Price and Allocation Models*. Amsterdam: North-Holland Publishing Company.
Tang, P.J.G. and K. Wälde, 2001. 'International Competition, Growth and Welfare', European Economic Review, Vol. 45, pp. 1439–59.
Tataru, M., 1999. 'Growth Rates in Multidimensional Spatial Voting', Mathematical Social Sciences, Vol. 37, pp. 253–63.
Teulings, C.N., 1995. 'The Wage Distribution in a Model of the Assignment of Skills to Jobs', Journal of Political Economy, Vol. 103, pp. 280–315.
Thoreau, H.D., 1910. *Walden, or, Life in the Woods*, 1992. London: David Campell Publishers.
Tirole, J., 1985. 'Asset Bubbles and Overlapping Generations', Econometrica, Vol. 53, pp. 1499–528.
Tobin, J., 1965. 'Money and Economic Growth', Econometrica, Vol. 33, pp. 671–84.
Trostel, P.A., 1993. 'The Effect of Taxation on Human Capital', Journal of Political Economy, Vol. 101, pp. 327–50.
Turnovsky, S.J., 1999. 'Fiscal Policy and Growth in a Small Open Economy with Elastic Labor Supply', Canadian Journal of Economics, Vol. 32, pp. 1191–214.
Turrini, A., 1998. 'Endogenous Education Policy and Increasing Income Inequality between Skilled and Unskilled Workers', European Journal of Political Economy, Vol. 14, pp. 303–26.
Uzawa, H., 1961. 'On A Two-Sector Model of Economic Growth', Review of Economic Studies, Vol. 29, pp. 47–70.
Uzawa, H., 1965. 'Optimal Technical Change in an Aggregative Model of Economic Growth', International Economic Review, Vol. 6, pp. 18–31.
Uzawa, H., 1968. 'Time Preference, the Consumption Function, and Optimum Asset Holdings', in *Capital and Growth: Papers in Honour of Sir John Hicks*. Ed. by J.N. Wolfe. Chicago: Aldine.

Valdés, B., 1999. *Economic Growth – Theory, Empirics and Policy*. Cheltenham: Edward Elgar.
Varga, A., 1998. *University Research and Regional Innovation: a Spatial Econometric Analysis of Academic Technology Transfers*. Boston: Kluwer Academic Publishers.
Veblen, T., 1898. *The Theory of the Leisure Class*. New York: MacMillan.
Vellutini, C., 2003. 'Capital Mobility and Underdevelopment Traps', Journal of Development Economics, Vol. 71, pp. 435–62.
Vendrik, M.C.M., 2003. 'Dynamics of Household Norm in Female Labor Supply', Journal of Economic Dynamics & Control, Vol. 27, pp. 823–41.
Voith, R., 1991. 'Capitalization of Local and Regional Attributes into Wages and Rents – Differences across Residential, Commercial and Mixed-Use Communities', Journal of Regional Science, Vol. 31, pp. 129–45.
Von Thadden, L., 1999. *Money, Inflation, and Capital Formation*. Berlin: Springer.
Waller, C.J., T. Verdier and R. Gardner, 2002. 'Corruption: Top Down or Bottom Up?', Economic Inquiry, Vol. 40, pp. 688–703.
Walz, U., 1999. *Dynamics of Regional Integration*. Berlin: Physica-Verlag.
Wang, J.Y., 1990. 'Growth, Technology Transfer, and the Long-Run Theory of International Capital Movements', Journal of International Economics, Vol. 29, pp. 255–71.
Wang, J.Y. and M. Blomström, 1992. 'Foreign Investment and Technology Transfer – a Simple Model', European Economic Review, Vol. 36, pp. 137–55.
Wang, P. and D.Y. Xie, 2004. 'Activation of a Modern Industry', Journal of Development Economics, Vol. 4, pp. 393–410.
Warner, J.T. and S. Pleeter, 2001. 'The Personal Discount Rate: Evidence from Military Downsizing Programs', American Economic Review, Vol. 91, pp. 33–53.
Webber, D.J., P. White and D.O. Allen, 2005. 'Income Convergence across U.S. States: an Analysis Using Measures of Concordance and Discordance', Journal of Regional Science, Vol. 45, pp. 565–89.
Weiss, Y. and C. Fershtman, 'Social Status and Economic Performance: a Survey', European Economic Review, Vol. 42, pp. 801–20.
Weiss, Y. and R. Gronau, 1981. 'Expected Interruptions in Labour Force Participation and Sex-Related Differences in Earnings Growth', Review of Economic Studies, Vol. 48, pp. 607–19.
Weizsäcker, C.C., 1966. 'Tentative Notes on a Two-Sector Model with Induced Technical Progress', Review of Economic Studies, Vol. 33, pp. 245–51.
Williamson, J.G. and P.H. Lindert, 1980. *American Inequality – a Macroeconomic History*. New York: Academic Press.
Winters, L.A., N. McCulloch and A. McKay, 2004. 'Trade Liberalization and Poverty: the Evidence So Far', Journal of Economic Literature, Vol. 42, pp. 72–115.
Wirl, F., 2004. 'Sustainable Growth, Renewable Resources and Pollution: Thresholds and Cycles', Journal of Economic Dynamics & Control, Vol. 28, pp. 1149–57.
Wolff, E.N., 1996. *Economics of Poverty, Inequality, and Discrimination*. Cincinnati: South-Western College Publishing.
Wong, K.Y., 1995. *International Trade in Goods and Factor Mobility*. Cambridge, Mass.: MIT Press.

Bibliography 427

Yamamoto, K., 2005. 'A Two-Region Model with Two Types of Manufacturing Technologies and Agglomeration', Regional Science and Urban Economics (in press).

Yang, G.F. and K.E. Maskus, 2001. 'Intellectual Property Rights, Licensing, and Innovation in an Endogenous Product-cycle Model', Journal of International Economics, Vol. 53, pp. 169–87.

Young, A., 1993. 'Invention and Bounded Learning by Doing', Journal of Political Economy, Vol. 101, pp. 443–72.

Zak, P.J. and Y. Feng, 2003. 'A Dynamic Theory of the Transition to Democracy', Journal of Economic Behavior & Organization, Vol. 52, pp. 1–25.

Zak, P.J., Y. Feng and J. Kugler, 2002. 'Immigration, Fertility, and Growth', Journal of Economic Dynamics and Control, Vol. 23, pp. 547–76.

Zamagni, S. and E. Agliardi, eds., 2004. *Time in Economic Theory*, in three volumes. Vermont: Edward Elgar Publishing Co.

Zhang, J.X., 2000jx. 'Public Services, Increasing Returns, and Equilibrium Dynamics', Journal of Economic Dynamics & Control, Vol. 24, pp. 227–46.

Zhang, W.B., 1990. *Economic Dynamics – Growth and Development*. Heidelberg: Springer-Verlag.

Zhang, W.B., 1991. *Synergetic Economics*. Heidelberg: Springer-Verlag.

Zhang, W.B., 1992a. 'Trade and World Economic Growth – Differences in Knowledge Utilization and Creativity', Economic Letters, Vol. 39, pp. 199–206.

Zhang, W.B., 1992b. 'A Two-Country Growth Model – Knowledge Accumulation with International Interactions', Journal of Scientific & Industrial Research, Vol. 31, pp. 187–94.

Zhang, W.B., 1994. 'Capital, Population and Urban Patterns. Regional Science and Urban Economics', Vol. 24, pp. 273–86.

Zhang, W.B., 1995. 'Leisure Time, Savings and Trade Patterns – a Two-Country Growth Model', Economic Modelling, Vol. 12, pp. 425–34.

Zhang, W.B., 1996a. 'Economic Growth, Housing and Residential Location', Umeå Economic Studies, No. 403, Umeå University.

Zhang, W.B., 1996b. 'Change of Economic Dynamics – Capital, Knowledge, Population and Pollution', Chaos, Solitons and Fractals, Vol. 6, pp. 2019–29.

Zhang, W.B., 1996c. 'Knowledge and Economic Growth with Research and Job Amenity', The Interdisciplinary Information Sciences, Vol. 2, pp. 1–10.

Zhang, W.B., 1996d. 'Knowledge and Value', Umeå Economic Studies, No. 408, Umeå University.

Zhang, W.B., 1998a. *Japan versus China in the Industrial Race*. London: Macmillan.

Zhang, W.B., 1998b. 'A Two-Region Growth Model – Competition, References, Resources, and Amenities', Papers in Regional Science, Vol. 77, pp. 173–88.

Zhang, W.B., 1999. *Capital and Knowledge – Dynamics of Economic Structures with Non-constant Returns*. Heidelberg: Springer-Verlag.

Zhang, W.B., 2000. *A Theory of International Trade – Capital, Knowledge and Economic Structures*. Berlin: Springer.

Zhang, W.B, 2001. 'Economic Growth with Creative Leisure', in *Singapore's Manpower Policy*. Ed. by Department of Economics, National University of Singapore. Singapore: McGraw-Hill.

Zhang, W.B., 2002a. *An Economic Theory of Cities – Spatial Models with Capital, Knowledge, and Structures*. Berlin: Springer.

Zhang, W.B., 2002b. 'Theory of Complex Systems and Economic Dynamics', <u>Nonlinear Dynamics, Psychology, and Life Sciences</u>, Vol. 6, pp. 83–101.

Zhang, W.B., 2002c. *Singapore's Modernization – Westernization and Modernizing Confucian Manifestations*. New York: Nova Science.

Zhang, W.B., 2003a. *A Theory of Interregional Dynamics – Spatial Models with Capital, Knowledge, and Structures*. Berlin: Springer.

Zhang, W.B., 2003b. *The American Civilization Portrayed by Ancient Confucianism*. New York: Algora Publisher.

Zhang, W.B., 2003c. *Taiwan's Modernization*. Singapore: World Scientific.

Zhang, W.B., 2003d. 'Complexity and Sustainable Development', in *Fundamental Economics* in *Encyclopedia of Social Sciences and Humanities* (http://www.eolss.com). Ed. by UNESCO (United Nations Educational, Scientific, and Cultural Organization).

Zhang, W.B., 2004. 'Mathematical Modeling in Social and Behavioral Science', in *Mathematical Models* in *Encyclopedia of Social Sciences and Humanities* (http://www.eolss.com). Ed. by UNESCO (United Nations Educational, Scientific, and Cultural Organization).

Zhang, W.B., 2005a. *Economic Growth Theory*. Aldershot, Hampshire: Ashgate.

Zhang, W.B., 2005b. *Differential Equations, Bifurcations, and Chaos in Economics*. Singapore: World Scientific.

Zhang, W.B., 2005c. 'A Discrete Economic Growth Model with Endogenous Labor', <u>Discrete Dynamics in Nature and Society</u>, Vol. 2, pp. 101–9.

Zhang, W.B., 2005d. 'Path-Dependent Economic Evolution with Capital Accumulation and Education', <u>Nonlinear Dynamics, Psychology, and Life Sciences</u>, Vol. 6, pp. 83–101.

Zhang, W.B., 2005e. 'A Two-Sector Growth Model with Labour Supply', <u>Australian Journal of Labor Economics</u>, Vol. 8, pp. 245–60.

Zhang, W.B., 2006a. *Discrete Dynamical Systems, Bifurcations and Chaos in Economics*. Elsevier: Amsterdam.

Zhang, W.B 2006b. *Hong Kong – the Pearl Made of the British Mastery and the Chinese Docile-Diligence*. New York: Nova Science.

Zhang, W.B., 2006c. 'A Multi-Region Model with Capital Accumulation and Endogenous Amenities', <u>Environment and Planning A</u> (to appear).

Index

Abel, A.B., 397
Abel-Rahman, H.M., 300
accessibility, 277
Acemoglu, D., 396
Acharyya, R., 400
additive comparison utility function, 269
agglomeration, 295, 313, 399
   economy, 299
   spatial, 400
   urban, 300
agricultural, 32, 299
   sector, 140
Aghion, P., 169, 395–7
Agliardi, E., 392
Aiyagari, R., 397–8
AK model, 123
Akerlof, G.A., 398
Alesina, A., 390, 396
Allen, D.O., 400
Aloi, M., 401
Alonso, W., 398
Alpizar, F., 398
Amato, J.D., 393
amenity, 276, 302, 311
   doing science, 385
   job, 140, 385, 395
   professional, 144
   regional, 283
   urban, 141
analytical economics, 384
Anderson, J.E., 380
Anderson, W.P., 399
Andersson, A.E., 399
Andersson, F., 400
APC, 103; *see also* average propensity to consume

APS, 103; *see also* average propensity to save
arbitrage
   opportunity, 83
   relation, 88
Aristotle, 384
Arnott, R., 398
Arrow, K.J., 2, 121, 124, 389, 394; *see also* Arrow–Debreu equilibrium theory
Arrow learning-by-doing model, 383
Arrow–Debreu equilibrium theory, 2, 383, 398; *see also* Walrasian system
asymptotic stability, 46–7
   global, 52
Atkinson, A.B., xii, 1, 176, 396
autarky, 96–9, 331, 372
Autor, D., 175, 396
average propensity to
   consume, 103
   save, 103
Ayong Le Kama, A.D., 393
Azariadis, C., 389, 391, 394, 397

Baffes, J., 399
Baierl, G., 397
Bajo-Rubio, O., 392
Baldwin, R.E., 400
Banerjee, A.V., 395
Bardhan, P.K., 401
Barreto, R.A., 392
Barro, R., 66, 165, 168, 391–2, 394, 396, 399
Barten, A.P., 394
Batten, D.F., 399
Baumol, W., 148

429

Bayindir-Upmann, T., 400
Becker, G. S., 71, 205, 269, 392–5
Becker, R.A., 23, 390
Beckmann, M.J., 398
Bell, C., 399
bell shape, 117
Bénabou, R., 396–7
Benhabib, J., 226, 392–3, 397
Benigno, G., 393
Benigno, P., 393
Berger, M.C., 399
Berliant, M., 399
Bernanke, B.S., 397
Bernoulli equation, 50
Bertinelli, L., 400
Bertola, G., 390
Bhagwati, J.N., 401
bifurcation, 173
birth rate, 82
Black, D., 400
Blanchard, O., 391
Blankenau, W.F., 395
Blaug, M., 391
Blinder, A., 395
Blomquist, G.C., 399
Blomström, M., 401
Blume, L., 391
Blundell, R., 393
Böhm, V., 390, 394
Boldrin, M., 394, 397
Bolton, P., 396
Borck, R., 400
bordered Hessian, 42, 45, 57
Borts, G.H., 398
Boucekkine, R., 393
bounded learning by doing, 168
Bourguignon, F., xii, 1, 176, 396
Bovenberg, A.L., 393
Boyer, M., 389
brain drain, 124

Brecher, R.A., 399
Brekke, K.A., 398
Bresnahan, T.F., 146
Bretschger, L., 123
Brezis, E.S., 394
Brito, P.M.B., 398
Browning, M., 393
Bruce, N., 401
Brueckner, J.K., 399
budget, 3, 54, 100, 125
 constraint, 55, 77, 178
 line, 41, 50
Bukenya, J.O., 399
bundle, 41, 100
Burbidge, J., 400
Burmeister, E., 212, 389

Cain, L.P., 394
Calvó-Armengol, A., 206
Campbell, J.Y., 392
capacity for supporting people, 80
capital, 8, 68, 193, 210
 accumulation, 12, 14, 27, 37, 71, 89, 108, 120, 124, 133, 141, 279, 399
 distribution, 72
 income, 68
 intensity, 219
 sector, 210, 214, 227
 variety, 386
capital–labor ratio, 45, 51, 55, 213, 356
capitalist, 22, 213
capitalization, 283
Cardia, E., 394
Carlino, J., 400
Carlsson, F., 398
Carroll, C., 398
Caselli, F., 24, 390
Cass, D., 14
CES, 64, 391; *see also* constant elasticity of substitution

Chakrabarti, R., 117, 394
Chakraborty, S., 392
Chamberlin, E., 377
Champ, B., 393
Chan, W., 392
Chang, W.Y., 392
changeable speed, 30-3, 391
characteristic equation, 18
Chari, V.V., 394, 397
Chasin, B.H., 396
Chatterjee, S., 390, 392
checking force of the population growth, 80
Chen, H.J., 395
Chen, Z.Q., 399
Chiang, A.C., 391
Chiappori, P.A., 392-3
China, 324, 354; *see also* mainland China
Chinese, 133
  societies, 133
Chipman, J.S., 328, 376, 401
Choudhri, E.U., 399
Christiano, L.J., 397
Ciccone, A., 397
circular causation, 299
city size, 300
Clark, A.E., 398
Clarke, H.R., 393
Club of Rome, 74
Cobb-Douglas, 47, 128, 279, 290
  production function, 47, 64, 68, 70, 93, 121, 151, 182, 189, 205, 219, 229, 252
  utility function, 47, 84, 93, 102, 144, 179, 252
Combes, P.G., 299, 399
comparative
  advantage, 301, 324, 329, 332, 377
  cost, 324, 363
comparative dynamic analysis, 224, 354

comparative statics analysis, 233
competition
  imperfect, 150, 159
  monopolistic 6, 150-8
  perfect 6, 114, 150, 277, 279, 299, 335, 343, 378, 383, 387
complementarity, 152
concave, 45; *see also* quasi-concave
Confucian regions, 395
Confucianism, 133
  classical, 133
conspicuous consumption, 269
constant elasticity demand curve, 154
constant elasticity of substitution, 64
consumer durable, 227, 251
consumption 15, 91, 269
  goods, 210, 251
  sector, 210, 214, 227
consumption set, 4, 100
convexity, 3, 45
Corden, W.M., 397
Corneo, G., 398
cost
  average, 300
  of living, 277-8
  of migration, 284
creative destruction, 169
creativity, 366
criteria of a theory, 7
Cropper, M.L., 393
Cuff, K., 400
cultural value, 134, 146
  education, 133
cumulative causation, 299
cumulative discount factor, 162
current account balance, 90
  balance, 90
  deficit, 90
  surplus, 90
current consumption expenditure, 103

current earning, 40; *see also* income
custom, 7

Das, M., 389
Das, S.P., 380, 401
Davis, L.S., 392, 396
Day, R.H., 394
De la Croix, D., 391, 393
Deardorff, A.V., 399
Debreu, G., 2, 102; *see also* Arrow–Debreu equilibrium theory
deflation rate, 83
demand complementarity, 397
demand function, 43, 162
  market, 43
  ordinary, 43
  Walrasian, 43
democracy, 383
democratic society, 175, 380
developed economy, 80
developed financial market, 112
developing country (economy), 112, 400
development, 150
Devereux, M.B., 334, 392
Diamond, D.B., 391, 399
Diamond, P.A., 397
diminishing return, 122, 124, 159
disamenity, 278
  noise and pollutant, 278
discounted utility, 37
discounting rate, 390
discrete dynamical systems, 391
disparity in regional wage, 275
disposable personal income, 120
distribution, 395
  income, xii, 174, 176, 199–203, 277, 323, 375, 389
  income and wealth distribution, xii, 205, 276, 376, 380, 383, 387, 395
  policy, 148
  wealth, 175, 193, 395

distributional justice, 383
disutility, 77
diversity in consumption, 159
division of labor, 124, 209, 269, 279, 305, 324, 331, 392
Dixit, A., 151, 160, 377, 392, 401; *see also* Dixit-Stiglitz
Dixit-Stiglitz
  approach, 300
  model, 379
  utility function, 270
Dixon, H.D., 401
Dixon, R.J., 400
Dobb, M., 401
Dobell, A.R., 212, 389
Dollar, D., 394
Domhoff, G.W., 396
Drandakis, E., 397
Dressing, M., 393
Drugeon, J.P., 397
Duczynski, P., 397
Duesenberry, J.S., 269
Duménil, G., 396
Duranton, G., 299, 396, 399
Durlauf, S.N., 396
dynamic game theory, 380
dynamics
  population 7
Dynan, K.E., 396
dynasty, 195

East Asian
  economies, 174
  thinker, 395
Easterlin, R.A., 269
Eaton, J., 333, 377, 399
Echevarria, C., 397
economic analysis, 32
economic geography, 124, 275, 279, 299, 305, 313, 398–9
economic globalization, 1

economic growth theory, xii, 1, 37
economic integration, 379
economic structure, 2, 124, 210, 391, 398
  transformation, 80
economic theory, 2, 7, 30–3, 313, 395, 401
economy of scale, 299–300, 366
education, 7, 43, 80, 124–9, 196, 200, 376
  cost, 200
  policy, 134
  sector, 124
  Western, 133
educational institution, 395
Eeckhout, J., 397
efficiency of knowledge utilization, 192
efficiency unit of labor, 169
Ehrlich, I., 392
Eicher, T.S., 397
eigenvalues, 18, 116, 190, 206
Einstein's theory of relativity, 146
Ekeland, I., 393
elasticity
  substitution, 199, 203, 205
  utility, 283
Elmslie, B., 400
endogenous discount rate, 389
endowment, 5, 113
  factor, 333
  nonhuman, 284
energy, 7
Englmann, F.C., 301
entrepreneurship, 124
entry, 150, 163
environment, 7, 74–8, 141, 278, 383
  improvement, 279
  sector, 75–8
Epstein, L.G., 389
equality, 384

equality of return on assets, 83
equilibrium, 5, 70, 180
  approach, 276
  competitive, 39, 85, 89, 124, 209
  theory, 279
equilibrium point, 70, 81, 94, 108, 172, 194, 234, 308, 340, 371
  multiple, 132, 397, 400
  stable, 70, 81, 94, 108, 132, 194
  two, 172, 194, 308, 371
  unstable, 70, 81, 194
Eswaran, M., 397
Ethier, W.J., 151, 160, 300, 331, 366, 378, 400–1
ethic diversity, 396
Euler equation, 25
Euler theorem, 10
Evans, G., 393
excess demand, 5
exchange, 3
exchange economy, 5
exit, 151
export-led, 299
external economy, 379
externality, 4, 6, 124, 201, 283
  consumer, 398
  education, 203

factor-price equalization theorem, 331
Fahr, R., 395
family, 71
  child, 72
  member, 71
  utility function, 71
Farmer, R.E., 397
fast variable, 2
Feng, Y., 396, 398
Ferrara, E.L., 396
Fershtman, C., 398
fertility, 112
Fielding, D., 399

Filatrella, G., 394
final good, 151, 155
Findlay, R., 332, 379, 399, 401
first-order condition, 16, 27, 41–2, 45, 153, 166
fiscal, 393
Fischer, S., 401
Fisher, A.C., 393
Fisher, E.O., 400
Fisher, I., xii
fixed point, 116
flip bifurcation, 117
Foley, D., 396
Forbes, 323
foreign
  asset, 89, 91
  borrowing, 333
Forslid, R., 400
Forster, B.A., 75
Forteza, A., 396
Fortin, B., 392
Francois, J.F., 378
Frank, R.H., 398
Franke, R., 396
Frederick, S., 26, 37, 390
Freeman, S., 393
French, 299
Frenkel, J.A., 334, 401
Friedman, J.W., 398
Friedman, M., 106
Froyen, R. T., 394
Fujita, M., 313, 398–400
Fukuzawa Yukichi, 395

Gale, D., 393
Galí, J., 393
Galor, O., 169, 393–4, 396–7
Gandolfo, G., 326, 401
García-Peñalosa, C., 397
Gardner, R., 392
GDP, 90, 109, 258; *see also* gross domestic product
general equilibrium analysis, 327, 396
Gerlagh, R., 393, 399
Germany, 395
Ghiglino, C., 390
Giannetti, M., 398
Gini coefficient, 175
Glachant, J., 390
Glaeser, E.L., 399
Glazer, A., 399
globalizing world economy, 323
Glomm, G., 393, 396
GNP, 90, 103, 108, 223; *see also* gross national product
Gobillon, L., 299, 399
Gollier, C., 390
Gomme, P., 392
Gong, G., 395
government, 66, 75, 127, 281, 386, 391
  budget, 77
  debt, 334
  expenditure, 67, 82
  growth, 392
  intervention, 66, 386
  spending, 392
Graham, F.D., 366
Gram, H.G., 397
Granstein, M., 399
Gray, J.S., 392
Green, J.R., 389, 391
Greenberg, E.S., 396
Greenhut, M.L., 398
Greenwood, J., 226, 392
Greiner, A., 395
Grilo, I., 398
Grinols, E.L., 377
Gronau, R., 395
gross domestic product, 90
gross national product, 90
Grossman, G.M., 159, 395–6, 401

Grossman, V., 395
group, 2, 22, 204, 248
   multiple, 191, 396–7
   two, 191–5
growth and income distribution, xii
growth rate, 53, 157
growth theory; 8, 204; *see also* neoclassical growth theory
   traditional, 8, 248
   new, 150, 155
growth with income and wealth distribution, 37, 276
Gruver, G.W., 393
Guo, J.T., 392

Haavelmo, T., 79, 393; *see also* Haavelmo model
Haavelmo model, 79
Hahn, F.H., 2, 389
Hale, J., 396
Hamiltonian, 166
happiness
   average, 269
   subjective, 269
Harris, J.R., 397
Hazan, M., 393
Head, A.C., 392
Heckman, J.J., 395
Heckscher, E., 331; *see also* Heckscher-Ohlin
Heckscher-Ohlin, 377
   model, 331, 334
   theorem, 331
   theory, 331
Helpman, E., 159, 377, 395–6, 401
Henderson, J. V., 398, 400
Hercowitz, Z., 226, 392
Hillman, A.L., 401
Hockman, O., 400
Hoehn, J.C., 399
Holländer, H., 398

home
   production, 71, 392–3
   sector, 392
Hommes, C.H., 394
homogeneous function, 9
homogeneous of degree
   one, 4, 9, 11, 39, 152, 9
Hong Kong, 395
Honkaponja, S., 393
Hopenhayn, H., 394
household 23, 396; *see also* groups
   capital, 392
   heterogeneous, 23, 186–91, 248, 343, 376, 390–1, 399
   one type, 38–99
   production function, 71
   sector, 392
   two-types, 177–86
housing, 72, 282, 392
Howarth, R.B., 398
Howitt, P., 169, 395–6
Hughes, J., 394
human capital, 7, 122, 124, 150, 153, 178, 184, 189, 195, 260, 356, 367, 395
   accumulation, 6, 67, 121, 199
   growth, 121
Hung, C.S., 398
Hynes, J.A., 389

I Ching, 402
ideology, 401
Ikeda, S., 334, 401
impatience, 26, 334
implicit function theorem, 42
import, 327
Imrohoroglu, S., 397
Inada condition, 15, 122
income, 40, 103, 270
   absolute, 269, 384
   current, 40, 59, 84, 89, 122, 125, 192,

214, 239, 251, 282, 335, 344
disposable, 40, 48, 54, 59, 84, 90, 102, 125, 144, 178, 214, 251, 270, 282, 336, 344
potential, 170
potential disposable, 60
increasing return, 80, 151
India, 324, 354
indifference curve, 47
inducement through factor price, 124
industrial, 32, 72
sector, 132, 140, 145, 148, 302, 309
industrialization, 141, 299, 397
industrializing process, 209
inequality, 175, 199, 313, 323, 384, 396, 400
income, 174
income and wealth, 174, 205, 275
inferior good, 270
inflation taxation, 88
infrastructure, 6, 9, 66, 141, 277, 304, 385
government-financed, 150
innovation, 124, 146, 299
industrial, 150
input–output, 161
input–output system, 209, 248, 276
institution, 7, 68, 281, 387
institutional
economics, 7
friction, 396
intellectual property right, 380
interaction between wealth and the population, 81
interest income, 14
intermediate product, 378
intermediate-goods sector, 151
internal structure, 73
international, 277
economics, 150, 391, 398

trade, 323–80
trade theory, 277, 324, 391
interregional, 400
economics, 150, 398
dynamics, 398
interaction, 276
macroeconomic growth model, 279
trade and income distribution, 277
transport infrastructure, 301
intraregional, 300
Ioannides, Y.M., 205
Iooss, G., 396
Isard, W., 276, 398–9

Jackson, M.O., 206
Jacobian, 42, 206, 212
Japan, 324, 354, 395
Japanese, 133
Jeanne, O., 398
Jehle, G.A., 389
Jellah, M., 394
Jensen, B.S., 401
Jha, R., 392
job information, 205
Johansson, B., 399
Johansson-Stenman, O., 398
Johnson, H.G., 333
Jones, L.E., 392
Jones, R.W., 333, 397, 400–1
Joseph, D.D., 396
Jouini, E., 390
Jovanovic, B., 394, 397
Judd, K.L., 151, 395
Judge, G.G., 399
justice and fairness, 383

Kaas, L., 390
Kaiyama, M., 397
Kaldor, N., 21, 299, 389; *see also* Kaldor model
Kaldor model, 22

Kanemoto, Y., 399
Karp, L., 394
Katz, L., 396
Keister, L.A., 176
Keller, W., 323
Kemp, M.C., 333, 377
Kenen, P.B., 401
Kennedy, C., 124, 393-4
Kennedy, P.W., 393
Keynes, J.M., 33, 103, 391
Keynesian consumption function, 102-5
  average propensity to consume, 103
  generalized, 104
  marginal propensity to consume, 103
Keyzer, M.A., 399
Kim, S.J., 401
Kim, Y.J., 401
Kimmel, J., 393
King, R.G., 392
Knapp, D.J., 397
Knell, M., 398
Kniesner, T.J., 393
Knight, F.H., 366
knowledge, 7, 9, 142, 147, 151, 159, 191, 195, 302, 391, 394
  accumulation, 240, 305, 307, 310
  common, 394
  creation, 6, 121, 147, 194, 301, 385
  diffusion, 385
  dynamics, 368
  new, 124
  nontrivial, 151
  society, 32
  stock, 141, 153, 367
  utilization, 121, 141, 192, 194, 301, 303, 307, 366, 375
knowledge-based, 301
Koçak, H., 396
Koomann, R., 393
Koopmans, T.C., 14, 37

Korean, 133
Kostiuk, P.F., 399
Kotwal, A., 397
Krawczyk, J.B., 401
Krueger, A., 175
Krugman, P., 300, 313, 377, 394, 398-9, 400-1
Krusell, P., 392, 394
Kugler, J., 398
Kuhn, T.S., 7
Kuncoro, A., 398
Kuznets, S., 174, 397; *see also* Kuznets' hypothesis
Kuznets' hypothesis, 174
Kuznetsov, Y.A., 396
Kydland, F.E., 393

labor distribution, 128, 138, 214, 252
labor supply, 201
Labys, W.C., 399
Lacroix, G., 392
Ladrón-de-Guevara, S., 392
Lagrangian, 42
Laitner, J., 397
Lambertini, L., 391
Lancaster, K.J., 71, 177
land, 169, 276, 285, 399
  ownership, 281
  price, 283
  rent, 279
  revenue, 281
  use distribution, 141
Lane, P.R., 393
Lanfranchi, J., 399
Lapham, B.J., 392
Laslier, J.F., 396
Latz, L., 175
Laubach, T., 393
Layner-Farrar, A., 395
learning, 43, 124
  by doing, 124, 140-4, 150, 193, 204

240, 299, 378, 383, 394, 401
  through education, 121
  through leisure, 43
  through producing, 121, 125
  through trading, 124
  through working, 43
Lee, H., 394
leisure, 58, 80, 204, 227, 392
  time, 59–64, 228, 282, 393, 395
Leontief, W.W., 209, 248, 398; *see also* input–output system
Lerner, A.P., 331
Lévy, D., 396
Levy, P.I., 401
Lewis, W.A., 174, 397
life cycle hypothesis, 105–6
  average labor income, 106
lifetime budget constraint, 16
Lindbeck, A., 396
Lindert, P.H., 174
linearized system, 116
Lisandro, O., 393
Liso, N.D., 394
Liu, W.F., 392
Ljungquist, L., 398
Lloyd-Braga, T., 401
lobbying, 380, 396
local interaction, 284
location, 392
location theory, 279
Loewenstein, G., 26, 36, 390
logistic model, 79
lot size, 282
Loury, L.D., 205
Love, D.O., 399
low-growth trap, 203
Lucas, R.E., 150, 205, 400
Ludvigson, S., 392
Lui, F.T., 392
luxury good, 270

Lyapunov's theorem, 46

MacDougall, G.D.A., 333
macroeconomics, 150
mainland China, 133, 395
Maital, S., 21, 108
Maital, S.L., 21, 108
Mäler, K.G., 393
Malthusian
  population model, 79
  regime, 169
  stagnation, 169
Manasse, P., 400
Manuelli, R.E., 392, 397
Maoz, Y.D., 393
Maré, D.C., 399
marginal
  condition, 89, 227, 281, 367
  cost, 154, 168
  variables, 2
marginal rate of substitution, 47
Marglin, S.A., 389
Marjit, S., 400
market, 3, 71
  capital, 114
  competitive, 281
  domestic, 337
  labor, 114, 146
  structure, 378
market good, 71
markup, 154, 166
Markusen, J.R., 377
Marshall, A., 332, 363, 401
Martin, P., 399
Marx's economic system, 2
Mas-Colell, A., 389, 391
Maskus, K.E., 380
mathematical economics, 42
Matsuyama, K., 379, 393–4, 396–7
Matthews, R.C.O., 377
Maurer, R., 401

Mayer, W., 401
McCann, P., 399
McCombie, J.S.L., 300, 400
McCulloch, N., 323
McGrattan, E., 393
McKay, A., 323
median voter, 380
Meghir, C., 393
Meier, G.M., 396
Melvin, J.R., 377
Meng, Q.L., 397
mercantilism, 324
Michel, P., 391, 394
Michi, D., 396
microeconomics, 42
migration, 299, 301, 343, 387
Milesi-Ferretti, G.M., 397
Milikovic, D., 399
Mill, J.S., 328, 332, 401
Mills, L., 400
Mino, K., 397
Moav, O., 195, 396
mobility
   capital, 279, 334, 387, 401
   factor, 300, 327
   labor, 279
modeling strategy, 147
modern economic regime, 169
modern industrial competition, 151
Modigliani, F., 105, 390
Monacelli, T., 393
Monastiriotis, V., 399
monetary, 393
   economy, 82–8
   expansion, 88
   policy, 393
   variable, 2, 6, 387
money, 82–8
   fiat, 82, 393
   inside, 86

   outside, 82, 86, 393
   stock, 82
monopolistic
   competition, 150, 168–9, 300, 366, 377, 400
   power, 24
monopoly, 6, 148, 165
   pricing, 154
monotonicity, 41
Montouri, B.D., 400
Moomaw, R.L., 299
Morishima, M., 397, 400
MRS, 47; *see also* marginal rate of substitution
Mulligan, C.B., 397
multi-
   nation (country), 210, 276, 343, 399
   region, 210, 275–313, 399
   sector, 209, 397
Murata, Y., 398
Murphy, K., 205, 269, 393–4
Mussa, M., 333
Myrdal, G., 299

Nahuis, R., 400
Nakajima, T., 401
Napp, C., 390
Nardini, F., 394
natural
   climate, 277
   endowment, 277, 386
   resource, 74, 79, 133, 277
natural purification, 76
Neary, J.P., 400
Negishi, T., 377, 391, 401
Nelson, R.R., 302, 394
neoclassical
   economics, 299
   growth theory, 2, 7, 14, 158, 209, 214, 275, 279, 300, 333, 389, 399
   production theory, 14

trade theory, 279, 328, 331, 334
neoclassical model, 8, 88, 141; see also neoclassical growth theory
neo-Ricardian, 301
network, 385
new trade theory, 378, 401
newly industrializing economy, 132
Newman, A.F., 395
Newton's mechanics, 146
Ng, Y.K., 398
Ni, S., 401
Niehans, J., 393
Nikaido, H., 397
Nishimura, K., 390, 394, 397, 401
Nocco, A., 399
nonconvex production possibility, 377
nondurable consumer good, 165
nonhome economic activities, 58
nonmarket good, 71
nontraded good, 277
normal good, 270
Norman, G., 398
Norman, V., 401
Nourzad, F., 397
number of
  commodity, 5
  firm, 5
  service, 5
Nyarko, Y., 394
Nybergw, S., 396

Obstfeld, M., 334, 393
occupational choice, 395
O'Donoghue, T., 26, 37, 390
Ohlin, B., 331, 377; see also Heckscher-Ohlin model
Ohlsson, H., 399
old age support, 112
OLG model 27, 112, 169, 398, 400; see also overlapping generations model
oligopoly, 151

one-sector growth model, 37, 47, 67, 209
Oniki, H., 333, 383, 399
Oniki-Uzawa trade model, 383
Ono, Y., 334, 401
OPEC, 74
open economy, 380, 393
opportunity cost, 164
Ortigueira, S., 392, 397
OSG model, 37, 102, 108, 177, 334, 397, 401–2; see also one-sector growth model
  capital accumulation and education, 124–39
  consumption function, 104
  endogenous human capital, 125–39
  discrete time, 53
  home production, 71–3
  learning by doing and research, 140–4
  population growth, 79–82
  public good, 67–71
  trade, 376
  two-sector, 214–23
Oswald, A.J., 398
Ottaviano, G.I.P., 399–400
Oulton, N., 397
output, 90
  net, 90
Overland, J., 398
overlapping generations model, 27
ownership, 40, 396
  land, 281
  resource, 278

Panagariya, A., 377
Parente, S., 394
Pareto, 102
Pasinetti, L.L., 22, 209, 383, 389–90, 397
path-dependent, 124, 132, 400
patient, 48
Peng, S.K., 399

Pereira, A.M., 398
periodic solution, 117
  period 2, 117
Perli, R., 392
permanent income hypothesis, 106–8
  permanent income, 107
Persson, T., 390
Peterson, F.A., 393
Pflüger, M., 400
phase diagram, 17
Picard, N., 396
Piketty, T., 396
Pines, D., 400
Pitchford, J.D., 393
Pleeter, S., 26
Plourde, G.C., 75
political, 134, 380
pollutant stock, 75
pollution, 74
population, 263, 383
  distribution, 284
  dynamics, 43, 79
    endogenous, 80, 385
    exogenous, 43
  economies, 7
  growth rate, 112
  structure, 257
portfolio, 82, 397
post-industrial, 142, 386
post-Keynesian growth model, 3, 21–3
poverty, 323
  trap, 195, 198, 401
preference, 7, 48, 84, 96, 138, 155, 184, 189, 257, 327, 330, 394, 397–8
  change, 263, 270, 386, 398, 401
  completeness, 101
  continuity, 101
  Dixit-Stiglitz, 160
  intertemporal, 159
  order, 101
  indifference, 101
  preferred, 102
  recursive, 334
  reflexibility, 101
  structure 99, 194, 386, 389, 394
  transitivity, 101
present-value Hamiltonian, 16
price
  competition, 301
  elasticity, 160
  equalization, 280, 302
  index, 161
pricing strategy, 162
product differentiation, 300
product variety, 159
production function, 8, 67, 89, 211, 243, 257, 303; *see also* Cobb–Douglas
  CES, 64, 114, 182
  constant return to scale, 113
  intensive form, 10
  Leontief form, 391
  neoclassical, 8, 14, 38, 57, 89, 187, 344
production possibility, 3
production sector, 140
productivity, 66, 75, 95, 275, 293, 301
professional choice, 142
profit, 3, 162
  maximization, 279
  present discounted value, 162
progressive taxation, 24
propensity to
  consume goods, 60, 77, 84, 142, 179, 214, 229, 283
  consume lot size, 283
  enjoy environment, 77
  own wealth, 23, 48, 60, 71, 77, 84, 95, 97, 110, 138, 142, 144, 179, 214, 229, 263, 283
  use consumer durable, 229

use leisure, 60, 64, 229, 283
proportional consumption tax, 25
public
    consumption, 66
    good, 66–9, 283, 366
    infrastructure, 67
    sector, 68
purification efficiency, 76

qualified labor force, 191
quality of product, 169
quality upgrading, 159
quasi-concave, 5, 9, 42

R&D, 121, 140, 159, 163, 166, 201, 366
    policy, 124
Rader, T., 102, 390
Ralf, K., 397
Ramsey, F., 14, 23
Ramsey growth model, xiii, 3, 13–21, 27, 111–12, 177, 275, 390, 392, 399, 401
    OSG model, 111
    time preference, 111
Rangazas, P., 394
Ranjan, P., 399
Rankin, N., 401
rational
    household, 20
    individual, 108
    mechanism, 13, 276
Rauch, J.E., 394, 396, 398
Raut, L.K., 394
Ravikumar, B., 392, 396
Razin, A., 334
RC theory, 26; *see also* representative consumer approach
real disposable income, 103
real variable, 2
Rebelo, S., 392
Reed, W.J., 393
regional, 275, 400

amenity, 283
attractiveness, 283
culture, 277, 283, 304
economics, 276
difference in income and wealth, 275
distribution of labor and capital, 279
development with learning, 400
dwelling, 282
infrastructure, 283
mobility, 276
science, 141
tax competition, 313
two, 400
relative
    consumption, 269
    income, 269
    social status, 269–70
    standing, 398
    wealth, 269
relative maximum, 42
Ren, L.Q., 394
Reny, P.J., 389
representability of a preference relation, 101
representative consumer, 390
    approach, 23
research, 140, 150, 153, 200, 376
    industrial, 159
    sector, 151
return of wealth, 111
return to scale, 66, 68, 130, 147, 193, 397
    constant, 9, 71, 88, 147, 161, 299
    decreasing, 9, 71, 124, 131, 147, 194, 305, 308, 366, 370
    external, 378
    increasing, 3, 9, 71, 124, 131, 147, 150, 194, 305, 307, 363, 366, 370, 397
    nonconstant, 378
Rey, H., 393
Rey, S.J., 400

Ricardian, 377
  model, 326, 331, 383
  theory, 328, 363
Ricardo, D., 324, 332, 362, 400; *see also* Ricardian
Richardson, H. W., 398
Riezman, R.G., 401
Rios-Rull, J.V., 392, 394
Rivera-Batiz, F., 400
Rivera-Batiz, L.A., 300, 379, 400
Roback, J., 283
Robson, A.J., 398
Rodrik, D., 390
Roemer, J.E., 384
Rogerson, E., 393
Rogerson, R., 226, 392-3
Rogoff, K., 393
Romer, D., 107, 389, 400
Romer, P.M., 124, 150-1, 379; *see also* Romer model
Romer model, 151, 159
Rosenzweig, M.R., 392
Rossi, P.E., 397
Rossi-Hansberg, E., 400
Rostow, W.W., 397
Roubini, N., 397
Roy, J.R., 399
Ruffin, R.J., 399
Rupert, P., 392-3
Rybczynski, T.M., 331; *see also* Rybczynski theorem
Rybczynski theorem, 331
Ryder, H.E., 393, 401

saddle point 19, 87, 117
saddle-path stable, 18
Sahota, G.S., 389
Sakoulis, G., 392
Sala-I-Martin, X., 165, 168, 391-2, 396-7, 399
Salvadori, N., 390

Samuelson, L., 394
Samuelson, P.A., 21, 37, 331, 333, 383, 390-1, 394, 399; *see also* Stolper-Samuelson theory
Santos, M.S., 392, 397
Sato, K., 22, 289-90, 398
Sato, R., 394
Sattinger, M., 398
saving, 15, 43, 73, 91, 140, 282
  rate, 109, 133
saving class, 174
scarce resource, 1
Schmitt, J., 396
Schmitt-Grohé, S., 393
Schultz, T.W., 124, 394
Schumpeter, J.A., 33, 151, 169, 391
science, 140
Scotchmer, S., 277
Seckin, A., 393
second-order condition, 42
Sedgley, N., 400
seigniorage, 82
self-reinforcing, 299
Semmler, W., 395
service, 277, 299, 301, 344
  sector, 140, 302
shadow price, 16
Shell, K., 151
Shi, S., 334, 389
Shields, K., 399
Shigoka, T., 394, 397
Shimomura, K., 390, 401
Shleifer, A., 392
Shone, R., 394
Siebert, H., 398
Simon, C.P., 391
Simon, J.L., 399
Simpson, N.B., 395
Singapore, 395
sink, 117

situation-dependent, 301; *see also* path-dependent
Sivitanidou, R., 399
Skalli, A., 399
skill, 7
  composition, 284
skilled, 199
Skinner, J., 396
small open economy, 89–99, 401
Smith, A., 31, 66, 124, 324
Smith, V.K., 393
Smulders, S.A., 393
social
  class, 2; *see also* group
  norm, 205
  security program, 112
  structure, 205
  welfare, 69, 363
Solow, R., 8, 12, 18, 389; *see also* Solow growth model
Solow capital accumulation equation, 13
Solow growth model, xiii, 3, 8, 12, 19, 38, 82, 108–11, 158, 213, 275, 383, 389–90, 399, 401
  extended, 80
  framework, 168
  saving rate, 110
Song, E.Y., 392
Song, X.C., 397
Sorger, G., 390, 399, 401
spatial, 275, 279, 387
  economics, 32
  differential in labor productivity, 330
spatiotemporal scale, 32
specific-factor trade model, 331
specification, 269, 299
speculative, 83
Spence, M., 396
spillover effect, 378

Sraffa, P., 397
Srinivasan, T.N., 394
stability, 132, 309
  competitive economy, 6
Stark, O., 392
status, 141, 269, 396, 398
Stein, J.L., 398
Stephens, J.K., 393
Stiglitz, J.E., 151, 160, 248, 377, 390, 397, 401; *see also* Dixit-Stiglitz
Stokey, N.L., 394
Stolper, W., 331; *see also* Stolper-Samuelson theory
Stolper-Samuelson theory, 331
store of value, 83
structure of the economy, 75
study, 125
Suarez-Villa, L., 400
subjective discount rate, 159
subsistence, 170
substitutability, 152
Suen, W., 392
survivorship function, 12
sustainability, 74
sustainable development, 137
Svensson, L.E.O., 401
Swan, T.W., 8, 389

Tabellini, G., 390
Tabuchi, T., 398–9
Taiwan, 133
Takayama, A., 389, 397
Takayama, T., 399
Tamura, R., 393–4
Tang, P.J.G., 398
tariff, 280, 366
taste, 7, 100; *see also* preference
  change, 270
Tataru, M., 392
tax, 68, 75, 127, 148, 205, 386
  income, 69, 127, 200, 392

rate, 69, 75, 134, 141
teaching, 125
technical progress, 43, 124, 209, 396
technological
  change, 6, 64, 121, 141, 151, 169, 171, 199, 393, 396
  diffusion, 323
  possibility, 3
technology, 7, 96, 108, 151, 299, 301, 331, 335, 394
  choice, 394
Teulings, C.N., 398
Thirlwall, A.P., 400
Thisse, J.F., 277, 398–400
Thoreau, H.D., 384, 401
threshold
  income, 197
  pollution, 77
time
  discounting, 390
  distribution, 58
    between leisure and work, 58
  preference, 19, 21, 390
timescale, 30–3, 391
Tirole, J., 393
Tobin, J., 82, 393; *see also* Tobin effect
Tobin effect, 88, 393
Todaro, M.P., 397
Todd, P., 395
Tolley, G.S., 399
trade, 323–80, 398, 400
  balance, 286, 347
  cost, 380
  deficit, 285, 347
  gain from, 324, 363
  liberalization, 323
  pattern, 327, 332, 366
  policy, 378
  structure, 333
  surplus, 285, 347

theory, 327, 376, 379
Trajtenberg, M., 146
transaction cost, 387
transport cost, 280, 283, 300
  iceberg, 399
transportation and communication, 385
transversality condition, 16
treelike structure, 146
Trostel, P.A., 395
Tsai, H.F., 392
Tsiddon, D., 394
Tsutsui, S., 394
Tsyganov, E.N., 390
Turner, M., 398
Turnovsky, S.J., 392
Turrini, A., 395, 400
two-sector growth model, 210–13, 239–43, 249–52, 397, 400

Uhlig, H., 398
unskilled, 199
urban economics, 141, 279, 391
urbanization, 141, 299, 387
unemployment, 206, 386, 391, 402
unified theory, 1
university, 125, 140, 147
  budget, 127
  output, 127
  scientist, 143
  student, 125
  teacher, 125
Uribe, M., 393
US, 66, 324, 354, 400
  economy, 108, 119, 174, 400
  Great Depression, 1975
  low-skilled worker, 400
  productivity, 119
  region, 299, 400
utility, 277; *see also* preference
  discount rate, 158
  discounted, 21, 390

equalization, 284
function, 4, 77, 99, 101, 125, 193, 214, 269, 345, 394
   instantaneous, 15, 159
   lifetime, 23, 27, 107
   maximization, 42, 54, 82, 166, 279
   same level, 143
utility surplus, 72
Uzawa, H., 121, 125, 210, 243, 333, 383, 389, 394, 399; *see also* Uzawa two-sector model
Uzawa two-sector model, 210–13, 383, 398

Valdés, B., 401
value, 7
   locational attribute, 283
   wealth, 40
value and distribution, 401
Van der Zwaan, B.C.C., 393
Varga, A., 301
variety of goods, 159, 165
Veblen, T., 269; *see also* conspicuous consumption
Vellutini, C., 390
Venables, A.J., 398–400
Venditti, A., 397, 401
Vendrik, M.C.M., 393
Ventura, J., 24, 390
Verdier, T., 392
Violante, G.L., 396
Vishny, R.W., 392
Voith, R., 399
Von Thadden, L., 393

wage
   differential, 141
   disparity, 284
   equalization, 284
   regional, 280
   scientist, 146

Wälde, K., 398
Waller, C.J., 392
Walrasian system, 3, 14, 248; *see also* Arrow–Debreu equilibrium theory
   equilibrium, 5
   tâtonnement, 5
Walrasian theory, 7; *see also* Walrasian system
Walz, U., 301, 398
Wang, J.Y., 379, 401
Wang, P., 397, 399
Warner, J.T., 26
wealth, 40, 43, 73, 89, 125, 161
   accumulation, 55, 89, 91, 143, 284, 336, 397
   change, 43
   distribution, 142
   nonhuman, 107
   sold, 43
Weaver, N., 394
Webber, D.J., 400
Weibull, J.W., 396
Weil, D., 169, 393–4, 396, 398
Weiss, Y., 395, 398
Weizsäcker, C.C., 124, 394
well-being, 72
Werning, I., 205
Western civilization, 134
Wheaton, W.C., 399
Whinston, M.D., 389, 391
White, P., 400
Williamson, J.G., 174
Wincoop, E. van., 280
Winter, S.G., 301, 394
Winters, L.A., 323
Wirl, F., 393
Wolff, E.N., 396
Wong, K.Y., 401
work time, 59–64
worker, 22, 213

world economy, 89
Wright, R., 226, 392–3

Xie, D.Y., 397

Yamamoto, K., 400
Yang, G.F., 380
Yano, M., 394, 397
Yoshida, A., 399
Young, A., 168

Zak, P.J., 396, 398
Zamagni, S., 392
Zeckhauser, R., 390
Zeira, J., 396
Zeldes, S.P., 396
Zenou, Y., 394, 399
Ziad, A., 400
Zhang, J., 392
Zhang, J.X., 392
Zhang, W.B., xii, 70, 79, 168, 194, 333, 387, 389–98, 340–401